Sixth Edition

Bridges
Not Walls

A Book about
Interpersonal Communication

Edited by

JOHN STEWART
University of Washington

McGraw-Hill, Inc.
New York   St. Louis   San Francisco   Auckland   Bogotá
Caracas   Lisbon   London   Madrid   Mexico City   Milan
Montreal   New Delhi   San Juan   Singapore
Sydney   Tokyo   Toronto

Bridges Not Walls
A Book about Interpersonal Communication

Copyright © 1995, 1990, 1986, 1982, 1977, 1973 by McGraw-Hill, Inc. All rights reserved. Printed in the United States of America. Except as permitted under the United States Copyright Act of 1976, no part of this publication may be reproduced or distributed in any form or by any means, or stored in a data base or retrieval system, without the prior written permission of the publisher.

This book is printed on acid-free paper.

2 3 4 5 6 7 8 9 0 DOC DOC 9 0 9 8 7 6 5

ISBN 0-07-061549-7

This book was set in Goudy Oldstyle by Better Graphics, Inc.
The editors were Hilary Jackson and Tom Holton;
the production supervisor was Kathryn Porzio.
The cover was designed by Delgado Design.
R. R. Donnelley & Sons Company was printer and binder.

Cover: The Rower's Lunch
by Pierre Auguste Renoir/Superstock.

Library of Congress Cataloging-in-Publication Data

Bridges not walls: a book about interpersonal communication / edited by
    John Stewart. —6th ed.
        p.   cm.
    Includes index.
    ISBN 0-07-061549-7
    1. Interpersonal communication.   I. Stewart, John Robert, (date).
    BF637.C45B74   1995
    158'.2—dc20   94-33881

About the Author

John Stewart has been teaching interpersonal communication at the University of Washington since 1969. He attended Centralia (Junior) College and Pacific Lutheran University, then got his M.A. at Northwestern University and completed his Ph.D. at the University of Southern California in 1970. John coordinates the basic interpersonal communication course at the University of Washington and also teaches upper-division and graduate courses. He is married to Kris Chrey, a Seattle attorney. He has two children and two grandchildren and they have a son, Lincoln, who was two years old in 1994.

Books and People

Imagine yourself in a situation where you are alone, wholly alone on earth, and you are offered one of the two, books or [people]. I often hear [speakers] prizing their solitude, but that is only because there are still [people] somewhere on earth, even though in the far distance. I knew nothing of books when I came forth from the womb of my mother, and I shall die without books, with another human hand in my own. I do, indeed, close my door at times and surrender myself to a book, but only because I can open the door again and see a human being looking at me.

Martin Buber

Contents

v

Preface

This edition of *Bridges Not Walls* maintains the approach and basic format that have characterized the previous five editions. It also offers an entirely new four-chapter section on relationships, a new essay in the "approaches" section at the end, and twenty-four readings that either replace or supplement materials used before. The book continues to be designed primarily for college students enrolled in interpersonal communication classes. But the materials address topics also covered in social work, counseling, sociology and humanities courses, and much of what's here is suitable for off-campus communication workshops and seminars. Chapters treat most of the standard interpersonal communication topics, and readings are drawn from a range of disciplines, including communication, education, clinical and social psychology, philosophy, and organizational behavior. There are also excerpts from some of the more substantive self-help literature.

The communication theory that guided the selection of readings is a relational or transactional one. This means that the reader is urged to move beyond "sender-receiver" or "source-channel-message-receiver" views of communication. I argue in Chapters 1 and 2 that communication is best approached as a collaborative process rather than something one person does "to" another, and that it is a process in which personal identities are actually negotiated and changed. Most of the authors represented here also acknowledge that, although communication is often expressive and instrumental, it is also person-building, which is to say that who we are gets worked out in our verbal and nonverbal contact.

This is a book for persons who want practical ideas and skills that will help them communicate more effectively with their friends, partners, spouses, family, and coworkers. But unlike most self-help literature, it resists the tendency to ignore conceptual issues and to reduce interpersonal effectiveness to techniques or formulas. The authors represented here recognize that there is much more to effective communication than simply being "open and honest." For example, there are thought-provoking discussions of the nature of interpersonal contact, self awareness, person perception, listening, disclosure, gender styles, conflict, and intercultural communication in Chapters 1, 2, 5, 6, 7, 8, 9, 14, and 15, and three developed philosophies of communication in Chapters 16–18. The book also includes systematic treatments of verbal and nonverbal communicating, negotiating relationships, friendship, family communication, and contacts between intimate partners, but no reading claims to offer the definitive "six steps" or "twelve easy techniques" for guaranteed success. The authors emphasize that the unique situation, the constancy of change, and especially the element of human choice all make it impossible to design and execute a purely technical approach to *human* relationships.

This point is rooted in the book's definition of its subject matter. *Bridges Not Walls* does not define interpersonal communication as something that only happens in face-to-face settings, during discussions of weighty topics, or in long-term intimate relationships. Instead, the term "interpersonal" designates a quality, type, or kind of communication that emerges between people whenever they are able to highlight in their speaking and listening aspects of what makes them human. My introduction in Chapter 1 explains this definition and subsequent readings extend and develop it. Throughout the book the point is made that different qualities or kinds of interpersonal contact are possible or appropriate in different situations. "More" interpersonal communication is not *always* "better." I do believe, though, that in most cases people's personal, educational, and professional lives could profit from increased interpersonal contact.

Readings in Chapters 1, 2, 3, 5, 6, 9, 10, 15, and 18 also emphasize the point made earlier that communication is more than just a way to get things done, because it affects who we are. I introduce this idea in Chapters 1 and 2; James Lynch, William Wilmot, Ken Cissna and Evelyn Sieburg, and Carole Logan and I develop and extend the early discussions; and the person-building dimension of communication is discussed in detail by Martin Buber in Chapter 18.

These commitments to a relational or transactional theory of communication are complemented by my desire that the book be readable. As in all earlier editions, I have tried to select materials that develop this theory by speaking directly to the student reader. I continue to look especially for authors who "write with their ears," or *talk* with their readers. Selections from past editions by Virginia Satir, Carl Rogers, Hugh Prather, Neil Postman, Deborah Tannen, and John Amodeo and Kris Wentworth continue to be in this edition partly because they do this so well. I have also found this accessibility in some new authors including Stephen R. Covey, Gerald and Marianne Corey, Sam Keen, and C. Roland Christensen.

New Features

As I mentioned, the most significant addition to this edition is the new Part 4 on relationships. Readings in Chapter 10 explore the general processes of relationship negotiation. In the first reading, Carole Logan and I describe how communicators' explicit and implicit choices about what to disclose and what to attend to combine to define the quality of the contact between them. Then Ted Grove explains how social and personal dimensions of two-person relationships get worked out in talk and how people use both specific *tactics* and a general sense of *tact* to manage their interactions. This reading ends with an explanation of the power dimension of relationships and patterns of relational control. Chapter 10 concludes with Ken Cissna and Evelyn Sieburg's explanation of patterns of confirmation and disconfirmation, which has been included in earlier editions of *Bridges*.

The other three chapters making up Part 4 explore "Friendship" (Chapter 11), "Families" (Chapter 12), and "Intimate Partners" (Chapter 13). Chapter 11 begins with the Adelman, Parks, and Albrecht description of friendship included in the fifth edition of *Bridges*. Then Steve Duck introduces his concept of "relationshipping" in order to talk about the general *features* people expect friends to have, some general friendship *rules*, and what he calls the *provisions* of friendships—that is, what they provide or do for us. The final reading in Chapter 11 is a thought-provoking discussion of the ethics of personal relationships.

Chapter 12 is made up of two discussions of family communication: Virginia Satir's simple yet powerful description of family maps, and a more detailed outline of some common problems in family communication and their corresponding solutions. This reading ends with two exercises designed to help family members create and sustain a healthy communication climate.

The final chapter in Part 4 focuses on intimate partners. It begins with an excerpt from the fifth edition of a book by a husband-wife team with a unique ability to speak sensibly and directly to college-age readers. After rejecting the rule of *quid pro quo* in intimate relationships, Gerald and Marianne Corey describe nineteen characteristics of a meaningful relationship, several of which overlap with points made in earlier readings. Then they offer guidance in dealing with barriers to effective communication in intimate relationships. They close with a useful discussion of inauthentic and authentic love. The next two readings were part of the fifth edition of *Bridges*: Dolores Curran's report of her survey identifying characteristics of a healthy couple relationship and Hugh and Gayle Prather's advice about how to resolve conflicts "unmemorably." The chapter closes with an excerpt from Sam Keen's best-seller, *Fire in the Belly: On Being a Man*. As one might expect from an author with a theology degree from Harvard and a Ph.D. from Princeton, Keen believes that, if you're going to understand the mystery of sexual love, you'll need to recognize that "the language of sexuality and spirituality mingle." As he explains, in love we learn, just as we learn in our spiritual lives, "to respect and adore what is beyond understanding, grasping, or explanation." He also makes a strong argument for the importance of the intact, "nuclear" family, while noting that unmarried, childless, and gay men can participate in this dynamic, too. This is a provocative reading that should generate considerable discussion, and taken together, these four chapters provide considerable information about communication in the most consequential relationships we experience.

Several chapters have also been significantly updated in this edition. There are new readings in the introductory and verbal communicating chapters and considerably more material than before in the nonverbal chapter. In order to alert readers to the dangers of oversimplified pop-psychology writing about nonverbal communication, Chapter 4 concludes with a brief excerpt from Julius Fast's recent book, which is followed by some review questions and probes designed to help students exercise their critical thinking skills.

There is also a new description of person perception by Sarah Trenholm and Arthur Jensen in Chapter 6, a new skill-building reading by Judi Brownell in the "Listening" chapter, a new discussion of disclosure in Chapter 8, and two new descriptions of women's and men's expressive styles in Chapter 9.

Jack Gibb's description of defensive communication still anchors the "Conflict" chapter, but his ideas are fleshed out in a new introductory reading by Joseph Folger, Scott Poole, and Randall Stutman. The intercultural chapter also keeps two readings and adds two new ones, an overview by William Gudykunst and Young Yun Kim and a discussion of black language by Shirley N. Weber.

Harvard educator, C. Roland Christensen was gracious enough to let me add his approach to interpersonal communication to the concluding section of this edition of *Bridges*. The essay comes from a book called *Education for Judgment: The Artistry of Discussion Leadership*, and it eloquently describes the collaborative, transactional nature of communication in Christensen's classroom. Over his long and varied career, Christensen discovered that genuinely reciprocal learning was dependent on three basic communication activities: questioning, listening, and responding. In the major section of this essay he describes six main lessons that he has learned about this approach to teaching, including (1) *A teacher's openness and caring increase the student's learning opportunities*, (3) *Modest expectations are the most powerful of all*, and (5) *Faith is the most essential ingredient in good teaching practice*. This reading nicely complements the approaches by Carl Rogers and Martin Buber.

Plan of the Book

This edition maintains the basic structure of the last one, starting with "basic ingredients," treating the "inhaling" dimensions of communication separately from the "exhaling" dimensions—even though the breathing metaphor underscores their inseparability—discussing relationships and bridging differences, and then concluding with three overall "approaches." This structure makes the materials easy to adapt to each instructor's approach. Although it makes sense to me to assign readings in the order they are presented, both the sections and the chapters are self-contained enough to be read in whatever sequence fits the situation in which they're used.

My introduction tries to show that *Bridges Not Walls* is a little different from the standard, faceless, "objective" text. I want readers to think about the potential for, and the limits of, interpersonal quality communicating between writer and reader. I also want them to remember that a book or essay is always somebody's point of view. I'd like readers to respond to what's here not as "true because it's printed in black and white" but as the thoughtful speech of a person addressing them. In the introduction I explain the distinction I make between impersonal and interpersonal communicating and argue for the link between quality of communication and quality of life. I also preview the book.

Chapter 2 of the "Basic Ingredients" section introduces the book's transactional approach to or theory of communication, and the next two chapters focus on verbal and nonverbal communicating. The introduction to these two chapters underscores again the inseparability of the parts of this complex whole called interpersonal communication.

Part 2, "Openness as Inhaling," outlines the receiving dimensions of interpersonal contact. I explain why I've chosen the terms "openness," "inhaling," and "exhaling" in the Introduction. On the one hand, a book can only treat one topic at a time, while on the other hand, "sending" or "speaking" and "receiving" or "listening" sound like vestiges of a linear view of communication, not a relational or transactional one. My compromise is to use the profitably ambiguous term "openness" in both Part 2 and Part 3 and to highlight its "inhaling" meaning in Part 2 and its "exhaling" meaning in Part 3. As I noted, the allusions to breathing also emphasize the indivisibility of these two parts of the whole.

Chapter 5, "Self Awareness," begins with the discussion I mentioned earlier by Gerald and Marianne Corey and, after a brief, provocative comment by Hugh Prather, concludes with Robert Bolton's discussion of some important barriers to effective self-perception. Chapter 6 shifts focus to person perception via William Wilmot's account of the transactional nature of person perception and Sarah Trenholm and Arthur Jenson's outline of social cognition. Chapter 7 concludes Part 2 with three discussions of listening, one highlighting the links between listening and the rhetorical process, one focusing on active listening skill development, and one urging readers to move beyond active or empathic listening to a dialogic approach that is more fully consistent with the relational perspective of the rest of the book.

Part 3 consists of two chapters. Chapter 8 treats disclosure in three readings, the first two of which outline what it is and how it works, and the third reminds the reader that disclosure is not a panacea for every communication problem. Then Chapter 9 uses readings from Diana Ivy and Phil Backlund's new book, Deborah Tannen's best-seller, and Bernie Zilbergeld's *The New Male Sexuality* to distinguish men's and women's expressive styles.

Part 4, "Relationships," is described above in the "New Features" section.

Part 5, "Bridging Differences," begins with a chapter on conflict and concludes with a chapter on intercultural communication. Chapter 14 is introduced by a useful, recent overview of interpersonal conflict by Folger, Poole, and Stutman. This is followed by Jack Gibb's classic, "Defensive Communication," and some useful suggestions about how to deal with anger by John Amodeo and Kris Wentworth. The chapter closes with another pithy contribution from Hugh Prather.

Chapter 15 also begins with an overview, this one by Gudykunst and Kim. Then Letty Cottin Pogrebin discusses how to cross boundaries of color, culture, sexual preference, disability, and age. Shirley Weber outlines the sociocultural significance of black language, and the chapter closes with Paul Rabinow's account of his confrontation with Arabic culture personified in his friend, Ali.

As before, Part 5 collects three "approaches" to interpersonal communication, statements by noted writers that summarize their views of and ways of being-in-relation. Chapter 16 presents a teacher's approach, Chapter 17 a psychotherapist's approach, and Chapter 18 a philosopher's approach. I have already discussed the teacher, C. Roland Christensen. Carl Rogers is the psychotherapist and Martin Buber the philosopher. Let me mention again that I still hear some complaints that the final reading by Buber is "too confusing," "too hard to read," and "too heavy." Happily, I also hear and see what happens when students in my classes—and in classes taught by teaching assistants—actually begin to connect with this person and his ideas. When student readers are patient and diligent, they often begin to appreciate through Buber the depth and importance of interpersonal communication. Frequently this motivates them to apply these ideas, even in the face of hardships and challenges. All this makes teaching Buber rewarding for me and many of the people I work with. I agree that it's difficult to make Buber accessible to the basic course student, but I believe in the value of high expectations, and I continue to be surprised and delighted by the majority of my students' understanding of his ideas.

Other Features

As in the fifth edition, two sets of questions follow each reading. The first, "Review Questions," are designed to prompt the reader's recall of key ideas. If the student can respond to "Review Questions," there is some clear indication that he or she understands what's in the reading. Then "Probes" ask the reader to take additional steps by extending, criticizing, or applying the author's ideas. Some "Probes" also suggest links between readings in various chapters.

Many of the readings also include extensive bibliographies. There are lengthy reference lists, for example, of sources discussing verbal and nonverbal communicating, person perception and social cognition, language usage among women and men, relationship development, friendship, and intercultural communicating. Finally, a detailed index locates and provides cross references to authors and key ideas.

As before, I want to remind readers that this book *about* interpersonal communication cannot substitute for direct contact between persons in the concrete, everyday world. This is why I've again begun the book with Buber's comment about "Books and People" and ended with Hugh Prather's reflections on the world of ideas and the world of "messy mortals."

Acknowledgments

I want to express many thanks to the authors and publishers of material reprinted here. This book would not have been possible without their cooperation.

I am also grateful to reviewers of earlier editions. The following people offered insightful and useful comments that have guided the revision process: Richard Brynteson, Concordia College; Dudley Cahn, The State University of New York at New Paltz; Stephen Coffman, Eastern Montana College; Donald Darnell, University of Colorado at Boulder; Jackie Ganschow, Del Mar College; Dennis Garn, Spring Arbor College; David Valley, Southern Illinois University at Edwardsville; Melissa Wood, University of Iowa; and Mark Woolsey, Fresno City College.

Many people I am fortunate enough to contact regularly have also contributed in direct and indirect ways to what's here. I appreciate current and former interpersonal communication teachers in our program, including Milt Thomas, Karen Zediker, Jeff Kerssen, Lisa Coutu, Roberta Gray, Kathy Hendrix, Ruth Huwe, Kent Nelson, Laura Manning, and Beckie McCann. Among these, Karen Zediker has been especially influential. She has integrated a couple of generations of transactional thinking and teaching into a classroom approach to these ideas that won a Distinguished Teaching Award at the University of Washington, one of only two given to teaching assistants in 1994. Karen has also proved again to me the accuracy of Roland Christensen's point about the *reciprocal* gift of discussion teaching—I learn as much from her as she does from me.

I also appreciate the colleagues who support and challenge my ideas, including Robert Arundale, Isabelle Bauman, Gerry Philipsen, Jody Nyquist, and Carole Logan, and important friends like Ann Lukens, Fr. Ralph Carskadden, Walt Fisher, and John Angus Campbell who do the same. As before, my most important living relationships—with Kris, Lincoln, Lisa, Marcia, Mark, Jamie, Joshua, Helene, Mom, Bob, Barbara, Michael, and other family members—are still the central reasons for, and the ultimate tests of the ideas in this book.

Two things that have not changed through all editions of *Bridges Not Walls* are my awareness of the difficulty and the necessity of interpersonal communicating and my excitement about the challenge of working toward achieving it. I hope some of this excitement will rub off on you.

John Stewart

Part

1

The Basic Ingredients

Chapter 1

Introduction to the Editor and to the Rationale for This Book

"**W**riting about interpersonal communication, especially in a context like this one, is extremely difficult, primarily because it's almost impossible to practice what you preach." In 1972, I began the introduction to the first edition of *Bridges Not Walls* with this sentence, and it is as true for me now—in 1994—as it was twenty-two years ago. Now, as then, I could simply think of you as "reader" or "student" and of myself as "author," "editor," or "teacher" and proceed to "tell you what I want you to know." But if I did, we'd have something a lot closer to *impersonal* than *interpersonal* communication.

The reason that approach wouldn't work for this book is that I'm not simply "author," "editor," or "teacher," and you are not just "reader" or "student." Each of us is many-sided and unique. My name is John Stewart, I have been teaching college for more than twenty-five years, I like just about everything about my job, and right now I am in the midst of the most exciting and enjoyable activities I've ever experienced—being a 53-year-old parent of a 20-month-old son. This is my second time around as a dad. My daughters are 31 and 32, and my grandkids are 8 and 6. So Kris's and my son, Lincoln, is not only a miracle, he's also an uncle to a niece and nephew older than he, and a new grandchild to my mom who's already a great-grandparent. Lincoln's a toddler now—which means he explores everything, is learning to go to sleep on his own, feeds himself (sometimes), constantly communicates nonverbally, understands most of what he hears, and is learning many new words. Every day Kris and I learn something more about parenting.

I'm a native of the northwest corner of the United States and have been fortunate enough to spend most of my life near where I was born and grew up. I love the smell of salt water and the fizz it makes behind a sail or rowboat, the brisk, wet freshness of local winters, the exhilaration of downhill biking and skiing, the chatter of a crowded family holiday gathering, and the rainbow of faces in our church congregation. I don't like phony smiles, air pollution, pretentious academicians, rules that are vaguely stated but rigidly enforced, or machinery that runs rough. I also often get impatient with people who can't or won't say what they mean. I was raised in a small town and live in Seattle, near Lake Washington. I like the challenges of helping people in my classes learn new and old ideas, and translating philosophical research into communication theory. I feel incredibly fortunate to have the job I do and to live where I do with a healthy family.

The longer I study and teach interpersonal communication, the more I'm struck by how much the person I am today is a function of the relationships I've experienced. Some of the most important people in my life are no longer alive; for example, my dad, my father-in-law, my first real "boss" Marc Burdick, college teachers Peter Ristuben and Ted Karl, and Allen Clark, the friend who introduced me to Martin Buber's writings. Others, like high school and college teachers Frank Richardson, Loris Crampton, and Robert Harris, I've almost completely lost contact with. But many other relationships continue to teach and mold me, including those I have with Kris and Lincoln, my mom and new dad, Kris's mother, my sister Barbara, and close friends John Campbell, Dale Reiger, Walter Fisher, Jody Nyquist, and Karen Zediker. I've also been affected by relationships with several authors who have made themselves available in their writing, especially Martin Buber, Carl Rogers, Hans-Georg Gadamer, and Mikhail Bakhtin. Contacts with all these persons have helped shape me. At the same time I sense the presence of a continuous core self that's never static but that's firmly anchored in values, understandings, weaknesses, and strengths that make me who I am.

If I were just "writer" or "teacher" I could also conceal the fact that I am almost as excited about doing this sixth edition of *Bridges* as I was about the first edition, and that I'm a little amazed that this book continues to speak to so many different people. Each mention of the book by a student who's read it or a teacher who's used it is a delight, and I get especially excited by the young communication teachers and scholars who tell me that this was their first introduction to the field. It's a gift to be able to share some ideas and feelings about interpersonal communication in this way, and I'm pleased that readers continue to allow me to talk directly and personally instead of in the safe, sterile, and distant style of some "educational materials."

The impersonal attitudes I mentioned will also get in the way of the contact between you and me, because *you* are not simply "reader" or "student." Where were you born and raised, and how has that affected you? Are you reading this book because you want to or because somebody required it? If you're reading it as part of a college course, how do you expect the course to turn out? Challenging? Boring? Threatening? Useful? Inhibiting? Exciting? How do you generally feel about required texts? About going to school? What groups have you been in or are you a part of? A neighborhood gang? Natural Helpers? A band or rap group? A sorority or fraternity? Alateen? A church group? What important choices have you made recently? To end a relationship? Move? Change majors? Quit work? Make a new commitment?

I'm not trying to say that you have to pry into the intimate details of somebody's life before you can communicate with him or her, but I am saying that interpersonal communication happens between *persons*, not between roles, masks, or stereotypes. Interpersonal communication can happen between you and me only if and when each of us makes available some of what makes us a person *and* at the same time is aware of some of what makes the other a person, too.

One way to conceptualize what I'm saying is to think about what I call your Contact Quotient, or CQ. Your CQ is a measure of how well you *connect* with another person. It's the quotient that expresses the ratio between the quality of contact you experience and the quality of contact that's possible. In other words:

$$CQ = \frac{\text{Richness or quality of contact achieved}}{\text{Richness or quality of contact possible}}$$

A husband and wife who've been married for forty years have a huge CQ denominator—let's say 10,000. When one is giving the other the silent treatment, his or her numerator is painfully small—maybe 15. So their CQ in this instance would be 15/10,000—pretty low. But when they spend an afternoon and evening together in conversation, mutually-enjoyed activities, and lovemaking, their numerator is very high—perhaps 9500—and their CQ approaches

10,000/10,000. You and I, on the other hand, have a pretty small denominator. This means that the absolute quality of contact we can achieve by way of this book is relatively low. But we can still strive toward a CQ of unity—maybe 100/100—and this is my primary goal in this introduction and the other materials I've written for this book.

It's going to be difficult, though, to maximize the CQ between you and me. I can continue to tell you some of who I am, but I don't know whether what I write is what you need in order to know me as me. In addition, I know almost nothing about what makes you a person—nothing about your choices, feelings, hopes, fears, insights, blind spots—your individuality. This is why *writing* about interpersonal communication is sometimes frustrating. Interpersonal communication can be discussed in print, but not much of it can happen here.

More can happen, though, than usually does with a "textbook." Our relationship can be closer to interpersonal than it often is. I will work toward this end by continuing to share some of what I'm actually thinking and feeling in my introductions to the readings, the review questions and probes at the end of each selection, and the four essays I've authored or coauthored. I hope you'll be willing to make yourself available by becoming involved enough in this book to recognize clearly which of the ideas and skills are worthwhile for you and which are not. I also hope you'll be willing and able to make yourself available to other persons reading this book, so they can benefit from your insights and you can benefit from theirs.

Why Approach Interpersonal Communication This Way?

Before we begin breaking human communication down into some manageable parts, I want to talk about a couple of beliefs that guide my selection and organization of the materials in this book. I believe that when you know something about this book's rationale, it'll be easier for you to understand what's being said about each topic, and you'll be in a better position to accept what works for you while leaving aside the rest.

Quality of Communication and Quality of Life

One of my basic assumptions is that *there's a direct link between the quality of your communication and the quality of your life.* I can best explain this idea with a little bit more personal history.

After high school, I attended a community college for two years and then transferred to a four-year college to finish my degree. I took a "basic speech" course at both schools, and noticed that in each, something was missing. The teachers emphasized how to inform others and persuade them to do what you want. They showed the class how to research and outline ideas, how to gesture effectively, and how to use vocal variety to keep your listeners' attention. Students were required to write papers and give speeches to demonstrate that they'd mastered these skills. But the courses seemed to overlook something important. Neither the textbooks nor the instructors said anything about the connection between the quality of your communication and the quality of your life.

Other texts and teachers did. In my literature and anthropology classes I read that "No human is an island," and that "the human is a social animal." Psychology books reported studies of infants who suffered profoundly when they were deprived of touch, talk, or any other kind of contact. A philosophy text made the same point in these words: ". . . communication means life or death to persons. . . . Both the individual and society derive their basic meaning from the relations that exist between [persons]. It is through dialogue that [humans] accomplish the miracle of personhood and community."[1]

The speech communication texts and teachers promised students that they could help them learn to make ideas clear, be entertaining, and persuade others to agree with them. But they seemed to miss the communication impact of the point being made in literature, anthropology, psychology, and philosophy. If humans really are "social" beings, then *communication is where humanness happens*. In other words, although communication is definitely a way to express ideas, get things done, and entertain, convince, and persuade others, it's also more than this. It's the process that defines who we are. *As a result, if we experience mainly distant, objective, impersonal communicating, we're liable to grow up pretty one-sided, but if we experience mainly close, supportive, interpersonal communicating, we're likely to develop more of our human potential.* This is how the quality of your communication affects the quality of your life.

One reason I started teaching interpersonal communication is that I figured out the truth of this idea, and this same point has motivated me to edit this book. I've also been impressed with some recent research that supports this reason for studying interpersonal communication.

Medical doctors have done some of the most impressive studies. James J. Lynch is codirector of the Psychophysiological Clinic and Laboratories at the University of Maryland School of Medicine. He introduces one of his recent books with these words:

> As we shall see, study after study reveals that human dialogue not only affects our hearts significantly but can even alter the biochemistry of individual tissues at the farthest extremities of the body. Since blood flows through every human tissue, the entire body is influenced by dialogue.[2]

In other words, Lynch is saying that the quality of your communication affects the *physiological* quality of your life. One of his important discoveries is that blood pressure changes much more rapidly and frequently than we used to believe, and that some of the most radical blood pressure changes occur when we speak and are spoken to. Computerized instruments permit Lynch and other medical researchers to monitor blood pressure constantly and to map the effects of a person entering the room, nonverbal contact, reading aloud, and conversation. Speech appears to directly affect blood pressure; in one study the mean arterial pressure of healthy nurses went from 92 when they were quiet to 100 when they "talked calmly."[3] Listening has the opposite effect. Rather than just returning to baseline when a person stops speaking, blood pressure actually drops below baseline when one concentrates on the other person.[4] And this only happens when we talk with people; "conversation" with pets does not produce the same result.[5]

In an earlier book, Lynch discusses some of the more global effects of essentially the same phenomenon. There he reports the results of literally hundreds of medical studies that correlate loneliness and poor health. For example, people with few interpersonal relationships tend to die before their counterparts who enjoy a network of family and friends.[6] In fact, a study by two Swedish doctors of identical twins found that smoking habits, obesity, and cholesterol levels of the twins who had heart attacks were *not* significantly different from the twins with healthier hearts. But there were some other important differences, one of which was what the doctors called "poor childhood and adult interpersonal relationships." The twins with heart disease were the ones who had experienced more unresolved conflict, more arguments at work and home, and less emotional support.[7]

What conclusions can we draw from evidence like this? Lynch puts it this way:

> Human companionship does affect our heart, and . . . there is reflected in our hearts a biological basis for our need for loving human relationships, which we fail to fulfill at our peril. . . . The ultimate decision is simple: we must either learn to live together or increase our chances of prematurely dying alone.[8]

In other words, if you view quality of life physiologically, it becomes apparent that there's more to it than ample food, warm clothing, shelter, education, and modern conveniences. The quality of your existence is directly linked to the quality of your communication.

If you go beyond physiological quality of life, the same point can be made even more strongly. In fact, nonmedical people have been talking about the link between the quality of your communication and the quality of your life for many years. For example, the philosopher Martin Buber wrote,

> The unique thing about the human world is that something is continually happening between one person and another, something that never happens in the animal or plant world. . . . *Humans are made human by that happening.* . . . That special event begins by one human turning to another, seeing him or her as this particular other being, and offering to communicate with the other in a mutual way, building from the individual world each person experiences to a world they share together.[9]

Psychologist John Powell puts the same idea in simpler terms: "What I am, at any given moment in the process of my becoming a person, will be determined by my relationships with those who love me or refuse to love me, with those I love or refuse to love."[10]

"Okay," you might be saying, "I don't disagree with the lofty ideals expressed by all these people, and I can see how quality of life and quality of communication are related. But let's be a little *practical*. It's not always *possible* to treat everybody as a personal friend, and it's not always *wise*. Plus, you sure can't expect other people to treat you this way all the time. So you can't realistically expect your communication always to be friendly and supportive. Impersonal communicating happens all the time."

I agree. Many factors can and do make this kind of communication difficult or even impossible. Role-definitions, status relationships, cultural differences, physical surroundings, and the amount of time available can all be obstacles to interpersonal contact. Lack of awareness and lack of skills can also limit the quality of the communication you experience. One person may want to connect interpersonally with someone else, but may simply not know how to do it.

In still other situations it may be possible but, as you point out, it may not be wise. The power relationships or the level of hostility may make it too risky. For example, I know a guy who used to teach interpersonal communication as part of a Living Skills class in a prison work-release facility. Eric also worked there as a guard. His power as a guard—he had the authority to send people back to the County Jail—drastically affected what he could accomplish as an interpersonal communication teacher. Some people in his classes responded openly to his efforts to connect with them. Others, however, were so hardened by their years in various prisons that they could only think about maintaining their own power in the convict hierarchy and getting out as soon as possible—legally or otherwise. It simply didn't make good sense for Eric to try to communicate with all the persons in his class in consistently "interpersonal" ways.

Human Being Results from Human Contact

The second, closely related basic assumption behind the materials in this book is that *there is a basic movement in the human world, and it is toward relation, not division*. This may sound a little vague, but I think it'll get clearer if you bear with me for a couple of paragraphs. First, I believe that human life is a process and that the general kind of process we humans are engaged in is the process of growing into fully developed persons. So far, no big deal, right?

Second, humans are relational, not solitary, beings. We fundamentally or existentially need contact with other persons. If you could combine a human egg and sperm in a completely impersonal environment—an artificial womb, machine-assisted birth, mechanical feeding and changing, and so on—what you'd end up with would not be a person. Why? Because in order to become a person, you have to experience relationships with other persons. This point can't be proved experimentally, of course, because it'd be unethical to treat any human organism that way. But there is some empirical evidence to support this claim in the studies of "feral" or "wild" children—children discovered after they'd been raised for a time by wolves or other animals. One book tells about the Wild Boy of Aveyron, a "remarkable creature" who came out of the woods near a small village in southern France on January 9, 1800, and was captured while digging for vegetables in a village garden. According to the people who knew him, the "creature" was human in bodily form and walked erect. Everything else about him suggested an animal. He was naked except for the tatters of a shirt and showed no modesty, no awareness of himself as a human person related in any way to the people who had captured him. He could not speak and made only weird, meaningless cries. Though very short, he appeared to be a boy of about eleven or twelve. . . .[11]

The creature was taken to a distinguished physician named Dr. Pinel, one of the founders of psychiatry. The doctor was unable to help, partly because "the boy had no human sense of being in the world. He had no sense of himself as a person related to other persons."[12] The "savage of Aveyron" only made progress toward becoming human after he was taken on as a project by another medical doctor named Jean-Marc Gaspard Itard. Itard's first move was to give the boy a foster family and to put him in the care of a mature, loving mother, Mme. Guerin. In this household the boy was able to learn to "use his own chamberpot," dress himself, come when he was called, and even associate some letters of the alphabet with some pictures.

Itard's first report about his year of efforts to socialize the wild boy emphasizes the importance of human contact in becoming a person. Itard describes in detail events that demonstrate the significance of "the feeling of friendship" between him and the boy and especially between the boy and Mme. Guerin: "Perhaps I shall be understood if people remember the major influence on a child of those endless cooings and caresses, those kindly nothings which come naturally from a mother's heart and which bring forth the first smiles and joys in a human life."[13] Without this contact, the young human organism was a "creature," a "savage." With contact, he began to develop into a person.

Accounts like these help again make the point that *human being results from human contact*. Our genes give us the potential to develop into humans, but without contact, this potential cannot be realized. People definitely are affected by solitude, meditation, and quiet reflection, but mostly because those activities happen in the context of ongoing relationships. As many writers have pointed out, we are molded by our contacts with nature, our contacts with other humans, and our contacts with whatever supreme being, higher power, or god we believe in. This book focuses on the second kind—our contacts with people. This is *why* there's a direct relationship between the quality of your communication and the quality of your life. This is also why I encourage you to think about your communicating in terms of its Contact Quotient (CQ). You certainly can't have the same quality of contact with everybody you meet, in every situation. But you can recognize the quality of contact that's possible between you and the other person(s) and work toward a CQ of 1/1.

Again, I'm not saying that if everybody just relaxes, holds hands, smiles, and stares at the sunset, all conflict will disappear and the world will be a happy place. I've been around too long to be that naive. Sometimes the fear that prohibits interpersonal communication is legitimate; we are often acutely vulnerable to another person's gossip, lies, manipulation, or power moves. Our ignorance can also be devastating. If I don't know how to listen, how to talk about feelings, or how to clarify an abstract idea, my inability alone can inhibit our contact.

But the point is, the kind of communicating discussed in this book is not just a trendy, pop psychology, western white middle-class exercise in narcissism. It's grounded in some basic beliefs about who human beings are and what communication means in human life—regardless of ethnicity, culture, gender, or age. In the first reading of Chapter 2 I say more about this point by distinguishing among the expressive, instrumental, and person-building functions of communication. When you read those pages, you might want to refer back to these two assumptions.

Preview of the Book

So far I've tried to say that for me, interpersonal communication differs from impersonal communication in that it consists of *contact between* (inter)*persons*. This means that for interpersonal communication to happen, each participant has to be willing and able to make available some of what makes him or her a person and to be aware of some of what makes the other a person. This willingness and ability will happen only when the people involved (1) are familiar with the basic ingredients of the human communication process, (2) are willing and able accurately to perceive and listen to themselves and others, (3) are willing and able to make themselves and their ideas available to others, (4) recognize how the basic communication processes work in various relationships, (5) have some resources to deal with differences, and (6) can put the whole complex of attitudes and skills together into a human synthesis that works for them.

This is why I've organized *Bridges Not Walls* into five sections, or parts. The next three chapters explore the basic ingredients—your overall view of the communication process (Chapter 2), verbal communicating (Chapter 3), and nonverbal communicating (Chapter 4). Readings in Chapter 2 explain what it means to say that interpersonal communication means "contact between persons," lay out the connection between communication and health, and tell how communication in a variety of settings can be genuinely "synergistic." Then Chapter 3 discusses how words can help divide and bring people together, and in Chapter 4, several authors talk about how nonverbal communicating works.

Part 2 is also made up of three chapters. The first—Chapter 5—is made up of three selections about self-awareness. Chapter 6 shifts to the processes of perception and person perception, and Chapter 7 is about listening. Then the two chapters of Part 3 talk about self-disclosure (Chapter 8) and differences between men's and women's expressive styles (Chapter 9).

The last three sections, or parts, of the book focus on application. The four chapters of Part 4 discuss applications to relationships. Chapter 10 discusses how relationships are negotiated in verbal and nonverbal talk. Then there's a chapter that deals with friendship (Chapter 11), one talking about communication in families (Chapter 12), and a chapter discussing communication between intimate partners (Chapter 13).

Then the two chapters that make up Part 5 grapple with some of the most difficult situations where communication knowledge and skills are applied.

Chapter 14 focuses on conflict and Chapter 15 discusses communicating across cultures. The readings in these chapters can help equip you to cope with the challenges of hostility, defensiveness, anger, ethnocentrism, racism, and related tensions.

The final part of *Bridges Not Walls* consists of three overall approaches to communication described by C. Roland Christensen, a famous teacher, Carl Rogers, a famous psychotherapist, and Martin Buber, a famous philosopher. These readings illustrate how the individual insights, attitudes, and skills talked about in all the other chapters can be synthesized and condensed. They also suggest some additional ways to take this content out of the classroom and into your life.

Before each reading there are some introductory comments that pinpoint what I think are the key ideas that appear there. At the end of each reading I've also included two kinds of questions. "Review questions" prompt your recall of key ideas. "Probes" are questions intended to provoke your thinking and discussion, especially about how the ideas in the reading relate (1) to your own life experience and (2) to ideas in other readings.

So that's what's coming. I hope it will be helpful *and* fun.

One final note: a few of the essays that I have reprinted here were written before we learned about the destructive potential of the male bias in the English language. As a result, when these authors mean "humanity" "humans," or "humankind," they write "man," or "mankind." In addition, when they are using a pronoun to refer to a person in the abstract, it's always "he" rather than "she" or "his" rather than "hers." Since this is how some of these materials appear in print, it is illegal to change them without using brackets and ellipses to show where changes have been made. Part of the time I make such changes, despite the clutter that it creates on the page. But part of the time I also leave the original intact, and hope that you can read the section for the ideas behind the sexist language. This is especially a problem in the readings by Jack Gibb (Chapter 14) and Martin Buber (Chapter 18).

Notes

1. Reuel Howe, *The Miracle of Dialogue* (New York: Seabury, 1963), cited in *The Human Dialogue*, ed. F.W. Matson and A. Montagu (New York: Free Press, 1968), pp. 148–149.
2. James J. Lynch, *The Language of the Heart: The Body's Response to Human Dialogue* (New York: Basic Books, 1985), p. 3.
3. Lynch, pp. 123–124.
4. Lynch, pp. 160ff.
5. Lynch, pp. 150–155.
6. James J. Lynch, *The Broken Heart: The Medical Consequences of Loneliness* (New York: Basic Books, 1977), pp. 42–51.
7. E.A. Liljefors and R.H. Rahe, "Psychosocial Characteristics of Subjects with Myocardial Infarction in Stockholm," in *Life Stress Illness*, ed. E.K. Gunderson and Richard H. Rahe (Springfield, Ill.: Charles C. Thomas, 1974), pp. 90–104.
8. Lynch, *The Broken Heart*, p. 14.
9. This is a paraphrase of what Buber writes in *Between Man and Man* (New York: Macmillan, 1965), p. 203. Italics added.

10. John Powell, *Why Am I Afraid to Tell You Who I Am?* (Chicago: Argus Communications, 1969), p. 43.
11. Roger Shattuck, *The Forbidden Experiment: The Story of the Wild Boy of Aveyron* (New York: Farrar Straus Giroux, 1980), p. 5.
12. Shattuck, p. 37.
13. Shattuck, p. 119.

Chapter 2

Introduction to Interpersonal Communicating

O ne of the best courses I took during my first year of college was "Introduction to Philosophy." Part of the appeal was the teacher; he knew his stuff, and he loved to teach it. But as I discovered a few years later, I also enjoyed the course because I liked the kind of thinking that was going on in the materials we read and the discussions we had. It seemed as though I usually thought that way myself. As I continued through college, I supplemented my speech communication courses with other work in philosophy. The topics I talk about in this essay reflect that dual interest.

Originally, the Greek words for "philosophy" meant the love of wisdom, where "wisdom" was contrasted with the kind of knowledge it takes to do art, politics, or science. That meant that *philo-sophia* was concerned with "eternal truths" and such general questions as "What does it mean to be a 'good' person?" or, "How do you know that you really *know* something?" Later, philosophy was defined as the "systematic critique of presuppositions," which is another way of saying that it's concerned with first principles, basic understandings, underlying assumptions. If you've read much philosophy you may have the impression that it can be stuffy or even nit-picking to the point of irrelevance. But frequently it's exciting and important, because the philosopher says, "Hold it! Before you go off to spin a complicated web of explanations about human communication, or an economic system, or the history of culture, or the operation of a political system, or whatever, try to get clear about some *basic* things: When you're talking about human communication, what are you assuming, for example, about what actually gets passed between people when they communicate?" The philosopher might say, "If each human perceives the world in his or her own way, then I can only communicate with *my perception* of you; I can *never* really get in touch with you. All I can do, when it comes right down to it, is communicate with myself!"

Such basic issues intrigue me. I know that many potentially exciting conversations have been squelched by someone's dogmatic insistence that everybody "define the terms." But I also know that a great deal of fuzziness can be cleared up when a conversation starts with some shared understandings about what's being discussed.

In the following essay I describe my definition of the topic of this book— interpersonal communication. I talk mostly about what's meant by the two halves of the word "interpersonal," *contact between* (inter) and *person*. My main goal is to clarify how the approach to interpersonal communication taken in this book is a little different from what you might be expecting. Basically, it's different because it acknowledges and emphasizes the fact that communication is not only important for getting things done; it also affects *who we are*.

Interpersonal Communication: Contact Between Persons

John Stewart

The fact that you're reading this means that you've decided to think and hopefully to talk about the topic of interpersonal communication. You could have made many different choices. You could have decided to study public speaking, television production, or organizational communication. You could also have decided to read, think, and talk about geology, mathematics, English literature, or religion—in fact, you may be doing some of that now too. But what is this "interpersonal communication"? What does it mean to study *this* topic?

Does it just mean "two-person" communication? Or perhaps two- to five-person communication (but after five people it becomes "group discussion" or "small group decision making")? Or does the term mean informal, face-to-face communication? Or supportive communication? Or therapeutic communication? What *are* you using this book to study?

I don't want to make too big a deal out of "defining our terms," but I believe that interpersonal communication is more than any of the things I've mentioned so far. For me, when the term "interpersonal" is used to modify the word "communication," it means something more than just "two-person," "face-to-face," "informal," or "warm and supportive." The term "interpersonal" designates a type or quality of human contact that can characterize many different communication events, including a telephone conversation (which obviously isn't face to face), an intense argument (which is hardly ever warm and supportive), a ten-person committee meeting, and even a public speech. This definition or approach grows out of the two assumptions I discussed in this book's introduction, and it expands the study of interpersonal communication from just an expressive or instrumental enterprise to one with person-building implications. For me *interpersonal communication is the type, quality, or kind of contact that occurs when the persons involved talk and listen in ways that maximize the presence of the personal.*

So what does all *that* mean? "Expressive or instrumental"? "Type, quality, or kind"? "Contact"? "The presence of the personal"? Well, I mean all these terms to do more than just confuse or to generate jargon. My purpose in this first reading is to unpack this definition and to explain how the approach to interpersonal communication that's built on it influences everything that's in this book.

Persons

Let's start with "the presence of the personal." It seems to me that as you and I move through our daily family, work, social, and school lives, we tend to relate with others in two different ways: We treat others and are treated by them impersonally or personally. I don't mean that there is a sharp dichotomy; sometimes we treat others and are treated by them more personally than impersonally, and sometimes it's the other way around. But "personal" and "impersonal" seem to be two ends of a scale that describes how we relate with others. Communication with bank tellers, receptionists, registration clerks, and most other institutional representatives tends to be impersonal, and much of the time this is completely expected and legitimate; in fact, it's almost impossible to do anything else. Communication with family members, lovers, and spouses tends at least part of the time to be personal. One central theme of this book is that although all our communicating cannot be personal, *more of it could be*. If it were, things would be greatly improved both for us and for the people we contact.

In order to move in this direction, it's important to recognize what this impersonal-personal communication scale looks like. Early in this century a man named Martin Buber described this sliding scale in a little book that became a classic. The name of the book is *I and Thou*, and since its publication in 1922, it's been translated into more than twenty languages, sold millions of copies all over the world, and continues to be read, discussed, and cited by communication scholars and teachers, philosophers, psychologists, educators, sociologists, anthropologists, and theologians. You might think from its title that Buber's book is a religious work, but it's not just that. The "Thou" in the title is the English translation of the German word for the familiar form of the pronoun "you." Buber originally wrote the book in German and called it *Ich und Du*, which became *Je et Tu* in French, and since English used to include "thee" and "thou," it was translated into English as *I and Thou*. The most recent translation, as you will see in a minute, keeps this title but renders *Du* as "You" in the text of the book itself.

In this book and in virtually all the writings he did between 1922 and his death in 1965, Buber focused in one way or another on the impersonal-personal relationship scale or communication continuum. In a three-paragraph section near the end of the first part of *I and Thou*, Buber summarized the distinctions that were the foundation of his entire approach to interpersonal communication. Here's my paraphrase of what he says with some marginal notes I'll explain in a minute.

Humans can relate to the world in two different ways	Unlike other animals, persons live in a twofold world, because they have a twofold perspective or point of view. [This, by the way, is the same sentence as the first one in his book. Buber's signaling that these paragraphs are a summary of his main point.]
As interchangeable parts	One perspective works like this: Sometimes humans perceive the surrounding world as made up of plain things and beings they perceive as things. They perceive what happens in this world as a collection of processes and impersonal actions, as things that consist of qualities and processes that consist of moments, things recorded in terms of length, width, and height and processes recorded in terms of seconds, minutes, hours, and days, things and processes that are bounded by other things and processes and capable of being measured against and compared with these others.
As measurable	From this perspective what exists is an ordered world, a detached world. This world is somewhat reliable; it has density and duration, its structure can be surveyed; you can get it out again and again: You can recount it with your eyes closed and then check with your eyes open. There it stands—right next to your skin if you think of it that way, or nestled in your soul, should you prefer that: it is your object and remains that, according to your pleasure.
As controllable	But all this also means that it remains alien to you. You perceive it and take it for your "truth"; this world permits itself to be taken by

**As reacting only
as not addressable**

you, but it does not give itself to you. You can only come to an understanding with others *about* it: although it takes a somewhat different form for everybody, it is prepared to be a common object for you; but you cannot encounter others in it. Without this world you cannot remain alive; its reliability preserves you; but if you were to die into it, then you would be buried in nothingness.

Or as unique

As what happens *to* you
As unmeasurable

Or the human encounters the world in a decisively different way. He or she perceives things and people as present and always as only *one* being. What's in the world reveals itself as it occurs, and what occurs happens to you as a unique event. Nothing else is present but this one. . . . When this happens, measure and comparison have fled. It is up to you how much of the immeasurable becomes reality for you. . . . The world that appears to you in this way is unreliable, for it appears always new to you, and you cannot expect it to hold still. It lacks density, for everything in it permeates everything else. It lacks duration, for it comes even when not called and vanishes even when you cling to it. It cannot be surveyed: if you try to make it surveyable, you lose it. It comes—comes to fetch you—and if it does not reach you or encounter you it vanishes—but it comes again, transformed. It does not stand outside you, it touches your ground. . . . Between you and it there is a reciprocity of giving: you say Thou to it and give yourself to it; it says Thou to you and gives itself to you. You cannot come to an understanding *about* it with others . . .

As a choice maker

As addressable

The It-world hangs together in space and time.
The You-world does not hang together in space and time.[1]

As you can see, Buber's word for impersonal is "It," and personal is "Thou" or "you." His point is that as humans we have the twofold ability to relate to what's around us as either an "it" or as a "you." And the difference between these two modes of relating is very significant.

Unique

Consider for a minute the characteristics of Its and Yous that I've highlighted in the margins of the preceding quotation. Perhaps most important, persons are unique. Although a microscopic examination of the pencil I'm writing with right now might reveal some nicks, coloration, or erasure contours that are different from any other pencil, for all practical purposes, this pencil is the same as any other no. 2 pencil. The same can be said for all the other objects around me now—my computer, chair, lamp, paperweight, coffee cup, calculator, and so on. There might be some minute distinctions, but for all practical purposes this chair is interchangeable with others of the same model, and so are the other objects here.

Persons aren't that way. We can be treated as if we're interchangeable parts, but for *many* practical purposes it's important to remember that we are not; each of us is unique. I remember hearing of a geneticist who said that given the complexity of each individual's makeup of genes and chromosomes, the probability of two persons other than identical twins having the same genetic materials was one in ten to the ten-thousandth power. That's less than one chance in a billion trillion! In other words, each of us is virtually a genetic one of a kind. But even if we weren't—even when identical twins have the same biological raw material—each is still unique, because each experiences the world differently. If you doubt it, recall the differences between any twins you've known. Or you might check the uniqueness of others with a little experiment. After you finish this chapter, ask a friend who's also read it how he or she is experiencing this book, or this paragraph, or this sentence. Superficially, your experiences may be similar, but if you probe them even a little, it will be clear that they're unique. There's only one you.

"OK," you might be saying, "chairs might be interchangeable, and humans might be unique, but uniqueness by itself doesn't make something personal. Each dog, cat, and horse is unique, too, and so are a lot of other living beings." That's a good point. Although zoologists and even veterinarians might argue that animals aren't unique, it sure seems to me that our cat Pansy is different from every other cat I've ever known. So let's go a little further. Uniqueness may be part of it, but what else distinguishes the personal from the impersonal?

Unmeasurable

A second difference that Buber notes is that the impersonal world is completely measurable; it's a space-and-time (spatiotemporal) world, and the human world is not. Part of what he means is that even extremely complex objects, such as giant computers, well-equipped automobiles, and fifty-story buildings, can be described completely in terms of space and time. This is what blueprints do; they record all the measurements necessary to re-create the object—length, width, height, velocity, amperage, voltage, specific gravity, circumference, hardness, and so on. Although it's difficult to measure some things directly—the velocity of a photon, the temperature of a kiss, the duration of an explosion—no object has any parts that are unmeasurable, at least in theory.

The same can't be said for persons. Even if I accurately identify your height, weight, temperature, specific gravity, velocity, and electric potential, I will not have exhaustively accounted for the person who's you. Some cognitive scientists include in their model of the person components they call "schemata," "cognitive patterns," or "categories" that do not appear to have any space-and-time (measurable) existence but that can be inferred from observations of our behavior. Less scientifically inclined people call this unmeasurable part the human "spirit," "soul," "psyche," or "personality." But whatever you call it, it's there.

The clearest manifestations of this unmeasurable part of us are those phenomena we call "emotions" or "feelings." Although we can measure things related to feelings—brainwaves, sweaty palms, heart rate, paper and pencil responses—what the measurements record is a long way from the feelings themselves. "Pulse 110, respiration 72, Likert rating 5.39, palmar conductivity .036 ohms" might be accurate, but it doesn't quite capture all of what's going on in me when I greet somebody I love.

Another thing: these unmeasurable emotions or feelings can't be turned off or on at will; they're always part of what we are experiencing. Contemporary educators have given up the idea that an academic course can focus exclusively on the "intellectual" or "objective" side of some subject matter, because students—like other people—are always thinking *and* feeling. Emotions or feelings are part of all learning, even in mathematics and the hard sciences. Recently a philosopher put this same idea another way when he argued that we should get rid of our "prejudice against prejudice." If you think of a prejudice as a pre-judgment, an emotionally-laden conclusion that we reach before "all the facts are in," everybody is always prejudiced to some degree. This is because we never have "all" the facts, and we've always got some emotional response to the information we know. So rather than trying to do away with this kind of prejudice, he argued that we would be better advised to recognize that it's always present, label it for what it is, and work to reduce its negative effects.

The point of all this is that there is more to persons than just what's observable and measurable. Although the human "spirit" and human "feelings" are concretely *real* in the sense that we are experiencing them all the time, these elements of us cannot be completely accounted for in space-and-time terms.

But what about nonhuman animals? Don't they feel too? Again, some people might want to reserve the notion of feelings exclusively for human animals. But it is difficult not to attribute the horse's springtime friskiness and the cocker spaniel's eager greeting—and her sorrowful droop—to "feelings." The question, though, suggests again that there is more to say about what distinguishes the *personal*.

Choice

A third distinction Buber identifies is that the It world is "reliable" and the You world is unreliable. This means that impersonal things and processes occur in predictable patterns. If I leave my hammer outside for a week (in western Washington State), it will rust, because unprotected metal with a given iron content always oxidizes in a moist environment. *Always*. It can't choose not to. The difference between the reliability of the impersonal world and the unreliability of the human world is choice. My word processor can't choose to start spell-checking, and my calculator can't choose to start balancing my checkbook. Automatic pilots, photoelectric switches, and thermostats sometimes seem to "operate on their own" or "turn themselves off and on," but they too are dependent on actions initiated outside them. The pilot has to be programmed; the thermostat reacts to the temperature, which reacts to the sun's rays, which react to the earth's rotation, and so on. As a result, we have a considerable amount of *control* over impersonal things like gears, internal combustion engines, and electronic devices. Similarly, a ball can only react to the force of the foot that kicks it, and if you're good enough at body control and physics calculations, you can pretty much pinpoint how far and where it will go, based on weight, velocity, the shape of your shoe, atmospheric conditions, and so on.

But you can't predict or control what will happen if you kick your roommate, your teacher, or the grocery checker. The reason you can't is that when persons are involved, human choice intervenes between cause and effect, stimulus and response. If you tap my knee with a hammer, you may cause a reflex jerk, but the behavior that accompanies the reflex might be anything from giggles to a lawsuit, and there is no way that you can predict or control for sure what it will be.

One way Buber puts this idea is to say that events in the human world "happen to you as a unique event." Later he says that the human world "comes—comes to fetch you—and if it does not reach you or encounter you it vanishes—but it comes again, transformed. It does not stand outside you, it touches your ground." When we are aware of choice-making capabilities of the people we're communicating with, we are more likely to *let them happen to us* rather than trying to predict or control them. This is kind of an odd-sounding idea, but it has some very practical implications. Especially when I'm feeling defensive and ready to shut somebody off or deal with them by categorizing them into a neat little box, it often helps if I can remind myself to just be receptive and "let the other person happen to me."

It works the other way, too. The more we're aware of our own ability to choose, the more of our personal selves we're expressing. When I feel like, "I *had* to shout back, because he was making me look silly!" or "I just *couldn't* say anything!" or "Sure I withdrew, but she *made* me—she was always on my back about something!" I'm out of touch with part of what it means to be a person. Persons can act, not just react; persons can choose. And, as I'll clarify in a minute, interpersonal communication is in part communication that maximizes our ability to do these uniquely personlike things.

Have we reached a quality that completely distinguishes the impersonal and the personal yet? Well, we're getting closer. Our cat Pansy turns up her nose at some flavors of cat food; migrating salmon select just the right stream from the hundreds that empty into the ocean; and a horse may "decide" to stop running and return to its fallen rider, but many people would describe all those events as programmed by reinforcement rather than conscious choices. The salmon are programmed to find and follow the subtle chemical signature of the stream they were born in, Pansy is just temporarily reacting to the food's odor or temperature, and the horse is just going through a pattern it has learned, too; it can't "decide" only to return to short-haired riders wearing dirty boots. But others will say, "No, they're *choosing.*" So let's keep going and see if we can further sharpen the distinction.

Reflectiveness

A fourth distinguishing characteristic is that persons are reflective. Being reflective means that not only are we aware of what's around us but also that we can be aware of our awareness. Wrenches, rocks, and rowboats aren't aware at all. Dogs, cats, armadillos, and whales are all aware of their environments, but we don't have any evidence that they are reflective. As far as we know, only humans compose and preserve histories of their communities, explore their extrasensory powers, question the meaning of life, and speculate about the past and future.

Reflection is not a process engaged in only by philosophers, moody adolescents, or people with terminal illnesses. Healthy, ordinary people reflect, too. I wonder from time to time whether I am spending my work time wisely. Like me, sometimes you probably wonder what you'll be doing five or ten years from now. Before you make an important decision, you ask questions of yourself and others about priorities and probable consequences. On certain days you may notice the beauty of your surroundings and think about how fortunate you are to live where you do. Like all persons, you ask questions and reflect. And your ability to do this is another feature that helps distinguish the personal from the impersonal you.

When you ignore the fact that persons are reflective, your communication usually shows it. For example, you may stick with superficial topics—the weather, recent sports and news items, gossip. You will also probably miss noticing how your communication is affected by the identity negotiation process that's going on (see Chapter 10)—for example, the way you see yourself, the other person's self-image, and what the other person believes that you think of him or her. On the other hand, when you are aware of your own and others' reflectiveness, you can recognize, for example, that although you feel uneasy in this group, Bill sees you as a strong leader, and his view of you influences your communicating as much as your view of yourself.

Addressability

The fifth distinction Buber identifies is that persons are addressable and objects aren't; you can only talk *about* objects but you can talk *to* persons, or better yet, *with* them. Notice how he makes this point. An It, he says, "permits itself to be taken by you, but it does not give itself to you." A You, on the other hand, "comes to fetch you. . . . Between you and it there is a reciprocity of giving: you say You to it and give yourself to it; it says You to you and gives itself to you."

Addressability is the clearest difference between the kind of contact you can have with a person and the kind you can have with the "almost human" pet cat, dog, or horse. For example, you may have looked into the eyes of a pet animal and noticed what seemed to be a real glance of reciprocity—almost as if you were being addressed. Buber described an experience like this which he often had with a house cat.

> Undeniably, this cat began its glance by asking me with a glance that was ignited by the breath of my glance: "Can it be that you mean me! Do you actually want that I should not merely do tricks for you? Do I concern you? Am I there for you? Am I there? What is coming from you? What is that around me? What is that?!" . . . There the glance of the animal, the language of anxiety, had risen hugely—and set almost at once.[2]

Later he explained that cats are not "twofold," like humans; they cannot perceive both the it-world and the you-world. Especially tame animals can step up to the threshold of mutuality, but they cannot cross it. All the unasked "cat" questions that Buber paraphrased dissolved in a twitch of feline ears and tail, and the cat stayed an "it." Experiments with chimpanzees, dolphins, and whales have raised some questions about this phenomenon. But so far the evidence supports the point that animals are not addressable in the sense that persons are.

In short, addressability especially characterizes the human world. We certainly treat each other as objects and as animals—for example, in crowds, bureaucracies, and wars. But we also engage in fully mutual address-and-response. As you sit in an audience of several hundred, the speaker can say your name and single you out for immediate contact: "Jeff Peterson? Are you here? Your question is about abortion and I want to try to answer it now." Or even more commonly and more directly, you may sit across from a friend and know from the touch of the friend's eyes, her hand, and her voice that she means *you*; she "comes to fetch you" and "touches your ground."

In summary, when I say that interpersonal communication maximizes the presence of the personal, the word "person" means more than just a "rational animal," or "thinking biped." Persons are different from other beings in five special ways, and in order to contact them as persons, you need to keep these differences in mind.

1. Each person is a **unique**, noninterchangeable part of the communication situation.
2. A person is more than just a combination of observable, measurable elements; there are **unmeasurable parts** that we call "feelings," "emotions," or "spirit."
3. Persons can **choose**; we can respond rather than just react. We can't turn back the clock or beam ourselves to another planet, but our future is never completely determined by our past.
4. Persons are **reflective**. Not only are we aware of what's around us; we can also be aware of our awareness.
5. Persons are **addressable**, which means we can be talked *to* and *with*, not just *about*, and we can respond in kind with mutuality.

The first step toward communicating interpersonally, then, is to contact others in ways that affirm your "personness" and theirs. This means doing several things, and each chapter that follows is about one or more of these things. For example, it means looking for the uniqueness in each person (Chapter 6) instead of being satisfied with what makes this person "just like every other _____ (hunk, chick, sorority Sally, farm kid, etc.)." It also means remembering that even in a conflict situation, both you and the other person are *choosing* to feel as you do, so you both need to own your feelings, to be responsible for them (Chapter 14). Sharing some of your feelings (Chapter 8) and listening to the feelings of the other (Chapter 7) are also important, as is the process of sculpting mutual meanings (Chapter 7). The key is to be aware of your own and the other's humanness and to communicate in ways that demonstrate your awareness.

Contact

When I say that interpersonal communication is a type, quality, or kind of contact, I mean to emphasize that it's something that happens *between* people, not something one person does to someone else. Just as your ability to communicate interpersonally is affected by your recognition of what it is to be a *person*, it will also be affected by your recognition of what it means to say that communication occurs *between* persons.

There are several practical reasons why it's important to develop your ability to see the betweenness, or relational nature, of human communication. For one thing, until you do, it's hard to keep from getting mad at the person who criticizes you or to keep from feeling defensive whenever you're being evaluated or controlled. Until you see the betweenness, it's also hard to keep track of the complex, continually changing myriad of things that affect your communication with a person you are close to. Without a relational perspective that focuses on contact, it's also difficult not to let the past determine what's going on in the present. In fact, all the communication behaviors discussed in later chapters—touch, tone of voice, self-disclosure, interpretive listening, and so on—make real sense only when you see them relationally, as part of what's going on *between* persons.

The problem is, most people don't actually see communicating this way. If you were to ask the person on the street what communication means, he or she would probably say something like "getting your ideas across" or "making yourself understood." This is a common view of the communication process, a view that's operating every time someone says, "How did you screw that up? I *told* you what to do!" or "I'm sure they understood; I *explained* it three times." In these cases the conception that is operating is that communication is something I *do*. From this point of view, communication doesn't occur "between," but rather "in" the communicator. When things don't work out, it's because I didn't communicate well or because you didn't, the company didn't, the supervisor didn't, or whatever. From this point of view, in other words, communication is an *action*, something determined entirely by the communicator's choices. As the diagram below indicates, this point of view says that communication is like giving or getting an inoculation; ideas and feelings are prepackaged in a mental and physical syringe and then forced under pressure in a straight line into the receiver.

If you think about it for a minute, it becomes pretty clear why this view is inaccurate. When you see communication as just an action, you're ignoring feedback, something that's present whenever people communicate. Even on the phone, we make noises to indicate we're listening to a long comment or story. If you doubt the importance of this feedback, try being completely silent and see how soon the person on the other end asks, "Are you still there?"

Communication-as-action

Situation

Communicator | Presentation → | Audience

Situation

The model of communication as action is also oversimplified in another way. It suggests that when you speak, there can be "an audience"; that is, a group of persons who are homogeneous—whose backgrounds, thoughts, feelings, and attitudes toward the topic and communicator are more similar than different. It also implies that the communicator's identity is not greatly affected by what goes into, or goes on during, the communication experience. In other words, it implies that regardless of any changes in the situation, the communicator is, for example, always "teacher" and never "learner," always "boss" and never "friend."

The point is, the common view that communication is an *action*, something one person *does* to somebody else, is drastically oversimplified. All of our communication behavior is affected by not only our own expectations, needs, attitudes, and goals, but also the responses we are getting from the other person involved. So it's more accurate to view communication as an *interaction*, as a process of *reciprocal* influence.

The interactional point of view can account for quite a bit of complexity. This point of view emphasizes that communication involves not just action, but rather action and reaction; not just stimulus, but also stimulus and response. According to this perspective, a "good" communicator not only skillfully prepares and delivers messages, but also watches for significant reactions to his or her communication. The study of human communication becomes a study of how people "talk" and how they "respond."

Communication-as-interaction

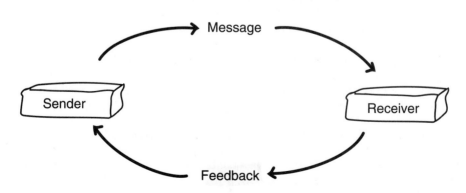

Message

Sender

Receiver

Feedback

Although the interactional viewpoint is an improvement over communication-as-action, it still has some weaknesses. The most serious one, it seems to me, is that although it's not as oversimplified as the action view, the interactional view still distorts human communication by treating it as a series of causes and effects, stimuli and responses. For example, think about the last time you had a conversation with someone you know. What was the stimulus that caused you to greet the other person? His or her greeting? His or her look? Your expectations about the other's eagerness to talk with you? Was your greeting a response, or was it a stimulus to his or her next utterance? Or was it both? What caused you to say what you said? What the other person said? What you thought the other's words *meant*? What you *felt* because of those words? What you felt because of *how* the other person said what she or he said? What you felt because of how the other *looked* when speaking? Are you able to distinguish clearly between the stimuli and responses in this conversation or between the actions, the hypotheses about the reactions, and the reactions?

Psychologist George Kelly reported that he had "pretty well given up trying to figure out" the relationship between stimuli and responses. He wrote, "Some of my friends have tried to explain to me that the world is filled with 'S's' and 'R's' and it is unrealistic of me to refuse to recognize them. But before they have talked themselves out they become pretty vague about which is which."[3]

What I'm saying is that it's more accurate to see communication as an interaction than to see it as just an action one person performs. But if you stick to an interactional view, you will still miss an important part of what it means to focus on the *contact* or the "between," and the part you will miss is the one part that makes the most difference, the part that can make interpersonal-quality communication happen.

Over the last twenty years I've found that helping students see this "part," helping them to see communication from this relational point of view, is one of the most important and most difficult things I do as a teacher. In my own life I am also continually reminded of how important it is to focus on the contact—every time I try to explain a concept in class, discuss a disagreement over a grade, pursue an idea with a colleague or student, or divide housekeeping responsibilities or plan a weekend with Kris. Every time my communication is really important, in other words, I rediscover how necessary it is to see that it's occurring *between* persons. Since this perspective is so vital, I want to talk about it in two different ways using two different terms: "transaction," and "relationship."

As I begin, notice how I've referred to this as a relational "point of view" and a transactional "perspective." I'm talking here about a way to look at or understand the communicating you experience. Historically, people first saw communication as an *action*, and then, when they realized the shortcomings of this perspective, they understood it as an *interaction*. Now we recognize that there is more to communication than either of these points of view enables us to see. So it's time to put on another pair of glasses, to use another lens to examine and understand the communication process. But importantly, this is different from saying that there are three different "kinds" of communication—some that is "actional," some that is "interactional," and some that is "transactional." This is not what I am saying. I don't believe that either God or Mother Nature made human communication a certain way and then sat back to see if we humans could figure out what it "really is." I believe, instead, that different lenses or points of view help you see different things. Just like a view from the top of a skyscraper enables you to see some things about a city that the view from the sidewalk doesn't, *and vice versa*. I'm suggesting that, if you view communication transactionally or relationally, you'll be able to see some important features of the process that you can't see otherwise.

A Transactional View

What important features? Specifically these:

1. The action and interaction lenses focus on individuals and individual behaviors, while the transactional lens focuses on what people do together. So the transactional view highlights what's *between* people, how they collaborate to construct meanings.
2. The action and interaction views treat people as if they had set identities *before their contact*, while the transactional view acknowledged that people's identities change *during their contact*.

A transactional view emphasizes that humans are not billiard balls or electrical sources sending and receiving current through a conduit. We are beings who are always "in process" or on the way. So long as we are alive, we are changing—replacing blood cells with new ones manufactured in our bone marrow, sloughing off old skin and replacing it with new, modifying old beliefs, learning new ideas, feeling new feelings, *changing*. Our view of communication needs to acknowledge this fact.

The way communication affects who we are became especially apparent in a conversation I had with a friend who was going through a painful divorce. "Mary Kay is not the person she used to be," Dale said. "Sometimes I hardly know her. I wish we could communicate and enjoy each other like we did when we were first married."

The times Dale was remembering were before Mary Kay was a mother, before she completed medical school, before she suffered through her residency in an urban hospital two thousand miles from home, before she joined a prestigious medical clinic, and before she became a full-fledged practicing physician. They were also before Dale was a dad, before he started his exporting business, before he developed relationships with his Japanese customers, before he became active in his state professional association, and before he began attending church regularly. Dale was forgetting that Mary Kay could not possibly still be "the person she used to be." Neither could he. Both of them have experienced many relationships that have changed them decisively. Mary Kay has been treated like a medical student—required to cram scientific information into her head and spout it on command—and like a first-year resident—forced to go without sleep, stand up to authoritarian doctors, and cope with hospital administrators. Now people treat her like a medical doctor—nurses obey her, many patients worship her for her skills, prestigious doctors treat her like an equal. And she's treated as a mom by her son. Dale has also experienced many different relationships, and he's changed, too. He's treated as a boss by his employees, for example, and as a "respected American businessman" by his Japanese customers. Because of the contacts both have experienced, each is a different person. And the process continues; both Mary Kay and Dale continue to be changed by their communication. *Who they are is a function of their contacts with others.*

Your changing may not seem as dramatic as Mary Kay's and Dale's. But consider, for example, who you were before you entered adolescence, who you were when you were 15 to 17, and who you are now. Think about how your first job changed the way you felt and acted around others. Recall how you have been changed by a significant success or failure in sports or academics, by going to jail, or by what happened the first time you fell in love or got dumped by a boy- or girlfriend.

The transactional view acknowledges that people are constantly being affected by their communicating. In fact, a transaction is defined as a process in which "all parts or aspects of the concrete event derive their existence and nature from active participation in the event."[4] In other words, when something is viewed as transactional, you can see that *who the participants are* (their "existence and nature") emerges out of the event itself. Communication can be viewed this way, and when you do, you can see how *our identities get negotiated between people.*

This is where the "expressive," "instrumental," and "person-building" terms I mentioned earlier come in. To say that communication is "expressive" is just to say that it's a way to get what's on the inside, outside—to express thoughts and feelings. To say that communication is "instrumental" is to say that it's a way to accomplish a goal or to produce a product or effect. Certainly communication *is* both expressive and instrumental. But it's more. If identities actually get changed (negotiated) as we communicate, then communication is also "person-building." It's a process that affects *who we are.* This is why, as I said in the introduction, there's a connection between quality of communication and quality of life, between the ways you speak and listen and who you are. To put it in other words, whenever humans communicate, part of what's going on between them is that they are collaborating on one another's identities.

Obviously, this defining process has some limits. I am male, 53, and brown-eyed. I can't define myself as female, 10, and blue-eyed. But I *can* offer a definition of myself that says I see myself as more masculine—or more feminine—than you and in some ways as younger or older than you. Then it's up to you to respond to the definition of self I offer. You may accept, partly accept, or reject it altogether. The point is, at a given moment, neither of us can change our identity absolutely, but we do change in relation to each other.

The only even nearly adequate "model" of this transactional perspective that I've ever seen is the "Bond of Union" print shown here by M. C. Escher. It graphically illustrates two persons whose "existence and nature" are intertwined. Each one is a "function," in the mathematical sense, of the other, so much so that not only are the bands that constitute each head joined at the top and bottom, but they also intersect at one additional point. This image does not highlight how communication accomplishes our relational being, but it does clearly illustrate many of the "transactional" points I've been making.

To review, then, you can see human communication as an action if you want to, but if you do you will miss a lot of what's happening. You can look at human communication as an interaction too, but you will still miss an important part of what's going on. The part you will miss is the ongoing process of self-definition-and-response-to-definition-of-the-other—the person-building part—and you won't see this clearly until you view communication transactionally.

The main reason is that when you see communication as an action you aren't focusing on the *contact between* the persons involved. All you're seeing is one person's choices, one person's behavior. When you see communication is an interaction, you still aren't seeing the contact between person A and person B. You see each person functioning something like a sophisticated billiard ball—reacting to forces from the other billiard balls, the table surface, cue stick, pads, and so on. From an interactional point of view, one's actions are affected by the others, but *who one is* doesn't change.

When you adopt a transactional point of view, though, you can't help but look

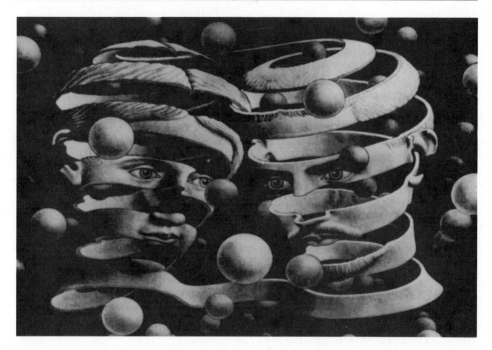

From M. C. Escher: His Life and Work by F. H. Boul, J. R. Kist, J. C. Loder, and F. Wjerda, ed. J. L. Loder (New York: Abrams, 1981). The print is #409, "Bond of Union," April 1956, Lithograph, 253 × 339 (10 × 13 $\frac{3}{8}$").

at the contact *between* the persons involved and the ways that their identities get defined and changed by their communicating. If you focus your attention on just Jack, for example, you realize that since Jack is who he is only in relation to Jill, you have to look immediately at what's happening *between* them. The same goes for Jill. Since *who the persons are*—their "existence and nature"—emerges out of their meeting with each other, you can't help but focus on the meeting itself rather than on the individual meeters.

Relationship

I want to shift vocabularies now and make the same point in slightly different terms. The authors of one of the two or three most influential communication books written in the last twenty-five years earned their well-justified fame in part by distinguishing between the *content* aspect of communication and the *relationship* aspect.[5] The authors' names are Paul Watzlawick, Janet Beavin, and Don Jackson. As they explain, the content aspect of communication is the information, the "facts," the data in the message. The difference between "I'll meet you here in twenty minutes" and "I'll meet you at the post office in an hour" is a difference in communication *content*. Up to the publication of their book, most communication studies focused on content. People concentrated on creating and researching ideas, organizing information systematically, and building persuasive arguments. If attention was paid to style or delivery, it was mainly to insure that the message had vitality, smoothness, or the right amount of ornamentation.

Watzlawick, Beavin, and Jackson argue persuasively that there's also another aspect of communication that most communication scholars and teachers have overlooked, the *relationship* aspect. They call it that because it has to do with the way the people communicating are relating with each other. The difference between "I'll meet you here in twenty minutes" and "Why the hell didn't you call before now? Get over here in twenty minutes or you're in deep trouble!" is a difference in *relationship* communication: It's a difference in how I perceive myself, how I see you, how I see you seeing me, and vice versa—how you perceive yourself, your perception of me, and how you see me seeing you. So whereas the information makes up the content aspect, the relationship aspect refers to the quality, type, or kind of *contact* that's occurring *between* the communicators.

Watzlawick, Beavin, and Jackson point out that the relationship aspect is a part of *all* human communicating. You cannot write, say, or respond to anything without at least implicitly offering a definition of the relationship between yourself and the other(s) involved. In addition, any response from the other will include his or her own definition-and-response-to-yours. For example, if you begin a letter with "Dear Professor Nichols:" the "Professor" title and the colon help define the relationship as more formal than a letter to the same person which begins, "Dear Marie." You decide which to use by noticing how the other person defines herself in relation to you. I've already mentioned in my discussion of basic assumptions how, in face-to-face contacts, the communicators' tone of voice, touch, distance, and eye contact also contribute to this process of relationship defining.

Another way we define the relationships we're in is by organizing—or what Watzlawick, Beavin, and Jackson call "punctuating"—the sequence of communication events we experience. For example, let's assume that a couple you are friends with has heard that you're studying interpersonal communication, so they ask you to help them out. Jill tells you that Jack withdraws all the time; he won't talk with her and it's driving her nuts. Jack tells you that Jill consistently nags him. "Sure I withdraw," he says, "You would too if she nagged you like she does me."

If you were going to apply this insight about relationship communication, you might diagram the couple's relationship as has been done this way.[6]

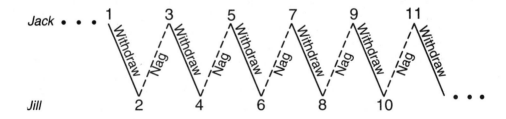

The diagram allows you to see that, for Jill, the sequence goes 1–2–3, 3–4–5, 5–6–7, and so on. She believes that Jack "starts" the pattern; it's his fault because he won't talk to her. As Jill says to you, "I'm just responding to him—like any normal person would."

Jacks sees it differently; for him the sequence goes 2–3–4, 4–5–6, 6–7–8, and so on. He thinks it starts with Jill's nagging, and he's just responding the way any normal person would—by withdrawing. For our purposes, the point is that Jack and Jill each define the relationship differently, depending on how they organize, or "punctuate," it—specifically, where each believes it "starts." The ellipses at the left and right of the diagram indicate that both Jack and Jill are "right" *and* "wrong." Things actually started before this nag–withdraw sequence got going, and they will continue beyond it. The definition of the *between*, the quality of the *contact*, or the *relationship* depends on how each person punctuates the ongoing flow of events.

I want to emphasize that both the relationship aspect of communication and the "punctuation" notion focus your attention not on the individual communicators but on their *contact*, what's *between* them, the *transaction* in which they're involved. It's like the "bridges" in the title of this book. The metaphor of *Bridges Not Walls* is meant to highlight not only the difference between separation and connection but also the importance of the *between*. Think of a bridge that spans a deep canyon. The structure of the bridge is that-which-connects the two sides. When you're focusing on the bridge itself, your attention is not on the forest on one side or the rocks on the other, but on the contact, the relationship, the between.

This is exactly where your attention needs to be if you're going to promote and enhance what this book means by interpersonal communication. As I've already indicated, our inability—or unwillingness—to see communication relationally or transactionally has the most impact when we're in the middle of a conflict. When you're really feeling attacked or arguing with someone, it *seems* obvious that he or she is "making you mad," that the argument is the other person's fault, and that you're "right" about important points and the other person is "wrong." But all these conclusions that *seem* so obvious come from *your point of view, not just from the situation itself.* "Fault" and "blame" loom large because of the lens you're using to look at and understand what's going on.

For example, when you say, "It's her fault that we missed that deadline; she didn't get me the information on time," you're saying that she *caused* the outcome just like a weight on one end of a seesaw causes the other end to rise. You're overlooking all the ways that *other* people's choices—including yours—also contributed to the outcome. The same kind of thing is happening in such common complaints as "That professor bores me," "He hurt my feelings," "She ruined the whole program," "We wouldn't have been confused if he had made it clear," and "Israel caused the current problems in the Mideast." All these statements make communication look and sound like a linear, causal process.

But when you view communication transactionally or relationally, all this has to change. You can't explain a relationship by referring only to one of the relaters. While it may be partly true that "She didn't get me the information on time," I also didn't ask for it until a day before I needed it, and my request wasn't very direct or clear. On my e-mail message asking for the information got lost in cyberspace. As for the Mideast conflict, the PLO, the governments in Syria, Lebanon, Egypt, and Iraq, and the U.S. President and Congress are as tied up in that mess as are the Israelis. Viewing communication as an action or interaction is like trying to explain the features or personality of a child by only referring to one of its parents. Each child is physiologically the product of its parents' sexual *relationship*, and its personality is the product of many different family and cultural *relationships*. There's no single, linear cause of events that happen between persons.

Does this mean that when there are problems, "Nobody's responsible"? Have we given up any possibility of accountability? No, not at all. Individual choices still make important differences, and some choices are definitely better than others—more efficient, ethical, appropriate, effective, or humane. But the transactional and relational viewpoints replace the oversimplified and distorted notions of fault and blame with a more complex and accurate focus on both or all "sides" of the communication process. I *don't* mean you should replace "It's his fault," or "It's her fault" with "It's both of their faults," or "It's nobody's fault." Instead, I encourage you to give up the notion of fault and blame altogether, at least when you're thinking or talking about human communication. It's like asking, "How tall was that baseball game?" The notion of height can't usefully be applied to baseball games. Similarly, the notion of linear causality and its outcomes "fault" and "blame" can't usefully be applied to human communication events.

Another way to put this point is to say that a transactional or relational perspective redefines what is meant by "responsibility." From an actional or interactional point of view, being responsible means being the one who *caused* something to happen. This is what people mean when they say that an ineffective manager is responsible for a drop in sales, or that a parent is responsible for his or her child's high self-esteem. But from a transactional or relational point of view, responsibility means *ability to respond,* not fault, blame, or credit. You are response-able when you have the willingness and the ability to "do something next," to contribute in some hopefully positive way to how things are unfolding. Being "irresponsible" is being unresponsive—ignoring what's going on or dropping out. "Irresponsible" people act without taking into account what else is going on or how their actions affect others. Responsible people may not always do what others want them to, but they are aware of how their choices are part of a larger whole. They (a) understand that they are part of the process, so their actions make a difference, and (b) have some sense of how their actions will affect what's going on.

This redefinition of responsibility is one important outcome of adopting a transactional, relational view of communication. You might want to keep it in mind as you read later in the book what some authors say about communication as "synergy" (this chapter), the transactional nature of person perception (Chapter 6), dialogic listening (Chapter 7), negotiating selves (Chapter 10), friendship (Chapter 11), family communicating (Chapter 12), communication with intimate partners (Chapter 13), and conflict (Chapter 14).

A final important result of giving up the notions of fault and blame is that you recognize that you cannot control or determine by yourself the quality of the communication you experience. In other words, you alone cannot make interpersonal quality communication happen. Since communication occurs *between* persons, all you can control is your part of the process.

Does this mean that you're powerless, that the quality of your communication will be determined by what others do? Again, not at all. Your choices, attitudes, and behaviors can and do contribute substantially to what goes on between you and others. You can promote, encourage, facilitate, or help interpersonal communication happen. You can also discourage it. But you yourself cannot *control* something that's understood to be transactional or relational.

Summary

In short, when I use the term *interpersonal communication* I mean "contact between persons." That sounds pretty simple, but both key concepts—*contact between* and *persons*—carry a lot of meaning in this statement. *Persons* are unique, unmeasurable, choosing, reflective, and addressable. The synonyms for *contact* are "union," "connection," "adhesion," "joining," and "touch." So *contact between* occurs outside of individuals, at the points where they intersect. This means that *contact between* persons is mutual and collaborative, even when it's the contact of an argument, a fistfight, or a lawsuit. (Fighters collaborate, for example, on where they're going to duke it out and whether kicking, biting, and weapons are part of the fight.) Contact requires at least two, and it can't be understood by paying attention only to one person or "side." You have to focus on where the people meet or "touch"—the "bridges" in this book's title. If you keep in mind what it is to be a person and what's meant by contact, you can come up with a fairly straightforward definition of interpersonal communication:

> Interpersonal communication is the kind, type, or quality of contact that happens when two or more humans are willing and able to meet as persons by making available some of their uniqueness, unmeasurable aspects, choices, reflectiveness, and addressability, and at the same time being aware of and responsive to some of the other's personness. Or more briefly, *interpersonal communication is the quality of contact that happens when each person involved talks and listens in ways that maximize the presence of the personal.*

As I suggested earlier, this means that you can think of interpersonal communication in terms of the following continuum or sliding scale:[7]

TYPES OR QUALITIES OF COMMUNICATION
Impersonal -**Interpersonal**

Sometimes people make available almost nothing of their uniqueness or choices by presenting themselves as "just another customer," for example, who wants to exchange these stockings for a different colored pair. In this instance, the customer may also see the person behind the counter as "just another clerk," and the clerk may reciprocate in kind by only making available his or her role definition and by perceiving the customer as just that and nothing else. When both persons make these choices, their communication (their contact) fits somewhere near the left-hand end of the Impersonal-Interpersonal continuum. And, importantly, that's often just fine. In many situations, there's nothing wrong with *impersonal* communication. It's exactly what's expected and needed.

In other situations, one person discloses a little bit of her uniqueness, feelings, choices, and uncertainties (reflectiveness), because she perceives the other person as an especially sympathetic and informed listener, and at the same time the other person listens in a generally supportive way, without responding in great detail. When both persons make these choices, their communication fits somewhere near the middle of the Impersonal-Interpersonal continuum.

In still other situations, both persons disclose in considerable breadth and depth what they think and feel about the topic they're discussing, and both listen with care and understanding to the other's thoughts and feelings, even though they may not agree with everything they hear. In this case, their communication fits somewhere near the right-hand end of the continuum.

So this definition and the continuum or sliding scale that goes with it can function, first, *descriptively*, as a simple but potentially detailed model of interpersonal communication. But they can also function *prescriptively*, as an indicator of what you *ought* to do when you want the communication you experience to be more impersonal or more interpersonal. The basic prescriptive message is this: When you want your communication to move toward the right-hand end of the sliding scale, (a) make available more of what makes you a person, and (b) pay more careful attention to what makes the other a person. If the other person does some of the same things, the contact between you will be more interpersonal than impersonal. On the other hand, when you want your communication to move toward the left-hand end of the sliding scale, (a) only disclose your impersonal features, and (b) only pay attention to the other's impersonal features. If he or she makes similar choices, the contact between you will be more impersonal than interpersonal. But remember, you can't *control* where your communication is on this continuum; your choices are only part of the whole.

"Wait a minute!" you might be saying. "This is getting complicated!" "How am I supposed to remember to do all of this at once, and what if I don't know what it means to 'disclose what makes me a person' or 'pay attention to the other's impersonal features'??"

My response is that this whole book is organized around this definition, and all of its readings are designed to help you do what I've outlined here. Part 1 is called "The Basic Ingredients," and it lays the foundation for this approach. The first of the two remaining articles in this chapter expands on the connection between quality of communication and quality of life, and the other one provides a second description of what it means for communication to be mutual and collaborative—"synergistic." The other two chapters in Part 1 treat the verbal parts of the process (Chapter 3) and the nonverbal basic ingredients (Chapter 4).

Part 2 and Part 3 lay out the skills that will enable you to affect where your communication is on the Impersonal-Interpersonal continuum. Part 2 is called "Openness as 'Inhaling,'" and Part 3 is called "Openness as 'Exhaling.'" I've labeled them this way for a couple of reasons. First, I want to acknowledge that communication contact is made up of two parts or "moves": "input and output," "receiving and sending," "listening and talking." But those labels are misleading, because they're not relational; they highlight the sides of the canyon rather than the bridge. So I've chosen two other language strategies.

First, I've used the word "openness," because it has two meanings. "Being open" can mean being both receptive to others' ideas and feelings *and* willing to disclose. A person can be open in the sense that he or she is tolerant, broadminded, and willing to listen (open to "input") and open in the sense that he or she does not hesitate to share ideas and feelings with others (open with "output"). So I use "open" in the titles of both Part 2 and Part 3.

My second language move is to use "exhaling" and "inhaling" to identify which sense of openness each Part deals with. I chose these words because each of us has first-hand experience with how inseparable they are. Try inhaling without exhaling or vice versa. I'd like you to think of "input and output" or "receiving and sending" this way too—as inseparable, *always* occurring together. The one disadvantage is that inhaling and exhaling can't happen simultaneously, but both senses of openness can and do. So my choice of labels is a bit of a compromise. But I hope that the titles for Parts 2 and 3 help reinforce the transactional, relational point I've been making.

Part 2, "Openness as 'Inhaling,'" treats the three skillsets that make up this element of the process: self-awareness (Chapter 5), awareness of the other (Chapter 6), and listening (Chapter 7). So the readings in these three chapters are designed to help you know better how to perceive, be aware, and listen in ways that can promote interpersonal, or, if you choose, impersonal communicating. The two chapters in Part 3, "Openness as 'Exhaling,'" focus on the other side of the equation. The readings in Chapter 8 discuss self disclosure, and those in Chapter 9 analyze the differences between women's and men's expressive styles. By the time you're through Chapter 9, you'll have an overview of the whole process and a sense of the basic interpersonal communication attitudes and skills.

Then the readings in Part 4, "Relationships", turn to application. There's a chapter on negotiating relationships generally (Chapter 10), which is followed by specific chapters on friendship (Chapter 11), families (Chapter 12), and intimate partners (Chapter 13). Part 5, Bridging Differences, then focuses on the most difficult kinds of application: conflict (Chapter 14), and communicating across cultures (Chapter 15).

The final three chapters in the book present three overall approaches to interpersonal communication that synthesize the ideas in all the previous readings. One approach comes from an experienced teacher, one from a counselor-psychotherapist, and one from Martin Buber, the philosopher I've quoted who spent most of his life encouraging people to communicate interpersonally.

So this is what's coming and how it fits together. I hope the ideas and suggestions in these readings work for you. They make a real difference to me!

Notes

1. Paraphrased from Martin Buber, *I and Thou*, trans. Walter Kaufmann (New York: Scribner, 1970), pp. 82–84.
2. Buber, p. 145.
3. George A. Kelly, "The Autobiography of a Theory," *Clinical Psychology and Personality: The Selected Papers of George Kelly*, ed. Brendan Maher (New York: Wiley, 1969), p. 47.
4. Horace B. English and Ava Champney English, *A Comprehensive Dictionary of Psychological and Psychoanalytical Terms* (New York: Longmans, Green, 1958), p. 561.
5. Paul Watzlawick, Janet Helmick Beavin, and Don D. Jackson, *Pragmatics of Human Communication* (New York: Norton, 1968), see especially Chapter 2.
6. Watzlawick, Beavin, and Jackson, pp. 54–59.
7. Carole Logan and I offer another description of this approach to interpersonal communication in the first two chapters of *Together: Communicating Interpersonally*, 4th ed. (New York: McGraw-Hill, 1993).

Review Questions

1. True or False: According to my definition, interpersonal communication can't happen between two people who are talking to each other on the telephone. Explain.
2. What does Buber mean when he says that humans have a "twofold perspective"?
3. What does it mean to say that humans can't be described completely in spatiotemporal terms?
4. What's the relationship between choice and fault/blame?
5. In your own words, describe the two features of communication that become evident when you look at the process transactionally.
6. According to Watzlawick, Beavin, and Jackson, what does it mean to "punctuate a communication sequence"?
7. Why do I use the terms *openness, inhaling,* and *exhaling* as I do in the divisions of this book?

Probes

1. Does this essay claim that people who experience a certain kind or quality of communication are actually "more human" or "more persons" than those who don't? If so, how can that be? What does it mean to be "more" or "less" *human?*
2. What's the relationship between the human characteristics of *choice* and *predictability?*
3. Give your own description of *addressability*. What does it mean to be able to talk *to* and *with* someone as contrasted with only being able to talk *about* him or her?
4. Squeeze together the thumb and index finger of your left hand. Now describe their *contact*— not what the thumb is doing or what the index finger is doing, but their *contact*. (You'll probably find that it's difficult to describe contact. This is one reason why I use two different terms—*transactional* and *relational*.)
5. Think back to the last argument you had. Try applying what I say about "fault and blame" and "response-ability" to this event. What do you notice? What happens to your understanding of the argument?

The following pages come from one of the books I quoted in the introductory essay. As I mentioned there, James Lynch is a professor and clinic director at the University of Maryland School of Medicine. Since the early 1980s, he's written extensively about the impact of dialogue on our physical health. His books contain a great deal of detailed evidence about how the quality of the communication we experience affects the quality of our lives.

This is the introduction to his most recent book, The Language of the Heart. He argues here that "human dialogue not only affects our hearts significantly but can even alter the biochemistry of individual tissues at the further extremities of the body." To some people, that probably sounds like eastern mysticism or New Age pseudoscience. But Lynch's documentation is impressive; in his book, he cites literally hundreds of medical studies that support his claims. He also points out that it is difficult for some people to accept the link between dialogue and physical health, because we've been taught for years that the human body is essentially a complex machine. We know that talk, human conversation, or dialogue is not reducible without remainder to the programmable, cause-and-effect elements of mechanics. And yet this nonmechanical phenomenon significantly affects our allegedly mechanical bodies. How can that be?

Without trying to provide an easy answer to this question, Lynch briefly describes what he believes are the historical ideas and attitudes that have led us to our current picture of the human body. And he tells how the discoveries he and his colleagues are making are beginning to provide the foundation for a new type of clinic that integrates medicine and speech communication.

I include this essay in order to encourage you to think about how the communication *you* experience is more than just a way to accomplish tasks, negotiate deals, and get your needs met. There's an important link between how you talk and *who you are*. No complete study of speech communication in any of its forms—public speaking, argumentation, organizational communication, media, or interpersonal relationships—should overlook this link.

The Language of the Heart

James J. Lynch

It is obvious that we human beings are distinguished from all other living creatures by the fact that we speak. Whether man or woman or child, we can share our desires, thoughts, plans, and—above all—feelings with each other through dialogue. Coupled to this is another simple yet sublime truth: that while we speak with words, we speak also with our flesh and blood. As we shall see, study after study reveals that human dialogue not only affects our hearts significantly but can even alter the biochemistry of individual tissues at the further extremities of the body. Since blood flows through every human tissue, the entire body is influenced by human dialogue. Thus, it is true that when we speak we do so with every fiber of our being.

This "language of the heart" is integral to the health and emotional life of every one of us. Yet this vital truth has been largely obscured by a scientific-philosophical perspective we all share and that leads us to think about the human body solely in terms of its mechanical functions. In an age dominated by dramatic images of heart transplants, artificial heart machines, and even the implantation of a baboon's heart into a human baby, it is all too easy to look on the human body solely as a machine incapable of either listening or speaking to others. Nonetheless, the essence of the human being is the body's involvement in dialogue—a process in which no machine can ever engage. For the human heart speaks a language that not only is vital to our well-being but makes possible human feelings and binds human beings together. . . .

To appreciate why we tend to think about the body as a machine, we need only recall an outstanding event of late 1982 and early 1983. For the first time ever, at the University of Utah's Medical Center in Salt Lake City, the life of a human being was sustained by an artificial heart machine. The public's response to this endeavor was electric, perhaps equaled only by the excitement over the first heart transplant operation performed by Christiaan Barnard in Capetown, South Africa, in 1969. And, as in that earlier operation, hourly news bulletins told the world of Dr. Clark's progress, as relentlessly and efficiently pulsating with the timed sighs of its own air compressors, a machine outside of his body kept the life-sustaining fluid—blood—flowing through it. For 112 days, the machine kept beating, pumping blood through his body, until with the failure of other organs, his circulatory system collapsed, and he died. Thirteen hundred mourners, including a personal representative of the President of the United States, attended his funeral in the town of Federal Way in the state of Washington.

Clearly, not only Dr. Clark but the medical profession had attempted, and accomplished, a heroic and extraordinary feat. Moreover, this feat, heralded all over the world, was the culmination of a belief on which medical scientists have acted for over three centuries: that is, that the human body is made up of a group of essentially mechanical organs that, when not running properly, can be tinkered with, like any mechanism, in the hope of setting it right again.

From *The Language of the Heart: The Human Body in Dialogue* by James J. Lynch. Reprinted by permission of Basic Books, Inc., Publishers.

At about the same time, my colleagues and I at the Psychophysiological Clinic at the University of Maryland Medical School, were seeing, also for the first time, quite a different aspect of the human cardiovascular system that would lead us to develop an entirely new type of clinic, one based on an understanding of the connection between human communication and the cardiovascular system. For computer technology allowed us to see that as soon as one begins to speak, one's blood pressure increases significantly, one's heart beats faster and harder, and microscopic blood vessels in distant parts of the body change as well. Conversely, when one listens to others speak or truly attends to the external environment in a relaxed manner, then blood pressure usually falls and heart rate slows, frequently below its normal resting levels.

Initially, this discovery seemed more a curiosity than a conceptual breakthrough, especially when contrasted with the human and technical drama in Utah. Yet the data were so clear and so predictably consistent that we could not ignore them. They showed us that centuries of religious, philosophical, literary, and poetic wisdom that had suggested links between words and the human heart contained the core of an astonishingly fertile truth, and one central to medicine. Once aware of this truth, we tested for it in a variety of cases and research studies. We examined thousands of individuals, from newborn babies crying in their cribs; to preschool children reciting their ABCs; to grade-school children reading aloud from textbooks; to nursing and medical students describing their daily work routine; to hypertensive patients in our clinic, and those waiting anxiously for cardiac by-pass surgery; to schizophrenics in psychiatric wards; to elderly patients in nursing homes describing their loneliness, and in patients close to death. In each and every one, the link between language and the heart was clear and undeniable.

Yet, as I shall discuss, there was a powerful force that made it initially difficult for us to appreciate fully that we were indeed creating a new type of clinic. That force had to do, as I have said, with an unexamined philosophical perspective we brought to our own research. It included a vision of the human body shared by virtually everyone in our society, and first formulated by the French philosopher René Descartes in the seventeenth century. Living in an era that witnessed the beginnings of modern science, Descartes harnessed the discoveries of scientists like Galileo, Copernicus, Kepler, Harvey, and Pascal and cast their findings into a new and comprehensive philosophical system. As Descartes himself stated, he intended to create a totally new medicine, one based on the idea that the human body is a machine. He accomplished his goal so brilliantly that his influence, though pervasive, is scarcely understood today. Rather, like the air we breathe, his perspective is simply taken for granted.

Descartes promulgated and defended the idea that the human body functions like all other bodies in nature, according to mechanical principles. He separated mental functioning from bodily mechanics, arguing that the capacity to think has to be the result of the existence of the human soul. While ostensibly innocent, it was an extraordinary vision, one that permeates the way we in the Western world came to understand the nature of human beings, the human body, human health, and the links between our individual bodies and our social existence. After Descartes, issues of health and illness were relegated strictly to medical science; while spiritual and social concerns came to be seen as having little in common with physical health.* Physicians

---

*Descartes's influence was every bit as pronounced in religious circles as in medicine. Thus, today no theological school—be it Catholic, Protestant, or Rabbinical—deems it necessary to teach its students elementary anatomy and physiology. The body is considered utterly irrelevant to religious questions, even though the Bible was rooted in such concerns (for example, Talmudic dietary regulations, or Christian and Judaic

would come to be trained much as were the highly skilled technicians who maintained the French water gardens where statues were cleverly designed to move by means of water pressure, and that helped to inspire Descartes's concept. Three centuries after him, it would make "perfect sense" to think about a heart transplant in a human being much as a mechanic thinks about replacing a faulty water pump in an automobile: heart disease had become a mechanical problem in a faulty hydraulic system. Indeed, as the doctor treating the baby girl with the transplanted baboon heart said, "The heart . . . 'is a muscular pump and is not the seat of the soul.'"[1]

The stage, thus, was set with Descartes. From then on, thinker after thinker, scientist after scientist—including, as we shall see, those seminal masters of modern times, Marx, Darwin, Freud, and Pavlov—thought about the human body in mechanical terms. Whether in social evolution or in social revolution, the body was uncritically accepted to be an isolated, self-contained group of organs functioning strictly according to mechanical principles. In the process, the emotional life of human beings came to be seen as a reflection of mechanical functions inside a well-regulated machine. Unique aspects of human emotional life and the unique nature of human speech were obscured by a scientific perspective that accepted the human body as mechanically similar to other animal bodies, and human emotional life as comparable to the emotional life of animals.

Our thinking about these issues has developed over two decades of research. When we originally began our journey, we sought to understand how human relationships and human loneliness affect cardiovascular health. In 1977, I summarized our findings in *The Broken Heart*.[2] That book was based on the fact that human loneliness is among the most important causes of premature death in modern America. In our studies, for virtually every cause of death—whether suicide, cancer, cirrhosis of the liver, automobile accident, or heart disease—the incidence of premature death was far higher among people who lived alone than among those who were married. While in certain cases—such as suicide, cirrhosis of the liver, or lung cancer—we could easily detect the factors that caused premature death, in others the mechanisms were far less clearcut, especially for heart disease, the leading cause of death in the United States. It was far from obvious why the single, the widowed, and the divorced were two to four times more likely than married people to die prematurely from hypertension, stroke, and coronary heart disease.

While human loneliness appeared to be the single most important and compelling emotional factor in these premature deaths, we were at a loss to explain how this feeling state influenced the heart. Though the statistics were unambiguous, we did not understand how a human experience such as loss or bereavement could lead to premature death from hypertension, stroke, or heart attack any more than we understood how loneliness caused elevations in blood pressure. While pondering this question, we were equally troubled about how to counteract this problem effectively, since many of the patients who appeared in the coronary-care unit recapitulated the very statistics we had uncovered linking loneliness to increased risk of heart disease.

---

notions about blood and the heart). Hospital chaplains are today trained so as to feel no need to understand even the most rudimentary aspects of physical disease; instead, they see their job as caring for the soul. Likewise, psychologists can go through college and graduate school without any training in anatomy and physiology. And even the most elementary introductory courses in psychology or philosophy are not required to gain entrance to medical schools, though such schools do require advanced training in calculus, physics, and chemistry.

These questions led us to explore loneliness in hypertensive patients. Since hypertension was, and still is, the single most important medical problem in modern America (it has been estimated that anywhere between forty million to sixty million Americans are hypertensive), we assumed that loneliness played an important role in the problem in at least a significant percentage of these cases.

Yet our efforts to examine the interlocking problem of human loneliness and hypertension quickly confronted us with a whole series of paradoxes. While it seemed intuitively obvious that human dialogue ought to be the best antidote to human loneliness, a large and well-documented literature had amply warned that certain types of social interaction can cause marked increases in the blood pressure of hypertensive patients. Even more to the point, the type of psychotherapeutic dialogue that seemed best suited to delve into issues surrounding the loneliness of hypertensive patients had already been shown to be precisely the type of encounter that would cause their blood pressure to rise to dangerous levels. This problem was compounded further when we discovered a striking relationship between speaking and blood pressure. While the blood pressure of almost everyone we tested rose during speech, that of hypertensive patients increased far more than that of any other group. Sometimes a hypertensive person's blood pressure would surge 50 percent above the resting baseline level as soon as he or she began to speak. Thus, we were forced to recognize that our psychotherapeutic "cure" could make hypertension worse. We began to wonder whether hypertensive patients were trapped inside their own bodies, damned if they withdrew from their fellow human beings and damned if they tried to relate to them.

Through our efforts to reconcile this dilemma, we uncovered a new dimension of the cardiovascular system which allowed us to develop an entirely new way to approach the treatment of vascular disorders, such as hypertension and migraine headaches. And we came finally to recognize that the human cardiovascular system does far more than change in response to internal and external demands: it also communicates. Since our hearts can speak a language that no one hears or sees and therefore cannot understand, we can get sick at heart. . . .

In machines created by humans, it is perfectly clear who and what controls the internal mechanisms and why a particular machine, such as the pump that replaced Barney Clark's heart, was created. That pump was designed to fill a particular purpose, and it was absolutely regulated by its creators. Yet who is in charge of, and what controls, the machinery of the human heart is another matter. Control is exercised from both inside and outside. This idea, though simple when it first occurred to us, gradually led us to understand that internal bodily mechanisms, such as blood pressure, long thought to be primarily regulated by the internal machinery of the human body, are also powerfully influenced by the force of human dialogue. Once this force was recognized, we came to understand that dialogue gives the body its very humanity.

Since human dialogue, and its relationship to our hearts and feelings, is the central issue of this book, let me define it as I did in *The Broken Heart*:

> In its most general meaning, dialogue consists of reciprocal communication between two or more living creatures. It involves the sharing of thoughts, physical sensations, ideas, ideals, hopes, and feelings. In sum, dialogue involves the reciprocal sharing of any and all life experiences. . . .
>
> Other characteristics of the process of dialogue are that it is reciprocal, spontaneous, often nonverbal, *and* alive.[3]

At the core of this book is the idea that we human beings are biologically inter-related—and that any attempt to maintain or restore health must be based on that reality. Scientific attempts to understand the human body apart from the most basic of all human traits—the fact that we speak—[are] all too likely to produce a medicine that brilliantly treats isolated parts of the human body, while it seriously neglects the individual as a whole and as part of nature. We can understand and cope with illness only when we are able to view ourselves as part of a complex world beyond the con-fines of our own individual skin. The response of our hearts, blood vessels, and muscles when we communicate with spouse, children, friends, colleagues, and the larger com-munity has as much to do with our cardiovascular health as do factors such as exercise or diet.

So vital to human health is the language of our hearts that—if ignored, unheard, or misunderstood—it can produce terrible physical suffering, even premature death. For the language of our hearts cries out to be heard. It demands to be understood. And it must not be denied. Our hearts speak with an eloquence that poets have always, and truly, sensed. It is for us to learn to listen and to understand.

Notes

1. *The New York Times*, October 31, 1984, p. A18.
2. James J. Lynch, *The Broken Heart: The Medical Consequences of Loneliness* (New York: Basic Books, 1977).
3. Lynch, pp. 217, 218.

Review Questions

1. Lynch claims that a "vital truth" has been "largely obscured" by our mechanistic scientific-philosophical perspective. What is this "vital truth"?
2. What is the primary distinctive feature of the approach to cardiovascular health that Dr. Lynch and his colleagues are taking in their clinic at the University of Maryland?
3. Lynch claims that a seventeenth-century philosopher named _____ is primarily responsi-ble for our current mechanical view of the human body.
4. Our mechanical view of the human body begins from the belief that there is a fundamental separation between what and what?
5. What has Dr. Lynch's research shown about the relationships between loneliness, heart dis-ease, and dialogue?
6. Lynch believes that, if our efforts to understand the human body don't pay attention to speech, what will occur? What problem will the neglect of speech create?

Probes

1. Based on your own experience with the medical profession, how do you think most medical doctors might be responding to Lynch's belief that doctors can learn from "centuries of reli-gious, philosophical, literary, and poetic wisdom"?
2. Is Lynch arguing that Descartes single-handedly established our modern view of the human body? What's his point here?
3. Lynch implies that Descartes' scientific-philosophical perspective especially affected the way we view *speech*? What does he say about this topic?
4. What does Lynch mean when he says that control of the human heart is exercised from both inside and outside"?
5. What's the relationship between Lynch's definition of dialogue and my definition of inter-personal communication?

T his reading is here because of the first three letters in its title. "Syn" is the Greek prefix that means "with," so "synergy" is energy that people create by working with one another or by collaborating. This means that "synergistic communication" is the positive form of what happens when people experience the kind of *contact* I talked about in this chapter's first reading.

Stephen R. Covey wrote these words near the end of his book called *The Seven Habits of Highly Effective People*. He calls synergy the "crowning principle" of all the habits, the dynamic that makes them all work together. If you can practice this kind of communication, Covey argues, you can become more effective both at work and with your family.

Importantly, synergy is different from compromise. As Covey puts, it, compromise means that $1 + 1 = 1\frac{1}{2}$. Each party to a compromise gets part of what he or she wants, but each also has to give up something. Synergy, though, means that "$1 = 1$ may equal 8, 16, or even 1,600." When people are working together in this way, they can achieve new insights and create new solutions that go well beyond their individual capabilities.

And this is more than pie-in-the-sky theorizing. Covey is obviously not naive enough to believe that everybody will always agree—or even agree to disagree. But he gives several concrete examples of how people who are committed to their relationship, trust each other, and are willing to collaborate can come up with creative, win/win solutions to actual problems they face.

He also talks about negative synergy, the kind that makes relationships worse instead of better. When people who are actually interdependent act as if they're independent, lots of time and energy go into "confessing other people's sins, politicking, rivalry, interpersonal conflict, protecting one's backside, masterminding, and second guessing." Sometimes these people also focus on trying to clone others, to mold them over into their own thinking, rather than accepting and working with the ways they're different. In fact, Covey believes that valuing differences between people is the essence of synergy. This means that the first step toward communicating productively with someone who's very different from you—in ethnicity, age, sexual preference, gender, or politics—is to see the differences as potential pluses rather than obstacles to creative agreement.

Covey doesn't focus on specific how-tos in this essay. They come in the articles that make up later chapters of *Bridges Not Walls*. But the mind-set he outlines here is vital for just about everything that follows.

Synergistic Communication

Stephen R. Covey

When you communicate synergistically, you are simply opening your mind and heart and expressions to new possibilities, new alternatives, new options. You're not sure when you engage in synergistic communication how things will work out or what the end will look like, but you do have an inward sense of excitement and security and adventure, believing that it will be significantly better than it was before. And that is the end that you have in mind.

You begin with the belief that parties involved will gain more insight, and that the excitement of that mutual learning and insight will create a momentum toward more and more insights, learnings, and growth.

Many people have not really experienced even a moderate degree of synergy in their family life or in other interactions. They've been trained and scripted into defensive and protective communications or into believing that life or other people can't be trusted. This represents one of the great tragedies and wastes in life, because so much potential remains untapped—completely undeveloped and unused. Ineffective people live day after day with unused potential. They experience synergy only in small, peripheral ways in their lives.

They may have memories of some unusual creative experiences, perhaps in athletics, where they were involved in a real team spirit for a period of time. Or perhaps they were in an emergency situation where people cooperated to an unusually high degree and submerged ego and pride in an effort to save someone's life or to produce a solution to a crisis.

To many, such events may seem unusual, almost out of character with life, even miraculous. But this is not so. These things can be produced regularly, consistently, almost daily in people's lives. But it requires enormous personal security and openness and a spirit of adventure.

Most all creative endeavors are somewhat unpredictable. They often seem ambiguous, hit-or-miss, trial and error. And unless people have a high tolerance for ambiguity and get their security from integrity to principles and inner values they find it unnerving and unpleasant to be involved in highly creative enterprises. Their need for structure, certainty, and predictability is too high.

Synergy and Communication

Synergy is exciting. Creativity is exciting. It's phenomenal what openness and communication can produce. The possibilities of truly significant gain, of significant improvement are so real that it's worth the risk such openness entails.

After World War II, the United States commissioned David Lilienthal to head the new Atomic Energy Commission. Lilienthal brought together a group of people who were highly influential—celebrities in their own right—disciples, as it were, of their own frames of reference.

This very diverse group of individuals had an extremely heavy agenda, and they were impatient to get at it. In addition, the press was pushing them.

But Lilienthal took several weeks to create a high Emotional Bank Account. He had these people get to know each other—their interests, their hopes, their goals, their concerns, their backgrounds, their frames of reference, their paradigms. He facilitated the kind of human interaction that creates a great bonding between people, and he was heavily criticized for taking the time to do it because it wasn't "efficient."

But the net result was that this group became closely knit together, very open with each other, very creative, and synergistic. The respect among the members of the commission was so high that if there was disagreement, instead of opposition and defense, there was a genuine effort to understand. The attitude was "If a person of your intelligence and competence and commitment disagrees with me, then there must be something to your disagreement that I don't understand, and I need to understand it. You have a perspective, a frame of reference I need to look at." Nonprotective interaction developed, and an unusual culture was born.

The following diagram illustrates how closely trust is related to different levels of communication.

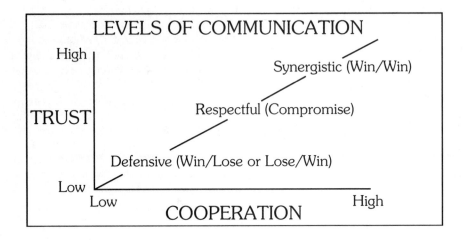

The lowest level of communication coming out of low-trust situations would be characterized by defensiveness, protectiveness, and often legalistic language, which covers all the bases and spells out qualifiers and the escape clauses in the event things go sour. Such communication produces only Win/Lose or Lose/Lose. It isn't effective . . . and it creates further reasons to defend and protect.

The middle position is respectful communication. This is the level where fairly mature people interact. They have respect for each other, but they want to avoid the possibility of ugly confrontations, so they communicate politely but not empathically. They might understand each other intellectually, but they really don't deeply look at the paradigms and assumptions underlying their own positions and become open to new possibilities.

Respectful communication works in independent situations and even in interdependent situations, but the creative possibilities are not opened up. In interdependent situations compromise is the position usually taken. Compromise means that $1 + 1 = 1\frac{1}{2}$. Both give and take. The communication isn't defensive or protective or angry or manipulative; it is honest and genuine and respectful. But it isn't creative or synergistic. It produces a low form of Win/Win.

Synergy means that $1 + 1$ may equal 8, 16, or even 1,600. The synergistic position of high trust produces solutions better than any originally proposed, and all parties know it. Furthermore, they genuinely enjoy the creative enterprise. A miniculture is formed to satisfy in and of itself. . . .

There are some circumstances in which synergy may not be achievable and No Deal isn't viable. But even in these circumstances, the spirit of sincere trying will usually result in a more effective compromise.

Fishing for the Third Alternative

To get a better idea of how our level of communication affects our independent effectiveness, envision the following scenario:

It's vacation time, and a husband wants to take his family out to the lake country to enjoy camping and fishing. This is important to him; he's been planning it all year. He's made reservations at a cottage on the lake and arranged to rent a boat, and his sons are really excited about going.

His wife, however, wants to use the vacation time to visit her ailing mother some 250 miles away. She doesn't have the opportunity to see her very often, and this is important to her.

Their differences could be the cause of a major negative experience.

"The plans are set. The boys are excited. We should go on the fishing trip," he says.

"But we don't know how much longer my mother will be around, and I want to be by her," she replies. "This is our only opportunity to have enough time to do that."

"All year long we've looked forward to this one-week vacation. The boys would be miserable sitting around grandmother's house for a week. They'd drive everybody crazy. Besides, your mother's not that sick. And she has your sister less than a mile away to take care of her."

"She's my mother, too. I want to be with her."

"You could phone her every night. And we're planning to spend time with her at the Christmas family reunion. Remember?"

"That's not for five more months. We don't even know if she'll still be here by then. Besides, she needs me, and she wants me."

"She's being well taken care of. Besides, the boys and I need you, too."

"My mother is more important than fishing."

"Your husband and sons are more important than your mother."

As they disagree, back and forth, they finally may come up with some kind of compromise. They may decide to split up—he takes the boys fishing at the lake while she visits her mother. And they both feel guilty and unhappy. The boys sense it, and it affects their enjoyment of the vacation.

The husband may give in to his wife, but he does it grudgingly. And consciously or unconsciously, he produces evidence to fulfill his prophecy of how miserable the week will be for everyone.

The wife may give in to her husband, but she's withdrawn and overreactive to any new developments in her mother's health situation. If her mother were to become seriously ill and die, the husband could never forgive himself, and she couldn't forgive him either.

Whatever compromise they finally agree on, it could be rehearsed over the years as evidence of insensitivity, neglect, or a bad priority decision on either part. It could be a source of contention for years and could even polarize the family. Many marriages that once were beautiful and soft and spontaneous and loving have deteriorated to the level of a hostility through a series of incidents just like this.

The husband and wife see the situation differently. And that difference can polarize them, separate them, create wedges in the relationship. Or it can bring them closer together on a higher level. If they have cultivated the habits of effective interdependence, they approach their differences from an entirely different paradigm. Their communication is on a higher level.

Because they have a high Emotional Bank Account, they have trust and open communication in their marriage. Because they think Win/Win, they believe in a third alternative, a solution that is mutually beneficial and is better than what either of them originally proposed. Because they listen empathically and seek first to understand, they create within themselves and between them a comprehensive picture of the values and the concerns that need to be taken into account in making a decision.

And the combination of those ingredients—the high Emotional Bank Account, thinking Win/Win, and seeking first to understand—creates the ideal environment for synergy.

Buddhism calls this "the middle way." *Middle* in this sense does not mean compromise; it means higher, like the apex of the triangle.

In searching for the "middle" or higher way, this husband and wife realize that their love, their relationship, is part of their synergy.

As they communicate, the husband really, deeply feels his wife's desire, her need to be with her mother. He understands how she wants to relieve her sister, who has had the primary responsibility for their mother's care. He understands that they really don't know how long she will be with them, and that she certainly is more important than fishing.

And the wife deeply understands her husband's desire to have the family together and to provide a great experience for the boys. She realizes the investment that has been made in lessons and equipment to prepare for this fishing vacation, and she feels the importance of creating good memories with them.

So they pool those desires. And they're not on opposite sides of the problem. They're together on one side, looking at the problem, understanding the needs, and working to create a third alternative that will meet them.

"Maybe we could arrange another time within the month for you to visit with your mother," he suggests. "I could take over the home responsibilities for the weekend and arrange for some help at the first of the week so that you could go. I know it's important to you to have that time.

"Or maybe we could locate a place to camp and fish that would be close to your mother. The area wouldn't be as nice, but we could still be outdoors and meet other needs as well. And the boys wouldn't be climbing the walls. We could even plan some recreational activities with the cousins, aunts, and uncles, which would be an added benefit."

They synergize. They communicate back and forth until they come up with a solution they both feel good about. It's better than the solutions either of them originally proposed. It's better than compromise. It's a synergistic solution. . . .

Negative Synergy

Seeking the third alternative is a major paradigm shift from the dichotomous, either/or mentality. But look at the difference in results!

How much negative energy is typically expended when people try to solve problems or make decisions in an interdependent reality? How much time is spent in confessing other people's sins, politicking, rivalry, interpersonal conflict, protecting one's backside, masterminding, and second guessing? It's like trying to drive down the road with one foot on the gas and the other foot on the brake!

And instead of getting a foot off the brake, most people give it more gas. They try to apply more pressure, more eloquence, more logical information to strengthen their position.

The problem is that highly dependent people are trying to succeed in an inter-dependent reality. They're either dependent on borrowing strength from position power and they go for Win/Lose, or they're dependent on being popular with others and they go for Lose/Win. They may talk Win/Win technique, but they don't really want to listen; they want to manipulate. And synergy can't thrive in that environment.

Insecure people think that all reality should be amenable to their paradigms. They have a high need to clone others, to mold them over into their own thinking. They don't realize that the very strength of the relationship is in having another point of view. Sameness is not oneness; uniformity is not unity. Unity, or oneness is comple-mentariness, not sameness. Sameness is uncreative . . . and boring. These essence of synergy is to value the differences.

I've come to believe that the key to interpersonal synergy is intrapersonal syner-gy, that is synergy within ourselves. . . . People who are scripted deeply in logical, ver-bal, left-brain thinking will discover how totally inadequate that thinking is in solving problems which require a great deal of creativity. They become aware and begin to open up a new script inside their right brain. It's not that the right brain wasn't there; it just lay dormant. The muscles had not been developed, or perhaps they had atro-phied after early childhood because of the heavy left-brain emphasis of formal educa-tion or social scripting.

When a person has access to both the intuitive, creative, and visual right brain, and the analytical, logical, verbal left brain, then the whole brain is working. In other words, there is psychic synergy taking place in our own head. And this tool is best suit-ed to the reality of what life is, because life is not just logical—it is also emotional.

One day I was presenting a seminar which I titled, "Manage from the Left, Lead from the Right" to a company in Orlando, Florida. During the break, the president of the company came up to me and said, "Stephen, this is intriguing. But I have been thinking about this material more in terms of its application to my marriage than to my business. My wife and I have a real communication problem. I wonder if you would have lunch with the two of us and just kind of watch how we talk to each other?"

"Let's do it," I replied.

As we sat down together, we exchanged a few pleasantries. Then this man turned to his wife and said, "Now, honey, I've invited Stephen to have lunch with us to see if he could help us in our communication with each other. I know you feel I should be a more sensitive, considerate husband. Could you give me something specific you think I ought to do?" His dominant left brain wanted facts, figures, specifics, parts.

"Well, as I've told you before, it's nothing specific. It's more of a general sense I have about priorities." Her dominant right brain was dealing with sensing and with the gestalt, the whole, the relationship between the parts.

"What do you mean, 'a general feeling about priorities'? What is it you want me to do? Give me something specific I can get a handle on."

"Well, it's just a feeling." Her right brain was dealing in images, intuitive feelings. "I just don't think our marriage is as important to you as you tell me it is."

"Well, what can I do to make it more important? Give me something concrete and specific to go on."

"It's hard to put into words."

At that point, he just rolled his eyes and looked at me as if to say, "Stephen, could you endure this kind of dumbness in your marriage?"

"It's just a feeling," she said, "a very strong feeling."

"Honey," he said to her, "that's your problem. And that's the problem with your mother. In fact, it's the problem with every woman I know."

Then he began to interrogate her as though it were some kind of legal deposition.

"Do you live where you want to live?"

"That's not it," she sighed. "That's not it at all."

"I know," he replied with a forced patience. "But since you won't tell me exactly what it is, I figure the best way to find out what it is is to find out what it is not. Do you live where you want to live?"

"I guess."

"Honey, Stephen's here for just a few minutes to try to help us. Just give a quick 'yes' or 'no' answer. Do you live where you want to live?"

"Yes."

"Okay. That's settled. Do you have the things you want to have?"

"Yes."

"All right. Do you do the things you want to do?"

This went on for a little while, and I could see I wasn't helping at all. So I intervened and said, "Is this kind of how it goes in your relationship?"

"Every day, Stephen," he replied.

"It's the story of our marriage," she sighed.

I looked at the two of them and the thought crossed my mind that they were two half-brained people living together. "Do you have any children?" I asked.

"Yes, two."

"Really?" I asked incredulously. "How did you do it?"

"What do you mean how did we do it?"

"You were synergistic!" I said. "One plus one usually equals two. But you made one plus one equal four. Now that's synergy. The whole is greater than the sum of the parts. So how did you do it?"

"You know how we did it," he replied.

"You must have valued the differences!" I exclaimed.

Valuing the Differences

Valuing the differences is the essence of synergy—the mental, the emotional, the psychological differences between people. And the key to valuing those differences is to realize that all people see the world, not as it is, but as they are.

If I think I see the world as it is, why would I want to value the differences? Why would I even want to bother with someone who's "off track"? My paradigm is that I am objective; I see the world as it is. Everyone else is buried by the minutia, but I see the larger picture. That's why they call me a supervisor—I have super vision.

If that's my paradigm, then I will never be effectively interdependent, or even effectively independent, for that matter. I will be limited by the paradigms of my own conditioning.

The person who is truly effective has the humility and reverence to recognize his own perceptual limitations and to appreciate the rich resources available through interaction with the hearts and minds of other human beings. That person values the differences because those differences add to his knowledge, to his understanding of reality. When we're left to our own experiences, we constantly suffer from a shortage of data.

Is it logical that two people can disagree and that both can be right? It's not logical: it's *psychological*. . . .

And unless we value the differences in our perceptions, unless we value each other and give credence to the possibility that we're both right, that life is not always a dichotomous either/or, that there are almost always third alternatives, we will never be able to transcend the limits of that conditioning.

All Nature Is Synergistic

Ecology is a word which basically describes the synergism in nature—everything is related to everything else. . . .

The relationship of the parts is also the power in creating a synergistic culture inside a family or an organization. The more genuine the involvement, the more sincere and sustained the participation in analyzing and solving problems, the greater the release of everyone's creativity, and of their commitment to what they create. This, I'm convinced, is the essence of the power in the Japanese approach to business, which has changed the world marketplace.

Synergy works; it's a correct principle. . . . It is effectiveness in an interdependent reality—it is teamwork, team building, the development of unity and creativity with other human beings.

Although you cannot control the paradigms of others in an interdependent interaction or the synergistic process itself, a great deal of synergy is within your Circle of Influence.

Your own internal synergy is completely within the circle. You can respect both sides of your own nature—the analytical side and the creative side. You can value the difference between them and use that difference to catalyze creativity.

You can be synergistic within yourself even in the midst of a very adversarial environment. You don't have to take insults personally. You can sidestep negative energy; you can look for the good in others and utilize that good, as different as it may be, to improve your point of view and to enlarge your perspective.

You can exercise the courage in interdependent situations to be open, to express your ideas, your feelings, and your experiences in a way that will encourage other people to be open also.

You can value the difference in other people. When someone disagrees with you, you can say, "Good! You see it differently." You don't have to agree with them; you can simply affirm them. and you can seek to understand.

When you see only two alternatives—yours and the "wrong" one—you can look for a synergistic third alternative. There's almost always a third alternative, and if you work with a Win/Win philosophy and really seek to understand, you usually can find a solution that will be better for everyone concerned.

Review Questions

1. What is "synergistic communication"?
2. Explain what it means to say that compromise means that $1 + 1 = 1\frac{1}{2}$ and synergy means that $1 + 1$ may equal 8, 16, or even 1,600.

3. What does Covey mean when he says that the "middle" way means the "higher" way?
4. What is "negative synergy"?
5. What is the difference between something making sense because it's "logical" and something making sense because it's "psychological"?

Probes

1. Some people desire a lot of *control* in their lives. They don't like surprises and want others to behave in ways that meet their standards. Why might synergistic communication be especially challenging for these people?
2. You can imagine the "highly influential celebrities" in the Atomic Energy Commission group getting very impatient about all the time David Lilienthal insisted that they spend creating a high Emotional Bank Account. It must have felt like they were wasting enormous amounts of very valuable time. If you were Lilienthal, how would you have responded to their impatience?
3. How do you respond to this statement: "Insecure people think that all reality should be amenable to their paradigms. They have a high need to clone others, to mold them over into their own thinking." What experiences do you have that either support or challenge this statement?
4. Covey gave some very general advice to the husband and wife who couldn't agree. If you were in Covey's place, what specific communication suggestions might you give each of them?
5. What specific insights do you get from Covey's point that synergy in nature can teach us about synergy in communication?

Chapter 3

Verbal
Communicating

Basic interpersonal communication texts typically devote one chapter to language, or verbal codes, and a separate one to nonverbal communication. This practice began in the late 1960s when communication researchers and teachers first discovered the importance of the nonverbal parts of communicating—eye contact, body movement, facial expression, tone of voice, touch, silence, and so on. So for about twenty-five years, most textbooks treated each subject as significant and distinct.

But now research is focusing more and more closely on conversations as people actually live them, and it has become obvious that you can't really separate the verbal and the nonverbal parts. In the words of two researchers, "It is impossible to study either verbal or nonverbal communication as isolated structures. Rather, these systems should be regarded as a unified communication construct."[1] And as speech communication teacher Wendy Leeds-Hurwitz puts it,

> In discussing communication as consisting of verbal and nonverbal modes . . . we leave ourselves open to the impression that the two are somehow distinct and should be studied separately. This is not at all the case, and there is now a current body of literature devoted to rejoining the two.[2]

Interestingly, almost this same point was made at the beginning of the twentieth century by Ferdinand deSaussure, one of the founders of linguistics. Saussure said that language is like a sheet of paper, where sound makes up one side of the page and concepts or thoughts make up the other. You can't pick up one side of the paper without picking up the other, and you can't cut one side without cutting the other. So it's best to think of them together.[3] I think the same way about the verbal and the nonverbal parts of communicating; they're like the two sides of one sheet of paper.

This is actually the way they occur in human experience. For example, consider this conversation:

> Scott: (*Smiling and nodding*) Hi John Paul. Howzit goin'?
>
> John Paul: (*Excited look*) Scott! (*Shaking hands*) It's good to see you! I heard you'd moved. Where've you *been*??
>
> Scott: (*Smiling knowingly*) Nowhere, really. I've just been working and going to school. But Heather and I have been hangin' around together quite a bit.
>
> John Paul: (*Teasing*) Yeah, I heard that. What's the story with you two anyway?
>
> Scott: (*Playful but cagey*) What do you mean 'What's the story'? We just like each other, and we spend a lot of time together.
>
> John Paul: (*Still teasing*) Yeah, like all weekend. And every night. And most of the rest of the time.
>
> Scott: (*Turning the tables*) Well, what about you and Bill?? I've heard you two are a duo . . . partners . . . an item.
>
> John Paul: (*A little shy*) Where'd you hear that? Yeah, it's pretty true. (*Brighter*) And it's kind of neat, actually. It's the first time I've felt like a part of a *couple*. We might even get an apartment together. But he's got to get a job that pays more. I can't support both of us.
>
> Scott: (*Friendly*) Sounds like you've got the same questions Heather and I have. But her folks are also a problem.
>
> John Paul: (*Serious*) *My* mom and dad are fine. But Bill's parents don't know any-

thing about us, and I'm trying to get him to change that. In fact, I was thinking that I'd like to talk with you about that. I also wonder how you and Heather plan to actually set up living together. But I've got to get to work now. Give me your new number so I can give you a call, Okay?

Several of the *verbal* parts of this conversation are significant. Scott says "Howzit goin'?" rather than "How is it going?" or the even more formal "I'm pleased to see you again." He uses the general phrase "spending a lot of time together" rather than a more specific description of his and Heather's activities. For John Paul the word *couple* is significant. The two also share an understanding of what it means, in this context, to say that parents are "a problem."

Nonverbal features of the conversation are also significant. Scott's initial tone of voice is pretty low-key, but John Paul sounds excited to see him. They touch as they shake hands. Their smiles "say" several different things—"It's good to see you." "I like you." "I'm teasing." "I'm teasing back." "We've got something in common." Since they're friends, they stand fairly close together.

But the important thing is that they experience all these verbal and nonverbal elements *together*. In this conversation, excited, friendly, and teasing tones of voice are integral parts of the words each person says. Facial expressions show that the words each speaks are genuine and not sarcastic. Space and touch go even further to frame the verbal messages as sincere and cordial. To put it in researcher's terms, "utterance meaning" and "nonverbal meaning" are not "discrete and independent."[4] This is even true of written words on a page. What you might consider to be "purely verbal" written words appear in a designed typeface, on a certain weight and color of paper, and surrounded by more or less white space. All these nonverbal elements affect how we interpret the written words. Similarly, even "purely nonverbal" behaviors like gestures or eye behavior occur in the context of some spoken or written words. One way to sort out these features is to think in terms of a continuum or sliding scale like this:

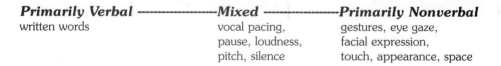

Primarily Verbal --------------------*Mixed* -----------------*Primarily Nonverbal*
written words   vocal pacing,   gestures, eye gaze,
                                    pause, loudness,   facial expression,
                                    pitch, silence   touch, appearance, space

Written words are classified as *"primarily verbal"* for the reasons I just gave. They appear in a nonverbal typeface surrounded by nonverbal space, but people primarily interpret their verbal content. Tones of voice—pacing, pause, loudness, pitch, silence—are labeled "mixed" because they almost always occur along with or are overlaid on spoken words. And gestures, facial expression, and so on are labeled "primarily *nonverbal*" because, for example, a smile, a frown, or a skeptical look can mean something without any accompanying words. They are labeled *"primarily* nonverbal" because most facial expressions (and gestures, touch, etc.) are interpreted in the context of spoken words.

One point to emphasize, though, is that the verbal and nonverbal elements of communication are completely interdependent, which means that the verbal affects the nonverbal and the nonverbal affects the verbal, but that neither *determines* the meaning of the other. In order to make this point, I considered putting articles about both kinds of communicating in the same chapter. But I realize that isn't the way most courses cover this material, so I decided to stick with tradition and have a chapter on each.

This chapter on verbal cues includes an overview of three ways of describing language, a family therapist's warnings about ten troublesome English words, and a Chinese-American woman's experiences with Chinese vs. English. It also includes a brief reminder about how words work interculturally, an example of an amazingly impersonal family letter, and a brief fable that highlights the connection between the words we speak and who we are.

In the first reading Carole Logan and I clarify the difference between "verbal" and "oral," and then explain what's been learned when language has been studied (1) as a system of symbols, (2) as an activity, and (3) as a soup. We show how each way of studying language reveals some of its complexities—and obscures some others—and how each also leads to some specific suggestions about how to use and treat language.

When you approach language as a system of symbols you can learn that "the word is not the thing," which can help you avoid stereotyping and using words to turn processes into static "things" (a process called "reifying"). When you notice the ways that language is an activity, you can become more aware of the speech acts you perform by using certain words. This can help you be more straightforward and less manipulative or strategic, and can help you diagnose some communication problems.

The third approach views language as a soup, a rich and thick broth that humans swim around in like bits of carrot or potato. This perspective emphasizes how language "uses" us as much as we "use" it—that we are born into a language world, are surrounded by it throughout our lives, and die while it's still functioning. In other words, this approach views language as closely related to *culture*. When you look at language this way, you can see how language and perception are closely interrelated and how the limits of a person's language mean the limits of his or her world.

In the final part of the reading we review six guidelines that emerge from these three ways of approaching language. The first is to look out for language traps, and the second is to resist the "proper meaning" fallacy. It's also helpful to build your vocabulary and to exploit the creative power of language, especially with metaphors. The fifth guideline is to develop inclusive and respectful language. This idea gets echoed in later chapters of *Bridges Not Walls* that focus on conflict (Chapter 14) and intercultural and interracial communication (Chapter 15). We explain what it means for your language to be inclusive and respectful, and distinguish this idea from "political correctness." Then our final guideline is to "care about your talk."

Overall, this reading should give you some general ways to think about the primarily verbal parts of your communicating. Spoken language is a powerful resource, and effective communicators manage it carefully.

References

1. D. J. Higginbotham and D. E. Yoder, "Communication Within Natural Conversational Interaction: Implications for Severe Communicatively Impaired Persons," *Topics in Language Disorders, 2* (1982), 4.
2. Wendy Leeds-Hurwitz, *Communication in Everyday Life* (Norwood, NJ: Ablex), p. 102.
3. Ferdinand de Saussure, *Course in General Linguistics,* ed. Charles Bally and Albert Sechehaye, Trans. Roy Harris (LaSalle, IL: Open Court, 1986), pp. 66-70. After making this point, de Saussure focused his attention on the *system* of language, in order to make linguistics a "science."
4. Robert E. Sanders, "The Interconnection of Utterances and Nonverbal Displays," *Research on Language and Social Interaction, 20* (1987), 141.

Verbal Communicating

John Stewart and Carole Logan

Just to make sure we start out talking about the same things, notice how Figure 1 shows that *verbal* is not the same thing as *oral*. *Oral* means "by mouth." So not only spoken words but also intonation, vocal quality, and nervous coughing are "oral" ways of communicating. *Verbal* comes from the Latin word for "word," so both written and spoken words are forms of "verbal" communicating. *Language* is the general term that's typically used to talk about the *verbal* parts of communicating. However, as we will explain, it's important to recognize that "language" can include both verbal and nonverbal cues. That's why there are dotted lines separating the four quadrants in Figure 1. The distinctions are not quite as simple as this diagram suggests.

As the figure also suggests, there are important differences between spoken language (oral-verbal) and written language (nonoral-verbal). For example, spoken language emphasizes what's *heard*, and written language what's *seen*. Spoken English tends to be made up of shorter sentences than written English and tends to use different verb forms (more active, less passive) and different pronoun patterns. In this book we're

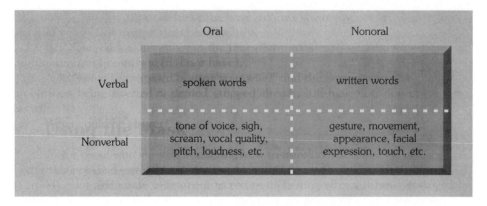

Figure 1
Kinds of messages.

obviously focusing most on spoken language. But many of the ideas in this chapter on verbal communicating apply to both spoken and written language. The next chapter on nonverbal communicating will discuss the bottom half of Figure 1—oral and non-oral modes of communicating.

One of John's students discovered the importance of the verbal parts of communicating when she worked as an intern in the sales department of a large mobile home dealership. Early in her internship she was struck by how important it seemed to be to use the right words as she talked with prospective customers. When Barbara asked her supervisor about this part of her job, he gave her the lists below.

Common Expressions	Improved Expressions
House	Home
Buy	Invest
Cost	Investment
Down payment	Initial investment
Deal	Offer or opportunity
Contract	Agreement
Lot	Homesite or location
Second Mortgage	Additional financing
Small	Cozy
Large	Expansive
Sound barriers	Acoustically engineered
Layout	Design concept
No, it's not included	Personal, optional feature
Sales lot	Display center
Dealer	Retailer
Salesperson	Consultant

Obviously Barbara's supervisor had given a lot of thought to the impact words have on the relationship between customer—or should we say, "client"—and the mobile home "consultant." And you don't have to be a communication genius to hear the obvious differences. Which of the following sounds less threatening and more inviting to you?

> With the offer we have outlined, your initial investment will require only a minimum of additional financing, depending on the optional features you decide to include in the design.

> OR

> With the deal we have outlined, your down payment will require only a small second mortgage, depending on how much you add to what's not included in the layout.

Barbara followed up her internship by taking a class called "Perspectives on Language in Speech Communication," which focused on how words work between people. In this course she learned that language can be studied in three different ways, each of which can help you communicate more effectively.

Preview

First, language can be studied as a system. Historically, this is the oldest point of view. From this perspective language is made up of different kinds of words and the rules governing their combinations. Grade school teachers emphasize the *systematic* features of language when they help students learn the different parts of speech and rules for making grammatical sentences. When you think of German, Mandarin, or Spanish as "a language," you're thinking of it as a language *system*. Dictionaries record a part of a language system and provide a record of, for example, word histories and new words like *ROM* (a computer's read-only memory), *herstory* (a feminist substitute for *history*), and *rapping*.

Second, language can be studied as an activity. The most influential version of this approach to language began early in the twentieth century. This perspective emphasizes that many utterances actually perform actions, for example, the words *I will* or *I do* in a marriage ceremony. These words aren't just "about" getting married; they are an important part of *the activity of marrying*. If they're not said at the right time by the right people, the marriage hasn't happened. Similarly, the words *I agree*, or *Okay, it's a deal* can perform the activity of buying, selling, or contracting for work, and *Howzitgoin'?* is not "about" a greeting; it's the activity of greeting itself.

Third, language can be studied as a soup in which humans swim like fish swim in water. This is also primarily a twentieth-century approach to language, and it emphasizes how the *cultures* we live in, the specific *contexts* we define, and the *roles* we play are all defined primarily by how we talk. From this point of view the human infant is born into a language world and stays immersed in it until he or she dies. As a surrounding soup, language is more than a "system" we use or an "activity" we perform. It is larger than any of us; it happens to us and we are subject to it. The language world we inhabit determines how we can successfully "make sense," "be polite," "act mature," and even "be a man" and "be feminine." For example, if you grow up in the blue-collar culture of South Chicago, you learn how a certain kind of talk shows that you're "a man,"[1] but if you're raised in East Los Angeles, New Orleans, or Fairbanks, maleness is communicated in significantly different ways. This language soup we live in conditions how we understand the meaning of our perceptions, our thoughts, and our experience. When studied from this perspective, language is made up of both verbal and nonverbal elements. This perspective also treats language as almost synonymous with communication.

Each of these ways of studying language teaches us something important about it, and each can also be translated into some practical applications and skills. In this chapter we will explain each of the three and describe how you can apply some of the insights each approach generates.

Language Is a System of Symbols

Those who study language as a system emphasize that it is preeminently a system of *symbols*. They develop a point made about twenty-five hundred years ago when the Greek philosopher Aristotle began one of his major works on language this way: "Spoken words are the symbols of mental experience and written words are the symbols of spoken words."[2] As a contemporary linguist explains, "This criterion implies that for anything to be a language it must function so as to *symbolize* (represent for the organism) the not-necessarily-*here* and not-necessarily-*now*."[3] In brief, since a symbol is something that stands for something else, this perspective emphasizes that units of language—words, usually—represent, or stand for, "chunks" or "pieces" of nonlinguistic reality. So in simplest terms, the word *cat* stands for the furry, purring, tail-twitching animal sitting in the corner.

One feature of symbols that's important to our understanding of language is that they're *arbitrary*. This means that there is no necessary relationship between the word and the thing which it symbolizes. Even though the word *five* is physically smaller than the word *three*, the quantity which *five* symbolizes is larger. That shows that there is no necessary relationship between the size—in this case—of the word and the "size" of what it means. Or consider the various words different people use to symbolize the dwelling where someone lives: *casa* in Spanish, *maison* in French, and *Haus* in German. This couldn't happen unless the relationship between the word and its meaning were arbitrary.

A classic book first published in 1923 elaborates just this point. Its authors, C. K. Ogden and I. A. Richards, diagramed this insight with their famous "triangle of meaning" (see Figure 2).[4] Ogden and Richards's triangle is meant to illustrate how words are related to both thoughts and things. The word-thought relationship is direct—that's why that line is solid. As Aristotle put it, words stand for thoughts. The relationship between thought and thing is also more or less direct. But the word-thing relationship is arbitrary; various patterns of written letters or spoken sounds can be used to refer to the same thing. The dotted line across the bottom of the triangle emphasizes this point.

The Word Is Not the Thing

The idea illustrated by Ogden and Richards's triangle was translated into an important insight about language, namely, that "the word is not the thing." This slogan emphasizes that words are arbitrary symbols that members of a culture agree to use to represent or symbolize things they sense and experience. But there's no necessary connection between word and thing.

Stated this way, the claim sounds pretty obvious. But we often behave as if it weren't true. For example, we sometimes give concrete labels to abstract entities or processes and then forget that we're dealing with the arbitrary label and not the abstraction or process itself. This process is called **reification**, from the Latin word *res*, which means "thing." To *reify* something is to "thingafy" it.

The term *communication* is an example. When a person first starts studying this subject matter, the tendency is to think about communication as a "thing" made up of certain parts. From this perspective, if there's something wrong with your communication, you can fix it by replacing or repairing the faulty parts. So if you get in an argument with someone important to you, you resolve to fix things by "never bringing up

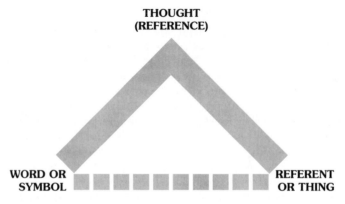

Figure 2
Triangle of meaning.

that subject again," "using different words," or "handling questions like this over the phone rather than face to face." You may figure that those moves will "repair your communication," somewhat like you would repair a car. But then you discover that you can't continue the relationship without bringing up that subject, or that even though you use different words, the person still misunderstands or gets angry. And the more you study communication, the more you recognize that it is not a "thing" made up of certain parts. It's a happening, a fluid event, a process that's continually in flux and that is more than the sum of its parts. This is one reason why we have called this reading "Verbal Communicating" rather than "Verbal Communication." We want to avoid reifying the word "communication." This move makes it more difficult to study the process, but it helps us avoid all the mistakes that come from treating communication as an identifiable thing.

There are at least three different kinds of reification. One is called *static evaluation*. It occurs when we overlook the fact that we're using the same, unchanging word to talk about a reality that's constantly changing. For example, when we were growing up, *home* took on some special meanings. Sometimes after living away from home for some time, we return expecting things to be just like they were. But as a classic novel puts it, you really can't "go home again." If we treat home as a static place which we expect will always remain the same, we're bound to be disappointed.

An example of static evaluation of a person concerns the words *mother*, or *my mom*. These are the labels you have been using ever since you can remember to symbolize or refer to an important person in your life. Yet that person has been constantly changing; she obviously isn't the same today as she was when you were five years old. The fact that her label hasn't changed even though she has can sometimes create problems. For example, you might expect the person you call "mom" to still clean up after you or always to be sympathetic when you screw things up—just because she's *mom*. But *she* may have decided that adults—especially her own children—can clean up after themselves and should be allowed to experience the consequences of their own foulups. When you treat her-the-person like an unchanging label—"mom"—instead of a changing person, you're forgetting an important sense in which *the word is not the thing*.

Another problem created when we forget that the word is not the thing is called *bypassing*. Bypassing means using different words with the same meaning or the same words with different meanings. It's called "bypassing" because, when it occurs, communicators pass by each other rather than making contact. For example, in their campaign ads two state politicians hammered away at each other because one wanted to "radically readjust the state budget" while the other wanted to "significantly increase the salaries of state employees." When they met face to face in a televised debate, they discovered that they were both talking about the same thing. This is one kind of bypassing—different words for the same meaning. The two politicians heard different words and assumed they meant different positions. But they didn't: the words were not the positions. There was only an arbitrary relationship between the words and the positions they symbolized. And in this case, the bypassing that happened in their radio, TV, and print communicating was reduced when they talked face to face.

Another kind of bypassing occurred when a high school basketball team from a small town in Idaho went on a special trip to Australia. The team members were asked to speak to the students in the Australian high schools they visited, and one team member named Randy kept wondering why everyone laughed so much when he began a conversation, "Hi! I'm Randy." It took him awhile to learn that in Australia, the word *randy* means "horny," wanting to have sex.

The most tragic example of bypassing we know of happened near the end of

World War II. Before the United States dropped atomic bombs on Hiroshima and Nagasaki, the Japanese government knew that they had lost the war. Government leaders were meeting almost constantly, and they had agreed to surrender; the only question was exactly when and how. Surrender negotiations were also under way with Russia, which meant the Japanese government had received detailed ultimatums from both Russia and the Allied Forces. So as not to upset the negotiations with Russia, the Japanese cabinet decided that their first response to the Allied ultimatum would be noncommittal. The key word in their reply was *mokusatsu*, a term which can be translated as "no comment." Unfortunately, the Japanese word is made up of two characters, one meaning "silence" and the other meaning "kill," so *mokusatsu* can also mean "kill with silence" or "ignore." Allied translators understood the Japanese to have "ignored" the ultimatum and were furious. The punishment came quickly, tens of thousands of people died, and the world was propelled into an age of weapons we still haven't completely figured out how to manage. This happened partly because of bypassing—a misunderstanding created by using a word with two different meanings and forgetting that the word is not the thing it symbolizes.

   Labeling is a third problem that's created when we forget that the word is not the thing. Labeling occurs when we respond to the particular word choice instead of the thing the word symbolizes or represents. Did you ever wonder why a restaurant menu will offer "mesquite broiled filet mignon" instead of "scorched piece of dead cow"? The main reason we don't want to read "dead cow" on a restaurant menu is that, even though we "know" that we're not going to eat the words on the menu, we still have a tendency to respond to the words as if they were the thing we have ordered for dinner. . . . This same phenomenon of labeling is also operating when people get angry because they're stereotyped as "nerd," "dweeb," airhead," "greaser," "jock," "sorority sally," "shyster lawyer," or "bitchy feminist." We're definitely not saying that stereotyping or name-calling is acceptable. But our point is that people who study language as a system of symbols argue that all these labels are *words* and not the realities they're used to talk about. It follows that when someone gets angry about a label, it may be because the person is forgetting that the word is not the thing.

Language Skills

   The general way to solve problems created by reifying, static evaluations, bypassing, and labeling is to remember that the word is not the thing. Words never completely or accurately capture the realities they're used to talk about. When people express their feelings or opinions, for example, they can never say *everything* they feel or believe. And perceptions differ. Your view of the reality symbolized by *hunk, bitch, homeboy,* or *jamoke* may be very different from the reality of the person using the word.

   There are also three more solutions for problems created by our tendency to forget that "the word is not the thing." The first is called *dating*, and it means that you put a date or time frame around some of the statements you make. It's a way of saying, "This is my perception for right now." So you move from "Mom will lend me the money" to "The last time I needed money, Mom lent it to me, but I don't know about this time." Or you replace "You can't drink in Salt Lake City" with "When we were in Salt Lake City two years ago, it was really inconvenient to find a place that served drinks." When you use dating, you also add to statements like "Professor Crowell is really enthusiastic" something like "—or at least she was last quarter in the group discussion class." Similarly, "Michelle seemed phony the other night" is a statement that's dated, in this sense, and "Michelle's a phony" isn't. You can use language to highlight rather than to obscure the fact that the realities your words symbolize are changing over time, even though your words aren't.

A second solution is called *indexing*. The term comes from mathematics where subscript or superscript numbers are used to distinguish one variable from similar ones—x_1, x_2, x_3; or z^1, z^2, z^3, and so on. These numbers index the variables. You index verbally when you use words to highlight individual differences. We can use the process of stereotyping that we talked about in the perception chapter by saying, "Since Seattle's supposed to be one of the most 'livable' cities, it's got to have lots of theater." The indexed statement could be, "Since Seattle's rated as one of the most 'livable' cities, it should have lots of good theater, but it may not—it's a long way from New York and Los Angeles." In this example, indexing highlights some possibly *unique* features of Seattle. Or you would replace the statement "You'll get seventy thousand miles out of those Michelin tires" with "I've gotten as high as seventy thousand miles out of Michelins, and if you do the kind of driving I do, you should get that, too." Two interpersonal communication teachers summarize their advice about indexing this way:

1. Before you make a statement about an object, person, or place, consider whether your statement is about that specific object, person, or place or whether it is a generalization about a class to which the object, person, or place belongs.
2. If your statement is a generalization, inform your listener that it is not necessarily accurate.[5]

A third cure is to make the fact that words are arbitrary work for you rather than against you by using a euphemism. *Euphemisms* are neutral, vaguely positive, or ambiguous words that are used to talk about negative things. When you use a euphemism, you are suspending the negative impressions that are likely to be associated with a particular term. For example, your hairdresser may insist that he or she doesn't ever "dye" hair, but that you can get a "tint" or "rinse." Or consider how parents responded to many middle and high school courses that cover such topics as the biology of human reproduction, causes and dangers of sexually transmitted diseases, and, in some cases, methods of contraception. When school authorities labeled the courses "sex education," they were frequently attacked for allowing such material to be taught to young people. But when they changed the labels to "social hygiene" or "family health," community members were much less worried, even though the content of the courses remained unchanged.

Euphemisms can also create problems. When government or military spokespersons use such euphemisms as "terminate with extreme prejudice" to talk about a murder or assassination, they are perceived by many as deceptive and manipulative. A similar thing can happen when your friend tells you that she had an "open" or "honest" conversation with someone you both know, and you discover that she was actually divulging several pieces of private information you asked her not to discuss with anyone.

So one approach to language studies it as a system of symbols. From this perspective the most important thing to remember is the word is not the thing it symbolizes. Several communication problems are created when people forget this point, and there are several language moves you can make to emphasize that the word is not the thing.

Language Is an Activity

It can be helpful to view language as a system of symbols, because it alerts us to several problems we create by the ways we use words. We can also learn from this perspective how to remember that the word is not the thing. But the symbolic view is also drastically oversimplified. The triangle of meaning assumes that language is essentially made up of nouns, labels for things in the world. It doesn't take much reflection to realize that language is much more complicated than that. How will the triangle help you understand the workings of words like *love, pride,* and *homelessness*? There are no "things" or "referents" which these terms are even arbitrarily related to. And what about words like *and, whether, however,* and *larger*? You can get really confused trying to figure out what "things" these words symbolize. Even more important, we don't usually experience language as individual words but as statements, utterances, messages, or parts of a conversation. So an approach that tries to explain language as people live it by focusing on individual words has to be limited. All this is why it's partly true to say that language is a system of symbols, but language is more than that.

Words can also perform actions. As we mentioned above, sometimes words don't refer to or symbolize anything; they *constitute* the act of marrying, promising, betting, contracting, greeting, and so on. This perspective can also be applied more generally. A group of researchers called *conversation analysts* carefully scrutinize naturally occurring conversations to determine what actions the participants are using language to perform.

One of the first important distinctions they make separates what talk "says" from what it "does." For example, even though the words *I'll bet you . . .* can mean that the speaker is making a wager, "I'll bet you didn't even *listen* to what I said!" doesn't have anything to do with gambling or wagering. Even though the meanings of the words in this utterance have to do with betting, the utterance itself is a *complaint* about the other person's listening behavior. So the utterance performs the *act of complaining.* This example shows that there's a clear difference between semantic meaning (what the words "say") and the action that is performed in the saying (what the words "do").[6] Conversation analysis focuses almost completely on what utterances do.

One conversation analyst identifies seven speech acts which have been clearly identified and described: the promise, request, threat, offer, command, compliment, and greeting.[7] Each of these acts is a "move" in a conversation game or language game. Speakers perform these acts by following certain culturally defined rules about (a) what must be said (*propositional content*), (b) how the situation is defined, and (c) the sincerity of the speaker. These three sets of rules can be used to analyze all the different speech acts.

So, for example, the propositional content of a *promise* must be about a future behavior of the speaker. If there's nothing in the speech act about the speaker's future behavior, then the act can't be a promise. Often this is explicit: "Okay, I'll call you tonight." But Laura also makes a promise in this sequence:

KATI: You will be there for my recital, won't you?
LAURA: Absolutely.

In this case, Laura's speech act is a promise in part because of the situation or context it fits into. Even though the dictionary meaning of the single word *absolutely* does not always make it a "promise," it is one *in this situation*, because of what Kati just said. Third, in order for an utterance to be a full and valid promise, it also has to reflect the speaker's sincere intent. Sometimes this can't be determined at the time. But utterances which could be promises but are spoken with heavy sarcasm obviously don't qualify.

This same analysis can be applied to each of the other speech acts. The propositional content of a *request* must be about the future behavior of the *hearer* rather than the speaker. The situation must be one in which the hearer is able and at least potentially willing to do what is requested. In addition, there must be reason to suppose that the speaker believes the hearer wouldn't normally do what's being requested without being asked. And in order to be a valid request, the speaker must actually want the hearer to comply. So, for example, "Say that one more time, and I'll . . ." would be something like a challenge rather than a request.

Does it sound like conversation analysts are viewing communication as an *action*, an *interaction*, or a *transaction*? So far, you probably have the impression that they look at it as an *action* not only because they emphasize that language is an "activity" but also because they focus on what *one person does* to craft an utterance that works as a threat, offer, command, and so on. Or you might say that they are viewing communication as if it were an *interaction*, because they notice what *each person separately contributes*. But so far it does not look like conversation analysis approaches communication *transactionally*, because (a) they haven't shown how conversation events are produced *collaboratively*, mutually, by both (or all) the people involved, and (b) they haven't discussed how the persons' *identities are affected* by their communicating. As our examples show, this is partly true. A big chunk of conversation analysis research has applied action or interaction perspectives.

But conversation analysts have also studied some ways conversation partners collaborate to mutually construct some conversation events. In these studies they have moved closer to a *transactional* view of communication. For example, an important line of conversation analysis work has focused on how, when one conversation partner produces a greeting, good-bye, invitation, apology, offer, congratulation, and so on, it helps create a situation where both partners expect the first utterance to be followed by another greeting or good-bye; an acceptance, questioning, or rejection of the invitation; an acceptance of the apology, and so on. As one conversation analyst puts it,

> As we shall see, when one of these first actions has been produced, participants orient to the presence or absence of the relevant second action. There is an expectation by participants that the second action should be produced, and when it does not occur, participants behave as if it should have.[8]

Conversation analysts call these collaborative conversational acts adjacency pairs. An *adjacency pair* is a sequence of two communicative actions usually occurring one after the other, each produced by a different speaker and related in such a way that when you have the first action, coherence or common sense indicates that some version of the second action needs to happen next. So "Hello there!" is part of an adjacency pair, because people expect the first utterance of this greeting to be followed by some type of reciprocal acknowledgment—"Oh, hi," "Howzitgoin," "Hello," or some such. Similarly, a compliment is part of an adjacency pair, because it's expected that the person complimented will respond with "Thanks" or with some self-deprecation—"It's not that great," "This old rag??" "It was nothing." . . .

In summary, conversation analysts have demonstrated the value of studying language as an activity. They have shown that every time we *say* something, we're also *doing* something—that speech is a kind of action. So they have exploited the value of looking at communication from an action point of view. But they have also gone beyond this point. Not only have they catalogued many of the actions that people perform by talking but they have also shown that some of these actions are produced collaboratively. In this way they have begun to look at conversation as an interaction and, to some degree, as a transaction. Their research is not yet fully transactional, because they have not studied how the self-definitions of conversation partners change during the conversation. But conversation analysts have acknowledged that, although researchers can identify patterns or sequences that occur in conversation, the actual conversation is made up of more than just the sequences. Every day we engage in greetings, good-byes, promises, threats, compliments, offers, commands, requests, and dozens of other conversation acts. But we also improvise and modify expected patterns.

Language Skills

So how can you apply the results of studying language as an activity? First, you can pay more attention to the relationship between what you're *saying* with your talk and what you're *doing*. This can help in several ways.

For example, if you want it to work this way, this knowledge can help you be more straightforward and less manipulative or strategic. People often say, "I'm not complaining, I'm just making an observation!" or "I don't mean to crit icize, but have you looked in the mirror today?" or "I'm not asking you to go, I'm just telling you that I can't go unless you do." In each of these cases, the activities that are performed by the "observation," "suggestion," and "telling" *are complaining, criticizing,* and *requesting.* So when the person says, "I'm not complaining," he or she actually is. And when the person claims, "I'm not asking you to go," this is exactly what is going on. Usually communication works best when people "own up" to what they're doing with their talk. So if you understand the connection between your spoken language and the actions it is performing, you can be more straightforward or candid.[9]

Recognizing the action your talk performs can also help you diagnose communication problems. If somebody doesn't understand you, it may be because they think you were just making an observation when you meant to be making a request. If a subordinate at work doesn't follow your directions, it may be because he or she thought you were making a suggestion rather than giving an order. If a person keeps talking when you want the conversation to end, it may be because he or she didn't notice that you were attempting to say good-bye. When a friend is offended by something you say, it may be because your comment was heard as criticism or sarcasm rather than as humor. If you can recognize the difference between the action you intended and the action others heard, you can adapt your talk to clarify things. . . .

Another way to apply these ideas is to recognize that conversation—face to face, over the telephone, and even in letters and papers—consists of equally important parts of *structure* and *surprise.* Effective communicators are sensitive to both. This means that improvisation is as important as following the rules. Don't expect to be able to predict with mathematical accuracy exactly what's going to happen in your conversations. But realize that you don't have to have that level of certainty in order to "do" conversation well. You already know how to manage most of the intricacies of conversation, at least in your native language. Let part of your flexibility show itself in spontaneity.

Language Is a Soup

Especially in the last thirty years, many scholars have recognized the limitations of both the system and action views of language. Both these views treat language as a tool humans manipulate—to arbitrarily stand for some referent or to perform an action. As we have explained, there's some truth to these views, and they can teach us some important things about language. But language is more than a tool. If it were a tool, we could lay it aside when we didn't need it and pick up some other tool. But we can't do that. As humans, we're always already immersed in language, like a fish in water. As one philosopher puts it,

> In all our knowledge of ourselves and in all knowledge of the world, we are always already encompassed by the language that is our own. We grow up, and we become acquainted with [people] and in the last analysis with ourselves when we learn to speak. Learning to speak does not mean learning to use a preexistent tool for designating a world already somehow familiar to us; it means acquiring a familiarity and acquaintance with the world itself and how it confronts us.[10]

As little as twenty weeks after conception, the human fetus has functioning ears and is beginning to respond to sounds.[11] Its mother's voice is clearly one sound the fetus learns to identify.[12] When the infant is born it typically enters an environment of exclamations and greetings. Then communication experiences fill the infant's life. Touch, eye contact, smiles, and a great deal of talk are directed to him or her. As infants develop, parents and other caregivers invite them into conversations by providing a context for talk, by encouraging them with positive attitudes toward talk, and by interpreting, modeling, and extending talk.[13] This process continues right up to the last tearful good-byes we hear at death. In between, we live like nutritious morsels in a broth of language. If all this sounds a little abstract, consider two practical implications of the fact that language is a soup: (a) Language and perception are interrelated, and (b) the limits of a person's language are the limits of his or her world.

Language and Perception Are Interrelated

One of the most important lessons learned from the twentieth-century study of language concerns the links between language and perception. . . . Part of this basic insight—the Language → Perception part—is usually called "the Sapir-Whorf hypothesis" after the two people who originally wrote about it, Edward Sapir and Benjamin Lee Whorf. It has been summarized by Whorf in these words:

> The background linguistic system (in other words the grammar) of each language is not merely a reproducing instrument for voicing ideas but rather is itself the shaper of ideas, the program and guide for the individual's mental activity, for his [or her] analysis of impressions. . . . We dissect nature along lines laid down by our native language.[14]

So if you have spent enough time on boats and around the water to learn a dozen different words for water conditions, you will perceive more differences in the water than will the person who was born and raised in Cheyenne, Oklahoma City, or Calgary. That person might distinguish between "waves" and "smooth water," but you will see and feel differences between cats' paws, ripples, chop, and swells that he or she won't even notice.[15] Or if you have learned important meanings for *latex, natural, lubricated,* and *spermicidal,* you can make distinctions among condoms that were impossible for the high school graduate of the 1970s or early 1980s.

As we try to write about communication as a transaction, we notice one partic-ular way our native language limits our perceptions. Unlike some languages, English maintains clear distinctions between subjects and predicates, causes and effects, begin-nings and ends. The word system of the Navajo doesn't do that. According to one researcher, Navajo speakers characteristically talk in terms of processes—uncaused, ongoing, incomplete, dynamic happenings. The word Navajos use for *wagon,* for exam-ple, translates roughly as "wood rolls about hooplike."[16] The Navajo words that we would translate "He begins to carry a stone" mean not that the actor produces an action but that the person is simply linked with a given round object and with an already existing, continuous movement of all round objects in the universe. The English language, on the other hand, requires us to talk in terms of present, past, future, cause and effect, beginning and end. But some things English speakers would like to discuss just can't be expressed in these terms. We would like to be able to talk more clearly about the everchanging, processlike, ongoing nature of communication and about the "betweeness" of the quality of communication we have labeled "interper-sonal". . . . But the English language makes it difficult to do this.

Our language also affects the way we perceive females and males. One accom-plishment of the feminist movement of the 1960s and 1970s is that we now recognize how the male bias of Standard American English has contributed to the ways English-speaking cultures perceive women and men. The fact that, until recently, there were no female firefighters, was not caused simply by the existence of the word *fireman.* It's not that simple. But changes in job titles have helped open several occupations to more equal male-female participation. Consider, for example, *parking checker* instead of *metermaid, chair* or *chairperson* instead of *chairman, salesperson* instead of *salesman,* and *server* instead of *waiter* or *waitress.* We have also just about stopped referring to female physicians as "woman doctors" and female attorneys as "lady lawyers," and it is more than a coincidence that these changes have been accompanied by significant increases in the numbers of women in these two professions. . . .

Our primary point, however, is that language both *reflects* and *affects* the ways we perceive both women and men. This is one important implication of the general point first made by Sapir and Whorf. There is an interdependence, a reciprocal relationship between language and perception: language affects what we perceive, and our percep-tions are reflected in our speaking and writing.

The Limits of My Language Are the Limits of My World

Within the last couple of decades, language researchers and teachers have become increasingly aware that "languaging" as people actually live it is less of a sys-tem or action and more of an event, process, or *transaction.* For these people, the term *language* encompasses both verbal and nonverbal cues. . . .

A philosopher named Ludwig Wittgenstein first wrote, "The limits of my lan-guage are the limits of my world" in a book published in 1953.[17] But one of the clearest expressions of what this sentence *means* appears in a book called *Hunger of Memory* by Richard Rodriguez, a Latino teacher and writer who grew up in Sacramento in the 1950s and 1960s. When Rodriguez talks about his childhood, you understand just how "the limits of my language are the limits of my world."

The first chapter of Rodriguez's book describes how he lived happily as a young boy in the Spanish-speaking world of his home, and then how he was forced into the world of *los gringos* as his parents, brothers, and sisters obeyed the request of his school-teachers to speak English at home rather than Spanish. Rodriguez tells the following story to illustrate how his father was at home in Spanish and a stranger in the world of English and to suggest the impact his homelessness had on his son, Richard:

> There were many times like the night at a brightly lit gasoline station (a blaring white memory) when I stood uneasily, hearing my father. He was talking to a teenaged attendant. I do not recall what they were saying, but I cannot forget the sounds my father made as he spoke. At one point his words slid together to form one word—sounds as confused as the threads of blue and green oil in the puddle next to my shoes. His voice rushed through what he had left to say. And, toward the end, reached falsetto notes, appealing to his listener's understanding. I looked away to the lights of passing automobiles. I tried not to hear anymore. But I heard only too well the calm, easy tones in the attendant's reply. Shortly afterward, walking toward home with my father, I shivered when he put his hand on my shoulder. The very first chance that I got, I evaded his grasp and ran on ahead into the dark, skipping with feigned boyish exuberance.[18]

Later Rodriguez contrasts that feeling of alienation with the warm comfort he felt when being spoken to in Spanish:

> A family member would say something to me and I would feel myself specially recognized. My parents would say something to me and I would feel embraced by the sounds of their words. Those sounds said: *I am speaking with ease in Spanish. I am addressing you in words I never use with los gringos. I recognize you as someone special, close, like no one outside. You belong with us. In the family. . . .*
>
> Walking down the sidewalk, under the canopy of tall trees, I'd warily notice the—suddenly—silent neighborhood kids who stood warily watching me. Nervously, I'd arrive at the grocery store to hear the sounds of the gringo—foreign to me—reminding me that in this world so big, I was a foreigner. But then I'd return. Walking back toward our house, climbing the steps from the sidewalk, when the front door was open in summer, I'd hear voices beyond the screen door talking in Spanish. For a second or two, I'd stay, linger there, listening. Smiling, I'd hear my mother call out, saying in Spanish [words]: "Is that you, Richard?" All the while her sounds would assure me: *You are home now; come closer; inside. With us.*[19]

Rodriguez's story poignantly illustrates that, although there's definitely some truth to the ideas that "language is a system of symbols," "the word is not the thing," and "people use language to perform actions," there is much more to language than these descriptions include. Language is an all-encompassing activity that we are born into and that constantly affects all we perceive. All this is what it means to say that "the limits of my language are the limits of my world." Perhaps the most important feature that marks us as humans is that we are born into a linguistic soup in which we simmer throughout our lives.

So What? Some Language Guidelines

We have already mentioned some language skills that emerge from viewing language as a system, an activity, and a soup. But we want to briefly mention four even more concrete suggestions.

Look Out for Language Traps

Beware of the natural tendency to reify abstractions, and look out for static evaluations. Remember that things and people change faster than words do, so you need to try to make your language reflect those changes. Beware of bypassing. Ask yourself whether you're contributing to a misunderstanding by using different words with the same meaning or the same words with different meanings. Look out for labeling. Try not to respond to the word as if it were the thing it labels. Recognize when you're hearing, reading, or using euphemisms. The fact that they're vague and indirect can sometimes help interpersonal communicating, and can sometimes hinder it. Especially when it's really important for you to be understood, consider using some forms of dating and indexing to increase the precision of your talk and writing.

Resist the "Proper-Meaning" Fallacy

Some people believe that each word has its own clear meaning and that the best way to solve problems of misunderstanding is to consult the dictionary or agree on definitions. Or even worse, they communicate as if they believed this fallacy, without realizing what they're doing. A person doing this might feel grossly mistreated when his partner says she will be home from work "soon," and then she arrives two hours later. "*Soon,*" *she* insists, means "as soon as possible," and that's just what she did: she left work as soon as she could and drove as fast as possible! That's *the meaning*, she insists, of the word, *soon*. From *his* point of view, though, *soon* means in less than an hour, so he thinks his anger is justified. This scenario illustrates the fact that meaning does not exist in words. Words are not simply bearers of dictionary definitions. Some people make this point by emphasizing that "meanings aren't in words; they're in people."

We would change the statement just a little. Meanings are not in words, but they're also not in people. If meanings exist anywhere at all, they exist *between* people. It's true that each unique individual has his or her own understanding of important terms, but if you're thinking about communication, the important thing is not what's in each individual's head but what's negotiated between them. The attitudes, feelings, opinions, and behavioral responses we label "meanings" are outcomes of negotiations between people. They are functions of the ways we engage in the all-encompassing activity that is languaging. Meaning making is a cultural, social, and interpersonal event we participate in with other people. When problems occur, it's not usually because someone doesn't understand *the* meaning of a word or phrase, but rather that *our* meaning differs from another person's or group's. So when someone misunderstands, don't condemn him or her for missing the "proper meaning." Instead, take the misunderstanding as an invitation to dialogue, a signal that you need to engage together in more talk so you can negotiate and agree upon an understanding between you.

Build Your Vocabulary

Since the limits of your language are the limits of your world, look for ways to expand and develop your language resources. . . . When you learn new vocabulary items, you broaden and deepen your perception skills and you increase your ability to converse with more groups of people who are informed about more topics. Vocabulary building is world expanding.

If you're superorganized, you might keep a small notebook of new words you read or hear, along with a short definition of each. But if, like us, you're not that organized, try one or more of the following:

> Buy a thesaurus and use it whenever you're writing—papers, memos, even letters to friends. Most word-processing programs include a thesaurus, so you can use it on the computer if that's the way you write. Notice which words you overuse, and use the thesaurus to discover other ways to say the same thing.

> Do some crossword puzzles—and be sure to compare the solution with your version. Some of the words you will discover there are so esoteric you will never use them, but many aren't. And this can be an entertaining way to expand your vocabulary.

> Browse in bookstores; give books as gifts (you will have to at least look them over before you buy them); and read a lot of different things—at least one newspaper, a news magazine or two, a magazine with stories that interest you. In addition, always try to be reading three to five different things at the same time. School obviously forces you to do that, but you can even supplement school reading with a novel or magazine full of stories at your bedside. Don't ever believe that just because you're deep into some long book you can't, at the same time, also be reading a couple of magazines and another book or two. Even if it takes weeks or months to finish them all, the variety can make each one more interesting.

> When you meet someone who has a job or hobby you're unfamiliar with, encourage him or her to talk about it. Listen for new words and expressions and check with the person for what they mean.

> Most important, use the new words you hear. Play with them; adapt them to your own concerns; roll them around in your thinking; teach them to your friends. It can be fun to think of new words like *reification, transaction, metamessages,* and *bypassing* as cocktail-party words—terms you drop into cocktail party conversation to impress your listeners. You can overdo this, of course, but the more you use a new word, the more you'll make it your own. This leads to our next suggestion.

Exploit the Creative Power of Language

Think of spoken language as living paint or clay. It's a resource for creativity, a medium you can use to think, to express yourself, to entertain yourself and others, and above all to make contact. Remember that language is first and foremost talk, speech between people. This means it's alive, it's in process. And you can squeeze it, mold it, form it, polish it, and work with others to cosculpt meanings in it. In fact, you can think of you and your conversation partner seated on opposite sides of a potter's wheel, each throwing bits of clay on to the wheel, and both using wet fingers, thumbs, and palms to shape the moving mass between you into "what the two of you mean." You can be as creative with language as you can be with clay. . . .

One of the most obviously creative parts of language is *metaphor.* As you probably know, a metaphor is language that links two dissimilar objects or ideas in order to make a point. "My love is a red, red rose," and "He's built like an NFL lineman" are both metaphors. The first links love and a rose in order to make a point about what love is. The second does the same thing with his physique and a pro football player's. Both speech and writing are filled with metaphors, and one of the best ways to exploit the creative potential of language is to learn to notice and play with them.

For example, one of John's colleagues, a Norwegian professor named Jan, recently complained that a meeting they had both attended was so painful and fruitless that he was reminded of an old Norwegian saying. "I felt," he said, "like I was throwing up woolen rags." The metaphor is pretty gross, but it captures a central part of the experience of gagging on dry, scratchy, useless information. John agreed in part, but he also disagreed some, and the metaphor triggered a conversation that was informative for both John and Jan. In this case the metaphor not only was creative, it also helped them check each other's perceptions and move toward more understanding. . . .

In short, try thinking of language as a living thing, a resource for creativity that you and others can play with in order to reach understandings and even solve problems. It can help to think of you and your conversation partner as cosculptors, cooperative participants in the process of sculpting mutual meaning.[20]

The four suggestions we have just made are important, but they also have a relatively narrow range of application. Now we want to offer two guidelines that affect all your language. So with these two suggestions, the stakes go up.

Develop Inclusive and Respectful Language

As we have said before, the talk people engage in helps shape the world they inhabit. Inclusive language broadens your world by recognizing people different from you; it is talk that acknowledges the legitimacy of diverse identities. For example, let's say you're talking with a group of friends, one of whom has a brother who's disabled. You are talking about a new person who's just moved near you, and you say something like, "Zack's great! He's a normal, healthy guy who likes to shoot hoops, go jogging, and eat pizza—my favorite activities. I really like him." It's likely that the person with a disabled brother will notice that your talk makes her brother invisible—only guys who can shoot hoops, go jogging, and go out for pizza are considered "normal," "healthy," and "likable." She knows you have been nice to her brother before, but she also knows that if he had heard what you just said, he would feel like he doesn't count, like he's invisible. Or a professor may be talking about a required textbook and say something like, "I know it's a little expensive, but you can just call home and get money for it," and those in class who cannot get more money from home feel they're invisible. They don't exist, and they are not important because they are struggling financially. Or the professor is talking about something that happened during the Korean war and says, "I know none of you were alive when this occurred," and the forty-five-year-old returning student in the second row feels invisible. Or a group is making jokes about homosexuals without realizing that someone in the group is gay. These examples show how talk can help make somebody invisible even when he or she is standing right in front of us. Whenever you want to promote interpersonal rather than impersonal communicating, it's important to acknowledge differences as completely as you can. How? By thinking inclusively and using inclusive language.

Sometimes the problem is more blatant and what's needed is respectful language. You've probably heard people use derogatory or offensive words that demean people different from themselves. This can be the effect of talk about "Jewing down the price," "shylocks," and "Christ-killers" on people who are Jewish. This can be the effect of talk about "dumb black jocks," "slant-eyes," and "Ay-rabs" on people of color. This can be the effect of talk about "homos," faggots," and "dykes" on people who are gay or lesbian. This can be the effect of talk about "bitchy broads," "his main squeeze," "suffering from PMS," and "respect all mankind" on women. This can be the effect of "dumb stud," "dick head," and "bull in a china shop" on men. This can be the effect of talk about "dumbo," "spastic Sam," "gimpy," or "scarface" on persons who are disabled or disfigured. This can be the effect of talk about "beanpole," "boobless," "blimpo," or "elephant-legs," referring to body size or characteristics. And this can be the effect of such age-related labels as "old hag," "senile," "over-the-hill," and "duffer."

Earlier in this chapter we noted that some language teachers tell people who have these labels applied to them that they should remember that these words are not the things they are used to talk about. If you remember that the word is not the thing, they argue, you won't be as offended. As we said, this is partly true. But it's also true that words help build worlds between people, and that negative labels help build toxic worlds. So both the label user and the label hearer have responsibility for what happens between them.

Inclusive and respectful language recognizes that all kinds of people have a great deal to contribute and that no one should be shut out arbitrarily. It's especially important to understand this, because the world is shrinking. Demographic changes mean that there will soon be no such thing as a majority culture. Diverse cultures will make up the societies in most countries. *Time* magazine writer Robert Hughes put the point this way in early 1992:

> The future of America . . . will rest with people who can think and act with informed grace across ethnic, cultural, linguistic lines. And the first step in becoming such a person lies in acknowledging that we are not one big world family, or ever likely to be; that the differences among races, nations, cultures and their various histories are at least as profound and as durable as the similarities; that these differences are not divagations from a European norm but structures eminently worth knowing about for their own sake. In the world that is coming, if you can't navigate difference, you've had it.[21]

Your language can reflect the mature awareness that people differ in important ways but that we also hold many beliefs and hopes in common—and we *all* have the right to be treated with respect. In other words, your language can demonstrate that you pay attention to . . . the *personal* rather than the *impersonal* features of those you talk with and about: how they are unique, the choices they make, their unmeasurable parts, their reflectiveness, and their addressability.

As we have said, we're not suggesting that you manage your language only when you believe that someone within earshot might be a member of a potentially offended group. That's what some people would call being "politically correct," and our point is different. We are suggesting that you try to make *all* your language inclusive and respectful. It's increasingly obvious that even a group of your friends who appear to be a lot like you may very well include one or two who could be negatively touched by something you say. So if you selectively use sensitive and respectful language as just a technique or communication strategy, you are definitely not following the suggestion we're making here. Our point is that you adopt this perspective as a part of your communicating all the time.

Specifically how can you follow this suggestion? We have tried to provide some illustrations throughout this book. As authors, when we give examples of conversations, we have tried to use names that are common to various ethnic and cultural groups. In the introduction to Part II we used an example of a conversation between a straight male and his gay friend, not to make a point about sexual orientation but to illustrate something about verbal and nonverbal communication that happens whenever human beings—not just certain human beings—communicate. We have also used "partner" instead of "spouse" to acknowledge that not all persons with permanent, intimate commitments are married. Earlier in this chapter we talked about gender-neutral communication, and throughout the book we have included both males and females in both positive and negative examples.

You can use language similarly. Keep in mind that people with identities different from yours are likely to be affected almost any time you speak. Recognize that, although you might sometimes want to communicate only with people who are like you, the real world isn't like that. Increasing diversity is a fact of life not only across the United States but also in most other countries.

When you want to use a respectful or inclusive term but you aren't sure which one is right, ask the person. The reason why *African-American* is better than *Negro*, and often better than the term *black*, is that many (although not all) African-Americans prefer it that way. The reason that *Latino* is often preferred over *Hispanic* and *Asian* over *Oriental* is that *Hispanic* and *Oriental* are terms Caucasians originally used as labels, and the people involved prefer to choose their own identifying terms. It's also good to remember that terms like *Asian* don't acknowledge the important differences between Chinese, Japanese, Filipino, Vietnamese, and others.

When you think and talk about someone who is disabled, the most important thing you can do is to acknowledge that his or her disability is only part of who he or she is. So it isn't that "there's a handicap in the group" but that "there's a person with a handicap who won't be able to do what we're planning." In other words, treat these individuals first as persons and only secondarily as persons with disabilities.

It can be difficult to make your language consistently inclusive. Patterns you have learned can be hard to break. And it can sometimes seem impossible to be completely sensitive and respectful. We can increase our flexibility, but we still will represent our own cultural perspective in whatever we say.

Care About Your Talk

Our point about inclusive and respectful language leads directly to this final guideline. Just about everything we have said about language emphasizes the close connection between what you say and who you are. So our final suggestion is that you "watch your tongue"; be careful about your speech; revere talk for what it is—a direct reflection and a clear indication of who you are and what's important to you. Talk is how you make yourself present to others.

Martin Buber had a way of expressing this idea that he discovered while living with the Hasidic people, an orthodox Jewish sect which originated in Eastern Europe. Part of Hasidic teaching emphasizes that human life has three primary parts: thought, speech, and action. They believe that our goal should be to unify them, to make them "all of a piece."[22] This means, among other things, that what you say—your spoken language—should as nearly as possible reflect what you're actually thinking and who you actually are. In other words, it's helpful to strive for a unity among your saying, being, and doing (see Figure 3). This is one way to operationalize the general suggestion that you "care about your talk." Of course none of us can achieve 100 percent success at this effort, but our communication can definitely improve if we work toward it.

Summary

The purpose of this chapter is to increase your awareness of the important role language plays in your efforts to promote interpersonal-quality communication.

We reviewed three ways language has been studied, each of which tells us something about how to improve our verbal communicating. First, language has historically been treated as a "system of symbols." One insight that has emerged from this perspective is that the relationship between words and their referents is arbitrary, which is to say that the word is not the thing. This insight, in turn, leads to warnings about reification, static evaluations, bypassing, and labeling and to suggestions about dating and indexing that can improve your language use.

Second, language has been treated as an activity. It isn't just a system of symbols representing nonlinguistic things; when people speak, they are both saying something and *doing* something. As conversation analysts have demonstrated, informal talk is made up in part of certain patterns or sequences of greeting, complimenting, requesting, commanding, complaining, threatening, interrupting, and so on. Each action requires certain propositional content, adaptations to the situation, and speaker intent. Some actions, for example, adjacency pairs, require that conversation partners collaborate. In these cases persons work together to accomplish, for example, a pre-request, or pre-announcement. But conversation analysts have also emphasized that everyday talk is made up of more than just predictable patterns or sequences. In actual conversation we muddle through just about as often as we engage in specifiable conversation acts.

This perspective on language can teach you to understand the relationship between what you say and what you do in your talk. This can help you reduce the extent to which others see you as manipulative or strategic. It can also help you diag-

Figure 3
Buber's circle of three primary goals.

nose or troubleshoot communication difficulties. The final payoff from this perspective is the insight that effective conversation requires both structure and improvisation. It's important to know the cultural and linguistic rules, but that's not enough by itself. You also need to be comfortable enough to adapt to unique circumstances.

Language has also been studied as a soup, an all-encompassing medium or environment which surrounds humans from birth to death. From this perspective, language is not simply a tool I use to accomplish certain goals, a tool I can lay down or replace with some alternative. Language isn't something I can "lay down" any more than I can lay down my ethnicity or my liver. It's part of who I am. The world each of us inhabits is, to a considerable extent, a linguistic world, a world made up of the language we hear, write, and speak. And when we thoroughly learn a second language, we actually come to inhabit a second world.

One insight that emerged from taking this perspective is that language and perception are interrelated. The Sapir-Whorf hypothesis underscores the ways language affects perception, and subsequent research has highlighted the impact of perception on language. Now we recognize that it goes both ways: What people sense is affected by and affects their language. We discussed two examples of this phenomenon—how language limits our ability to talk about communication processes, and how language can contribute to male-female stereotyping.

When language is viewed as a soup, we can also understand the sense in which the limits of my language are the limits of my world. This means that the best way to expand my horizons is to expand my language—to develop my vocabulary, get familiar with the terminology or jargon of a variety of occupations, learn a second or third language.

Finally, we ended with six suggestions, or language guidelines. All flow from what we have said about language before. First, look out for language traps, especially reification, static evaluation, and labeling. Second, resist the proper-meaning fallacy. Third, build your vocabulary. Fourth, exploit the creative power of language. Fifth, use inclusive and respectful language. And sixth, care about your talk.

Notes

1. Gerry Philipsen, "Speaking 'Like a Man' in Teamsterville," *Quarterly Journal of Speech* 61 (1975): 13–22.
2. Aristotle, *De Interpretatione*, trans. E. M. Edgehill, *The Basic Works of Aristotle*, edited by Richard McKeon (New York: Random House, 1941), p. 20.
3. Charles E. Osgood, "What is a Language?" in *The Signifying Animal*, edited by I. Rauch and G. F. Carr (Bloomington, IN: Indiana University Press, 1980), p. 12.
4. C. K. Ogden and I. A. Richards, *The Meaning of Meaning*, 8th ed. New York: Harcourt, Brace, 1986), p. 11.
5. Kathleen S. Verderber and Rudolf F. Verderber, *Inter-Act: Using Interpersonal Skills*, 6th ed. (Belmont, CA: Wadsworth, 1991), p. 94
6. Researchers call what an utterance "says" its *locutionary force* and what it "does" its *illocutionary force*. Some also distinguish between these two and a third, the utterance's *perlocutionary force*, or its effects. So, if you think of a simple act like flipping a coin, from one point of view you've thrown a coin in the air in a way to make it tumble. But at the same time, from another point of view, you've engaged in an action designed to randomly settle a two-

sided question ("heads or tails?"). And at the same time, from a third point of view, you may have disappointed your friend ("Why don't you just agree with me rather than flipping a coin?") If your coin flipping had been a verbal action, the simple act would have been the *locution*, the act you performed *in* flipping the coin would have been the *illocution*, and the action you performed *by* flipping the coin (the effect) would have been the *perlocution*. We don't discuss all these distinctions here, primarily because researchers have learned that there's too much overlap among them. This distinction was originally made by philosopher John L. Austin in *How to Do Things With Words*, edited by J. O. Urmson (Oxford: Oxford University Press, 1962). Robert E. Nofsinger provides a simplified discussion in *Everyday Conversation* (Newbury Park, CA: Sage, 1991), pp. 14–18.

7. Nofsinger, pp. 19–26.
8. Nofsinger, p. 51.
9. In the conflict chapter (Chapter 10), we will call this more straightforward and candid way of communicating "leveling."
10. Hans-Georg Gadamer, "Man and Language, " *Philosophical Hermeneutics*, edited by David E. Linge (Berkeley: University of California Press, 1976), pp. 62–63.
11. D. B. Chamberlain, "Consciousness at Birth: The Range of Empirical Evidence," in *Pre- and Perinatal Psychology: An Introduction*, edited by T. R. Verney (New York: Human Sciences, 1987), pp. 70–86.
12. A. Tomatis, "Ontogenesis of the Faculty of Listening," in Verney (ed.), pp. 23–35.
13. Beth Haslett, "Acquiring Conversational Competence," *Western Journal of Speech Communications* 48 (1984): 120.
14. John B. Carroll (ed.), *Language Thought and Reality: Selected Writings of Benjamin Lee Whorf* (New York: Wiley, 1956), pp. 212–213.
15. For over fifty years, linguistics, anthropology, and communication textbooks have used the example of Eskimo words for snow to illustrate how language and perception are interrelated. You may have seen it before. According to this account, the importance of snow in Eskimo culture is reflected in the many terms they have for "falling snow," "drifting snow," "snow on the ground," "slushy snow," and so on. Earlier editions of this text repeated this myth. But we now know it isn't true. The myth began in 1911 when an anthropologist working in Alaska compared the different Eskimo root words for "snow on the ground," "falling snow," "drifting snow," and "a snow drift" with different English root words for a variety of forms of water (liquid, lake, river, brook, rain, dew, wave, foam, and so on). The anthropologist's comment was popularized in a 1940 article and then found its way into literally hundreds of publications which confidently asserted that Eskimos had "nine," "twenty-three," "fifty," and even "one hundred" words for "snow." But they don't. The best available source, a *Dictionary of the West Greenlandic Eskimo Language*, gives just two: *quanik*, meaning "snow in the air" and *aput*, meaning "snow on the ground." So if you hear or read of the Eskimo-words-for-snow example, feel free to correct it. Or at least don't repeat it. See Geoffrey Pullum, "The Great Eskimo Vocabulary Hoax," *Lingua Franca* 14 (June 1990): 28–29.
16. Harry Hoijer, "Cultural Implications of Some Navajo Linguistic Categories," *Language* 27 (1951): 117.
17. Ludwig Wittgenstein, *Tractatus Logico-Philosophicus*, trans. D. F. Pears and D. F. McGuiness (London: Routledge & Kegan Paul, 1961).
18. Richard Rodriguez, *Hunger of Memory* (New York: Bantam, 1982), p. 15.
19. Rodriguez, pp. 16–17.
20. John Stewart and Milt Thomas, "Dialogic Listening: Sculpting Mutual Meanings," *Bridges Not Walls: A Book About Interpersonal Communication*, 5th ed. (New York: McGraw-Hill, 1990), pp. 192–210.
21. Robert Hughes, "The Fraying of America," *Time* (February 3, 1992): 47.
22. See Martin Buber, *Hasidism and Modern Man* (New York: Harper, 1958), pp. 154–157.

Review Questions

1. Review the differences among verbal, oral, nonverbal, and nonoral communication.
2. What is the point made by the fact that the bottom line of the triangle of meaning is dotted?
3. Explain how *dating* and *indexing* can help solve problems created by *reifying* and *bypassing*.
4. What is the *propositional content* of a speech act?
5. What is "transactional" about an *adjacency pair?*
6. Explain what it means to view language as a "soup."
7. Give one example of how the language you grew up around has affected the ways you perceive women and men.
8. Define *metaphor* and tell how it can function in everyday conversation.

Probes

1. On the one hand, it's obvious that there's no necessary relationship between words like "five" and "three." On the other hand, you *can't* call a CD player a "stepladder" or an "axe." There *does* seem to be something nonarbitrary about language. Explain.
2. The approach that views language as a system of symbols works best for concrete nouns—words like "cat," and "hat." How much of everyday conversation is made up of this kind of word? How well does this approach explain abstract nouns, like "love," and prepositions, conjunctions, and adverbs?
3. Explain the advantages and disadvantages or strengths and weaknesses of euphemisms.
4. What are the most consequential or high-impact speech acts that you've performed in the past two days? Did you make an important *promise* or *commitment?* Lay down a *threat?* Present an *offer?* What were the outcomes of these speech acts?
5. If you have studied a language other than English, give your own example of the point we make by referring to the Navajo way of talking about "wagon." If you don't, interview a nonnative English speaker to get an example from him or her.
6. This reading suggests that people change such statements as, "I don't mean to criticize, but have you looked in the mirror today?" to be more candid about what the statements actually are. How does this suggestion relate to the concept of *metacommunication?*
7. When you view language as a soup, you recognize that infants are learning *language* a long time before they speak their first word. Explain.
8. Based on your experience, have the changes from such words as "metermaid" to "parking checker," and "fireman" to "firefighter" had any noticeable impact on the ways women are perceived? Explain.
9. Explain how the "proper meaning fallacy" can help create interpersonal conflict.
10. Without telling anyone what you're doing, listen for one day to the disrespectful language around you. How often do you hear people use words like "faggot," "bitch," "dick head," or "blimpo"? Is this a common pattern in your speech community or an exception to the rule?
11. What's the difference between "political correctness" and "using inclusive and respectful language"?

Shortly after Thanksgiving, 1993, a friend showed me a letter that combined some pretty striking verbal and nonverbal cues. The letter was written by an attorney to his mother, sister, and brother-in-law. It is laser-printed on law-office letterhead. The name of the law firm is in the upper-left corner, and across from it are the words "Attorneys At Law" followed by the law office address, voice telephone number, and fax number. Across the bottom of the letter are listed all the attorneys in the firm. The rest of the letter looks like this (I've changed the names and addresses):

A Family Letter

November 16, 1993

Mrs. Elizabeth McPherron
3206 Hemlock Road #C-5
Portland, OR 97399

Mrs. Nancy James
Mr. Peter Lawrence
3424 So. 147th
Salem, OR 97522

Re: Thanksgiving!

Greetings:

As all of you know, I have been extremely busy the last few months with several major matters in my office. I am pleased to say that all of those matters have now been successfully concluded. I want to thank you for your patience and understanding.

There is also the matter of Thanksgiving. Dorothy plans to have Thanksgiving at our home and we are inviting everyone from our respective families. Please let me know whether you will be able to attend.

Very truly yours,

Charles T. Groves
hmf

    The letter struck me because of the amazingly impersonal way it addressed close family members about a family topic. How do you respond to this combination of verbal and nonverbal cues?

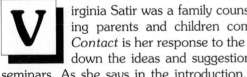

irginia Satir was a family counselor who spent over forty years helping parents and children communicate. Her small book *Making Contact* is her response to the many persons who asked her to write down the ideas and suggestions that she shared in workshops and seminars. As she says in the introduction, "The framework of this book is the BARE BONES of the possible, which I believe applies to *all* human beings. You, the reader, can flesh out the framework to fit you."

I like the simple, straightforward, no-nonsense way she talks about words, and I think she's pinpointed several insights that can help all of us communicate better. If we did, as she suggests, pay more attention to the ways we use the ten key words she discusses, I'm convinced that we'd experience considerably less conflict, misunderstanding, and frustration. See if you don't agree.

Paying Attention to Words

Virginia Satir

Words are important tools for contact. They are used more consciously than any other form of contact. I think it is important to learn how to use words well in the service of our communication.

Words cannot be separated from sights, sounds, movements, and touch of the person using them. They are one package.

However, for the moment, let's consider only words. Using words is literally the outcome of a whole lot of processes that go on in the body. All the senses, the nervous system, brain, vocal chords, throat, lungs, and all parts of the mouth are involved. This means that physiologically, talking is a very complicated process. . . .

If you think of your brain as a computer, storing all your experiences on tapes, then the words you pick will have to come from those tapes. Those tapes represent all our past experiences, accumulated knowledge, rules, and guides. There is nothing else there until new tapes are added. I hope that what you are reading will help you to add new tapes out of getting new experiences.

The words we use have an effect on our health. They definitely influence emotional relationships between people and how people can work together.

Words Have Power

Listen to what you say and see if you are really saying what you mean. Nine people out of ten can't remember what they said sixty seconds ago, others remember.

There are ten English words that it is well to pay close attention to, to use with caution and with loving care: *I, You, They, It, But, Yes, No, Always, Never, Should*.

If you were able to use these special words carefully it would already solve many contact problems created by misunderstanding.

I

Many people avoid the use of the word *I* because they feel they are trying to bring attention to themselves. They think they are being selfish. Shades of childhood, when you shouldn't show off, and who wants to be selfish? The most important thing is that

From Virginia Satir, *Making Contact* (Millbrae, Calif.: Celestial Arts, 1976). The excerpt covers twelve pages in the text of Satir's book. Courtesy of Celestial Arts Pub. Co., 231 Adrian Rd., Millbrae, Calif. 94030.

using "I" clearly means that you are taking responsibility for what you say. Many people mix this up by starting off with saying "you." I have heard people say "You can't do that." This is often heard as a "put-down," whereas "I think you can't do that" makes a more equal relationship between the two. It gives the same information without the put-down.

"I" is the pronoun that clearly states "me" when I am talking so it is important to say it. If you want to be clear when you are talking, no matter what you say, it is important to state clearly your ownership of *your* statement.

"I am saying that the moon is made of red cheese."
(*This is clearly your picture*)

instead of saying . . .

"The moon is made of red cheese."
(*This is a new law*)

Being aware of your clear use of "I" is particularly crucial when people are already in crisis. It is more clear to say "It is my picture that . . ." (which is an ownership statement). Whoever has the presence of mind to do this can begin to alter an escalating situation. When "I" is not clear, it is easy for the hearer to get a "you" message, which very often is interpreted as a "put-down."

You

The use of the word *you* is also tricky. It can be felt as an accusation when only reporting or sharing is intended.

"You are making things worse" can sound quite different if the words "I think" are added. "I think you are making things worse. . . ."

When used in clear commands or directions, it is not so easily misunderstood. For example, "I want you to . . ." or "You are the one I wanted to speak to."

They

The use of *they* is often an indirect way of talking about "you." It is also often a loose way of spreading gossip.

"They say . . ."

"They" can also be some kind of smorgasbord that refers to our negative fantasies. This is especially true in a situation where people are assessing blame. If we know who "they" are we can say so.

How many times do we hear "They won't let me." "They will be upset." "They don't like what I am doing." "They say . . ."

If someone else uses it, we can ask "Who is your *they*?"

The important part of this is to have clear who "they" are so that inaccurate information is not passed on and it is clear exactly who is being referred to. Being clear in this way seems to add to everyone's security. Information becomes concrete which one can get hold of, instead of being nebulous and perhaps posing some kind of threat.

It

It is a word that can easily be misunderstood because it often isn't clear what "it" refers to. "It" is a word that has to be used with care.

The more clear your "it" is, the less the hearer fills it in with his own meaning. Sometimes "it" is related to a hidden "I" message. One way to better understand your "it" is to substitute "I" and see what happens. "It isn't clear" changed to "I am not clear" could make things more accurate and therefore easier to respond to.

"It often happens to people" is a statement that when said straight could be a comfort message that says, "The thing you are talking about has happened to me. I know how feeling humiliated feels."

To be more sure that we are understood, it might be wiser to fill in the details.

But

Next is the word *but*.

"But" is often a way of saying "yes" and "no" in the same sentence.

"I love you *but* I wish you would change your underwear more often."

This kind of use can easily end up with the other person feeling very uncomfortable, uneasy, and frequently confused.

Try substituting the word "and" for "but," which will clarify the situation. Your body will even feel different.

By using "but" the speaker is often linking two different thoughts together, which is what causes the difficulty.

Thus "I love you, but I wish you would change your underwear more often" could be two expressions.

"I love you," and "I wish you would change your underwear more often."

It could also represent someone's best, although fearful, attempt to make an uncomfortable demand by couching the demand in a love context, hoping the other person would not feel hurt.

If this is the case, what would happen if the person were to say "I want to ask something of you that I feel very uncomfortable about. I would like you to change your underwear more often."

Yes, No

A clear "yes" and "no" are important. Too many people say "yes, but" or "yes, maybe" or "no" just to be on the safe side, especially if they are in a position of power.

When "yes" or "no" are said clearly, and they mean NOW and not forever, and it is further clear "yes" and "no" relate to an issue rather than a person's value, then "yes" and "no" are very helpful words in making contact.

People can get away with much misuse of words when trust and good feeling have been established and when the freedom to comment is around. However, so often people feel so unsure about themselves that the lack of clarity leaves a lot of room for misunderstanding and consequent bad feelings. It is easy to build up these bad feelings once they are started.

"No" is a word that we all need and need to be able to use when it fits. So often when people feel "no," they say "maybe" or "yes" to avoid meeting the issue. This is justified on the basis of sparing the other's feelings. It is a form of lying and usually invites distrust, which, of course, is death to making contact.

When the "no" isn't clear, the "yes" can also be mistrusted. Have you ever heard "He said yes, but he doesn't really mean it."

Always, Never

Always is the positive form of a global word. *Never* is the negative form. For example:

Always clean up your plate.
Never leave anything on your plate.

The literal meaning of these words is seldom accurate and the directions seldom applicable to life situations. There are few cases in life where something is always *or* never. Therefore to try to follow these demands in all situations will surely end up in failure like the rules I described earlier.

Often the use of these words is a way to make emotional emphasis, like . . .

"You *always* make me mad."

meaning really . . .

"I am NOW very mad at you."

If the situation were as the speaker states, the adrenals would wear out.

Sometimes the words *always* and *never* hide ignorance. For example, someone has spent just five minutes with a person and announces,

"He is always bright."

In most cases the literal use of these two words could not be followed in all times, places and situations. Furthermore, they are frequently untrue. For the most part they become emotionally laden words that harm rather than nurture or enlighten the situation.

I find that these words are often used without any meaning in any literal sense.

These words are related to the inhuman rules I talked about earlier, so they have the potential for the same unnecessary guilt and inadequacy feelings because they are almost impossible to apply.

Should

"Ought" and "should" are other trap words from which it is easy to imply that there is something wrong with you—you have failed somehow to measure up.

Often the use of these words implies stupidity on someone's part . . .

"You should have known better."

This is frequently heard as an accusation. Sometimes it merely represents some friendly advice. When people use the words "ought" and "should," often they are trying to indicate a dilemma in which they have more than one direction to go at a time—one may be pulling harder than the rest although the others are equally important . . .

"I like this, but I should get that."

When your words are these, your body often feels tight. There are no easy answers to the pulls which "ought" and "should" represent. Biologically we really can go in only one direction at a time.

When your body feels tight your brain often freezes right along with your tight body, and so your thinking becomes limited as well.

Hearing yourself use the words *ought* and *should* can be a tip-off to you that you are engaged in a struggle. Perhaps instead of trying to deal with these opposing parts as one, you can separate them and make two parts.

"I like this . . ." (one part)
"But I should get that"

translated into . . .

"I also need that . . ." (a second part).

Such a separation may be helpful in considering each piece separately and then considering them together.

When you do this your body has a chance to become a little looser, thus freeing some energy to negotiate a bit better.

When I am in this spot, I can help myself by asking whether I will literally die in either situation. If the answer is *no*, then I have a different perspective, and I can more easily play around with alternatives, since I am now out of a win-loss feeling in myself. I won't die. I may be only a little deprived or inconvenienced at most.

Start paying attention to the words you use.

Who is your *they?*
What is your *it?*
What does your *no* mean?
What does your *yes* mean?
Is your *I* clear?

Are you saying *never* and *always* when you mean sometimes and when you want to make emotional emphasis?

How are you using *ought* and *should?*

Review Questions

1. What reasons do people give for *not* using the word "I"?
2. What is similar about the problems Satir finds with the words "they" and "it"?
3. Does Satir suggest that we should not use the words "but," "yes," and "no"? What is she saying about these words?
4. How does a person's use of the words "ought" and "should" reflect that person's value system?

Probes

1. When you're in a conversation, can you recall what you said sixty seconds earlier? Try it. What do you notice?
2. Notice how, as Virginia Satir says, "it" and "they" both often work to hide the fact that some *I* is actually talking. When do you hear yourself using "it" and "they" that way?
3. What happens when you substitute "and" for "but"?
4. Do you experience your body responding as Satir describes to the words "ought" and "should"?

Amy Tan, a widely-published Chinese-American author, is impatient with some popular assumptions about how Chinese people in the United States communicate. In this reading she pays special attention to the belief among many that Chinese people are unfailingly "discreet and modest," so much so that there aren't even words in the Chinese language for "yes" and "no." As she writes, "That's not true. . .although I can see why an outsider might think that."

Tan reports, "I find there was nothing discreet about the Chinese language I grew up with. My parents made everything abundantly clear. Nothing wishy-washy in their demands, no compromises accepted." She points out how direct and unambiguous demands and rejections can be clearly expressed in a language without a single term for "yes" or "no," and how euphemisms and indirect language can smooth relationships. Along the way, Tan raises some interesting questions about some aspects of the Sapir-Whorf hypothesis.

In addition to helping correct some cultural stereotypes, this reading also provides support for the usefulness of viewing language as a soup (see Carole's and my essay at the start of this chapter). The language Amy Tan's parents and family spoke helped construct a particular world, with values and ways of relating that helped its members feel "at home' in that world.

The Language of Discretion

Amy Tan

At a recent family dinner in San Francisco, my mother whispered to me: "Sausau [Brother's wife] pretends too hard to be polite! Why bother? In the end, she always takes everything."

My mother thinks like a *waixiao*, an expatriate, temporarily away from China since 1949, no longer patient with ritual courtesies. As if to prove her point, she reached across the table to offer my elderly aunt from Beijing the last scallop from the Happy Family seafood dish.

Sau-sau scowled. "*B'yao, zhen b'yao!*" (I don't want it, really I don't!) she cried, patting her plump stomach.

"Take it! Take it!" scolded my mother in Chinese.

"Full, I'm already full," Sau-sau protested weakly, eyeing the beloved scallop.

"Ai!" exclaimed my mother, completely exasperated. "Nobody else wants it. If you don't take it, it will only rot!"

At this point, Sau-sau sighed, acting as if she were doing my mother a big favor by taking the wretched scrap off her hands.

My mother turned to her brother, a high-ranking communist official who was visiting her in California for the first time: "In America a Chinese person could starve to death. If you say you don't want it, they won't ask you again forever."

My uncle nodded and said he understood fully: Americans take things quickly because they have no time to be polite.

I thought about this misunderstanding again—of social contexts failing in translation—when a friend sent me an article from the *New York Times Magazine* (24 April 1988). The article, on changes in New York's Chinatown, made passing reference to the inherent ambivalence of the Chinese language.

Chinese people are so "discreet and modest," the article stated, there aren't even words for "yes" and "no."

That's not true, I thought, although I can see why an outsider might think that. I continued reading.

If one is Chinese, the article went on to say, "One compromises, one doesn't hazard a loss of face by an overemphatic response."

My throat seized. Why do people keep saying these things? As if we truly were those little dolls sold in Chinatown tourist shops, heads bobbing up and down in complacent agreement to anything said!

I worry about the effect of one-dimensional statements on the unwary and guileless. When they read about this so-called vocabulary deficit, do they also conclude that Chinese people evolved into a mild-mannered lot because the language only allowed them to hobble forth with minced words?

Something enormous is always lost in translation. Something insidious seeps into the gaps, especially when amateur linguists continue to compare, one-for-one, language differences and then put forth notions wide open to misinterpretation: that Chinese people have no direct linguistic means to make decisions, assert or deny, affirm or negate, just say no to drug dealers, or behave properly on the witness stand when told, "Please answer yes or no."

Yet one can argue, with the help of renowned linguists, that the Chinese are indeed up a creek without "yes" and "no." Take any number of variations on the old language-and-reality theory stated years ago by Edward Sapir: "Human beings . . . are very much at the mercy of the particular language which has become the medium for their society. . . . The fact of the matter is that the 'real world' is to a large extent built up on the language habits of the group."

This notion was further bolstered by the famous Sapir-Whorf hypothesis, which roughly states that one's perception of the world and how one functions in it depends a great deal on the language used. As Sapir, Whorf, and new carriers of the banner would have us believe, language shapes our thinking, channels us along certain patterns embedded in words, syntactic structures, and intonation patterns. Language has become the peg and the shelf that enables us to sort out and categorize the world. In English, we see "cats" and "dogs"; what if the language had also specified *glatz*, meaning "animals that leave fur on the sofa," and *glotz*, meaning "animals that leave fur and drool on the sofa"? How would language, the enabler, have changed our perceptions with slight vocabulary variations?

And if this were the case—of language being the master of destined thought—think of the opportunities lost from failure to evolve two little words, *yes* and *no*, the simplest of opposites! Ghenghis Khan could have been sent back to Mongolia. Opium wars might have been averted. The Cultural Revolution could have been sidestepped.

There are still many, from serious linguists to pop psychology cultists, who view language and reality as inextricably tied, on being the consequence of the other. We have traversed the range from the Sapir-Whorf hypothesis to est and neurolinguistic programming, which tell us "you are what you say."

I too have been intrigued by the theories I can summarize, albeit badly, ages-old empirical evidence: of Eskimos and their infinite ways to say "snow," their ability to *see* the differences in snowflake configurations, thanks to the richness of their vocabulary, while non-Eskimo speakers like myself founder in "snow," "more snow," and "lots more where that came from."

I too have experienced dramatic cognitive awakenings via the word. Once I added "mauve" to my vocabulary I began to see it everywhere. When I learned how to pronounce *prix fixe*, I ate French food at prices better than the easier-to-say *à la carte* choices.

But just how seriously are we supposed to take this?

Sapir said something else about language and reality. It is the part that often gets left behind in the dot-dot-dots of quotes: ". . . No two languages are ever sufficiently similar to be considered as representing the same social reality. The worlds in which different societies live are distinct worlds, not merely the same world with different labels attached."

When I first read this, I thought, Here at last is validity for the dilemmas I felt growing up in a bicultural, bilingual family! As any child of immigrant parents knows, there's a special kind of double bind attached to knowing two languages. My parents, for example, spoke to me in both Chinese and English; I spoke back to them in English.

"Amy-ah!" they'd call to me.

"What?" I'd mumble back.

"Do not question us when we call," they scolded me in Chinese. "It is not respectful."

"What do you mean?"

"Ai! Didn't we just tell you not to question?"

To this day, I wonder which parts of my behavior were shaped by Chinese, which by English. I am tempted to think, for example, that if I am of two minds on some matter it is due to the richness of my linguistic experiences, not to any personal tendencies toward wishy-washiness. But which mind says what?

Was it perhaps patience—developed through years of deciphering my mother's fractured English—that had me listening politely while a woman announced over the phone that I had won one of five valuable prizes? Was it respect—pounded in by the Chinese imperative to accept convoluted explanations—that had me agreeing that I might find it worthwhile to drive seventy-five miles to view a time-share resort? Could I have been at a loss for words when asked, "Wouldn't you like to win a Hawaiian cruise or perhaps a fabulous Star of India designed exclusively by Carter and Van Arpels?"

And when this same woman called back a week later, this time complaining that I had missed my appointment, obviously it was my type A language that kicked into gear and interrupted her. Certainly, my blunt denial—"Frankly I'm not interested"—was as American as apple pie. And when she said, "But it's in Morgan Hill," and I shouted, "Read my lips, I don't care if it's Timbuktu," you can be sure I said it with the precise intonation expressing both cynicism and disgust.

It's dangerous business, this sorting out of language and behavior. Which one is English? Which is Chinese? The categories manifest themselves: passive and aggressive, tentative and assertive, indirect and direct. And I realize they are just variations of the same theme: that Chinese people are discreet and modest.

Reject them all!

If my reaction is overly strident, it is because I cannot come across as too emphatic. I grew up listening to the same lines over and over again, like so many rote expressions repeated in an English phrase-book. And I too almost came to believe them.

Yet if I consider my upbringing more carefully, I find there was nothing discreet about the Chinese language I grew up with. My parents made everything abundantly clear. Nothing wishy-washy in their demands, no compromises accepted: "Of course you will become a famous neurosurgeon," they told me. "And yes, a concert pianist on the side."

In fact, now that I remember, it seems that the more emphatic outbursts always spilled over into Chinese: "Not that way! You must wash rice so not a single grain spills out."

I do not believe that my parents—both immigrants from mainland China—are an exception to the modest-and-discreet rule. I have only to look at the number of Chinese engineering students skewing minority ratios at Berkeley, MIT, and Yale. Certainly they were not raised by passive mothers and fathers who said, "It is up to you, my daughter. Writer, welfare recipient, masseuse, or molecular engineer—you decide."

And my American mind says, See, those engineering students weren't able to say no to their parents' demands. But then my Chinese mind remembers: Ah, but those parents all wanted their sons and daughters to be *pre-med*.

Having listened to both Chinese and English, I also tend to be suspicious of any comparisons between the two languages. Typically, one language—that of the person doing the comparing—is often used as the standard, the benchmark for a logical form of expression. And so the language being compared is always in danger of being judged deficient or superfluous, simplistic or unnecessarily complex, melodious or cacophonous. English speakers point out that Chinese is extremely difficult because it relies on variations in tone barely discernible to the human ear. By the same token, Chinese speakers tell me English is extremely difficult because it is inconsistent, a language of too many broken rules, of Mickey Mice and Donald Ducks.

Even more dangerous to my mind is the temptation to compare both language and behavior *in translation*. To listen to my mother speak English, one might think she has no concept of past or future tense, that she doesn't see the difference between singular and plural, that she is gender blind because she calls my husband "she." If one were not careful, one might also generalize that, based on the way my mother talks, all Chinese people take a circumlocutory route to get to the point. It is, in fact, my mother's idiosyncratic behavior to ramble a bit. . . .

I worry that the dominant society may see Chinese people from a limited—and limiting—perspective. I worry that seemingly benign stereotypes may be part of the reason there are few Chinese in top management positions, in mainstream political roles. I worry about the power of language: that if one says anything enough times—in *any* language—it might become true.

Could this be why Chinese friends of my parents' generation are willing to accept the generalization?

"Why are you complaining?" one of them said to me. "If people think we are modest and polite, let them think that. Wouldn't Americans be pleased to admit they are thought of as polite?"

And I do believe anyone would take the description as a compliment—at first. But after a while, it annoys, as if the only things that people heard one say were phatic remarks: "I'm so pleased to meet you. I've heard many wonderful things about you. For me? You shouldn't have!"

These remarks are not representative of new ideas, honest emotions, or considered thought. They are what is said from the polite distance of social contexts: of greetings, farewells, wedding thank-you notes, convenient excuses, and the like.

It makes me wonder though. How many anthropologists, how many sociologists, how many travel journalists have documented so-called "natural interactions" in foreign lands, all observed with spiral notebook in hand? How many other cases are there of the long-lost primitive tribe, people who turned out to be sophisticated enough to put on the stone-age show that ethnologists had come to see?

And how many tourists fresh off the bus have wandered into Chinatown expecting the self-effacing shopkeeper to admit under duress that the goods are not worth the price asked? I have witnessed it.

"I don't know," the tourist said to the shopkeeper, a Cantonese woman in her fifties. "It doesn't look genuine to me. I'll give you three dollars."

"You don't like my price, go somewhere else," said the shopkeeper.

"You are not a nice person," cried the shocked tourist, "not a nice person at all!"

"Who say I have to be nice," snapped the shopkeeper.

"So how does one say 'yes' and 'no' in Chinese?" ask my friends a bit warily.

And here I do agree in part with the *New York Times Magazine* article. There is no one word for "yes" or "no"—but not out of necessity to be discreet. If anything, I would say the Chinese equivalent of answering "yes" or "no" is dis*crete*, that is, specific to what is asked.

Ask a Chinese person if he or she has eaten, and he or she might say *chrle* (eaten already) or perhaps *meiyou* (have not).

Ask, "So you had insurance at the time of the accident?" and the response would be *dwei* (correct) or *meiyou* (did not have).

Ask, "Have you stopped beating your wife?" and the answer refers directly to the proposition being asserted or denied: stopped already, still have not, never beat, have no wife.

What could be clearer?

As for those who are still wondering how to translate the language of discretion, I offer this personal example.

My aunt and uncle were about to return to Beijing after a three-month visit to the United States. On their last night I announced I wanted to take them out to dinner.

"Are you hungry?" I asked in Chinese.

"Not hungry," said my uncle promptly, the same response he once gave me ten minutes before he suffered a low-blood-sugar attack.

"Not too hungry," said my aunt. "Perhaps you're hungry?"

"A little," I admitted.

"We can eat, we can eat," they both consented.

"What kind of food?" I asked.

"Oh, doesn't matter. Anything will do. Nothing fancy, just some simple food is fine."

"Do you like Japanese food? We haven't had that yet," I suggested.

They looked at each other.

"We can eat it," said my uncle bravely, this survivor of the Long March.

"We have eaten it before," added my aunt. "Raw fish."

"Oh, you don't like it?" I said. "Don't be polite. We can go somewhere else."

"We are not being polite. We can eat it," my aunt insisted.

So I drove them to Japantown and we walked past several restaurants featuring colorful plastic displays of sushi.

"Not this one, not this one either," I continued to say, as if searching for a Japanese restaurant similar to the last. "Here it is," I finally said, turning into a restaurant famous for its Chinese fish dishes from Shandong.

"Oh, Chinese food!" cried my aunt, obviously relieved.

My uncle patted my arm. "You think Chinese."

"It's your last night here in America," I said. "So don't be polite. Act like an American."

And that night we ate a banquet.

Note

1. Edward Sapir, *Selected Writings*, ed. D. G. Mandelbaum (Berkeley and Los Angeles, 1949).

Review Questions

1. What does it mean to say that "social contexts" can "fail in translation"?
2. What is the Sapir-Whorf hypothesis? What does it say about interpersonal communication?
3. What point is Amy Tan making about "respect" when she uses the examples of telephone calls about a time-share resort or a Hawaiian cruise?
4. Amy Tan admits that the Chinese language does not have one word for "yes" or "no," but she insists that speakers of Chinese are *not* wishy-washy or noncommittal. As she explains it, how do they affirm or deny without these words?

Probes

1. Amy Tan wants to correct a stereotype about Chinese communication. She makes the point of her first example in these words: "Americans take things quickly because they have no time to be polite." Is this a stereotype, too? Discuss.
2. As Carole and I explained in the first reading in this chapter, the Sapir-Whorf hypothesis says that language affects perception. On the one hand, Amy Tan rejects the idea that vocabulary determines behavior—that "Chinese people evolved into a mild-mannered lot because the language only allowed them to hobble forth with minced words." On the other hand, she says, "Sapir was right about differences between two languages and their realities." What do you understand her position to be on this idea about the relationship between language and perception?

3. If you know at least two languages, you can respond to this question on your own. If not, interview someone who does before you respond to it. Here's the question: What does it mean to say that the "worlds" inhabited by people who speak different languages "are distinct worlds, not merely the same world with different labels attached"?

Hugh Prather's insights have been an important part of every edition of *Bridges Not Walls* since the first edition was printed in 1973. In *Notes to Myself* and other books, he captures important insights succinctly and memorably. Recently he and his wife, Gayle, have collaborated on several books, including one they call *Parables from Other Planets: Folktales of the Universe.* It's made up of a number of short stories, each of which subtly makes an insightful point.

What feature or function of language is highlighted in this selection called "The Salesman"?

The Salesman

Hugh and Gayle Prather

A passage from one of the holy scriptures of the planet Zigtara reads: *If the mind of the child has one honest thought, truth will take root in the heart. If the eye of the child has a single tear, that tear will become a river that will float the child back to the heart of the Divine. Therefore, do not despair for anyone.*

A salesman who once lived in Zigtara went from door to door selling computerized holy men for home inspiration. He was not sincere. But he knew a good product when he saw one. Gradually he learned when to say "Praise A!" and when to say "Praise B!" Gradually he learned what passages from the various scriptures to call up on his wristband monitor. Sometimes he encountered people who were truly devout and he had to speak words that would be of interest to them. What he didn't realize was that these words contained true goodness that echoed within the forgotten goodness of his heart. The more he spoke the words of truth, the more conscious he became of the truth within him. In the end, he did not attain devoutness itself, but he did become harmless. And on the planet of Zigtara, where arguments are concluded by exchanging bites, this is a substantial accomplishment.

Chapter 4

Nonverbal
Communicating

This chapter from a recent interpersonal communication text begins with the same point we made at the start of the last chapter: In actual communicating, you can't really separate the verbal and the nonverbal. As Ted Grove puts it, in real life, "There are no separate chapters." Grove also emphasizes that another distinction we use for thinking and talking about communication is difficult to apply in practice—the distinction between the expression or production of cues ("exhaling") and the reception or experience of cues ("inhaling"). But this distinction can help organize some of what we know about nonverbal communicating into an understandable whole.

Grove uses the 'expressive functions" heading to talk about kinds or types of nonverbal communicating, including "vocalics"—the rate, pitch, volume, and tone variations in the human voice—and "kinesics," or body movement. He also distinguishes among kinds of cues by the function they perform—illustrating, adapting, displaying emotions, etc. He concludes this section with a discussion of five characteristics of nonverbal cues which helps explain how they work.

Then he shifts perspective from the "exhaling" side to "inhaling" and talks about how nonverbal communicating gets interpreted. For example, we draw conclusions from nonverbal cues about how responsive a person is and about what the power balance is between us and them. We also use nonverbal cues to give us insights into how the other person is feeling. Grove talks about how "nonverbal leakage" works in communication, and how we interpret nonverbal cues to detect when someone is lying. He concludes the chapter by emphasizing that no nonverbal cue "means" anything by itself, because each has to be interpreted in relation to the context in which it's experienced.

This reading provides a general overview of the nonverbal cues that affect conversations the most. The other selections in this chapter focus more on specifics.

Nonverbal Elements of Interaction

Theodore G. Grove

. . . In ongoing dyadic interaction, verbal and nonverbal behavior occur together and influence one another. There are no separate chapters. Nonverbal and verbal behavior are *produced* concurrently as part of the holistic larger pattern of individuals' behavior and are *experienced* as integrated patterns by the actor and observer alike.

Similar to the verbal elements, nonverbal behavior forms part of both the *expressive* and *interpretive* domains of dyadic interaction. As such, nonverbal elements contribute in a powerful way to the course of interaction episodes and, thereby, to the texture of conversations and the definition of relationships. However, in many fundamental respects, the nonverbal codes differ greatly from the verbal. . . .

Expressive Functions of Nonverbal Behavior

The Domains of Nonverbal Behavior

Similar to the verbal dimension, nonverbal behavior is a primary element of dyadic interaction. Nonverbal interactional behavior has been classified into 1) *vocalics* and 2) *kinesics*. Other nonverbal categories, having an important but somewhat less direct connection with interaction are physical appearance or *person-objects*, use of time or *chronemics*, and physical objects and their arrangements or *artifacts*.

Vocalics refers to the sound of our voice in the production of utterances and other nonlinguistic vocalizations like yawns, throat-clearing, and vocalized pauses (Traeger 1958). Vocalic factors include voice quality, rate of speech, pitch, loudness, duration of phonation, latency of reply, hesitations, dialects, regionalisms, and others. Many of these vocalic variables combine to produce what is popularly known as "inflection."

Kinesics (Birdwhistell 1955; 1970) refers to movement and can be extended to a broad range of behaviors that rely on movement for their effects. These include *postural-gestural* behavior, *face displays*, *gaze*, *proxemics*, and *haptics*. Postural-gestural behavior generally includes position and movement of the head, limbs, hands, torso, hips, as well as overall posture, postural shifts, and orientation of head and shoulders with respect to the conversational partner.

Face displays refers to all of those expressions, both large and subtle, which we produce by manipulating the network of facial musculature as we interact, including the so-called "impassive" expression where the face is very still. To the reader, the term "display" may suggest a self-conscious manipulation of these expressions to create a kind of window dressing. But, as we shall see, that is not necessarily the case. Facial displays frequently occur quite automatically in connection with the experiencing and expression of various feelings and emotions.

Gaze refers to the way we use our eyes during conversation: where we look, how frequently we maintain eye contact or mutual gaze with the other person, the duration of our gaze, and conditions associated with changes in gaze behavior. Gaze has been examined in infants and young children and mother/infant interactions as well as in adult conversational settings (Argyle and Cook 1976; Cappella 1981).

Proxemics has to do with the use of space and the physical distance between interactants (Burgoon and Jones 1976; Patterson 1968). It has been observed that the distance between people varies as a function of their immediate engagement level in the conversation, their relationship, and a number of situational factors.

Haptics refers to the study of touching behavior and has been found to function in concert with specific contexts to elicit a wide variety of meaning in the interacting parties. Twelve distinctly different meanings of touch have been identified and include support, appreciation, inclusion, sexual interest or intent, affection, playful affection, playful aggression, compliance, attention-getting, announcing a response, greetings, and departure (Jones and Yarbrough 1985).

Another well-known set of distinctions classifies nonverbal behavior on the basis of the kind of meanings it functions to create—what it *does* in the interaction (Ekman and Friesen 1969). The five categories in this scheme are *illustrators, regulators, emblems, adaptors,* and *affect displays. Illustrators* are those gestures that support or complement the meaning of the utterance. For example, one uses an illustrator when one points while saying, ". . .then you take a left. . . ." *Regulators* refer to the way we use the whole body, even the head, eyes, and voice, to regulate the flow of our interaction. For example, when we touch someone to get their attention, turn toward someone as we interrupt, or back away as we terminate a conversation, we are using regulators.

Emblems consist mainly of head, shoulder, arm, and hand signals that have precise, usually quite specific meanings, such as waving "good-bye," shrugging "I don't know," and nodding "yes." Emblems differ from the rest of interactive nonverbal behavior in that, like language symbols, they have a specific denotative value—a relatively stable designated meaning, regardless of context. More on this, later.

A fourth category in this functional classification scheme is *adaptors.* Adaptors bear little consistent relationship to the content of conversation; however, occasionally they have been observed being used to emphasize some point. Some adaptors are widely used. Examples are rubbing the back of one's neck while pondering a verbal response and touching one's chin or forehead during interaction. Other adaptors are idiosyncratic behaviors, perhaps habituated by the individual as nervous habits and eventually incorporated into their interactive behavior. Television talk-show host Johnny Carson has offered a virtual encyclopedia of adaptors with his stylized, jerky, roosterlike head movements, tie-touching, pencil play, and other behaviors.

Finally, *affect displays* refers to nonverbal expression of emotions, utilizing primarily facial expressions (Ekman and Friesen 1975). Studying facial affect displays in several cultures, investigators have identified some universally observed patterns of facial movements during expression of the emotions of happiness, fear, surprise, sadness, anger, and disgust. While public facial displays of each of these emotions may vary across cultures, private expressions of each are quite similar. Four display rules that seem to govern when particular emotions are publicly displayed within specific cultures have been identified (Ekman and Friesen 1971).

One display rule is to *intensify*—make the emotional involvement bigger than it really is. For example, facial displays of pleasure as we greet invited guests in our own culture suggest the "intensify" rule. "We're just *sooo* happy you could come!" In contrast, we seem to *de-intensify* our public disappointment or sadness upon being passed over for some sought-after honor or prize and, in some situations, de-intensify our joy when we gain the honor. Some situations and some publicly visible roles prescribe that individuals *neutralize* their facial affect displays for certain emotions. For example, the behavior of judges in the courtroom and of referees at athletic contests rarely include expressions of glee at the outcomes of the trials and games over which they preside, even though privately they must be happier over some outcomes than others. Finally, some situations seem to call for suppressing displays of a particular emotion by *masking* it with a different one. Losers of Miss America "talent" contests smile brightly while the winner cries and, in the presence of a girlfriend or comrades, teenage American boys and "macho" men have been observed to mask fear with anger.

While many emotions are expressed as *full* facial displays, those rules sometimes influence the way emotions are displayed on the face. For example, de-intensification as well as inept attempts to neutralize sometimes lead to *partial* facial involvement. As a small boy I recall swinging furiously and futilely, trying to hit another in the stomach, while my much larger adversary calmly held me at bay at arm's length with one hand on the top of my head. To my humiliation, the teacher who broke up the "fight" ineptly neutralized her amusement, resulting in a partial facial display. In similar fashion, inept attempts at masking may lead to facial *blends*, a merging of the suppressed and the superimposed emotions. For example, part of the face may reflect surprise, while another part reveals the anger one is actually feeling.

Five Characteristics of Nonverbal Codes

Contrasting nonverbal behavior with our linguistic interactive behavior will illustrate several fundamental properties of how the nonverbal codes function. First, unlike verbal behavior, we engage in nonverbal action constantly throughout a conversation, when we are not talking as well as when we are talking. We wrinkle the nose, scratch, turn our head toward or away from the other person, nod, stop nodding, and the like. Therefore, each party to a conversation is *unceasingly engaged in nonverbal behavior,* regardless of whether one is talking or is listening to the utterances of the other person.

Second, except for some noninteractive aspect like physical appearance and artifacts, one's nonverbal behaviors are produced more thoughtlessly and, therefore, are largely *out of the behavior's awareness,* relative to the more consciously selected verbal behavior. This characteristic has a number of important implications for observing the partner's nonverbal behavior, discussed in a later section.

There is some indication that we are even less aware of some of our nonverbal behaviors than of others. We tend to be more aware of our face and head than of what we are doing with the rest of our body. For example, we are able to produce "social smiles" at appropriate times in the interaction. Moreover, generally low self-awareness seems to be even lower with respect to the lower regions of the body, being lower in the legs and extremities (feet and hands) than in the head and arms.

A third difference is that while our words bear an arbitrary relationship to what they are supposed to represent, with a few exceptions (like emblems) individual nonverbal behaviors do not have arbitrarily assigned denotative meanings. They are *iconic* (Burgoon 1985) representations of meaning and do not possess the designated character of spoken words. For example, the spoken word "chair" is a designated set of sounds and could be replaced by "spurk" or any other equally arbitrary set of sounds, as long as members of our language community all agreed upon that usage. The meaning is *outside of* the actual behavior. On the other hand, if I motion to a chair as you enter the room, the gesture I make literally models the action it represents.

Fourth, while the meanings elicited by spoken words and language utterances are dependent, to some extent, on the context in which they are uttered, the meaning of nonverbal behavior is *more exclusively a function of contextual factors* just because they do lack conventional definition. Even the variety of meanings associated with the simple act of touching or being touched are heavily dependent on the context, including the verbal and other nonverbal behaviors as well as relational and situational factors (Jones and Yarbrough 1985).

Regardless of the different connotations elicited in different listeners, the word "father" refers to a fixed biological relationship; that designated core of meaning is relatively stable irrespective of connotation or context. But a particular nonverbal act lacks such linguistically conferred stability—lacks a core of consistent meaning. The same behaviors are used in connection with quite different, sometimes opposite, meanings, and those meanings are rooted in the context where the behavior occurs. For example, given a slight shift in context, my pointing toward the door could convey, "Godspeed!" or, "Get out of my office!" With the exception of emblems, each little movement does *not* have a meaning of its own. For that and other reasons, scholars have little faith in the *body-language* view of nonverbal behavior (Burgoon and Saine 1978). This contextual feature of nonverbal behavior will be elaborated in the next section interpreting nonverbal behavior.

Fifth, specific nonverbal behaviors are always produced as one part of a larger pattern along with other nonverbal behaviors; that is, they are *integrated*. That means we tend to produce nonverbal behaviors in concurrent *sets* and coordinated *sequences* rather than as single isolated behaviors. For example, typical smiling behavior may involve, in addition to an upturned mouth, crinkling the skin at the temples, cheek movements, and the like. Laughing may be accompanied by total bodily involvement including postural changes and momentary withdrawal of eye contact. Although the words in our utterances also follow combinational patterns prescribed by rules of syntax, we are able to select and utter any given single word or verbal expression in isolation from all others. We can select language segments to include in our utterances. But we would have a hard time segmenting our muscles to produce only a "lip smile." Try as we might, our cheek, nose, jaw and chin muscles, perhaps our eyes, would join in. All of these ways in which nonverbal behavior differs from verbal behavior have important consequences for interpreting the nonverbal behavior of one's interactional partner.

The Interpretive Functions of Nonverbal Behavior

As indicated in the introductory discussion of this chapter, nonverbal behavior may be viewed both in terms of its expressive role and its interpretive role in dyadic interaction. The immediately preceding material introduced nonverbal functioning from the perspective of the actor. Here, we shift gears to interpretive processes by exploring those important topics from the perspective of the observer. These explorations are organized into sections on strong nonverbal messages, nonverbal leakage, clues to deception, and the contextual interpretation of nonverbal behavior.

Strong Nonverbal Messages

Our interpretations of nonverbal behavior are certainly a crucial part of the interpersonal communication process. Based on an analysis of results from twenty-four studies comparing verbal and nonverbal behavior, Philpott found verbal interaction was associated with only 31 percent of elicited meaning, while nonverbal interaction, alone and coupled with verbal, accounted for the remaining 69 percent (Burgoon 1985). While the linguistic aspect of others' utterances can provide us with very precise information and distinctions not available through observation of nonverbal behavior alone, the latter seems to outstrip the contributions of verbal behavior with respect to a number of interpretive functions. Three of these include responsiveness, dominance relations, and expression of feelings.

Responsiveness Interpretations   "Responsiveness interpretations" refer to our sense of how engaged the partner is in our interaction—to what extent the other is *lis-*

tening to and *involved in* the give-and-take of our exchange. How do you know whether someone is listening carefully to what you are saying—listening at the very peak of their effort? There are several clues provided by your *own* listening function. For example, when your conversational partner asks a targeted question, one which required careful attention to your previous remarks, you know they have been listening attentively. Or if the partner paraphrases what you just said or asks you to elaborate on or repeat something you ineptly expressed, you know he or she has been attentive at some level. Certainly, numerous "yeah's," "I see's," and other verbal prompts and acknowledgments (or lack of them) add to one's sense of how well the other is listening. But more often and with great accuracy, we interpret how well someone is listening from our observation of their nonverbal behavior.

Behaviors called *backchanneling* (Duncan 1975) are indicative that one is continuing to listen. These may include head nods, eye contact, vocalic cues, leaning in, sitting close, standing close, direct shoulder and head orientation, alert body posture, and the like. People vary somewhat in their propensity to provide such backchannels when listening and to need them when talking. An acquaintance required constant and direct eye contact in all circumstances, whether talking or listening. Once, it was my misfortune to be in the backseat of his car as he chatted constantly, shooting frequent glances at me as we careened along at high speeds over narrow winding country roads. Despite my increasingly desperate "uh-huh's," "right's," and "yeah's," he seemed to need, above all else, the sign of responsiveness that only my eye contact could provide.

Unlike my friend, most of us are content to observe whatever nonverbal signs of responsiveness the situation permits. These interpretations of another's responsiveness pertain not only to the other's listening, but to whether the other is interested in continued interaction or even starting a conversation in the first place. We rarely need to talk about these things, because we usually can observe the partner's eye gaze, head orientation, body posture and movement, and vocalics, and draw our own fairly accurate conclusions at a given moment.

Interpretations of Dominance Relations   "Dominance relations" refers to the power relationship between the partner and oneself. . . . One tends to convey a sense of being a subordinate, a peer, or one of superior status by eye behavior, postural attitude, use of space, and the like. For example, while speaking we tend to gaze most at partners with moderate positional power, somewhat less toward high-power partners, and least toward low-power partners (Knapp 1978).

One's nonverbal behavior may be *deference-demanding, deferential,* or *neutral* with respect to dominance relations (Dovidio and Ellyson 1982). Observing a conversation from afar, one obtains a pretty accurate idea of how the interacting parties perceive their own dominance pattern. For example, individuals who perceive themselves as lower status or subordinate to the interaction partner tend to maintain more tense musculature and more erect, less relaxed postural attitudes. This feature has been recognized for thousands of years in the military services and ritualized in the command of *"attention!"* and its historical precursors, directed at lower ranking individuals and groups.

Gaze behavior also conveys different power impressions. Both large amounts of gaze while speaking and small amounts of gaze while listening convey the impression of high power (Dovidio and Ellyson 1982). With these and many more signs of dominance relations available, it is rarely necessary to be told, "I feel we are equals," or, "I am your boss," or even, "I feel that I am not in control here." Careful observation of the other's nonverbal behavior in a few seconds of interaction usually tells you all you need to know about deference and other trappings of dominance relations in a given dyad.

Interpretations of Feelings   Our judgments concerning the immediate feelings of the other party usually rely more on our observation of nonverbal behavior than on what the other is saying. We arrive at these judgments through observation of facial affect displays, postural cues, and the like. Words need to be decoded into symbolic meaning denoted in our language system. But, as discussed earlier, nonverbal signals do not require such processing. Our reactions to combinations of gestures, bodily posture, tones of voice, and facial expressions provide instantaneous clues to the feeling states of the partner (Burgoon 1985). As one begins to tell us how they feel about something, we most frequently have a pretty good idea of their emotional state, even before the utterance has been completed. Additional bases for the nonverbal contribution to our capacity to interpret one another's feelings are examined in the subsequent discussion of "nonverbal leakage."

Summary

Judee Burgoon (1985) characterizes the difference between how we use the verbal and nonverbal codes as follows. We place more importance on verbal cues for factual, abstract, and persuasive meanings, but place more importance on nonverbal cues for relational, attributional, emotional, and attitudinal meanings. In general, we are influenced more by our partner's language behavior with respect to *objective, denotative information*, and more by his or her nonverbal behavior with respect to *relational, connotative information*. In large part, that division of labor reflects the different limitations of the nonverbal and verbal codes.

Nonverbal Leakage

The spontaneous, out-of-awareness way in which nonverbal behavior is produced also provides a *direct* indicator of the other's feelings. This is in contrast to our interpretation of verbal behavior, which is dependent on the other's awareness of and willingness to verbally express his or her emotional states. Through such *nonverbal leakage*, subtle feelings may be accurately perceived and much faster than it takes to utter a short sentence (Ekman and Friesen 1969). Although we do talk about our feelings more than, for example, our dominance relations, by the time we say, "I'm happy" or, "I'm angry," those words are often unnecessary. The other often knows just how happy or angry we are through observation of our nonverbal behavior. Although the emotional states of some people are more guarded or impassive than others, at some level we all wear our spleens, as well as our hearts, on our sleeves.

Nonverbal leakage is presented through those nonverbal signs which are outside of the awareness of the behavior and which may contain information about the internal state (thoughts, feelings, attitudes) of the one who exhibits the behavior. The professor who frequently misses or is late for student appointments but who is unceasingly punctual for meetings with the Dean of the College may be "leaking" his or her orientation about dominance relations and what he or she feels is appropriate behavior there. "Yeah, I'm listening" may be uttered in a tone of voice and with facial affect that suggests the opposite would be a more accurate statement.

This leakage exerts a strong influence on how we view the interacting partner. When what the other says is clearly discrepant with what he or she does and how he or she says it, the nonverbal interpretation is the more credible of the two interpretations. On those occasions when what the partner *says* seems disparate with what the partner *does* with body and voice, the observer trusts his or her nonverbal behavior interpretation over the verbal. However, as the correspondence between verbal and nonverbal behavior increases toward the point of no discrepancy, we give more and more weight to the verbal implications (Burgoon 1985).

Sometimes someone intentionally displays discrepant verbal/nonverbal behavior to achieve some effect. For example, old friends meeting after a long separation have been observed directing the most unflattering remarks at one another ("you old so-and-so") with voices and facial expressions that leave no doubt they are indeed good friends. In the other direction, coupling verbal expressions of positive evaluation with nonverbal behavior that suggests negative feeling is such a frequent occurrence that we have a special term for it—"sarcasm."

In instances where we observe discontinuity between verbal and nonverbal behavior, it is not certain why we place greater trust in our interpretations of the nonverbal. It may be we sense the difficulties we all have in monitoring our own nonverbal behavior and, therefore, find the nonverbal behavior of others more credible than their words. Perhaps, without even thinking about it in any orderly fashion, we register that nonverbal behavior is more automatic and out-of-awareness than one's language utterances and is, therefore, less subject to control.

Clues to Deception

Clues to deception are a special kind of nonverbal leakage. These are instances where observed discrepancies between utterance and nonverbal behavior or other observations suggest the speaker may be actively attempting to conceal or misrepresent something during interaction. Again these are instances where the words say one thing, but the nonverbal behavior does not seem to "fit." Some features that have been found to occasionally accompany deceitful utterances include shortened response latency to questions and increases in adaptor gestures and in foot, hand, and leg movement, and decreases in eye contact, in physical directness in head and shoulders, and in illustrator gestures (Knapp and others 1987).

Most investigators believe that the most reliable cues to deception exist in those nonverbal behaviors over which we have the least self-conscious control and which are therefore most subject to leakage. John Hocking and Dale Leathers' (1980) ideas have guided several recent efforts to isolate reliable clues to deceptive intent during interaction. They suggest that deceivers who are motivated to avoid detection 1) *suppress controllable behaviors* stereotypical of liars in an attempt to avoid appearing like liars, 2) while at the same time *increasing less controllable behaviors* that are also indicative of anxiety during lying. Controllable behaviors might include various head, foot, leg, and hand-to-face movements, and gaze avoidance. Liars have been observed exhibiting increased vocal nervousness and dysfluencies, shorter response latencies (pre-reply pauses), shorter hesitation pauses (within-turn pauses), and briefer answers than truth-tellers (Cody and O'Hair 1983). In addition, during falsification individuals have been observed to decrease the stereotyped and controllable liar behaviors such as postural shifts. Among other effects, such adjustments result in an abnormally still body during interaction.

It is likely that individuals who rely almost exclusively for their interpretations on the partner's utterances place themselves at a disadvantage in a few of their important encounters. At the same time, the reader needs to be aware that none of the above are infallible indicators of intentional deceit, for reasons discussed in the next section.

Contextual Interpretation of Nonverbal Behavior

Notwithstanding the immediately preceding discussions of leakage deception, *contextual* interpretations of another's nonverbal behavior are n be valid than single-cue "body language" interpretations. Observers' judgments of what behaviors represent are more likely to be accurate when observers take into account the total context in which the behavior occurs and when those judgments are based on observation of whole sets or sequences of nonverbal behaviors. Stated another way, our judgments are likely to be wrong when they are based on interpretation of a single behavior in isolation from its context.

With few exceptions (like *emblems*), individual nonverbal acts do not have conventional assigned meanings. They are produced in combination with other nonverbal and verbal behaviors in holistic patterns. Some important contextual features include what has been and is being said in the interactional episode, the setting of the interaction, why it is taking place, the relationship between the parties, and how the partner usually behaves. Several reasons compel this emphasis on the wisdom of contextual interpretations of nonverbal behavior.

1. *First,* the same behavior supports very different interpretations in different contexts. For example, arm-stretching could be indicative of relaxation, of dominance, of boredom or even represent a nervous adaptor, given specific situations. There is ample evidence that the one-meaning-for-every-behavior fallacy is likely to mislead our attempts to interpret accurately. For example, among other things decreased eye gaze can represent dislike or submissiveness or rejection, and complete withdrawal of gaze can be associated with extreme anxiety. Heightened gaze can reflect liking or can intensify either the positive or the negative values of uttered sentiments (Bowers and others 1985). Steady eye gaze during a plea for help calls for a very different interpretation than a steady gaze accompanied by "Stop it!" As indicated earlier, the simple act of touching the other person can represent a very large number of different meanings (Jones and Yarbrough 1985), all rooted in the specific interactional context in which the touching occurred.

   A class of senior law students once sought support for the *body language* fallacy from a guest who had been invited to speak on nonverbal signs of deception in deposition-taking and witness-stand behavior. These future attorneys were understandably interested in learning about behaviors that could "tip off" a witness's deceptive utterances, and they were particularly interested in eye gaze behavior. But they learned that withdrawal of eye gaze is also frequently associated with stressful moments. Testifying in a legal proceeding would be very stressful for most people Undoubtedly, observation of nonverbal leakage may provide information that enhances interactional effectiveness, but there are no shortcuts across the terrain of contextual interpretation.

2. *Second,* reasonably accurate interpretations must be based on several behaviors, because any single behavior occurs within a framework of many other behaviors. For example, the presence of any one of the behaviors associated with active listening does not automatically mean the partner is responsive to your comments. At one time or another all of us have faked attention by maintaining eye contact and throwing in an occasional head not.

   By the same reasoning, absence of a specific sign of responsivity does not necessarily indicate poor listening. The grade school student who is admonished to "sit up and listen" may actually have been listening very carefully. Some of us slouch our way through school. Because a friend stands farther away while talking to you does not mean he/she likes you any less at the moment. But, if the same friend simultaneously talks impersonally with lower-than-normal eye contact while facing less directly than usual and unexpectedly ends the conversation without explanation, one is probably justified in concluding that all is not well.

3. *Third,* even if you interpret the behavior correctly, you may be wrong in your inference about the implications of that interpretation, until you fully understand the context. For example, laughter ranks among the most unequivocal nonverbal behaviors one will ever observe; it usually means the laugher thinks something is funny. Yet, one still must infer the source of the laugher's amusement. On one occasion, a professor made what he thought was a witty remark before turning to the blackboard. Sensing something was amiss when the anticipated chuckle gave way to a roar, he turned to face the class, clearly puzzled. A sympathetic student pointed out the professor's V-neck sweater was on backwards.

   Sometimes information required for accurate inferences is simply not available at the time the nonverbal behavior occurs. A graduate student and mother of two small children was taking an independent study from her professor/adviser. During one of their meetings, she was markedly more responsive and cheerful than usual. She smiled frequently, was more animated, and her voice conveyed pleasure and excitement throughout. At the end of the meeting the professor asked if she thought the material covered held promise for her dissertation topic. She replied she would "think about that later when I calm down." Just before the meeting, she had received a check for over a year of delinquent child support. When a behavior is viewed in isolation from the context in which it occurred, one's interpretations are more likely to be inaccurate. Sometimes one simply does not know enough about the context.

Summary

Some nonverbal elements of interaction are described, first from the point of view of expressive behavior, then from the perspective of one who is interpreting the nonverbal expressions of the interactional partner. Several common classification schemes are used to describe the domain of nonverbal interactional behavior, and five interrelated characteristics of nonverbal behavior are discussed. During interaction nonverbal behaviors 1) are unceasingly produces, 2) are produced relatively out-of-awareness, 3) are nonarbitrary, 4) have contextually determined meanings, and 5) are produced in integrated sets.

References

Argyle, M., and Cook, M. 1976. *Gaze and mutual gaze.* London: Cambridge University Press.

Birdwhistell, R. L. 1955. Background to kinesics. *ETC*13: 10–28.

Birdwhistell, R. L. 1970. *Kinesics and context: Essays on body motion communication.* Philadelphia: University of Pennsylvania Press.

Bowers, J. W., Metts, S. M., and Duncanson, W.T. 1985. Emotion and interpersonal communication. In *Handbook of interpersonal communication*, eds. M.L. Knapp and G. R. Miller, 500–550. Beverly Hills, CA: Sage Publications.

Burgoon, J. K. 1985. Nonverbal signals. In *Handbook of interpersonal communication*, eds. M. L. Knapp and G. R. Miller, 344–390. Beverly Hills, CA: Sage Publications.

Burgoon, J. K., and Jones, S. B. 1976. Toward a theory of personal space expectations and their violations. *Human Communication Research* 2: 131–146.

Burgoon, J. K., and Saine, T. 1978. *The unspoken dialogue: An introduction to nonverbal communication*. Boston: Houghton Mifflin Co.

Cappella, J. N. 1981. Mutual influence in expressive behavior: Adult-adult and infant-adult interaction. *Psychological Bulletin* 89: 101–132.

Cody, M. J., and O'Hair, H. D. 1983. Nonverbal communication and deception: Differences in deception cues due to gender and communicator dominance. *Communication Monographs*: 176–192.

Dovidio, J. F., and Ellyson, S. L. 1982. Decoding visual dominance: Attributions of power based on relative percentages of looking while speaking and looking while listening. *Social Psychology Quarterly* 45: 106–113.

Duncan, S. 1975. Interaction units during speaking turns in dyadic, face-to-face conversations. In *Organization of behavior in face-to-face interaction*, eds. A. Kendon, R. M. Harris, and M. R. Key, 199–213. The Hague: Mouton.

Ekman, P., and Friesen, W. V. 1969. Nonverbal leakage and clues to deception. *Psychiatry* 32: 88–106.

Ekman, P., and Friesen, W. V. 1971. Constancy across cultures in the face and emotion. *Journal of Personality and Social Psychology* 17: 124–129.

Ekman, P., and Friesen, W. V. 1975. *Unmasking the face*. Englewood Cliffs, NJ: Prentice-Hall.

Hocking, J. E., and Leathers, D. 1980. Nonverbal indicators of deception: A new theoretical perspective. *Communication Monographs* 47: 119–131.

Jones, S. E., and Yarbrough, A. E. 1985. A naturalistic study of the meanings of touch. *Communication Monographs* 52: 19–56.

Knapp, M. L. 1978. *Nonverbal communication in human interaction*. New York: Holt, Rinehart, and Winston.

Knapp, M. L., Cody, M. J., and Reardon, K. K. 1987. Nonverbal signals, In *Handbook of communication science*, eds. C. R. Berger and S. H. Chaffee, 385–418. Beverly Hills, Ca: Sage Publications

Patterson, M. L. 1968. Spatial factors in social interactions. *Human Relations* 21: 351–361.

Traeger, G. L. 1958. Paralanguage: A first approximation. *Studies in Linguistics* 13: 1–12.

Review Questions

1. Explain the difference between the terms *expressive* and *interpretive* as used here.
2. Define the following jargon terms from this chapter: *vocalics, kinesics, proxemics, haptics, illustrators, regulators, emblems, adaptors, affect displays, iconic cues, dominance relations, nonverbal leakage.*
3. What's the difference between "arbitrary" communication cues (Chapter 3) and "iconic" cues (this reading)?
4. What's the significance of Grove's point that nonverbal cues tend to be produced in "sets" or "sequences"?
5. Grove says that you can't rely on specific nonverbal cues to tell whether a person is lying. How come?

Probes

1. Sometimes people tell how someone "stopped communicating," or how a problem was caused by communication being "terminated." Does Ted Grove believe that people can "stop" communicating nonverbally? Explain.
2. Give an example from your own experience that illustrates how "strong" nonverbal messages can be.
3. Why do you believe nonverbal leakage can exert such a strong influence on how we view our interacting partner?
4. Grove discusses four ways context can affect the interpretation of nonverbal cues. What practical advice for your own communicating do you draw from this discussion?

This next reading illustrates the significant differences in nonverbal cues used by various cultural groups. It was assembled from the experiences a number of U.S. businesspeople had with customers and clients from other cultures.

You may believe that "everybody understands" such common gestures as the "A-OK" sign or the "Hello" or "Goodbye" wave. But you'll discover that even these common gestures mean very different things in other cultures.

This collection of examples is anecdotal rather than rigorously systematic or scholarly. But I still think it makes its point pretty effectively.

Dos and Taboos Around the World

Roger E. Axtell, ed.

A Risky Language
or
Actions Speak Louder Than Words—and Often Say All the Wrong Things

"I knew I'd committed a monumental goof. But I just couldn't imagine how".

A young computer salesman from New Jersey is remembering his first overseas sales pitch. The scene was his company's offices in Rio, and it had gone like a Sunday preacher's favorite sermon. As he looked around the table, he knew he had clinched the sale. Triumphantly, he raised his hand to his Latin customers and flashed the classic American okay sign—thumb and forefinger forming a circle, other fingers pointing up.

The sunny Brazilian atmosphere suddenly felt like a deep freeze. Stony silence. Icy stares. Plus embarrassed smirks from his colleagues.

Calling for a break, they took him outside the conference room and explained. Our hero had just treated everyone to a gesture with roughly the same meaning over there as the notorious third-finger sign conveys so vividly here. Apologies saved the sale, but he still turns as pink as a Brazilian sunset when retelling the tale.

It is only natural when you find yourself at sea in the local language to use gestures to bail yourself out. Anyway, even when you can be understood, isn't it friendlier and more endearing to say it with a hand, an eye, or some other intentional body language? Yes. But only if you know what the sign is really saying. Gestures pack the power to punctuate, to dramatize, to speak a more colorful language than mere words. Yet, like the computer salesman, you may discover that those innocent winks and well-meaning nods are anything but universal. . . .

Be Prepared for Incoming Messages, Too

On his maiden trip to the Middle East, a Midwestern public relations man stepped from the cool of an ultramodern conference center into the dust and glare of an ancient roadway. Donkey carts rustled up whirlwinds of stinging sand. The air rang with a mullah's bullhorned call to prayer. Without a word, a Saudi who had attended the same conference reached down and gently took his hand. The word exotic was taking on new meaning, and the meaning set off a panic button in the visitor's brain. "What does this Arab think . . .?" "What will all the *other* Arabs think . . .?" Etc., etc. Finally, common sense set in. Of course, the gesture was just a simple signal of trust: silent Arabic for friendship and respect.

Even unconscious gestures can be unsettling to the uninitiated. Just back from a tour of several Arabian Gulf countries, a woman recalls how jumpy she felt talking to men there. "Not because of what they said," she explains, "but what they did with their eyes." Instead of the occasional blink, Arabs lower their lids so slowly and languorously that she was convinced they were falling asleep.

In Japan, eye contact is a key to the way you feel about someone. And the less of it, the better. What a Westerner considers an honest look in the eye, the Oriental takes as a lack of respect and a personal affront. Even when shaking hands or bowing—and especially when conversing—only an occasional glance into the other person's face is considered polite. The rest of the time great attention should be paid to fingertips, desk tops, and the warp and woof of the carpet.

"Always keep your shoes shined in Tokyo," advises an electronics representative who has logged many hours there. "You can bet a lot of Japanese you meet will have their eyes on them."

On the other hand (or foot), Arabs flinch at the sight of shoe soles. Hence, feet are best kept flat on the floor—never propped up on a table or desk or crossed over the knee.

From Do's and Taboos Around the World, ed. Roger E. Axtell. Compiled by the Parker Pen Company. A Benjamin Book, John Wiley & Sons, Inc.

Bye-Bye No-No

In Europe, the correct form for waving hello and goodbye is palm out, hand and arm stationary, fingers wagging up and down. The common American wave with the whole hand in motion means no—except in Greece, where it is an insult that is likely to get you into big trouble. In many countries, hitchhiking with a thumb stuck out is also a very rude gesture. However, it is easy for a traveler to lapse into old habits, in which case—as long as you are recognized as an American—the reaction will probably be nothing worse than a frown.

International Gesture Dictionary

Gestures Using the Face

Eyebrow Raise: In Tonga, a gesture meaning "yes" or "I agree." In Peru, means "money" or "Pay me."

Blink: In Taiwan, blinking the eyes at someone is considered impolite.

Wink: Winking at women, even to express friendship, is considered improper in Australia.

Eyelid Pull: In Europe and some Latin American countries, means "Be alert" or "I am alert."

Ear Flick: In Italy, signifies that a nearby gentleman is effeminate.

Ear Grasp: Grasping one's ears is a sign of repentance or sincerity in India. A similar gesture in Brazil—holding the lobe of one's ear between thumb and forefinger—signifies appreciation.

Nose Circle: The classic American "okay" sign—the fingers circle—is placed over the nose in Colombia to signify that the person in question is homosexual.

Nose Tap: In Britain, secrecy or confidentiality. In Italy, a friendly warning.

Nose Thumb: One of Europe's most widely known gestures, signifying mockery. May be done double-handed for greater effect.

Nose Wiggle: In Puerto Rico, "What's going on?"

Cheek Screw: Primarily an Italian gesture of praise.

Cheek Stroke: In Greece, Italy, and Spain, means "attractive." In Yugoslavia, "success." Elsewhere, it can mean "ill" or "thin."

Fingertips Kiss: Common throughout Europe, particularly in Latin countries (and in Latin America). Connotes "aah, beautiful!," the object of which may be anything from a woman or a wine to a Ferrari or a soccer play. Origin probably dates to the custom of ancient Greeks and Romans who, when entering and leaving the temple, threw a kiss toward sacred objects such as statues and altars.

Chin Flick: "Not interested," "Buzz off," in Italy. In Brazil and Paraguay, "I don't know."

Head Circle: In most European and some Latin American countries, a circular motion of the finger around the ear means "crazy." In the Netherlands, it means someone has a telephone call.

Head Nod: In Bulgaria and Greece, signifies "no." In most other countries, "yes."

Head Screw: In Germany, a strong symbol meaning "You're crazy." Often used by drivers on the autobahn to comment on the driving skills of other travelers, this gesture can get you arrested! The same gesture is used in Argentina, but without the consequences.

Head Tap: In Argentina and Peru, "I'm thinking" or "Think." Elsewhere it can mean "He's crazy."

Head Tilt: In Paraguay, tilting the head backward means "I forgot."

Head Toss: In Southern Italy, Malta, Greece, and Tunisia, a negation. In Germany and Scandinavia, a beckoning motion. In India, "yes." Unfamiliar elsewhere.

Hand and Arm Gestures

Horizontal Horns: A gesture of self-protection against evil spirits in most European countries. In some African countries, a variation — pointing the index and third finger toward someone — can be interpreted as putting the "evil eye" on him. Use with discretion.

Vertical Horns: In Italy, signifies that you are being cuckolded. But in Brazil and other parts of Latin America, can be a sign of good luck.

V Sign: In most of Europe, means victory when, as Churchill did, you keep your palm facing away from you. Margaret Thatcher has been known to forget this — and to get roundly hooted for it, for the same gesture palm *in* means, roughly, "Shove it." In non-British-oriented countries, it generally means two of something as in "Two more beers, please." It was, by the way, not an Englishman but a Belgian who first made the V synonymous with victory in World War II.

Beckon: To use finger(s) to call someone is insulting to most Middle and Far Easterners. It is proper in most of these countries, and in Portugal, Spain, and Latin America, to beckon someone with palm down, fingers or whole hand waving.

Fingers Circle: Widely accepted as the American "okay" sign, except in Brazil, where it's considered vulgar or obscene. The gesture is also considered impolite in Greece and the USSR, while in Japan, it signifies "money," and in southern France, "zero" or "worthless."

Fingers Cross: In Europe, crossed fingers have several meanings, most commonly "protection" or "good luck." In Paraguay, the gesture may be offensive.

Fingers Snap: In France and Belgium, snapping the fingers of both hands has a vulgar meaning. In Brazil, it connotes something done long ago or for a long time.

One-Finger Point: In most Middle and Far Eastern countries, pointing with the index finger is considered impolite. The open hand is used instead, or, in Indonesia, the thumb.

Two-Finger Tap: In Egypt, this means a couple is sleeping together and, true or false, is always rude. Can also mean, "Would you like to sleep together?"

Third-Finger Thrust: Not nice in any language, this old favorite has survived for more than 2,000 years. (The Romans called the third finger the "impudent" finger.)

Third-Finger Reverse: Same meaning as executed by an Arab.

Fist Slap: "———you" in Italy, Chile, and many other places.

Forearm Jerk: Another way of saying the above or some variation thereof, especially in Mediterranean

countries. In England, however, it connotes a sexual compliment, equivalent to a wolf whistle.

Thumbs Up: In Australia, a rude gesture; in almost every other place in the world simply means "okay."

Flat-Hand Flick: The universal flicking of the fingers toward the source of irritation, meaning "Go away" or "Get lost."

Palm Push: In Nigeria, pushing the palm of the hand forward with fingers spread is a vulgar gesture.

Hand Pat: In Holland, "He/she is gay."

Hand Purse: Can signify a question or good or fear. Considered almost the national gesture of Italy.

Hand Saw: When you make a deal in Colombia and intend to share the profits, the gesture is: one palm facing down with the other hand making a sawing motion across the back of the hand facing down.

Hand Sweep: In Latin America and the Netherlands, a sweeping or grabbing motion made toward your body, as though you were sweeping chips off a table, means that someone is stealing or "getting away with something." The same gesture in Peru means "money" or "Pay me."

Waving: Called the *moutza* in Greece, this is a serious insult, and the closer the hand to the other person's face, the more threatening it is considered. Same in Nigeria. Never use it to get a waiter's or cabdriver's attention. In Europe, raise the palm outward and wag the fingers in unison to wave "goodbye." Waving the whole hand back and forth can signify "no," while in Peru, that gesture means, "Come here."

Height: In Colombia and much of Latin America, only an animal's height is indicated by using the whole hand, palm down. It is polite to hold the palm facing the observer to show human height, or, in Mexico, to use the index finger.

The Wai: Traditional greeting in Thailand. Called the *namaste* in India.

Arms Fold: In Finland, folded arms are a sign of arrogance and pride. In Fiji, the gesture shows disrespect.

Elbow Tap: In Holland, "He's unreliable." In Colombia, "You are stingy."

The Fig: In some European and Mediterranean countries, an obscene gesture of contempt. In Brazil and Venezuela, a symbol of good luck reproduced in such diverse forms as paper weights and golden amulets worn around the neck.

Review Questions

1. When you're in a foreign culture and you don't know the language, it only makes sense to rely on gestures. But what does this reading say about this strategy?
2. Which categories of nonverbal cues (see the previous reading) are emphasized here?

Probes

1. What patterns do you notice in nonverbal cues used by northern Europeans versus southern Europeans versus South Americans versus Asians?
2. What advice about your own communicating in other countries do you take away from this reading?
3. What do you notice about the prevalence in most cultures of gestures suggesting sexual intercourse?

Partly because of the views toward sex and sexuality that are prevalent in the United States and some other Western cultures, touch and talk about it have become almost taboo. We know that touch is important in greeting, giving support, and conflict, but its sexual meanings all but overshadow everything else. Young persons learn very clearly where and when they can legitimately touch their parents, their friends, and themselves without being branded as "effeminate" or "aggressive" if they are male or as "masculine" or "easy" if they are female. Touch, in brief, is the one mode of nonverbal communication with which most of us are the least comfortable.

James Hardison tries to remedy this in the next reading. He notes that our genuine desires to express warmth and caring are often frustrated by our awkwardness and inability to use touch to communicate. His goal is to suggest how we can, in small ways, use touch to build more gestures of caring into our day-to-day relationships.

Hardison emphasizes how touch can build trust, even in a completely nonsexual context. Doctors, dentists, and beauty operators, for example, can enhance or reduce trust by the ways they touch their patients or clients. Trust is also obviously important in intimate relationships, and a great deal of it—or its opposite—is communicated by touch.

Touch is also an important part of our contact with strangers and with persons from other cultures. In both contexts we can profit from the recognition of (1) the reality of legitimate differences, (2) the desirability of adding appropriate touch to our repertoire of communication skills, and (3) the effectiveness of a "progressive, slowly developing, step-by-step pattern of touching behavior for specific purposes. . . ."

Hardison suggests that we begin our efforts to change with those closest to us. It's easiest to control the level or risk in these relationships and to make progress toward more effectively communicating the genuine feelings of warmth, support, and caring that we experience.

I hope this essay will at least prompt you to consider your touching attitudes and behaviors. There is no need for all of us to turn into exuberant huggers, especially if that kind of behavior violates cultural norms we've been taught. But even a little more touch could humanize our communication contacts substantially.

Touching for Improving Interpersonal Relationships

James Hardison

Interpersonal relationships form the bases of what we perceive as our state of being. Yet a common complaint today is the alienation workers feel for management, students express about teachers, youth experience with parents, and spouses sense with each other. It seems that despite our efforts to the contrary, our interactions often result in conflict and misunderstanding. On the other hand, our good intentions abound. We wish to give and receive warmth through physical affection. We desire to aid one another in emotional development and self-actualization. We try to maintain an atmosphere in which one individual cares about another's needs and welfare. In short, we care about one another and wish to convey the warmth we feel.

Warmth is a measurable physical quality; however, the type of warmth we are talking about has an internal dimension. How do we derive the concept of "warmth"? In our earliest years, particularly in that period before we developed verbal skills, we depended on tactual senses for a large portion of our learning, coping, and experiencing. We were touched by our parents for consolation, companionship, and protection. Their warm bodies provided us with a feeling of security allowing us to move about with less fear and more emotional strength. Our behavior and adjustment in later life were fundamentally influenced by the degree of emotional warmth we received through our parents' touching. In feeding, bathing, clothing, comforting, and entertaining us, our parents gave us our first concept of love and affection—warmth.

Each of us has the potential for giving physical affection and communicating warmth as we truly seek to improve our interpersonal relations. Our associates, colleagues, and friends also have the need to be touched. They subconsciously have the desire to make human contact, but they may be held back because many of them feel that "it's not nice to touch," or that touching will imply or lead to "something sexual." As individuals in search of a better way to relate to others, we must take the initiative, be slightly daring, and transcend the taboos and unreasonable social restrictions placed on us. We must turn to one of our most natural instincts, the tendency to touch in a caringly human way.

Touching in Times of Crisis

Have you ever noticed how interpersonal relationships take on more importance in times of crisis? Little children might feel independent as they play outside with their buddies, but an injury will quickly bring them to their parents in search of reassurance and care. Even the momentary crisis experienced by young lovers descending the steepest drop on a roller coaster is enough to trigger the need (or at least the pretext of it) to hold each other securely until the danger passes. Other minor crises include fender-bender auto accidents, final exams, and major business transactions. In any one of these crises, significant persons frequently give us verbal consolation as well as tactual reassurances.

Accordingly, interpersonal relationships are intensified in times of severe crisis, as in interactions between survivors after a death or even between distraught individuals who are separated by long-term physical barriers or divorce. Our friends seek us out more readily when they know we have experienced a crisis. They want us to know that they are close by to help, and they often signal this through touch. Through loving and supportive touches, a person can help to heal a friend's deepest wounds. Touching in such circumstances is something most of us do naturally. Why should we reserve our capability to use touch effectively only for times of crisis? Why not try, in small ways, to build such caring gestures into our day-to-day relationships!

Touch in Everyday Relationships

If we consider everyday activities in interpersonal relationships, we may see that we have friends and associates with whom we feel more comfortable in communication and touching exchanges. We may not even be aware of the exchanges we engage in; moreover, we may be unconscious of the messages we send our through touch. A case of unconscious touching occurred in the lounge outside a board of trustees' meeting room in a community college in Southern California. Two large lounge chairs were situated side by side, with high armrests close together. A close personal colleague and I sat in the adjoining chairs, placing our hands, parallel and palms down, on the front of each armrest. An active observer, I counted twenty-two contacts from my colleague as we conversed. He would emphasize a point in conversation or assure himself that he had my full attention by reaching over and patting the back of my hand, my forearm, or wrist. During a brief recess in our conversation, I asked him if he had been aware of any touching exchanges while we had been talking. He was surprised to learn that he, a forceful and very masculine character, had been touching the hand of another male. When I explained that I had accepted his touching as a catalyst to communication, he became aware that he could touch another male's hand to improve communication and interpersonal relationships. He later admitted that he had heretofore locked himself (as most Americans do) into the stereotyped role in which touching is generally taboo—especially between males—because of the "sexual overtones" or "sexual connotations." I have a high regard for my colleague because of his ability to accept his natural tendency to touch as a wholesome and useful behavior pattern.

Many of us have similar unconscious habits. If we become more aware of our touching practice, we can learn to use our natural inclinations in a deliberate way to improve interpersonal relationships.

Touch Can Build Trust

Touching can facilitate a sense of trust and empathy. From early childhood, we begin leaning how much we can trust people by the way they touch us. We affix a supreme trust to our parents as we feel their tender and caring touch in feeding, bathing, clothing, and rocking us. Our trust in them stabilizes in proportion to how often they touch us and how often their contact satisfies our needs. Basically, the same commitment to touch is carried forward throughout life; we tend to trust those people whose touching either satisfies our needs or brings us pleasure. The greater the satisfaction received, the greater interest we have in maintaining the touching.

The same dynamics of trust come into play in adult touching experiences. This is particularly true in the helping professions. If we examine very closely why we go to a certain doctor, dentist, or chiropractor, we may find that we are highly influenced by the way these people have touched us and by how much trust they inspired.

Consider your dentist. When you are in the office, seated in the dental chair, you must at least be able to trust that the hands about to treat you will be clean and gentle.

I believe that dentists are acutely aware of the need to communicate trust through touch. They know that patients don't return to dentists who squeeze the inside of their lips to their teeth. Nor do they return to dentists whose novocaine needle hurts more than they imagine the treatment would.

I experienced two contrasting examples of dentists' touching activities. One dentist entered the examination room, shook hands with me warmly, and proceeded to wash his hands in front of me before touching my mouth. Both tactually and visually, his behavior inspired trust. Another dentist neglected both these steps and cleaned my teeth so brusquely that he cut my gum tissues unnecessarily; they bled considerably. Touch and the trust it fosters accounted for the distinctly different impressions these dentists made.

Making a similar point, a woman told me of her experience at a beauty salon over a period of three years. The owner combed and set her hair each week with great care. While the owner washed the woman's hair, she took special interest to see that the strands did not become entangled; she made sure that the roots were not being pulled, nor the ends split, as she combed her hair, and she used a light touch in setting her hair. Mainly in response to the owner's touch, the patron had complete trust in her abilities. Then the owner sold the salon and moved away. The new owner, less cautious, showed little regard for the patron's comfort as she handled her hair. She failed to communicate trustworthiness to her customer and soon lost her.

The effective use of touch to improve relationships requires sensitivity and discretion. As we have seen, though touch has the potential to convey warmth and build trust, it can just as easily produce a tremendous "turn-off."

Trust in Opposite-Sex Friendships

Clearly, the trustworthiness we communicate can alter our relationships. Our trust in ourselves with regard to touch can also alter relationships. When establishing a new friendship, can you trust yourself to be just friendly and not to expect sexual intimacy with a member of the opposite sex? That's a difficult task for a lot of us. We are so bound by cultural mores that many of us are locked into believing that persons of the opposite sex are not capable of being just good friends; we assume they must eventually become intimate if they maintain a close relationship. In actuality, many people form relationships with members of the opposite sex that do not lead to sexual relations.

A woman account executive of my acquaintance in San Francisco had an experience of this type. She and her friend did not follow the "expected" pattern between men and women. She had attended a business cocktail party where she met a charming man with a lot to say; he startled her with his witty comments, unusual thoughts, and sensitivity. The two later found themselves in her apartment. It was six-thirty in the morning, the sun rising, before they both realized that they had spent the whole night talking, occasionally touching and hugging, experiencing a profound interchange of conversation. They also realized and reflected on the fact they had not performed the standard antics of a brief conversation followed by a jump into bed, not an uncommon routine for either of them. They agreed to maintain a relationship characterized by the meaningful combination of talking and touching they had enjoyed on their first meeting. Such a relationship requires a high degree of mutual trust and respect. Seven years later, these two people are still enjoying what they consider a most rewarding friendship. . . .

Touch in Other Cultures

Tactual expressions are a component of interpersonal relations in all cultures. Every group exhibits some form of touching to express feelings of friendship and love. North and South Americans kiss on the lips, touch cheek to cheek, kiss each other on the cheek, and round it off with hugs. Eskimos, on the other hand, hug rarely and touch noses to express their love. They lightly tap nose to nose, or one partner moves his or her nose in a circular motion around that of the mate, touching it lightly.

Samoans express their most profound love, not by prolonged kissing or touching noses, but by one partner pressing his or her flattened cheek to the cheek of the other party and taking impassioned staccato breaths that cause airjet sounds to emanate from the nose. The staccato pattern also characterizes their sexual relations. Samoans copulate in an abrupt, rapid manner, involving direct contact only between the genitals and almost never including a hug. . . .

Some African tribes use an arm grasp in greetings. Participant A extends both forearms, with the hands in a palm-up position and the elbows slightly bent. Meanwhile, participant B places an arm over each of the forearms of A. B's hands then grasp A's forearms at the inside elbow joint. This African arm clasp might well be considered as an alternative to the standard Western handshake to avoid some of its disadvantages. The standard handshake appears to have little meaning other than a cursory recognition of the individual. We might bring about a benevolent revolution by examining the various ways of revealing warmth, determining the effects of passivity in the exchange, measuring the relationship between the pressure applied and the meanings given (or received), and determining the significance of varying types of grasps and embraces. Such a study could give us some new insights and a refreshing perspective on how to use touch to express friendship and love. . . .

Difficulties in Touching Strangers

Touching to improve interpersonal relations cannot occur so easily between strangers. Most of us are not very open to touch as part of our communicating, a limitation that is even more pronounced among strangers. Basically, we are not a touching society, and tend to feel discomfort in most touching interactions. Factors that contribute to this are (1) our basic lack of trust in strangers and (2) our resistance to being observed in touching interactions. We frequently have unverified suspicions about strangers, so we tend to proceed very cautiously with them, especially when it comes to touching. Although the handshake is generally an acceptable opening gesture in meeting a stranger, some people are reluctant to extend a hand to someone they do not know. This reluctance can be seen in churches where a handshake is part of the ritual; resistance is sometimes expressed as an actual refusal. Whatever the reasons for this resistance, it is clear that interpersonal relating must be entered into willingly; moreover, the imposition of a touching exchange can have an adverse effect. In some areas, congregational resistance to shaking hands has brought about a compromise from the pulpit. Religious leaders are asking their congregations to recognize their fellow church members by alternate modes: smiling or simply verbalizing a greeting.

We resist being observed in touching actions, perhaps mostly because we envision a sexual link to touching. Our cultural mores prohibit us from observing the most intimate form of touching—sexual intercourse. We extend our reluctance to being observed to many signs of affection, whether or not they are sexual in intent. As mature adults, we shy away from hugging or embracing in public, even for expressing friendship.

Modern psychologists have sought out ways through encounter group sessions to modify our behavior to allow us to feel more open to nonverbal touching behavior. Conflicting views have been presented. Some psychologists tell us that most touching techniques used in encounter groups are of little benefit, perhaps even harmful, since they foster defensiveness, produce stress, and have a potential for being psychologically disturbing. Their position underscores our cultural trait of little openness to touching strangers. It also points to a reluctance to have touching activities observed. I strongly recommend, however, that we consider a progressive, slowly developing, step-by-step pattern of touching behavior for specific purposes that would allow us to transcend the discomfort associated with touching strangers in general, while enabling us to relax just a bit about our touching behavior.

Understandably, most of us are not ready to embrace a complete stranger on the first meeting. If we are interested in developing a relationship, we want more information to go on. The information can generally be gained through verbal exchanges, which are more distant, less threatening, and more easily controlled than tactual contact. We can generally determine, through conversation, if we wish to move closer to others, and we can slowly assess their trustworthiness as they simultaneously determine ours.

If we are consistent in the meanings of our touching behavior, and others are similarly consistent with us, an unthreatening progression will follow. We will know, as will they, that a light touch by a hand on the arm is an act of friendliness and an expression of interest, not one of hostility or aggression. We can progressively work out understandings, such as whether a pat on the knee is used to show playfulness, to emphasize a point, or even to express a greeting. We can communicate that a hug or a full embrace means a warm greeting (a commitment of the entire self to it, so to speak), not sexual aggression. All touching transactions, in order not to threaten the relationship, must proceed with moderation and clearly expressed intentions.

Begin with Those Closest to You

A healthy improvement in the ability to be comfortable about touching might be brought about through slow, progressive, deliberate acts. This certainly doesn't mean that we become touching exhibitionists, ready to show everybody that we are the world's greatest touchers. A good place to begin could be in our homes. How many friends have confided that they never saw their parents hold hands, hug, or kiss each other? This state of affairs obviously encourages the children's future reticence to express themselves through touch. I suggest that couples begin to express their caring through touch in their homes freely, regardless of who is watching. Children or others who observe might be surprised or possibly ill at ease about what they see, viewing it as a departure from "dignified" behavior; but after several observations, they will probably be able to regard it as the honest expression of affection and caring it is. Don't hesitate on this; it is worth the risk. It can gradually make your life richer with meaning and expressed feelings.

Let's start with those people who are very significant in our lives. If they are a part of the family, very close friends, or loving mates, they will be more accepting of this new idea. . . .Without giving notice, take your mate's hand. Say nothing. Just hold the hand as unobtrusively as possible for a few minutes; then go back to doing whatever you were doing before. Or take your child lightly in your arms at intervals during the day. Let the child return to play or study without entering into verbal exchanges. The next time you are with a colleague you admire, dare to go over and give the associate a light pat on the back, saying, "You know, I really enjoy working with you" or "It's really great to be here with you." All these recommendations are designed to aid in improving interpersonal relationships. If our honest intent is to improve, we will do so. To gauge our progress, we might make "before" and "after" assessments of our relationships during a six-month period; a greater trust will surely emerge.

Touching behavior can have a significant impact on interpersonal relationships. Our touches and tactual expressions, when applied appropriately and tactfully, can carry with them a sense of warmth and companionship. Touches tend to improve interactions and communications. They cement our social and personal bonding with those people who are special to us.

Review Questions

1. How does Hardison suggest we try to counter the automatic link that tends to be made between touching and "inappropriateness" or "something sexual"?
2. Hardison argues that touch is more common in everyday relationships than we sometimes think. What evidence does he give to support his claim?

3. Hardison tells a story about a San Francisco couple who spent a night together in "profound . . . conversation" without having sex. What point does this story make about touch and communication?
4. What does Hardison say we should do about the difficulties we have touching strangers?

Probes

1. On a 10-point scale where 1 means "painfully awkward" and 10 means "utterly confident," where would you rank yourself on the following: (a) Your use of touch in your communication with family members? (b) Your use of touch in your job? (c) Your use of touch in your intimate relationships?
2. In a group of five to seven persons, discuss specific times when genuine feelings of caring or warmth were not communicated because of the person's inability to use touch appropriately and effectively.
3. What is your memory of touching in your family as you were growing up? What touch norms did you learn there?
4. Give an example from your own experience of the touch communication of a dentist, doctor, hair stylist, or other professional.
5. What are some specific differences that you've observed between white and nonwhite members of your community?
6. What is the most embarrassing experience involving touch that you can recall? (You don't need to share it with anyone, just recall it privately.) What did that experience reveal about the touch norms or values for touching that are most important to you?
7. How *consistent* is your touching? How might you increase its consistency?

Julius Fast was one of the first authors to call the general public's attention to the importance of nonverbal communication. In 1971, his book *Body Language* warned readers that a person with his or her arms folded across the chest is "closed," and advised men to watch for the signals women used to indicate that they're available. Serious students of nonverbal communication strongly criticized Fast's book because it was based on anecdotal observations rather than careful research, and because it drastically oversimplified the processes it discussed. Fast also tended to emphasize the manipulative potential of strategically managed nonverbal cues, and some of his critics rejected what they thought was inappropriate cynicism.

Subtext is Julius Fast's 1990s version of his 1970s best-seller. This time he focuses on how to "make body language work in the workplace." He includes chapters called "Touchy Situations," "Body Language: Gestures, Posture, and Space," "Aspects of Power," and "The Magic Behind the Sale." As you might gather from the chapter titles, this author was apparently not very moved by his critics. He still relies on anecdotes rather than careful observations, he emphasizes generalizations rather than specifics, and, as you'll read, he claims that "civilization, to a large degree, is based on masking, or its first cousin, control."

As the title of this reading suggests, Fast's main goal is to enable his readers to effectively manipulate the nonverbal "subtext" of their communication in order to meet their own goals. There isn't much interest in collaboration here, or in paying attention to the *other* person's interests or goals. In fact, Fast seems to view communication as an action rather than a transaction, a process where one person's choices and behaviors can pretty much control the interpretations of everybody involved. As he puts it in the final sentence, "Learning, understanding, and using these techniques will allow us to manage life better and control the subtext we send out to others, changing the way others see us and enabling us to successfully handle our jobs and make our way up the corporate ladder."

It's not surprising that Fast sells a lot of books. Everybody in the workforce wants to "successfully handle our job and make our way up the corporate ladder."But the reason I include this selection in *Bridges Not Walls* is to suggest that *things may not be as simple as this reading makes them sound*. I think it's helpful to be aware of what's out there in the "self-help" and "pop psychology" literature, so you can read it with a liberal grain of salt. As Ted Grove emphasizes in the first reading in this chapter, nonverbal elements of interaction are often inseparable from verbal elements, they operate both expressively and interpretively, and their meaning is significantly affected by the context in which they occur. This means that human communication is more than a simple process of managing behavior to, as Fast puts it, "change the way others see us," and nonverbal cues make up more than what Fast calls a person's "image." As a serious student of interpersonal communication, I think you might want to distinguish between careful and thoughtful analysis of communication topics and pleasant-sounding but poorly-substantiated advice that panders to some readers' desires to find simple, sure-fire solutions to difficult problems.

In short, on the one hand, Julius Fast raises some legitimate and helpful points in this reading. Like the selection from *Dos and Taboos Around the World*, you can learn something about nonverbal communicating from the anecdotes he includes here. On the other hand, Fast also makes some incompletely-supported claims and writes in an overall tone that you might want to be wary of.

What You See Is Not What You Get

Julius Fast

Making An Impression

Sometimes, it's not what's on the inside, but what is on the outside that counts in projecting a subtext. External techniques can be just as important as inner personality traits in producing an image, especially when it comes to interviewing for a job, making a sale, or closing a deal.

A winner of the prestigious Westinghouse Science Award came up with a very clever project which illustrates the point. Mina Chow, a young Korean-American girl who attended Cardozo High School in New York City, noticed that teachers base a lot of grades on a student's image, on what students look like. Mina originally looked like a typical "punk" kid with spiked hair and blue lipstick. Her grades were slipping until she decided on an image change. She toned herself down to a more average appearance, and her grades went up. "I figured that the teachers' perceptions had a lot to do with it," Mina realized.

Mina elaborated on her own perceptions for a science project. She collected "neutral" pictures of black, white, and Asian students, male and female, and distributed them along with a questionnaire to eighty-seven teachers in New York City high schools.

The results scored a big point for the subtext behind image projection. Asian students were rated highest for motivation, blacks the lowest. Blacks were rated highest for physical activity, Asians the lowest. Mina concluded that Asians might do better in school simply because teachers had preconceived notions about them.

We all carry preconceived notions around with us. Certainly, in an ideal world, we would judge people by what they do, not by their race or clothes or social status, but this is not an ideal world, and we judge others by the images they project.

Nowhere is this more true than in television. In 1987, during the Senate confirmation hearings of Judge Robert H. Bork for the U.S. Supreme Court, John Dancy, a TV correspondent, said of the Bork hearings, "The wind blows from the image." According to John Corry, the *New York Times* television critic, Judge Bork "looks like a Reform rabbi, and speaks like an Oxford don." He went on to note that Bork's constitutional interpretation is "as interesting as origami folding. How one looks, however, is something else. Appearance is what counts."

In business, as well as in television, how one looks becomes all important. There are lessons that businesspeople can learn from television techniques.

Creating the Right Image For Any Situation

A statement by Michael K. Deaver, who used to manage President Reagan's news conferences, holds a key to projecting an image with a serious and dramatic subtext. Deaver had Reagan stand in front of the open doors of the East Room for press conferences, because it made the president appear livelier and more substantive. "The open doors with the light coming across the hall makes a much better picture," Mr. Deaver told reporters. Moving the lectern away from the open door was, in Mr. Deaver's opinion, unwise—telegenically speaking.

In politics, we see an example of subtext at work. How the president looks sends a strong subtext to the television viewer no matter what he says! Margaret Mead, the great anthropologist, was aware of this. She once told me that her advice to President Carter was, "It doesn't matter what you say. What's important is how you look."

Television critic John Corry recognized the importance of subtext in politics. He pointed out that Reagan's campaign used visual effects that were very strong and sent a clear image of patriotism. There were flags, waving placards, balloons rising up in clouds, and, at his 1981 inaugural, the Mormon Tabernacle Choir singing "The Battle Hymn of the Republic." President Reagan himself was so moved that he cried. It worked!

The paradox of television campaigning, according to John Corry, is that what is real always works better than artifice. The president's tears worked. However, combine reality with carefully planned presentation, and you have a compelling subtext!

Unfortunately, television can create an artificial subtext that is often accepted as real. Viewers can be moved, not by the issue, but by the projected image. The candidate may be an empty shell, but that doesn't matter. Is the candidate too cold, too remote? Let that person appear before the camera as one of us, as a common man or woman. Is there some doubt about the candidate's patriotism? Let that candidate appear before the memorial of the flag raising at Iwo Jima, or even in a flag factory. The strong subtext will carry him or her through.

In the business world, the same rules apply. Is the boss seen as too cold, too far removed? Let him or her appear at a plant inspection in work clothes and a hard hat—a warm, caring subtext!

The Janus Factor

Civilization, to a large degree, is based on masking, or its first cousin, control. When people live together and work together, a great deal of their day is spent covering up what they really feel and in controlling their real emotions. It may seem surprising, but sometimes it is very important to mask the subtexts we send out, to keep what we really feel hidden.

Sometimes the masking is consistent, but more often than not it is based on what I call the Janus Factor. Janus, you will remember, was the Roman god represented with two opposite faces. Jake is a perfect example of the Janus Factor in action.

Jake's job is to supervise a dozen workers in his department. "One thing about Jake," one of the people under him said, "he's consistent. A grade-A bully every time!"

The executives above Jake couldn't believe the occasional negative reports they heard about him. "This is a very sweet guy," his immediate superior insisted. "He's always ready to do a favor, always helpful and pleasant. Gets his job done quickly. There must be a couple of bad apples in that crew of his."

Was Jake two different people? A dual personality? Not at all. He simply used the Janus Factor to cope with life. In essence, the Janus Factor says that every man or woman in a corporation has two faces. One face is turned toward the people higher up in the corporate structure, and sends out one type of subtext. Another face is turned toward those lower down, with quite a different subtext.

A corollary of the Janus Factor is that the more secure the person is in the corporate structure, the less difference there is between the two faces and the two subtexts. The president of Jake's company seems to have only one face, but of course no one at work sees the face he presents to his wife and children.

The Janus factor is best observed in industry, but it also applies to politics. In the Watergate affair, the nation saw one face of President Nixon and received one subtext—a calm, rational man in control. The secret tapes disclosed a completely different face—vulgar and out of control. Were the two faces one man? Certainly. It was the Janus Factor in action.

Wearing the Mask

What is important about the Janus Factor in business, in politics, and even in the family is learning when and how to mask, to cover up your real emotions and the subtexts they send out. Politicians must learn this lesson early on. Edmund Muskie was destroyed as a possible presidential candidate by crying in public, letting the mask drop. On the other hand, when television evangelist Tammy Faye Bakker cried openly, she was using tears as a mask.

Doctors must learn to mask in front of patients; lawyers must wear a mask in court. The higher you climb on the corporate ladder, the more important the mask becomes. The simplest mask is the noncommittal look, the expressionless face. But expression itself is a much better masking device.

Lack of expression sends a negative subtext—"No one is home." An expression of any kind sends a positive subtext: joy, anger, fear, hate, whatever. A smile is the easiest way to mask unhappiness, anger, or disappointment. It sends a pleasant subtext. A grim look can mask joy and elation; a frown can cover up happiness.

Some of us use more than expressions to mask. Women use makeup to emphasize their lips and eyes, create a blush on their cheeks. Men use hair to mask: a full moustache can be a virility mask; a beard can change the contour of the face, strengthen a receding chin, add a subtext of wisdom, of cool.

When does masking start? As far as we know, it is present in early childhood. Most children approach strange adults with solemn faces and wary eyes, giving little of themselves, holding back their true feelings. The bright child learns quickly what adults expect and masks accordingly.

When children discover that their own feelings are not acceptable to society, they have the choice of changing those feelings or covering them up—masking. In most cases feelings can't be changed, so the child covers them up and creates a secret, inner world of emotions and fantasies.

Teenagers become even more adept at masking as their changing bodies release a flood of hormones that sharpens their desires and needs. They don't dare reveal those needs, and yet they are not nearly as adept at masking as grown-ups. As a compromise, they usually dredge up the noncommittal mask of childhood, or hide behind a sullen look. Unfortunately, the subtexts sent out are not *I'm upset, I'm in trouble!* but *I don't give a damn!*

Parents and teachers write off teenage sullenness as typical of the child at that age, but behind the sullen mask there may be a sensitive person—too tender, frightened, and vulnerable to face the world. The mask and its subtext are a way of protecting that fragile interior.

Using the Mask

If we consider all the situations in which we use the masking technique, we can realize what a universal device it is to send out subtext, or rather, not send a subtext. Politeness, something we think of as a civilized pleasure of our culture, is simply an elaborate form of masking. We use masking constantly in business, at school, at home, with our enemies, and with our friends. When it comes right down to it, very few of us will dare to expose our inner selves by sending out the subtext of our true feelings.

This inner self is the most sacred part of us, and we are not expected to reveal it. Masking these feelings is important, provided the masking is kept within reasonable limits. In fact, showing our true feelings can be wrong and selfish.

Sandy, in charge of training in the computer department of her firm, explained this in terms of her relationship to her trainees. "I can't tell them the truth about their work in the beginning. It would be counterproductive. Sure, they make some stupid mistakes and I point out the obvious ones, but I can't let them see how exasperated I get. I must encourage them, and as long as they understand the subtext of encouragement behind what I say, they'll keep on trying. If they think they're doing well, they'll go on to do better."

Sandy's training technique was a form of masking. Sid, a foreman on the production line, used a similar technique. "I never tell the new guys how klutzy they are. I tell them they're doing fine, build them up, and they lose their nervousness and actually do better. I guess I put on an act, but it encourages them to keep at it. I turn out some good people that way."

Control

Another aspect of masking is control, something we need in order to adapt to life in a civilized society. We need to control our basic desires to take what we want, to do what we want, even to live and work as we want. The modification of want is what control is all about.

We learn control at an early age. Hungry babies scream until the bottle comes, but gradually they learn to control their hunger, to wait for food at appropriate times. They learn to control their bladder and bowels as they grow up, then learn to control their desires and suppress those that are antisocial.

The act of learning control can be pleasant, because along with control the growing child learns anticipation with all its joys. The gradual refinement of control and the suppression of drives and desires are steps to maturity. We even define the subtext of immaturity as a lack of control.

Immature children who can't or won't learn control are hard to live with. When they want something, they want it at once. When they feel angry, they cry or yell or throw a tantrum. When they're hungry, they beg for food. If they're old enough to get their own food, they eat erratically with no regard for regular hours.

Gavin was that kind of a child, and not much better as an adult. He was unlucky enough to have parents who gave in easily and catered to his lack of control. When he moved out on his own, his apartment became as messy as his room at home, junk and clothes everywhere.

For a brief period he shared his apartment, and his life, with a young woman, but it didn't last. "I can't live like that. I'm not that neat, but to just drop everything everywhere and wonder where it is when you want it! And meals. I plan dinner at seven and at six you're hungry so you fill up on junk food!"

Gavin shrugged. "Why not eat when you're hungry? I'm hungry at six. Why wait till seven?"

"Because I go to a lot of trouble to prepare dinner at seven! Can't you control your hunger?"

Obviously Gavin couldn't, and finally his girlfriend moved out. He was upset, but not enough to change. "Why do I have to be uptight about everything? It's not my life-style!"

But his life-style spilled over into his work. He started a good job with an outfit making documentaries for cable television, but he could no more control his work than he could control his life. He misplaced important documents, neglected dull projects, failed to change scripts, and eventually lost his job.

It's difficult, he discovered, to be controlled on one level while you're out of control on another. To be effective, control must be exhibited in most areas of your life.

Sometimes we find a deceptive charm about uncontrolled people. The subtext they send out is romantic, above commonplace demands, even primitive and natural, but they are difficult to live with and next to impossible to work with—or, worse still, to work for!

Few people are controlled in every area, but most people use degrees of control to send out a subtext of sensibility and order. The ones who can't or won't are the gamblers who never resist a long shot: the person who buys the too-expensive car because "even if I don't need it, it looks great"; the thief who can't resist an easy setup; or the dieter who must have that extra piece of cake.

All the World's a Stage

A strong link exists between your ability to "act" a certain way and the subtext you send out to the world. A successful businessman told me, "I choose my clothes each day depending on the way I feel. When I'm low, for one reason or another, and I feel I'm going to have a hard time of it, I'll wear something upbeat, a tie with a little life to it, one of my brighter shirts. I try to perk up my image."

When I pressed him about this, he said, "It's not so much to change the way I feel as it is to convince everyone else that I'm really dealing with things. The trouble is, no matter how I dress, it's not too hard for people to read me, to see the subtext, 'I can't handle things today!' Thank God it doesn't happen often."

Another friend, the director of a national foundation, says she faces the same problem. "There are times when I simply can't cope with things, and usually they are the exact times I don't want the people who work for me to know I can't manage."

"What do you do?"

She shrugged. "I become someone else. If I have a meeting and I want to look very efficient, I decide I'll be a Sigourney Weaver type. That takes a smart suit and a beautiful blouse and pin. If I have to coax a donation out of a big shot, I'll be Blanche DuBois with a few ruffles, and if I go from the office right to someone's house for dinner, I can be Doris Day. I use pretenses to send out a particular image."

Selecting an image and trying to live up to it may not help much in actually dealing with the problem at hand, but it could send out a subtext that you are dealing just fine, thereby gaining the confidence of those around you. Still, there are better ways. While playacting can work for some, other methods are necessary for people who often have problems dealing with situations, and therefore send out a subtext of inadequacy.

Today's world is an overwhelming one, and many people find it difficult and often impossible to handle the economic and political upheavals of our time, the turmoil of our troubled cities—and, on a more intimate level, the difficulties of the workplace or personal life.

All these problems create anxieties which we may often feel helpless to handle. Others then sense a subtext of helplessness in us. So, it is important to reduce the anxieties, to deal realistically with life, and change the subtext that others read in us.

Each of us is different, thus each has a different method of coping with life. We all, however, use certain basic external techniques. Learning, understanding, and using these techniques will allow us to manage life better and control the subtext we send out to others, changing the way others see us and enabling us to successfully handle our jobs and make our way up the corporate ladder.

Review Questions

1. How much control does Fast suggest one person has over the image others have of him or her?
2. What is the "Janus Factor"?
3. According to Fast, *why* do people learn to wear a "mask"?
4. What point does Fast make about control and nonverbal communication?
5. What point about nonverbal communication does Fast make with his example of Gavin?
6. What specific advice does Fast offer about controlling your clothing and other aspects of your appearance?

Probes

1. Given your knowledge of and experience with nonverbal communication, what would you say are the most legitimate and helpful ideas in this reading? One might be this comment: "Certainly, in an ideal world, we would judge people by what they do, not by their race or clothes or social status, but this is not an ideal world, and we judge others by the images they project." Do you agree? What other key ideas do you find here?
2. Fast talks a lot about image in politics. How much of this information is also applicable to everyday work and family situations?
3. Do you agree that there's a "Janus Factor," that is, that "When people live together and work together, a great deal of their day is spent covering up what they really feel and in controlling their real emotions"? If you agree, do you believe that this is a situation we ought to accept and live with, or one that we ought to try to change? If you disagree, how do you support or substantiate your disagreement?
4. Fast argues that "masking" starts in early childhood and peaks in teenagers. Do you agree with his implication that adults continue sending out the subtext, "I don't give a damn!"?

Part 2

Openness as "Inhaling"

Chapter 5

Self-Awareness

T he readings in chapters 5, 6, and 7 all focus on the awareness, input, or perception side of "inhaling-exhaling." This chapter discusses self-awareness, the next explores how we perceive others, and Chapter 7 is about listening.

Everybody spends some time in self-awareness. As adolescents we compare our bodies and our looks to the people around us and worry about the ways we're labeled. At one time or another most people have had the experience of feeling completely "strange," "out-of-it," unlike anybody else we know. These feelings underscore one of the most important qualities of "the self": it is *not* fundamentally an internal thing, a composite of genetic makeup and individual attitudes. Rather, the self is interpersonal and social, which means it's made up of and affected by the ways we relate with and to others. Each of us develops a sense of who we are primarily by comparing and contrasting ourselves with others—parents, siblings, and other family members; friends; schoolmates; bosses, teachers; and other influential people.

This fact was demonstrated in a famous experiment that was carried out a number of years ago, before there were regulations that prevent social scientists from treating experimental subjects this way. A teacher asked several males to change the ways they behaved toward a woman in their class who was thought of as "plain." They lavished attention on her in class, took turns dating her, and generally responded to her as if she were very attractive. In a few weeks, it was clear that the woman was paying more attention to her appearance and was becoming more pleasant and outgoing. By the time the last male asked her out, he was informed that she was booked up for some time in the future. As one report put it, "It seems that there were more desirable males around than those 'plain' graduate students."[1]

In this experiment the woman's self changed dramatically, and it changed because of the relationships she had with others. Your self—and mine—are the same. Genetics and heredity give us the raw material, but we become who we are in relationships with others. This means that our communication is not only *affected by* our selves, it also *affects* who we are. Our selves are built primarily in relationships with the persons we're communicating with.

This first reading comes from a book written to help college students of all ages who want to expand their self-awareness and explore the choices available to them in significant areas of their lives. It is a personal reading, partly because it asks you to focus on yourself as you read it, and partly because its authors, Gerald Corey and Marianne Schneider-Corey, write personally about their own experiences. This chapter encourages you to look critically at the *why* of your existence and to clarify the sources of your values. The authors emphasize the importance of listening to your own inner desires and feelings as you ask three key questions, Who am I? Where am I going? and Why? But they also make the point that "meaning in life is found through intense relationships with others, not through an exclusive and narrow pursuit of self-realization."

Jerry and Marianne encourage you to reflect on your philosophy of life, your response to religion, and your values. You might think a discussion of religion is out of place in a textbook, but, as they point out, religious faith can be a powerful source of meaning and purpose. Even reflection that begins with the question, "Is there a God?" is religious, and as you extend your exploration of some of the related questions they suggest, you can often learn a great deal about your self. When I grew up, for example, church was just something the family automatically did on Sunday, and my responses were predictable. I didn't hate it, but I also didn't get much out of it. For a time I didn't have much connection with religion, but when I attended a church-sponsored college and developed some religious friends, I discovered some deep resonances between my fundamental values and those I saw being lived out by some of the religious people I knew. Since then I've profited a whole lot from the academic writings of some theologians and from friendships with people with a variety of religious commitments. My spiritual life is important to me, and I define myself in part as a "religious" person.

Your experience might be totally different. But the point these authors reinforce is that, as part of your study of interpersonal communication, it can be helpful to reflect on your own philosophy, values, and religious beliefs. Why? Because (a) they have been developed in your past communication experiences, (b) they will be changed by communication you experience in the future, and (c) your philosophy, values, and religious beliefs affect how you communicate with others today.

Note

1. John W. Kinch, "A Formalized Theory of the Self-Concept," in *Symbolic Interaction,* 2nd ed. Jerome Manis & Bernard N. Meltzer (eds.). (Boston: Allyn & Bacon, 1972), pp. 245–252.

Meaning and Values

Gerald Corey and Marianne Schneider-Corey

In this chapter we encourage you to look critically at the *why* of your existence, to clarify the sources of your values, and to reflect on questions such as these: In what direction am I moving in my life? What do I have to show for my years on this earth so far? Where have I been, where am I now, and where do I want to go? What steps can I take to make the changes I have decided on?

Many who are fortunate enough to achieve power, fame, success, and material comfort nevertheless experience a sense of emptiness. Although they may not be able to articulate what is lacking in their lives, they know that something is amiss. The astronomical number of pills and drugs consumed to allay the symptoms of this "existential vacuum"—depression and anxiety—is evidence of our failure to find values that allow us to make sense of our place in the world. In *Habits of the Heart*, Bellah and his colleagues (1985) found among the people they interviewed a growing interest in finding purpose in their lives. Although our achievements as a society are enormous, we seem to be hovering on the very brink of disaster, not only from internal conflict but also from societal incoherence. Bellah and his associates assert that the core problem with our society is that we have put our own good, as individuals and as groups, ahead of the common good.

The need for a sense of meaning is manifested by the increased interest in religion, especially among young people in college. A student told us recently that in her English class of twenty students, four of them had selected religion as a topic for a composition dealing with a conflict in their lives. Other signs of the search for meaning include the widespread interest in Eastern and other philosophies, the use of meditation, the number of self-help and inspirational books published each year, the experimentation with different lifestyles, and even the college courses in personal adjustment!

The paradox of our contemporary society is that although we have the benefits of technological progress, we are still not satisfied. We have become increasingly troubled about ourselves and our place in the world, we have less certainty about morality, and we are less sure that there is any meaning or purpose in the universe (Carr, 1988, p. 167). It seems fair to say that we are caught up in a crisis of meaning and values.

Our Search for Identity

The discovery of meaning and values is essentially related to our achievement of identity as a person. The quest for identity involves a commitment to give birth to ourselves by exploring the meaning of our uniqueness and humanity. A major problem for many people is that they have lost a sense of self, because they have directed their search for identity outside themselves. In their attempt to be liked and accepted by everyone, they have become finely tuned to what *others* expect of them but alienated from their *own* inner desires and feelings. As Rollo May (1973) observes, they are able to *respond* but not to *choose*. Indeed, May sees inner emptiness as the chief problem in contemporary society; too many of us, he says, have become "hollow people" who have very little understanding of who we are and what we feel. He cites one person's succinct description: "I'm just a collection of mirrors, reflecting what everyone expects of me" (p. 15).

Moustakas (1975) describes the same alienation from self that May talks about. For Moustakas, alienation is "the developing of a life outlined and determined by others, rather than a life based on one's own inner experience" (p. 31). If we become alienated from ourselves, we don't trust our own feelings but respond automatically to others as we think they want us to respond. As a consequence, Moustakas writes, we live in a world devoid of excitement, risk, and meaning. . . .

Achieving identity doesn't necessarily mean stubbornly clinging to a certain way of thinking or behaving. Instead, it may involve trusting ourselves enough to become open to new possibilities. Nor is an identity something we achieve for all time; rather, we need to be continually willing to reexamine our patterns and our priorities, our habits and relationships. Above all, we need to develop the ability to listen to our inner selves and trust what we hear. To take just one example, some students for whom academic life has become stale and empty have chosen to leave it in response to their inner feelings. Some have opted to travel and live modestly for a time, taking in new cultures and even assimilating into them for a while. They may not be directly engaged in preparing for a career and, in that sense, "establishing" themselves, but they are achieving their own identities by being open to new experiences and ways of being. For some of them, it may take real courage to resist the pressure to settle down in a career or "complete" their education.

Our search for identity involves asking three key existential questions, none of which has easy or definite answers: Who am I? Where am I going? Why?

The question Who am I? is never settled once and for all, for it can be answered differently at different times in our life. We need to revise our life, especially when old identities no longer seem to supply a meaning or give us direction. As we have seen, we must decide whether to let others tell us who we are or to take a stand and define ourselves.

Where am I going? This issue relates to our plans for a lifetime and the means we expect to use in attaining our goals. Like the previous question, this one demands periodic review. Our life goals are not set once and for all. Again, do we show the courage it takes to decide for ourselves where we are going, or do we look for a guru to show us where to go?

Asking the question Why? and searching for reasons are characteristics of being human. We face a rapidly changing world in which old values give way to new ones or to none at all. Part of shaping an identity implies that we are actively searching for meaning, trying to make sense of the world in which we find ourselves. . . .

Finding Meaning by Transcending Personal Interests

Carr (1988) concludes that what most of us want is to make a difference in the world. The process of becoming self-actualizing begins as a personal search. Although self-acceptance is a prerequisite for meaningful interpersonal relationships, there is a quest to go beyond self-centered interests. Ultimately, we want to establish connections with others in society, and we want to make a contribution. Likewise, Bellah and his colleagues (1985) conclude that meaning in life is found through intense relationships with others, not through an exclusive and narrow pursuit of self-realization. In their interviews with many people they found a desire to move beyond the isolated self. Our common life requires more than an exclusive concern with material accumulation. These authors maintain that a reconstituting of the social world is required, involving a transformation of consciousness.

Developing a Philosophy of Life

A philosophy of life is made up of the fundamental beliefs, attitudes, and values that govern a person's behavior. Many students have said that they hadn't really thought much about their philosophy of life. However, the fact that we've never explicitly defined the components of our philosophy doesn't mean that we are completely without one. All of us do operate on the basis of general assumptions about ourselves, others, and the world. Thus, the first step in actively developing a philosophy of life is to formulate a clearer picture of our present attitudes and beliefs.

We have all been developing an implicit philosophy of life since we first began, as children, to wonder about life and death, love and hate, joy and fear, and the nature of the universe. We probably didn't need to be taught to be curious about such questions; raising them seems to be a natural part of human development. If we were fortunate, adults took the time to engage in dialogue with us, instead of discouraging us from asking questions and deadening some of our innate curiosity.

During the adolescent years the process of questioning usually assumes new dimensions. Adolescents who have been allowed to question and think for themselves as children begin to get involved in a more advanced set of issues. Many of the adolescents we've encountered in classes and workshops have at one time or another struggled with questions such as the following:

- Are the values that I've believed in for all these years the values I want to continue to live by?
- Where did I get my values? Are they still valid for me? Are there additional sources from which I can derive new values?
- Is there a God? What is the nature of the hereafter? What is my conception of a God? What does religion mean in my life? What kind of religion do I choose for myself? Does religion have any value for me?
- What do I base my ethical and moral decisions on? Peer-group standards? Parental standards? The normative values of my society?
- What explains the inhumanity I see in our world?
- What kind of future do I want? What can I do about actively creating this kind of future?

These are only a few of the questions that many adolescents think about and perhaps answer for themselves. However, a philosophy of life is not something we arrive at once and for all during our adolescent years. The development of a philosophy of life continues as long as we live. As long as we remain curious and open to new learning, we can revise and rebuild our conceptions of the world. Life may have a particular meaning for us during adolescence, a new meaning during adulthood, and still another meaning as we reach old age. Indeed, if we don't remain open to basic changes in our views of life, we may find it difficult to adjust to changed circumstances.

Keeping in mind that developing a philosophy of life is a continuing activity of examining and modifying the values we live by, you may find the following suggestions helpful as you go about formulating and reforming your own philosophy:

- Frequently create time to be alone in reflective thought.
- Consider what meaning the fact of your eventual death has for the present moment.
- Make use of significant contacts with others who are willing to challenge your beliefs and the degree to which you live by them.
- Adopt an accepting attitude toward those whose belief systems differ from yours, and develop a willingness to test your own beliefs. . . .

Religion and Meaning: A Personal View

Religious faith can be a powerful source of meaning and purpose. Religion helps many people make sense out of the universe and the mystery of our purpose in living. Like any other potential source of meaning, religious faith seems most authentic and valuable when it enables us to become as fully human as possible. This means that religion helps us get in touch with our own powers of thinking, feeling, deciding, willing, and acting. You might consider reflecting on the following questions about your religion to determine whether it is a constructive force in your life:

- Does my religion provide me with a set of values that is congruent with the way I live my life?
- Does my religion assist me in better understanding the meaning of life and death?
- Does my religion allow tolerance for others who see the world differently from me?
- Does my religion provide me with a sense of peace and serenity?
- Is my religious faith something that I actively choose or passively accept?
- Do my religious beliefs help me live life fully and treat others with respect and concern?
- Does my religion help me integrate my experience and make sense of the world?
- Does my religion encourage me to exercise my freedom and to assume the responsibility for the direction of my own life?
- Are my religious beliefs helping me become more of the person I'd like to become?
- Does my religion encourage me to question life and keep myself open to new learning?

As you take time for self-examination, how able are you to answer these questions in a way that is meaningful and satisfying to you? If you are honest with yourself, perhaps you will find that you have not really critically evaluated the sources of your spiritual and religious beliefs. Although you may hesitate to question your belief system out of a fear of weakening or undermining your faith, the opposite might well be true: demonstrating the courage to question your beliefs and values might strengthen them. As we have mentioned, increasing numbers of people seem to be deciding that a religious faith is necessary if they are to find an order and purpose in life. At the same time, many others insist that religion only impedes the quest for meaning or that it is incompatible with contemporary beliefs in other areas of life. What seems essential is that our acceptance or rejection of religious faith come authentically from within ourselves and that we remain open to new experience and learning, whatever points of view we decide on.

It is perhaps worth emphasizing that a "religion" may take the form of a system of beliefs and values concerning the ultimate questions in life rather than (or in addition to) membership in a church. People who belong to a church may not be "religious" in this sense, and others may consider themselves religious even though they are atheists or agnostics. Like almost anything else in human life, religion (or irreligion) can be bent to worthwhile or base purposes.

In my own experience, I (Jerry) have found religion most valuable when it is a challenge to broaden my choices and potential, rather than a restrictive influence. Until I was about 30, I tended to think of my religion as a package of ready-made answers for all the crises of life and was willing to let my church make many key decisions for me. I now think that I was experiencing too much anxiety in many areas of life to take full responsibility for my choices. My religious training had taught me that I should look to the authority of the church for ultimate answers in the areas of morality, value, and purpose. Like many other people I was encouraged to learn the "correct" answers and conform my thinking to them. Now, when I think of religion as a positive force, I think of it as being *freeing*, in the sense that it encourages me to trust myself, to discover the sources of strength and integrity within myself, and to assume responsibility for my own choices.

Although as an adult I've questioned and altered many of the religious teachings with which I was raised, I haven't discarded many of my past moral and religious values. Many of them served a purpose earlier in my life and, with modification, are still meaningful for me. However, whether or not I continue to hold the beliefs and values I've been taught, it seems crucial to me that I be willing to subject them to scrutiny. If they hold up under challenge, I can reincorporate them; by the same token, I can continue to examine the new beliefs and values I acquire.

My (Marianne's) religious faith has always been a positive force in my life. Sometimes people who are religious suffer from feelings of guilt and fears of damnation. This saddens me greatly, for if this is the case, religion ceases being a positive and powerful force in one's life. For me, religion helps me with an inner strength on which I can rely and that helps me to overcome difficulties that life presents. Although religion was encouraged in my childhood, it was never forced on me. It was a practice that I wanted to emulate because I saw the positive effects it had on the people in my life. Religion was practiced more than it was preached. The questions that we asked you to reflect on earlier are ones that I pose to myself as well. I want to be sure that I am aware of my beliefs and the necessity for making changes if I am not satisfied with my answers. . . .

Becoming Aware of How Your Values Operate

Your values influence what you do; your daily behavior is an expression of your basic values. We encourage you to make the time to continue examining the source of your values to determine if they are appropriate for you at this time in your life. Furthermore, it is essential that you be aware of the significant impact your value system has on your relationships with others. In our view, it is not appropriate for you to push your values on others, to assume a judgmental stance toward those who have a different world view, or to strive to convert others to adopt your perspective on life. Indeed, if you are secure in your values and basic beliefs, you will not be threatened by those who have a different set of beliefs and values.

In *God's Love Song*, Maier (1991) wonders how anyone can claim to have found the only way, not only for himself or herself but also for everyone else. We strongly agree with his view that there is a unique way for each person, however different that may be from the way of anyone else. As a minister, Sam Maier teaches that diversity shared not only is beautiful but also fosters understanding, caring, and the creation of community. He puts this message in a powerful and poetic way:

> It is heartening to find communities where the emphasis is placed upon each person having the opportunity to:
>
> - share what is vital and meaningful out of one's own experience;
> - listen to what is vital and meaningful to others;
> - not expect or demand that anyone else do it exactly the same way as oneself. (p. 3)

Reverend Maier's message is well worth contemplating. Although you might clarify a set of values that seem to work for you, we would hope that you respect the values of others that may be quite different from yours. It is not that one is right and the other is wrong. The diversity of cultures, religions, and world views implies a necessity not only to tolerate differences but also to embrace diverse paths toward meaning in life.

Whatever your own values are, they can be further clarified and strengthened if you entertain open discussion of various viewpoints and cultivate a nonjudgmental attitude toward diversity. You might raise questions such as:

- Where did I develop my values?
- Are my values open to modification?
- Have I challenged my values, and am I open to being challenged by others?
- Do I insist that the world remain the same now as it was earlier in my life?
- Do I feel so deeply committed to any of my values that I'm likely to push my friends and family members to accept them?
- How would I communicate my values to others without imposing those values?
- How do my own values and beliefs affect my behavior?
- Am I willing to accept people who hold different values?
- Do I avoid judging others if they think, feel, or act in different ways from myself? . . .

Where to Go from Here: Continuing Your Personal Growth

. . . As you consider what experiences for continued personal growth you are likely to choose at this time, be aware that your meaning in life is not cast in concrete. As you change, you can expect that what brings meaning to your life will also change. The projects that you were deeply absorbed in as an adolescent may hold little meaning for you today. And where and how you discover meaning today may not be the pattern for some future period.

You can deliberately choose experiences that will help you actualize your potentials. Perhaps you remember reading a book or seeing a film that had a profound impact on you and really seemed to put things in perspective. Certainly, reading books that deal with significant issues in your life can be a growth experience in itself, as well as an encouragement to try new things.

Often, we make all sorts of resolutions about what we'd like to be doing in our life or about experiences we want to share with others, and then we fail to carry them out. Is this true of you? Are there activities you value yet rarely get around to doing? Perhaps you tell yourself that you prize making new friendships; yet you find that you do very little to actually initiate any contacts. Or perhaps you derive satisfaction from growing vegetables or puttering in your garden and yet find many reasons to neglect this activity. You might tell yourself that you'd love to take a day or two just to be alone and yet never get around to arranging it. When you stop to think about it, aren't there choices you could be making right now that would make your life a richer one? How would you really like to be spending your time? What changes are you willing to make today, this week, this month, this year?

In addition to activities that you enjoy but don't engage in as often as you'd like, there are undoubtedly many new things you might consider trying out as ways of adding meaning to your life and developing your potentials. You might consider making a contract with yourself to start now on a definite plan of action, instead of putting it off until next week or next year. Some of the ways in which many people choose to challenge themselves to grow include the following:

- finding hobbies that develop new sides of themselves
- going to plays, concerts, and museums
- taking courses in pottery making, wine tasting, guitar playing, and innumerable other special interests
- getting involved in exciting work projects or actively pursuing forms of work that will lead to the development of hidden talents
- spending time alone to reflect on the quality of their lives
- initiating contacts with others and perhaps developing an intimate relationship
- enrolling in continuing-education courses or earning a degree primarily for the satisfaction of learning
- doing volunteer work and helping to make others' lives better
- experiencing the mountains, the desert, and the ocean—by hiking, sailing, and so on
- becoming involved in religious activities or pursuing a spiritual path that is meaningful to them
- traveling to new places, especially to experience different cultures
- keeping a journal in which they record feelings and dreams
- sharing some of their dreams with a person they trust

Any list of ways of growing is only a sample, of course; the avenues to personal growth are as various as the people who choose them. Growth can occur in small ways, and there are many things that you can do on your own (or with friends or family) to continue your personal development. Perhaps the greatest hindrance to our growth as a person is our failure to allow ourselves to imagine all the possibilities that are open to us.

References

Bellah, R. N., Madsen, R., Sullivan, W.M., Swidler, A., & Tipton, S. M. (1985). *Habits of the Heart: Individualism and Commitment in American Life*. New York: Harper & Row.

Carr, J. B. (1988). *Crisis In Intimacy: When Expectations Don't Meet Reality*. Pacific Grove, CA: Brooks/Cole.

Maier, S. (1991). *God's Love Song*. Corvallis, OR: Postal Instant Press.

May, R. (1973). *Man's Search for Himself*. New York: Dell

Moustakas, C. (1975). *Finding Yourself, Finding Others*. Englewood Cliffs, NJ: Prentice-Hall.

Review Questions

1. What do these authors mean by "existential vacuum"?
2. What does it generally mean to "find meaning by transcending personal interests"?
3. According to these authors, how much of a person's philosophy of life is stable, and how much changes?
4. What rationale do the Coreys give for including the topic of religion in this chapter?
5. What's the difference between religious influences and values?
6. How do these authors view individual choice? How important is it?

Probes

1. Do you agree that there is a widespread need for a sense of meaning among people you know, or do you think that these authors exaggerate the problem?
2. Before you read this essay, did you believe you had a "philosophy of life"? Do you now believe you do? What's it made up of?
3. What feelings are generated in you by this reading's discussion of religion? What experiences with others (family, friends, etc.) do those feelings grow out of?
4. How do you respond to Jerry's and Marianne's individual discussions of the roles of religion in their lives?
5. Do you agree that you can make conscious choices to change the directions of your personal growth? What examples from your own experience reinforce your view?

Compared to the Earth's sun, Zui 3 is very large, giving off more than a hundred times the light and heat. However, the orbit of Yadonasora is sufficiently removed that the planet is eminently habitable. The two seasons of its solar year, which is approximately twenty-eight Earth years long, trigger an unusual water cycle below the planet's surface. As the cooler season begins, water rises from thousands of spout holes and Yadonasora becomes all ocean. During the warm season the planet returns to a predominantly dry-land state. Yadonasora's sage and adviser is So-To-Lo-Cho, Jewel of the Twinkling Planet, who is reputedly five and a half. As would be expected, many of his sayings involve boats, of which there are far more than people.

One day a man named Pe-Te-Leet came seeking help with his moodiness.

"Give me an example of this 'moodiness,'" said Cho.

"No one looks where he's going," said Leet. "Last night a family in a swamp boat almost ran into us. I stood on our bow and watched for twenty harsecs as the helmsman, a doddering three-year-old, left and returned to his post six times. He didn't even seem to notice us, and at the last moment I had to turn to avoid him. I, of course, became furious."

"Of course," said Cho, and fell silent.

"But what can I do about my anger?"

"You can do nothing," said Cho, "because you believe that your anger is caused." And again he fell silent.

"But, O Jewel of the Twinkling Planet, surely there is something I can do. Not all men are as volatile as I."

"You could escape from your moods only if they were not caused. Do you not see that the three-year-old did not cause you to become angry?"

"But his swamp boat almost drifted into us. My whole family could have perished as a result of his negligence."

Cho smiled and gently placed his hand on Leet's arm. "My friend, are there not many abandoned boats on the ocean? If from your bow you had noticed that the boat was empty, and yet it had drifted toward you in exactly the same manner, what would you have done?"

"I would have turned out of its way."

"And would you have been angry?"

"No, it couldn't have helped doing what it did."

"Ah!" said Cho. "Boats are innocent! You give the most important gift of all to a mere boat. And yet boats are not even your brothers and sisters.

"Your anger came not from the boat almost ramming you, but from the fact that it was occupied by a living soul. You know that empty boats cannot help what they do, and yet you believe that people can. Last night, you could not have helped getting angry. But now that you are no longer empty, you have a choice."

—HUGH AND GAYLE PRATHER, *The Innocence of Boats*

S oon after it was published, I discovered Robert Bolton's book, *People Skills: How to Assert Yourself, Listen to Others and Resolve Conflicts.* It contains a wealth of interpersonal communication insights and advice, almost all of which is as relevant and applicable today as it was when the book was first published. This chapter catalogs a number of what Bolton calls "barriers" or "roadblocks" to communication that often create problems in friend, family, and work relationships. I include this reading here because it shifts your self-awareness from a general consideration of your philosophy and values to specific reflection on communication patterns that might be helping to cause problems for you.

As Bolton explains, each of these barriers or roadblocks is a high-risk response because its "impact on communication is frequently (though not inevitably) negative." These communication moves function as roadblocks especially when people are under stress, and they can diminish the other person's self-esteem, trigger defensiveness and resentment, lead to dependency or feelings of defeat, and decrease the likelihood that the other person will find his or her own solution to whatever problem is being discussed. Bolton lists twelve such responses, and discusses them under three general headings: judging, sending solutions, and avoiding the other's concerns.

With the help of communication theorist and psychotherapist Carl Rogers, Bolton describes how judging may be the most toxic of these responses. As Rogers pointed out, often our first inclination is to respond to someone's statement with a criticism, label, or diagnosis—"What a dumb thing to say," "Sounds just like a punk kid," or "She always talks that way when she's depressed." Even positive judgments can hurt when they're used manipulatively. This is one reason why many people try to protect themselves from praise with such responses as "I don't think it's that good," or "I could have done a lot better."

Communicators "send solutions" by ordering, threatening, moralizing, asking excessive or inappropriate questions, and giving advice. In some cases, each of these can be helpful. But when used excessively or inappropriately, they make the giver of orders or advice superior to the incompetent or hapless person on the other end. These communication moves can short circuit the other person's efforts to solve his or her own problem, and at the worst they can represent a kind of "interfere-iority complex."

In situations of stress, diverting, logical argument, and reassuring can be ways to "avoid the other's concerns." Each of these tactics works to shift the focus away from the other and can sharply unbalance conversations. "Even reassurance?" you might ask. Yes, because the target of reassurance is often a part of a person's self-image, and self-images resist most direct change efforts. For example, if you're feeling clumsy, unattractive, or foolish, is your self-image actually likely to be changed by your mom's reassurance that you "look just fine," or your friend's well-intentioned reassurance that "Everybody makes mistakes"? Often the best response is simple acceptance, which can free the person to move *through* the feeling, rather than trying to deny or avoid it.

The final section of this reading talks about "guilt, remorse, [and] regret," which can arise when you realize that you sometimes do throw up these barriers to communication. Bolton reminds his readers that diagnosis is the first step toward recovery and that these ineffective conversational habits can be corrected. Many of the readings that follow this one offer ways to correct them.

Barriers to Communication

Robert Bolton

Common Communication Spoilers

Sue Maxwell, a woman in her mid-thirties, sighed as she said, "Well, I blew it again. We took the family to visit my parents over Thanksgiving weekend. They have been under heavy emotional and financial pressure this year, and I resolved to be very gentle and caring with them. But they started criticizing the way I handle the kids and I got mad. I told them they didn't do such a great job with me and my brother. We argued for half an hour. All three of us felt very hurt.

"This type of thing happens each time I return home," Sue continued. "Even though they have no right to say some of the things they do, I love them and want our visits to be pleasant. But somehow, we almost always say things that hurt each other."

Sue's experience is, unfortunately, a common one. Whether it is with parents, children, bosses, employees, colleagues, friends, or "all of the above," people usually long for better interpersonal results than they commonly achieve.

Since there is in most of us a strong desire for effective communication, why is it so rare and difficult to establish? One of the prime reasons is that, without realizing it, people typically inject communication barriers into their conversations. It has been estimated that *these barriers are used over 90 percent of the time* when one or both parties to a conversation has a problem to be dealt with or a need to be fulfilled.[2]

Communication barriers are *high-risk responses*—that is, responses whose impact on communication is frequently (though not inevitably) negative. These roadblocks are more likely to be destructive when one or more persons who are interacting are under stress. The unfortunate effects of communication blocks are many and varied. They frequently diminish the other's self-esteem. They tend to trigger defensiveness, resistance, and resentment. They can lead to dependency, withdrawal, feelings of defeat or of inadequacy. They decrease the likelihood that the other will find her own solution to her problem. Each roadblock is a "feeling-blocker"; it reduces the likelihood that the other will constructively express her true feelings. Because communication roadblocks carry a high risk of fostering these negative results, their repeated use can cause permanent damage to a relationship.

What specific barriers are apt to hinder a conversation? Experts in interpersonal communication like Carl Rogers, Reuel Howe, Haim Ginott, and Jack Gibb[3] have pinpointed responses that tend to block conversation. More recently, Thomas Gordon[4] devised a comprehensive list that he calls the "dirty dozen" of communication spoilers. These undesirable responses include:

Criticizing: Making a negative evaluation of the other person, her actions, or attitudes. "You brought it on yourself—you've got nobody else to blame for the mess you are in."

Name-calling: "Putting down" or stereotyping the other person "What a dope!" "Just like a woman. . . ." "Egghead." "You hardhats are all alike." "You are just another insensitive male."

Diagnosing: Analyzing why a person is behaving as she is; playing amateur psychiatrist. "I can read you like a book—you are just doing that to irritate me." "Just because you went to college, you think you are better than I."

Praising Evaluatively: Making a positive judgment of the other person, her actions, or attitudes. "You are always such a good girl. I know you will help me with the lawn tonight." Teacher to teenage student: "You are a great poet." (Many people find it difficult to believe that some of the barriers like praise are high-risk responses. Later, I will explain why I believe repeated use of these responses can be detrimental to relationships.)

Ordering: Commanding the other person to do what you want to have done. "Do your homework right now." "Why?! Because I said so. . . ."

Threatening: Trying to control the other's actions by warning of negative consequences that you will instigate. "You'll do it *or else* . . ." "Stop that noise right now or I will keep the whole class after school."

Moralizing: Telling another person what she *should* do. "Preaching" at the other. "You shouldn't get a divorce; think of what will happen to the children." "You ought to tell him you are sorry."

Excessive/Inappropriate Questioning: Closed-ended questions are often barriers in a relationship; these are those that can usually be answered in a few words—often with a simple yes or no. "When did it happen?" "Are you sorry that you did it?"

Advising: Giving the other person a solution to her problems. "If I were you, I'd sure tell him off." "That's an easy one to solve. First . . ."

Diverting: Pushing the other's problems aside through distraction. "Don't dwell on it, Sarah. Let's talk about something more pleasant." Or; "Think you've got it bad?! Let me tell you what happened to me."

Logical argument: Attempting to convince the other with an appeal to facts or logic, usually without consideration of the emotional factors involved. "Look at the facts; if you hadn't bought that new car, we could have made the down payment on the house."

Reassuring: Trying to stop the other person from feeling the negative emotions she is experiencing. "Don't worry, it is always darkest before the dawn." "It will all work out OK in the end."

Why Roadblocks Are High-Risk Responses

At first glance, some of these barriers seem quite innocent. Praise, reassurance, logical responses, questions, and well-intentioned advice are often thought of as positive factors in interpersonal relations. Why, then, do behavioral scientists think of these twelve types of responses as potentially damaging to communication?

These twelve ways of responding are viewed as *high-risk* responses, rather than *inevitably* destructive elements of all communication. They are more likely to block conversation, thwart the other person's problem-solving efficiency, and increase the emotional distance between people than other ways of communicating. However, at times, people use these responses with little or no obvious negative effect.

If one or two persons are experiencing a strong need or wrestling with a difficult problem, the likelihood of negative impact from roadblocks increases greatly. A useful guideline to follow is, "Whenever you or the other person is experiencing stress, avoid all roadblocks." Unfortunately, it is precisely when stress is experienced that we are most likely to use these high-risk responses.

The twelve barriers to communication can be divided into three major categories: judgment, sending solutions, and avoidance of the other's concerns:

1. Criticizing
2. Name-calling } JUDGING
3. Diagnosing
4. Praising Evaluatively

5. Ordering
6. Threatening
7. Moralizing } SENDING SOLUTIONS
8. Excessive/Inappropriate Questioning
9. Advising

10. Diverting
11. Logical Argument } AVOIDING THE OTHER'S CONCERNS
12. Reassuring

Let's look in greater detail at each of these major categories of high-risk responses.

Judging: The Major Roadblock

Four roadblocks fall into this category—criticizing, name-calling, diagnosing, and praising. They are all variations on a common theme—judging the other person.

Psychologist Carl Rogers delivered a lecture on communication in which he said he believes the *major barrier* to interpersonal communication lies in our *very natural tendency to judge*—to approve or disapprove of the statements of the other person.[5]

Few people think of themselves as judgmental. Yet in that lecture, Rogers convinced many of his listeners that the tendency to judge was more widespread than they realized:

> As you leave the meeting tonight, one of the statements you are likely to hear is, "I didn't like that man's talk." Now what do you respond? Almost invariably your reply will be either approval or disapproval of the attitude expressed. Either you respond, "I didn't either. I thought it was terrible." Or else you tend to reply, "Oh, I thought it was really good." In other words, your primary reaction is to evaluate what has just been said to you, to evaluate it from *your* point of view, your own frame of reference.
>
> Or, take another example. Suppose I say with some feeling, "I think the Republicans are behaving in ways that show a lot of good sound sense these days." What is the response that arises in your mind as you listen? The overwhelming likelihood is that it will be evaluative. You will find yourself agreeing, or disagreeing, or making some judgment about me such as "He must be a conservative," or "He seems solid in his thinking."

In that same speech, Rogers made another important point about the human inclination to be judgmental:

> Although the tendency to make evaluations is common in almost all interchange of language, it is very much heightened in those situations where feelings and emotions are deeply involved. So, the stronger our feelings, the more likely it is that there will be no mutual element in the communication. There will be just two ideas, two feelings, two judgments missing each other in psychological space. I'm sure you recognize this from your own experience. When you have not been emotionally involved yourself, and have listened to a heated discussion, you often go away thinking, "Well, they actually weren't talking about the same thing." And they were not. Each was making a judgment, an evaluation from his own frame of reference. There was really nothing which could be called communication in any genuine sense. This tendency to react to any emotionally meaningful statement by forming an evaluation of it from our own point of view is, I repeat, the major barrier to interpersonal communication.[6]

Criticizing

One of the judgmental roadblocks is criticism. Many of us feel we ought to be critical—or other people will never improve. Parents think they need to judge their children or they will never become hard-working, mannerly adults. Teachers think they must criticize their students or they will never learn. Supervisors think they must criticize their employees or production will slip. In later chapters we will see how some of the objectives we are trying to accomplish with criticism (and the other roadblocks) can be achieved more effectively by other means.

Meanwhile, it is worth observing our interactions with others to see how frequently we are critical. For some people, criticism is a way of life. One husband described his wife as being on a constant fault-finding safari. An admiral once gave White House aide Harry Hopkins the title of "Generalissimo of the Needle Brigade"[7] because of the latter's critical nature.

Name-Calling and Labeling

Name-calling and labeling usually have negative overtones to both the sender and receiver. "Nigger," "Wasp," "intellectual," "brat," "bitch," "shrew," "autocrat," "jerk," "dope," "nag"—these all attach a stigma to the other. Some other labels, however, provide halos: "bright," "hard worker," "dedicated," "a chip off the old block," "a real go-getter."

Labeling prevents us from getting to know ourselves and other individuals: there is no longer a person before us—only a type. The psychologist Clark Moustakas says:

> Labels and classifications make it appear that we know the other, when actually, we have caught the shadow and not the substance. Since we are convinced we know ourselves and others . . . [we] no longer actually see what is happening before us and in us, and, not knowing that we do not know, we make no effort to be in contact with the real. We continue to use labels to stereotype ourselves and others, and these labels have replaced human meanings, unique feelings and growing life within and between persons.[8]

Diagnosing

Diagnosis, a form of labeling, has plagued mankind through the centuries, but has been even more prevalent since the time of Freud. Some people, instead of listening to the substance of what a person is saying, play emotional detective; probing for hidden motives, psychological complexes, and the like.

A secretary who went to work for a psychologist resigned within a month. When a friend asked why she left the job, she explained, "He analyzed what motives were behind everything I did. I couldn't win. If I came to work late, it was because I was hostile; if I came early, it was because I was anxious; if I arrived on time, I was compulsive."

Perhaps you have found, as I have, that communication tends to be thwarted when one person informs another that she is being defensive, or self-deceiving, or that she is acting out of guilt or fear or some other unconscious motive or "complex."

Praising Evaluatively

There is a common belief that all honest praise is helpful. Many parents, teachers, managers, and others endorse praise without reservation. Praise "is supposed to build confidence, increase security, stimulate initiative, motivate learning, generate good will and improve human relations," says Haim Ginott.[9] Thus, at first sight, praise seems to be an unlikely candidate to qualify as a roadblock. However, positive evaluations often have negative results.

Praise is often used as a gimmick to try to get people to change their behavior. When someone with ulterior purposes offers praise, there is often resentment, not only of the effort to control, but also of the manipulativeness experienced. David Augsburger says that it is not always true that to be praised is to be loved. "To be praised more often is to be manipulated. To be praised is often to be used. To be praised is often to be outsmarted, outmaneuvered, out-sweet-talked."[10]

Even when it is not used manipulatively, praise often has detrimental effects. Have you ever noticed how people defend themselves against praise as though they were protecting themselves against a threat? Their guardedness and defensiveness cause them to come up with stock denials such as:

"I don't think it's that good."
"It wasn't much, really."
"I can't take the credit for it; my assistant, Charlie, thought it up."
"It was mainly luck."
"I could have done a lot better."

When people hear about the perils of evaluative praise, they often think behavioral scientists believe *all* forms of encouragement are detrimental. This is far from the case. Expressing positive feelings toward people is an important element of interpersonal communication. . . .

Sending Solutions Can Be a Problem!

Another group of roadblocks involves sending solutions to other persons. The solutions may be sent caringly as advice, indirectly by questioning, authoritatively as an order, aggressively as a threat, or with a halo around it as moralizing. Some ways of sending solutions obviously carry higher risks than others. *All* of these ways of sending solutions, however, are potential barriers to communication, especially when one or both of the persons is experiencing a need or a problem. Sending a solution often compounds a problem or creates new problems without resolving the original dilemma.

Ordering, threatening, moralizing, advising (and often asking closed-ended questions), are ways of sending solutions. I am not suggesting that sending solutions is never appropriate, but sending solutions can erect barriers and can thwart another person's growth.

Ordering

An order is a solution sent coercively and backed by force. When coercion is used, people often become resistant and resentful. Sabotage may result. Or people who are constantly given orders may become very compliant and submissive. Orders imply that the other's judgment is unsound and thus tend to undermine self-esteem.

Threatening

A threat is a solution that is sent with an emphasis on the punishment that will be forthcoming if the solution is not implemented. Threats produce the same kind of negative results that are produced by orders.

Moralizing

Many people love to put a halo around their solutions for others. They attempt to back their ideas with the force of social, moral, or theological authority. Moralizing speaks with "shoulds" and "oughts" but it chooses other wordings, too. "It's the right thing to do." "You don't visit me enough." "Shoulds" are often implied, even when they are not stated directly.

"Moralizing is demoralizing." It fosters anxiety, arouses resentment, tends to thwart honest self-expression, and invites pretense.

Excessive or Inappropriate Questioning

Some kinds of questions have their place in communication. But questions can be real conversation-stoppers, as illustrated in this familiar question-and-nonresponse routine:

> "Where did you go?"
> "Out."
> "What did you do?"
> "Nothing."

Day after day, parents in American homes ask, "How was school today?" and day after day they hear the droned nonresponse. "OK."

Some people ask questions constantly. When this happens, they experience an almost total drying up of conversation. When loved ones share so little with them, these questioners desperately resort to more questions to keep at least a trickle of disclosure coming from the other person. But the added questions retard the communication even more.

A large percentage of the population is addicted to questioning. While there are constructive ways of asking *occasional* questions . . . , extensive questioning usually derails a conversation. Jacques Lalanne, president of the Institut de Developpement Humain in Quebec, says, "In everyday conversation, questions are usually a poor substitute for more direct communication. Questions are incomplete, indirect, veiled, impersonal and consequently ineffective messages that often breed defense reactions and resistance. They are rarely simple requests for information, but an indirect means of attaining an end, a way of manipulating the person being questioned."[11]

Advising

Advice is another of the most commonly used of the roadblocks. At its worst, it represents an "interfere-iority complex." Though I have known and taught others many of the important reasons why advice is rarely constructive, and though I have decreased my advice-giving enormously, I still find myself dispensing advice inappropriately. The advice-giving trap is a rather constant temptation to me, and I find I am most apt to give in to it when someone I love talks over a problem with me.

Well, what's wrong with advice? Advice is often a basic insult to the intelligence of the other person. It implies a lack of confidence in the capacity of the person with the problem to understand and cope with his or her own difficulties. As Norman Kagan puts it, "In essence, we implicitly say to someone, 'You have been making a "big deal" out of a problem whose solution is immediately apparent to me—how stupid you are!'"[12]

Another problem with advice is that the advisor seldom understands the full implications of the problem. When people share their concerns with us, they often display only the "tip of the iceberg." The advisor is unaware of the complexities, feelings, and the many other factors that lie hidden beneath the surface. Dag Hammarskjold, the introspective Swedish diplomat, said:

> Not knowing the question,
> It was easy for him
> To give the answer.[13]

Avoiding the Other's Concerns

A journalist once commented that the first law of conversation is that if there is any possible way to derail the train of dialogue, someone will do it. The remaining three roadblocks—diverting, logical argument, and reassurance—are notable for getting conversations off the track.

Diverting

One of the most frequent ways of switching a conversation from the other person's concerns to your own topic is called "diverting." The phrase "Speaking of . . ." often signals the beginning of a diversion. Much of what passes for conversation is really little more than a series of diversions. For example, I overheard this interchange between four elderly ladies visiting a friend in a hospital:

PATIENT: This was such a painful operation! I didn't think I would be able to stand it. It was just . . .

PERSON A: Speaking of operations, I had my gallbladder out in Memorial Hospital in 1976. What a time I had . . .

PERSON B: That's the hospital my grandson was taken to when he broke his arm. Dr. Beyer set it.

PERSON C: Did you know that Dr. Beyer lives on my street? They say he has an alcohol problem.

PERSON D: Well, alcohol is not nearly so bad as drugs. The son of the principal of the high school is really messed up by drugs. He shouldn't deal with other people's kids if he can't manage his own.

Whoa! What happened to the patient's concerns?

Sometimes people divert a conversation because they lack the awareness and skills to listen effectively. Sometimes they are grabbing the focus of attention for themselves. At other times people resort to diversion when they are uncomfortable with the emotions stimulated by the conversation. Many people dislike talking about affection, anger, conflict, death, sickness, divorce, and other topics that create tension in them. When these topics are the focus of conversation, they divert the conversation to a topic more comfortable for them.

Logical Argument

Logic has many important functions. When another person is under stress, however, or when there is conflict between people, providing logical solutions can be infuriating. Though it may seem that those are the very times we most need logic, it nevertheless has a high risk of alienating the other person.

One of the main problems with logic in situations of personal or interpersonal stress is that it keeps others at an emotional distance. Logic focuses on facts and typically avoids feelings. But when another person has a problem or when there is a problem in the relationship, feelings are the main issue. When persons use logic to avoid emotional involvement, they are withdrawing from another at a most inopportune moment.

Reassuring

"What on earth can be wrong with reassurance?" is a question we get from many people.

Like the other eleven barriers, reassurance can drive a wedge between people. Haim Ginott writes:

> Once in a blue moon, almost every parent hears his son or daughter declare, "I am stupid." Knowing that *his* child cannot be stupid, the parent sets out to convince him that he is bright.

SON: I am stupid.
FATHER: You are not stupid.
SON: Yes, I am.
FATHER: You are not. Remember how smart you were at camp? The counselor thought you were one of the brightest.
SON: How do you know what he thought?
FATHER: He told me so.
SON: Yeah, how come he called me stupid all the time?
FATHER: He was just kidding.
SON: I am stupid, and I know it. Look at my grades in school.
FATHER: You just have to work harder.
SON: I already work harder, and it doesn't help. I have no brains.
FATHER: You are smart, I know.
SON: I am stupid, *I* know.
FATHER: (loudly) You are not stupid!
SON: Yes, I am!
FATHER: You are not stupid, Stupid!

Ginott goes on to explain:

> When a child declares that he is stupid or ugly or bad, nothing that we can say or do will change his self-image immediately. A person's ingrained opinion of himself resists direct attempts at alteration. As one child said to his father, I know you mean well, Dad, but I am not *that* stupid to take your word that I am bright.[14]

Reassurance is a way of seeming to comfort another person while actually doing the opposite. The word *comfort* comes from two Latin words, *con* and *fortis*. The combination literally means "strengthened by being with." Reassurance does not allow the comforter to really be with the other. It can be a form of emotional withdrawal. Reassurance is often by people who like the idea of being helpful but who do not want to experience the emotional demand that goes with it.

Roadblock Number Thirteen

When people are introduced to the roadblocks, a fairly typical reaction is, "That's just what my husband has been doing all these years! Wait till I tell him about all the roadblocks he sends." Or, "Gosh, my boss uses just about all of these barriers. The next time he does it, I'm going to point out how he's roadblocking me." This is Roadblock Thirteen: telling other people they are sending roadblocks. Roadblock Thirteen belongs in the judgment category. If you want to improve your communication, pointing the finger of judgment at others is a poor place to begin.

Guilt, Remorse, Regret

After hearing a presentation on the roadblocks, many people experience pangs of guilt. They suddenly become aware that some patterns of their communication are barriers in important relationships and have probably caused needless distance between them and other people. After presentations on communications barriers in our workshops, people typically make comments like these:

> Awareness of the three major groupings of roadblocks was like a stab and I cringe for all the situations that I "blew" that could have been productive had I known how to respond properly. . . .
>
> It's like suddenly knowing the enemy and finding out that it's *me!* . . .
>
> I had always thought of myself as a "good listener," never realizing that I was often guilty of actually shutting off communication by the way I was listening. . . .
>
> The responses you identified as barriers were things I'd always felt *helped* conversation, and I've been using many of them pretty consistently! As I listened to you talk about the roadblocks, I felt remorse and regret. These thoughts flew into my mind: "I've failed as a parent and a teacher." "I wish I could have learned this fifteen years ago" "How did I get to be forty years old without discovering that these were roadblocks?" After the guilt, however, I became hopeful. After all, it is practically impossible to counter a negative approach unless you know that it is destructive. Learning about the roadblocks is the first step to positive action for me.

We all use roadblocks sometimes. Their occasional usage rarely does much harm to a relationship. When employed frequently, however, there is a high probability that roadblocks will do considerable harm.

These conversational bad habits can be corrected. The awareness that comes from reading a chapter like this can help greatly. You can figure out which roadblock you most want to eliminate and concentrate on eradicating that one. It is difficult and discouraging work at first because roadblocks are habitual ways of responding and it requires time and effort to change any habit. At the same time that you try to eliminate the roadblocks, you can use the communication skills described in the remainder of this book. Several thousand years ago, a sage taught that it is much easier to stamp out a bad habit by supplanting it with a good one than it is to try to stamp out negative habits by willpower alone.[15] That wisdom still holds today. As you learn to listen, assert, resolve conflict, and solve interpersonal problems more effectively, your use of the roadblocks will inevitably diminish.

Summary

Certain ways of verbalizing carry a high risk of putting a damper on the conversation, being harmful to the relationship, triggering feelings of inadequacy, anger, or dependency in the other person, or all of these things. As a result of one or more of the twelve roadblocks, the other may become more submissive and compliant. Or she may become more resistant, rebellious, and argumentative. These barriers to conversation tend to diminish the other's self-esteem and to undermine motivation. They decrease the likelihood that the other will be self-determining—they increase the likelihood that she will put the focus of evaluation outside herself. Roadblocks are prevalent in our culture; they are used in over 90 percent of the conversations where one or both persons have a problem or a strong need. Yet these conversational bad habits can be corrected, primarily through the use of the skills taught in the remainder of this book.

Notes

1. Reuel L. Howe, *The Miracle of Dialogue* (New York: The Seabury Press, Inc., 1963), pp. 23–24. Copyright © 1963 by the Seabury Press, Inc.
2. Thomas Gordon, *Parent/Effectiveness Training: The "No-Lose" Program for Raising Responsible Children* (New York: Peter H. Wyden, 1970), pp. 44, 108.
3. Carl Rogers, *Client-Centered Therapy: Its Current Practice, Implications, and Theory* (Boston: Houghton Mifflin, 1951); note especially 31. See also Carl Rogers, *On Becoming a Person: A Therapist's View of Psychotherapy* (Boston: Houghton Mifflin, 1961). Copyright © 1961 by Carl R. Rogers. Reprinted by permission of Houghton Mifflin Co. Howe, *The Miracle of Dialogue*, pp. 18–35. Haim Ginott, *Between Parent and Child: New Solutions to Old Problems* (New York: Macmillan, 1965). See also Ginott's *Between Parent and Teenager* (New York: Avon, 1969) and *Teacher and Child: A Book for Parents and Teachers* (New York: Macmillan, 1972). Jack Gibb "Defensive Communication," in *Leadership and Interpersonal Behavior*, edited by Luigi Petrullo and Bernard M. Bass (New York: Holt, Rinehart and Winston, 1961), pp. 66–81.
4. Gordon, *Parent Effectiveness Training*, pp. 41–47, 108–117 and 321–27.
5. Rogers, *On Becoming a Person*, p. 330. Copyright © 1961 by Carl R. Rogers. Reprinted by permission of Houghton Mifflin Co.
6. Ibid., pp. 330–31. Copyright © 1961 by Carl R. Rogers. Reprinted by permission of Houghton Mifflin Co.
7. Quoted in Robert Sherwood, *Roosevelt and Hopkins* (New York: Harper, 1948), p. 282.
8. Clark Moustakas, *Individuality and Encounter: A Brief Journey into Loneliness and Sensitivity Groups* (Cambridge, Mass.: Howard A. Doyle, 1971), pp. 7–8.
9. Ginott, *Between Parent and Teen-ager, p. 113.*
10. David Augsburger, *The Love Fight* (Scottsdale, Pa.: Herald Press, 1973), p. 110.
11. Jacques Lalanne, "Attack by Question," *Psychology Today*, November 1975), p. 134.
12. Norman Kagan, *Interpersonal Process Recall: A Method of Influencing Human Interaction* (Ann Arbor: Michigan State University Press, 1975), p. 29.
13. Dag Hammarskjold, *Markings* (New York: Alfred A. Knopf, 1964), p. 190.
14. Ginott, *Between Parent and Child*, pp. 29–20.
15. Luke 11:24–25.

Review Questions

1. Bolton is not talking about all communication in this chapter, but only about communication under what conditions?
2. What are some of the justifications people often give for being critical?
3. What does it mean to "play emotional detective"?

4. How can praise backfire?
5. What is an "interfere-iority complex"?
6. In the last paragraph before the summary, Bolton reminds his readers of the key to "getting rid of a bad habit." What is it?

Probes

1. Pay attention to your own responses for a day. How often do you respond to a feeling-laden comment or statement with an evaluation or judgment? What other options do you have?
2. Bolton is certainly not suggesting that you should never give anyone praise or advice. What is he saying about these kinds of communication?
3. Bolton quotes Jacques Lalanne's comment that questions are often "a poor substitute for more direct communication." What are some examples of questions that are actually indirect statements or judgments?
4. In his section on logical argument, Bolton is also not saying that we should throw reason out the window. What point is he making about the relationship between logic and psychologic?

Chapter 6

Awareness of Others

This excerpt challenges a commonsense belief which is outlined in the first sentence of the essay. It's the conviction that we perceive and observe other people "in a correct, factual, unbiased way." In other words, many people believe that perception is fundamentally a process of soaking up sense data. There's a "real world" out there waiting to be sensed, and we see, hear, smell, taste, and touch it in more or less "objective" ways.

The problem with this commonsense belief is that it is not supported by the psychological and communication research that's been designed to test it. Even more importantly, it's not supported by everyday experience. Consider, for example, the widely recognized problems with eyewitnesses in the courtroom. Two people who both witness an auto accident or a mugging can perceive it in significantly different ways. And even when lawyers and juries compare eyewitness accounts with photographs and videotapes, they find that "what happened" and "what that meant" depend on whom you ask. Except perhaps for the simplest of events, what we call "reality" and the lawyer calls "the facts" is a transaction between perceiver and perceived. That's why Bill Wilmot labels this excerpt "The Transactional Nature of Person Perception."

First Bill introduces what he means by "transactional." The basic idea is that perception is a *mutual* process, it happens *between* perceiver and perceived, it is a *two-way* phenomenon. This is true basically because human beings live not in a world of things but in a world of *meanings*. We don't respond to objects and persons but to what they *mean* to us. So even in the case of nonhumans, as Bill puts it, "The meaning attached to an object is a function of (1) the perceiver, (2) the object, and (3) the situation."

When we move from the perception of objects to the perception of persons, four elements are added to the process. The first is the-perception-of-being-perceived. When you smell a rose, your smelling is not affected by any thoughts about the how the rose feels about being smelled. But when you smell a person, it is. Person perception is significantly affected by the perception-of-being-perceived. We know that people can or do see us seeing them, feel us touching them, notice us smelling them. Our recognition of this fact affects how we perceive them. Bill discusses this phenomenon.

The second feature person perception adds to object perception is what Bill calls "the imposition of structure." We don't just perceive isolated aspects of persons; we notice some features and then we put other features with them. So if we perceive a person to be warm and approachable rather than cold and aloof, we are also likely to perceive him or her as intelligent and competent. This is how we operate with what are called "implicit personality theories." Interestingly, Bill notes, our imposition of structure leads us to see not only "more than what's there" but also "less than what's there." If we label someone, for example, we can stop noticing what's unique about him or her and perceive the person simply as a representative of that label—"professor," "jock," "nurse," and so on.

Third, we assume consistency on the part of the others we're perceiving. Thus, although we might accept in theory the idea that people change, we are often shocked when people we know do things we don't expect. Bill relates some interesting stories about how this tendency to assume consistency can produce humorous results.

The fourth feature of person perception that Bill discusses is the attribution of causality and responsibility. When we see a rock roll down a slope, we don't believe that the rock "meant" to move that way. But we do make this assumption about people. Whatever we perceive them to be doing, we assume that some choice-making process prompted the action. Sometimes we attribute the action primarily to causes "inside" the individual, and sometimes we attribute it to "outside" causes. But in both cases we are viewing human activity as purposeful.

There are obviously several important ideas in this reading. I've put it at the beginning of this chapter because it overviews most of what it is vital to know about person perception. The other readings in this chapter will develop, elaborate, and illustrate several of the points Bill Wilmot makes here.

The Transactional Nature of Person Perception

William W. Wilmot

The psychologically naive individual operates under the assumption that he or she "perceives and observes other people in a correct, factual, unbiased way" [14]. If Charlie perceives Sam as dishonest, that means for him that Sam is dishonest. Such an approach, although it makes "reality" easy to deal with, ignores the transactional nature of perception. There is no objective world of persons. We each interpret others in different ways. To be sure, there is much agreement over evaluations. Two women may both agree, after each had to fight her way home, that Sam is "handy with the hands." But what does it mean? Sam needs affection? Sam is a male chauvinist? Sam's mother rejected him? Sam is overreacting because he's afraid of women? Sam would make a bad husband? Sam would make a good husband? Just as we can never know the real or ultimate self, we cannot know what Sam is really like. We can say, however, that "This was my experience and this is how I reacted," recognizing that others experience a different aspect of Sam and attach their own meanings. The following anecdote illustrates the point that our meaning for another's behavior is subject to error.

The small son of upper-class parents worried them considerably. In the presence of strangers, the boy stammered, withdrew, and became quiet. When around other children he became afraid and nervous. The parents felt the need to secure some professional help for the boy but wanted to do it so that the boy would not be embarrassed or feel singled out. Finally they hit upon an idea. An old college friend of the father was a clinical psychologist, so they invited him to dinner. After the meal, they revealed the real reason they had asked him over—to diagnose the son's problem. He accepted the task of observing the boy the next day (after, of course, collecting appropriate information on history and behavior).

> He watched, unseen, from a balcony above the garden where the boy played by himself. The boy sat pensively in the sun, listening to neighboring children shout. He frowned, rolled over on his stomach, kicked the toes of his white shoes against the grass, sat up and looked at the stains. Then he saw an earthworm. He stretched it out on the flagstone, found a sharp-edged chip, and began to saw the worm in half. At this point, impressions were forming in the psychologist's mind, and he made some tentative notes to the effect: "Seems isolated and angry, perhaps overaggressive, or sadistic, should be watched carefully when playing with other children, not have knives or pets." Then he noticed that the boy was talking to himself. He leaned forward and strained to catch the words. The boy finished the separation of the worm. His frown disappeared, and he said, "There. Now you have a friend." [23]

The transactional nature of perception occurs in both the perception of objects and perceptions of people. You might think that objects, since they are "real" and objective facts, can be observed without interference of our own views. However, as Bateson says, "objects are my creation, and my experience of them is subjective not objective" [3]. The meaning attached to an object is a function of (1) the perceiver, (2) the object, and (3) the situation. For an illustration of this, look at Figure 1.

Figure 1
Disappearing dot.

Hold the book level with your eyes and close your left eye. With your right eye look directly at the asterisk and then move the book back and forth slowly about 12 inches away. You will notice that the spot, which you can first see, disappears at a certain point. The "disappearance" of the spot on the right occurs because we have an absence of photo receptors (rods and cones) at that point on the retina [30]. But this physical "blind spot" makes an important point as well. We all have "blind spots" in our perceptions of both objects and people, and even if we had all the physical equipment, we could not "objectively" perceive objects. For purposes of illustration, look at Figure 2 [29]. What do you see?

•   •   •

•   •   •   •

Figure 2
Arrangement of dots.

Probably dots arranged in the forms of a triangle and a square. Look again! On the left are three dots and on the right are four dots. Why did they not produce the following shapes in your mind?

Or why were they not seen as totally unrelated to one another? Clearly, what you perceived was as much a function of you as of the arrangement of dots.

If the perception of objects is a "transaction between the brain and the environment" [22], the process of person perception is certainly no less a transaction. As a *minimum* in person perception, there is (1) the perceiver, (2) the person, and (3) the situation. In addition, some important elements are added in a dyadic relationship that are not present in the perception of objects. To begin with, there is a *mutually shared field* [28]. You see him and he sees you. The person you are perceiving is engaging in the same process you are. The complexity of the situation is described by Tagiuri [27]:

> The perceiver, in some sense aware of many of the general properties of the other person (consciousness, mind) or his specific attributes (for example, generosity), has to allow for the fact that he himself, with similar properties, is also the object of perception and thought and that, as such, he influences his own object of perception. Observer and observed are simultaneously observed and observer. Their reciprocal perceptions [move] in a continuous recycling but varying process during which each person uses the variations in himself and the other person as a means of validating his hypothesis about the other.

Your own behavior in a dyadic transaction produces reactions in the other, which you then use as the basis of your perception. And the same process is occurring for the other participant. The process of person perception is obviously more complex than is object perception because the object is not adjusting to our presence. Often the conclusion that another person's behavior is consistent simply means that we provide a "self-picture which remains relatively stable and coherent," which has consistent effects on the other's behavior [11]. The personality characteristics you perceive in a person may depend in part on the characteristics he or she perceives in you [18].

We can never perceive the "real" person because the concept of the "real" person is a myth. The other person's behavior is just as relationship-bound as ours is. For example, if you perceive a person to be acting in a hostile manner, her perception of your behavior as hostile could have triggered her response. Furthermore, we often project onto others. We see things in them that are not in them, but in us [14]. For instance, if you are feeling alone and bitter because of the recent loss of a romantic partner, you may tend to perceive other people as being lonely. And conversely, "when you're smiling, the whole world smiles with you."

At the very least, person perception is a transactional process because what we see *is as much a function of us* as it is of the qualities of the other person. For example, when you are really angry at someone, your reaction may say more about you than it does him. There is no "immutable reality" [9] of the other person awaiting our discovery. We attribute qualities to the other based on the cues we have available, and the unique way that we interpret them. Our perception of the other, while seeming certain, is grounded in permanent uncertainty.

Research dealing with person perception is beginning to recognize more fully the transactional nature of the process. For instance, Delia's work argues that the communicative transactions influence perceptions of others [7]. At this point, we can specify that there are some general principles about the process of attaching meaning to another's behavior, and they will be discussed under the topic of perceptual regularities. Two of the most important perceptual regularities occurring in dyadic contexts are (1) the imposition of structure and (2) the attribution of causality and responsibility.

Perceptual Patterns

Perceptual Sets

There are certain patterns that regularly occur in our perceptions of others. These "perceptual sets" arise because of our desire to "make sense" out of others' behavior—to place it in a category with a label. Perceptual sets are the result of these regularities: (1) imposing structure, (2) assuming consistency on the part of the other.

Just as we impose structure upon objects, such as seeing the dots of Figure 3.2 in a pattern, we impose a structure upon a person's behavior. We always have to act on the basis of incomplete information, and we make sense of the incomplete information *by going beyond it* [5]. We take the initial and incomplete information and use it to define the person, to place her in a particular category. We do this because our world of experience has (1) structure, (2) some stability, and therefore (3) meaning [12]. The Asch [1] study is one of the best examples of how we structure impressions of others based on partial information. Subjects were given a list of traits of an individual and were asked to write a paragraph describing the person. They also chose from a list of opposing traits those they felt characterized the person. Subjects formed overall impressions of persons based on such terse descriptions as *intelligent, skillful, industrious, warm, determined, practical,* and *cautious*. And furthermore, when the word *warm* was replaced by the word *cold*, impressions were considerably altered. Overall impressions of others are based on partial evidence; we translate the partial evidence, whether it comes from a list of words or from a short transaction with the other, into a meaningful structure. Once we construct this model of the other, we guide our responses appropriately [19]. For instance, if you interpret a new acquaintance's acts as generally morose, you will use this overall structure as the basis for your reactions.

The structure that we impose upon situations is uniquely ours. As Kelly [16] noted, we interpret information within the realm of our personal constructs. We "make sense" out of the other through our own personal experiences and ways of viewing the world [8]. In fact, the person's behavior is understandable to *us only to the extent that we can tie it back to our own experience* [31]—only to the extent that we have a construct for it. While the way each of us construes events is personal, there is enough commonality between two peoples' constructs to allow overlap in constructs. [10]. Therefore, if you and Sharon both observe Bob in the same situation, your interpretations of his behavior may have enough commonality that you "agree" on what you perceive to be his personality.

The meaning that we impose on the behaviors of others has been termed the "implicit personality theory" that each of us has [6]. We each have an intuitive notion about which traits are likely to go together and use those ideas as a basis for judgment of others. If a car salesperson misrepresents some of the information about a car to you,

you may well refer to him as a "shyster," imputing a definite personality trait. But some other person may say, "Hey, the person isn't a shyster. He is just required to turn the best profit possible. It's all part of the job." Each of you is imposing a different implicit personality theory on the behavior of the other. One research study in communication demonstrates that implicit personality judgments are made early in the course of our interactions with others. Berger [4] found that if people act somewhat consistently both early and late in their interactions with others, they are judged to have traits that carry on through the other interactions. If you meet your college roommate and she acts "warm and outgoing" toward you, you will probably conclude that she is a "friendly person." This early attribution will carry forth until there is compelling evidence to cause you to alter your attribution—such as her moving all your belongings out into the hall and changing the lock on the door.

As noted earlier, our perceptual sets about others involve imposing structure and "going beyond" the information about another. Paradoxically, not only do we "see more than is there," but we also "see less than is there." Once we impose a perceptual structure on another, it blocks us from seeing other attributes of the person. For instance, one man when asked what his ex-wife's name is says "FANG!" Such a label short-circuits our thinking about her, blocking us from seeing her other qualities as a mother, friend, or co-worker. I once had an experience of being stranded on a lonely Montana back road, about 20 miles from the nearest town. There was almost no traffic, it was dark, and the car engine had just had a major seizure. One car finally came over the horizon, and I managed to stand in the middle of the road and get the man to stop. As I sat in the back of the car, the driver said, "Hi—what do you do?" I said, "I'm a professor at the university." There was a silence, and "Oh," and then the conversation ended. The rest of the ride to Townsend was filled with the sounds of silence while I wondered what his perceptual set was for college professors.

One fascinating study with mental health workers also illustrates perceptual sets in action—blocking people from seeing other information. Over 100 mental health workers were shown a videotape of a therapy session with a female client. Half of the professionals was told that the client was lesbian and the other half was told that she was heterosexual. When the professionals were asked to assess her psychological adjustment, those who thought she was lesbian saw her as being more defensive, less nurturant, and less confident and having less self-control and more negative attitudes toward men. On the other hand, those who believed her to be heterosexual reacted to her in a totally positive way and even wondered why she was in therapy [17]. The label of *lesbian* activated a perceptual set that did not allow the mental health workers to see the behavior they could see in the case of someone else.

Perceptual sets permeate perceptions of others, and the imposed structure both adds and misses important information. These processes are so pervasive that you can be assured that someone's description of another person will not be accurate. The perceiver's imposed structure will not present an accurate picture to you of the other person no matter how hard they try. Our language gives us shortcuts for explanations, but unfortunately, it also guarantees misrepresentation of another.

A related aspect of our imposition of structure is that we assume personal consistency on the part of others. Because we attribute a "definiteness of attitudes, sentiments, and views" to others [14] when it is not there, we are often surprised. The young woman who had been a serious student shocks her parents by quitting her job and traveling alone around the world. The boy who had been a juvenile delinquent suddenly breaks his habits and spends his next few years helping others. And the freewheeling, loose bachelor joins the monastery. Research evidence does not support the notion that people are consistent in their behavior, yet we are often dismayed when they act inconsistently. As Mischel [20, 21] has pointed out, our behavior is a product of the unique combination of the people we are around and our adjustment to them and is not due to any inherent personality trait.

Often our expectation for consistency in others' behavior can produce humor. Joe was a semiserious student in one of my classes (he attended and participated, but did not study very hard). He was older than the other students, about thirty, and was the father of four children. All in all, I saw him as a responsible, hard-working student. One day during a rather rigorous final examination, he was sitting in the back of the room and like the other students, was intensely involved in the test. All of a sudden, when I looked his way his hand shot into the air with a huge middle finger extended—and a grin on his face. His gesture was so unexpected and so disruptive to my view of him that all I could do was laugh in front of a very puzzled class.

We often punish people who violate our conceptions of what they are. When we label someone's behavior as insincere or label her as a fake, we are only saying that she violated how we expect to perceive her. One study demonstrated that predictable people tend to be liked more than unpredictable ones [11]. Because (1) we want consistency in the other, (2) our behavior often produces consistency in the other's response, and (3) we construct a consistent view of the other, we have a tendency to evaluate him in terms of particular personality traits [14]. If someone always acts intelligently around us, we tend to ascribe it as a personality trait, when in fact it as well as all his other behaviors are situationally determined. The total mix of (1) your meaning and behavior and (2) his meaning and behavior produces the "personality" you perceive. There may be certain tendencies for response—he may wish to be a happy person—but the situation has to be appropriate in order to observe that quality in him.

Attribution of Causality and Responsibility

The second perceptual regularity characteristic of person perception is the attribution of causality. As human beings, we want to come to grips with our environment; we want to make sense out of the world. One of the techniques we utilize to this end is the attribution of causality. From the general view that events are caused, we view human behavior as being caused. Most of us feel we are in part responsible for our actions, and we impose this same perspective on others. We see them as at least partly responsible for their actions [27].

When we mentally attach causes to the behaviors of others, we essentially have two choices: attribution to *external* causes or attribution to *internal* causes; that is, we ascribe the behavior of another either to the actor (internal locus) or to the circumstances surrounding him or her (external locus) [24]. We tend to attribute the person's actions to external causality under the following conditions [2]:

1. *High consensus*. Other people also act in this manner in this kind of situation. For instance, if we think that most people will suffer depression when they lose a loved one, then person A's depression is seen as being caused by the loss of a loved one.
2. *High consistency*. If the person acts similarly to the way she is acting in this situation on other occasions, then we assume that the situational constraints produce the behavior.
3. *High distinctiveness*. If this person acts differently in other situations, then we

assume that her depression has been produced by circumstances of this situation. For instance, if someone lies when interviewed by the police for a drug charge but does not lie in other situations, we would tend to see the lying as produced by the strong arm of the law, and not by some personality trait.

The conditions leading to an attribution of internal causality are the opposite of those cited earlier. If there is low consensus (others in this situation do not act this way), then we attribute the behavior to a personality, or internal state of the person. Suppose that an out-of-work, recently divorced friend of yours has been evicted by his landlord. During the process of moving, he physically harms his ex-wife because she had come over to claim some of the furniture. You will see your friend as "aggressive" or "hostile," because most people would not act violently in such a situation. Therefore, whenever attributing causes to the other, the more unique or bizarre the behavior, the more likely we are to attribute it to some internal state. If there is low consistency (the person is in the situation often, but acts differently), we tend to attribute the behavior to internal states that are unpredictable. Take the evicted friend again. If he has been with his former mate many times before in dealing with the property, but this one time he assaults her, we are likely to conclude that he "has gone off the deep end," or some similar situation. Finally, if there is low distinctiveness (the person acts similarly in a number of situations), then we assume it is a function of personality not of the situation. If our friend has been in many physical spats with others before, we would see him as an aggressive person and would see his assault on his ex-wife as just fitting a firmly established pattern.

The key to attribution of causality is, as Kelley [16] notes, the amount of covariation. If the behavior occurs with the presence of the person and not when the person is not present, then we conclude that the person has caused it. With the man who assaulted his former mate, if the woman has been physically assaulted many times by many former romantic partners, we would conclude that something in her behavior toward men contributes to the responses that they have toward her [16].

When attributing causality, the judgment centers on whether we think the other has the power to create the effects. In most situations, we also attribute responsibility—where we impose an emotional or moral judgment along with the notion of causality. Researchers in attribution theory separate the two processes, but the preceding examples combine the notions of causality and responsibility because in most reactions to others, the two are intertwined.

The degree of responsibility we place on others for events depends on a number of factors. If external forces are not very strong or if the ability to withstand those forces is regarded as high, we tend to place causality and responsibility in the lap of the other. If the person has the ability to create effects, he is typically held responsible for those effects [26]. When observing a disintegrating marriage, for example, if we feel that one of the partners had it in his power to cause the demise of the marriage by having an outside relationship, we place the responsibility on him. Furthermore, if we see the person intending to gain the desired goal, we are more likely to assign responsibility to him. In sum, people are held responsible for the effects they intend to create and for effects they have the ability to create [13].

The crux of the matter is that in analyzing social situations, we usually have two choices. We can ascribe the effects either to the person or to the environment. If we see another fail at a task, we can attribute it to a lack of ability, "a personal characteristic, or to the difficult task, an environmental factor" [13]. Whichever path we choose has consequences for our transactions. If, in the preceding case, we see the person as failing because of a lack of ability, we may concomitantly perceive him as a weak-willed, nonpowerful person. Our tendency will be to blame him and to take the "he-had-it-coming" attitude toward his misfortunes. This attribution often follows the "belief in a just world" notion that many people have [25]. If a person is fired, has children in trouble with the law, or is experiencing any other difficulty, this belief allows people to conclude that if bad things happen to a person, he or she somehow deserves it. This attribution pins the effects of behaviors solely upon the person.

If, on the other hand, we ascribe his failure to environmental causes ("Anyone would have failed at that."), then we will see him in a friendlier light and be sympathetic to his plight. A special form of attributing causes to environmental forces occurs in the case of unconscious motivation. If you see someone's behavior as caused by circumstances beyond his understanding and control ("He had a bad childhood and that is why he is insane."), you will absolve him of blame. Our courts of law recognize that environmental forces may be so overwhelming in some cases that the individual should not be tried.

The attribution process is central to the ongoing communication transactions we have with others. If we see someone as "trustworthy" and "having to slightly bend the truth," our communication behavior toward her will be markedly different than if we view her as a "liar who cannot be trusted in any situation." In our communicative transactions with others, we make attributions, attach meanings to their communicative behaviors, and take action based on them. The process of attribution, therefore, occurs constantly in our communication with others.

References

1. Asch, Solomon E., "Forming Impressions of Personality." *Journal of Abnormal and Social Psychology* 41 (1946): 258–290.
2. Baron, Robert A., and Donn Byrne, *Social Psychology: Understanding Human Interaction*, 2d ed. Boston: Allyn and Bacon, 1977.
3. Baxter, Leslie A., Personal correspondence, March 22, 1978. Department of Communications, Lewis and Clark College, Portland, OR.
4. Berger, Charles R., "Proactive and Retroactive Attribution Processes in Interpersonal Communications." *Human Communication Research* 2 (Fall 1975): 33–50.
5. Bruner, Jerome S., David Shapiro, and Renato Tagiuri, "The Meaning of Traits in Isolation and in Combination," in *Personal Perception and Interpersonal Behavior*, Renato Tagiuri and Luigi Petrullo (eds.). Stanford, Calif.: Stanford University Press, 1958, pp. 277–288.
6. Cronbach, Lee J., "Processes Affecting Scores on 'Understanding of Other,' and 'Assumed Similarity.'" *Psychological Bulletin* 52 (2955): 177–193.
7. Delia, Jesse G., "Change of Meaning Processes in Impression Formation," *Communication Monographs* 43 (June 1976): 142–157.
8. Delia, Jesse G., Andrew H. Gonyea, and Walter H. Crockett, "Individual Personality Constructs in the Formation of Impressions," Paper presented to Speech Communication Association Convention, Chicago, 1970.
9. Dettering, Richard, "The Syntax of Personality." *ETC: A Review of General Semantics* 26 (June 1969): 139–156.
10. Duck, Steven, *Personal Relationships and Personal Constructs*. New York: Wiley, 1973.
11. Gergen, Kenneth J., "Personal Consistency and the Presentation of Self," in *The Self in Social Interaction*, vol I: *Classic and Contemporary Perspectives*, Chad Gordon and Kenneth J. Gergen (eds.). New York: Wiley, 1968, pp. 299–308.
12. Hastorf, Albert H., David J. Schneider, and Judith Polefka, *Person Perception*. Reading, Mass.: Addison-Wesley, 1970.

13. Heider, Fritz, *The Psychology of Interpersonal Relations*. New York: Wiley, 1958.
14. Ichheiser, Gustav, *Appearances and Realities: Misunderstanding in Human Relations*. San Francisco: Jossey-Bass, 1970.
15. Jacobson, N. S., "A Component Analysis of Behavioral Marital Therapy: The Relative Effectiveness of Behavior Change and Communication/Problem-Solving Training." *Journal of Consulting and Clinical Psychology* 52 (1984), 295–305.
16. Kelley, Harold H., "Attribution in Social Interaction," in *Attribution: Perceiving the Causes of Behavior*, Edward E. Jones et al. Morristown, N.J.: General Learning Corporation, 1972.
17. Lewis, Robert A. (ed.), *Men in Difficult Times*. Englewood Cliffs, N.J.: Prentice-Hall, 1981.
18. Marlowe, David, and Kenneth J. Gergen, "Personality and Social Interaction," in *The Handbook of Social Psychology*, vol. III: *The Individual in a Social Context*, Garner Lindzey and Elliot Aronson (eds.). Reading, Mass.: Addison-Wesley, 1969, pp. 590–665.
19. McGuire, Michael T., "Dyadic Communication, Verbal Behavior, Thinking, and Understanding, vol I: Background Problems and Theory," *Journal of Nervous and Mental Disease* 152 (April 1971): 223–241.
20. Mischel, T., *Personality and Assessment*. New York: Wiley, 1968.
21. Morton, Teru L., and Mary Ann Douglas, "Growth of Relationships," in *Personal Relationships*, vol. II, Steve Duck and Robin Gilmour (eds.). New York: Academic Press, 1981, pp. 3–26.
22. Parry, John, *The Psychology of Human Communication*. New York: American Elsevier, 1967.
23. Schlien, John M., "Phenomenology and Personality," in *Concepts of Personality*, Joseph W. Wepman and Ralph W. Heine (eds.). Chicago: Aldine-Atherton, 1963, pp. 291–330.
24. Schopler, John, and John C. Compere, "Effects of Being Kind or Harsh to Another on Liking," *Journal of Personality and Social Psychology* 20, no. 2 (1971): 155–59.
25. Shaver, Kelly G., *An Introduction to Attribution Processes*. Cambridge, Mass.: Winthrop Publishers, 1975.
26. Taguiri, Renato, "Social Preference and Its Perception," in *Person Perception and Interpersonal Behavior*, Renato Taguiri and Luigi Petrullo (eds.). Stanford, Calif.: Stanford University Press, 1958, pp. 316–336.
27. Taguiri, Renato, "Person Perception," in *The Handbook of Social Psychology*, vol. III: *The Individual in a Social Context*, Gardner Lindzey and Elliot Aronson (eds.). Reading, Mass.: Addison-Wesley, 1969, pp. 395–449.
28. Taguiri, Renato, and Luigi Petrullo (eds.), *Person Perception and Interpersonal Behavior*. Stanford, Calif.: Stanford University Press, 1958.
29. Vernon, Glen M., *Human Interaction: An Introduction to Sociology*, 2d ed. New York: Ronald Press, 1972.
30. Von Foerster, Heinz, *Observing Systems*. Seaside, Calif.: Intersystems Publications, 1981.
31. Walster, Elaine, "The Effect of Self-Esteem on Liking for Dates of Various Social Desirabilities," *Journal of Experimental Social Psychology* 6 (1970): 248–253.

Review Questions

1. What does Bill Wilmot mean by the term "transactional"? How does it relate to what I wrote about this process in Chapter 1?
2. In this article Bill claims that "We can never perceive the 'real' person because the concept of the 'real' person is a myth." What does he mean?
3. What does Bill mean when he says that we make sense of the incomplete information we sense by "going beyond it"?
4. Define the term "implicit personality theory."
5. How does the example of the mental health workers perceiving the heterosexual/lesbian woman illustrate the idea that we sometimes perceive "less than what's there"?
6. Give an example from your own experience of a problem you had making sense of an inconsistent action of a friend.

7. We can attribute choices to _____ causes or _____ causes.
8. Explain the operation in the attribution process of "high consensus," "high consistency," and "high distinctiveness."

Probes

1. If you were to keep walking across the room you're in, eventually you'd run into a piece of furniture, window, door, or wall. If someone stomped on your bare toes, it would hurt. What's "transactional" about these perception processes? Don't they involve perceiving a "real" obstacle and "real" pain?
2. Give an example from your own experience where your perception of a person said as much about you as it did about that person.
3. Bill claims that we make sense of incomplete information by "going beyond it." Don't we sometimes make sense of something by going more deeply into it rather than beyond it? Give an example of this phenomenon.
4. If perception is as transactional as Bill claims, how can he account for perceptual similarities and regularities? For example, everybody agrees that ex-President Reagan is male, a conservative Republican, and an effective public speaker. What's transactional about our perception of Reagan?
5. In your own communicating, how do attribution processes affect your communication success?

This reading remakes some points Bill Wilmot made, but it also extends his introduction to perception and person perception by explaining how we perceive not only individuals but also relationships and social events. In addition, it integrates some ideas that have emerged from recent research. In the past decade, research on what's called "social cognition" has exploded. Increasing numbers of communication scholars have been figuring out how interpersonal communication is affected by such things as cognitive scripts, episodes, prototypes, and self-monitoring. But the authors of this selection don't bore you with details of the studies. Instead, Sarah Trenholm and Arthur Jensen translate the key findings into understandable principles and tell how they can be applied to your communication.

They summarize the information into four processes that people engage in before, during, and after communicating: (1) identifying the situation, (2) defining the other person, (3) defining yourself and your relationship with the other, and (4) figuring out why things unfold the way they do. This reading describes each.

First, they describe how we orient ourselves to the situations we're in by defining what kind of an *episode* it is. Definitions vary from culture to culture. Examples of Western middle-class episodes include the big family dinner, the parent-teacher conference, TV-viewing, and such less-enjoyable episodes as avoiding dad or mom when they're drunk, and apologizing to the neighbor whose property you've damaged. Communication within various episodes often follows a script. The major way we make overall sense of the situations we're in is to define the episode, figure out the script, and then identify the *consequences* of being in the middle of this episode and following this script.

Second, we size up the people we're around. Again, we use several strategies, including personal constructs, implicit personality theory (Bill Wilmot discussed this, too), self-fulfilling prophecies, and cognitive complexity. Trenholm and Jensen explain each of these jargon terms and give examples of them, so you can see how they operate in your own communication life. For example, they point out how people tend to group certain personality traits together, so if we perceive someone as "friendly" and "quiet," we may also believe them to be "intelligent," even though we have no evidence of how smart they are. This is how we apply an overall "implicit personality theory" as we perceive others.

Third, we size up relationships. We start with perceptions of ourselves (as were discussed in the readings in Chapter 5), and then we develop perceptions of who we are in relation to the person or people we're communicating with. In this section, Trenholm and Jensen explain briefly the identity-negotiation process that is described much more completely in Chapter 10. They talk about how we label relationships and manage our responses to fit the label.

Finally, we use communication to answer the question, "Why did I do what I did?" and "Why did he/she do that?" Trenholm and Jensen discuss this process under the heading of "attribution theories." These theories explain how we *attribute* reasons or causes to the events we experience. They distinguish between attributing events to surrounding situations (external) versus attributing them to somebody's personality traits (internal). They also describe some of the biases that affect people's attributions.

By the end of this reading you should have a pretty good overview of how perception processes affect your interpersonal communicating.

Social Cognition: How We Perceive Individuals, Relationships, and Social Events

Sarah Trenholm and Arthur Jensen

Four Processes in Interpersonal Perception

To interact with others successfully requires a wealth of social knowledge. You must be able to perceive the information in your social environment accurately enough to know which of the hundreds of schemata in your memory banks are the best ones to pull out of the vault. This is, of course, a very complicated operation. Cognitive psychologists are just beginning to understand how we do it. We have tried to simplify the problem by highlighting four perceptual processes that people engage in before, during,

Excerpted from pp. 67–83 of *Interpersonal Communication*, 2/e by Sara Trenholm and Arthur Jensen. © 1992. Wadsworth Publishing Company. Reprinted by permission.

and after social interaction. These include identifying (1) what the situation is, (2) who the other person is, (3) who you are and what kind of relationship between self and other is implied, and (4) why things unfold the way they do. Let's examine each of these processes more closely.

Sizing up Situations

The more we know about the particular situations in which we interact with others, the more likely we are to produce effective messages. We propose three useful ways to manage situations: (1) identifying episodes, (2) knowing scripts, and (3) perceiving potential consequences of following scripts.

Orienting Ourselves: Episode Identification

At one time or another, we have all been in situations where we didn't know what was going on or what to do. Visiting a foreign culture or being initiated into a sorority or fraternity are examples of situations that are not very well defined for us. Knowing the situation can make interactions much easier. In its simplest form a situation is "a place plus a definition."[1] When we enter a place, our first task is to orient ourselves or get our bearings. One way to do this is to ask the simple question "Where am I?" We find ourselves in a variety of places every day: in the car, at home or work, in the shopping mall, at the zoo, church or bus station, and so on. Where we are determines to a large extent what we can do socially. But identifying the place alone is not enough. For instance, a church building can serve as a place for worship, weddings, ice cream socials, even bingo. To communicate appropriately requires that we recognize the physical and social cues that define the episode or activity that is taking place.

Each culture has an array of social episodes or activities for its members to follow. For the individual, **social episodes** are "internal cognitive representations about common, recurring interaction routines within a defined cultural milieu."[2] Some typical social episodes? Having a big family dinner, attending a parent-teacher conference, planning a party, gossiping. How do we know which episodes to enact? Often we have a particular episode in mind when we initiate a conversation with someone. Perhaps you know someone who likes to "pick fights" or tease a brother or sister in order to get him or her riled up. Often enacting an episode is a process of negotiation—one person suggests an activity, only to have the other counter with another option, as in this conversation:

LAURA: I noticed that Kmart is having a sale on lawn mowers.
BUD: This is the only evening I'm free all week. I don't want to spend it shopping for a lawn mower. Besides, the Battle of the Mack Trucks is going on at the fairgrounds tonight.

Social interaction is a continuous dance in which participants accept and decline each other's invitations to enact different episodes. For instance, when two old friends have a chance meeting on the street, the question "Can I buy you a drink?" is an invitation to engage in the episode of "talking over old times." Refusing the drink because you are not thirsty would be missing the point—it would reflect a failure to recognize the other's definition of the situation.

Using Scripts to Guide Interaction:
Open, Closed, and Defined Episodes

When people play out an episode, they may also follow a script. As we have seen, a script is a highly predictable sequence of events. Some classroom learning episodes are highly scripted; others are not. For example, you may be able to predict (from experience) that every Wednesday morning your history professor will call the roll, hand out a quiz, collect the quizzes, lecture for 20 minutes, and end the class with a humorous anecdote. The more predictable the sequence of events, the more scripted the interaction is. Another class may be taught so differently that you never know for sure what will happen in a given class period. Both examples are classroom episodes, but only the first one follows a script.

Scripts and episodes are useful guides to interaction. Identifying the episode narrows the range of possible actions and reactions. Knowing the script makes social life even more predictable. Michael Brenner has proposed that the vast majority of social episodes fall into one of three types: closed, open, and defined.[3]

Closed Episodes   When a situation is almost completely scripted, it is a **closed episode**. Rules for proper behavior are well known in advance and govern the flow of interaction. Rituals such as greetings and religious observances are closed episodes. Many business organizations tightly script interactions within their doors by training their personnel to follow carefully devised sets of procedures. If you've ever applied for a loan at a bank, you have probably participated in a closed episode. You have a standard set of questions you want answered (the loan rate, fixed or variable, length of repayment, and so on) and so does the loan officer (income, collateral, address, credit references, and so on). Other, less formal interactions are also somewhat scripted. The episode of "small talk" has a limited range of topics although the sequence in which they are discussed may vary.

Open Episodes   When participants enter a situation without any preconceived plan or with a very general one, they are involved in an **open episode.** In such situations there is greater freedom to create new forms of interaction and to change episodes midway through. Episodes such as "hanging out with friends" are sometimes scripted, but not always. When almost anything can be introduced as a topic of conversation or an activity to perform, the episode is an open one. An orchestra performing a John Philip Sousa march is clearly following a musical script, but a group of musicians having a "jam session" is not. The freedom to improvise or break the rules is typical of an open episode. Some open episodes may be unsettling, since there is no clear idea of what should be done next. Perhaps you have been in situations where nobody seemed to know what to do. We know of an instructor whose routine on the first day of class was to walk into the room, assume the lotus position on top of his desk, and say nothing for the first half of the class. His point was to show how communication is used to define ambiguous situations. Eventually, students would begin talking to one another, trying to figure out what he was doing. From the students' point of view, this was an open episode.

Defined Episodes   While closed episodes are known to be such in advance as a result of expectations, many situations are defined "in progress" as participants follow their own personal goals and plans to achieve a working consensus. Even so, the consensus is often temporary—definitions of the situation may fall apart as quickly as they develop. A **defined episode** is an open episode in which the participants are trying to negotiate some closure. The difference is that open episodes are experienced as creative and liberating; defined episodes are competitive attempts to control the activity. Brenner suggests that defined episodes are often ambiguous and unstructured interactions because each partner may be proposing alternative directions for the episode. For example, a not-very-good salesperson might initiate a "sales episode" but eventually succumb to a clever-but-unwilling-to-buy customer's definition of the situation as "shooting the breeze." A romantic evening can be spoiled quickly when a candlelight dinner becomes redefined as an episode of "stilted conversation" or "talking about the kids." In closed relationships people may spend a lot of time just deciding what episode to enact next. We know of four friends who, in the course of one evening, proposed over 20 different activities for that evening. Needless to say, they ended up doing nothing but talking about what they could be doing. Chances are none of the persons involved planned to spend the evening that way, but our observations lead us to believe that these two couples frequently end up playing this "what do you want to do tonight" episode.

Although we may think that closed episodes are too limiting and value open ones for the freedom they provide, stop and think how chaotic social life would be without any well-defined or scripted episodes. The important thing, of course, is that we recognize the types of episodes others propose so that we can accept the invitation or decline gracefully.

Identifying Consequences of Episodes and Scripts

Sometimes it is just as important to perceive the possible outcomes of a situation, like the chess player who sees several moves ahead, as it is to properly label that situation. We can avoid detrimental outcomes if we can see them coming.

Salespeople often use the tried-and-true "yes technique" to set up unwitting customers. They ask questions that seem unrelated to selling their product, such as "Are those lovely photographs of *your* children?" or "I've had a hard time catching you at home. You must work awfully long hours." The customer's automatic "yes" in response to each question or comment establishes a habitual pattern that could cost a lot of money at the end of the episode.

Following a script can lead to positive or negative outcomes. Sometimes we know the script so well that we can tell our friends what they are going to say next. If we finish the sentence for them, they may be gratified that we understand them so well or offended that we cut them off. Another negative consequence is that scripted interactions can become boring or even damage a relationship if repeated too often. Researchers who study marital conflict patterns often comment that couples get caught up in "conflict scripts" that neither person intended to start but both felt compelled to see to the bitter end once the episode began. . . . Expecting the interaction to follow a script can prevent us from perceiving important messages the other may be sending our way. Following the script can also limit creativity, but only if we remain tied completely to the script. Minor alterations, improvisations, and other forms of playing with the script can add some spice to everyday interactions.

Sizing Up People

As we interact, we come to an understanding of what other people are like. Knowing how to size up the individual is another way to reduce our uncertainty about communication. In studying the process of impression formation, researchers have discovered several factors that influence our judgment. We will discuss four of these factors: (1) the use of personal constructs, (2) implicit personality theory, (3) self-fulfilling prophecies, and (4) cognitive complexity.

The Use of Personal Constructs to Judge Others

. . . Personal constructs [are] mental yardsticks for evaluating objects, events, and people. . . . We use those constructs to form impressions of those people we communicate with. Since constructs are "personal," no two people will use them in exactly the same way. You and I may both observe Bill eating a sandwich in two bites, mustard dribbling down his chin. You may think he is "aggressive" while I argue that he is "messy" and "impolite." What we see in others is a combination of their actual behavior and our personal construct of their behavior. These constructs say as much about you and me as they do about Bill.

Even though we each use different constructs to judge others, we do use them in similar ways. Steven Duck has noted a typical pattern in the use of four different kinds of constructs.[4] The four types are:

- Physical constructs (tall–short, beautiful–ugly)
- Role constructs (buyer–seller, teacher–student)
- Interaction constructs (friendly–hostile, polite–rude)
- Psychological constructs (motivated–lazy, kind–cruel)

Our initial impressions are frequently based on physical attributes—we take stock of how people are dressed or how attractive they are. These are quickly followed by the formation of role constructs as we try to make sense out of each other's position in the social world. As we talk, we may focus attention on interaction constructs, or aspects of the other's style of communication. Finally, we use these observations to infer what makes the other tick (psychological constructs)—we begin to guess at motivations and build a personality for the other. When we reach this last stage, we have gone beyond simply interpreting what we see and hear; we've begun to assume that we know things about the person that we can't see.

Implicit Personality Theory: Organizing Trait Impressions

We don't simply form isolated opinions of other people; rather, we organize all of our individual perceptions into a more complete picture by filling in a lot of missing information. One of the ways we do this is through what is referred to as an **implicit personality theory.** This is the belief on our part that certain individual traits are related to other traits. If we observe a trait that we think is part of a cluster, we will assume that the person also has the rest of those traits. Each of us has our own notions of what traits go together. For some, the traits (or constructs) "intelligent," "quiet," and "friendly" may cluster together.[5] If we observe behavior that we interpret as friendly and quiet, we may then attribute intelligence to that person without any firsthand evidence. The formation of trait impressions depends on several factors: (1) the perception of central traits, (2) the order in which traits are observed, and (3) the influence of prototypes and stereotypes.

Central Traits Some traits may carry more weight than others in forming impressions and can be described as *central traits*. When present, a central trait changes the way we perceive the whole cluster of traits. In a classic study social psychologist Harold Kelley presented two groups of students with the following list of adjectives describing a new instructor they were about to meet. One group was told the new instructor was *"warm,* industrious, critical, practical, and determined"; the other group was told the instructor was *"cold,* industrious, critical, practical, and determined."

Which description do you think led students to form a more favorable impression? If you said the first description, you are in agreement with most of the students in this study. The central trait (warm-cold) changed the way the perceiver judged the other traits, which in turn affected the overall impression.[6]

Primacy Versus Recency Effect Another factor that makes some traits stand out is *when* they are first perceived. The tendency for first impressions to be lasting ones is known as the **primacy effect.** When more recent observations change our initial impression, we have the **recency effect.** Which effect is more likely to prevail? Generally, the primacy effect rules—we tend to form impressions quickly and hold on to them. For example, you attend a social mixer and see Pete, whom you do not know, placing a whoopee cushion on the chair of some unsuspecting person. You surmise that he must have gone to a lot of trouble to bring the cushion and waited anxiously for the right moment to play his practical joke. You quickly form an impression of him as a "clown," and you are not overly impressed by such people. Your impression is likely to stick, especially if you later hear him laughing at someone who recoiled from a piece of plastic vomit. Even if he spends the rest of the evening in a rather docile mood, your impression is unlikely to change. Psychiatrist Leonard Zunin estimates that the first impression is formed solidly within the first four minutes of interaction with a stranger, followed by a decision to continue or terminate the episode.[7]

Prototypes and Stereotypes Prototypes and stereotypes may also affect the emerging impression. Physical traits or key words and phrases used by a person may be so similar to our image of the prototypical "sales manager type" that we have trouble describing that person in any other way. Furthermore, if you have an associated stereotype that all salespeople have loose morals and tell offensive jokes, you can flesh out a complete impression in a matter of a few seconds. Once the impression is formed, you may only notice behaviors that are consistent with the image and ignore those that do not fit. Suppose someone other than Pete leaves the party with the whoopee cushion in tow. Objectively, this may call into question your belief that Pete planned a series of practical jokes for the evening. But you will probably not give it much thought now that you are convinced you know what kind of person he is. In this way we reinforce stereotypes even in the face of contradictory evidence.

Interpersonal Self-Fulfilling Prophecies

Another important perceptual tendency is the self-fulfilling prophecy. Unlike the more passive implicit personality theory (in which traits are associated in the mind), the **self-fulfilling prophecy** involves both perception *and* behavior. It starts when one person—the observer—believing something to be true about another person—the target—begins acting toward the target as if the belief were fact. This action prompts the target to behave in line with the observer's expectations. If you believe your friend is "touchy," you are likely to avoid sensitive topics and be more hesitant in what you say. The effect of your behavior? Your friend becomes oversensitive because *you* are acting oversolicitous. Unaware that you helped create the prickly atmosphere, you say to yourself, "My God, it's true. You can't say anything to him." . . .

Sizing Up Relationships

As we read the situation and form impressions of the other, we also face the perceptual task of determining what relevant aspects of *self* fit the situation and how the emerging *relationship* between self and other should be interpreted.

Self-Monitoring: Deciding Who to Be

. . . It is important to realize that our self-concept is frequently connected to our definition of the situation. Just as we form impressions of others, we form and present images of ourselves to others. The awareness of and ability to adapt images of self to the situation at hand has been referred to as **self-monitoring.**[8] A high self-monitor tends to read the social situation first and then present an appropriate face, as opposed to simply presenting a consistent image of self in every situation.

Mark Snyder characterizes the difference between a high and low self-monitor in the form of the question each might ask in defining the situation.

> The high self-monitor asks, "Who does this situation want me to be and how can I be that person?" In so doing, the high self-monitoring individual reads the character of the situation to identify the type of person called for by that type of situation, constructs a mental image or representation of a person who best exemplifies that type of person, and uses the prototypic person's self-presentation and expressive behavior as a set of guidelines for monitoring his or her own verbal and nonverbal actions. [The low self-monitor asks] "Who am I and how can I be me in this situation?"[9]

Instead of calling on a prototype to guide his or her actions, the low self-monitor behaves in accordance with an image of his or her "real" self.

To test yourself, make a short list of five or six very different social situations you frequently take part in. Write down how you typically behave in each situation, or better yet, have someone observe you in each of those situations and write down what you do. Then compare your actual behavior to Snyder's self-monitoring questions. Do you normally present a consistent self-image, or do you alter your self-presentation for each situation?

Our culture often sends us mixed messages. For instance, we are told to "be ourselves" and "remain true to self," messages that seem to endorse the low self-monitor's position. On the other hand, research demonstrates that being adaptable (being a high self-monitor) is one of the keys to social success. It is probably best to recognize that either extreme can be limiting. If we always try to maintain a consistent self-concept, we will be less versatile and probably less human because we won't experience the full range of human emotions and potentials. But if we are always changing to fit the situation or someone else's conception of us, we may compromise important standards and values. The best course is to ask ourselves which is more important in a given situation—being adaptable or being consistent. On one occasion it may be important for you to exert your individuality and violate the family rule that "everyone comes home for Christmas." The next year you might pass up a wonderful ski trip just to be home and fit in again.

Defining Relationships: Self in Relation to Others

When people interact, each presents an image of self to the other. These images, are, however, usually quite fluid. We are responsive to the feedback of the other and begin quickly to negotiate a definition of the relationship between self and other. Thus, one important perceptual process is the identification of the type of relationship that applies in a given situation. Office workers at a company picnic may perceive that the superior—subordinate relationship with the boss no longer applies during a game of softball. As long as the boss sees things the same way, there is no problem. But what if the boss assumes he or she is still in charge and wants to pitch? The difference in perceptions may lead to negative feelings that were never intended.

A wide range of relationship labels are available to us. We can be casual or long-time acquaintances, friends, close friends, almost friends, just friends, coworkers, neighbors, bowling partners, platonic lovers, husbands and wives, ex-husbands and wives, blood brothers or sisters, business associates, straight man and funnyman, roommates, counselor and advisee, master and slave, even student and teacher. The list could go on.

Once a relational label is firm in our mind, it tends to limit our perception of what we can do together. Most American couples who have just begun dating probably don't even think about drawing up and signing prenuptial agreements about finances, children, property, and so on. These actions are not perceived as having anything to do with "real" romantic relationships.

Although no empirical studies that we know of have demonstrated the existence of relational prototypes, they probably do exist. In the same way that we have mental images of typical personalities, we may have a cognitive model of the best example of a romantic relationship or a good friendship. No doubt you have heard the phrases "all-American couple" or "Barbie and Ken" to describe prototypical male—female relationships.

Robert Carson has used the term **master contract** to refer to the worked-out definition of a relationship that guides the recurring interaction of any dyad.[10] This means that as relationships develop, perceptions that were originally guided by a prototype eventually give way to an understanding based on verbalized agreements or silent acceptance of established patterns of behavior. . . . Identifying what type of relationship you're involved in may be just as crucial as knowing the situation or forming a useful impression of the other.

Explaining Behavior: Attribution Theories

When all is said and done, we are frequently left with the question "Why did he (or she) do that?" or "Why did I do that?" Most of the time we are quick to offer some type of explanation. If we think we understand what motivated our own or another's actions, we have reduced some uncertainty and made our world a little more predictable. Theories concerned with how the average person infers the cause(s) of social behavior have been called *attribution theories*. Before we examine some of these theories, let's look at a typical conversation and try to explain each person's behavior.

Imagine that you've been visiting your friends Angela and Howie for a few days. You are sitting at the kitchen table with Howie when Angela comes home from work. She looks very tired. The following conversation ensues:

HOWIE: *(looking up from the plastic model car kit he has been putting together)* Hi, honey. How was work?

ANGELA: *(after saying hello to you, she scans the room)* Howie! You haven't done the dishes yet? They're left over from last night. Can't you do anything you're asked to do?

HOWIE: It's been a busy morning. I just haven't had time.

ANGELA: No time! You don't have a job. You're not looking for work. And you can't find 15 minutes to do a dozen dishes?

HOWIE: I've been looking through the classifieds, for your information.

ANGELA: Did you send out any resumes?

HOWIE: No, not really . . .

ANGELA: Here we go again. Do I have to physically *force* you to sit down and write letters of application and send your resume out?

HOWIE: I'll do it. I'll do it.

ANGELA: You'll do what? The dishes or the resumes? . . .

How would you explain the communication behavior of your two friends? Is Angela the kind of person who constantly nags and belittles others? Or did Howie provoke this tirade? What other explanations could there be?

Attribution theorists have discovered several different ways that you and I infer the causes of each other's behavior. We will look at two of the more prominent attribution theories—correspondent inference theory and covariance theory—and see how they explain our perceptions of Angela and Howie's interaction. . . .

When we observe another person's behavior, we generally attribute that behavior to one of two types of causes: internal dispositions or external situational factors. Anytime we explain someone's actions in terms of his or her personality, motivation, or personal preferences, we are making an *internal attribution*. For instance, you might believe that Howie's behavior stems from his innate laziness. When we perceive behavior to be the result of social pressure, unusual circumstances, or physical forces beyond the individual's control, we are making a *situational attribution*. What if you knew that Angela had just arrived home from work, where she had been informed that she was in danger of losing her job due to impending budget cuts? You might perceive her behavior as being caused by temporary frustration or anxiety, not her personality.

Identifying Attributional Biases

If all the causes of behavior we attribute were clearly logical and made use of all the relevant information, our social lives would be much easier to manage. Unfortunately, we humans are notoriously irrational at times. A number of perceptual biases affect how we arrive at causal attributions. We rely on some of these biases when we don't have any prior knowledge of the persons being observed, and at other times the biases just override whatever knowledge we do have.

Personality Bias Toward Others   The most common bias is to explain other people's behavior in terms of their personality dispositions.[11] We are especially prone to this **personality bias** when we observe strangers. We just naturally assume that a stranger who throws a shoe at the television screen lacks self-control or is mentally unstable. The bias is even stronger if the person's behavior is contrary to our expectations.[12] Since we expect people in a restaurant to be eating or drinking, we probably think that only a buffoon would start singing in that setting. Rarely do we look for other explanations—such as the possibility that someone offered him $50 to do it or that the woman he was with accepted his proposal of marriage. Cognitively complex individuals may be less susceptible to this bias, perhaps because of their tendency to engage in role-taking. When we try to see a situation from the other person's point of view, we may see more situational or relational causes.

Situational Bias Toward Self   When we're asked to explain our own behavior, the story is somewhat different—we're more likely to rely on **situational bias.** If I throw a shoe at the television, I can explain that it was because of tension built up at the office, a stupid call by the referee, or the loose morals of television producers. There are several reasons why we tend to attribute our own behavior to situational factors. In the case of negative behavior, blaming it on the situation can serve as an excuse or justification for that behavior. Another reason is that we simply have more information about our own past and present experience than an observer would. We know if we've had a bad day; an observer probably doesn't. Finally, our visual vantage point makes a difference. When we behave, we don't see ourselves performing the action. What we do see is other people and external circumstances. It's much more likely that we will reference the situation as the cause of our behavior.

Bias Toward Groups   In addition to these two biases, perceived group membership also produces a bias. We explain the behavior of members of highly stereotyped *out-groups* (groups we do not belong to) differently than the behavior of *in-group* members (such as our own friends, associates, or ethnic group). In general, researchers have found that we attribute positive behavior by in-group members to their personal dispositions, while negative behavior is explained in terms of situational factors. We explain the behavior of out-group members in exactly the opposite manner. Positive behavior is explained away as situationally produced, while negative behavior is seen as the product of personality or group culture.[13] For example, suppose you are watching a close friend play in a tennis tournament when she screams at the referee for calling her shot out of bounds. You turn to the person next to you and say, "She's been under a lot of pressure lately. I think she just needed to blow off some steam." Moments later, her opponent (from an arch-rival institution) heatedly disputes another out-of-bounds call. "Why do they let people without manners play this game?" you think to yourself.

Why are we so prone to discriminate in favor of friends and against members of other social groups? We usually think of friends as being similar to us in many ways, but apparently perceive them to be even more similar when compared to an outsider. This in-group/out-group comparison seems to set in motion a role-taking process in which we identify closely with the in-group member and view things from his or her perspective. As a result, we often seek a situational account for the behavior. In contrast, we tend to view the out-group member with very little empathy or understanding. This makes it easier to assume the person would behave this way regardless of the situation.

Bias Toward Cultures   Culture also plays a significant role in producing attributional bias. Our culture is a very individualistic one. As a result, we have a greater tendency to believe that the individual person is responsible for his or her behavior. In collectivist cultures such as Japan or India, situational attributions are more common.[14] A *collectivist culture* is one in which group goals have a higher priority than individual goals; loyalty to the group is usually expressed by behaving according to the rules in different situations. Thus, in collectivist cultures people are more aware of situational constraints and less aware of individual differences.

How can knowledge of these causal schemata and attributional biases help improve interpersonal communication? The first step is to realize that our past interactions with a person influence how we decide to communicate in the present. To a large extent, what we remember about past interactions is stored in the form of attributions. If you have a tendency to explain interactions in terms of single causes (such as personal or stimulus attributions), your communication may frequently take the form of complaining about or blaming the other. You may even do this without realizing it. It may be beneficial to sit down occasionally and evaluate how you've been explaining the events that have happened in your important relationships.

This chapter has focused on the ways we process information about social situations and the people involved in them. This processing of information leads to perceptions that strongly influence the way we communicate with others. With a growing awareness of these perceptual processes, we will be better able to improve interpersonal communication.

Notes

1. Stanley Deetz and Sheryl Stevenson, *Managing Interpersonal Communication* (New York: Harper & Row, 1986), p. 58.
2. Joseph Forgas, "Affective and Emotional Influences on Episode Representations," in *Social Cognition: Perspectives on Everyday Understanding,* ed. Joseph Forgas (London: Academic Press, 1981), pp. 165–180.
3. Michael Brenner, "Actors' Powers," in *The Analysis of Action: Recent Theoretical and Empirical Advances,* ed. M. von Cranach and Rom Harre (Cambridge: Cambridge University Press, 1982), pp. 213–280.
4. Steven Duck, "Interpersonal Communication in Developing Acquaintances," in *Explorations in Interpersonal Communication,* ed. Gerald R. Miller (Beverly Hills, CA: Sage, 1976), pp. 127–147.
5. Seymour Rosenberg and Andrea Sedlak, "Structural Representations of Implicit Personality Theory," in *Advances in Experimental Social Psychology* 6, ed. Leonard Berkowitz (New York: Academic Press, 1972).
6. Harold H. Kelley, "The Warm-Cold Variable in First Impressions of Persons," *Journal of Personality* 19 (1950), 431–439.
7. Leonard Zunin, *Contact: The First Four Minutes* (Los Angeles: Nash, 1972).
8. Mark L. Snyder, "The Self-Monitoring of Expressive Behavior," *Journal of Personality and Social Psychology* 30 (1974), 526–537.
9. Mark L. Snyder, "Self-Monitoring Processes," in *Advances in Experimental Social Psychology* 12, ed. Leonard Berkowitz (New York: Academic Press, 1979), pp. 86–131.
10. Robert Carson, *Interactional Concepts of Personality* (Chicago: Aldine, 1969).
11. For a review, see Lee Ross, "The Intuitive Psychologist and His Shortcomings: Distortions in the Attribution Process," in *Advances in Experimental Social Psychology* 10, ed. Leonard Berkowitz (New York: Academic Press, 1977).

12. E. E. Jones and D. McGillis, "Correspondent Inferences and the Attribution Cube: A Comparative Reappraisal," in *New Directions in Attribution Research* 1, ed. J. H. Harvey, W. J. Ickes, and R. F. Kidd (Hillsdale, NJ: Lawrence Erlbaum, 1976).

13. J. Jaspars and M. Hewstone, "Cross-Cultural Interaction, Social Attribution, and Intergroup Relations," in *Cultures in Contact*, ed. S. Bochner (Elmsford, NY: Pergamon Press, 1982); B. Park and M. Rothbart, "Perceptions of Outgroup Homogeneity and Levels of Social Categorization: Memory for the Subordinate Attributes of In-Group and Out-Group Members," *Journal of Personality and Social Psychology* 42 (1982): 1051–68.

14. J. Miller, "Culture and the Development of Everyday Social Explanations," *Journal of Personality and Social Psychology* 46 (1984): 961–78.

Review Questions

1. These authors make some of the same points Bill Wilmot made in the previous reading, and they also extend Bill's analysis and add some new concepts. Where do they extend his discussion? What new concepts do they introduce?
2. List the four perception processes this reading explains.
3. How are scripts related to episodes?
4. What's the difference between closed episodes and defined episodes?
5. What's the relationship between personal constructs and implicit personality theory?
6. What's an "interpersonal self-fulfilling prophecy"?
7. Explain the difference between a high self-monitor and a low self-monitor.
8. People use attribution theories to infer the _____ of other people's behavior.

Probes

1. Trenholm and Jensen say at one point that "social interaction is a continuous dance in which participants accept and decline each other's invitations to enact different episodes." Extend their metaphor to explain your experience. In what ways are your conversations, say at work, like a "dance"?
2. What principle is exemplified by the salesperson's "yes technique"? What do you hear Trenholm and Jensen saying about this technique? Do they think it's a good tactic to use?
3. Do you agree or disagree with the claim that first impressions are formed solidly within the first four minutes of interaction with a stranger, and that we use these hastily-formed impressions to decide whether to continue conversing or not?
4. Do you tend to be a high self-monitor or a low self-monitor? How does your tendency affect your communicating?
5. Give an example of a bias toward groups and a bias toward cultures that affects how you perceive people you're communicating with.

Chapter 7

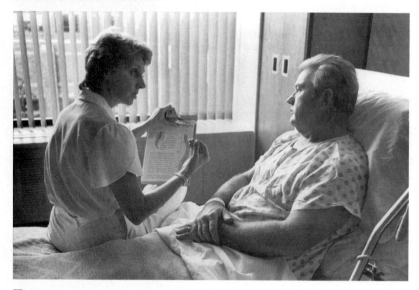

Listening

A s the authors of this reading point out, most treatments of listening begin by arguing for the importance of good listening and then try to convince you that you're probably not an effective listener. But if you're studying listening, chances are you already know it's important and believe you could do it better. So rather than telling you what you already know, these authors begin their book on listening by discussing three misconceptions people commonly have about the listening process. Their idea is that it will be easier to improve your listening if you begin with an accurate rather than a distorted understanding of what's involved.

The first misconception is that listening is natural. The authors explain that hearing is the natural process, and that listening takes some thought, training, and effort. I've always believed that one of the most ironic things about listening is that, according to several surveys, we spend much more time listening than we spend reading, writing, or speaking, but we get almost no organized training in listening. So we are taught the least about the communication activity we engage in the most! Roach and Wyatt discuss this phenomenon.

The second misconception they discuss is the belief that listening is a passive act, a process of simply being open to what's available. This misconception exists primarily because we associate "work" with *visible* effort, and the effort you invest in listening is sometimes not very visible. But *every* person who listens for a living—therapist, lawyer, doctor, accountant, business consultant—has personally experienced the crushing fatigue that can come from working hard at listening.

The third misconception is that "I'm a good listener when I try." Some early listening research indicated that the average white-collar worker remembers about 25 percent of what he or she hears. So most of us start with a pretty low efficiency rate. Raw effort can improve that number, but not very permanently. It's most effective to get some listening training aimed at both attitudes and skills and then to practice what you learn long enough to make it habitual.

My primary purpose for including this brief reading is to set up the more developed articles that follow. If you're well informed about misconceptions, you'll be prepared to take on some new understandings and skills.

Listening and the Rhetorical Process

Carol A. Roach and Nancy J. Wyatt

Most texts on listening begin by establishing that listening skills are important to you in school, on the job, and in your personal relationships. Then they go on to convince you that you're not a very good listener. While these two observations may be true, we believe that you already know you could benefit by improving your listening skills or you wouldn't be taking this course. We will not, therefore, bore you by telling you what you already know. Instead, we will introduce you to some common misconceptions about listening and refute those misconceptions. . . .

Misconception Number One: Listening Is Natural

The misconception that listening is natural arises partly because we confuse the process of listening with the process of hearing. Hearing is certainly a natural process. Unless you have organic damage to some part of your ear you will have been hearing since before you were born. Hearing is a matter of perception of small changes in atmospheric pressure, which goes on continuously, even when you are sleeping. How else would the alarm wake you in the morning? . . .

Humans can "hear" changes in air pressure in an effective range of frequencies from 20 to 20,000 cycles per second. Changes in air pressure impact the eardrum and are transmitted through the middle ear to the inner ear, where they are transformed into electrochemical messages and sent to the hearing center in the brain. That process is natural and automatic and outside conscious control. Problems start when we confuse this purely automatic physical process with the consciously purposeful psychological process of listening.

Listening is largely a process of discriminating and identifying which sounds are meaningful or important to us and which aren't. We actually focus our hearing in the same way we focus our sight. You can probably remember a time when you didn't "see" something that was in plain sight. Maybe you even fell over it. You have probably also had the experience of talking to someone—a parent, a teacher, a colleague, even a friend—who was thinking about something else and didn't "hear" what you said. In fact, they did hear in the sense that the sounds reached their ears, but they didn't hear what you said because they were paying attention to something else at the time. If you're sufficiently candid, you may also remember some times when you didn't hear something that was said to you because you weren't paying attention. We are all guilty of thinking about other things sometimes. The point is, you did hear, but you weren't listening.

> "Excuse me, Dr. Simpson, I'm having trouble thinking of a good attention getter for my speech."
> "What's your topic?"
> "I'm talking about Cambodia and the Khmer Rouge, all that killing."
> "In that case why don't you use the technique I just illustrated in class, the one from the acid rain speech?"
> "I didn't hear that one. I guess I wasn't listening."

The importance of distinguishing between hearing and listening is that we don't need training to hear well, but we do need training to listen well. In fact, if the hearing mechanism is damaged, no amount of training will improve its function. Real deafness can't be cured by trying harder. Faulty listening, on the other hand, can't be cured by medical science or by magic. To learn to listen more effectively, you have to try harder. You have to learn how to listen.

The idea that we learn to listen as children is partially true. Before they start to school, children learn many things by listening. But they only learn as well as they were trained. Unfortunately most of the training children receive in listening skills comes largely in the form of injunctions. "Now, you listen to me!" they are told, or "Listen carefully!" The usefulness of such training can be illustrated by comparing it to a similar injunction to a child to "Catch the ball!" Not very useful advice. It's more useful to show children how to hold their hands and tell them to keep their eyes on the ball. Then give them plenty of supervised practice and explain to them what they are doing right and what they're doing wrong, so they can improve. Without supervised practice, children can pick up bad habits of listening which serve them indifferently as they grow up. Learning to listen is a matter of training; it doesn't come naturally any more than playing ball does.

In one very interesting study, Nichols and Stevens (1957) found evidence that younger children listen better than older children. When the researchers stopped teachers in the middle of lectures and asked the students what the teachers were talking about, they found that 90 percent of the first graders could answer correctly, 80 percent of the second graders could answer correctly, but only 28 percent of the senior high school students could answer correctly. These results might even lead us to believe that we become worse listeners as we grow up. Far from being a natural process, listening is clearly a consciously purposive activity for which we need systematic training and supervision to learn to do well.

Another way to look at listening is as one part of the communication process, like speaking. While we could agree that speaking is a natural human function, no one could deny that children have to be taught how to speak. Certainly no one was born speaking standard English. If you have forgotten the process of learning to speak, spend a couple of hours in a supermarket listening to mothers talk to toddlers as they shop. You will hear careful and constant instruction, reiteration, correction, and reinforcement of correct language patterns and usage. Or, if you have studied a second language, remember how much time you had to spend memorizing, listening, and practicing to become fluent.

Listening and speaking are both consciously purposive activities for which we need training to do well. The idea that some people are born listeners or born speakers is a fiction. It's a copout for people who don't want to try harder.

Misconception Number Two: Listening Is Passive

One of the most common misconceptions we have in our American way of life is the idea that work is always active. We seem to think that if we don't "see" something happening, work is not being done. So thinking is not often defined as work. Children are encouraged to "do something"—join the Little League, scouts, clubs. They are enrolled in camps, dancing lessons, junior business associations, and extracurricular activities. Students are encouraged to "get involved"—join the students' government, join a club or fraternity or association, contribute time to charities, and attend social events. Time spent "doing nothing" is assumed to be time wasted. In businesses and corporations people spend much of their working day going to meetings, having lunch, traveling, doing anything to look busy. Employees learn very quickly how to "look busy" when the boss comes around, even though no specific action is required at the moment. Also, scholars, whose business is thinking, have to list specific activities to their administrators to prove they really are working. In our culture, movement is equated with work.

This American orientation toward a definition of work with visible activity leads us to view listening as passive. After all, you can't see anyone listening, so they must not be "doing" anything. What we have done instead is to define the visible signs of listening as the activity itself. You will understand this statement if you think back to when you were in high school. Think about the most boring class you had in high school. You didn't want to be caught daydreaming, so what did you do! You perfected the "student's stare." You put your chin in your hand, opened your eyes real wide, and nodded periodically as though you were agreeing with what was being said. If you were clever, you remembered to throw in a frown once in a while to show you were trying to understand something particularly difficult. You smiled occasionally to show you were glad to have something so interesting to listen to in school. Meanwhile your mind went on vacation. It worked perfectly. You had learned that activity equates with work.

> When I began teaching I learned very quickly that I couldn't tell by looking who was listening and who wasn't. I had one student who always sat in the back, tilted his chair against the wall, and seemed to go to sleep. Finally one day I got fed up and challenged him. I told him that if he only meant to sleep, he could do it at home on his own time. He sat up, pushed his hat back, and recited to me the last ten minutes of my lecture. Boy, was I embarrassed.

One consequence of defining listening by its visible signs is to deny the active nature of real listening. When you are listening, your mind is extremely busy receiving and sorting out new ideas and relating them to what you already know and making new connections with old information. Real listening involves taking in new information and checking it against what you already know, selecting important ideas from unimportant ideas, searching for categories to store the information in (or creating new categories), and predicting what's coming next in order to be ready for it. The explanation of hearing and listening in the next chapter will help to make the active nature of listening clearer. When you're listening, your brain is busy actively reconstructing what the speaker is saying into meaningful units in terms of your own experience. But all this activity takes place in your brain; none of it necessarily shows itself outwardly. So it often looks like nothing is being done.

> One of the things I found most frustrating about working in a group was that no one ever seemed to be listening to me. It was like I was always talking to myself. But then when it came time to prepare the final report, I discovered that the other group members knew a lot of the things I had been talking about. I was surprised to find out they had been listening after all. Especially John. I had thought he was a total deadhead.

Misconception Number Three: I'm a Good Listener When I Try

Most people vastly overestimate their own listening skills. One clever educator illustrates this to people who take his workshop on listening skills by having each person introduce herself to the class. Then he asks each of them to name the person who is sitting to her left. Most people can't do it.

If you ask most people what their listening efficiency is, they will tell you that they remember about 75 to 80 percent of what they hear. Most people think they are good listeners. Research findings directly contradict this perception. The research finding most often cited to illustrate this poor listening efficiency comes from the work of Nichols (1957) who found that the average white-collar worker demonstrates only about 25 percent listening efficiency. This means that the average person only remembers about one-quarter of what he or she hears. Both these percentages are in comparison to the ideal of 100 percent recall, a feat only accomplished by fictional detectives and a few unusual persons who have perfect auditory recall (like some people have photographic memories).

The real test of listening skills is, of course, not what you can do on a listening test, but how well you understand and remember the things you have to understand and remember to get along in your daily life. When the television news broadcast is over, how much of what you heard do you remember? Can you pick out the main points when someone is giving a speech? Can you understand and remember oral instructions? How good are you at discovering people's feelings when they are talking to you? Can you distinguish between a genuinely good business deal and a scam? Can you pick out the arguments and evidence in a political speech? Can you pick out the different instruments in a band or identify the theme of a symphony? All these tasks are related to your ability to listen effectively, and skill at these tasks is important to your welfare. But most people are only partially successful at any of these tasks.

The fact is that most of us would like to think we are better listeners (more intelligent, more sensitive, more beautiful) than we really are. Listening is hard work, and we don't apply ourselves to the task unless there is a clear payoff. But unless we practice and sharpen our listening skills and develop good listening habits, it may be too late when opportunity knocks. When you're in the middle of a business deal or in the middle of a physics lecture is not the time to start practicing listening skills.

References and Recommended Reading

Barbara, Dominick A. *How to Make People Listen to You.* Springfield, Ill.: Charles C. Thomas, 1971.

Barker, Larry L. *Listening Behavior.* Englewood Cliffs, N.J.: Prentice-Hall, 1971.

Hirsh, Robert O. *Listening: A Way to Process Information Aurally.* Dubuque, Iowa: Corsuch Scarisbrich, 1979.

Nichols, Ralph G. "Factors in Listening Comprehension." *Speech Monographs* 15 (1948): 154–163.

Nichols, Ralph G., and Leonard A. Stevens. *Are You Listening?* New York: McGraw-Hill, 1957, pp. 12–13.

Phillips, Gerald M., and Julia T. Wood. *Communication and Human Relations.* New York: Macmillan, 1983.

Steil, Lyman, Larry L. Barker, and Kittie W. Watson. *Effective Listening.* Reading, Mass.: Addison-Wesley, 1983.

Wolff, Florence I., Nadine C. Marsnik, William S. Tracy, and Ralph G. Nichols. *Perceptive Listening.* New York: Holt, Rinehart and Winston, 1983.

Review Questions

1. What are the primary differences between hearing and listening?
2. What kind of listening training do we typically get as young children?

3. How is our attitude about listening affected by the typically North American belief that "movement is equated with work"?
4. What do your lecture notes say about your listening efficiency? Do they indicate that you're retaining more or less than 25 percent of what you hear in class?

Probes

1. Assume for a minute that human activities can be divided into the *physiological* (nerve impulses, skin reactions to chemicals, bleeding, etc.), *psychological* (attitudes, beliefs, fears, etc.), and *communicative* (involving coordination with at least one other person). Which type or types of activity are involved in *hearing*? Which ones characterize *listening*?
2. How would you describe some of the "invisible" activities that are involved in effective listening? What specifically is going on that can't be seen?
3. Think about your own listening efficiency. Do you remember more than 25 percent of what you hear in class? At a party? Around the dinner table at home? When talking to your boss at work? In the past, what factors have increased or decreased your listening efficiency?

T he first reading in this chapter gave you an overview of listening, and this one begins with the point that "the proof of good listening is an appropriate response." So Judi Brownell explains eight responses that help make up effective listening, and six that you probably want to *avoid*. These are the *visible* parts of the hard work of listening that, as the authors of the first reading explained, is also partly invisible. Judi Brownell offers the eight as a kind of salad bar—you don't use every one all the time, but it would be good to have all eight in your repertoire of possible responses.

The first response—the paraphrase—is probably the best way to tell the other person that you're tuned in. The second, questions and perception checks, are designed to avoid the problems created by listeners who mechanically nod and smile but can't remember what they just heard. Constructive feedback is the third response, and Brownell lays out five rules to guide you. She also provides specific wording, so you can get a clear sense of how this response works.

Response number four is physical alertness, and number five has to do with eye contact. I agree with Brownell about the crucial importance of eye contact, but I think she should have also mentioned that the form and meaning of this response varies in important ways from culture to culture. For example, in some Hispanic homes, children are taught *not* to look into the eyes of their elders, because it is impolite. Eye contact is also considered inappropriate for all but the most intimate relationships in some Asian cultures, and many urban gang members treat direct eye contact as an overt challenge or threat. If you apply Brownell's advice in a conversation with a member of a gang subculture, you could have a fight on your hands.

Brownell's other suggestions involve body posture, gestures and movement, and what she calls "minimal reinforcers."

The best way to use the information in this reading is as a checklist to draw on when you're at school, on the job, or dealing with the public in a culture that values direct contact. In those instances, responses like these can significantly improve your effectiveness as a listener.

Responding to Messages

Judi Brownell

The Process of Responding

The proof of good listening is an appropriate response. To a large extent speakers judge the effectiveness of your listening by what you say or do in response to their message. Communication is a dynamic, reciprocal process. When you listen, you share responsibility for the accurate exchange of meanings. In fact, it would be helpful to think that as listeners, we take on 51 percent of this obligation!

An important part of your role as a receiver, then, is to respond appropriately, in a manner that will result in satisfying relationships and improved understanding. Most of us, through the years, have developed habitual patterns of response. Instead of analyzing each situation and determining the most effective course of action (as we would if the problem belonged to someone else), we rely on habits developed early in our relationships. These almost automatic response styles may, in fact, serve us well most of the time. They make conversations and verbal exchanges effortless. The problem arises when we are confronted with a new or particularly difficult situation, or when we are dissatisfied with the way a relationship is progressing. We sense a need for analysis and change when what we are doing for some reason doesn't work.

This section is not prescriptive. Its purpose is not to give you rules, but to acquaint you with the range of alternatives for any given listening situation so that you may choose your response wisely. As a listener, you cannot underestimate the control you have over the direction and quality of your encounters. Now that you have become more sensitive to all aspects of the communication situation, your response will reflect your understanding both of the nonverbal and contextual aspect of the encounter as well as the words exchanged. The greater variety of response styles at your command, the more likely you will be to select one that accomplishes your purpose. In this section we will discuss several response styles. . . . We will also examine some of the variables affecting the communication environment. . . .

The Paraphrase or Understanding Response

When you want to communicate empathy—that is, show you understand a speaker without judging his ideas—the paraphrase may be an effective response. The paraphrase does not "lead" the speaker in any particular direction. Rather, it allows him to take responsibility for his own problems and decisions. When an individual is under stress, uncertain, or emotionally involved, the paraphrase can be an effective listening tool. Guidelines for an effective paraphrase include:

- The listener must have a sincere interest in the speaker.
- The listener must put the speaker's ideas and feelings into his own words rather than repeating verbatim what was said.

- The paraphrase reflects the listener's understanding of the situation as a whole.
- The paraphrase reflects the tone of the original message.
- The paraphrase does not add or omit content; it should be as simple and clear as possible so that the speaker can recognize that it is complete and accurate.

A paraphrase is most effective if the listener also practices nonverbal attending skills that communicate his involvement. As a listener, strive to maintain eye contact, assume a forward posture, and provide minimal reinforcers such as head nods, "uh-huh," and so forth. But don't be misled—*these cues alone do not represent an effective response*. It is your attitude and sincere interest in the speaker that will ultimately determine the effectiveness of your efforts.

Questions and Perception Checks

Of course you understand what I'm saying! Your smile, the nod of your head, the periodic vocal reinforcers all tell me that I'm a very exciting, intelligent speaker and that you're interested and following what I have to say. Right? Surprise! The art of "smile and nod" seems, at times, to be almost second nature to listeners. Most of us can't even remember when or how we learned to provide these cues that keep a conversation running smoothly—or at least keep the speaker talking constantly! Imagine this typical situation.

> Your supervisor comes into your office and begins to explain what he needs done during the week he'll be out of town. You're not familiar with some of the names of his associates or the terms he's using, but you hesitate to interrupt. He seems in a hurry, and the information seems important to him. You don't want him to think that you're slow to catch on or that you're not familiar with some of the people you probably should know by now. So you remain quiet, thinking that you'll certainly be able to put the pieces together once he leaves. Finally, he's finished. As he shuts the door your phone rings. You pick it up and discover that there's a serious problem in manufacturing that needs your immediate attention. The next several hours are spent troubleshooting. By the time you get a chance to think about your earlier conversation, you have forgotten much of the information. Very little makes sense. Suddenly, you wish you had done a better job of listening.

In situations like these, there are two responses that may be helpful: questioning, and an application of the paraphrase called a perception check. Both are easy to use, but our fear of interrupting and our desire to create the impression that we "know a lot" sometimes prevents us from applying them.

Perception Checks   One way to make sure you understand the speaker's message is to restate its essential components. Perception checking is particularly useful when accuracy is essential, such as when a task has just been delegated to you. Restating procedures, dates, and final outcomes makes it less likely for misunderstandings to occur. In our everyday encounters, it often is difficult to avoid jumping to conclusions. We are in a hurry—we seldom stop to confirm our understandings. As a result many unnecessary mistakes are made. Perception checking is a useful application of the paraphrase, and it greatly improves our listening comprehension and recall.

Questions Questions are just that—a way to seek additional information from the speaker. Often a person makes inaccurate assumptions about what you already know or neglects to provide important details. Since he is familiar with his subject, it is difficult for him to make wise choices about what to communicate. Your questions let him know how your background compares with his. They provide an opportunity for you to receive clarification on points that seem vague or ambiguous. They prevent you from making inaccurate assumptions when you try to put together incomplete

Responses to Avoid

Clichés
Inappropriate clichés are often worse than not responding at all. They create distance between people, particularly if the individual had hoped for some honest information.

Ignoring
This often means the listener is trying to avoid a confrontation. To simply say nothing or change the subject after listening leaves the speaker frustrated. It is better to disagree, let a person know that you didn't understand, anything (almost!) is better than no response at all.

Long-windedness
Monologues are deadly. The other person is apt to lose interest. Long-winded messages might just as well be delivered to large numbers of people, since they do not incorporate any of the advantages of two-way communication.

Advice
You may feel that giving advice is helpful. In reality, however, it puts you in the higher status position. Nothing is worse than getting unwanted and unsolicited advice. Be careful that you don't express your "helpfulness" by telling people what *you* think they should do without giving them an opportunity to take responsibility for their own actions.

Blaming
Avoid a preoccupation with finding fault. Take a positive approach whenever possible and focus on problem-solving. Generate solutions to a conflict and focus on constructive action. Blaming quickly creates defensiveness.

Joking
It's good to have a sense of humor, but joking about serious matters can frustrate your colleagues. Try to face conflicts and other matters squarely. There are times when being serious is most appropriate, and it is important to be able to recognize these times.

information. Don't be discouraged by speakers who seem annoyed or impatient with your questions. Your goal is accurate communication, and your effectiveness in carrying out directions will be proof of the importance of getting all the facts.

Constructive Feedback

Your roommate's sloppiness annoys you.

You promised an eleven-year-old neighbor you'd help her with her tumbling routine.

Your best employee has been less productive lately and you don't know why.

Each of the above situations calls for constructive feedback. If you think about it, you'll discover endless instances where you need to let others know what you think of their actions or ideas. Through the use of constructive feedback we provide information to another person in a serious, planned, straightforward manner. Yet, a recent survey of Fortune 500 companies revealed that poor feedback accounts for a large percentage of internal communication breakdowns. Why? Because giving constructive feedback isn't easy, and it seldom comes naturally. It's tempting to resort to indirect cues which are easily misinterpreted, to make judgments which quickly create defensiveness, or to avoid the confrontation completely.

Clearly, the ability to provide accurate feedback is essential for productive interpersonal relationships and greater organizational health. Employees must feel comfortable providing their supervisors with relevant information; supervisors must learn to share their perceptions of subordinates' job performance clearly and honestly. These skills only develop if they are implemented and practiced on a regular basis.

Rules of Constructive Feedback

1. Constructive feedback is descriptive, not evaluative. When you evaluate, you tell someone that his performance is "good" or "bad," that he is "terrific" or "sloppy" or "slow." This type of information does not give the individual specific pointers. It is difficult for him to change because he doesn't know exactly what behaviors need modification. Be descriptive. Let the person know exactly what he did, and how his behavior compares to what you expect.
2. Helpful comments focus on those aspects of a person's behavior that he can improve and that are relevant to the situation at hand. When your subordinates perform a new task, comment on the effectiveness of their performance in terms of behaviors over which they have control.
3. Own your opinions by phrasing them appropriately. Acknowledge that your comments are made from your point of view—others may have a different opinion. Appropriate phrases include "to me," "as far as I know," "from what I've observed during the past week," or simply, "I think."
4. Feedback must be given as soon after the behavior occurs as possible. If you observe one of your workers performing a task incorrectly, don't wait until her next evaluation interview to tell her! It will be much more meaningful if you provide instruction right after your observation. Be careful, however, to avoid embarrassing someone by giving her constructive criticism in front of colleagues. The two of you should be alone, and have sufficient time to discuss issues that might arise.
5. Information is more readily acknowledged and acted on if it is seen as useful. Ideally, the person you direct your comments to has some desire to know what you think of his performance. Unwanted information will seldom be appreci-

Rules of Constructive Feedback

1. *It is descriptive* . . .

   Tim, I like your report. The style was clear and concise and your ideas were organized logically. The documentation you used made the problem credible and vivid.

   . . . not evaluative.

   Tim, that was a terrific report.

2. *It focuses on behavior* . . .

   Tim, try to slow down a little bit, and I think you can reduce the number of errors.

   . . . not on personal characteristics.

   Tim, you could be a lot faster on that machine if you were better coordinated.

3. *It is specific* . . .

   Tim, I couldn't hear you from where I was sitting.

   . . . not general.

   Tim, your voice isn't effective.

4. *It is timed appropriately* . . .

   Tim, let's get together around 2:00 and talk about your progress on the AMF.

   . . . not delayed or left to chance.

   Let's get together sometime.

5. *It is offered* . . .

   Tim, perhaps my reactions to your report would help you in preparing for next week's meeting. Would you like to get together sometime this afternoon?

   . . . not imposed.

   Tim, I've got to talk with you about that report before you give it at our meeting next week.

ated or acted on. It is only likely to make the person upset and defensive. Your relationship to him and his motivation to perform well are both influencing factors.

The atmosphere created in your department and the attitude of your colleagues make a big difference in the ease with which feedback is exchanged. Keep in mind that it is an important and useful way to provide individuals with information about their behavior—things they may not discover in any other way. . . .

Why are some people easier to talk with than others? Why do some individuals seem more approachable, more interested, more enthusiastic? In your efforts to become a better listener, the importance of your nonverbal cues cannot be overlooked. Your nonverbal response is just as important to effective communication as your verbal message; in fact, nonverbal cues are perceived as more significant indicators of effective listening than the verbal response. Speakers infer from your head nodding, posture, and eye contact that you are "with" them. Chances are if you act like a good listener the speaker will assume that you also hear, understand, and accurately evaluate what he has to say. His perception of you is significant, because it influences the quality and frequency of his interactions. Individuals are more likely to seek out those they perceive as good listeners for help and advice. Although you are not encouraged to simply manipulate nonverbal cues so that you appear to be listening (called faking attention), you do need to recognize how interaction is encouraged through appropriate nonverbal behaviors. Let's look at some of the ways in which our body communicates the message: "I'm listening."

Be Physically Alert

Imagine you are preparing for a race. Your body anticipates a certain stimulus and is poised to respond. Just as a runner waits for the go signal, so too a listener must be physically ready to perceive aural stimuli. If someone says to you, "Listen, if you need to use my credit card, you first have to . . ." Notice how you respond! Your muscles tense, your ears literally perk up. All of this, however, takes energy—so much energy that you can't possibly hold this level of attention for long. Still, it is important to remember that listening begins with this physical set, and unless we keep reasonably alert, we are likely to miss out on some of what goes on around us.

Maintain Eye Contact

Your supervisor says he wants you to come with your problems, but whenever you discuss something with him you get the impression that he doesn't really care about what you have to say. His mind seems elsewhere. Why? Perhaps it is because he doesn't focus on you but looks at the papers on his desk or rummages through his briefcase.

Eye contact is one of the most significant nonverbal cues. Averting the eyes signals a lack of interest or removal from the situation. Consider the following:

> You are sitting in someone's office and the phone rings. The person answers it and begins a conversation with the calling party. Where do you focus?

Few of us will sit and stare at the individual on the phone. Rather, we try to be polite by looking at the bookshelves or staring at the floor. Does looking away make you hard of hearing? Do you eavesdrop less when your eyes are averted? Of course not. But, socially, we learn that removing our gaze is the next best thing to leaving the room.

By eye contact we are not talking about a penetrating stare that makes the speaker uncomfortable and nervous. Concentrated eye contact can be threatening. A general focus that maintains a regular exchange of ideas and allows the listener to pick up important nonverbal cues is desired. This type of eye behavior allows for taking turns in conversation, as we have seen earlier. It also provides recognition, while communicating interest and empathy.

Use Appropriate Body Posture

Postures may be either "open" or "closed." The open posture is characterized by arms to the sides and legs uncrossed, whereas the closed posture is tighter with crossed arms and legs. Warmth and receptiveness, as you may have guessed, are communicated through open postures. A comfortable, relaxed, yet attentive pose lets the speaker know that you are ready to listen. Remember that listening is active. Although assuming a comfortable posture, the attentive listener does not slouch or appear tired or bored. Rather, he leans forward slightly and, although relaxed, looks physically alert. Both in speaking and listening, avoid bringing your hand to your face or covering your mouth by leaning on your elbow. Any of these manners indicate boredom and make your speech muffled and difficult to understand.

Minimize Gestures and Random Movement

Gestures can be overused easily. Random movements and fidgeting, whether conscious or unconscious, communicate impatience, boredom, or nervousness. Once the speaker becomes distracted by these nonverbal behaviors, he may lose his train of thought or modify his message, because he interprets your behavior to mean that you are not involved in the encounter or that you're not interested in what he has to say.

Some listeners explain that they intentionally use nonverbal cues to regulate or terminate a conversation that seems to be dragging on. Although a few people use such cues effectively, it is far better to verbalize your needs than to rely on indirect indicators. Rather than just glancing at your watch, tell the speaker that although you'd like to continue the conversation, you need the next few minutes to prepare for an important interview. The speaker will appreciate your directness.

Provide Minimal Reinforcers

Both verbal and nonverbal behaviors are used to show that a listener is involved and following the speaker's thoughts. In addition to "Uh-huh," "Oh," and "I see," the listener shows his understanding by facial expressions, nodding, and even tilting the head to one side. Minimal reinforcers are an important element in conversations, for unless the speaker receives some cue that the listener has heard and understood what he said, he will have no basis by which to judge whether his message needs modification.

Review Questions

1. What does Brownell mean when she says that as listeners, we take on 51 percent of the obligation to make communication successful?
2. What does Brownell say is the relationship between listening attitude and listening skills?
3. What does it mean to say that constructive feedback is "descriptive" not "evaluative"?
4. At one point Brownell asks, "Why are some people easier to talk with than others?" What's her answer to this question?

Probes

1. When you place an order over the telephone, which listening techniques does the person taking the order often use?
2. How is Brownell's treatment of advice-giving similar to Bolton's comments about advice in the last reading in Chapter 5?

3. Brownell draws several examples from the business world. What is your experience of listening on the job? Do your supervisors and the people you work with listen poorly or well? How does listening affect you at work?
4. Give an example of some body posture, gestures, and/or movement that mean different things in different cultures.
5. Can you think of any exceptions to Brownell's suggestion to give feedback as soon as possible after the behavior occurs?

In this next reading, Milt Thomas and I describe an approach to listening that's grown out of our reading and teaching. I first wrote about this approach in the October 1983 issue of a journal called *Communication Education*. While I was writing that article, I discussed it in a class Milt was taking, and he really picked up the ideas and ran with them. He began applying them in his own teaching and encouraging me to do the same. So when I decided to include a discussion on this approach in *Bridges Not Walls*, I knew that Milt could contribute a great deal to the effort.

The most exciting thing about our collaboration on this piece—and we are both still smiling about it—is that our work together was an example of what we were writing about. Each time we talked, we seemed to get more evidence of the value of this approach to listening. In fact, after we were finished, when I discovered that I needed to cut thirty-five pages from this book before sending it to the publisher, I asked Milt to discuss the issue with me, because I knew that the ways we had learned to listen to each other would make that conversation very productive. I wasn't disappointed; the difficult decisions that emerged from that discussion still strike me as right.

So we encourage you to give dialogic listening a try. It's different from the kind of listening that Judi Brownell discusses, but only in the sense that it broadens and goes beyond her advice. We feel confident about it because we know it's solidly grounded in some well-developed philosophy of communication. But more important, we also know it can *work*.

Dialogic Listening: Sculpting Mutual Meanings

John Stewart and Milt Thomas

The two of us have recently had a number of communication experiences that have led us to substantially rethink our attitudes toward listening. In conversations with each other and in many of our contacts with students, family, friends, and co-

John Stewart, "Interpretive Listening: An Alternative to Empathy," *Communication Education*, 32 (October 1983): 379–391.

workers, we have rediscovered in a concrete and exciting way the *productive* quality of interpersonal communication. In other words, we've experienced how in the most fruitful and satisfying conversations, our listening is focused less on reproducing what's "inside" the other person and more on co-producing, with the other person, mutual meanings *between* us. As a result, we've rediscovered how a good conversation can create insights, ideas, and solutions to problems that none of the conversation partners could have generated alone. It seems to us that a certain kind of listening has helped that happen.

For example, Milt was recently involved with two other people in an effort to design and conduct a training program for beginning university teachers. Jack, one of Milt's partners, came to the planning sessions with very definite ideas about the design and operation of the program. He assumed that Milt and Susan would also have their definite ideas and that their meeting times would be spent with each trainer bargaining for his or her own plan. You could say that Jack was mainly content-focused. Susan's primary concern was the quality of learning experienced by the beginning university teachers; she focused more on outcome or goals. She was willing to bargain with Jack, to advocate her own ideas, or to engage in whatever process seemed to lead to the outcomes she valued.

Although Milt wasn't fully aware of the contrast at the time, his main concern was neither the content of the program nor outcomes for the participants, but the quality of the contact among the three planners. He was *not* just functioning as a "pure process" person; he brought his own ideas—for example, about how the new teachers could learn to handle the grading and the cross-cultural communication problems they might encounter in their classrooms. But Milt found his ideas about content and outcomes entering the conversation somewhat like "counter-punches" in the sense that they were responses to Jack's or Susan's contributions. He seemed to use the momentum of the ongoing talk to create "holes" that his contributions helped fill.

Milt's efforts were not always greeted cheerfully. He often slowed down the planning process as he made sure that he understood the others, that they understood him, and that they comprehended one another. When Susan and Jack presented their ideas, he would often raise questions or offer countersuggestions in order to build more talk about the ideas. Milt wasn't merely playing "devil's advocate" to stir things up; he was trying to help engage all three persons in a mutual building process. They were building conversation-texts, "chunks" of talk that developed ideas and suggestions, teased out nuances, and helped mold incomplete suggestions into refined ones.

While Jack's strength was content and Susan's strength was her outcome-focus, Milt's contribution to this effort came primarily from the way he *listened.* His attitudes and expectations, the questions he asked, the way he paraphrased others' comments, and even his nonverbal behavior—posture, tone of voice, rate of speaking, and so on—were all aimed not just toward *reproducing* what Jack or Susan said but toward *producing* with them a full response to the issues they faced.

We've come to call the kind of listening Milt engaged in *dialogic listening*. We use this term to label listening that values and builds mutuality, requires active involvement, is genuine, and grows out of a belief in and commitment to synergy—the idea that the whole actually can be greater than the sum of its parts. There are some important differences between dialogic listening and what's usually called "active listening" or "empathic listening." Let's start by briefly reviewing them.

"Active" or "Empathic" Listening

Recall for a minute some of what you've read or heard about listening, perhaps from a listening text,[1] from your teacher, or in a listening seminar or workshop. For one thing, you may well have read or discussed some of the ironies of listening. For example, we spend much more time listening than we spend speaking, reading, or writing, but we're taught the most about writing and reading, a little about speaking, and almost nothing about listening.[2] Another irony is that we are worst at the activity we engage in the most. As Robert Bolton notes, researchers claim that we usually remember only about one quarter of what we hear, and many people miss almost 100% of the feeling content of spoken communication.

To help remedy this situation, most books and articles emphasize that listening differs from hearing. Hearing is the physiological part of the process—the reception of sound waves. Good listening is traditionally defined as effective sensing, interpreting, and evaluating the other person's meanings. That definition is reflected in the anonymous maxim, "I know you believe you understand what you think I said, but I'm not sure you realize that what you heard is not what I meant." The idea behind this maxim is that listening involves *one* person grasping the *other* person's meanings, and since we can't get inside the other person's experience, the listening process is inherently flawed.

When people discuss empathic listening, they generally begin from this same basic understanding. Empathy is the process of "putting yourself in the other's place," or as Carl Rogers puts it,

> It means entering the private perceptual world of the other and becoming thoroughly at home in it. It involves being sensitive, moment by moment, to the changing felt meanings which flow in this other person. . . . To be with another in this way means that for the time being, you lay aside your own views and values in order to enter another's world without prejudice. In some sense it means that you lay aside yourself. . . .[3]

One of the most important skills for achieving empathic understanding is paraphrasing. As Bolton puts it, "a *paraphrase* is a *concise response* to the speaker which states the *essence* of the other's *content* in the *listener's own words*."[4] Most traditional treatments of active or empathic listening also discuss several other parts of the process, including attending skills, clarifying skills, and perception checking.[5]

These traditional accounts are useful in several ways. For one thing, they call our attention to the fact that most of us don't listen as well as we could. We think of listening as a passive process, like "soaking up sense data," and as a result we often don't work at it. Good listening takes real effort and traditional listening texts and workshops almost always include helpful suggestions about how to do it better. There's also something intuitively appealing about discussions of empathic listening. Each of us knows what it's like to "walk a mile in the other person's moccasins," and we've also had the opposite experience where someone is so self-centered that he or she never really connects with any else's thoughts or feelings. Empathizing with someone's fear or pain—or having someone empathize with yours—can be very confirming and reassuring, and when it doesn't happen, it can hurt.

But there are also some problems with this view of listening. For one thing, it's based on a kind of fiction. As we mentioned, you cannot actually "get inside" the other person's awareness, and it can be confusing to try to think, feel, and act as if you could.

It's also impossible to, as Rogers puts it, "lay aside your own views and values" or to "lay aside yourself." Any decision or effort to make that kind of move would be the decision or effort of a "self" and it would be rooted in that self's views and values. In other words, you cannot put yourself on the shelf because that move is an active choice that keeps yourself involved. "Laying aside yourself" is as literally impossible as lifting yourself by your ears—or your own bootstraps. So you may well decide to focus on the other person and to do your best to sense her meanings or feel his happiness, but these efforts will always be grounded in your own attitudes, expectations, past experiences, and world view. You *can't* "lay aside yourself." Neither can we.

A second problem is that empathic listening can get distorted into a frustrating or even manipulative process of parroting. The generally recognized "father" of empathic listening, Carl Rogers, often commented on how vulnerable to distortion the process can be. Consider, for example, how you'd feel if you were the client in this counselor-client conversation:

CLIENT: I really think he's a very nice guy; he's so thoughtful, sensitive, and kind. He calls me a lot. He's fun to go out with.
COUNSELOR: You like him very much, then.
CLIENT: Yeah, and I think my friends like him too. Two of them have asked me to double-date.
COUNSELOR: You are pleased that your friends accept him.
CLIENT: Yeah, but I don't want to get too involved right now. I've got a lot of commitments at school and to my family.
COUNSELOR: You want to limit your involvement with him.
CLIENT: Yeah. . . . Is there an echo in here?

When your conversation partner—whether counselor, lover, parent, or friend—is focusing only on sensing your meanings or feeling your feelings, it can begin to seem like you are talking to yourself. The contact between you is sacrificed to serve the other person's desire to "understand fully."

This brings us to a third shortcoming of many of the traditional approaches to active or empathic listening: They emphasize the "psychology" of the situation rather than the *communication*. By this we mean that these approaches make each person's "psyche" or internal state the focus of attention rather than the verbal and nonverbal transaction that's going on *between* them. As we've already said, it can be very helpful to try to sense another's feelings, and it is confirming and reassuring when someone does that for you. But we think there's more to effective listening than that. You definitely do not need to stop trying to listen actively or empathically, but we do think it can be helpful to broaden your repertoire by also learning to listen dialogically.

Dialogic Listening

In our thinking and talking we've identified four distinctive features of dialogic listening. In this section we want to outline them and to offer five suggestions for practicing this approach. We'll conclude with a brief discussion of some problems you might encounter as you try to apply what we suggest here.

Focus on "Ours"

The first distinctive feature of dialogic listening is that it focuses on "ours" rather than "mine" or "yours." Without listening training of any kind—and sometimes even with it—many of us fall into a pattern of communicating as if we were talking to ourselves—we focus on "mine." Sometimes this monologic communication "just happens"; we're not aware of the fact that we are only discussing our topic from our point of view, or we're not conscious of how long we've been talking or how few real questions we've asked. At other times we get caught up in our own agendas; we get so involved in and enthusiastic about our project or opportunity that we lose track of—and hence contact with—the other person. That happens often to one of John's friends. The friend's wife urges him to "be more sensitive," but he often can't seem to help himself. He gets going on his most recent idea or project and fifteen minutes pass before he takes a breath. Then he'll abruptly notice what he's done and apologize for "monopolizing the conversation—again."

Other persons concentrate on "mine" simply because they believe that their agenda is more significant than anyone else's. They fall into a "me focused" pattern when their excitement or worry about their own concerns overshadows everything else. And in still other cases a person sticks with his or her agenda because of the belief that "I can say it my way better than you can say it your way," and the possibility that *we* could say it even more effectively never occurs to them. In short, unconsciousness, honest enthusiasm, and a sense of superiority can all help us keep our communication focused on "mine."

The preceding quotations from Rogers and Bolton illustrate how treatments of empathic listening concentrate on "yours." A paraphrase states the essence of the *other's* content in the listener's own words, and empathizing means "entering the private conceptual world of the *other*." As we have already said, this can be a useful move for the very self-centered person, but it can also lead to the kind of communication illustrated in our counselor–client example.

The third alternative is to focus on *ours*. This is what we had in mind when we subtitled this discussion "Sculpting Mutual Meanings." The metaphor is Milt's and he uses it to suggest a concrete, graphic image of what it means to listen dialogically. Picture yourself sitting on one side of a potter's wheel with your conversation partner across from you. As you work (talk) together, each of you adds clay to the form on the wheel, and each uses wet fingers, thumbs, and palms to shape the finished product. Like clay, talk is tangible and malleable; it's out there to hear, to record, and to shape. If I am unclear or uncertain about what I am thinking or about what I want to say, I can put something out there and you can modify its shape, ask me to add more clay, or add some of your own. Your specific shaping, which you could only have done in response to the shape I formed, may move in a direction I would never have envisioned. The clay you add may be an idea I've thought about before—though not here or in this form—or it may be completely new to me. Sometimes these "co-sculpting" sessions will be mostly playful, with general notions tossed on the wheel and the result looking like a vaguely shaped mass. At other times, the basic shape is well defined and we spend our time on detail and refinement. Our efforts, though, are almost always productive and frequently very gratifying. Sometimes I feel that our talk helps me understand myself better than I could have alone. At other times we produce something that transcends anything either of us could have conceived separately. This is because the figure we sculpt is not mine or yours, but *ours*, the outcome of both of our active shapings.

Open-ended and "Playful"

The second distinctive feature of dialogic listening in its open-ended, tentative, playful quality. We notice that when we are listening dialogically, we actually do not know what the outcome of the conversation will be. For example, John initiated the collaboration on this chapter because he knew that Milt had done a lot of thinking about this approach to listening and had worked with these ideas in the interpersonal communication courses he teaches. Our first conversation about this essay occurred in the hallway outside the Speech Communication Department office, where we set a time to meet and talk about the project. At that point neither of us knew what the outcome of our longer conversation would be. One option was for John to write the essay and for Milt to read it and suggest changes and additions. Another possibility was that Milt would write it, based on his recent classroom experience, and then John would edit and polish it. A third was that each of us would draft different sections and then comment on what the other person wrote. In our meeting, we didn't discuss any of those options until after an hour and a half or so, when our tentative strategy emerged from our talk. We agreed that we would start by having John take the ideas that developed in our conversation—most of which Milt had initiated and given examples of—and would begin organizing the whole, and Milt would draft certain sections that he knew best. As the process has developed, Milt has written several sections, John has integrated Milt's contributions into the text, and Milt has critiqued, raised questions, and made additions to each draft. Our point is that this kind of open-endedness is one of the primary prerequisites for—and one of the greatest challenges of—dialogic listening.

It's a challenge especially because a great deal of what we learn in twentieth-century Western culture pushes us in the opposite direction, toward closure and certainty. In his book on creativity, Roger von Oech addresses those concerns when he discusses "soft and hard thinking."[6] "Hard" thinking is logical, analytical, critical, propositional, digital, focused, concrete, and "left-brain." "Soft" thinking is speculative, divergent, symbolic, elliptical, analogical, ambiguous, metaphoric, and "right-brain." Both are vital to effective problem-solving. Yet von Oech describes how, especially in the twentieth-century Western world, we are taught that there is only one kind of *real* thinking that leads to *real* knowledge, and that's the "hard" kind. This same bias makes it difficult to practice the kind of openness and tentativeness that dialogic listening requires.

What von Oech calls "hard" thinking is thinking that values the three c's: certainty, closure, and control. Much of the "hard" sciences, like physics and chemistry, concentrate on the development of lawlike generalizations that apply with certainty in all situations.[7] Whether it's morning or evening, winter or summer, at General Motors or General Mills, H_2O will always boil at 100°C and freeze at 0°C. If you know these laws you can confidently *control* the "behavior" of water, and you can be sure that on these matters inquiry is *closed*; we know what we need to know.

Obviously, the hard sciences and the hard thinking that develops them are enormously powerful and effective. Holography and the space shuttle, to say nothing of diet soft drinks and word processing, would be impossible without them. But certainty, closure, and control are not always possible, and especially where persons are involved, they're often not even desirable.

In order to listen dialogically you need, in place of the three c's, a combination of some modesty or humility and some trust. The modesty comes from remembering that persons are choosers, choice-makers. That means that you cannot predict with certainty what they will think, feel, or do in any situation. We just don't have that power over people, although habits and patterns sometimes make it seem as if we do. John's grandmother "always" cries at weddings, and politicians "always" like publicity. So it seems that we could predict what they'll do in these situations "every time." But all you have to do is pay attention to the people around you, and you will discover how those "always" predictions turn into "usually" or "sometimes." So there's an inverse relationship between this kind of humility and your desire for conversational certainty and control. When you can acknowledge and affirm your partner's power, as a person, to choose, you can relax your grip on two of the three c's.

There's also an inverse relationship between conversational trust and the two c's of closure and control. By trust we don't mean a naive belief that the world is a completely friendly place and that nobody in it means you any harm. That's obviously foolish. What we do mean is that you trust the potential of the conversation to produce more than you could on your own, and that, at least until you're proven wrong, you trust the other person's presence to you. For us, the cognitive part of this trust seems to be a decision to let the talk work, a choice in favor of what William S. Howell calls the "joint venture" quality of the conversation.[8] The feeling part seems to be a combination of a relaxing-letting-go and a deep-breath-leap-of-faith. That may overstate things a bit; the point is that you relax whatever white-knuckled grip you might have on the conversation's direction or outcome—"How can I be sure she doesn't think I am being silly?" "What if he won't give me the time off?"—and trust it to work.

Playfulness is the icing on the cake. If you and your conversation partner can manage to be tentative and experimental and can manifest a sense of open-endedness, you'll frequently find yourself literally playing with the ideas. In the past couple of decades scholars from several disciplines have emphasized the "seriousness" of play, the many senses in which play isn't just for fun. Psychotherapists discuss "games people play," defense analysts engage in war games, and play therapy is one way to help both troubled and normal children. Even a couple of philosophers have discussed the "playful" nature of conversation.[9] They emphasize that the "to-and-fro" is the basic form of everything we call "play," including sporting events, board games, and even the play of light on the water. Another characteristic is indeterminacy, that is, that play constantly renews itself. No Super Bowl or World Series game is ever the definitive or final instance of the play of football or baseball; these activities are constantly renewed in each playing. In addition, we don't completely control our playing; in an important sense we are played by the game as much as we play it. This quality becomes clear if you think of the way the rules, the tempo, the setting, and the spectators all affect your playing of racquetball, chess, baseball, or poker.

The point is, when we are engaged in spontaneous conversation, the form of the to-and-fro itself can generate insight and surprise—if we are listening dialogically. No un-self-conscious conversation is ever simply outward *replay* of your inner intentions and meanings. Instead, you and your partner actually play together; the two of you enter a dynamic over which you do not have complete control, and the outcome of your talk can be a surprise to you both, a creation of your play. It's difficult to write down an example of open-ended playfulness, but we think the following conversation at least points in the directions we mean:

KIM: Can I talk to you, Professor Carbaugh?

DON: Sure, "Student Wells," what's up? Oh, yeah, you missed the exam on Friday, didn't you.

KIM: Yeah. That's why I came by. And since you said at the beginning of the term that you didn't have a set policy on makeups, I don't know what to do about it.

DON: Well, you're doing it exactly right! There's no set policy, because the situation is a little different in each case. So we definitely *do* have to do something about it, or you will end up with a zero. But I don't know yet what that should be. Sit down and let's talk about it.

KIM: Can I take the exam now?

DON: Right now? I don't know. . . . let's back off a little and talk about what happened when the rest of the class was writing the exam.

KIM: I was sick. Well, not exactly *sick*, sick, but I couldn't do it. I was really not physically or mentally able to do it.

DON: Keep talking. . . .

KIM: Well, I don't want to give you a pile of excuses.

DON: I don't want you to give me a pile either—(*smiling*) of anything. But I do want to hear what was happening with you.

KIM: We had a big party on Thursday at the house I'm in, and I was in charge of all the arrangements, and I stayed up most of Wednesday night getting ready for it, and then in the middle of the party my boyfriend and I had a big fight, and he left, and I fell apart that night and couldn't even get out of bed Friday until after noon. Actually, I knew the fight was coming; I wouldn't have gotten so upset except I was so tired. Anyway, I just blew it.

DON: Okay. I appreciate your honesty. Hmmm . . . so you didn't have a certified, diagnosed disease, but it sounds like you *were* fairly well incapacitated—and probably a little hung over too.

KIM: I don't drink.

DON: I apologize. A dumb assumption on my part. I'm sorry.

KIM: It's okay. So what are we going to do?

DON: Well, what do you suggest? Sounds like you ought to be able to take a makeup, but that you aren't exactly in the same position as somebody who had the flu or who had to attend a funeral.

KIM: I don't know; I think it's the same. I don't know why I should be penalized at all. But you're the teacher.

DON: Yeah, and *both* of us are involved in this—as is the rest of the class, indirectly. I'm concerned that the exam was Friday and now it's Monday.

KIM: And I could have talked about it with other people in the class.

DON: Yeah, that's possible; and that would be less fair to the others. I don't care to put you "on the stand" to testify about that; I don't like playing judge and jury. So what if I modify the exam, you take it this afternoon, and we knock fifteen points off the top because, as you put it, you did kind of "blow" it.

KIM: All of that's fine but the fifteen-point penalty. I think I was as sick as anyone who has the twenty-four-hour flu.

DON: Okay, let's run that part of it briefly by the class. I'll keep you anonymous and see how they feel about makeups under these general circumstances—whether they feel any unfairness.

KIM: Well, if you feel you have to do that.

DON: Sounds like you don't. What are you thinking?

Don's open-endedness is evident here in his unwillingness to set a rigid policy in advance, his concern that the two of them discuss the situation before arriving at a conclusion, and his willingness to admit his own errors and to acknowledge the validity of Kim's viewpoint. Obviously, he does have principles here, and the fact that he is open to play does not mean he's wishy-washy. In this case, his position is clear: "We definitely *do* have to do something about it, or you will end up with a zero," but he is willing to let the conversation guide the two of them toward their specific solution. There's also a little play here around titles—"professor" and "student"—and the "pile of excuses" metaphor. In addition, once Don enters into a discussion that is this open, he cannot not take Kim's arguments seriously. He has to at least listen to her; in that sense Don is "being played by the game." The same is obviously true for Kim. We end the example before a final resolution is reached to emphasize that even after this much talk it may still be important to stay open.

In Front Of

The third distinctive feature of dialogic listening is that it emphasizes what's in front of or between the conversation partners rather than what's "behind" them. One influential definition of empathy includes this sentence: "It is an experiencing of the consciousness 'behind' another's outward communication, but with continuous awareness that this consciousness is originating and proceeding in the other."[10] That's the opposite of dialogic listening. Instead of trying to infer internal "psychic" states from the talk, when you are listening dialogically you join with the other person in the process of co-creating meaning *between* you.

Again, we don't mean to be making an artificial dichotomy. "Internal states" cannot be separated from external ones, and thoughts and feelings are obviously a part of all communication. But it makes a big difference whether you are *focusing* on those internal states, trying to make an educated guess about where the other person is coming from, or focusing on building talk between the two of you. In other words, it can make a big difference whether your metaphor is "figuring out where she's coming from" or "sculpting mutual meanings." When your focus is "behind" you spend your time and mental energy searching for possible fits between what you're seeing and hearing and what the other person "must be" meaning and feeling. In other words, you're engaging in a form of psychologizing, treating the talk as an indicator of something else that's more reliable, more important, more interesting.

On the other hand, when you're listening dialogically, your focus, as we said before, is on the communication not the psychology. We don't mean that you are insensitive to the other person's feelings. In fact your sensitivity may well be heightened, but it is focused *between* rather than behind. You concentrate on the verbal and nonverbal text that the two of you are building together. In one sense you take the talk at face value; you attend to it and not to something you infer to be behind it. But this doesn't mean you uncritically accept everything that's said as the "whole truth and nothing but the truth." You respond and inquire in ways that make the mutual text as full and reliable as possible. You work to co-build it into a text you *can* trust. That leads us to the final distinctive feature we want to mention.

Presentness

When you're listening dialogically, you focus more on the present than on the past or future. Once again, please don't hear an absolute; the future is not irrelevant and neither is the past. When we met to discuss our collaboration on this essay, we felt the pressure of a future deadline, and we were encouraged by the success of past interactions. But as we talked, our attention was on the present; we were open to what *could* be co-built, we focused on the "ours" *between* us, and all that helped keep us in the here-and-now.

The philosopher of communication, Martin Buber, was once described by his friend and biographer Maurice Friedman as a person with a unique ability to be "present to the presentness of the other and able to call the other into presence with him." Friedman speaks of how, when he met Buber, he first noticed his eyes. Others mentioned too how Buber's look was penetrating but gentle. His gaze and his look seemed both to demand presentness and to reassure. One person said that the message from Buber's eyes was always, "Do not be afraid." And it was difficult not to respond in kind, with as much presentness as one could muster. This quality of Buber's communication is what we mean by this characteristic of dialogic listening.

Buber also had another way of making the point as we are making here: he talked of the desirability of working toward a unity of one's saying, being, and doing. In one of his books, Buber wrote that human life can be thought of as consisting of three realms: thought, speech, and action. "Whoever straightens himself out in regard to all three will find that everything prospers at his hand."[11] Later in the same book he added, "The root of all conflict between me and my fellow man is that I do not say what I mean and I do not mean what I say."[12]

It seems to us that if you are going to work toward unifying your saying, being, and doing, you are going to have to focus on the present. You can't connect and coordinate your actions, speech, and being in any other way. It also seems that when we focus on the present as a way toward unifying these three realms, our efforts tend to make it easier for the other person to do the same thing. So the whole process can spiral in a very positive way.

"But," you may be asking, "what if the other person is lying? What if the 'present talk' *cannot* be trusted? Isn't your advice a little naive?" Our response, as we mentioned earlier, is that we are not suggesting blind naiveté. If you allow us one other personal example, trust was an issue for us as we collaborated on this essay. John is clearly "one up" on the power scale in this partnership, because he's a professor and Milt is a teaching assistant. In order for us to be able to practice what we are preaching about dialogic listening, John has to be willing and able to participate in genuine power *sharing*, and Milt has to *trust* him to do that. It isn't enough for John just to "give Milt power" by letting him have his say while reserving the right to make the final decision. He has to actually share responsibility, to leave the outcomes genuinely open. Both of us also need to trust each other to work constructively with incomplete, fuzzy, and sometimes off-the-point ideas. Especially because he's power-down, Milt needs to trust John, first to criticize rather than just to superficially agree with everything, and second, to criticize in constructive ways and not to ridicule unfinished ideas. We've been excited by the power sharing and trust that's been generated. We think it's materially improved the finished product.

If you aren't that fortunate and find that you mistrust the other's presence or his truthfulness, you can make that fact part of your conversation. There are ways to raise this issue without ridiculing or rejecting the other person. You can describe your reservations or ask your questions in ways that keep the conversation going, and this brings us to our "how to do it" section.

Applications

When we first began to think seriously about dialogic listening, we both moved almost immediately to this point. "What behavioral differences," we asked ourselves and each other, "are there between active or empathic listening and dialogic listening? What do you *do* differently?" For a while we felt like we'd run up against a brick wall. We could identify two or three important behaviors, "moves" or "techniques," but (1) there seemed to be much more to the process than just those behaviors and (2) strictly speaking, there was at least a mention in a "traditional" treatment of listening of each behavior on our list. After about two years of periodic thinking, discussing, and classroom experimenting, we began to understand our struggle. There are at least five ways of applying this approach to listening, but the most important element is the listener's *attitude, intent, awareness,* or *perspective.*

The first and most important application advice is that you define your specific listening situation as "ours," "open-ended," "between," and "present." Try not to focus your attention on "mine" or "his/hers," "control," "what's behind," or the past or future. When you're able to do that you will notice how "attitudes" and "behaviors" are not really separate. What you do—the behaviors—will *feel* different as your attitude or perspective shifts. At least that is our experience. For example, the ways we paraphrase (we'll discuss that skill in a minute) actually change as we shift from empathic to dialogic listening. We believe you may well discover the same. The point is, if you can genuinely achieve the mind-set we've discussed here, you'll have gone a long way toward listening dialogically.

"Say More"

One communication behavior that seems to be an application of that mind-set is the response, "Say more." As we explained when we discussed the sculpting metaphor, talk is tangible and malleable, and one of the primary goals of dialogic listening is to build more "chunks" of talk that develop ideas and suggestions, tease out nuances, and help define incomplete ideas. As a listener, you can most directly contribute to this process by simply encouraging your conversation partner to keep talking.

One common situation where "say more" can help is when someone makes a comment that sounds fuzzy or incomplete. Frequently, our inclination is to try to paraphrase what's been said or to act on that information even though we don't feel like we have the materials to do so. When Milt is in this situation, he finds himself feeling frustrated because he seems to have a disproportionate share of the burden to "make things clear." When he feels that frustration, he uses it as a signal to ask the person to "say more." The indirect message is that Milt wants the other person's help; he's saying, in effect, "I can't continue our sculpture until you add some definition to the form you began."

In this situation and in others, you might expect that your "say more" will just promote repetition and redundancy, but that's not been our experience. We find that if our encouragement is genuine, we frequently get talk that clarifies ideas, gets more specific, and substantially reduces misunderstanding. Like each of our suggestions, this one has to be used appropriately. It'd be pretty ridiculous to respond to "Could you tell me what time it is?" with "Say more about that." But each time you hear a new idea, a new topic, or an important point being made, we suggest you begin your listening effort at that moment not by guessing what the other person means but by asking them to tell you. "Say more," "Keep talking," or some similar encouragement can help.[13]

Run with the Metaphor

Our second suggestion is that you build more conversation-text, in part by extending whatever metaphors the other person has used to express his or her ideas, developing your own metaphors, or encouraging the other person to extend yours. As you know, a metaphor is a figure of speech that links two dissimilar objects or ideas in order to make a point. "My love is a red, red rose," "He's built like King Kong," and "The table wiggles because one leg is shorter than the others" all include metaphors. The first links my love and a rose in order to make a point. The second links his build and King Kong's, and the third links a table support with the appendage an animal uses to walk. As the third example suggests, metaphors are more common than we sometimes think. In fact, some people argue that virtually *all* language is metaphoric.[14]

We use the example, though, to encourage you to listen for both subtle and obvious metaphors and to weave them into your responses. We've found that when people hear their metaphors coming back at them, they can get a very quick and clear sense of what's being heard. For example, notice how the process works in this conversation:

VICE PRESIDENT: This is an important project we're going after. Water reclamation is the wave of the future, if you'll pardon the pun, and we want to do as much of it as we can.

PROJECT MANAGER: I agree completely. But I am not sure the people from the other firms on our team are as enthusiastic as you and I are.

VICE PRESIDENT: Well, if they aren't, part of your job as quarterback is to get them charged up and committed. We can't go into this with a half-hearted attitude and expect to do well.

PROJECT MANAGER: Okay, I realize I am quarterbacking the effort, but it seems to me that the coach can also help "fire up the troops," and I haven't heard you doing much of that yet. Are you willing to help me increase their enthusiasm?

VICE PRESIDENT: Sure. What do you want me to do?

PROJECT MANAGER: I think part of the problem is they already think they've won the game. I don't. We haven't got this contract yet, and we won't get it unless we convince the city we *want* it. You could help by giving sort of half-time talk before the kickoff.

VICE PRESIDENT: Sure, no problem. I'll talk to everybody at the start of tomorrow's meeting.

In this situation the project manager develops her boss's "team" and "quarterback" metaphors by talking about what a "coach" can do with a "half-time talk." On the other hand, sometimes the process is more subtle.

CHIP: You look a lot less happy than when I saw you this morning. What's happening?

THERESE: I just got out of my second two-hour class today, and I can't believe how much I have to do. I'm really feeling squashed.

CHIP: "Squashed" like you can't come up for air, or "squashed" as in you have to do what everybody else wants and you can't pursue your own ideas?

THERESE: More like I can't come up for air. Every professor seems to think this is the only class I'm taking.

Again, the purpose of running with each other's metaphors (notice that "running with" is a metaphor too) is to co-build talk between you in order to produce as full as possible a response to the issues you face together. In addition, the metaphors themselves reframe or give you a new perspective on the topic of your conversation. A project manager who sees herself as a "quarterback" is going to think and behave differently from one who sees himself as a "general," a "guide," or a "senior-level bureaucrat." And the work stress that "squashes" you is different from the pressure that "keeps you jumping like a flea on a griddle." Listen for metaphors and take advantage of their power to shape and extend your ideas.

Paraphrase Plus

Our third suggestion is that you apply that most useful of all communication techniques, paraphrasing, but that you do it in a couple of new ways: Paraphrase not to *reproduce* the other's meaning but to *produce* a fuller conversation-text between you, and ask the other person to paraphrase you. As we've noted, paraphrasing is usually defined as restating the other person's meaning in your own words. It's an enormously useful thing to do in *many* communication situations, including conflict, parent-child contacts, classroom, and on the job.

In a way, though, if you only spend your conversational time checking to see if you are following the same path as the other person, you aren't fully carrying your share of the conversational load. To do more of that, you can add to your paraphrase your own response to the question, "Now what?" In other words, you start by remembering that the meanings you are developing are created between the two of you, and individual perspectives are only a part of that. So you follow your perception-checking with whatever your good judgment tells you is your response to what the person said. The spirit of a paraphrase plus is that each individual perspective is a building block for the team effort.

When we suggest that paraphrasing can include new information—your contribution—we are not implying that the person listening dialogically has license to poke fun at or to parody the other person. Notice the difference among these three responses:

RITA: I like being in a "exclusive" relationship, and your commitment to me is important. But I still sometimes want to go out with other people.

MIKE'S RESPONSE: So even though there are some things you value about our decision not to date others, you're still a little uncertain about it.

TIM'S RESPONSE: Oh, so you want me to hang around like a fool while you go out and play social butterfly! Talk about a double standard!

SCOTT'S RESPONSE: It sounds like you think there are some advantages and disadvantages to the kind of relationship we have now. I like it the way it is now, but I don't like knowing that you aren't sure. Can you talk some more about your uncertainty?

Mike responded to Rita's comment with a paraphrase. This tells us that Mike listened to Rita, but not much more. Tim made a caricature of Rita's comment, masking an editorial in the guise of a paraphrase. Scott offered a paraphrase plus. He made explicit his interpretation of what Rita was saying, then he moved the focus of the conversation back to "the between," back to "the middle" where both persons could work on the problem together. Because of what Rita said, Scott may have felt hurt or mad or both, and maybe he wouldn't have been so constructive as we've made him sound, but the point is that he not only paraphrased but also interpreted and responded to her comments. When this happens both the paraphrase and the interpretation keep understanding growing between the individuals, instead of within them.

Another way to think about the paraphrase plus is that you're broadening your goal beyond "fidelity" or "correspondence." If you're paraphrasing for fidelity or correspondence, you're satisfied and "finished" with the task as soon as you've successfully reproduced "what she means." Your paraphrase is a success if it corresponds accurately to the other person's intent. We're suggesting that you go beyond correspondence to creativity, beyond reproducing to co-producing. It's the same point we've made before.

It's easy to see that this kind of listening takes energy, even more so if only one person in a conversation is committed to dialogue. One way to elicit help from the other participants in a conversation is to *ask for paraphrasing* from them. Whenever you're uncertain about whether the other person is listening fully, you can check their perceptions by asking them for talk. This works best if you don't demand a paraphrase, and if you don't say, "Ha! Gotcha!" if the other person cannot respond well. The other person's paraphrase can, however, let both of you check for mutual understanding, and it can also keep the other's interpretations and responses in the talk between you where they can be managed productively.

Context-Building

We've mentioned that your conversation partner(s) may sometimes not be as eager or as willing as you are to work toward shared understanding. Their indifference sometimes surfaces in semi-messages, such as a blank stare or a dirty look, an indistinct blob of words, or silence. Paraphrasing and asking for a paraphrase can help produce more talk to build on between you, but what else can you do? We've found that what we call context-building can help.

By "context" we mean the circumstances that surround or relate to a topic, idea, opinion, or statement. When someone says something, it is spoken in a particular context or situation, which is made up of at least the physical location, feelings and thoughts, and the comment it is a response to. When you are listening dialogically, you can thematize and help develop or flesh out this contextual information so it can become part of the material you are co-sculpting.

For example, often ideas come out initially as vague judgments such as "That's stupid!" or, "What a jerk!" That's like slamming some clay down hard onto the potter's wheel. But there is potential value in a move like that, if you are willing to initiate talk that helps turn the clay from a blob into a more distinct shape. As difficult as it sounds, one of the best ways to respond to comments like these is to say, "What do you mean by 'stupid'?" or "Tell me more," or, "Where did that come from?" These contributions all help elicit additional talk.

Although many discussions of communication suggest that skillful communicators need to learn to describe their feelings, there is nothing particularly enlightening about, "I feel like hell!" thrown into the middle of a conversation. Feelings are accompanied by circumstances and desires—their context—and you can help sculpt mutual meanings by trying to find out what preceded the feelings, what they are a response to, and what desires accompany them. Try, "Are you disappointed by what she did to you or are you angry?" "I notice that whenever I offer a suggestion, you dismiss it. Do you see that happening too?" or, "What do you want to have happen?"

Of course, it's not always just the other person who offers de-contextualized comments. You too will catch yourself throwing out cryptic judgments and incomplete exclamations that contribute little to shared understanding. In fact, sometimes all of us do this on purpose. But when you are not trying to be vague, you can follow an "I'm bored," with talk about the parts of the context that you feel bored about and what you would like to have happen. These individual contributions can be part of a text of conversation that can help all the participants create shared meanings.

Potential Problems

We don't want to stop without at least mentioning some of the negative responses we've gotten to our efforts to listen dialogically. We assume that if you are actually going to try what we've outlined here, you may appreciate being forewarned about some potential difficulties.

Time   The first is most obvious: It takes *time*. Dialogic listening is not efficient. Open-endedness and play, a commitment to developing full conversation-texts and even presentness all extend and prolong talk-time. When you ask someone to "Say more," they usually do. Running with metaphors can fill up the better part of an afternoon. Be ready for that increased time commitment, and realize that when there just *isn't* time, most of your efforts to listen dialogically will be frustrated.

On the other hand, we've also found that the time issue becomes less important when we recognize (1) that the gain in quality of contact can more than balance the "loss" of time, (2) that dialogic listening generates "economies of clarity" that can increase subsequent communication efficiency, and (3) that it often doesn't take all *that* much time. By (1) we mean that yours and your conversation partner's feelings of confirmation, comfort, and even intimacy can be enhanced enough by dialogic listening that the time investment is more than worth it.

This kind of listening can also help a group handle misunderstanding before it gets serious and can help a couple build a firm foundation of mutual agreement under their relationship. Both those outcomes are examples of "economies of clarity." Our parallel here is the "economies of scale" that manufacturers get. As they get into larger-scale production—they build more widgets—their cost per widget goes down, and that's an example of "economy of scale." Similarly, as your listening builds clearer and clearer foundations, you can move through more fuzzy or problematic issues faster. That's what we mean by an "economy of clarity."

We've also found that though dialogic listening definitely takes time, it doesn't need to go on forever. A ten-minute conversation may be extended to fifteen minutes, and a one-hour meeting to an hour and twenty minutes. And usually that's not too much to pay for what you can get.

What Are You Up To?   After experiencing some openness, some presentness, a few "Keep talking'" and "Paraphrase what I just said" responses, some people want to stop the conversation to find what's going on. They perceive those communication behaviors as a little unusual, and they jump to the conclusion that we must be up to something. "Is this a study of some kind?" "Are you just answering every question with a question, or what?" Some people may perceive your efforts to co-build more talk as disruption just for the sake of disruption. Others may even hear this kind of listening as manipulative.

We believe there are two ways to respond to this challenge. The first is to examine your own motives. *Are* you "listening for effect"? *Are* you obstructing or manipulating? In order for this kind of listening to work, your attitude needs to be one of genuine open-endedness focusing on ours, and so on.

The second way is to give a brief account of what you're doing, to *meta*communicate. Metacommunication simply means communication about your communication, talk about your talk, and it can help facilitate your dialogic listening, especially where someone's feeling manipulated. Try, "I want us to talk about this more before we decide," or, "I'd really like to hear more talk; I don't think we've gotten everything out on the table yet and I'd like us to play with as full a deck as we can." You may even want to go into more detail about the value of focusing on the between and staying present—expressed in your own words, of course. Or in other situations you may want to begin a discussion with something like, "Let's just play with this question for a while. We don't have to come up out of this discussion with a solid decision or conclusion." The point is, if your motives are genuine and you can metacommunicate or give an account of your motives, you should be able to diminish much of the other person's defensiveness and sense of being manipulated.

"Give Me a Break!"   Sometimes when one of us asks another person to paraphrase what he just said or when we slow down a group discussion with metacommunication or a request for someone to "Say more," others respond with exasperation. "Ease up," they might say, "Give me a break," or "Get off my back." Dialogic listening both takes and demands effort, and sometimes people don't feel like they have the energy to invest in it. During the group experience Milt described at the beginning of this essay, his dialogic listening efforts were sometimes met with responses that indicated that Susan and Jack were just "tolerating Milt's little digressions." And that can be frustrating; it can even hurt. At other times people can simply refuse to engage with you—they ignore your request to "Say more" or they simply stop talking.

There is no easy solution to this set of problems. Another dose of self-examination can help: *Are* you coming across like a pushy true-believer? Have you let your efforts to listen dialogically become a new task that you're trying to force on the group? Sometimes "give-me-a-break" responses really mean, "Let me be lazy," and you need to gently persevere. But at other times you need to remember that all you can do is all you can do, and it's time to back off a bit.

Conclusion

We believe that dialogic listening is little different from some other approaches to listening. We experience the focus on "ours" as an actual shift of awareness, the open-ended playfulness as a real challenge, and the concentration on the between and on presentness as ways to highlight the productive, co-creating that we are engaging in with our conversation partners. We also notice some different communication behaviors, although they feel different mainly because of our shift from an empathic to a dialogic perspective, attitude, or point of view. Of the five we've discussed here, the commonest and most useful behaviors for us are "Say more," running with the other's metaphor, and the paraphrase plus.

But we don't want to overemphasize the differences. The communication attitudes and behaviors that are discussed under the headings of active and empathic listening can also promote genuine understanding. Even more important, though we've discussed these ideas and skills as an approach to dialogic *listening*, they can also serve as the guidelines for a complete approach to interpersonal communicating. This is because they are based on the works of two philosophers of dialogue, Martin Buber and Hans-Georg Gadamer. Buber's and Gadamer's writing and teaching offer an approach to all your communicating that is only partly developed and applied in what we say here about listening. It's the approach that's behind this entire book, and we hope that by the time you've read through all these materials, you'll see how these fit together. (We especially recommend that you compare this essay with the final one in the book, Buber's "Elements of the Interhuman.")

Listening is only part of the entire communication process. But if it's dialogic listening, it can promote the richest kind of interpersonal-quality contact. Listening dialogically involves focusing on what you share with the persons you are talking with, playing with the conversation in an open-ended way, concentrating mostly on the ideas talked about together, and maintaining an emphasis on "Here and now," Some ways to instill in your communication these aspects of a dialogic approach to listening are to encourage others to "Say more," to run with metaphors, to include new information in paraphrasing (and request paraphrasing from others), and to build in as much contextual information as you can to facilitate clarity. We encourage you to develop the attitudes and skills associated with a dialogic perspective in listening and see if you find them helpful.

References

1. See, for example, Lyman K. Steil, Larry L. Barker, and Kittie W. Watson, *Effective Listening: Key to Your Success* (Reading, Mass.: Addison-Wesley, 1983); Madelyn Burley-Allen, *Listening: The Forgotten Skill* (New York: Wiley, 1982); and Florence I. Wolff, Nadine C. Marsnik, William S. Tracey, and Ralph G. Nichols, *Perceptive Listening* (New York: Holt, Rinehart & Winston, 1983).
2. Steil, Barker, and Watson, p. 5.
3. Carl R. Rogers, *A Way of Being* (Boston: Houghton Mifflin, 1980), pp. 142–143.
4. Robert Bolton, "Listening Is More than Merely Hearing," in *People Skills: How to Assert Yourself, Listen to Others, and Resolve Conflicts* (Englewood Cliffs, N.J.: Prentice-Hall, 1979), p. 51.
5. See, e.g., Lawrence M. Brammer, *The Helping Relationship: Process and Skills*, 2nd ed. (Englewood Cliffs, N.J.: Prentice-Hall, 1979), Chapter 4.
6. Roger von Oech, *A Whack on the Side of the Head: How to Unlock Your Mind for Innovation* (Menlo Park, Calif.: Creative Think, 1982), pp. 29–39.
7. There is, however, a large and important "metaphoric" or "soft" side of physics, especially theoretical and nuclear physics, and of mathematics.
8. William S. Howell, *The Empathic Communicator* (Belmont, Calif.: Wadsworth, 1982), pp. 9–10.
9. We're thinking of Hans-Georg Gadamer and Paul Ricoeur. See, e.g., Gadamer's *Truth and Method* (New York: Seabury Press, 1975), pp. 91ff. and Ricoeur, "Appropriation," in *Hermeneutics and the Human Sciences*, ed. and trans. by John B. Thompson (Cambridge: Cambridge University Press, 1981), pp. 182–186.
10. G. T. Barrett-Lennard, "Dimensions of Therapist Response as Casual Factors in Therapeutic Change," *Psychological Monographs*, 76 (1962), cited in Rogers, *A Way of Being*, p. 144.

11. Martin Buber, "The Way of Man," in *Hasidism and Modern Man*, ed. and trans. Mauricₑ Friedman (New York: Harper & Row, 1958), p. 155.
12. Ibid., p. 158.
13. Our suggestion here is similar to Step 2 of Robert Bolton's discussion of "door openers."
14. Paul Ricouer, *The Rule of Metaphor: Multi-Disciplinary Studies of the Creation of Meaning in Language*, trans. Robert Czerny with Kathleen Mclaughlin and John Costello, SJ (London: Routledge and Kegan Paul, 1978).

Review Questions

1. In your own words, describe the essential features of what has been called "empathy."
2. What shortcomings of the concept of "empathy" do Milt and I discuss?
3. Paraphrase the difference we discuss between *reproductive* listening and *productive* listening.
4. Develop an example of the potter's wheel image we describe. Choose a person who's "seated at the wheel" with you (i.e., a person you're having a conversation with). Describe what the "clay" is (the conversation topic; what each of you says). Continue in this way until you've described a hypothetical conversation about this topic between the two of you using our "sculpting" metaphor.
5. What are the "three c's" we discuss? How do the three c's relate to dialogic listening?
6. Describe the distinction we make between psychology and communication.
7. What does it mean to "unify your saying, being, and doing"?
8. Describe the basic difference between a "paraphrase" and a "paraphrase plus."
9. What's "context-building"?

Probes

1. "I know you believe you understand what you think I said, but I'm not sure you realize that what you heard is not what I meant." It strikes us that dialogic listening is a good *solution* to the *problem* that this quotation describes. Do you agree? Discuss.
2. Paraphrase our point that it's impossible to "lay aside yourself." Give an example from your own experience of this impossibility.
3. How well does the "sculpting" metaphor work for you? In what ways is it especially illuminating? In what ways does it seem inappropriate? What alternatives or additional metaphors would you suggest for the process we discuss here?
4. The idea that you can work with talk itself, that it is tangible and malleable and can be productively shaped, is a little unusual for some people. How is that idea different from some of what you've been taught in the past about human communication?
5. Do you agree that there are many pressures on us today pushing us toward the three c's—certainty, closure, and control? How do they affect your communicating?
6. Give an example from your own experience of conversational *play*. Discuss it with others. Which of the characteristics of play that we discuss do you notice in your own communicating?
7. Assume you are talking with a group of friends and one of them makes a racist or sexist remark that you don't like. In this situation how might you "unify your saying, being, and doing"?
8. What happens when you try the "Say more" response we suggest?
9. Identify two metaphors in this essay that we did not discuss as examples of metaphorizing. Notice how many there are to choose from.
10. Explain what it means to shift your paraphrasing-goal from fidelity or correspondence to creativity. (And, if you want to, pinpoint which previous Probe in this set asks essentially this same question.)
11. Which of the three potential problems that we discuss seems to you to be the most difficult?

Part 3

Openness as "Exhaling"

Chapter 8

Self-Disclosure

J ohn Amodeo and Kris Wentworth are family counselors who've writ- ten a book called *Being Intimate*. This chapter of their book focuses on what they call self-revealing communication. They first repeat a very useful distinction others have made between "I statements" and "You statements." They point out that, while the difference might be obvious, the effect of using one versus the other can be profound. "You statements" are almost always heard as blaming, fault-finding, or self-centered acting-out. None of that contributes much to interpersonal communication. "I statements," on the other hand, can be heard as clean, self-revealing comments that promote inter- personal contact.

It's important to note that "I statements" aren't always heard that way. One person's "I statements" can be heard by another person as thinly-disguised criti- cisms. When this happens, the conversation partners need to work harder to develop mutual understanding. The point is, your word choice is important, but it won't guarantee success.

The second section of this article discusses several benefits of self-revealing communication. The authors describe how it can, among other things, deescalate interpersonal tension, heal the wounds between oneself and a friend or partner, and invite others to change their behavior while respecting their autonomy.

The final section focuses on an important paradox of self-disclosure that these authors call "the power of vulnerability." Many people—for example, macho males—believe that aggressive, loud posturing will always be interpreted as a sign of confidence and strength. But just a little reflection will remind you that the reverse is often true. When we see someone acting aggressive, we often understand that he or she is actually trying to mask insecurity. Belligerence is often a cover-up for fear. Vulnerability, on the other hand, can be an extremely strong posture. As John and Kris point out, "a special kind of inner strength is required to 'hold our own' as we experience and assert our genuine feelings, as opposed to aggressively reacting with blame, attacks, moralizing, or other forms of manipulation. . . ." They make some very useful points about this paradox in this article.

The essay concludes by encouraging you to consider how you might take the risk of revealing more about yourself in order to build some relationships that move toward genuine intimacy.

Self-Revealing Communication: A Vital Bridge Between Two Worlds

John Amodeo and Kris Wentworth

Structuring Our Language to Invite Contact

The complex art of verbal communication is a learned skill that can enhance intimacy and mutual understanding when the structure of our language conveys the trust-promoting attitudes of honesty, acceptance, caring, and respect. The ability to state our experience in a simple, direct, noncoercive manner can serve the dual purpose of communicating what is happening in our inner world while honoring other people's right to respond to us in a manner that preserves the integrity of their own felt experience. Integrating this respectful attitude into the very structure of our language can do much to promote trust and create genuine contact between two autonomous individuals.

Thomas Gordon, in a landmark book entitled *Parent Effectiveness Training*, describes how communication is more effective when we express ourselves using "I statements" as opposed to "you statements." "I statements," or what we will call "self-revealing communications," are those that disclose our experience without attacking others, invalidating their feelings, or criticizing them for not meeting our needs or conforming to our point of view. Self-revealing communications invite others into our tender world of feelings and meanings. They reflect a willingness to risk being vulnerable, rather than resort to strategies of control or manipulation in order to get what we want.

For example, we might say, "I'm feeling frustrated about our conversation because I imagine that I'm not being understood." This way of expression effectively says how we feel ("frustrated") and gives the additional input of sharing what this feeling means to us ("being misunderstood").

Instead of this self-disclosing communication, we could resort to a variety of what Gordon calls "you statements," or what we prefer to call "intrusive communications." For example, instead of cleanly communicating that we feel frustrated or sad, we could blame the other person for not understanding us by saying something such as, "We're not resolving our conflict because you don't listen to my side of the story!" We could also criticize the other by a hostile statement such as, "You never want to listen to me!" Or, we may wage a personal attack by responding, "You're really selfish, childish, and stupid!"

The above reactions are impulsive ways of acting out our feelings, as opposed to simply sharing them. This can quickly lead to a downward spiral in the communication process. Mistrust grows and communication falters (if it ever existed in the first place), because people then feel judged rather than respected, criticized instead of accepted, intruded upon rather than invited to openly explore disagreements. Feeling less safe to be open and vulnerable, individuals will tend to react by either increasing

Excerpts from "Self-Revealing Communication: A Vital Bridge Between Two Worlds," from *Being Intimate: A Guide to Successful Relationships* by John Amodeo and Kris Wentworth. 1986 Viking Penguin.

their verbal attacks, which can further escalate a counter-productive power struggle, or withdrawing entirely in order to protect themselves from further hurt.

Self-revealing communications reflect a wise willingness to take responsibility for how we feel, rather than transfer blame or make judgmental decrees that infringe upon people's basic humanness. For instance, we may say, "I feel hurt when you joke about my weight. That's a sensitive area because people have kidded me about it all of my life." This statement is a simple, open description of how we feel. It also offers information to the other person that may assist him or her in understanding how past experiences have contributed to our present feeling. It does not counter-attack by saying, "Well, you're pretty flabby, too!" It does not criticize by exclaiming, "You're always nagging me about my weight." It does not place demands or pose threats as by stating, "If you don't stop, you'll be sorry!" All of these intrusive statements are manipulations in that they are intended to coerce the other to change his or her behavior, rather than to simply express our feelings. Such assertions represent a lack of trust in the other person's propensity to respond favorably to us if we reveal our more tender, vulnerable feelings. And, practically speaking, these intrusive statements rarely, if ever, produce lasting changes. Although one or the other may temporarily give in, resentments will continue to mount. As the basic humanness of the organism is wounded by this judgmental, coercive process, a cycle of damaging communications is generated. Allowing this to continue, a relationship can degenerate to the point where all openness and warmth are crushed. The two vulnerable and hurting human beings then take care of themselves the best way they know how—by retreating behind walls of self-protection and defense. However, the periodic eruption of vindictive, embittered fights will reveal the layer upon layer of unresolved resentment, hurt, and mistrust. . . .

Learning to communicate in a more reflective, self-revealing manner can halt a painful escalation of interpersonal tension by removing the fuel that has been intensifying the conflict. Hostilities may then cease long enough for us to explore what is really going on—that is, the unacknowledged feelings, meanings, and unmet needs that are at the source of the difficulties. As these are openly shared, some trust may re-emerge.

Whether we long to heal the wounds with a friend or partner, improve a satisfying relationship, or initiate a new one, self-revealing communications can be instrumental in eliciting responses from others that lead to greater love and intimacy in our lives. Such expressions shine a gentle light on our inner world, offering a glimpse of what we really feel and how we see things. This more self-searching and self-disclosing approach to interpersonal relating holds the prospect that another will treat us with loving care and human sensitivity as we become willing to be transparent. Lowering our defensive shield, we open ourselves to the possibility of being seen and warmly embraced, which is our quiet hope, although we risk being hurt, which is an ever-present possibility.

Focusing attention on the dimensions of disclosing our feelings, instead of on the nearly impossible task of trying to change others' behavior, can drastically shift the typical interactional scenario. By simply sharing how we feel in response to people's words or actions, we reveal our hurt, fear, anger, or other vulnerable feelings that are evoked by their words or deeds. Communicating in this way becomes an invitation for others to sensitively respond to our feelings and concerns, and, perhaps, to voluntarily modify their behavior.

A basic assumption behind self-revealing expressiveness is that if people see who we really are, how we really feel, and what we really need, they will tend to respond to us in an accommodating manner; at ground level, people do care about one another, and wish to be helpful if they can. . . .

In order for others to care about us they need to know what we are feeling. And, rather than assume that they already understand or "should" know how we feel, it is our responsibility to tell them. Self-revealing statements can be an empowering, effective way to communicate feelings and needs. An honest self-disclosing expression of our real feelings can make the crucial difference that leads to greater trust. Being non-manipulative, such expressions encourage others to concretely express their caring for us by allowing themselves to be touched by our feelings, and, as a result, respond to us in a more loving, cooperative way.

By communicating in a more vulnerable, self-revealing manner, we give people a chance to change while respecting their autonomous right to choose whether or not they want to change or give us what we are asking for. If they minimize our concerns, resist communicating about them, or refuse to be touched by our experience, then, of course, we may not feel very safe to continue exposing our vulnerable feelings. Our sense of trust will most likely diminish because we are not receiving caring in the way we need it. A vital, growing relationship requires two individuals who are willing and able to be touched by one another's feelings and be responsive to each other's felt concerns.

The communication of feelings is best done when others have the time and interest to hear what we have to say, rather than trying to make contact during a football game or after a tiring day at work. Eliminating or minimizing the distracting influences of the television, telephone, children, or pets enables us to attend more carefully to our subtle feelings and understand each other's concerns. It is often helpful to set aside time on a regular basis, such as one evening each week, in order to discuss ongoing issues or share recent upsets so that they may be resolved before they grow into more serious conflicts.

Creating undistracted time to open to each other's feelings, can create a refreshingly safe environment in which to become better acquainted with one another, and, as trust builds, to enjoy the flourishing of love and intimacy.

The Power of Vulnerability

Although using self-revealing statements to sensitively share our feelings and needs may appear to reduce us to a weaker position in terms of getting what we want from a relationship, in reality, the opposite is true. On the surface, it may seem that we rise to a stronger position by fighting for the changes we would like to see in the other person. We often fool ourselves by thinking that if only we could assert ourselves a little more convincingly or forcefully, then the other person would finally change.

Those who have discovered the hidden power of vulnerability realize that being vulnerable does not mean being weak. In fact, a special kind of inner strength is required to "hold our own" as we experience and assert our genuine feelings, as opposed to aggressively reacting with blame, attacks, moralizing, or other forms of manipulation that create an adversarial position. Even the intense emotion of anger can be expressed "cleanly" without being contaminated by blame, criticism, or self-righteousness.

As we learn to caringly accommodate our softer feelings, we can breathe more deeply and take greater risks in relation to others. Feeling strong and confident within ourselves, our communications can embody an integrity that respects another's freedom of response while affirming our right to our feelings and to make crucial life decisions based upon our growth needs.

Responding from a confident center within our vulnerable inner world reflects a special kind of inner strength. Reacting in a demanding or hostile way usually masks a personal sore spot or long-term unexpressed and unsatisfied need. What is sometimes considered to be a "strong" or courageous position often camouflages a host of unacknowledged fears or unexplored areas within ourselves that we have yet to understand, accept, or befriend.

For example, Rose, who wanted the best for her son, Ira, pressured him to enter medical school, which he reluctantly agreed to do. Finding the stresses of school overwhelming, he wanted to drop out, a decision his mother found difficult to accept. Needing her love and respect (and having an undeveloped inner caretaker), he agreed to push ahead in school. Shortly thereafter, Ira died of cancer. Only then was Rose able to acknowledge her fear of being embarrassed or ashamed if her son did not enter a prestigious profession.

What seemed a strong position by Rose was actually a reaction to her unexplored fears of being an inadequate parent. Unskilled at contacting and communicating her more vulnerable feelings, and unwilling to trust Ira to make decisions consistent with his own best interests, she remained invested in her own decision regarding what he should do. This led to pressuring him in ways that she later regretted.

Trying to achieve resolution on the dimension of feelings, rather than being preoccupied with what we think is the "right" thing for someone to do (the dimension of behavior), is more likely to produce the changes we want. For example, Lynn became very upset when Gary became attracted to another woman and was considering becoming more deeply involved with her. Lynn was aware of her hurt while maintaining respect for his choices. She expressed her hurt and allowed herself to cry without being accusatory or demanding, although she reserved the option to move out in case she needed to take care of herself in this way.

Gary was touched by her vulnerable sharing and appreciated not being criticized or told that he was acting immaturely or insensitively—invalidating accusations that had hurt him in previous relationships. Allowing himself to be affected by her hurt, he experienced a shift from being confused about what to do to feeling a deeper sense of intimacy with her. Lynn also discovered that expressing her real feelings produced an outcome in which she felt closer to Gary. Interestingly, it is this feeling of closeness that each of them had really been wanting, and which never would have resulted had she tried to make him feel guilty or change his behavior in some coercive way. It is likely that he would have then simply rebelled against the threat to his autonomy. In other words, her willingness to be vulnerable (and not controlling) had a surprisingly powerful effect that, indirectly, led to the deeper commitment she had been wanting.

Self-revealing statements create a climate in which it is vastly easier for another to remain attentive and interested in what we are saying. Reflecting an open-handed approach, they act as a gesture of goodwill and trust. Rather than condemn, insult, or defy, they open a door through which our real selves can be seen and empathetically understood. Consequently, conflicts or differences can be more easily resolved because the other is invited to visit and participate in our inner world of feelings and meanings. . . .

As human beings we possess the unique capacity to discover a serene territory that exists somewhere beneath the biologically programmed "fight or flight" response. The key to that territory lies in our capacity to simply experience the threatening feelings that exist immediately prior to our impulse to attack or flee. The major ones, as we have been mentioning throughout, are fear (or terror), sadness (or grief), hurt (or woundedness), anger (or rage), embarrassment (or shame), loneliness (or isolation), and longing (or intense desire). Personal growth is largely a function of our capacity to be with these feelings in an accepting, sensitive manner. The goal is to befriend them, not transcend them.

The ability to be caretakers for ourselves in regard to these feelings—that is, to simply be with them in an allowing way—can have a surprisingly transformative effect upon our lives and relationships. When we become capable of welcoming and being with these feelings as they arise within ourselves, our hearts and minds can remain open as we experience difficulties in relation to another person. As we face the "demons" (scary unwanted feelings) within ourselves and communicate these feelings to another, an interesting thing tends to happen. Being with and sharing intense feelings with another person are two essential ways of moving toward a deep place of restful contact within ourselves and in relation to another being. As we learn to stabilize in our capacity to identify and be present to a full range of human feelings, we become more and more at home with ourselves. From this base we can then openly communicate our experience to another person. Doing so, we come to know and understand one another more deeply. Communication becomes the bridge between our two separate worlds.

Those moments during which basic emotions, insistent needs, and personal concerns and dissatisfactions are no longer coursing through us are rare ones. However, these quiet moments are often the most rich and meaningful ones of our lives. We sometimes experience this after a poignant sharing of threatening or tender feelings. Engaging one another in a real, honest manner, we may find that communication at times, progresses into a non-verbal sense of contact or intimacy that can be referred to as a state of union or an experience of love. Free of unsettling feelings or undercurrents of dissatisfaction, we simply become present with one another—two beings free of struggle and pretensions, simply breathing and being together. . . .

Review Questions

1. When John and Kris discuss how to structure our language to invite contact, which linguistic element do they focus on?
2. According to the authors, how can you-messages lead to "a downward spiral in the communication process"?
3. List the benefits of self-revealing communication that the authors discuss.
4. What is the paradox of power and vulnerability?
5. What do the authors mean when they say that self-revealing communication can help us respond in ways that involve neither "fight nor flight"?

Probes

1. Some people argue that you cannot actually change other people; the only person you can change is yourself. Do John and Kris appear to agree or disagree with this generalization? How does their position on this issue affect what they say about self-revealing communication?
2. Recount an example that you either experienced or observed where vulnerability was powerful. What features of the communication situation helped it be interpreted that way?

3. How realistic do you think these authors are about self-revealing communication? Is the position they take a naive one? Or do you think you can apply their advice in communication situations you experience?

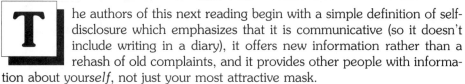 he authors of this next reading begin with a simple definition of self-disclosure which emphasizes that it is communicative (so it doesn't include writing in a diary), it offers new information rather than a rehash of old complaints, and it provides other people with information about your*self*, not just your most attractive mask.

They use a well-known diagram called the "Johari window" to describe what they mean by your "self." This diagram clarifies how each of us is made up of open, blind, hidden, and unknown components, and that disclosure consists in moving information from the hidden to the open quadrant.

McKay, Davis, and Fanning then briefly sketch five rewards of self-disclosure and several blocks that inhibit it. This part of their discussion can help you see that your disclosure decisions can often be made by balancing what you believe are the rewards and costs of your choice.

The chapter also points out that self-disclosure is more of a state than a trait phenomenon. This just means that, although people have general tendencies to disclose a lot or a little (traits), most of our choices are strongly affected by the persons we're talking with and the situations we're in (states). The authors also suggest that from age 17 to 50 most people increase the amount they disclose, and from age 50 on, they decrease it.

The heart of this reading is a discussion of five "rules for effective expression." As you can gather from the title, this is a pretty prescriptive list. McKay, Davis, and Fanning have some opinions about how disclosure can help or hinder good communication, and they aren't bashful about sharing them. I don't agree with everything they say, but I respect their clarity and directness, and I think it can be very useful to read, think about, and discuss their advice, even if you end up disagreeing with some of it.

For example, their first rule is that disclosure should be direct, which means that you don't assume people know what you think or want; you try to *tell* them. They admit that directness can be risky, but they explain how it's less risky than indirectness.

The second rule is that messages should be immediate, rather than delayed or "gunnysacked." And the third is that disclosure should be clear rather than vague or abstract. They offer six tips for achieving the kind of clarity they advise. Don't ask questions, they say, when you need to make a statement. I've made this same point in another book when I've discouraged people from using "pseudoquestions"—statements masquerading as questions. But I've also been reminded by students reading my book that sometimes strong statements can be heard less defensively when they're couched tentatively, as questions. So this is one piece of McKay, Davis, and Fanning's advice I'd take with a grain of salt.

I like the authors' suggestions to "keep your messages congruent" and "avoid double messages." I also think it's helpful, as they put it, to "be clear about your wants and feelings." But I've found that it's not easy to do this, and you may have discovered this, too. It takes a great deal of mature self-awareness to constantly know for sure what one wants and feels.

I agree with the idea behind their suggestion to "distinguish between observations and thoughts," but I don't think it's literally possible to do what they say. As the readings in Chapter 6 emphasize, our perceptions are always affected by our backgrounds and agendas—always. We can't really follow these authors' advice to separate what we "see and hear" from our judgments, theories, and beliefs. They're always mixed together. On the other hand, I think it *is* helpful to try to stick as closely as possible to what we've observed and to be aware of the ways our perceptions are biased.

I also think these authors' notion of "straight messages" is helpful. It's not easy to make the stated purpose of your talk "identical with the real purpose," but it is a worthy goal to work toward. In order to succeed, you need to know at each point along the way *why* you are saying what you're saying in the way that you're saying it. Most of us aren't perfect at this kind of clarity. But when we move in this direction, our communication is more understandable and "clean."

Their final suggestion is that messages should be supportive. They remind us of some of the pitfalls of win/lose communicating, and underscore the value of avoiding, for example, global labels, sarcasm, threats, and dragging up the past.

Like me, you may find yourself agreeing with some of what these authors suggest and disagreeing with the rest. But I think you'll find that the time and effort you invest in working with these ideas will be well-spent.

Self Disclosure and Expressiveness

Matthew McKay, Martha Davis, and Patrick Fanning

Self disclosure may be as scary to you as skydiving without a parachute. You hold back because you anticipate rejection or disapproval. But you miss a lot. Self disclosure makes relationships exciting and builds intimacy. It clarifies and enlivens. Without self disclosure, you are isolated in your private experience.

You can't help disclosing yourself. You do it whenever you're around other people. Even if you ignore them, your silence and posture are disclosing something. The question isn't whether to disclose yourself, but how to do it appropriately and effectively.

For the purposes of this chapter, self disclosure is simply *communicating information about yourself*. Contained in that short definition are some important implications.

First of all, communication implies another human being on the receiving end of your disclosure. Introspection and writing about yourself in a journal or diary won't pass as self disclosure. Communication also implies disclosure by nonverbal language such as gestures, posture, and tone of voice. Nonverbal language tends to include a lot of unintentional slips.

Information in the definition implies that what is disclosed is new knowledge to the other person, not a rehash of old themes and stories. The information can take the form of facts you have observed and are pointing out, feelings you had in the past or are experiencing now, your thoughts about yourself or others, and your desires or needs in the past or present.

The key word in the definition is *yourself*. This means your true being. Self disclosure is not a cloud of lies or distortions, or an attractive mask.

To better understand this "self" that is being disclosed, imagine that your entire being is represented by a circle, divided into quadrants like this:

The first quadrant is your Open Self. It contains all your conscious actions and statements. The second is your Blind Self, which is comprised of things others can find

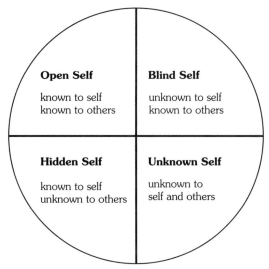

(Adapted from the Johari Window, presented in Luft, Joseph. *Group Process: An Introduction to Group Dynamics.* Palo Alto: National Press Books, 1970. p11.)

out about you that you are unaware of: habits, mannerisms, defense mechanisms, flight strategies. The third quadrant is your Hidden Self. This includes all your secrets— everything you think, feel, and desire that you keep to youself. The fourth quadrant is your Unknown Self. Since this self is by definition unknown, we can only assume its existence and give it names like the unconscious or subconscious. Dreams, drug trips, and mystical experiences are the strongest evidence for the existence of the Unknown Self.

These are not rigid compartments. Observations, thoughts, feelings, and wants are constantly moving from one area to another as you go about your daily routine. Everything you see and hear and touch in the outside world is taken into the Hidden

Self. Some is forgotten, which may mean that it goes down into the Unknown Self. Some experiences contribute to your continuing unconscious habits, and thus move into your Blind Self. Some things you remember but never reveal, just leaving them in the Hidden Self. And some things that you notice you pass on to others, moving them into the Open Self. When you have an insight about how you operate in the world, you move it from the Blind to the Hidden Self. Sharing the insight with someone moves it into the Open Self.

The movement that this chapter studies is the shift of information about your observations, feelings, thoughts, and needs from the Hidden to the Open Self. This is self disclosure. If you are good at self disclosure, your Open Self quadrant is large compared to the other quadrants. The larger your Open Self, the more likely you will be to reap the rewards of self disclosure.

Rewards of Self Disclosure

Accurately revealing who you are is hard work. Sometimes you think, "Why struggle to explain? Why risk rejection?" And yet the need to be close to others, to let them inside keeps reemerging. Some of the things that make self-disclosure worth the trouble are:

Increased Self-Knowledge

It's paradoxical but true that you know yourself to the extent that you are known. Your thoughts, feelings, and needs often remain vague and clouded until you put them into words. The process of making someone else understand you demands that you clarify, define, elaborate, and draw conclusions. Expressing your needs, for example, gives them shape and color, adds details, and points up inconsistencies and possible areas of conflict that you need to resolve.

Closer Intimate Relationships

Knowledge of yourself and the other person is basic to an intimate relationship. If you are both willing to disclose your true selves, a synergistic deepening of the relationship develops. If one or both of you keep large parts withheld, the relationship will be correspondingly shallow and unsatisfying.

Improved Communication

Disclosure breeds disclosure. As you make yourself available to others, they are encouraged to open up in response. The range of topics available for discussion broadens, even with those who are not particularly intimate with you. The depth of communication on a given topic deepens too, so that you get more than mere facts and opinions from others. They become willing to share their feelings, their deeply held convictions, and their needs.

Lighter Guilt Feelings

Guilt is a hybrid emotion composed of anger at yourself and fear of retribution for something you have done, failed to do, or thought. Guilt is often unreasonable and always painful. One thing that can relieve the pain a little is disclosure. Disclosing what you have done or thought lightens the guilt feeling in two ways: (1) You no longer have to expend energy to keep the transgression hidden. (2) When the thing you feel guilty about is disclosed, you can look at it more objectively. You can get feedback. Here is an opportunity to examine whether the guilt is justified, or whether your rules and values are too strict, too unforgiving.

Disclosure as first aid for guilt is institutionalized in several forms: Catholics confess, Protestants witness, AA members declare themselves alcoholics, and those in therapy relive traumatic events. But you don't need a priest or a therapist to experience the healing effects of disclosure. A good friend will do.

More Energy

It takes energy to keep important information about yourself hidden. Suppose you quit your job and go home to your family as usual, making no mention of your impending poverty. Here's what happens: you don't notice that your wife has a new haircut, that your favorite dinner is on the table, or that the bathroom has been painted. In fact, you're so concerned with keeping your secret, you can barely notice anything. You are silent, withdrawn, grouchy. Nothing is fun. Life is a burden. All your energy is drained. Until you unburden yourself, you are a walking corpse.

When a conversation seems dead, boring, and hard to keep going, ask yourself if there's something you're withholding. Unexpressed feelings and needs tend to simmer. They build up inside you until you lose spontaneity and your conversation takes on all the liveliness of a funeral oration. That's one way to tell if you should reveal a secret: if withheld feelings or needs keep cropping up to deaden your relationship.

Blocks to Self Disclosure

Since self disclosure is so rewarding, why doesn't everybody tell everybody else everything all the time? In fact, there are some powerful sources of resistance to self disclosure that often keep you huddled in your Hidden Self.

There is a societal bias against self disclosure. It isn't considered "nice" to talk about yourself too much, or to discuss your feelings or needs outside a narrow family circle.

You often don't disclose yourself out of fear: fear of rejection, fear of punishment, fear of being talked about behind your back, or fear that someone will take advantage of you. Someone might laugh, or say no, or leave. If you reveal one negative trait, they will imagine you're all bad. If you reveal something positive, you might be accused of bragging. If you take a stand, you might have to do something about it—vote, contribute, volunteer, or get involved in other people's troubles. Finally, you may be afraid of self-knowledge itself. You instinctively know that by disclosing you will come to know yourself better. You suspect that there are some unpleasant truths about yourself that you would rather not be aware of.

Optimal Levels of Self Disclosure

Some people are just more extroverted and forthcoming about themselves than others. Their Open Selves are relatively larger:

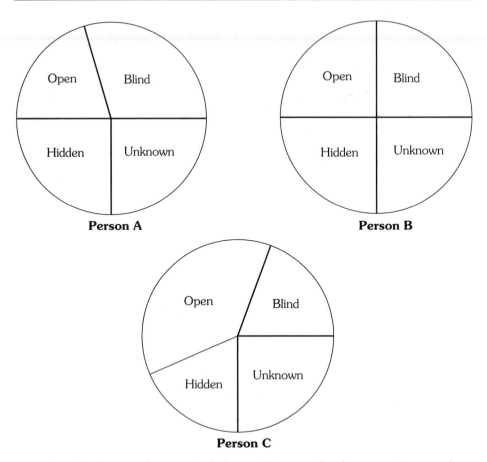

Person A

Person B

Person C

Actually, how much you reveal of yourself is not a fixed quantity. You may have a constant tendency to be more open or reserved than the next guy, but within your range of openness you fluctuate depending on your mood, whom you're talking to, and what you're talking about. The following diagrams represent the same person in different conversations:

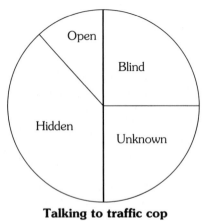

Talking to traffic cop

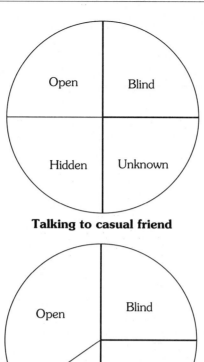

Talking to casual friend

Talking to lover

Research in self disclosure confirms what common sense suggests. You are more open with your mate, certain family members, and your close friends. You are more willing to disclose your preferences in clothes and foods than your financial status or sexual preferences. In some moods you don't want to tell anyone anything. As you age from seventeen to fifty you'll probably increase your average level of self disclosure, and become more reserved after fifty.

Healthy self disclosure is a matter of balance, of learning when to tell what to whom. Generally speaking, the more information you consistently move into the Open Self, the better your communication will be. The more you keep hidden or remain blind to, the less effective your communication will be. Beware of extremes. If your Open Self is too large, you'll be a garrulous, inappropriate blabbermouth; if too small, you'll be closed and secretive. If your Blind Self is too large, you'll be oblivious to how you appear in the world. Unknown to you, you'll get a reputation as a bully, a "space cadet," a "tight wad," and so on. If your Blind Self is too small, you'll be an over-analyzed self-awareness addict. If your Hidden Self is too large, you will be withdrawn and out of reach; if too small you will be untrustworthy—no secret will be safe with you.

Rules for Effective Expression
Messages Should Be Direct

The first requirement for effective self-expression is knowing when something needs to be said. This means that you don't assume people know what you think or want.

Indirectness can be emotionally costly. Here are a few examples. One man whose wife divorced him after fifteen years complained that she had no right to call him undemonstrative. "She knew I loved her. I didn't have to say it in so many words. A thing like that is obvious." But it wasn't obvious. His wife withered emotionally without direct expression of his affection. A woman who had been distressed by her child's performance in school stopped nagging when his grades went up. She was surprised to learn that her son felt unappreciated and wanted some direct approval. A man who had developed a chronic back problem was afraid to ask for help with gardening and household maintenance. He suffered through these tasks in pain and experienced a growing irritation and resentment toward his family. A fifteen-year-old retreated to her room when her divorced mother became interested in a new man. She complained of headaches and excused herself whenever the boyfriend arrived. Her mother, who once told the children they would always come first, assumed that her daughter was just embarrassed and would soon get over it.

These are all examples of people who have something important to communicate. But they don't know it. They assume others realize how they feel. Communicating directly means you don't make any assumptions. In fact, you should assume that people are poor mind readers and haven't the faintest idea what goes on inside you.

Some people are aware of the times when they need to communicate, but are afraid to do so. Instead they try hinting, or telling third parties in hope that the target person will eventually hear. This indirectness is risky. Hints are often misinterpreted or ignored. One woman kept turning the sound down on the TV during commercials. She hoped her husband would take the hint and converse a little at the breaks. Instead he read the sports page until she finally blew up at him. Third-party communications are extremely dangerous because of the likelihood that your message will be distorted. Even if the message is accurately delivered, no one wants to hear about your anger, disappointment, or even your love secondhand.

Messages Should Be Immediate

If you're hurt or angry, or needing to change something, delaying communication will often exacerbate your feelings. Your anger may smoulder, your frustrated need become a chronic irritant. What you couldn't express at the moment will be communicated later in subtle or passive-aggressive ways. One woman was quite hurt at the thought of not being invited to Thanksgiving at her sister's house. She said nothing, but broke a date they had to go to the planetarium and "forgot" to send a Christmas card.

Sometimes unexpressed feeling is gunnysacked to the point where a small transgression triggers a major dumping of the accumulated rage and hurt. These dumping episodes alienate family and friends. A hospital ward secretary had a reputation with peers for being dangerous and volatile. For months she would be sweet, considerate, and accommodating. But sooner or later the explosion came. A slight criticism would be answered with megatons of gripes and resentments.

There are two main advantages to immediate communication: (1) Immediate feedback increases the likelihood that people will learn what you need and adjust their behavior accordingly. This is because a clear relationship is established between what they do (for example, driving too fast) and the consequences (your expressed anxiety). (2) Immediate communication increases intimacy because you share your responses now. You don't wait three weeks for things to get stale. Here-and-now communications are more exciting and serve to intensify your relationships.

Messages Should Be Clear

A clear message is a complete and accurate reflection of your thoughts, feelings, needs, and observations. You don't leave things out. You don't fudge by being vague or abstract. Some people are afraid to say what they really mean. They talk in muddy, theoretical jargon. Everything is explained by "vibes" or by psychological interpretations. One woman who was afraid to tell her boyfriend she was turned off by public petting said that she felt "a little strange" that day and thought that her parents' upcoming visit was "repressing her sexuality." This ambiguous message allowed her boyfriend to interpret her discomfort as a temporary condition. He never learned her true needs.

Keeping your messages clear depends on awareness. You have to know what you've observed, and then how you reacted to it. What you see and hear in the outside world is so easily confused with what you think and feel inside. Separating these elements will go a long way toward helping you express yourself clearly.

Here are some tips for staying clear:

1. Don't ask questions when you need to make a statement.   Husband to wife: "Why do you have to go back to school? You have plenty of things to keep you busy." The statement hidden in the question is "I'm afraid if you go back to school I won't see you enough, I'll feel lonely. As you grow in independence I'll feel less control over the direction of our lives."

Wife to husband: "Do you think we need to make an appearance at your boss's barbeque today?" Imbedded in the question is the unexpressed need to relax and putter in the garden. By failing to plead her case clearly, her husband can either miss or safely ignore her needs.

Daughter to father: "Are we going to have a little three-foot tree this year?" What she thinks but doesn't say is that she likes the big trees seen at friends' houses— the ones full of lights and tinsel around which the family gathers. She wishes that her family did more things together, and thinks Christmas decorating would be a good place to start.

Father to son: "How much did that paint job cost?" He really wants to talk about the fact that his son lives above his means, and then borrows from mom without any intention of paying back. He's worried about his son's relationship to money and angry because he feels circumvented.

2. Keep your messages congruent.   The content, your tone of voice, and your body language should all fit together. If you congratulate someone on getting a fellowship, his response is congruent if the voice, facial gestures, and spoken message all reflect pleasure. Incongruence is apparent if he thanks you with a frown, suggesting that he doesn't really want the compliment.

Incongruence confuses communication. Congruence promotes clarity and understanding. A man who spent the day in his delivery truck arrived home to a request that he make a run to the supermarket. His response was, "Sure, whatever you want." But his tone was sarcastic and his body slumped. His wife got the message and went herself. But she was irritated by the sarcastic tone and later started a fight about the dishes. A model asked soothingly to hear about her roommate's "boyfriend in trouble." But while the story unfolded, her eyes flitted always to the mirror and she sat on the edge of her chair. Her voice said "I care" but her body said, "I'm bored, hurry up."

3. Avoid double messages.   Double messages are like kicking a dog and petting it at the same time. They occur when you say two contradictory things at once. Husband to wife: "I want to take you, I do. I'll be lonely without you. But I don't think the convention will be much fun. Really, you'd be bored to death." This is a double message because on the surface the husband seems to want his wife's company. But when you read between the lines, it's evident that he's trying to discourage her from coming.

Father to son: "Go ahead, have a good time. By the way, I noticed your report card has some real goof-off grades. What are you doing about them?" This is a rather obvious double message, but the effect is confusing. One message undercuts the other, and the son is left unclear about his father's real position. The most malignant double messages are the "come close, go away" and "I love you, I hate you" messages. These communications are found in parent-child and lover relationships, and inflict heavy psychological damage.

4. Be clear about your wants and feelings.   Hinting around about your feelings and needs may seem safer than stating them clearly. But you end up confusing the listener. Friend to friend: "Why don't you quit volunteering at that crazy free clinic?" The clear message would be "I'm afraid for you struggling in that conflict-ridden place. I think you are exhausting yourself, and I miss the days when we had time to spend an afternoon together. I want you to protect your health and have more time for me."

Husband to wife: "I see the professors and their wives at the faculty party, and I shudder at some of the grotesque relationships." The real message that couldn't be said was "When I see that terrible unhappiness, I realize what a fine life we have and how much I love you."

Mother to daughter: "I hope you visit grandma this week." On the surface this seems straightforward, but underneath lurks the guilt and anxiety she feels about grandma's loneliness. She worries about the old woman's health and, without explaining any of this, badgers her daughter to make frequent visits.

Two lovers: "I waited while you were on the phone and now our dinners are cold." The underlying statement is "I wonder how much you care about me when you take a phone call in the middle of dinner. I'm feeling hurt and angry."

5. Distinguish between observations and thoughts.   You have to separate what you see and hear from your judgments, theories, beliefs, and opinions. "I see you've been fishing with Joe again" could be a straight-forward observation. But in the context of a longstanding conflict about Joe, it becomes a barbed conclusion. Review the section on contaminated messages for more discussion of this issue.

6. Focus on one thing at a time. This means that you don't start complaining about your daughter's Spanish grades in the middle of a discussion about her boyfriend's marijuana habits. Stick with the topic at hand until both parties have made clear, whole messages. If you get unfocused, try using one of the following statements to clarify the message: "I'm feeling lost . . . what are we really talking about?" or "What do you hear me saying? I sense we've gotten off the track."

Messages Should Be Straight

A straight message is one in which the stated purpose is identical with the real purpose of the communication. Disguised intentions and hidden agendas destroy intimacy because they put you in a position of manipulating rather than relating to people. You can check if your messages are straight by asking these two questions: (1) Why am I saying this to this person? (2) Do I want him or her to hear it, or something else?

Hidden agendas are dealt with at length in another chapter. They are usually necessitated by feelings of inadequacy and poor self-worth. You have to protect yourself, and that means creating a certain image. Some people take the *I'm good* position. Most of their communications are subtle opportunities to boast. Others play the *I'm good but you aren't* game. They are very busy putting everyone down and presenting themselves, by implication, as smarter, stronger, more successful. Agendas such as *I'm helpless, I'm fragile, I'm tough*, and *I know it all* are good defensive maneuvers to keep you from getting hurt. But the stated purpose of your communication is always different from your real purpose. While you are ostensibly discoursing on intricate Middle East politics, the real purpose is to show how knowledgeable you are. We all succumb to little vanities, but when your communications are dominated by one such agenda, you aren't being straight.

Being straight also means that you tell the truth. You state your real needs and feelings. You don't say you're tired and want to go home if you're really angry and want more attention. You don't angle for compliments or reassurance by putting yourself down. You don't say you're anxious about going to a couples therapist when actually you feel angry about being pushed to go. You don't describe your feelings as depression because your mate prefers that to irritation. You don't say you enjoy visiting your girlfriend's brother when the experience is one step below fingernails scraping on the chalkboard. Lies cut you off from others. Lies keep them from knowing what you need or feel. You lie to be nice, you lie to protect yourself, but you end up feeling alone with your closest friends.

Messages Should Be Supportive

Being supportive means you want the other person to be able to hear you without getting blown away. Ask yourself, "Do I want my message to be heard defensively or accurately? Is my purpose to hurt someone, to aggrandize myself, or to communicate?"

If you prefer to hurt your listener with your messages, use these six tactics:

1. Global labels. Stupid, ugly, selfish, evil, asinine, mean, disgusting, worthless and lazy are a few of the huge list of hurtful words. The labels are most damaging when used in a "You're a fool, a coward, a drunk" and so on format. Making your point that way creates a total indictment of the person, instead of just a commentary on some specific behavior.

2. Sarcasm.   This form of humor very clearly tells the listener that you have contempt for him. It's often a cover for feelings of anger and hurt. The effect on the listener is to push him away or make him angry.

3. Dragging up the past.   This destroys any chance of clarifying how each of you feels about a present situation. You rake over old wounds and betrayals instead of examining your current dilemma.

4. Negative comparisons.   "Why aren't you generous like your brother?" "Why don't you come home at six like other men?" "Sarah's getting A's and you can't even get a B in music appreciation." Comparisons are deadly because they not only contain "you're bad" messages, but they make people feel inferior to friends and family.

5. Judgmental "you messages."   These are attacks that use an accusing form. "You don't love me anymore." "You're never here when I need you." "You never help around the house." "You turn me on about as much as a 1964 Plymouth."

6. Threats.   If you want to bring meaningful communication to a halt, get out the big guns. Threaten to move out, threaten to quit, threaten violence. Threats are good topic changers, because instead of talking about uncomfortable issues you can talk about the hostile things you plan to do.

Communicating supportively means that you avoid "win/lose" and "right/wrong" games. These are interactions where the intention of one or both players is "winning" or proving the other person "wrong" rather than sharing and understanding. Your intention is communication will guide you toward a predictable result. Real communication produces understanding and closeness while "win/lose" games produce warfare and distance. Ask yourself, "Do I want to win or do I want to communicate? Do I want to be right or do I want mutual understanding?" If you find yourself feeling defensive and wanting to criticize the other person, that's a clue that you're playing "win/lose."

Win/lose interactions can be avoided by sticking rigidly to the whole-message structure. You can also get around the win/lose pattern by making clear observations on your process: "I'm feeling pretty defensive and angry right now, and it looks like I've fallen into the old win/lose syndrome."

Review Questions

1. Paraphrase the points these authors make when they define self-disclosure as "communicating information about yourself."
2. What do the authors say is an example of moving some information from the Blind to the Hidden Self?
3. What is the movement among Johari quadrants that this chapter studies?
4. Paraphrase this statement: "You know yourself to the extent that you are known."
5. According to these authors, what is the relationship between disclosure and energy—personal energy and conversational energy?
6. What are the advantages to making messages immediate?
7. Add two examples from your own recent communication experience to the authors' list of questions that really make statements.
8. What's a "double message"?

Probes

1. Draw a Johari window that represents your self in your communication with one of your parents. Draw another one that shows what your self looks like in your relationship with a dating partner, lover, or spouse. What do you notice about the differences?
2. "Disclosure breeds disclosure," these authors note. This is obviously true much of the time. When does it work the other way around? When can disclosure *inhibit* reciprocal disclosure?
3. These authors don't discuss the block to self-disclosure that's sometimes stated this way: "If I tell people too much about who I am, pretty soon I'll be all 'out there' or 'used up'; there won't be anything left that's uniquely and privately *me*." How do you respond to this block?
4. In what ways is your disclosure a trait (a feature of your permanent personality) and in what ways is a state (a response to specific situations)?
5. "Communicating directly," the authors write, "means you don't make any assumptions." How do you respond to this claim? *Is* it desirable to reduce the assumptions you make? Is it possible not to make *any* assumptions?
6. In my introduction to this reading, I note my reservations about these authors' advice to "distinguish between observations and thoughts." What do *you* think about this advice?
7. How culturally limited are these authors' communication suggestions? Are "being clear," "being straight," and "being supportive" really only appropriate in Western white cultures? Or does this advice apply in other cultures, too?

I n this reading Neil Postman presents the viewpoint of "the opposition." Postman offers a sensible and compelling argument *against* the notion that all we have to do to solve our problems is to communicate more effectively. Better communication, he says, is *not* a panacea, especially if by better communication we mean self-disclosing, that is, "saying what's on your mind," and "expressing your feelings honestly."

Postman reminds us, as do some communication researchers, that one of the important functions of speech communication is concealment.[1] Civility is a necessary part of society, he argues, and civility sometimes requires that we keep our feelings to ourselves. It's pretty hard to ignore the way he makes his point; as he puts it in one place, "There is no dishonesty in a baboon cage, and yet, for all that, it holds only baboons."

Postman maintains that when people disagree fundamentally—for example, about racial issues—"honest openness may not help at all." He writes, "There is no good reason . . . for parents always to be honest with their children."

You may find it tempting to dismiss Postman as some kind of communication bigot and to reject his remarks as inflammatory hate-mongering. Try not to take that *easy* way out. His main point is, as he puts it, "that 'authentic communication' is a two-edged sword," and I think that's an idea that's well worth thinking about and discussing.

I feel frustrated and disappointed when my students—or readers of this book—conclude that the main message in all of this is just that we need to "be open and honest." That's a vast oversimplification, and it's also a dangerous one. One of Postman's most important points is that in any given situation we do not have *an* "honest feeling" but a complex of often conflicting "authentic" feelings.

So the expression of one may be no more or less "honest" or "dishonest" than the expression of another.

I hope this essay will prompt the kind of reflection and discussion that can move well beyond a simplistic belief in the universal value of "being open and honest."

Reference

1. Malcolm Parks, "Ideology in Interpersonal Communication: Off the Couch and into the World," *Communication Yearbook 5*, ed. Michael Burgoon (New Brunswick, N.J.: Transaction Books, 1982), pp. 79–107.

The Communication Panacea

Neil Postman

In the search for the Holy Grail of complete harmony, liberation, and integrity, which it is the duty of all true Americans to conduct, adventurers have stumbled upon a road sign which appears promising. It says in bold letters, **"All problems arise through lack of communication."** Under it, in smaller print, it says: "Say what is on your mind. Express your feelings honestly. This way lies the answer." A dangerous road, it seems to me. It is just as true to say, This way lies disaster.

I would not go so far as Oliver Goldsmith, who observed that the principal function of language is to *conceal* our thoughts. But I do think that concealment is one of the important functions of language, and on no account should it be dismissed categorically. As I have tried to make clear earlier, semantic environments have legitimate and necessary purposes of their own which do not always coincide with the particular and pressing needs of every individual within them. One of the main purposes of many of our semantic environments, for example, is to help us maintain a minimum level of civility in conducting our affairs. Civility requires not that we deny our feelings, only that we keep them to ourselves when they are not relevant to the situation at hand. Contrary to what many people believe, Freud does not teach us that we are "better off" when we express our deepest feelings. He teaches exactly the opposite: that civilization is impossible without inhibition. Silence, reticence, restraint, and yes, even dishonesty can be great virtues, in certain circumstances. They are, for example, frequently necessary in order for people to work together harmoniously. To learn how to say no is important in achieving personal goals, but to learn how to say yes when you want to say no is at the core of civilized behavior. There is no dishonesty in a baboon cage, and yet, for all that, it holds only baboons.

Now there are, to be sure, many situations in which trouble develops because some people are unaware of what other people are thinking and feeling. "If I'd only *known* that!" the refrain goes, when it is too late. But there are just as many situations which would get worse, not better, if everyone knew exactly what everyone else was thinking. I have in mind, for example, a conflict over school busing that occurred some time ago in New York City but has been replicated many times in different places. Whites against blacks. The whites maintained that they did not want their children to go to other neighborhoods. They wanted them close at hand, so that the children could walk home for lunch and enjoy all the benefits of a "neighborhood school." The blacks maintained that the schools their children attended were run-down and had inadequate facilities. They wanted their children to have the benefits of a good educational plant. It was most fortunate, I think, that these two groups were not reduced to "sharing with each other" their real feelings about the matter. For the whites' part, much of it amounted to, "I don't want to live, eat, or do anything else with niggers. Period." For the blacks' part, some of it, at least, included, "You honky bastards have had your own way at my expense for so long that I couldn't care less what happens to you or your children." Had these people communicated such feelings to each other, it is more than likely that there could have been no resolution to this problem. . . . As it was, the issue could be dealt with *as if* such hatred did not exist, and therefore, a reasonable political compromise was reached.

It is true enough, incidentally, that in this dispute and others like it, the charge of racism was made. But the word *racism*, for all its ominous overtones, is a euphemism. It conceals more than it reveals. What Americans call a *racist* public remark is something like "The Jews own the banks" or "The blacks are lazy." Such remarks are bad enough. But they are honorifics when compared to the "true" feelings that underlie them.

I must stress that the "school problem" did not arise in the first place through lack of communication. It arose because of certain historical, sociological, economic, and political facts which could not be made to disappear through the "miracle of communication." Sometimes, the less people know about other people, the better off everyone is. In fact, political language at its best can be viewed as an attempt to find solutions to problems by circumventing the authentic hostile feelings of concerned parties.

In our personal lives, surely each of us must have ample evidence by now that the capacity of words to exacerbate, wound, and destroy is at least as great as their capacity to clarify, heal, and organize. There is no good reason, for example, for parents always to be honest with their children (or their children always to be honest with them). The goal of parenthood is not to be honest, but to raise children to be loving, generous, confident, and competent human beings. Where full and open revelation helps to further that end, it is "good." Where it would defeat it, it is stupid talk. Similarly, there is no good reason why your boss always needs to know what you are thinking. It might, in the first place, scare him out of his wits and you out of a job. Then, too, many of the problems you and he have do not arise from lack of communication, but from the nature of the employer-employee relationship, which sometimes means that the less money you make, the more he does. This is a "problem" for a labor organizer, not a communication specialist.

Some large American corporations have, of late, taken the line that "improved communication" between employees and management will solve important problems. But very often this amounts to a kind of pacification program, designed to direct attention away from fundamental economic relationships. It is also worth noting that a number of such corporations have ceased to hold "communication seminars" in which executives were encouraged to express their "true" feelings. What happened, apparently, is that some of them decided they hated their jobs (or each other) and quit.

Whether this is "good" or not depends on your point of view. The corporations don't think it's so good, and probably the families of the men don't either.

The main point I want to make is that "authentic communication" is a two-edged sword. In some circumstances, it helps. In others, it defeats. This is a simple enough idea, and sensible people have always understood it. I am stressing it here only because there has grown up in America something amounting to a holy crusade in the case of Communication. One of the terms blazoned on its banners is the phrase *real* (or *authentic*) feelings. Another is the motto "Get in touch with your feelings!" From what I have been able to observe, this mostly means expressing anger and hostility. When is the last time someone said to you, "Let me be *lovingly* frank"? The expression of warmth and gentleness is usually considered to be a facade, masking what you are really thinking. To be certified as authentically in touch with your feelings, you more or less have to be nasty. Like all crusades, the Communication Crusade has the magical power to endow the most barbarous behavior with a purity of motive that excuses and obscures just about all its consequences. No human relationship is so tender, apparently, that it cannot be "purified" by sacrificing one or another of its participants on the altar of "Truth." Or, to paraphrase a widely known remark on another subject, "Brutality in the cause of honesty needs no defense." The point is that getting in touch with your feelings often amounts to losing touch with the feelings of others. Or at least losing touch with the purposes for which people have come together.

A final word on the matter of "honesty." As I have said before, human purposes are exceedingly complex—multileveled and multilayered. This means that, in any given situation, one does not have *an* "honest feeling," but a whole complex of different feelings. And, more often than not, some of these feelings are in conflict. If anger predominates at one instant, this does not mean it is more "authentic" than the love or sorrow or concern with which it is mingled. And the expression of the anger, alone, is no less "dishonest" than any other partial representation of what one is feeling. By *dishonesty*, then, I do not merely mean saying the opposite of what you believe to be true. Sometimes it is necessary to do even this in the interests of what you construe to be a worthwhile purpose. But more often, dishonesty takes the form of your simply not saying *all* that you are thinking about or feeling in a given situation. And, since our motives and feelings are never all that clear, to our own eyes in any case, most of us are "dishonest" in this sense most of the time. To be aware of this fact and to temper one's talk in the light of it is a sign of what we might call "intelligence." Other words for it are discretion and tact.

The relevant point is that communication is most sensibly viewed as a means through which desirable ends may be achieved. As an end in itself, it is disappointing, even meaningless. And it certainly does not make a very good deity.

Review Questions

1. What does Postman mean by "civility"?
2. Some persons insist that *whenever* humans disagree, to *some* extent there's a communication problem. Postman clearly doesn't agree. What is his position on this issue?
3. True or false: Postman urges the reader *not* always to "be honest." Explain.
4. What does Postman mean by "the Communication Crusade?" Where have you experienced this "crusade"?

Probes

1. Postman may sound like he is disagreeing with everything written by the other authors in this chapter. But I'm not so sure. What specific comments and suggestions by John Amodeo and Kris Wentworth is Postman emphasizing and developing? Where is he agreeing with points that they make?
2. In your experience is what Postman calls "civility" more a function of keeping feelings to one's self or expressing them in "constructive" ways? How so?
3. Do you agree or disagree with Postman's characterization of the perceptions and feelings that are "really" behind racist remarks? Discuss.
4. What's an example from your own experience of the accuracy of Postman's claim that "sometimes, the less people know about other people, the better off everyone is"?
5. In what specific ways do you agree or disagree with what Postman says about parenting?
6. What does Postman mean when he says that authentic communication is a two-edged sword? What are the two "edges"? How can the sword "cut" two ways?
7. Discuss an example from your own experience where you felt a complex of inconsistent or perhaps contradictory "honest feelings." How did you handle them in that situation?

Chapter 9

Men's and Women's Expressive Styles

T he chapter before this one talks about the "exhaling" side of the inhaling-exhaling process as it occurs in all relationships. This chapter focuses on differences in the ways men and women express themselves. Especially in the past ten years, a number of researchers, teachers, and mass-market authors have been making the point that the people-on-the-street have known for a long time: Men and women talk differently. One way to improve your effectiveness as a communicator is to be aware of these differences. Since many of them are embedded in our culture, they aren't easy to change. But it can help greatly to understand how gender roles get played out in talk.

This first reading is from the middle of a 1994 book called *Exploring Gender Speak: Personal Effectiveness in Gender Communication*. It's written by two speech communication teachers who want their readers to understand some ways that language usage differs between women and men. They base what they say on a great deal of research—they cite almost forty studies in the twelve pages I've reprinted here—but, like the other authors included in *Bridges Not Walls*, they translate research findings into simple and practical explanations.

Diana Ivy and Phil Backlund start by discussing some of the ways that women's generally higher-pitched voices can affect their communicating. Then they review the research on tentativeness. In 1975 a well-known language and gender scholar named Robin Lakoff argued that women introduce considerable tentativeness into their speech with such patterns as upward intonation, so-called "tag questions"—"This is really a beautiful day, don't you think?"—and various hedges and disclaimers—"well," "kind of," "sort of," "possibly," etc. In 1979 another woman found data that refuted some of Lakoff's claims about intonation patterns, and other studies raised questions about Lakoff's conclusions regarding tag questions. This dispute led still other scholars and teachers to warn against sex-role stereotyping even among academics. Today the general belief is that Lakoff's original findings were accurate in some ways, but that the early research greatly oversimplified these differences between women's and men's speech. You can use the information in this section to reflect on your own speech style and that of the women and men you know. When people fall into the patterns the research describes, they can be stereotyped negatively.

In the next section, Ivy and Backlund review what's known about word selection. Historically, women have been found to use more terms for colors that men, but this may be changing. It's also been historically assumed that men use much more profanity than women, but some studies have raised questions about this conclusion. In at least one study it was found that women *believed* men used more profanity than they actually did, and the reverse was true of women—men *believed* that women used less profanity than they actually did. This feature of conversation also changes with context—women seem to talk "dirtier" around other women, and men do the same thing around other men.

The final section discusses how women and men manage the structure of ordinary conversation differently. Researchers have studied such things as who starts a conversation, who interrupts, who talks more, who asks more questions, and who uses pauses and silence more. Ivy and Backlund discuss these questions in terms of two different "floors," as in "You now have the floor to speak." A "Floor 1 interaction" moves in the usual orderly, one-at-a-time pattern of many meetings and follows a generally competitive structure. Ideas get offered and tested to see which ones come out on top. A "Floor 2 interaction" includes more simultaneous talk and is characterized by more cooperation than competition. As Ivy and Backlund describe it, this kind of conversation "is full of give and take, riddled with interruption and overlapping talk, sporadic in its constant topic switching, and almost mystical in how the interactants finish each others' thoughts and sentences." You might guess the gender differences between these two different styles of conversation: men tend to engage in Floor 1 talk and women in Floor 2 talk. One of the conclusions from this line of research is that *both* styles are productive, and that the assumption that only the Floor 1 style is "organized" and "efficient" is evidence of another gender stereotype.

As this reading shows, the research on men's and women's expressive styles has generated a fair number of contradictory findings. There are some data that support gender stereotypes, but there is also evidence that we need to be careful about labeling talk "typically male" or "typically female." I encourage you to test what's discussed here against your own experience.

Language Usage Among Women and Men

Diana K. Ivy and Phil Backlund

. . . The information presented in this section is divided into three parts, vocal properties and linguistic constructions, word selection, and conversation management. For some topics, the research has produced contradictory results regarding linguistic patterns of the sexes, but a general, unsettling trend is for the research to label the feminine patterns as weaker, passive, and less commanding of respect when compared to masculine styles. Some sources of information view linguistic sex differences as being profound enough as to form "genderlects," variations of dialects indicative of men's and women's speech patterns (Cameron, 1985, p. 29).

Vocal Properties and Linguistic Constructions

Vocal *properties* are aspects of the production of sound that are related to the physiological voice-producing mechanism in humans. Some researchers argue that these properties are biologically determined; others believe that the differences are more influenced by social norms than by physiological attributes. We use the heading *linguistic constructions* to refer to choices people make when they communicate, such as using tag questions, hedges, and disclaimers. More specifically, linguistic constructions reflect speech patterns or habits, but they do not relate to specific word selections.

Excerpted from Chapter 5 of *Exploring Gender Speak: Personal Effectiveness in Gender Communication* by Diana K. Ivy and Phil Backlund, 1994 McGraw-Hill.

Pitch

The pitch of a human voice can be defined as the highness or lowness of a particular sound as air causes the vocal chords to vibrate. It is a generally accepted belief that physiological structures related to voice production are configured so that women produce higher pitched sounds, while men produce lower pitched sounds. Thus women's speaking voices tend to be higher in pitch than men's—a conclusion that is probably nothing new to you. But scholarly evidence, especially in the area of singing voices, has uprooted some notions about physiological sex differences and voice production. Current thinking suggests that sex differences in voice production have more to do with social interpretations than with physiology alone (Brownmiller, 1984; Graddol & Swann, 1989; Steinem, 1983).

Gender scholar Dale Spender (1985) believes that pitch can be seen "as an index for the measurement of women's language inferiority" (p. 38). Spender draws from research which indicates that women and men have equal abilities to produce high pitches, but men have been socialized not to use the higher pitches for fear of sounding feminine. If this were not the case, what would be the cause for men's ability to flip their voices into a falsetto (an extremely high-pitched singing voice)? Research has discovered that men actually have a greater range of pitches at their disposal than women, but they choose not to use these "feminine" pitches (Brend, 1975; Henley, 1977; Kramer, 1977; Pfeiffer, 1985).

The so-called high-pitched female whine has drawn longstanding societal criticism, in comparison to the low, rumbling, melodic tones that men are able to produce (McGonnell-Ginet, 1983). In a patriarchal society such as ours, men's lower pitched voices are viewed as being more credible and persuasive than women's, leading to what Cameron (1985) terms "a widespread prejudice against women's voices" (p. 54). Recall in Chapter 4 our discussion of the fact that men significantly outnumber women in the production of voiceovers for television and radio commercials. Women who possess lower than average-pitched voices have begun to make it into the voiceover ranks. But women who possess typically higher pitched, feminine voices most often portray silly, dependent, helpless women in commercials.

Men who possess higher pitched voices are often ridiculed for being effeminate. Their "feminine" voices detract from their credibility and dynamism, unless another physical or personality attribute somehow overpowers judgments made because of the feminine voice. (Mike Tyson, former heavy-weight boxing champion, is one example of this.) However, women whose voices are lower than the expected pitch norm are not generally derided for possessing "masculine" voices. Women whose voices generate comparisons to men have supposedly received a compliment rather than an insult. Spender (1985) asserts, "It is not a mystery why men choose not to speak in the high pitched tones which are available to them in a society which links low pitch and masculinity, and high pitch and femininity; males who did produce high pitched utterances would be venturing into that negative realm and violating the gender demarcation lines. They would be ridiculed—as many adolescents whose voices have been late in breaking could testify" (p. 39).

Indications of Tentativeness

There are several ways that humans indicate tentativeness in their communication. One of these involves a property of the voice, while the others involve linguistic constructions. Well-known language and gender scholar Robin Lakoff suggested in the 1970s that these linguistic forms offer a way that "a speaker can avoid committing himself [herself], and thereby avoid coming into conflict with the addressee" (1975, pp.

16–17). The problem is, according to Lakoff and other scholars, women use far more tentative constructions and vocal properties in their communication than men. The tentative means of expression undermines the messages that women convey, making them appear uncertain, insecure, unstable, incompetent, and not to be taken seriously (Graddol & Swann, 1989; Lakoff, 1975; McConnell-Ginet, 1983).

One vocal property that indicates tentativeness is *intonation*, described by sociolinguist McConnell-Ginet (1983) as "the tune to which we set the text of our talk" (p. 70). Research has produced contradictory findings on whether the use of statements ending in a rising intonation (typically associated with asking questions) is more indicative of a female style than a male style. Lakoff (1975) contended that the rising intonation pattern was unique to English-speaking women, with the effect being the seeking of confirmation from others. An example of rising intonation can be found in a simple exchange such as the question, "What's for dinner tonight?" followed by the answer, "Spaghetti?" The intonation turns the statement or answer into a question, as if to say, "Is that okay with you?"

Not long after Lakoff (1975) labeled tentative vocal properties and constructions elements within "women's language" (p. 53), research conducted by language and education expert Carole Edelsky (1979) refuted Lakoff's findings. Edelsky's study of intonation patterns of male and female speakers indicated that the interpretation of a rising intonation depended on the context in which it was used. In certain contexts within her research, female subjects used the rising intonation pattern more than men. But in other contexts, no patterns of sex differences emerged. Contradictory findings produced by research led feminist scholar Julia Penelope (1990) to conclude the following: "Women are said to use . . . structures that are servile and submissive ('polite'), tentative, uncertain, emotionally exaggerated, and self-demeaning. These alleged traits represent a stereotype of how women talk, *not* the way we do talk" (pp. xxii–xxiii).

A linguistic construction related to intonation, which some research views as indicative of feminine uncertainty, is the *tag question* (Fishman, 1980; McMillan, Clifton, McGrath, & Gale, 1977; Zimmerman & West, 1975). Lakoff (1975) described the tag question as being "midway between an outright statement and a yes-no question: it is less assertive than the former, but more confident than the latter" (p. 15). An example of a tag question would be, "This is a really beautiful day, don't you think?" Rather than asserting an opinion in the form of a statement about the day, the speaker attaches the question onto the end of the statement. The primary use of the tag question is to seek agreement or a response from a listener, or, as Lakoff suggested, to serve as an "apology for making an assertion at all" (p. 54). Lakoff attributed the use of tag questions to a general lack of assertiveness or confidence about what one is saying, a usage that her research indicated was more related to a female style than a male style. While Lakoff assigned certain linguistic practices to certain sexes, she was also perturbed by the tendency of people to "form judgments about other people on the basis of superficial linguistic behavior that may have nothing to do with inner character, but has been imposed upon the speaker" (p. 17).

Other research investigating Lakoff's claims found no evidence that tag questions occurred more in female speech than in male speech or that tag questions necessarily functioned to indicate uncertainty or tentativeness (Baumann, 1979; Dubois & Crouch, 1975; Holmes, 1990). Tag questions may operate as genuine requests or to "forestall opposition" (Dubois & Crouch, 1975, p. 292). As Spender (1985) points out, it is inappropriate to view tag questions as always indicating hesitancy, as evidenced by her example " 'You won't do that again, *will you?* ' " (p. 9).

Another linguistic construction generally interpreted to indicate tentativeness and stereotypically associated with women's speech is the reliance on such devices as *qualifiers, hedges, disclaimers, intensifiers,* and *compound* versus *simple requests.* Lakoff (1975) claimed that women's speech incorporated more of these constructions, indicating women's general uncertainty and inability to "vouch for the accuracy of the statement" (p. 53). Qualifying terms include *well, you know, kind of, sort of, really, perhaps, possibly, maybe,* and *of course.* Hedging devices include such terms as *I think/believe/feel, I guess, I mean,* and *I wonder* (Holmes, 1990; Lakoff, 1975; Spender, 1985). Disclaimers are typically longer forms of hedges which act as prefaces or defense mechanisms when one is unsure or doubtful of what one is about to say (Beach & Dunning, 1982; Bell, Zahn, & Hopper, 1984; Bradley, 1981; Hewitt & Stokes, 1975). Disclaimers generally weaken or soften the effect of a message. Examples of disclaimers include such statements as "I know this is a dumb question, but. . ." and "I may be wrong here, but I think that. . .." (Researchers label some of these devices qualifiers and others hedges or disclaimers; thus examples we provide here may not correspond to discrete categories.) Compound requests typically involve a negative construction and are the longer, more complex requests for action or assistance more characteristic of women's speech than men's, according to Lakoff (1975). The question "Won't you please come with me tonight?" is a compound request, compared with the simple or direct construction "Come with me tonight." Again, compound requests signal tentativeness or that "the speaker is not committed as with a simple declarative or affirmative" (Lakoff, 1975, p. 19).

Documentation of intensifiers by language scholars dates back as far as 1922 when linguist Otto Jespersen studied women's use of exaggeration, specifically in the form of the term *vastly.* His studies led him to conclude that women are much more prone to hyperbole in their communication than men. Lakoff (1975) focused on the word *so,* claiming that women use such constructions as "I like him *so* much" (p. 55) more than men. Penelope (1990) adds *so much, such,* and *quite* as ways of signaling a feeling level or intensifying what one is saying (p. xxii).

Two linguists, Janet Holmes (1990), who studied male and female speech patterns in New Zealand, and Deborah Cameron (1985), who studied tentativeness in the speech patterns of London natives, as well as researchers in the United States, have concluded that sex-typed interpretations of a range of linguistic devices, including qualifiers, hedges, disclaimers, intensifiers, and compound requests, must be made within the given context in which the communication occurs (Bradley, 1981; Kramarae, 1982; Mulac & Lundell, 1986; O'Barr & Atkins, 1980; Ragan, 1989; Sayers & Sherblom, 1987).

Holmes (1990) discovered, for example, that men and women were equally likely to use tentative linguistic devices, depending on the needs or mandates of the particular situation. Female subjects in her study demonstrated regular uses of tentative communication when in the presence of men, but less often when with other women. Cameron (1985) found that male subjects exhibited tentative communication when placed in certain roles, such as facilitators of group interaction. Male and female subjects alike in O'Barr and Atkins's ((1980) study of courtroom communication used the entire range of features constituting what Lakoff (1975) called "women's language" with equal frequency, with the exception of tag questions.

We grant that an overabundance of tentative forms of expression in one's communication can be interpreted as a sign of uncertainty and insecurity. But there may also be positive, affiliative uses of tentative language; these kinds of expressions need not be identified with one sex or the other. For example, a manager holding a higher status position within an organization might use disclaimers or hedges in an attempt to even out a status differential, to foster a sense of camaraderie among staff members, and to show herself or himself as open to suggestion and ideas from employees. While research suggests that women use more forms of tentativeness in their communication, other research indicates that both sexes may actually use tentative forms of expression at certain times and in a variety of contexts to convey affiliation and to facilitate inter-action with others. As an example, a male friend explains that he often uses compound requests, tag questions, and disclaimers when dealing with a range of people—cowork-ers, subordinates, friends, and so on—to convey a nondogmatic, supportive, and less dominant attitude to others. It's a good idea to use caution, to consider the context, and to avoid stereotypes when interpreting tentative communication.

Word Selection

The discussion in this section has to do with men's and women's preferences in their choice of words. The most interesting information surrounds the use of color terms, profanity, and sexual slang.

Color Language

In one episode of *Designing Women*, Julia Sugarbaker, one of the main female characters, and a man she had begun to date reported to Julia's coworkers the results of their shopping expedition. The male character explained that he had tried to talk Julia into buying a "mauve" suit that had a figure-enhancing "peplum." Later, Julia's female cohorts suggested that the man was probably homosexual, based on two key words he had mentioned, mauve and peplum—terms that they insisted no heterosexual man would use (or be able to define). (How many of you reading this are wondering, "Just what *is* a peplum?") We use this example for two purposes: (1) to emphasize what we said earlier in this text, that a man who exhibits what society deems "feminine" behav-ior is often demeaned and accused of being homosexual, an unfortunate trend often highlighted in media; and (2) to dramatize the research conducted on women, men, and the language of color.

Very little is written about this topic, but most often "colorful" language is rele-gated to women's realm. Lakoff (1975) contended, "Women make far more precise dis-criminations in naming colors than do men; words like beige, ecru, aquamarine, lavender, and so on are unremarkable in a woman's active vocabulary, but absent from that of most men" (pp. 8–9). One of our friends remarked recently that she gave her husband a nice "dusty plum" shirt for his birthday. Ask yourself if you've ever heard a man describe something as being "dusty plum." Probably not, but do you wonder why that is so? Research provides few explanations of why women tend to use more dis-crepant categories for colors than men. One explanation relates to the tendency for more men than women to be color blind. But this doesn't seem to have much practi-cal value if, in your experience, men who aren't color blind don't tend to use many variations of color terms. Another explanation is simply that the whole topic of color may be more important to women than to men, given that women have traditionally been more closely linked with home decoration and fashion. In this view, women have developed microdistinctions between colors and the words to go with them out of necessity.

Lakoff (1975) asserted that men relegate colors to the realm of the "unworldly," which they equate with a woman's realm. She argued that "since women are not expected to make decisions on important matters, such as what kind of job to hold, they are relegated to noncrucial decisions, . . . whether to name a color 'lavender' or 'mauve' " (p. 9). In *Basic Color Terms* sociologists Berlin and Kay (1969) explain that designations of color are closely connected to one's culture. As a final note, some students believe that the trend for women to use more color terms than men is changing among persons of their generation. They assert that as more men and women enter professions stereotypically associated with the opposite sex, such as men entering interior and fashion design fields, terminology tendencies will continue to change. Do you agree with this prediction?

Profanity and Sexual Slang

. . . What about profanity and sexual slang in interpersonal communication? Are there sex-typed tendencies for these kinds of language usage? Even in the 1990s, is it more acceptable for men than women to say shit, damn, hell, son of a bitch, and other colorful metaphors and profane terms?

Use of profanity has long been considered a man's behavior (if it's considered *anyone's* behavior), thus the conventional reference to "cursing like a sailor." Lakoff (1975) contended that women's language encouraged them to remain "little ladies" (p. 11). A woman violates this ladylike demeanor if she uses an overabundance of slang or profanity. In support of this argument, Lakoff offered two versions of the same statement, asking readers to label them as being spoken by a man or a woman. The statements were: "Oh dear, you've put the peanut butter in the refrigerator again," and "Shit, you've put the peanut butter in the refrigerator again" (p. 10). Lakoff believed that the gender labeling of these statements would be obvious, despite the fact that more women were feeling comfortable using profanity as a result of the women's movement occurring at the time. However, she also anticipated that most of "Middle America" would still flinch and disapprove of female cursing (p.10). If profanity made one's opinions more forceful and believable, but such usages were unacceptable for women, then the acceptance of their use of profanity only enhanced men's position of strength, according to Lakoff.

A fascinating study of male and female college students' uses of profane and hostile language was conducted in 1978 by a gender linguist named Constance Staley. A most interesting perceptual discrepancy emerged from Staley's data. Female subjects held the perception that men used profanity and hostile language to a much *greater* degree than male subjects indicated they did. In contrast, male subjects thought that women used *far less* profanity than female subjects reported actually using. So, even during a liberated decade like the 1970s when women experimented with profanity, they still placed profanity and "rough talk" predominantly into a male domain. At the same time, men expected women to talk like ladies, not sailors.

In a classic article concerning the use of sexual language, linguist Otto Jespersen (1922) wrote that "women in all countries are shy of mentioning certain parts of the human body and certain natural functions by the direct and often rude denominations which men, especially young men, prefer when among themselves" (p. 24). According to Jespersen, women's distaste for blunt, graphic terminology leads them to develop euphemisms which then become more common usages in everyday language. in this way, Jespersen believed that "women exercise a great and universal influence on linguistic development through their instinctive shrinking from coarse and gross expressions" (p. 246).

You might argue that a lot has changed since Jespersen's research in the 1920s. But has it really changed all that much? Are women really that much freer to use sexual language that is typically reserved for men? Research published in 1990 by gender and language expert Julia Penelope specifically addressed forms of language she termed "the slang of sexual slurs" (p. 46). Penelope concluded (with significant resentment) that it appears to be unacceptable even in our modern society for women to use sexual slang or to hear it used. Men are permitted to use such language, but with one restraint: "They rarely exhibit the full range of it in the company of women" (p. 46).

An interesting sex difference emerged from gender researcher Rinck Simkins's (1982) study of preferred language in discussions of male and female genitalia and sexual intercourse. Both female and male undergraduates reported that in mixed company they would use more formal, clinical terminology for genitalia and intercourse. However, when in the company of same-sex friends, men were more likely to use sexual slang while women still preferred the more formal terminology.

One of the problems people face when they have discussions about sex—with a dating or marital partner, with their children, with *anyone*—is that the language describing body parts and sexual activity is either completely clinical or "gutter" (Potorti, 1992). In other words, it's sometimes hard to talk frankly about sex-related topics, even though those kinds of discussions are important, because the embarrassing choices are (1) to use awkward medical-book terminology that may not be understandable to both speaker and listener; (2) to use "gutter terms" or graphic slang which may be offensive and is likely to demean the very topic you are discussing; or (3) to keep the discussion vague, by using inferences rather than specific language, thus risking misunderstanding. If people in general, and women in specific, have difficulty expressing themselves on sexual topics, it's somewhat understandable when you consider the language that currently exists for our use. . . .

Women and Men in Conversation

The final element within this discussion of how language is used in gender communication relates to the basic structure of ordinary conversation. Have you ever considered how conversation is organized or how it gets "managed"? The elements that make conversations appear to be organized are typically subsumed in research under the heading "conversation management." If you were to read about conversation management in other sources, you might see descriptions of the following: conversation initiation and maintenance; talkativeness; turn-taking; topic control and gossip; interruptions and overlaps; question asking versus answering; and the use of pauses and silence. Most of these areas would probably be discussed in terms of the contradictory research findings produced by studies that have attempted to isolate sex differences.

We choose a different approach to this topic, one that examines conversational management from the standpoint of research on two divergent types of interactions or "floors." We draw information for this section primarily from the work of Carole Edelsky, an educator and scholar who became interested in male and female communication styles within groups. In an article entitled "Who's Got the Floor?" Edelsky (1981) describes her participation in a series of university committee meetings in which two very different types of discussions occurred (Floor 1 and Floor 2). Edelsky became fascinated by sex differences that emerged in these committee meetings, in relation to aspects of conversation management, for example, turn-taking, topic control, interruptions or overlaps, and talk time (which she termed "floor holding"). Let's first review some definitions of these terms, then describe how they function in conversation.

Conversation Management Terminology

Conversation typically occurs in *turns*, meaning that one speaker takes a turn, then another, and so on, such that interaction is socially organized (Sacks, Schegloff, & Jefferson, 1978). A speaker's interjection into a conversation is her or his "turn at talk." *Topic control* is fairly self-explanatory; it occurs when a speaker initiates a topic and works to see that that topic continues to be the focal point of discussion. Part of that work involves fending off *interruptions*, defined by West and Zimmerman (1983) as "violations of speakers' turns at talk," and *overlaps*, defined as "simultaneous speech initiated by a next speaker just as a current speaker arrives at a possible turn-transition place" (pp. 103–104). The range of interpretations of interruptions and overlaps includes the following: they indicate disrespect and restrict a speaker's rights, they serve as devices to control the topic, and they indicate an attitude of dominance and authority (Marche & Peterson, 1993). *Talk time*, sometimes referred to as *air time* or *verbosity*, refers to how long a speaker takes to accomplish one turn at talk (Eakins & Eakins, 1976; Edelsky, 1981).

Edelsky's Floor 1

A Floor 1 interaction is described by Edelsky as "the usual orderly, one-at-a-time type of floor" (p. 384), characterized by "monologues, single-party control and hierarchical interaction where turn takers stand out from non-turn takers and floors are won

---

What if?

What if you could be a fly on the wall, eavesdropping on a conversation between a group of women or men? Have you ever wondered what an all-opposite-sex discussion sounds like? If you're a female reader, *what if* you were able to be a fly on the wall in the men's locker room to overhear a group of guys talking about women? Think for a moment about what that conversation would be like, in terms of the language that would be used, the topics that would be discussed, and the signs of male competitiveness that would be evident from the "flow" of the conversation. If you're a male reader, *what if* you were invisible and sat in on a conversation between a group of female friends over happy hour? Do you suspect that they'd talk more about their jobs or the men in their lives? Recent research indicates that conversation looks and sounds quite different for all-female versus all-male groups of people. Would a difference be noticeable to you, and would it make you uncomfortable? Would you find women's conversation to be disorganized and chaotic, or more fun and free-flowing than a typical conversation among men? Think about those times when you may have overheard a conversation between two or more people of the opposite sex. Were there elements to the way the conversation was conducted that surprised you? It's interesting to think about these experiences, or to imagine *what* your reactions would be *if* you were that fly on the wall.

or lost" (p. 416). Certain speakers (usually men, if the group is mixed sex) dominate discussion by imposing a hierarchical or status-based order to turns at talk; taking longer turns at talk; offering more statements than questions; interrupting other speakers; and using vocal devices to ward off interruptions to their own talk. Conversation exemplifies competition rather than cooperation. In Edelsky's experience with Floor 1 discussions, men's turns were four times as long as women's turns. Noted feminist Gloria Steinem (1983) calls this behavior a "policing of the subject matter of conversation" (p. 179).

Floor 1 discussions do not necessarily occur only within group settings; two people might have a Floor 1 conversation. For example, think about a conversation you may have had in which you became very aware that "conversational rules" were operating. Such a conversation might have arisen between you and your employer over an issue at work, or between you and a friend who comes to you for a favor, or between you and a parent, sibling, or spouse. Several things affect how the conversation will go, such as the nature or sensitivity of the topic being discussed, any status differentials between the participants, or the history of interaction between the two people. Later we discuss sex as one of the variables that has the potential to affect how a conversation will go. In a Floor 1 conversation, the tone or shape of the conversation is likely to be dominated by one person's interaction style. If your boss speaks in declaratives rather than with language that invites response, if she or he indicates that interruptions or overlaps are not welcome, if his or her talk consists of minimonologues rather than even exchanges—all aspects of conversation management—then those tendencies may configure the conversation into the Floor 1 type or profile.

Edelsky's Floor 2

Floor 2 interactions are characterized by cooperation rather than competition. Cooperation is evidenced by simultaneous talk, or "free-for-alls" as Edelsky termed them, the "joint building of an answer to a question," and by "collaboration on developing ideas" (p. 391). Floor 2 discussions may also contain a good deal of laughter, as well as flows of turn-taking and overlapping talk, indicative of members being "on the same wave length" (p. 391). In Edelsky's experience with Floor 2 discussions, participation was more balanced for the sexes, with men participating significantly less than they did in Floor 1 discussions and women participating more. Steinem (1983) contends that the "rotating style of talk and leadership" that emerges in a discussion of the Floor 2 variety is a predominant characteristic of women-only group discussions (p. 183).

Think of other conversations you've participated in that fit Edelsky's description of Floor 2. It may be that, on another day about another topic, the same employer you considered an exemplar of Floor 1 interactions will converse with you in a manner indicative of a Floor 2 variation. Have you been in conversations in which the rules and organizing, managing structures seem to be left outside the door? Such conversations might appear to an eavesdropper to be completely incoherent. As a personal example, your female co-author's conversations with her mother almost without exception take the form of Edelsky's Floor 2, to the amazement of her father. The two get teased for "going from Los Angeles to Seattle via Dallas," but the pattern of conversation makes perfect sense to them. Such a conversation is full of give and take, riddled with interruptions and overlapping talk, sporadic in its constant topic switching, and almost mystical in how the interactants finish each others' thoughts and sentences. This kind of discussion—a Floor 2 discussion—accomplishes its goals and has structure and management properties within it, but it just doesn't seem to match many people's versions of an "orderly" conversation.

Floor Comparisons

Edelsky explains that both types of floors may arise within a single discussion, but the main distinguishing characteristic is that Floor 1 develops singly, while Floor 2 develops jointly. It is important to understand that Edelsky contrasts the two floors by the *style* of interaction that emerges, not by what gets accomplished during each type of discussion. For example, Edelsky does not conclude that Floor 1 discussions are more conducive to getting tasks accomplished, while Floor 2's make interactants feel more positively toward one another. Edelsky reports that almost all of her meetings began socially, with joking, idle chitchat, and refreshments. What signaled the type of floor were who spoke first and how he or she spoke, the topics discussed in the first series of turns, the composition of the particular group (in terms of who was present and who was absent), and so on. These characteristics define a floor as well as move a group from one kind of floor to the other.

Conversational Management and the Sexes

The research on conversational management styles of men and women has produced such contradictory findings that presenting them one by one in this chapter would likely irritate more than enlighten. Another indictment of the conversation management research is that most of it is based on only one format for interaction—the "one-at-a-time" format that equates to Edelsky's Floor 1—as the model by which standards are determined and sex differences are measured. Many women and men alike have come to expect that a mixed-sex discussion will take the format of a Floor 1, with masculine individuals dominating the conversation, controlling what gets talked about and by whom. Edelsky sums up this faulty expectation: "One-at-a-time is not a conversational universal, nor is it essential for the communication of messages. Moreover, the unquestioning adoption of this premise causes researchers to see more-than-one-at-a-time as degenerate, a breakdown, or something requiring repair" (p. 397). She argues that researchers should question what conditions must exist for the sexes to interact as equals, rather than to question how the sexes demonstrate a power differential in one format of interaction.

Edelsky discovered some sex-related trends among her research findings. Women in the study tended to participate more and experience more satisfaction from Floor 2 than Floor 1 conversations because these informal, cooperative discussions provided "both a cover of 'anonymity' for assertive language use and a comfortable backdrop against which women can display a fuller range of language ability" (p. 416). As language and gender scholar Pamela Fishman (1983) put it, women in cooperative conversations don't have to accomplish the "conversational shitwork" that they typically do in competitive conversations (p. 99). In Edelsky's research, men talked less in Floor 2 discussions than they did in Floor 1's, but they still talked at a rate even with women in Floor 2's. Their participation did not appear to be hampered by the cooperative, free-flowing style. Edelsky also made no mention of a higher level of satisfaction from male subjects participating in Floor 1 versus Floor 2 discussions. Edelsky concludes that men can benefit from the "high-involvement, synergistic, solidarity-building interaction" characteristics of Floor 2 discussions (p. 417). Women and men alike could certainly benefit from the knowledge that they can indeed experience satisfying, power-equalizing interactions—an experience that many would probably welcome.

To conclude this section on conversational management, we encourage you to think about some of the more recent discussions you've been in and to assess your involvement in them. Did you display communication behaviors stereotypically connected to your sex and gender? Do you think that such dominant behaviors as interrupting and controlling the topic are necessarily male or masculine conversational devices? Is it "just like a woman" to wait for her turn at talk, rather than speak up and offer her input? Are the sexes somehow limited by such designations of "appropriate" behavior? What happens when the conversational expectations of women and men are violated? Consider the kind of condemnation a man who never speaks up might receive. What might be the response to a woman who interrupts others' comments and changes the topic, without the use of a disclaimer? It's fairly safe to say that the sex typing that may accompany conversational style is as debilitating as other forms of sex and gender stereotyping. Even to the point of expecting conversations to take certain forms because of women and men involved in them, gender stereotyping gets in the way of successful, effective gender communication.

Conclusion

We've given you a lot to think about in this chapter for one main reason—so that you'll more fully consider how communication occurs *between* women and men. Studying how it occurs empowers you to apply this information when you go about the business of initiating and developing all sorts of relationships. Knowing what you now know about varying approaches to communication, how would you describe your own approach, relative to that of someone of the opposite sex? Consider whether you typically approach communication as serving more of a relational or a content function, or whether you select an approach based on the needs or demands of the situation. Think about a special person—a past love, someone you're currently seeing, your spouse, or your best friend. How would you describe this person's style and approach to conversation? If it is significantly different from your own style, perhaps you find the contrast workable. But is it possible that the difference in your very purposes for having conversations has caused you significant relational problems?

Consider also your preferences for the management of conversation. Are you equally comfortable in Floor 1 and Floor 2 interactions? If you have set rules about things like interrupting and turn-taking in conversations, where did those rules come from? What happens if someone, perhaps someone who's on an inner ring of your relational concentric circles, has a set of rules vastly different from yours? It is well worth the energy to think about these things. especially if you feel that your current relational profile could use some improving. And this knowledge is critical as you prepare to initiate new relationships.

References

Baumann, M. (1979). Two features of "women's speech"? In B. L. Dubois & I. Crouch (Eds.), *The sociology of the languages of American women* (pp. 33–40). San Antonio, TX: Trinity University Press.

Beach, W. A., & Dunning, D. G. (1982). Pre-indexing and conversational organization. *Quarterly Journal of Speech, 67,* 170–185.

Bell, R. A., Zahn, C. J., & Hopper, R. (1984). Disclaiming: A test of two competing views. *Communication Quarterly, 32*, 28–36.

Berlin, B., & Kay, P. (1969). *Basic color terms: Their universality and evolution.* Berkeley: University of California Press.

Bradley, P. H. (1981). The folk-linguistics of women's speech: An empirical examination. *Communication Monographs, 48*, 73–90.

Brend, R. (1975). Male-female intonation patterns in American English. In B. Thorne & N. Henley (Eds.), *Language and sex: Difference and dominance* (pp. 84–87). Rowley, MA: Newbury House.

Brownmiller, S. (1984). *Femininity.* New York: Simon & Schuster.

Cameron, D. (1985). *Feminism and linguistic theory.* New York: St. Martin's Press.

Dubois, B. L., & Crouch, I. (1975). The question of tag questions in women's speech: They don't really use more of them, do they? *Language in Society, 4*, 289–294.

Edelsky, C. (1979). Question intonation and sex roles. *Language in Society, 8*, 15–32.

Edelsky, C. (1981). Who's got the floor? *Language in Society, 10*, 383–421.

Fishman, P. M. (1980). Conversational insecurity. In H. Giles, W. P. Robinson, & P. M. Smith (Eds.), *Language: Social psychological perspectives* (pp. 127–132). New York: Pergamon Press.

Fishman, P. M. (1983). Interaction: The work women do. In B. Thorne, C. Kramarae, & N. Henley (Eds.), *Language, gender, and society* (pp. 89–101). Rowley, MA: Newbury House.

Gilligan, C. (1982). *In a different voice.* Cambridge, MA: Harvard University Press.

Graddol, D., & Swann, J. (1989). *Gender voices.* Cambridge, MA: Basil Blackwell.

Henley, N. M. (1977). *Body politics: Power, sex, and nonverbal communication.* Englewood Cliffs, NJ: Prentice-Hall.

Hewitt, J. P., & Stokes, R. (1975). Disclaimers. *American Sociological Review, 40*, 1–11.

Holmes, J. (1990). Hedges and boosters in women's and men's speech. *Language and Communication, 10*, 185–205.

Jespersen, O. (1922). *Language: Its nature, development, and origin.* New York: Holt.

Kramarae, C. (1982). Gender: How she speaks. In E. Bouchard Ryan & H. Giles (Eds.), *Attitudes toward language variation: Social and applied contexts* (pp. 84–98). London: Edward Arnold.

Kramer, C. (1977). Perceptions of female and male speech. *Language and Speech, 20*, 151–161.

Lakoff, R. (1975). *Language and woman's place.* New York: Harper & Row.

Marche, T. A., & Peterson, C. (1993). The development and sex-related use of interruption behavior. *Human Communication Research, 19*, 388–408.

McConnell-Ginet, S. (1983). Intonation in a man's world. In B. Thorne, C. Kramarae, & N. Henley (Eds.), *Language, gender, and society* (pp. 69–88). Rowley, MA: Newbury House.

McMillan, J. R., Clifton, A. K., McGrath, D., & Gale, W. S. (1977). Women's language. Uncertainty or interpersonal sensitivity and emotionality? *Sex Roles, 3*, 545–559.

Mulac, A., & Lundell, T. L. (1986). Linguistic contributors to the gender-linked language effect. *Journal of Language and Social Psychology, 5*, 81–101.

O'Barr, W. M., & Atkins, B. K. (1980). "Women's language" or "powerless language"? in S. McConnell-Ginet, R. Borker, & N. Furman (Eds.), *Women and language in literature and society* (pp. 93–110). New York: Praeger.

Penelope, J. (1990). *Speaking freely: Unlearning the lies of the fathers' tongues.* New York: Pergamon Press.

Pfeiffer, J. (1985). Girl talk, boy talk. *Science, 85*, 58–63.

Potorti, P. (1992). Personal communication, October.

Ragan, S. L. (1989). Communication between the sexes: A consideration of sex differences in adult communication. In J. F. Nussbaum (Ed.), *Life-span communication: Normative processes* (pp. 179–193). Hillsdale, NJ: Lawrence Erlbaum Associates.

Sacks, H., Schegloff, E. A., & Jefferson, G. (1978). A simplest systematics for the organization of turn taking for conversation. In J. Schenkein (Ed.), *Studies in the organization of conversational interaction* (pp. 7–55). New York: Academic Press.

Sayers, F., & Sherblom, J. (1987). Qualification in male language as influenced by age and gender of conversational partner. *Communication Research Reports, 4*, 88–92.

Simkins, R. (1982). Male and female sexual vocabulary in different interpersonal contexts. *Journal of Sex Research, 18*, 160–172.

Spender, D. (1985). *Man made language* (2nd ed.). London: Routledge & Kegan Paul.

Staley, C. (1982). Sex related differences in the style of children's language. *Journal of Psycholinguistic Research, 11*, 141–152.

Steinem, G. (1983). *Outrageous acts and everyday rebellions*. New York: Signet Books.

West, C., & Zimmerman, D. H. (1983). Small insults: A study of interruptions in cross-sex conversations between unacquainted persons. In B. Thorne, C. Kramarae, & N. Henley (Eds.), *Language, gender, and society* (pp. 102–117). Rowley, MA: Newbury House.

Zimmerman, D. H., & West, C. (1975). Sex roles, interruptions, and silences in conversation. In B. Thorne & N. Henley (Eds.), *Language and sex: Difference and dominance* (pp. 105-129). Rowley, MA: Newbury House.

Review Questions

1. Do sex differences in voice production have more to do with physiology—shorter vocal cords and smaller resonators—or social interpretations?
2. Describe how rising intonation functions in Standard American English. How does it function in a language other than English?
3. Give an example from your own experience of each of the following: tag question, hedge, disclaimer, qualifier.
4. Research indicates that talk about sex tends to use one of two very different sets of vocabulary. What are the two extremes?
5. Who interrupts more, men or women?

Probes

1. How would you summarize the somewhat contradictory findings about tentativeness in women's and men's communicating?
2. In your experience, do women use more color terms than men? How, if at all, does this affect their communicating?
3. Respond to the same question about profanity. Does it make a difference in your communication whether men or women use more profanity? Explain.
4. Do you believe that gender stereotypes lead people to make certain language choices or that the language choices of women and men help generate gender stereotypes? Explain.
5. Respond to the questions Ivy and Backlund ask in the "What If?" box.

ince the first reading in this chapter was coauthored by a woman and a man, it seemed only fair to follow it with one that discusses expressive styles from a woman's point of view, and to conclude the chapter by giving equal time to a male perspective. This next selection is by Deborah Tannen, a sociolinguist who has become famous as a lecturer and talk-show guest. Tannen has written a couple of books that have showed up on the *New York Times* best-seller list because of the insights they contain into what she calls "asymmetries" that often lead to men and women talking "at cross-purposes." This selection is from her best-seller called *You Just Don't Understand*.

As she points out, an "asymmetry" is a pattern that is imbalanced—like when a tree planted too close to a power line is pruned by the power company into an off-balanced or asymmetrical shape. The asymmetry Tannen discusses here is the one created by the different conversational goals and expectations that men and women have, especially when they're talking about troubles. The women she has studied often want and expect understanding and confirmation. When they talk about their troubles, they are interested in responses that say, "I know what you mean; I've felt that way, too," or "What you did makes perfect sense—everybody in your shoes feels that way." By contrast, when men talk about troubles, they are interested in solutions or strategies for fixing whatever's wrong. They hope to hear suggestions for change and advice about what to do next. Neither the male nor the female pattern is always "right" or "wrong," but they certainly differ, and—this is the key point—when you put them together in the same conversation, they're asymmetrical.

As Tannen notes, there are exceptions to these patterns. Some effective teachers and managers, for example, can adapt their responses to fit the needs of both males and females. But in many situations women want and give "rapport talk" while men desire and prefer to offer "report talk." "Rapport" versus "report" is the main asymmetry Tannen discusses, not only in this chapter but throughout her book.

One problem with the different patterns is that each seems completely reasonable, but only to the person who favors it. From a woman's point of view, what could be more "logical" and appropriate than expressing support and confirmation for a person talking about her troubles? When you're hurting, the most important thing to know is that you're not alone. From a man's viewpoint, on the other hand, problems need solutions, and the most sincere and appropriate kind of response is advice about how to deal with whatever's troubling you. Because of this asymmetry, many women discussing troubles want the gift of understanding, and many men discussing troubles want the gift of advice.

In this excerpt, Tannen shows how this pattern surfaces in talk between tenth-graders, but she emphasizes that this analysis can be applied across the spectrum of ages. She also suggests that it's rooted in a difference between what male and female messages say about *status*. One reason many women resist men's suggestions and advice is that it puts the woman in a one-down position, as a person who needs to be helped because she apparently can't help herself. If "teaching" needs to be done, many women would prefer being instructed by someone who diminishes the power differential by minimizing technical terms and other signs of superiority and asking regularly for feedback. In other words, many men experience pleasant feelings of power when they come across as having superior *expertise*, while many women feel their power enhanced if they can be of *help*. So as Tannen summarizes, "the difference between. . .report-talk and rapport-talk can be understood in terms of status and connection."

You may find yourself agreeing with some things Tannen says and disagreeing with others. If so, you're in good company. Some scholars criticize the research she uses to support her claims, and some feminists believe she has distorted some of the differences between women and men. But if you test what she says against your own experience and discuss this essay and the two other articles in this chapter with others, you'll come to understand more about men's and women's expressive styles.

Asymmetries: Women and Men Talking at Cross-Purposes

Deborah Tannen

Eve had a lump removed from her breast. Shortly after the operation, talking to her sister, she said that she found it upsetting to have been cut into, and that looking at the stitches was distressing because they left a seam that had changed the contour of her breast. Her sister said, "I know. When I had my operation I felt the same way." Eve made the same observation to her friend Karen, who said, "I know. It's like your body has been violated." But when she told her husband, Mark, how she felt, he said, "You can have plastic surgery to cover up the scar and restore the shape of your breast."

Eve had been comforted by her sister and her friend, but she was not comforted by Mark's comment. Quite the contrary, it upset her more. Not only didn't she hear what she wanted, that he understood her feelings, but, far worse, she felt he was asking her to undergo more surgery just when she was telling him how much this operation had upset her. "I'm not having any more surgery!" she protested. "I'm sorry you don't like the way it looks." Mark was hurt and puzzled. "I don't care," he protested. "It doesn't bother me at all." She asked, "Then why are you telling me to have plastic surgery?" He answered, "Because you were saying *you* were upset about the way it looked."

Eve felt like a heel: Mark had been wonderfully supportive and concerned throughout her surgery. How could she snap at him because of what he said—"just words"—when what he had done was unassailable? And yet she had perceived in his words metamessages that cut to the core of their relationship. It was self-evident to him that his comment was a reaction to her complaint, but she heard it as an independent complaint of his. He thought he was reassuring her that she needn't feel bad about her scar because there was something she could *do* about it. She heard his suggestion that she do something about the scar as evidence that *he* was bothered by it. Furthermore, whereas she wanted reassurance that it was normal to feel bad in her situation, his telling her that the problem could easily be fixed implied she had no right to feel bad about it.

Eve wanted the gift of understanding, but Mark gave her the gift of advice. He was taking the role of problem solver, whereas she simply wanted confirmation for her feelings. . . .

Excerpted from *You Just Don't Understand: Women and Men in Conversation* by Deborah Tannen. 1990 Random House.

This explains why men are frustrated when their sincere attempts to help a woman solve her problems are met not with gratitude but with disapproval. One man reported being ready to tear his hair out over a girlfriend who continually told him about problems she was having at work but refused to take any of the advice he offered. Another man defended himself against his girlfriend's objection that he changed the subject as soon as she recounted something that was bothering her: "What's the point of talking about it any more?" he said. "You can't do anything about it." Yet another man commented that women seem to wallow in their problems, wanting to talk about them forever, whereas he and other men want to get them out and be done with them, either by finding a solution or by laughing them off.

Trying to solve a problem or fix a trouble focuses on the message level of talk. But for most women who habitually report problems at work or in friendships, the message is not the main point of complaining. It's the metamessage that counts: Telling about a problem is a bid for an expression of understanding ("I know how you feel") or a similar complaint ("I felt the same way when something similar happened to me"). In other words, troubles talk is intended to reinforce rapport by sending the metamessage "We're the same; you're not alone." Women are frustrated when they not only don't get this reinforcement but, quite the opposite, feel distanced by the advice, which seems to send the metamessage "We're not the same. You have the problems; I have the solutions."

Furthermore, mutual understanding is symmetrical, and this symmetry contributes to a sense of community. But giving advice is asymmetrical. It frames the advice giver as more knowledgeable, more reasonable, more in control—in a word, one-up. And this contributes to the distancing effect. . . .

Parallel Tracks

These differences seem to go far back in our growing up. A sixteen-year-old girl told me she tends to hang around with boys rather than girls. To test my ideas, I asked her whether boys and girls both talk about problems. Yes, she assured me, they both do. Do they do it the same way? I asked. Oh, no, she said. The girls go on and on. The boys raise the issue, one of them comes up with a solution, and they close the discussion.

Women's and men's frustrations with each other's ways of dealing with troubles talk amount to applying interpretations based on one system to talk that is produced according to a different system. Boys and men do not respond to each other the way women respond to each other in troubles talk. The roots of the very different way that men respond to talk about troubles became clear to me when I compared the transcript of a pair of tenth-grade boys talking to each other to the transcripts of girls' conversations from videotapes of best friends talking, recorded as part of a research project by psychologist Bruce Dorval.

Examining the videotaped conversations, I found that the boys and girls, who expressed deep concerns to each other, did it in different ways—ways that explain the differences that come up in daily conversations between women and men. The pairs of girls at both the sixth grade and tenth grade talked at length about one girl's problems. The other girl pressed her to elaborate, said, "I know," and gave supporting evidence. The following brief excerpts from the transcripts show the dramatic difference between the girls and boys.

The tenth-grade girls are talking about Nancy's problems with her boyfriend and her mother. It emerges that Nancy and Sally were both part of a group excursion to another state. Nancy suddenly left the group and returned home early at her mother's insistence. Nancy was upset about having to leave early. Sally reinforces Nancy's feelings by letting her know that her sudden departure was also upsetting to her friends:

NANCY: God, it was *bad.* I couldn't believe she made me go home.
SALLY: I thought it was kind of weird though, I mean, one minute we were going out and the next minute Nancy's going, "Excuse me, gotta be going." [Both laugh] I didn't know what was going *on,* and Judy comes up to me and she whispers (the whole place knows), "Do you know that Nancy's going home?" And I go, "What?" [Both laugh] "Nancy's going home." I go, "*Why*" She goes, "Her mom's making her." I go [makes a face], "Ah," She comes back and goes, "Nancy's left." Well, I said, "WELL, that was a fine thing TO DO, she didn't even come and say goodbye." And she starts boiling all over me. I go [mimicking yelling], "*All right!!*" She was upset, Judy. I was like "God"—

Sally's way of responding to her friend's troubles is to confirm Nancy's feelings of distress that her mother made her leave the trip early, by letting her know that her leaving upset her friends. In contrast, examining the transcript of a conversation between boys of the same age shows how differently they respond to each other's expressions of troubles.

The tenth-grade boys also express deep feelings. Theirs too is troubles talk, but it is troubles talk with a difference. They don't concentrate on the troubles of one, pursuing, exploring, and elaborating. Instead, each one talks about his own troubles and dismisses the other's as insignificant.

In the first excerpt from these boys' conversation, Richard says he feels bad because his friend Mary has no date for an upcoming dance, and Todd dismisses his concern:

RICHARD: God, I'm going to feel so bad for her if she stays home.
TODD: She's not going to stay home, it's ridiculous. Why doesn't she just ask somebody?

Yet Todd himself is upset because he has no date for the same dance. He explains that he doesn't want to ask Anita, and Richard, in turns, scoffs at his distress:

TODD: I felt so bad when she came over and started talking to me last night.
RICHARD: Why?
TODD: I don't know. I felt uncomfortable, I guess.
RICHARD: **I'll never understand that**. [Laugh]

Far from trying to show that he understands, Richard states flatly that he doesn't, as shown in boldface type.

Richard then tells Todd that he is afraid he has a drinking problem. Todd responds by changing the subject to something that is bothering him, his feelings of alienation:

RICHARD: When I took Anne home last night she told me off.
TODD: Really?
　　　. . .

RICHARD: You see when she found out what happened last Thursday night between Sam and me?

TODD: Mhm.

RICHARD: She knew about that. And she just said—and then she started talking about drinking. You know? . . . And then she said, you know, "You, how you hurt everybody when you do it. You're always cranky." And she just said, "I don't like it. You hurt Sam. You hurt Todd. You hurt Mary. You hurt Lois."

. . .

I mean, when she told me, you know I guess I was kind of stunned. [Pause] I didn't really drink that much.

TODD: **Are you still talking to Mary, a lot, I mean**?

RICHARD: Am I still talking to Mary?

TODD: Yeah, 'cause that's why—that's why I was mad Friday.

RICHARD: Why?

TODD: Because.

RICHARD: 'Cause Why?

TODD: 'Cause I didn't know why you all just wa- I mean I just went back upstairs for things, then y'all never came back. I was going, "Fine. I don't care." I said, "He's going to start this again."

As the lines printed in boldface show, when Richard says that he is upset because Anne told him he behaved badly when he was drunk, Todd responds by bringing up his own concern: He felt left out, and he was hurt when Richard disappeared from a party with his friend Mary.

Throughout the conversation, Todd expresses distress over feeling alienated and left out. Richard responds by trying to argue Todd out of the way he feels. When Todd says he felt out of place at a party the night before, Richard argues:

RICHARD: **How could you feel out of place? You know Lois, and you knew Sam.**

TODD: I don't know. I just feel really out of place and then last night again at the party, I mean, Sam was just running around, he knew everyone from the sorority. There was about five.

RICHARD: **Oh, no, he didn't.**

TODD: He knew a lot of people. He was—I don't know.

RICHARD: **Just Lois. He didn't know everybody.**

. . .

TODD: I just felt really out of place that day, all over the place. I used to feel, I mean—

RICHARD: Why?

TODD: I don't know. I don't even feel right at school anymore.

RICHARD: I don't know, last night, I mean—

TODD: I think I know what Ron Cameron and them feels like now. [Laugh]

RICHARD: [Laugh] **No, I don't think you feel as bad as Ron Cameron feels.**

TODD: I'm kidding.

RICHARD: Mm-mm. **Why should you? You know more people—**

TODD: I can't talk to anyone anymore.

RICHARD: **You know more people than me.**

By telling Todd that his feelings are unjustified and incomprehensible, Richard is not implying that he doesn't care. He clearly means to comfort his friend, to make him feel better. He's implying, "You shouldn't feel bad because your problems aren't so bad." . . .

When women confront men's ways of talking to them, they judge them by the standards of women's conversational styles. Women show concern by following up someone else's statement of trouble by questioning her about it. When men change the subject, women think they are showing a lack of sympathy—a failure of intimacy. But the failure to ask probing questions could just as well be a way of respecting the other's need for independence. . . .

Women tend to show understanding of another woman's feelings. When men try to reassure women by telling them that their situation is not so bleak, the women hear their feelings being belittled or discounted. Again, they encounter a failure of intimacy just when they were bidding to reinforce it. Trying to trigger a symmetrical communication, they end up in an asymmetrical one.

A Different Symmetry

The conversation between Richard and Todd shows that although the boys' responses are asymmetrical if looked at separately—each dismisses the other's concerns—they are symmetrical when looked at together: Todd responds to Richard's concern about his drinking in exactly the same way that Richard responds to Todd's feeling of alienation, by denying it is a problem:

RICHARD: Hey, man, I just don't feel—I mean, after what Anne said last night, I just don't feel like doing that.
TODD: **I don't think it was that way. You yourself knew it was no big problem.**
RICHARD: Oh, Anne—Sam told Anne that I fell down the levee.
TODD: **It's a lie.**
RICHARD: I didn't fall. I slipped, slid. I caught myself.
TODD: **Don't worry about it.**
RICHARD: But I do, kind of. I feel funny in front of Sam. I don't want to do it in front of you.
TODD: **It doesn't matter 'cause sometimes you're funny when you're off your butt.**

Todd denies that Richard was so drunk he was staggering ("It's a lie") and then says that even if he was out of control, it wasn't bad; it was funny.

In interpreting this conversation between tenth-grade boys, I initially saw their mutual reassurances and dismissals, and their mutual revelations of troubles, in terms of connection and sameness. But another perspective is possible. Their conversation may be touching precisely because it was based on asymmetries of status—or, more precisely, a deflecting of such asymmetries. When Todd tells his troubles, he puts himself in a potentially one-down position and invites Richard to take a one-up position by disclaiming troubles and asymmetrically offering advice or sympathy. By offering troubles of his own, Richard declines to take the superior position and restores their symmetrical footing, sending the metamessage "We're just a couple of guys trying to make it in a world that's tough on both of us, and both of us are about equally competent to deal with it."

From this perspective, responding as a woman might—for example by saying, "I can see how you feel; you must feel awful; so would I if it happened to me"—would have a totally different meaning for boys, since they would be inclined to interpret it through the lens of status. Such a response would send a metamessage like "Yes, I know, you incompetent jerk, I know how awful you must feel. If I were as incompetent as you, I'd feel the same way. But, lucky for you, I'm not, and I can help you out here, because I'm far too talented to be upset by a problem like that." In other words, refraining from expressing sympathy is generous, insofar as sympathy potentially condescends.

Women are often unhappy with the reactions they get from men when they try to start troubles talk, and men are often unhappy because they are accused of responding in the wrong way when they are trying to be helpful. But Richard and Todd seem satisfied with each other's ways of reacting to their troubles. And their ways make sense. When men and women talk to each other, the problem is that each expects a different kind of response. The men's approach seeks to assuage feelings indirectly by attacking their cause. Since women expect to have their feelings supported, the men's approach makes them feel that they themselves are being attacked. . . .

"I'll Help You If It Kills You"

Martha bought a computer and needed to learn to use it. After studying the manual and making some progress, she still had many questions, so she went to the store where she had bought it and asked for help. The man assigned to help her made her feel like the stupidest person in the world. He used technical language in explaining things, and each time she had to ask what a word meant she felt more incompetent, an impression reinforced by the tone of voice he used in his answer, a tone that sent the metamessage "This is obvious; everyone knows this." He explained things so quickly, she couldn't possibly remember them. When she went home, she discovered she couldn't recall what he had demonstrated, even in cases where she had followed his explanation at the time.

Still confused, and dreading the interaction, Martha returned to the store a week later, determined to stay until she got the information she needed. But this time a woman was assigned to help her. And the experience of getting help was utterly transformed. The woman avoided using technical terms for the most part, and if she did use one, she asked whether Martha knew what it meant and explained simply and clearly if she didn't. When the woman answered questions, her tone never implied that everyone should know this. And when showing how to do something, she had Martha do it, rather than demonstrating while Martha watched. The different style of this "teacher" made Martha feel like a different "student": a competent rather than stupid one, not humiliated by her ignorance.

Surely not all men give information in a way that confuses and humiliates their students. There are many gifted teachers who also happen to be men. And not all women give information in a way that makes it easy for students to understand. But many women report experiences similar to Martha's, especially in dealing with computers, automobiles, and other mechanical equipment; they claim that they feel more comfortable having women explain things to them. The different meanings that giving help entails may explain why. If women are focusing on connections, they will be motivated to minimize the difference in expertise and to be as comprehensible as possible. Since their goal is to maintain the appearance of similarity and equal status, sharing knowledge helps even the score. Their tone of voice sends metamessages of support rather than disdain, although "support" itself can be experienced as condescension.

If a man focuses on the negotiation of status and feels someone must have the upper hand, he may feel more comfortable when he has it. His attunement to the fact that having more information, knowledge, or skill puts him in a one-up position comes through in his way of talking. And if sometimes men seem intentionally to explain in a way that makes what they are explaining difficult to understand, it may be because their pleasant feeling of knowing more is reinforced when the student *does not* understand. The comfortable margin of superiority diminishes with every bit of knowledge the student gains. Or it may simply be that they are more concerned with displaying their superior knowledge and skill than with making sure that the knowledge is shared.

A colleague familiar with my ideas remarked that he'd seen evidence of this difference at an academic conference. A woman delivering a paper kept stopping and asking the audience, "Are you with me so far?" My colleague surmised that her main concern seemed to be that the audience understand what she was saying. When he gave his paper, his main concern was that he not be put down by members of the audience—and as far as he could tell, a similar preoccupation was motivating the other men presenting papers as well. From this point of view, if covering one's tracks to avoid attack entails obscuring one's point, it is a price worth paying.

This is not to say that women have no desire to feel knowledgeable or powerful. Indeed, the act of asking others whether they are able to follow your argument can be seen to frame you as superior. But it seems that having information, expertise, or skill at manipulating objects is not the primary measure of power for most women. Rather, they feel their power enhanced if they can be of help. Even more, if they are focusing on connection rather than independence and self-reliance, they feel stronger when the community is strong.

Rapport-Talk and Report-Talk

Who talks more, then, women or men? The seemingly contradictory evidence is reconciled by the difference between what I call *public* and *private speaking*. More men feel comfortable doing "public speaking," while more women feel comfortable doing "private" speaking. Another way of capturing these differences is by using the terms *report-talk* and *rapport-talk*.

For most women, the language of conversation is primarily a language of rapport: a way of establishing connections and negotiating relationships. Emphasis is placed on displaying similarities and matching experiences. From childhood, girls criticize peers who try to stand out or appear better than others. People feel their closest connections at home, or in settings where they *feel* at home—with one or a few people they feel close to and comfortable with—in other words, during private speaking. But even the most public situations can be approached like private speaking.

For most men, talk is primarily a means to preserve independence and negotiate and maintain status in a hierarchical social order. This is done by exhibiting knowledge and skill, and by holding center stage through verbal performance such as storytelling, joking, or imparting information. From childhood, men learn to use talking as a way to get and keep attention. So they are more comfortable speaking in larger groups made up of people they know less well—in the broadest sense, "public speaking." But even the most private situations can be approached like public speaking, more like giving a report than establishing rapport.

Private Speaking: The Wordy Woman and The Mute Man

What is the source of the stereotype that women talk a lot? Dale Spender suggests that most people feel instinctively (if not consciously) that women, like children, should be seen and not heard, so any amount of talk from them seems like too much. Studies have shown that if women and men talk equally in a group, people think the women talked more. So there is truth to Spender's view. But another explanation is that men think women talk a lot because they hear women talking in situations where men would not: on the telephone; or in social situations with friends, when they are not discussing topics that men find inherently interesting; or, like the couple at the women's group, at home alone—in other words, in private speaking. . . .

Sources as lofty as studies conducted by psychologists, as down to earth as letters written to advice columnists, and as sophisticated as movies and plays come up with the same insight: Men's silence at home is a disappointment to women. Again and again, women complain, "He seems to have everything to say to everyone else, and nothing to say to me."

The film *Divorce American Style* opens with a conversation in which Debbie Reynolds is claiming that she and Dick Van Dyke don't communicate, and he is protesting that he tells her everything that's on his mind. The doorbell interrupts their quarrel, and husband and wife compose themselves before opening the door to greet their guests with cheerful smiles.

Behind closed doors, many couples are having conversations like this. Like the character played by Debbie Reynolds, women feel men don't communicate. Like the husband played by Dick Van Dyke, men feel wrongly accused. How can she be convinced that he doesn't tell her anything, while he is equally convinced he tells her everything that's on his mind? How can women and men have such different ideas about the same conversations?

When something goes wrong, people look around for a source to blame: either the person they are trying to communicate with ("You're demanding, stubborn, self-centered") or the group that the other person belongs to ("All women are demanding"; "All men are self-centered"). Some generous-minded people blame the relationship ("We just can't communicate"). But underneath, or overlaid on these types of blame cast outward, most people believe that something is wrong with them.

If individual people or particular relationships were to blame, there wouldn't be so many different people having the same problems. The real problem is conversational style. Women and men have different ways of talking. Even with the best intentions, trying to settle the problem through talk can only make things worse if it is ways of talking that are causing trouble in the first place. . . .

Avoiding Mutual Blame

The difference between public and private speaking, or report-talk and rapport-talk, can be understood in terms of status and connection. It is not surprising that women are most comfortable talking when they feel safe and close, among friends and equals, whereas men feel comfortable talking when there is a need to establish and maintain their status in a group. But the situation is complex, because status and connection are bought with the same currency. What seems like a bid for status could be intended as a display of closeness, and what seems like distancing may have been intended to avoid the appearance of pulling rank. Hurtful and unjustified misinterpretations can be avoided by understanding the conversational styles of the other gender.

When men do all the talking at meetings, many women—including researchers—see them as "dominating" the meeting, intentionally preventing women from participating, publicly flexing their higher-status muscles. But the *result* that men do most of the talking does not necessarily mean that men *intend* to prevent women from speaking. Those who readily speak up assume that others are as free as they are to take the floor. In this sense, men's speaking out freely can be seen as evidence that they assume women are at the same level of status: "We are all equals," the metamessage of their behavior could be, "competing for the floor." If this is indeed the intention (and I believe it often, though not always, is), a woman can recognize women's lack of participation at meetings and take measures to redress the imbalance, without blaming men for intentionally locking them out.

The culprit, then, is not an individual man or even men's styles alone, but the difference between women's and men's styles. If that is the case, then both can make adjustments. A woman can push herself to speak up without being invited, or begin to speak without waiting for what seems a polite pause. But the adjustment should not be one-sided. A man can learn that a woman who is not accustomed to speaking up in groups is *not* as free as he is to do so. Someone who is waiting for a nice long pause before asking her question does not find the stage set for her appearance, as do those who are not awaiting a pause, the moment after (or before) another speaker stops talking. Someone who expects to be invited to speak ("You haven't said much, Millie. What do you think?") is not accustomed to leaping in and claiming the floor for herself. As in so many areas, being admitted as an equal is not in itself assurance of equal opportunity, if one is not accustomed to playing the game in the way it is being played. Being admitted to a dance does not ensure the participation of someone who has learned to dance to a different rhythm.

Review Questions

1. Tannen talks briefly about the "metamessages" in Mark's talk to Eve about her breast surgery. What's a "metamessage"?
2. Explain what Tannen means when she says that "mutual understanding is symmetrical. . . but giving advice is asymmetrical."
3. What does Tannen say is *supportive* about Richard telling Todd that his feeling "out of place" is unjustified and incomprehensible?
4. Why, according to Tannen, are Richard and Todd satisfied with their conversation, even though each *dismisses* some of the other's concerns?

Probes

1. Explain how, for the person looking for understanding, advice might not seem like a "gift," and for the person looking for advice, understanding might not seem like a "gift."
2. If you were Tannen, what would you say to the man who was about to tear his hair out over a girlfriend who continually told him about problems she was having at work but refused to take any of the advice he offered?
3. Richard indicates that he's worried about having a drinking problem, and Todd changes the subject. What do you believe is happening at this point of their conversation?

4. Paraphrase the main differences between "report" and "rapport" talk, an
each from your own experience.
5. How does Tannen respond to the "So What?" question? In other words
your communicating does she offer, as a way to deal with the differences
and rapport talk?

T hese next pages describe some of the cultural pressures on men that
affect the ways many men express themselves. The author, Bernie
Zilbergeld, is a psychotherapist who specializes in sex therapy for
men. The book this selection comes from is a 650-page guide to
enhancing sexual relationships, especially by helping men focus on pleasure
rather than performance. But I'll warn you in advance that this reading is not
directly about sex. I've included these pages because of what Zilbergeld says about
how culture and socialization help distort many men's communication with
women.

Zilbergeld describes the competing pressures that, on the one hand, drive
young boys to be "macho" and, on the other, insist that men should be more
interested in relationships, better able to express their feelings, and more involved
in household chores and childcare. He catalogs some of the media images that
help teach young boys what it means to "be a man," and contrasts them with
media images for girls. He points out that, although neither boys nor girls are supposed to look or act like their opposites, the label "sissy" when applied to a boy
has much more of a negative punch than "tomboy" applied to a girl.

This article also repeats the point made by Deborah Tannen, that girls learn
to focus on building connections with others while boys emphasize solving problems and accomplishing tasks. Ask girls about their best friends and you're likely
to hear, "Janie is my best friend because we talk and share secrets." Ask boys and
they will often say, "Robert is my best friend because we play baseball and do lots
of other things." As Zilbergeld notes, "These separate emphases set the stage for
huge problems in adult relationships" grounded in fundamentally different definitions of intimacy.

Dads tend to reinforce the cultural stereotypes that fill the media, not
because they mean to, but because this is what they got from their own fathers.
As Zilbergeld summarizes, "The socialization of males provides very little that is
of value in the formation and maintenance of intimate relationships." In most
Western cultures boys learn strong messages about the value of *competition*, and
these dominate the communication styles they take on later in life. But even the
boy or young man who competes effectively is in a bind when he's confused,
frightened, or needs help. If he admits his problem, he's not who he ought to be.
But if he doesn't, he can do worse at the task he's working on, or even make
himself sick. It's not surprising that men generally self-disclose much less than
women. In short, according to this author, "Being a male is like living in a suit of
armor, ready for battle to prove himself. The armor may offer protection
(although it's not clear against what), but it's horribly confining and not much
fun."

In the final section, Zilbergeld extends this analysis to the messages boys ²arn about sex. Developmental pressures, media images, and cultural stereotypes conspire to focus boys almost exclusively on the physical side of sex. Girls' sexuality, on the other hand, is channeled or filtered more through personal connection. And this difference persists into adult life.

In this part of his book, Zilbergeld doesn't offer many solutions for the problems he outlines. But he does help us understand something about *why* men and women communicate differently.

The Making of Anxious Performers

Bernie Zilbergeld

"I hear girls had it rougher, but you couldn't prove it by me. Growing up was the pits. Incredible pressures all the time, everywhere. Had to do well in school, had to do well in sports, had to maintain my manly image and couldn't walk away from a fight, and later had to do well with girls and pretend I knew all about sex and was getting it regularly. I often wished the whole world would just go away and leave me alone. I don't know what I would have done, but it couldn't have been any worse."

—MAN, 36

"It took me half a century to realize that I'd been living a half life, that I had buried important feelings and parts of myself. I was a shit father and husband. Not abusive or anything like that, but I wasn't even home most of the time. Aside from money and fixing things around the house, I didn't contribute anything. Only when my grandson arrived did I make a shift. With him, I am a whole person. I can love him, cuddle him, listen to him, and really talk to him. Sounds funny, listening and talking to a four-year-old, but it's true. His expression of emotion has allowed me to unblock my own feelings. I'm sad that my wife died before I could be a real partner to her. I'm sad that I didn't give more to my own children and that I missed out on so much."

—MAN, 54

Making The Man

Men in our culture walk a thin line. Like their fathers and grandfathers, they must be sure their behavior conforms to what is considered manly. It takes very little—maybe as little as one failure or one sign of weakness—to lose one's place in the charmed circle of men. . . .But if a man isn't a man, what then is he? The answer most men seem to believe is: Nothing at all. For their identities are inextricably linked to their gender role.

The concern of being considered a non-man keeps men in a state of almost perpetual vigilance and anxiety. It also makes for a certain inflexibility. If the results of changing one's behavior can be so dire as a loss of identity, one doesn't take change lightly. There is nothing new about this situation for men; it has existed in Western societies for hundreds of years. What is new is that the traditional definition of masculinity has come under scrutiny and attack and that the messages men get have become quite confused. Men are still supposed to exhibit all the manly virtues, but now they should also be sensitive and emotionally expressive, attributes that used to be considered feminine. Being a man has become more difficult than ever before.

What follows, is in my mind, not a pretty story. It shows how we transform male babies into adult beings who are somewhat less than human, who are cut off from huge portions of themselves, the parts that have to do with caring, nurturing, and expressing, who must wear a suit of armor almost all day and night, and who in a very real sense are only pale reflections of who they might be. At least in the old days, they were heavily rewarded for succeeding at being who society wanted them to be. But in recent times, men have come under unrelenting criticism for being who they were trained to be and for not being who they were discouraged from being. The cry is heard on media talk shows, in countless books and articles, in therapy offices, and in bedrooms and kitchens throughout the land: "Why aren't men more interested in relationships, why aren't they softer, why don't they express feelings, why aren't they more interested in household chores and childcare?" The questions are of course not really questions, but accusations.

But why should men be these ways? Where did they learn to focus on relationships, to express emotion, to be interested in children? The answer is: Nowhere at all.

By the age of three or so, boys and girls are aware that they are not just children—they are boy children and girl children, and these distinctions are extremely important. Later learning is always filtered through their gender-colored lenses. Even such neutral-seeming activities as cooking, soccer, and math are influenced by these lenses. Very early on, the child has a notion that soccer and math are things boys are interested in, while cooking is for girls. These notions are easily modifiable at early ages—a boy whose father takes pride in his culinary skills may well conclude that cooking is for males—but the point remains that everything is seen in terms of gender. This is especially true for areas such as sexuality, which is always and everywhere seen in genderlinked ways; in every culture, the rules for male and female sexual behavior are different.

What a culture teaches its boys and girls is dependent on its images of men and women, what it wants these youngsters to grow up to be. Although in recent years we have been reevaluating what we want from men and women, the traditional definitions still exert a very strong pull. A number of researchers have found that a small number of characteristics comprise most of what we expect from our men: strength and self-reliance, success, no sissy stuff (in other words, don't be like women), and sexual interest and prowess. Here's a description from a Harold Robbins novel: "This was a strong man. . . . The earth moved before him when he walked, men loved and feared him, women trembled at the power in his loins, people sought his favors." That may seem a bit outdated, but here's how a recent Sidney Sheldon novel describes the hero: "He was like a force of nature, taking over everything in his path." In a 1989 novel titled *Sophisticated Lady*, we read of the hero (who had, or course, a "tall, powerfully built body"): "Just standing there, he radiated a quiet kind of strength and authority. . . ." And it goes without saying that he was a very successful businessman. He's the modern version: less raucous, more sophisticated, but still strong and successful. Over and over, the descriptions of admired men in books and movies convey, implicitly or explicitly, strength, power, and independence.

Of course there are contrary images: weak men, passive men, and general bunglers like Dagwood Bumstead. But we know they aren't what's wanted, that their bungling is precisely what makes them funny. Real men don't behave like this.

Little boys and little girls are certainly not the same—boys, for example, are on the average more active and aggressive—but they are more similar than adult men and women. Boys, like girls, are playful, warm, open, expressive, loving, vulnerable, and all the other things that make children so attractive. But when we look at adult men, we may wonder what happened to all these wonderful qualities. As adults, men display them to a far lesser degree, if at all. A lot of their best stuff has been trained out of them. In addition, some of their worst and most dangerous tendencies—toward aggressiveness and even violence—have been overdeveloped.

Although I emphasize the role of learning or socialization in the discussion that follows, I do not mean to imply there are no biological differences between the sexes. There certainly are. Nature had different purposes in mind for males and females and programmed them accordingly. Nonetheless, the training given to boys and girls is strikingly different and has an important influence. While we may not be able totally to undo a genetic disposition, we can shape it to some extent. It is probably true, for instance, that males are genetically more aggressive than females, but how frequently and in what ways aggressiveness is manifested are significantly influenced by societal messages boys and men get about it.

For the last seven years I've been involved in helping to raise a boy named Ian, who is now eight. He and his friends are nothing like any man I know. Expressing feelings? No problem. When I've hurt his feelings, Ian doesn't beat around the bush: "Bernie, you hurt my feelings and that isn't very nice." When we go into a room that contains strangers, he takes my hand and says: "I'm scared. You know how shy I am." He has no trouble saying he's sad or apologizing when he has offended someone. He cries, he laughs, he smiles in a way that lights up the sky for everyone around, and he literally jumps for joy.

Little boys present a huge problem for all societies, because the societies don't want men to be like these boys. The question is how to make these open, expressive boys who wear their vulnerabilities and fears on their sleeves into strong, decisive performers who will be able to do whatever the society deems manly. We may think it's cute for a young boy to say, trembling, "I'm scared a monster is gonna get me," but we don't want a twenty- or thirty-year-old to act that way. Instead, we want him to deny his fear ("Monsters don't scare *me!*") and announce he's going to kick some monster ass.

Training in masculinity begins as soon as the child is born and continues for the rest of his life. By the age of six or seven, important lessons have already taken hold. An image of this process comes from a scene in a recent novel about a shooting at an elementary school. There was the usual mass confusion, shots, and a dead body being carried out; in short, a trauma. How did the kids react? A "little girl burst into tears. A chubby boy, five or six, cried. The boy next to him was older, maybe eight. Staring straight ahead and biting his lip, straining for macho." Between the ages of five and eight, he has learned lessons about being male. He will not cry, maybe never again. Nor will he show fear or dependency or tenderness, and he may not even be able to ask for directions when he's lost. He will lose his ability not only to show feelings, but also to experience and know them. He won't understand why his girlfriend or wife just wants to cuddle, to hear his fears and express hers, simply to talk. . . .

An important ingredient of the socialization of boys is the message "Don't be like a girl." Since females of all ages are the softer ones—the people who express feelings, who cry, who are more people oriented—not being like them is an effective way to suppress the softer side of males. Girls and women are allowed far greater leeway. *Tomboy* has nowhere near the derogatory punch of *girl* or *sissy*. Girls can play boys' games and with boys' toys, wear boys' clothes. But can you imagine what others will call a boy after the age of four or five who wears a dress or plays house or with dolls?

The primary focus of males and females is very different. Connection to others is the name of the game for females of all ages, even in their play. Dolls (the typical plaything of girls) are more conducive to intimacy training than the toy trucks and weapons boys get. You can cuddle a doll, comfort it, feed it, talk to it, sleep with it. But what can you do with a fire truck that has anything to do with relationships?

Ask little girls about their best friends, and this is what you get: "Janie is my best friend because we talk and share secrets." Research shows that girls spend much more time than boys in one-to-one interaction with their friends, in what one researcher called "chumships." Boys go in a different direction. They learn that the primary thing in life is doing or performing in the world out there, not in the family in here. When little boys are asked about their best friends, their answers usually are about activities: "Robert is my best friend because we play baseball and do lots of other things." Much more so than girls, boys spend time in large groups, often playing games. By the ages of six or seven, the differences that plague adult couples are already in evidence. The boys stress action and the girls talking.

These separate emphases set the stage for huge problems in adult relationships. Both men and women say they want love and intimacy, but they mean different things by these terms. Women favor what has been called face-to-face intimacy: They want to talk. Men prefer side-by-side intimacy: They want to do.

In almost all societies, femininity is given by having the right genitals. Masculinity or manhood is not. It is conditional. Having the right genitals is necessary but not sufficient. As Norman Mailer put it: "Nobody was born a man; you earned your manhood provided you were good enough, bold enough." . . .

Early on the boy gets the idea that he can't be like the person who means the most to him, his mother. No longer is it acceptable to bask in her warmth and nurturance, except occasionally, and no longer is it possible to think that he, as she did, will someday give birth to babies. She's a woman, and he can't be like her or any other woman. In effect he's wrenched away from the closest relationship he's had and may ever have. In most primitive societies, boys were also wrenched away from Mom, but they were entrusted to the care of one or more men who guided their development. In our society, there is no such arrangement.

There is only Dad, or whoever is playing that role for the boy. It is from him that the boy will learn his most important lessons about masculinity. Unfortunately, that relationship is rarely nurturing or positive in our society. Fathers are often not physically present and when they are, often are not emotionally present. Physical affection, emotional sharing, expression of approval and love—these are the human experiences that very few boys get from their dads. It is a tragedy of the greatest magnitude for men not to have been respected, nurtured, loved, and guided by their fathers.

Martial arts expert Richard Heckler recalls what happened when he was a child and his sailor father returned from a yearlong cruise:

> I felt proud of him, proud that he was my father, proud that after not seeing him for a year and not even sure what he looked like, I still had a father. He came up to me and extended his hand in his stiff, formal way. "Hello son. Have you been taking care of your moth-

er and sister while I was away?" I was nine years old and I wanted him to hold me and have him say that he loved me. But he didn't then or ever. . . .

What boys do get from their dads, if anything at all, is reinforcement of macho tendencies (Dad much more than Mom is the one who teaches the necessity for toughness) and the necessity for performance and achievement. Therapist Terrance O'Connor relates this story:

> I was struggling in my first year of high school. My father had just given me holy hell for the scores I had received on a standardized test. I felt terrible. In my room, I went over the results again and again. . . . Suddenly I realized that the numbers were raw scores. They needed to be converted. I was astonished. In percentiles, my scores were in the nineties. Vastly relieved, I rushed out to show my father. "Then why in hell don't you get better grades?" he yelled. It was a dagger in my heart. Never a word of love. Never a word of praise. Back in my room, teeth and fists clenched, I said a prayer: "Dear God, never, never, never, let me grow up like that son of a bitch."

This is not to blame our fathers, who were only doing what was done to them. Nonetheless, the wounds opened by this lack of care run deep and are rarely healed. And few men can find ways to express this primal pain and to heal the wounds. If you want to see grown men cry, give them a safe setting and get them talking about their fathers. That's all it takes.

Because the boy is wrenched away from his first real intimate relationship, does not get to experience one with his father, and is taught a body of attitudes, beliefs, and behaviors that are in fact not conducive to intimacy, he will arrive at adulthood quite unprepared for the requirements of a mature relationship. The point is simple and frightening: The socialization of males provides very little that is of value in the formation and maintenance of intimate relationships.

Since so much of male training is in opposition to female qualities, males come to believe that these qualities, and therefore femaleness as a whole, are strange and inferior. The result is the development of a habit of not taking women seriously. Although a man may dearly love a woman and want very much to be considerate, fair, and respectful, he has years of training pulling in the other direction. Women are icky, weird, and disgusting; they're weak and dependent rather than strong and independent as he's supposed to be; they're overly emotional and not logical; they're at the mercy of their hormones (as if they were the only ones with hormones and cycles); and, well, they just don't see thing the way men do. Since the boy had to break away from his mother and feminine ways to establish his masculinity, there's also a fear of once again coming under the domination of a woman. To be in this situation is too much like childhood, when he was a non-man. The last thing any man wants is to be "pussy-whipped" or "henpecked" because that's a clear indication that he's not man enough to keep "the little woman" under control. This, too, often leads men, no matter how much they love their partners, to be not quite able to treat them as full human beings with equal rights. This inability to take women seriously can cause much friction in adult relationships and negatively affects sex itself, as we will see later.

Since strength and self-reliance are the primary goals we have for our males, they are trained to mistrust and dislike the more vulnerable and expressive side of themselves. When the boy watches the adults around him, he sees that men are very different from women. Men are rougher and gruffer, they don't express many feelings, they don't talk about personal matters, they don't touch the way women do, and they're admired and rewarded for accomplishments that have nothing to do with what he loves in his mother.

Boys are rewarded for "toughing it out," "hanging tough," not crying, not being weak. By the time Ian was four, he was using the words *tough* and *strong* in an admiring way. By the time he was five, *wimp* and *sissy* had entered his vocabulary as negative terms for males. Sometimes when he was angry at me, he would explode, "You're just a wimp."

Part of being tough is not getting or needing the loving touching that all babies get. Parents stop touching their boys early on; it seems somehow feminine or treating him like a baby or sissy. Girls, on the other hand, continue to be touched and hugged. We end up with women who understand touch as a basic human need and like to touch and be touched as a way of reinforcing contact and demonstrating affection; men, in contrast, lose sight of their need for touching except as a part of roughhousing or sex.

Boys learn that competition is an aid in proving oneself. If you're as good as or better than other males then at least you're some kind of man. Maybe not the man you could or should be, but at least you're not out of the running.

Most of us experienced no choice: We had to demonstrate our masculinity no matter how ill equipped and ill prepared we felt. In his essay "Being a Boy," Julius Lester captures the agony so many of us felt. Comparing himself to girls, he says:

> There was the life, I thought! No constant pressure to prove oneself. No necessity always to be competing. While I humiliated myself on football and baseball fields, the girls stood on the sidelines laughing at me, because they didn't have to do anything except be girls. The rising of each sun brought me to the starting line of yet another day's Olympic decathlon, with no hope of ever winning even a bronze medal.

Competitiveness turned out to be one of the uglier manifestations of male upbringing. First, because so few of us could win and therefore feel good about ourselves. After all, how many boys can excel at baseball, basketball, and football? And what are the others supposed to do? Countless men have stories to tell about how humiliated they felt as boys when they weren't successful on the athletic field, couldn't even do well enough to be chosen when teams were selected. They felt bad not only because they didn't get to play, but because their very personhood or manhood was questioned.

Second, competition is antithetical to intimacy. As psychologist Ayala Pines points out, in competition the question is "Who's on top?" or "Who's in front?" In intimacy the question is "How close are we or do we want to be?" Closeness is tied to openness, how much we can share of ourselves. But it's difficult to be open if you have a competitive mental set, for the fear is that what is revealed can be used to the other person's advantage.

Because of the emphasis on strength and self-reliance, men have trouble admitting to unresolved personal problems. It's not that problems don't come up, but you handle them, solve them, master them without help and without complaint. That's a large part of what being tough and independent—of being a man—means.

Like so many of the other ideas that men learn, this one puts them in a bind. What is a man supposed to do when he's confused, when he's frightened, when he needs help? Almost by definition, if he acknowledges his confusion or fear and asks for help, there's something wrong with him. He's not as tough as he ought to be. If, on the other hand, he doesn't acknowledge what's bothering him and get help, he may literally make himself sick and do worse at the task he's working on. On a mundane level, this belief results in the ridiculous behavior of men driving around endlessly in their cars because to stop and ask for directions would suggest they need help, which they do.

Many men do not acknowledge their worries and fears to their partners. They simply try to handle everything on their own. I have been involved in many cases where the man was confronted with a major crisis that involved his whole family—the possible loss of a job or a move to another part of the country—but didn't say a word about it to his partner. She knew something was wrong because of the man's distance or irritability, but feared upsetting him by bringing it up: "I told you everything is fine. Leave me alone!" Yet, if she doesn't bring it up, she has to suffer with the man's behavior and may blame herself as well. . . .

Another consequence of being unable to express problems is that men often don't get what they need. They are slow to admit to illness and other physical problems, and they are even slower to admit to emotional distress. And the idea of needing to go to an expert for help in dealing with personal or relationship problems is anathema to many of them. Men are changing in this respect—more men, for example, are coming to therapists' offices—but the change is slow, and men are still nowhere near as willing as women to admit to personal problems.

It's not easy for boys and men. It's not easy to give up the warm, tender side of themselves. It's not easy to squelch feelings of dependency, love, fear, and anxiety. It's not always easy to be posturing, pretending to be more knowledgeable, more self-reliant, more confident, and more fierce than you really are. There are many times when a man feels fearful or defeated and wants nothing more than to be held and comforted, just as his mother held and comforted him long ago. But he can't get it. He can't admit his feelings and he can't ask to be held. And that is very sad. Like some men, he may choose to drown his feelings in alcohol or sex; at least in sex he will get some body contact and a distraction from his feelings. But neither the alcohol or the sex is the same as real physical and emotional comforting. Too bad he can't get what he really needs and wants.

It's not easy to always have to perform and succeed, whether on the athletic field, in the boardroom, or in the bedroom. Although the whole process has been romanticized, the fact is that boys and men often make themselves sick and crazy in getting ready to perform. It's not unusual for athletes to throw up in locker rooms before competition (romanticize that if you can) and to get themselves into a murderous rage that under any other circumstances would rightfully be considered psychotic. This process, by the way, is often called "getting it up." It's not easy for a man to go into a sexual situation believing that everything rides on how well he performs (especially with a part of himself that he can't control), but what else is he to do?

Being a male is like living in a suit of armor, ready for battle to prove himself. The armor may offer protection (although it's not clear against what), but it's horribly confining and not much fun. In fact, fun is exactly what it's not. Maybe this is why so many men take to alcohol and other ways of deadening themselves. And it may help explain men's fascination with sports.

In sports many of the usual prohibitions on males are lifted. A man can be as emotional and expressive about his favorite team and players as he wants. He can cheer them on with unabashed enthusiasm and what might even pass for love. He can be ecstatic and jump up and down when they win and he can feel despair and weep when they lose. Playfulness and creativity are allowed. He can dress up in ridiculous hats and shirts, make up posters and poems and songs, and just be plain silly. There's even a lot of physical contact: back- and butt-slapping, shoulder- and arm-touching, and hugging. And one can express anger without much risk, cursing a bad call, a decision, or a mistake. Sports is one of the few places where men can safely become boys again, where they can drop the facade of Mr. Uptight-and-in-Control and just play. Sports, whether watching or participating, is one of the few places that adult men display the expressiveness and playfulness of Ian and his friends. Is it any wonder they love it so?

Learning About Sex

"Through no fault of my own I reached adolescence. While the pressure to prove myself on the athletic field lessened, the overall situation got worse—because now I had to prove myself with girls. Just how I was supposed to go about doing this was beyond me. . . . Nonetheless, duty called, and with my ninth-grade gym-class jockstrap flapping between my legs, off I went."

—JULIUS LESTER

Between the ages of eleven and fourteen, children enter puberty. The brain signals the pituitary gland to increase its production of growth hormones and, in males, of testosterone. One of the first outward signs of puberty is a spurt in the rate of physical growth, unmatched since the first few years of life. During the next few years, in boys the penis and scrotum enlarge to adult size, facial and pubic hair appear, and sperm and semen are manufactured. By the age of fifteen or so, boys (and girls as well) are capable of sexual reproduction. And they feel differently than before, trying to get accustomed to their new bodies, trying to make sense of new sensations they experience, trying to deal with the hormonal gush. Testosterone in boys and estrogen in girls make a crucial difference, causing the boys and girls to seek each other out, but also propelling them along the separate paths already well developed.

Before they start having sex with partners or even themselves, boys know that sexual interest and prowess are crucial to being a man. The message permeates our culture. Here's how the hero of a romance novel thinks of himself: "He was, after all, a very physical man with a highly active sex drive. He enjoyed women, all kinds of women. . . ." All kinds: apparently short ones, tall ones, young ones, old ones, fat ones, thin ones, smart ones, dumb ones. He likes to get it on and presumably isn't too particular with whom. Can't be a hero if you don't have a highly active sex drive. When Jerry Brown was governor of California, one of the biggest questions concerned his sex life. That he didn't seem to have one was intolerable. The whole state felt greatly relieved when we learned he was going out with Linda Ronstadt.

It's interesting that in the liberated '90s we still have a double standard for males and females regarding sex. Boys will be boys, after all, and how can you be against a boy sowing his wild oats? We tend to admire males who get around. No one I know thought any the less of John F. Kennedy after learning that he had bedded almost every woman in town; in fact, most men I know seemed to think more of him. But although women are no longer expected to be virgins, God help any of them who has had sex with too many men, however many that might be.

Since sexuality is such a crucial component of masculinity, males feel pressured to act interested in sex whether or not they really are. They have to join in the jokes and banter. "Getting any, Fred?" "Oh yeah, more than I know what to do with." And they have to face the derision of their peers if they're still—God forbid—virgins at the advanced ages of eighteen or twenty-three. This is a great setup for faking, lying, and feeling inadequate. . . .

Girls go in a different direction. Perhaps because their genitals are internal and less obvious and obtrusive than boys', their attention isn't constantly drawn downward. Probably of greater importance is that nature had a different task in mind for women than for men (to find a mate to help to care for and raise the children they produced). . . .

Teenage girls aren't as focused on physical sex as boys. . . . Girls' sexuality is channeled or filtered through personal connection. They want to have sex with Prince Charming or Mr. Right in the context of a relationship. The idea of a group of girls getting together to have sex with Joe Dork just because he's willing to put out is almost unthinkable. More so than men's, women's first sexual experience with a partner is likely to be with someone they love. And women are far less likely than men to seek sex for its own sake. It's not surprising that when Lonnie Barbach and Linda Levine asked women what qualities make for a good sexual experience, relationship factors were mentioned most often. "Women talked about the security, comfort, and sharing that took place in the emotional relationship as being necessary prerequisites for good sex."

Here we see a male-female difference that persists into adult life. For women, sex is intertwined with personal connection. For men, sex is more a thing in itself, an act to be engaged in with or without love, with or without commitment, with or without connection. Although in surveys men agree with women that the best sex occurs in loving relationships, much more so than women they'll take it any way they can get it.

That the sex boys learn about is performance oriented goes without saying. What else could it be for a person who has already had over a decade of training in becoming a performance machine?

Review Questions

1. Describe three currently-popular television shows or media personalities that are helping define what it means today to be "male" and "female."
2. Some people would say that differences between males and females are genetically, not culturally, determined. What does Zilbergeld say about this point?
3. Explain the difference Zilbergeld makes between "face-to-face" and "side-by-side" intimacy.
4. What does Zilbergeld mean when he says that boys are "wrenched away" from their first really intimate relationship—the one they have with their moms?
5. What is the "double standard" for males and females about sex? Do you agree with Zilbergeld that it still exists?

Probes

1. Think back to the first memory you had about what it means to be a boy or a girl. Where did you get this message? How much impact did it have? Is it still part of your definition of your own sex role?
2. Zilbergeld describes his young friend Ian, who can communicate in some ways that are atypical for males. What point is he making here?
3. Analyze the favorite toys of some girl and boy children you know (1-6 years old). Which toys promote connection and help teach intimacy attitudes and skills? Which work against or ignore these teachings?

4. It's easy to cite examples of activities that teach boys competition. What activities, if any, also teach young girls to be competitive? Do you think Zilbergeld's analysis of the effects of competition applies to both sexes?
5. In your own experience, what communication problems have you experienced that seemed rooted in the demand on the males involved that they *perform*?

Relationships

Chapter 10

Negotiating
Relationships

In my introduction to interpersonal communication in Chapter 2, I emphasized the importance of recognizing that every time you or I communicate with anybody, one thing we're doing is negotiating our identity, which means mutually working out definitions of ourselves and each other. This is one reason why there's such a direct connection between quality of communication and quality of life—who we are is continually affected by the communication we experience. This is also why I emphasize that communication doesn't just function to express thoughts and feelings publicly or to get things done instrumentally. Communication is expressive and instrumental, but it's also a *person-building* process.

One way to talk about how the person-building part of communication works is to use the vocabulary of "Negotiating Selves." This vocabulary describes how, early in every relationship, the people involved directly and indirectly jockey for position with each other, sometimes competitively, but most of the time collaboratively. This process of negotiating selves happens when employees meet their bosses for the first few times, when couples work through the early stages of a dating relationship, and when teachers and students first get together. In all these situations the people *negotiate* who they are in relation to each other. Then, as relationships develop, this negotiation of selves process continues, although usually not so overtly. Sometimes very subtle events mark the change from a strict superior-subordinate relationship to a work-team, or from acquaintances to friends to sexual partners. Throughout the history of all the different kinds of relationships, people negotiate selves. This is part of what's going on *whenever* humans communicate.

In the basic interpersonal communication text I coauthored, Carole Logan and I discuss the process of negotiating selves in a fair amount of detail. The following reading is the first half of the chapter dedicated to this topic. After some examples to illustrate what we're talking about, we offer a definition of the process. We emphasize that people don't decide *whether* to engage in this process—it goes on all the time, in every culture. But people do continually make important decisions about *how* to engage in it. By the same token, there are no universally "right" or "wrong" ways to negotiate selves. There are just *outcomes*—fairly predictable results of the choices each person makes.

We point out that the label "negotiation" means that this process is ongoing and mutual. People collaborate to establish their identities, even when they're arguing or in conflict with each other. The process is mutual in the sense that one person's choices are affected by the other person's and vice versa. It's also a process that involves both "input" and "output," "inhaling" and "exhaling," or "giving" and "getting." We help define who we are in part by what we express verbally and nonverbally, and partly by what we notice, sense, or perceive about the other person(s) involved.

The "selves" part of the label emphasizes how identities are altered as we communicate. Carole and I acknowledge that everybody has some stable features of who they are, and we all follow some predictable patterns. But we emphasize how relationships change these identities, sometimes subtly and sometimes significantly. We note how selves are molded in our family of origin and how they change, for example, by how we experience criticism.

So this reading introduces two ideas: (a) that relationships are made up in part of ongoing negotiation processes, and (b) that one of the most important things we negotiate is *who we are*. The next two readings in this chapter extend and apply these basic ideas.

Negotiating Selves

John Stewart and Carole Logan

Notice the differences between the following two conversations:

Conversation 1

RICARDO: I've got some ideas about what we could do Sunday afternoon.
CHERYL: What do you want to do?
RICARDO: I'd like to find that new park we read about. I heard it has some good trails for biking or walking. Why don't you pack a lunch, and we'll spend the afternoon there.
CHERYL: Sounds great. When will you pick me up?
RICARDO: I'll be by about one.

Conversation 2

DERECK: I have some ideas about what we could do Sunday afternoon.
MARIA: Good. I'd like to spend the time together, but I'd rather not be with your friends. Let's just the two of us do something.
DERECK: Okay. Why don't we go down to the mall for a while and then see a movie? It's not very crowded on Sunday.
MARIA: Well, there are usually lots of little kids there. Let's do something more active.
DERECK: Okay, you want to walk or bike around Green Lake?
MARIA: That sounds great! What time can I pick you up?
DERECK: How about one?

How would you describe Ricardo in conversation 1? As active? Assertive? Creative? A leader? Decision maker? Or as passive? Agreeable? Accepting? A follower? How about Cheryl? Which of these labels fit her? What are the differences between Cheryl in conversation 1 and Maria in conversation 2? And what kind of person is Dereck in relation to Maria?

The answers are pretty obvious. In conversation 1, Ricardo comes across as active, assertive, and the primary decision maker ("I'd like to find a new park. . . ." "Why don't you pack a lunch. . . ." "I'll be by about one.") while Cheryl is more passive, accepting, and agreeable ("What do you want to do?" "Sounds great."). In this conversation, Ricardo defines himself as "leader," Cheryl accepts this definition, and she defines herself as "follower." Importantly, these may be the typical ways they define themselves in this relationship, or there very well may be other times when Cheryl is leader and Ricardo is follower.

Excerpted from Chapter 9 of *Together: Communicating Interpersonally*, 4/e by John Stewart and Carole Logan. 1993 McGraw-Hill.

When you compare the two conversations, Maria defines herself as much more of a decision maker than Cheryl. She wants to have an equal say in the plan for Sunday afternoon, rather than letting Dereck make all the decisions. And in conversation 2, Dereck appears to be comfortable with this equality. He accepts Maria's definition of herself and defines himself as agreeable and cooperative. Again, these may or may not be the typical ways these two people define themselves and each other.

The reason it's fairly obvious how to describe the four people is that their selves or identities are present *in their talk*. When Cheryl says to Ricardo, "What do you want to do?" she defines herself as, at this moment, a follower and encourages Ricardo to lead their decision making. On the other hand, when Maria says, "I'd like to spend the time together, but I'd rather not be with your friends," she defines herself as an equal participant in the process of deciding what to do on Sunday. Then when Dereck responds, "Okay, Why don't we go down to the mall . . . ," this comment contains his acceptance of Maria's definition of herself. So their definitions of themselves and of each other aren't just "in their heads"; their identities appear and are worked out in their talk.

Our comments about these brief conversations should make it clear how these four people are involved in a process of constructing and responding to definitions of themselves and definitions of the other persons communicating with them. This is negotiating selves.

We want to emphasize that nobody in these two conversations is negotiating selves "correctly," and nobody is doing it "wrong." In one sense, there is no right or wrong way to participate in this process. There are just *outcomes* of how you do it, *results* that you may or may not want. In these two brief conversations, it appears that the results are all positive. Ricardo and Cheryl seem to be perfectly satisfied with the definitions of each other they're constructing, and Maria and Dereck do, too. But if any of the four wanted to change his or her identity—how he or she is being defined in relation to the other person—it might help them to know more about negotiating selves.

We also want to underscore the point that these four people could not avoid negotiating selves. It's a process that happens whenever people communicate. No matter how brief or extended the contact, whether it's written or oral, mediated or face to face, impersonal or interpersonal, the people involved will be directly or indirectly constructing definitions of themselves and responding to the definitions offered by others. The person who writes a letter longhand on colorful stationery is defining him- or herself differently from the person who writes the same letter on a word processor or typewriter. The person who answers the telephone, "Yeah?" is defining him- or herself differently from the one who answers, "Good morning. May I help you?" This process goes on even when there seems to be no topic or subject matter.

Conversation 3

JAN: Hey, how's it goin', Paul?
PAUL: (*Silence and a scowl*)
JAN: What's the matter?
PAUL: Nothing. Forget it.
JAN: What are you so out of shape about?
PAUL: Forget it! Just drop it.
JAN: Well, all right! Pout! I don't give a damn!

Here, even though Paul and Jan are not talking about any object, issue, or event, they are definitely negotiating selves. In this conversation Paul's definition of himself and of Jan goes something like this:

> I see myself as independent of you (*silence*—"Nothing. Forget it."). I don't choose to do much self presentation in words. I see you as feeling superior to me; you seem to see me as crabby or unreasonable. But I know better. I have good reasons for my anger.

On the other hand, Jan's definition of himself and of Paul is something like this:

> I see myself as friendly and concerned (*"Hey, How's it goin'?"* *"What's the matter?"*). I'm willing to stick my neck out a little, but I see you as unreasonable and isolating. So there's a limit to how long I'll *stay* friendly and concerned. (*"Well all right! Pout! I don't give a damn!"*).

Some intercultural communication research shows how negotiating selves occurs all over the world. For example, in a bar in Nairobi, Kenya, a researcher observed three trilingual middle-class Kenyans negotiating identities in part by switching among the three languages each of them knew—English, Swahili, and Luyia, a native dialect. Two of the speakers used Swahili for "How did things go today?" "Things went well for me," and ". . . I'm waiting for you to order me a bottle of [beer]." But then one switched to Swahili-English to say, "Forget it, *bwana*," and into Luyia to add, "I found you here, so you're the one to buy for me first." This speaker used a language switch to help redefine himself as guest rather than buyer of the drinks. After a response from the other which also relied on Luyia, the third man offered in English to mediate their argument over who would buy. The researcher points out that one of the main ways he defined himself as mediator was to use English.[1] So these three people used language choice as one of their ways to negotiate selves.

A similar process often happens in the United States when African-Americans switch between black English and standard American English to define themselves differently in "informal" versus "official" communication contexts. Sometimes black grammar, vocabulary, intonation, and posture will be used among family and friends, and white language, intonation, and posture will be used with administrative officials. This process operates in other cross-cultural situations, too. For example, "much of the Spanish-English code switching by Hispanic-American bilinguals" functions to change self-definitions.[2] The main point of these intercultural studies is that speakers use language choices "imaginatively, that a range of options is open to them within a normative framework, and that taking one option rather than another is the *negotiation of identities*."[3]

So two reasons why it's important to understand negotiating selves are (a) that you're doing it whenever you communicate—and everybody else is, too—and (b) that the process affects your identity, who you are in relation to others. The third reason why it's important is that *your negotiation choices affect where your communication is on the Impersonal ——— Interpersonal continuum*. . . . When you make some negotiation choices, you just about guarantee that your communication will be impersonal. Other choices lead to more interpersonal communicating. So if you want to help make your contacts with your dating partner, employer, roommate, sister, or parent either more impersonal or more interpersonal, you need to learn as much as you can about this process.

Understanding the Terms

Negotiation

One widely respected book defines negotiation as "back-and-forth communication designed to reach an agreement when you and the other side have some interests that are shared and others that are opposed."[4] A writer who reviewed twenty different discussions of negotiation came up with a similar definition. She found that all twenty accounts dealt with situations marked by three characteristics: (1) the people involved are creating or building relationships, (2) their relationships move along a scale from competitive or confrontational to cooperative or collaborative, and (3) the people arrive at decisions mutually.[5]

These definitions capture much of what we mean by the term. First, we use the term *negotiation* to underscore the point that this process happens between people. You clearly can't negotiate by yourself. Whether you're trying to agree on the cost of a used car, the conditions of a legal settlement, or definitions of yourself and someone else, negotiation always involves two or more people.

Our second reason is closely related; negotiation is an active, not a passive, process. It isn't something that just happens to you. You act on the basis of choices you make. Again, this applies to all kinds of negotiation, including negotiation of selves. Before reading this discussion of the process, you may not have thought much about the self-definitions you are continually constructing and responding to. But we hope that the three conversations above help demonstrate how you have been making negotiation choices all along. . . . Part of what it means to be a person is to make choices like this. We also hope the conversations suggest that the more aware of the process you become, the more you will be able to choose effectively.

The term *negotiation* also suggests that the outcome of the process is not predetermined. When everybody knows how it's going to come out, you're not really negotiating; you're just going through the motions. Genuine negotiation requires at least the possibility of movement on both or all sides. So the term *negotiation* labels a process that involves two or more people making choices that affect a more or less open-ended set of outcomes.

We also want to make the point that, like communication, negotiation is made up of two activities: receiving and sending, getting and giving, listening and presenting, inhaling and exhaling. Because they happen as part of a transaction, these two processes get combined into the sense or meaning that communicators build together. In this particular sense *negotiation* is synonymous with *communication*.[6] Whenever you're either communicating or negotiating with someone else, you're both giving off cues and taking them in, sharing and being aware, giving and getting, listening and presenting. In a face-to-face situation, you're watching the person you're communicating with and interpreting what he or she is saying (listening), and at the same time you're gesturing, moving, nodding, and talking (presenting). On the phone the same two basic operations occur. Even written communication, radio, and television involve both processes. In these cases the journalist's or announcer's listening is limited; they have to rely on assumptions about who will read what they're writing, what their market research tells them about their audience, and what they learn from the people who call in. Sometimes their response is delayed until they receive an evaluation of what they have written or a letter from a listener or viewer. But what they "get" still affects what they write or say and how they write or say it. These same two processes characterize all the communicating humans do.

It's probably obvious from our examples that people are sometimes more aware of the negotiating that's going on, and at other times it happens below the level of awareness. For example, in some Arab countries it is very insulting to show someone the sole of your shoe. That act defines one person as not being worthy of respect. Someone who doesn't know the cultural meaning of this gesture could prop a shoe on a chair or desk and unwittingly insult his or her Arab conversation partner. This would be a significant negotiation event, but one person would be unaware of it. Other times people are unaware of the scowl on their face, the harshness of their tone of voice, or the bluntness of their words. But as research . . . demonstrates, people who are more aware of the negotiation that's going on are perceived as more competent and more effective communicators.[7] So it's worth your while to become as aware as possible of a process that often goes on outside our awareness.

Selves

Multidimensional and Changing   At the beginning of this chapter we said that each time you communicate, you are affecting yourself—your identity, who you are. This might sound a little strange. "I am who I am," you might say, "and that doesn't change every time I talk with somebody. In fact, if I didn't have a stable core self, people would think of me as confused, two-faced, or even schizophrenic."

"Well," we would say, "yes and no." On the one hand, there are some stabilities or patterns. Your genetic makeup is stable, and your gender and racial identity also probably haven't changed, and probably won't. In addition, you've developed some deeply ingrained habits. Someone who has known you all your life can probably identify some features you had when you were four or five years old that you still have—your optimism, for example, or your interest in mechanical things. And as you look at old photographs of yourself when you were a young child, you might recognize how the identity of the person in the picture is in some ways the same as who you are today.

On the other hand, you are different in at least as many ways as you are the same. Think, for example, of who you were at age nine or ten and who you were at age fourteen or fifteen. Adolescence is a time of *significant* change in our selves. Or think of yourself before you were married and after, or your identity before and after you had children. Our point is that the human self is not simply a unified chunk of unchanging traits, beliefs, and values.

We're more like an artichoke or, some people believe, an onion. An artichoke has a central core, but it's mostly made up of layers of overlapping leaves. An onion is even a more radical model: it is made up of layers all the way down, and there's no central core. Humans are similar. For example, one of John's good friends has all of the following characteristics:

athletically active	mechanically awkward	poor listener
high energy	extremely well-read	ambitious
deeply religious	happily childless	cares about others
loves dark beer	protective of his wife	loves to perform
selfish	tight-fisted with money	concerned about health

This list could include hundreds of more entries, all of which help make up this person's self. And even though some of John's friend's characteristics seem contradictory—for example, "selfish" and "cares about others"—they are both part of who this person is *in different situations and different relationships*. When he's with people who let him decide the topic of conversation, he will focus almost exclusively on his own concerns, but when he's working with the people from his church, he's very concerned about their well-being.

Some version of the same thing is true of you. You may think of yourself as consistently easy-going, goal-oriented, friendly, athletic, and intelligent, while someone who has known you for many years may agree that you're friendly and intelligent but also know that you are stressed in work situations and not very athletic when the sport involves throwing or catching a ball. So from their point of view, your identity changes in different situations. The important thing to remember is that neither of you is wrong. Selves are multidimensional and *living*, and to be alive means to change. So our selves change over time, and different dimensions surface in different situations.

Impersonal and Personal Aspects . . . The self you bring to the negotiation of selves process is made up of a combination of impersonal or "social role" features and personal, idiosyncratic characteristics. No person is simply a "student," "brother," "mechanic," "club president," or "retail clerk." No one is simply "shy," "friendly," "stubborn," "assertive," "cooperative," "brave," "phony," "a leader," or "a follower." Each of us is both "student" and "stubborn," sometimes "shy" and sometimes "friendly," sometimes "phony" and sometimes "cooperative," sometimes "a leader" and sometimes "a follower." The only sensible response to the question, "Who are you?" is "In what situation?" or "For whom?" Our identity is continually in flux, and it's made up of both impersonal and personal features or characteristics.

Developed in Past and Present Relationships   The reason our selves change over time is that we develop who we are in relationships with the people around us. This process begins at birth or even before. Some research suggests that the fetus can be affected by music or conversation it hears before it's born.[8] But some of the most important parts of each person's identity are established in one's *family of origin*, the unit in which you spend the first six to ten years of your life. For example, one of your parents may have consistently introduced you to new people from the time you were old enough to talk, and today you may still find it easy to make acquaintances. Or you may have moved around a lot when you were young, and today you feel most secure when you have your own "place" and you prefer to spend holidays close to home. You may remember always hearing that you were physically attractive, and you still enjoy having your picture taken. Or you may have had the opposite kind of experience:

> My father is an alcoholic. He has never admitted to that fact. He and my mom used to get in lots of fights when I lived at home. The six of us kids were used as pawns in their war games. I always wondered whether or not I was responsible for his drinking. When the fights were going on, I always retreated to my room. There I felt secure. Now, I am 22, and have been married for two years. I have this affliction that, whenever the slightest thing happens, I always say I am so sorry. I am sorry when the milk is not cold, sorry that the wet towel was left in the gym bag. I just want to take the blame for everything, even things I have no control over.[9]

Many current studies about dysfunctional families emphasize how people with addictions to alcohol, cocaine, prescription drugs, and other chemicals developed the behavior patterns that reinforce these addictions in their families of origin.[10] Other research focuses on how addictions affect the children or other family members of addicted persons. One review of studies about adult children of alcoholics concludes that, regardless of gender, socioeconomic group, or ethnic identity, these people develop thirteen common features. For example, many adult children of alcoholics "have difficulty following a project through from beginning to end," "lie when it would be just as easy to tell the truth," "judge themselves without mercy," "take themselves very seriously," "constantly seek approval and affirmation," and "are extremely loyal, even in the face of evidence that the loyalty is undeserved."[11] These books and articles illustrate how much our family of origin contributes to our self-identity and self-esteem. Past relationships contribute a great deal to the patterns that help make up our present selves.

Present relationships are also important. When you realize that a new friend really likes you, it can do great things for your self-definition. Getting an A from a teacher you respect can affect how you see yourself. At work, a positive performance evaluation from your supervisor or a raise can improve not only your mood and your bank account but also your perception of yourself. And again, the reverse can also happen. As one illustration, a counselor named Jennifer James compiled *The Slug Manual*, a collection of criticisms that can do major damage to a person's self-definition. As she explains some people put criticism into "sandwiches" that combine praise and blame:

> "You have a nice figure for someone your age."
> "That's a great looking dress, dear. Too bad they didn't have your size."
> Fifty-three-year-old divorced man to a widow on her first date after 32 years of marriage: "I used to see some of the guys in the department store with their fat wives, and I always wondered how they could love somebody like that! But now that I've met you, I know it is the person's personality that is important."

Other criticisms can only come from or to in-laws or step-parents:

> Mother says sadly, "A loving daughter wouldn't see her father if he and I split."
> Mother-in-law comments, "Now that Thom has remarried and is so happy, he doesn't need to take drugs anymore as he did when he was married to you."
> Six-year-old to step-mother: "Do you ever think of me as Cinderella?" "No." "Well, I sure think of you as the old ugly step-mother."

And still other criticisms are "classics":

> "Who wants to go to the party tonight?" I said, "I'll go," rather meekly. Question is repeated and I say again, louder, "I'll go." Reply: "I know you'll go, but doesn't anyone else want to go?"
> Co-worker about another co-worker: "I don't like her mouth. The lower teeth are set farther in than the upper, and the upper teeth are too large. . . . You know, like your mouth."[12]

All these examples illustrate interpersonal influences that affect who you are. Your current work, school, and living situations affect how you define yourself. So does your current social life. In fact, each person's identity is always being affected by the communicating he or she experiences. Genetic makeup has some influence on who you are, but *the primary forces that define the self are communication forces*. One recent book describes these forces in a section called "The Discursive Construction of Identities."[13] Here *discursive* means "in discourse," so this part of the book talks about how identities are constructed or built in discourse, conversation, talk. One contributor to this section summarizes his main message in these words:

> I want to repudiate the traditional . . . starting-point for psychological research located in the "I" of the individual . . . and to replace it by taking as basic not the inner subjectivity of the individual, but the practical social processes going on "between" people. In other words, I want to replace a starting-point in a supposed "thing" . . . located within individuals, with one located (if "located" is now at all the right word) within the general communicative commotion of everyday life at large. . . .[14]

As this researcher emphasizes, individual identities are relational and transactional; that is, they are built out of what goes on between people. They grow out of "the general communicative commotion of everyday life." Who we are today is a combination of patterns from the past that were established in relationships we experienced when we were children and young people and present patterns which emerge from relationships we experience today. Both past and present communication experiences affect our identity. **"Negotiation of selves" is our label for the communication process that produces these identities.**

Notes

1. Carol Myers Scotton, "The Negotiation of Identities in Conversation: A Theory of Markedness and Code Choice," *International Journal of Sociological Linguistics* 44 (1983): 119–125.
2. Scotton, pp. 122–123.
3. Scotton, p. 133.
4. Roger Fisher and William Ury, *Getting to Yes: Negotiating Agreement Without Giving In* (Boston: Houghton Mifflin, 1981), p. xi.
5. Mary E. Diez, "Negotiation Competence: A Conceptualization of the Rules of Negotiation Interaction," *Contemporary Issues in Language and Discourse Processes*, ed. Donald G. Ellis and William A. Donohue (Hillsdale, N.J.: Lawrence Erlbaum, 1986), p. 225.
6. But obviously not in all senses. The definitions of negotiation show how it is a particular kind of communicating.
7. Barbara J. O'Keefe, "The Logic of Message Design: Individual Differences in Reasoning about Communication," *Communication Monographs* 35 (1988): 30–103.
8. See, for example, W. E. Freud, "Prenatal Attachment and Bonding," in *Pre- and Perinatal Psychology: An Introduction*, ed. T. R. Verney (New York: Human Sciences, 1987), pp. 68–87.
9. "Sharon R.," quoted in Claudia Black, *It Will Never Happen to Me! Children of Alcoholics As Youngsters—Adolescents—Adults* (Denver: M.A.C., 1982), p. 9.
10. J. R. Milam and K. Ketcham, *Under the Influence: A Guide to the Myths and Realities of Alcoholism* (Seattle: Madrona, 1981); Donald Goodwin, *Is Alcoholism Hereditary?* (New York: Oxford, 1976).
11. Janet Geringer Woititz, *Adult Children of Alcoholics* (Pompano Beach, FL: Health Communications, 1983). Also see Melody Beattie, *Codependent No More* (New York: Harper/Hazelden, 1984); Beattie, *Beyond Codependency* (New York: Harper/Hazelden, 1989); Anne Wilson Schaef, *Co-Dependence: Misunderstood-Mistreated* (New York: Harper & Row, 1986).
12. Jennifer James, ed., *The Slug Manual: The Rise and Fall of Criticism* (Seattle: Inner Cosmos, 1983), pp. 9–10, 14–15, 44.
13. This is the title of Part II in John Shotter and Kenneth J. Gergen, eds., *Texts of Identity* (London: Sage, 1989), pp. 82–151.
14. John Shotter, "Social Accountability and the Social Construction of 'You,'" in Shotter and Gergen, eds., p. 137.

Review Questions

1. Negotiating selves means _____ and _____ to definitions of our-selves and definitions of _____ _____ _____ communicating with us.
2. There are no "right" or "wrong" ways to negotiate selves. There are just _____.
3. Are humans more like artichokes or onions?
4. What is your family of origin? Who was/is in your family of origin?

Probes

1. Test the claim that selves get negotiated *whenever* people communicate. How is this process working when you exchange "Hellos" with someone on the street? How is it working when you order a catalogue item over the telephone?
2. Draw on your experience in another culture to describe some ways selves are negotiated there.
3. What specific communication patterns did you learn in your family of origin?
4. If negotiation is really a collaborative or mutual process, then you alone can't control its out-come. This implies that you can't completely control *who you are* as you communicate. Discuss.

This reading is longer than some of the others. One reason is that it discusses a complex topic—how relationships get negotiated, coor-dinated, and repaired. Its author, Ted Grove, is a speech communi-cation professor at Portland State University in Oregon. This is a chapter from his book about two-person relationships, and it touches on several topics.

Grove starts by distinguishing between the social and the personal dimen-sions of two-person relationships. Communication is generally framed by the role definitions each person accepts and assigns to the other, but the specifics grow out of the unique norms and expectations that guide the individuals' communi-cating. As Grove points out, these social and personal influences get worked out in moment-to-moment conversational behavior.

The reading also describes generally how conversational partners manage meaning collaboratively, and how they collaborate to repair specific breakdowns. Researchers have identified three kinds of "fix-up" work we do in conversations: wording repairs, error repairs, and ambiguity repairs. Grove describes how each works and how they affect the ongoing relationship.

Then he develops a distinction between *tact* and *tactics,* partly to under-score the importance of different conversational motives. People use tactful state-ments like pre-apologies ("I hate to intrude, but. . . "), pre-interpretations ("You won't like this, but. . . "), and other statements to qualify or soften the impact of what they say. But these same conversational moves can also be made to serve the speaker's own immediate needs; in these cases they are functioning as *tac-tics* rather than *tact.* Grove warns against the dangers of tactics that misrepre-sent one's intentions, ones that are overused, and ones that set up a self-fulfilling prophecy.

Then the author turns his attention to the power dimension of relationships and patterns of relational control. He describes the differences between conver-sational moves that are responsive to the other and those that are autonomous.

He follows this section with a discussion of ways that power affects communication among friends, spouses, and coworkers. He notes that there are several kinds of power and that relationships are characterized by *patterns* of power exchange. He speculates at the end of the reading that it might be most desirable for relational partners to keep the various kinds of power asymmetrical, rather than completely balanced.

When you finish this reading, you should have a good general sense of some of the dynamics that make up the process of negotiating relationships.

Regulating Conversation: Relationships

Theodore G. Grove

. . . In interpersonal communication, a relationship involves expectations concerning how each will think, feel, and act toward the conversational partner. Expectations may be divided into two classes. Social role expectations are categorical ways of relating to strangers, spouses, people with more or with less power, younger or older people, and the like. These expectations are learned in the course of growing up in a particular society. On the other hand, expectations within personal relationships are built up through a unique history of prior interaction. Some of the impact that social role relationships have on our daily conversations are now considered.

Social Role Relationships

. . . Social roles comprise an important part of the impact our relationships have on conversation. In American culture we learn to enact certain roles as we develop into mature adults. When we go to a doctor for medical care, we normally expect to respond to questions, ask some questions of our own, and comply with instructions. At the same time, the doctor behaves according to certain constraints with respect to behavior toward the patient. Both doctor and patient have a set of expectations to guide the conversation. All of us have certain rights and responsibilities defined by the social role relationship between doctor and patient.

In a conversation between a supervisor and employee at work, the employee normally expects to adapt his or her behavior according to what the supervisor says and does. And the supervisor has certain responsibilities toward the employee. Similarly, social role guidelines exist and help to regulate conversations between student and teacher and within many other dyads.

Of course, these are not arbitrary role prescriptions but serve to further functional interaction. Whenever we consult with anyone about a problem, we tend to adjust to the initiations of that person. In terms of the task-at-hand, it may matter little whether the expert is a plumber, a tax accountant, an employment interviewer, the custodian in one's apartment building, a psychological counselor, or a neurosurgeon. We are very adept at fitting our behavior to the interaction-leader or interaction-follower roles as prescribed by a particular relationship. As an aside, there is some evidence that we may be "too good for our own health" in playing the role of submissive patient. Research increasingly indicates that patients who are more autonomous and "pushy" in physician/patient conferences receive better medical care than docile and compliant patients (Waitzkin 1984).

At any rate, both parties usually behave as prescribed by their respective roles. The social role of "employee" prescribes that we be responsive to initiations of those with higher rank in the organization. And one enters an interview expecting that the interviewer will direct and influence one's conversational behaviors much more extensively than one will influence the interviewer's behavior. We both make it happen that way. These social role enactments depend on our tacit agreements to treat one another in certain predictable ways. Such predictability reduces the uncertainty of both parties and imbues our conversations with some guiding structure.

Thus far all examples of social role relationships have referred to dyads involving a specialist and a layperson. But there are also general interaction guidelines for partners of the same social rank. Certainly, one observes certain differences in interactions between little-known acquaintances and those between familiar friends, between interactions at the work place, and those between spouses and romantic partners. And those differences exist independently from the unique expectations surrounding *specific* personal relationships. In these and many other encounters, social role prescriptions exist that help to regulate our conversation, even when the other person is a stranger; perhaps we should say, *especially* when the other is a stranger.

Personal Relationships and Intimacy-Equilibrium

We began discussion of the impact of relationship on conversations through this brief focus on social role relationships. Now, switch over to consider *personal relationships*. A personal relationship exists when two people have developed a unique set of norms and expectations shaped over a number of conversations. Conversation between two acquaintances, work associates, pals, antagonists, relatives, close friends, and romantic partners takes place within the framework of a personal relationship that exists at some stage of development.

Each of our personal relationships influences conversation with those relational partners at a number of different levels. For example, we may think of one of our relationships as that of "friends," "best friends," "acquaintances," "lovers," or "co-workers." Even those common *labels* we put on a relationship can influence our expectations for the behavior in that relationship and, thereby, serve as a guide for appropriate questioning, disclosure, and other behavior (Hecht 1984; Knapp and others 1980). The mere act of thinking in terms of those relationship labels helps people to select appropriate conversational behavior.

The nature of a personal relationship regulates conversations at another level. *Relational knowledge* contributes to our capacity to regulate conversations with a specific relational partner. In one study of conversational memory, *behavior-specific* relational knowledge accounted for over 80 percent of our memory of verbal dominance patterns (Planalp 1985). Situational-specific and other forms of relational knowledge may also play a part in guiding us to structure conversational messages to fit a given relationship. . . .

Combinations of behavior that give a sense of more or less intimacy include amount of mutual eye gaze, smiling, physical proximity, touching or lack thereof, amount and depth of verbal self-disclosure, and the like. As a conversation unfolds, each party may be seen making adjustments in all of those and other behaviors in order to maintain interaction at what each feels to be the appropriate, preferred level of intimacy.

Example #1.   Kate and Alexis are acquaintances who know one another because they are mutual friends with a third party. Both Kate and Alexis view the relationship as cordial on the few occasions when they interact and, without giving it any thought, relate to one another at a low intimacy level. Other than perfunctory handshakes upon meeting, they never touch one another. While interacting they stand at a distance of about four feet, maintain just enough mutual gaze to conduct polite, friendly conversation, and talk mostly about impersonal subjects and only at low levels of self-disclosure when they do venture into personal subjects. They are both comfortable at this intimacy level.

Occasionally during Alexis and Kate's conversations, mundane circumstances result in their mutual smiling or laughing, unexpected delving into personal topics, interacting in cramped physical space, or accidentally touching one another. During those occurrences their level of interaction intimacy is momentarily driven higher than what their present relationship prescribes. When this happens, they immediately and without reflection compensate by reducing gaze, by shifting torso and head slightly away from the head-on position, or by other *distancing* behaviors. Each reciprocates just enough of these distancing behaviors and intimacy is restored to the level each feels appropriate to their relationship. Similar adjustments in the opposite direction may be observed when circumstances momentarily drive the interaction intimacy lower than is expected or comfortable in their relationship.

Example #2.   Kerry and Anna are sisters as well as close personal friends and maintain a relationship with a commensurately high intimacy level. While interacting, frequently about highly personal topics involving much self-disclosure, they stand very close, exhibit a high frequency and duration of mutual gaze, occasionally use expressive touches on the partner's hand or arm, and sit and stand head-on with parallel shoulders.

Occasionally, circumstances or temperament momentarily reduces this high level of interaction intimacy. Perhaps they are interacting across a wide restaurant table, and they compensate for the reduced proximity by increased gaze or forward leaning. Or perhaps Anna is irritated with Kerry and reduces eye contact, amount of talking, and self-disclosure level. Automatically, Kerry adjusts by seeking more eye contact, moving in closer and perhaps touching Anna's arm or hand while asking for a personal disclosure of feelings. As with Kate and Alexis, such adjustments may be seen as an almost continuous feature of their conversational behavior.

Example #3.   Jeff and Kathy are co-workers in their employer's office. Unlike the other two relationships, they have not arrived at a compatible definition of the intimacy attribute of their relationship. Jeff just arrived a few weeks ago and almost immediately began interacting with Kathy at a somewhat more intimate level than Kathy prefers. Jeff stands closer, with more direct body orientation, uses more constant gaze, and asks about and discloses more personal topics than Kathy considers appropriate. Jeff is continually pressing forward with intimacy behaviors. Kathy responds by distancing in both her verbal and kinesic behaviors. And Jeff is adjusting to that behavior by further attempts to close the gap.

While interacting, their dance of move and countermove is continuous, and both are distracted by failure to arrive at a common interpretation of the intimacy level in their relationship. Because of the the the disparity between what each construes as a comfortable mode of interaction, both experience some amount of interaction strain. Eventually they will probably arrive at some behavioral accommodation or cease interaction altogether. Such differences in the parties' implicit relational definitions are difficult to sustain indefinitely.

The reader can certainly think of other "real-life" examples of how our implicit definitions of relational intimacy translate into moment-to-moment conversational behavior, and how they influence our joint efforts toward interpersonal communication. These processes represent just one of many ways in which the all-pervasive reciprocity and compensatory effects are influenced by one's interpersonal relationship and impinge on our daily conversations.

The Coordinated Management of Meaning

A perspective termed "the coordinated management of meaning" emphasizes how several *contexts* set the framework for meaning coordination between people (Cronen, Pearce, and Harris 1982). One of the most important contexts in this view is the specific *personal relationship* between two individuals. In short, people interpret one another's behavior and respond to those interpretations according to the meanings that are supported by their *relationship context*. Behavior takes on significance according to the *rules* nested within each particular relationship.

The following discussion relies on the previously mentioned hypothetical relationships of Kate and Alexis, Kerry and Anna, and Jeff and Kathy. Conversation within each relationship is governed by *rules of meaning* and *rules of action*, roughly paralleling the interpretive and behavioral aspects, respectively, of the interaction elements discussed in earlier chapters. We apply rules of meaning to understand what is going on, and we apply rules of action to guide our response to that understanding.

For example, Kate, Kerry, and Jeff each say to their respective relational partners, "I like that jacket; is it new?" Within their cordial and not very intimate relationship, Alexis' relational rule of meaning might run, *Kate has found a comfortably impersonal topic for us to discuss*. Alexis' relational action rule would follow, *When one of us finds a comfortable topic, it is expected that the other will enter in and extend that topic*. Kate does so.

In contrast to Kate and Alexis, Kerry and Anna are sisters and very close and mutually supportive. Their relational rules for meaning and action with respect to the same utterance are very different from those of Kate and Alexis. Anna's relationally embedded interpretation of Kerry's comment runs, *When we show interest in an article of the other's apparel, it often means we'd like to have one*. The action rule is to offer shopping help and companionship, and Anna responds, "I got it at Nordstrom's on sale just yesterday. They might have some more in that size. I'm free at ten tomorrow if you want to look and then have lunch."

The relational context for Jeff and Kathy supports still different meaning and action rules. As described above, they have not arrived at compatible relational definitions, so their rules will probably be disparate and their meaning interpretations poorly coordinated. In reaction to Jeff's jacket comment, Kathy thinks *Another ploy to stare at my anatomy or a lead-in to making his usual over-personal comments.* She replies, "Yes, I just bought it," and turns away. Jeff thinks, *She's gorgeous, and still playing hard-to-get, which means she really is interested in me. Think I'll ask her out again.* "Hey, Kathy. . . ."

According to the coordinated management of meaning view, as relationships develop, rules evolve for derivation of meaning from one another's behavior and for acting in response to those meanings. In turn, those responses elicit rule-governed interpretations by the other party who then applies the appropriate relational action rule, and so on. The rules comprise the expectations within a specific personal relationship. The two relating parties apply those rules to guide interpretations and behavioral responses, resulting in the management of their conversations according to the context supplied by their relationship.

Repair of Conversation

While the previous discussion described how conversation can be regulated with respect to relationship rules, the immediate concern is to demonstrate one way among the many in which *having any personal relationship at all* with the conversational partner invokes different regulatory behaviors. In order to do that, we first need to introduce some background on a category of interaction-regulating sequences. . . .

It has been increasingly recognized that *talk sequences* which address the ambiguities in our utterances, which correct various errors of speaking, and which relate to turn-taking and coherence, are embedded throughout our conversations. These corrective sequences have been termed "conversational repairs" (Schegloff, Jefferson, and Sacks 1977). They consist of single utterances or short segments of conversation that address problems of utterance, problems like misstatements, memory lapse resulting in omission of crucial information, logical errors, and ambiguous utterances of various kinds. When successful, these repair sequences serve to *align* the conversants and their meanings on common topics, themes, and motives.

Among other reasons, conversational repairs are important to maintaining coherent conversation because they *fix* problems of utterance so that meaningful exchange can proceed. Sometimes the person who made the utterance (self) notices a problem and *initiates* a repair:

LOU: It just wasn't there when I looked.
JEANNIE: Oh.
LOU: That isn't what I mean.

Sometimes the listener initiates the repair:

LOU: It just wasn't there when I looked.
JEANNIE: Sure it was.

After a repair is initiated, either the person committing the error *makes* the repair:

LOU: What I mean is, I just must have looked right at it and didn't see it.

Or the other person makes the repair:

JEANNIE: Oh yeah, you mean it just didn't register. I know what you mean.

When the person who erred initiates the repair, he or she does the repair work far more frequently than the listener. However, it has been found that when listeners initiate the repairs, they make repairs about equally as often as those who uttered the problematic statements (Zahn 1984).

More important to our examination of relationship influences on the course of conversation were Zahn's (1984) comparisons of talkers in an initial interaction (strangers) with talkers that had a history of previous interaction (a personal relationship) with respect to three kinds of repairables. He observed *wording* (problems of mispronunciation, grammar, word slips, and phrasing), *errors* (problems of logic or pragmatics; utterances viewed as inappropriate, irrelevant, or untrue), and *ambiguities* (problems of understanding and comprehension; utterances perceived as uninformative, unclear, or incomplete, including problems of hearing and attention). The performance of conversants with a personal relationship was comparable to that of strangers with respect to recognizing and repairing *error* category problems. However, the two groups differed markedly with respect to recognition and repair of *wording* and *ambiguity* problems. Couples with personal relationships were very active in the repair of ambiguous utterances, but were minimally involved in repair of wording problems, in direct contrast to the pattern of repairs made by strangers.

	Wording Repairs	*Error Repairs*	*Ambiguity Repairs*
Personal Relationship	6	14	25
Strangers	24	10	1

Apparently individuals with a history of prior interaction do not hesitate to identify and repair *ambiguous* utterances. That is, we are quite willing to deal overtly with problems that affect meaning—problems of clarity, attention, and hearing—when we are conversing with people we know. On the other hand, when interacting with a person for the first time, we expend our repair efforts on the problems of *wording*, problems like mispronunciation, and other miscues that 1) *are immediately apparent to both parties* and 2) *have little impact on understanding one another's meanings*.

This relatively increased focus on *appearance* at the sacrifice of attention to *meaning* in initial interactions suggests strangers must commit more undetected misunderstandings than conversants who do have a personal relationship, however minimal. This picture is compatible with a general conclusion that parties in initial conversation are more concerned with maintaining a *semblance of agreement* than conversants who know one another. Due to our sense of social delicacy or other reasons, in initial interactions we expend little effort on problems of ambiguity that do interfere with interpretation and *that are all the more likely to occur when talking with someone for the first time!* These findings suggest a course of action that talkers and listeners alike could take to improve interpersonal communication in the initial conversation with another. Namely, we could all probably choose to forsake *appearance* just a bit and turn more of our efforts to the *intended meanings* of our utterances.

On the other hand, it is probably beneficial for our various personal relationships that we do attend more to meaning management in those conversations. This care we take in our personal relationships is reflected in behaviors well beyond the correction of ambiguous utterances. When a personal relationship is important enough, and we need to open up a sensitive topic or convey negative information or criticism, we are often observed to insert tactful language into our conversational utterances. But that same language may be used in support of other motives, as well. That is, we may use the same *tactful* language for *tactical* purposes, as when we do not want to be blamed for the content of our utterance, or when we wish to say something without accepting the responsibility for having said it. This language of tact and tactics is yet another example of how, in different conversations, the identical behavior may represent very different motives. But it also represents another way in which our personal relationships influence our expressions and the course of entire conversations.

Language of Tact and Tactics

When conversing with those with whom we have a personal relationship, we all have experienced difficulties in expressing ourselves on sensitive matters or on issues that have implications for our feelings of mutual esteem and identity. Certain regulating devices surface with the introduction of potentially disturbing utterances into the conversation. Erving Goffman (1959) noted our continuing willingness and ability to cooperate with one another in the face of the many sensitive issues and divisive circumstances. Based on what he observed, he maintained that much of what we do in our interactions functions to hold our working relationships together and to support our continuing daily cooperation—to maintain the fragile *working consensus*.

If Goffman is correct, certain elements that support the working consensus should be present in the utterances of day-to-day conversations (Weinstein 1966). Such devices would be used frequently enough to be recognized as commonplace. Furthermore, they would be associated with sensitive, divisive, or face-threatening, conversational topics, and they would have the potential to ease the *interaction strain* that could dismantle our cooperative arrangements and existing relationships. These devices would be aimed at smoothing the way in uncertain matters or on highly reactive issues and, when successful, have the effect of pushing an interaction through to conclusion with minimal damage to the working consensus between the relating parties.

Upon examination of many interaction episodes, Weinstein identified several classes of just such "tact-full" devices attached to the beginning or the end of conversational utterances. Four of the most common of these forms are *pre-apologies*, *pre-interpretations*, *depersonalized motive revelations*, and *altruistic motive revelations*.

Pre-Apologies
I'm not quite sure of this . . .
I hate to intrude, but . . .

I don't mean to disagree with you . . .
Off the top of my head, I would say . . .

Pre-Interpretations
Now, be sure not to take this the wrong way . . .
You won't like this, but . . .
Don't think I'm silly when I say . . .
Promise me you won't get angry if I . . .

Depersonalized Motive Revelations
It's no reflection on you, but . . .
It's nothing personal, however I'm going to . . .
It's part of my job to tell you . . .
Look, just to keep them off my back, you need to . . .

Altruistic Motive Revelations
Because we're friends, I have to tell you that . . .
If we weren't so close, I couldn't say this to you . . .
This is very hard for me, but somebody's got to tell you . . .
So you won't build up false hopes, you need to know . . .

Pre-apologies are probably easiest to spot. They consist of expressions of apology or excuses preceding the sensitive or face-threatening part of the utterance. Pre-interpretations tell the conversational partner how badly the other will probably feel about or react to the sensitive material even before it has been uttered, and often asks the partner to refrain from the anticipated reaction. Both pre-apologies and pre-interpretations have been examined more recently by some writers under the single label of "disclaimers" (Eakins and Eakins 1978; Hewitt and Stokes 1975) and been considered as types of announced conversational rule violations termed "preventatives" by still others (e.g., McLaughlin 1984).

Depersonalized motive revelations either precede or follow the sensitive part of the utterance, and reveal that the speaker's motive is objective, neutral, not meant to be personally damaging, and (frequently) out of the speaker's control. "Nothing against you personally, Elaine, but due to the company's cutback in your department. . . ." Conversely, altruistic motive revelations assert the speaker's motive is wholly personal and "for your own good," with the suggestion the speaker is risking a great deal by caring enough to tell you at all. Television's breath mint, mouthwash, and toothpaste advertisements occasionally still use this device. "Look, Bill, we've been friends for a long time now, and somebody needs to tell you that Janet left you because you have . . . bad breath." . . .

These tactful utterances are a special kind of qualifying message that comment on, provide the context for, and modify the rest of the utterance. They typically refer to the speaker's intention, feelings, or situation, the listener's potential feelings or situation, or the relationship between the speaker and listener. When used to preserve good faith and cooperative attitudes, they can function to placate the listener, keep the listener from jumping to damaging conclusions, "buy time" until full explanations can be expressed, and lay the groundwork for *repair* of negative effects elicited by the sensitive material. When they are used sparingly, they can provide a kind of social grease that reduces the friction between the parties on those occasions when they deal with bad news or reactive issues that could threaten trust, mutual esteem, cooperative spirit, and their entire working consensus.

However, the reader may have noticed that some of the examples listed above do not fit easily into the picture of constructive, well-intentioned management of conversation depicted to this point. There are at least three matters that justify that reaction:

1. *Tactics*. Some of those examples may not evoke warm feelings in the reader because we all can recall occasions where others have pre-apologized, pre-interpreted our feelings, and revealed their motives in a way that seemed to serve their own immediate needs, instead of attending to the needs of the listener or furthering the objective of interpersonal communication. The identical language structures can be used in service of the speaker's narrow self-interest—can be used as *tactics* instead of *tact*. That is not a condemnation of tactics; the reader is urged to use a variety of tactics throughout this book. But when those devices *misrepresent* the speaker's intention and are used to maneuver for emotional advantage over the conversational partner, such behavior frequently damages the interaction process, rather than enhancing it.

   For example, pre-apologies can be an empty gesture inserted into the conversational "record" to which the speaker can later point. Pre-interpretations of listener's feelings can represent a speaker's attempt to shield him- or herself from the inconvenience of dealing with a listener's reasonable and normal emotional reactions to disturbing information. And labeling one's motives can be used as a blank check to say the most hurtful and damaging things without taking responsibility for saying them. In short, it is when such motives are passed off as *tact* that the course of conversation may be altered for the worse.

2. *Overuse*. But even when used in the interests of tact, those utterances may defeat communication processes. When overused, they may begin to sound like empty gestures and can dismantle the credibility of the user. You may know someone who daily begins at least one utterance with a pre-apology like "Off the top of my head . . ." even when it is not important to know how much thought was behind the comment or when the content itself makes that quite clear. And sometimes a person is surprised when someone else gets the credit for an idea he or she expressed earlier in the same conversation. That may be an uncomfortably frequent experience for people who consistently delay in getting to the point. In the case of pre-apologies, such overuse can cause the listener to misjudge the content and think, "Well, here comes another half-baked idea." Or equally dysfunctional, you may not bother to listen carefully for whatever merit the comment might have. Sometimes we tend to "tune out" on these prefacing qualifiers and then fail to tune in again and, consequently, miss useful information from that conversational partner.

3. *Self-fulfilling prophecy*. [Earlier] we described self-fulfilling prophecies as perceptions that *set up* the very behavior they prophesy. For example, you may know someone who all too frequently pre-interprets your emotional reactions with "Now don't be upset [angry, hurt, disgusted, confused], but I want you to know that. . . ." Such seemingly tactful behavior may trigger the very reaction the speaker claims to be trying to prevent. When forewarned by such a person that what we are about to hear may be good cause for a particular emotional reaction, the likelihood that we will comply with the prediction is probably increased. "You're right. I'm very upset!" When someone else chooses our reaction for us, it is easy to go along with that advance prescription. . . .

To this point, our discussion of the impact of personal relationships on the course of conversations has been confined to specific behaviors and interpretations of specific behaviors and sequences of behavior. But personal relationships produce patterns of initiation and response between the relating parties that impose their influence on whole conversations and even on entire conversational histories within a given relationship. It is to such large-scale relationship influences that we now turn.

Patterns of Relational Control

. . . With the possible exception of process comments and tactful language, the vast majority of regulatory behaviors discussed so far in this chapter are performed without our self-awareness. Here, we describe ways in which the attributes of the interpersonal relationship regulate whole conversations as well as minute segments of interaction. In this examination of large patterns of influence that typify entire conversations, conversation will be described at a level that will be quite familiar to the reader. . . .

Depending on the particular interpersonal relationship, conversations seem to vary widely regarding how much response contingency is in evidence. At one extreme, we have all participated in conversations where our own behavior seemed *completely* driven by the other's preceding behaviors. One might have felt like a puppet whose strings were being manipulated by the other person. For example, we may have felt, during interaction in the personal relationship with a domineering parent or relative, that the other party exclusively was calling the conversational shots. Or at work, one might recognize that a dictatorial supervisor tightly controls all conversations you have with him or her.

In other relationships extreme dependency of responses may be equally pervasive, but spread more evenly between the parties. We have all observed and participated in conversations that resembled Ping-Pong matches, where the behavior of *both of us* seemed to depend almost exclusively on where the other placed the last shot. For example, two lovers or two co-workers may have an argument in which each turn at talk represents a push-button response to the last comment by the other, with little evidence of thoughtful choice of responses. Here, as with the one-sided exchange with the domineering parent or dictatorial supervisor, the conversation may seem to "have a life of its own."

At the other extreme, all of us have participated in conversations that seemed to involve *minimal* response contingency. These have been characterized with phrases like "talking past each other" and "on different wave-lengths." These conversations exhibit a kind of behavioral anarchy where neither party seems to respond to the partner or be the least influenced by the other's previous behavior. One example of this can be seen when two people are so involved in rehearsing their own next comment that they do not bother to listen carefully to what the partner is saying. In those conversations, topic shifts occur with almost every speaking turn, and turn-taking is a function of interruption and volume rather than the usual regulatory features.

But most conversations probably range between those extremes of *extreme* responsiveness and *extreme* autonomy. Such exchanges exhibit some behavioral interdependence with the associated topical continuity and orderly turn-taking, but occasionally exhibiting behaviors that show some independence from the other's last response, suggesting the parties are deliberately choosing behaviors in each turn from among a number of alternatives. Viewed in this way, both parties continually adapt to the tension between the two polarities in a single conversation, exhibiting varying degrees of dependence on one another's behavior (say, from "5" to "95" percent) at different points in the conversation. These [are] fluctuations between *autonomy and responsiveness*—between independence and interdependence. . . .

Symmetrically contingent interactions refer to encounters where both parties' behaviors are roughly equivalent in the extent to which they depend on the partner's behavior. Sometimes, conversations between co-workers, friends, strangers, and others talking in a *status-equal* circumstance exhibit this pattern. But sometimes they do not. For example, when you help your friend with his income tax, his conversational behavior may depend much more on you than yours does on him. On those occasions our interaction is asymmetrically contingent.

Asymmetrically contingent interactions refer to those encounters where there is some observable imbalance between the parties' influence on one another. Here, one person's behavior is seen to depend more on the other's behavior than vice versa. Some dominant/submissive spousal and romantic relationships exhibit that contingency pattern, as do most conversations between supervisors and their subordinates at work. Your conversations with your classroom instructor usually reflect that imbalance of influence, as well. And as previously discussed, patients take their cues more from what the doctor says and does than the reverse.

We all have observed or participated in conversations where the behavior did not fit what one would expect from the parties' social role relationship. Explanation for those outcomes can be found in a different class of conversational regulators; namely, *relational power*.

Relational Power

. . . Friends, spouses, and co-workers who have developed interpersonal relationships possess an array of personal information about one another. They have a history of conversational experience with one another to guide their expectations and regulate their conversations. Accumulating episodes of talk provide expectations for future conversations and, thereby, work to structure the interaction, for better or worse. Norms emerge regarding such matters as who initiates certain topics and ideas and how each person is expected to respond to the initiations of the other. Together, the parties fashion behavioral expectations for their self and for the other—habituated ways of dealing with one another that produce a conversation that is more or less symmetrical or asymmetrical. Upon initiating a conversation, each has an idea about how he or she is expected to behave and how the partner will probably behave—expectations concerning what is and what is not appropriate for their specific personal relationship.

There is some advantage to viewing these observable dependency patterns as defining *relational power*. Here, we are not talking about one's relative rank in some organization or the *legitimate power* of a formal position. Rather, we refer to patterns of talking and behaving that indicate who is more in charge, if anybody, of a particular conversation or segment of conversation. In this perspective, it is the one who makes more adjustments to the behavior of the other, that has relatively lower relational power in that particular conversation.

What are the *sources* of relational power? In large part, relational power is a manifestation of the way two people *perceive* the power dimension in their personal relationship. . . . People react to the idea of "power" in very different ways. That is, we tend to have highly personalized notions of what power is. In one study, combinations of six different ingredients of how people view power were identified as *good, instinctive drive, charisma, resource dependency, political,* and *control and autonomy* (Goldberg and others 1983). The way an individual thinks of power in a specific relationship may reflect more or less of any of those elements.

For example, relational power can be reviewed as a kind of conversational resource dependency. One resource upon which we depend are all of those verbal and nonverbal behaviors of the other party to which we adapt and adjust, behaviors which constrain our range of potential responses. At the same time, those instances in which we behave with some degree of autonomy from those constraints, consciously selecting our own course with an awareness of alternatives, introduces a measure of control and autonomy into our conversational behavior.

Patterns of relational power may be seen operating in personal relationships where differences in rank or position, forms of contextual power, already exist. For example, the contrasting experiences the same supervisor has with two subordinates may be related to the differences in relational power associated with the two respective relationships. While the supervisor may be clearly in charge of interaction with the one employee, the other subordinate may exhibit relatively more control over the interaction process in conversations with that same supervisor, even though response dependencies are still somewhat asymmetrical. Some people seem to "get what they want" from their bosses; others fare worse.

Differences from one dyad to another in patterns of relational power may explain the wide variance in conversational outcomes different people of the same rank experience in their respective encounters with an identical superior or subordinate. For example, as I emerge from conferences with the boss, I see her as a person with strength of conviction and demandingly high standards. You emerge from your conference feeling she is arbitrary and intimidating. Different relational definitions give rise to different patterns of dyadic interaction, which, in turn, promote feelings of more or less goal achievement and satisfaction. These feelings may then influence our perceptions of the conversational partner, which come full circle to re-form or entrench our relational power pattern with a specific other. This sequence describes another way in which our relationships constantly influence the content and the course of our conversations. In addition it represents another important expression of the *self-fulfilling prophecy,* introduced in an earlier chapter. To a certain extent, each of us possesses the power in a given relationship that we imagine we have.

From all of this, one might expect relational power to be relatively balanced in a relationship between peers. There, one might reason, response contingency should even out in the short run. Your and my behaviors would be observed to be about equally adaptive to one another's behavior. But we all have observed conversations between friends, spouses, and co-workers where that is not the case.

The reader might compare relationships with different friends with respect to relational power. For example, your relational definition with one friend may be expressed in alternating patterns of relational power in your various encounters. You exhibit relatively more power in some encounters and relatively less in others. In still other conversations with the same friend, alterations in response dependency are so frequent that you would be hard-pressed to distinguish such overall differences. Indeed, the pattern of relational power in such a relationship could be described as evenly balanced.

However, you probably have relationships with other friends, acquaintances, or equal-status co-workers that lack that symmetry. Most of us have some relationships in which our own concerns and conversational initiatives consistently seem to supercede those of the partner. Conversely, most of us experience still other relationships where our responses consistently seem to depend more on the leads of the other than vice versa.

One might speculate that keeping such asymmetries in a relationship within tolerable limits may comprise one criterion for maintaining a friendship for an extended period. But that is only speculation, because the power patterns observed in our conversations reflect the differing definitions of our various relationships. . . .

Summary

Features of the relationship between two people regulate their conversations in a variety of ways. In the process of growing up in a particular culture, individuals learn about the conduct of conversation partly through the conventional behavior going on around them. They learn when deference is expected, and about other conversational responses that current practice defines as appropriate to specific kinds of social role relationships. These general expectations for conversational conduct serve to regulate all conversations, particularly those where the parties have had no previous contact whatsoever.

For other conversations, the parties have had some amount of previous contact and have developed habits of relating and responding to one another that are based on their unique relational history. Conversations in these personal relationships may center primarily around work activities, socializing activities, intimate partner activities, or some combination of those three. In these personal relationships, expectations about what is an appropriate level of intimacy give rise to behavioral adjustments aimed at maintaining the desired level.

The meanings that conversational behavior has for the relating parties are considerably influenced by their perceptions of the nature of the relationship. The parties to a specific relationship frequently manage conversations in repetitively patterned ways. Some of these relational characteristics involve how they repair conversations, the language they use to negotiate delicate matters, and the control and power aspects of the relationship that are expressed in the structure of their conversations.

References

Argyle, M., and Dean, J. 1965. Eye-contact, distance, and affiliation. *Sociometry* 28: 289–304.

Cappella, J. N. 1985. The management of conversations. In *Handbook of interpersonal communication*, eds. M. L. Knapp and G. R. Miller. Beverly Hills, CA: Sage Publications.

Capella, J. N. 1987. Interpersonal communication: Definitions and fundamental questions. In *Handbook of communication science*, eds. C. R. Berger and S. H. Chaffee, 184–238. Beverly Hills, CA: Sage Publications.

Cronen, V., Pearce, W. B., and Harris, L. 1982. The coordinated management of meaning. In *Comparative human communication theory*, ed. F. E. X. Dance, 61–89. New York: Harper & Row.

Eakins, B. W., and Eakins, R. G. 1978. *Sex differences in human communication.* Boston: Houghton Mifflin Co.

Goffman, E. 1959. *The presentation of self in everyday life*. Garden City, NY: Doubleday & Company.

Goldberg, A. A., Cavanaugh, M. S., and Larson, C. E. 1983. The meaning of power. *Journal of Applied Communication Research* 11: 89–108.

Hecht, M. L. 1984. Satisfying communication and relationship labels: Intimacy and length of relationship as perceptual frames of naturalistic conversations. *The Western Journal of Speech Communication* 48: 201–216.

Hewitt, J. P., and Stokes, R. 1975. Disclaimer. *American Sociological Review* 40: 1–11.

Jones, E. E., and Thibaut, J. W. 1958. Interaction goals as bases of inference in interpersonal perception. In *Person perception and interpersonal behavior*, eds. R. Tagiuri and L. Petrullo, 151–178. Stanford, CA: Stanford University Press.

Knapp, M. L., Ellis, D. G., and Williams, B. A. 1980. Perceptions of communication behavior associated with relationship terms. *Communication Monographs* 47: 262.

McLaughlin, M. L. 1984 *Conversation: How talk is organized*. Beverly Hills, CA: Sage Publications.

Piaget, J. 1955. *The language and thought of the child*. Cleveland, OH: The World Publishing Company.

Planalp, S. 1985. Relational schemata: A test of alternative forms of relational knowledge as guides to communication. *Human Communication Research* 12: 3–29.

Schegloff, E. A., Jefferson, G., and Sacks, H. 1977. The preference for self-correction in the organization of repair in conversation. *Language* 53: 361–382.

Waitzkin, J. 1984. Doctor-patient communication. *Journal of the American Medical Association* 252: 2441–2446.

Weinstein, E. A. 1966. Toward a theory of interpersonal tactics. In *Problems in social psychology*, eds. C. W. Backman and P. F. Secord, 394–398. New York: McGraw-Hill.

Zahn, C. J. 1984. A reexamination of conversational repair. *Communication Monographs* 51: 56–66.

Review Questions

1. What is the difference between the social and the personal dimensions of a relationship?
2. What is "relational knowledge"?
3. What is the distinction between "rules of meaning" and "rules of action"?
4. What does it mean to say that repair serves to "align" conversation partners?
5. Give an example from your own experience of each of the four "tact-full devices" that Grove summarizes—pre-apologies, pre-interpretations, depersonalized motive revelations, and altruistic motive revelations.
6. What is relational power? What are the main sources of relational power?

Probes

1. Pick one of the three relationships Grove describes—between Kate and Alexis, Kerry and Anna, or Jeff and Kathy. In the terms introduced in the reading before this one (Carole's and my essay), how would you describe the ways these partners are negotiating selves?
2. Test the data reported about wording, error, and ambiguity repairs against your own experience. Think about how you communicate in a close relationship and how you communicate with a new acquaintance. Do your repairs follow the pattern indicated here?
3. What do you think Grove's main point is in his discussion of "tact" and "tactics"? Is he suggesting that we should avoid "tactics"? Are there dangers of being "tactful"?

4. Some people who study communication believe that power and control are parts of *every* relationship. Others believe that only *some* relationships are marked by power and control. What do you think?
5. In most of your communication with your friends, do you tend to operate from the "autonomy" end of the autonomy-responsiveness continuum, or the "responsiveness" end?

The human person needs confirmation. . . . An animal does not need to be confirmed, for it is what it is unquestionably. It is different with [the person]. Sent forth from the natural domain of species into the hazard of the solitary category, surrounded by the air of a chaos which came into being with him, secretly and bashfully he watches for a Yes which allows him to be and which can come to him only from one human person to another. It is from one [person] to another that the heavenly bread of self-being is passed.*

MARTIN BUBER

Confirmation and its opposite—disconfirmation—are important elements of the process of negotiating selves. As the quotation by Martin Buber suggests, confirmation or disconfirmation exists to some degree or another in *every* relationship, and they distinguish the most positive relationships from the most toxic ones.

Confirmation means actively acknowledging a person as a person, recognizing him or her as a subject, a unique, unmeasurable, choosing, reflective, and addressable human. The authors of this next reading point out that Buber was the first to use the term in this interpersonal sense. In the words quoted above, Buber identifies confirmation as a phenomenon that distinguishes the human world from the nonhuman. His point is that we discover our personhood or humanness as we make contact with others. I learn that I am a person when I experience confirmation from another person. This is one of the crucial functions of communication: to confirm others and experience confirmation myself.

Ken Cissna and Evelyn Sieburg are two speech communication teachers who've been studying confirmation for several years. This essay is nicely organized into a section that defines and describes confirmation, a section that identifies its four main dimensions, and then a longer section that talks systematically about confirming and disconfirming behaviors.

The authors describe and illustrate how what they call indifferent responses, impervious responses, and disqualifying responses are all disconfirming. Indifference denies the other's existence, while imperviousness means responding only to my image of you, even if it contradicts your perception of yourself. We communicate indifference, for example, by avoiding eye contact or physical contact or by ignoring topics the other person brings up. Imperviousness can be communicated, for example, with "Don't be silly—of course you're not afraid," or, "Stop crying, there's nothing the matter with you!" Disqualification is the technique of denying without really saying "no," as we do when, for example, we

---

* Martin Buber, "Distance and Relation," in *The Knowledge of Man,* ed. Maurice Friedman, trans. Maurice Friedman and R. G. Smith (New York: Harper & Row, 1965), p. 71.

utter the "sigh of martyrdom," respond tangentially to the other person, or say something like, "If I were going to criticize, I'd say your haircut looks awful, but I wouldn't say that."

Responses that confirm, the authors point out, are less clearly defined than disconfirming ones. However, they identify three clusters of confirmation: recognition, acknowledgment, and endorsement. They also emphasize that "confirming response is dialogic in structure; it is a reciprocal activity involving shared talk and sometimes shared silence." This echoes the points about contact and the between that I've made and that have been made by several other contributors to this book.

Patterns of Interactional Confirmation and Disconfirmation

Kenneth N. Leone Cissna and Evelyn Sieburg

The term "confirmation" was first used in an interpersonal sense by Martin Buber (1957), who attributed broad existential significance to confirmation, describing it as basic to humanness and as providing the test of the degree of humanity present in any society. Although Buber did not explicitly define confirmation, he consistently stressed its importance to human intercourse:

> The basis of man's life with man is twofold, and it is one—the wish of every man to be *confirmed* as what he is, even as what he can become, by men; and the innate capacity in man to confirm his fellow men in this way. . . . Actual humanity exists only where this capacity unfolds. [p. 102]

R. D. Laing (1961) quoted extensively from Buber in his description of confirmation and disconfirmation as communicated qualities which exist in the relationship between two or more persons. Confirmation is the process through which individuals are "endorsed" by others, which, as Laing described it, implies recognition and acknowledgment of them. Though Laing developed confirmation at a conceptual level more thoroughly than anyone prior to him, his focus remained psychiatric: he was concerned with the effects of pervasive disconfirmation within the families of patients who had come to be diagnosed as schizophrenic. In such families, Laing noted, one child is

From Kenneth N. Leone Cissna and Evelyn Sieburg, "Patterns of Interactional Confirmation and Disconfirmation," *Rigor and Imagination*, Carol Wilder-Mott and John Weakland, eds. (Praeger Publishers, an imprint of Greenwood Publishing Group, Inc., Wesport, CT, 1981), pp. 230–239. Copyright © 1981 by Praeger Publications. Abridged and reprinted with permission.

frequently singled out as the recipient of especially destructive communicative acts by the other members. As Laing explained it, the behavior of the family "does not so much involve a child who has been subjected to outright neglect or even to obvious trauma, but a child who has been subjected to subtle but persistent *disconfirmation*, usually unwittingly" (1961:83). Laing further equated confirmation with a special kind of love, which "lets the other be, but with affection and concern," as contrasted with disconfirmation (or violence), which "attempts to constrain the other's freedom, to force him to act in the way we desire, but with ultimate lack of concern, with indifference to the other's own existence or destiny" (1967:58). This theme of showing concern while relinquishing control is common in psychiatric writing and is an important element in confirmation as we understand it. Although Laing stressed the significance of confirmation, he made no attempt to define it in terms of specific behaviors, noting only its variety of modes:

> Modes of confirmation or disconfirmation vary. Confirmation could be through a responsive smile (visual), a handshake (tactile), an expression of sympathy (auditory). A confirmatory response is *relevant* to the evocative action, it accords recognition to the evocatory act, and accepts its significance for the other, if not for the respondent. A confirmatory reaction is a direct response, it is "to the point," "on the same wavelength," as the initiatory or evocatory action. [1961:82]

In 1967, Watzlawick, Beavin, and Jackson located confirmation within a more general framework of human communication and developed it as a necessary element of all human interaction, involving a subtle but powerful validation of the other's self-image. In addition to its content, they said each unit of interaction also contains relational information, offering first, a self-definition by a person (P) and then a response from the other (O) to that self-definition. According to Watzlawick *et al.*, this response may take any of three possible forms: it may confirm, it may reject, or it may disconfirm. The last, disconfirmation, implies the relational message, "You do not exist," and negates the other as a valid message source. Confirmation implies acceptance of the speaker's self-definition. "As far as we can see, this confirmation of *P's* view of himself by O is probably the greatest single factor ensuring mental development and stability that has so far emerged from our study of communication" (p. 84). The descriptive material provided by Watzlawick *et al.* to illustrate disconfirmation includes instances of total unawareness of the person, lack of accurate perception of the other's point of view, and deliberate distortion or denial of the other's self-attributes.

Sieburg (1969) used the structure provided by Watzlawick as well as the concept of confirmation/disconfirmation to begin distinguishing between human communication which is growthful, productive, effective, functional, or "therapeutic," and communication which is not. She developed measurement systems for systematically observing confirming and disconfirming communication (1969, 1972); she devised the first scale which allowed for measurement of an individual's feeling of being confirmed by another person (1973). She has continued to refine the basic theory of confirmation (1975), and has recently used the concepts to describe both organizational (1976) and family (in preparation) communication systems. During this time, a growing body of theoretical development and empirical research has attempted to explore these important concerns (cf. Cissna, 1976a, 1976b). . . .

Dimensions of Confirmation

In the few direct allusions in the literature to confirmation and disconfirmation, several different elements are suggested. Confirmation is, of course, tied by definition to self-experience; our first problem, therefore, was to identify the specific aspects of self-experience that could be influenced positively or negatively in interaction with others. Four such elements seemed significant for our purpose:

1. The element of existence (the individual sees self as existing)
2. The element of relating (the individual sees self as a being-in-relation with others)
3. The element of significance, or worth
4. The element of validity of experience

Thus, it was assumed that the behavior of one person toward another is confirming to the extent that it performs the following functions in regard to the other's self-experience:

1. It expresses recognition of the other's existence
2. It acknowledges a relationship of affiliation with the other
3. It expresses awareness of the significance or worth of the other
4. It accepts or "endorses" the other's self-experience (particularly emotional experience)

Each unit of response is assumed to evoke relational metamessages with regard to each of the above functions, which can identify it as either confirming or disconfirming:

Confirming	Disconfirming
"To me, you exist."	"To me, you do not exist."
"We are relating."	"We are not relating."
"To me, you are significant."	"To me, you are not significant."
"Your way of experiencing your world is valid."	"Your way of experiencing your world is invalid."

In attempting to find behavioral correlates of these functions, we acknowledge that it is not possible to point with certainty to particular behaviors that universally perform these confirming functions for all persons, since individuals differ in the way they interpret the same acts; that is, they interpret the stimuli and assign their own meaning to them. Despite this reservation about making firm causal connections between the behavior of one person and the internal experience of another, we have followed the symbolic interactionist view that certain symbolic cues *do* acquire consensual validation and therefore are consistently interpreted by most persons as reflecting certain attitudes toward them on the part of others. Such cues thus have message value and are capable of arousing in the receiver feelings of being recognized or ignored, accepted or rejected, understood or misunderstood, humanized or "thingified," valued or devalued. This assumption was borne out in a very general way by our research to date (Sieburg & Larson, 1971). . . .

Systematizing Disconfirming Behavior

A variety of specific acts and omissions have been noted by clinicians and theoreticians as being damaging to some aspect of the receiver's self-view. We have arranged these behaviors into three general groupings, or clusters, each representing a somewhat different style of response:

1. Indifferent response (denying existence or relation)
2. Impervious response (denying self-experience of the other)
3. Disqualifying response (denying the other's significance)

These clusters include verbal/nonverbal and vocal/nonvocal behaviors. Since they encompass both content and process features of interaction, it meant that scorers must be trained to evaluate each scoring unit in terms of its manifest content, its transactional features, and its underlying structure. In either case, no single utterance stands alone since it is always in response to some behavior or another, and is so experienced by the other as having implications about his or her self.

Disconfirmation by Indifference

To deny another's existence is to deny the most fundamental aspect of self-experience. Indifference may be total, as when presence is denied; it may imply rejection of relatedness with the other; or it may only deny the other's attempt to communicate.

Denial of Presence   The absence of even a minimal show of recognition has been associated with alienation, self-destructiveness, violence against others, and with psychosis. Laing used the case of "Peter," a psychotic patient of 25 to illustrate the possible long-term effects of chronic indifference toward a child who may, as a consequence, come to believe that he has no presence at all—or to feel guilty that he *does*, feeling that he has no right even to occupy space.

> Peter . . . was a young man who was preoccupied with guilt *because* he occupied a place in the world, even in a physical sense. He could not realize . . . that he had a right to have any presence for others . . . A peculiar aspect of his childhood was that his presence in the world was largely ignored. No weight was given to the fact that he was in the same room while his parents had intercourse. He had been physically cared for in that he had been well fed and kept warm, and underwent no physical separation from his parents during his earlier years. Yet he had been consistently treated as though he did not "really" exist. Perhaps worse than the experience of physical separation was to be in the same room as his parents and ignored, not malevolently, but through sheer indifference. [Laing, 1961:119]

That such extreme indifference is also devastating to an adult is evident in the following excerpt from a marriage counseling session (Sieburg, personal audiotape). It is perhaps significant that throughout his wife's outburst, the husband sat silent and remote:

THERAPIST: . . . and is it okay to express emotion?
WIFE: Not in my house.

THERAPIST: Has he [the husband] ever *said* it's not okay to talk about feelings?

WIFE: But he never *says* anything!

THERAPIST: But he has ways of sending you messages?

WIFE: [loudly] Yes! And the message is *shut out*—no matter what I say, no matter what I do, I get no response—zero—shut out!

THERAPIST: And does that somehow make you feel you are wrong?

WIFE: Oh, of course not wrong—just *nothing!*

THERAPIST: Then what is it that makes you feel he disapproves of you?

WIFE: Because I get nothing! [tears] If I feel discouraged—like looking for a job all day and being turned down—and I cry—zero! No touching, no patting, no "Maybe tomorrow"—just *shut out*. And if I get angry at him, instead of getting angry back, he just walks away—just nothing! All the time I'm feeling shut out and shut off!

THERAPIST: And what is it you want from him?

WIFE: [quietly] Maybe sometimes just a pat on the back would be enough. But, no!— he just shrugs me off. Where am I supposed to go to feel real? [tears]

Avoiding Involvement   Extreme instances of indifference like those above are presumed to be rare because even the slightest attention at least confirms one's presence. Lesser shows of indifference, however, still create feelings of alienation, frustration, and lowered self-worth. Although recognition is a necessary first step in confirming another, it is not in itself sufficient unless accompanied by some further indication of a willingness to be involved.

The precise ways in which one person indicates to another that he or she is interested in relating (intimacy) are not fully known, but several clear indications of *unwillingness* to relate or to become more than minimally involved have emerged from research and have been included in our systemization of disconfirming behaviors. Of particular significance are the use of:

- Impersonal language—the avoidance of first person references (I, me, my, mine) in favor of a collective "we" or "one," or the tendency to begin sentences with "there" when making what amounts to a personal statement (as, "there seems to be . . .")
- Avoidance of eye contact
- Avoidance of physical contact except in ritualized situations such as handshaking
- Other nonverbal "distancing" cues

Rejecting Communication   A third way of suggesting indifference to another is to respond in a way that is unrelated, or only minimally related, to what he or she has just said, thus creating a break or disjunction in the flow of interaction.

Totally irrelevant response is, of course, much like denial of presence in that the person whose topic is repeatedly ignored may soon come to doubt his or her very existence, and at best will feel that he or she is not heard, attended to, or regarded as significant. Perhaps for this reason Laing called relevance the "crux of confirmation," noting that only by responding relevantly can one lend significance to another's communication and accord recognition (Laing, 1961:87).

The most extreme form of communication rejection is monologue, in which one speaker continues on and on, neither hearing nor acknowledging anything the other says. It reflects unawareness and lack of concern about the other person except as a socially acceptable audience for the speaker's own self-listening. A less severe communication rejection occurs when the responder makes a connection, however slight, with what the other has said, but immediately shifts into something quite different of his or her own choosing.

Disconfirming by Imperviousness

The term "imperviousness" as used here follows Laing's usage refers to a lack of accurate awareness of another's perceptions (Watzlawick *et al.*, 1967:91). Imperviousness is disconfirming because it denies or distorts another's self-expression and fosters dehumanized relationships in which one person perceives another as a pseudo-image rather than as what that person really is. Behaviorally, the impervious responder engages in various tactics that tend to negate or discredit the other's feeling expression. These may take the form of a flat denial that the other *has* such a feeling ("You don't really mean that"), or it may be handled more indirectly by reinterpreting the feeling in a more acceptable way, ("You're only saying that because . . ."), substituting some experience or feeling of the *listener* ("What you're trying to say is . . ."), challenging the speaker's right to have such a feeling ("How can you *possibly* feel that way after all that's been done for you?"), or some similar device intended to alter the feeling expressed. . . .

A slightly different form of imperviousness occurs when a responder creates and bestows on another an inaccurate identity, and then confirms the false identity, although it is not a part of the other's self-experience at all. Laing calls this pseudo-confirmation (1961:83). Thus a mother who insists that her daughter is always obedient and "never any trouble at all" may be able to interpret her daughter's most rebellious aggression in a way that fits the placid image she holds of her daughter, and the parents of even a murderous psychopath may be able to describe their son as a "good boy." Such a false confirmation frequently endorses the fiction of what the other is *wished* to be, without any real recognition of what the other is or how he/she feels. As noted earlier, this form of disconfirmation also appears as simply a well-meaning attempt to reassure another who is distressed, which too is usually motivated by the speaker's need to reduce his or her own discomfort.

> "Don't be silly—of course you're not afraid!"
> "You may think you feel that way now, but I know better."
> "Stop crying—there's nothing the matter with you!"
> "How can you possibly worry about a little thing like that?"
> "No matter what you say, I know you still love me."

Such responses constitute a rejection of the other person's expression and often identity, raising doubts about the validity of his/her way of experiencing by suggesting, "You don't really feel as you say you do; you are only imagining that you do."

A subtle variation of the same tactic occurs when the speaker responds in a selective way, rewarding the other with attention and relevant response *only* when he or she communicates in an approved fashion, and becoming silent or indifferent if the other's speech or behavior does not meet with the responder's approval. This may mean that the speaker limits response to those topics initiated by self, ignoring any topic initiated by the other person.

Imperviousness is considered disconfirming because it contributes to a feeling of uncertainty about self or uncertainty about the validity of personal experiencing.

Imperviousness occurs when a person is told how he or she feels, regardless of how he or she experiences self, when a person's talents and abilities are described without any data to support such a description, when motives are ascribed to another without any reference to the other's own experience, or when one's own efforts at self-expression are ignored or discounted unless they match the false image held by some other person. . . .

Disconfirmation by Disqualification

According to Watzlawick (1964) disqualification is a technique which enables one to say something without really saying it, to deny without really saying "no," and to disagree without really disagreeing. Certain messages, verbal and nonverbal, are included in this group because they (a) disqualify the other speaker, (b) disqualify another message, or (c) disqualify themselves.

Speaker Disqualification   This may include such direct disparagement of the other as name-calling, criticism, blame, and hostile attack, but may also take the indirect form of the sigh of martyrdom, the muttered expletive, addressing an adult in a tone of voice usually reserved for a backward child, joking "on the square," sarcasm, or any of the other numerous tactics to make the other appear and feel too incompetent or unreliable for his message to have validity. This creates a particularly unanswerable put-down by evoking strong metamessages of insignificance or worthlessness. The following examples are spouses' responses from conjoint counseling sessions:

- "Can't you ever do anything right?"
- "Here we go again!" [sigh]
- "We heard you the first time—why do you always keep repeating yourself?"
- "It's no wonder the rear axle broke, with you in the back seat!" [laughter]
- "Why do you always have to get your mouth open when you don't know what you're talking about?"

Message Disqualification   Without regard to their content, some messages tend to discredit the other person because of their irrelevance—that is, they do not "follow" the other's prior utterance in a transactional sense. (This is also a tactic of indifference and may serve a dual disconfirming purpose.) Such disjunctive responses were studied by Sluzki, Beavin, Tarnopolski, and Veron (1967) who used the term "transactional disqualification" to mean any incongruity in the response of the speaker in relation to the context of the previous message of the other. A relationship between two successive messages exists, they noted, on two possible levels: (a) continuity between the content of the two messages (are both persons talking about the same subject?), and (b) indication of reception of the prior message (what cues does the speaker give of receiving and understanding the previous message?). If a message is disjunctive at either of these levels, transactional disqualification of the prior message is said to have occurred.

A similar form of message disqualifica   occurs when a speaker reacts selectively to some incidental clue in another's speech, but ignores the primary theme. Thus the responder may acknowledge the other's attempt to communicate, but still appears to miss the point. This "tangential response" was identified and studied by Jurgen Ruesch (1958), who noted that a speaker often picks up on a topic presented, but then continues to spin a yarn in a different direction. The response is not totally irrelevant because it has made some connection, although perhaps slight, with the prior utterance. Because it causes the first speaker to question the value or importance of what he or she was trying to say, the tangential response is reported to affect adversely a speaker's feeling of self-significance, and is therefore included as a form of disconfirmation.

Message Disqualifying Itself

A third way in which a speaker can use disqualification to "say something without really saying it," is by sending messages that disqualify themselves. There are many ways in which this may be done, the commonest devices being lack of clarity, ambiguity, and incongruity of mode. These forms of response are grouped together here because they have all been interpreted as devices for avoiding involvement with another by generating the metamessage "I am not communicating," hence "We are not relating."

Systematizing Confirming Behaviors

Responses that confirm are less clearly defined than disconfirming behaviors because there has been less motivation to study them. In fact, identification of specific acts that are generally confirming is difficult unless we simply identify confirmation as the absence of disconfirming behaviors. More research in this area is clearly needed, but, in general, confirming behaviors are those which permit people to experience their own being and significance as well as their interconnectedness with others. Following Laing (1961), these have been arranged into three clusters: recognition, acknowledgment, and endorsement.

The Recognition Cluster Recognition is expressed by looking at the other, making frequent eye contact, touching, speaking directly to the person, and allowing the other the opportunity to respond without being interrupted or having to force his or her way into an ongoing monologue. In the case of an infant, recognition means holding and cuddling beyond basic survival functions; in the case of an adult, it may still mean physical contact (touching), but it also means psychological contact in the form of personal language, clarity, congruence of mode, and authentic self-expression. In other words, confirmation requires that a person treat the other with respect, acknowledging his or her attempt to relate, and need to have a presence in the world.

The Acknowledgment Cluster Acknowledgment of another is demonstrated by a relevant and direct response to his or her communication. This does not require praise or even agreement, but simple conjunction. Buber (Friedman, 1960) recognized this aspect when he wrote that mutually confirming partners can still "struggle together in direct opposition," and Laing (1961) made a similar point when he said that even rejection can be confirming if it is direct, not tangential, and if it grants significance and validity to what the other says. To hear, attend, and take note of the other and to acknowledge the other by responding directly is probably the most valued form of confirmation—and possibly the most rare. It means that the other's expression is furthered, facilitated, and encouraged.

The Endorsement Cluster This cluster includes any responses that express acceptance of the other's feelings as being true, accurate, and "okay." In general, it means simply letting the other *be*, without blame, praise, analysis, justification, modification, or denial.

Confirming response is dialogic in structure; it is a reciprocal activity involving shared talk and sometimes shared silence. It is interactional in the broadest sense of the word. It is not a one-way flow of talk; it is not a trade-off in which each speaker pauses and appears to listen only in order to get a chance to speak again. It is a complex affair in which each participates as both subject and object, cause and effect, of the other's talk. In short, confirming response, like all communication, is not something one does, it is a process in which one shares.

References

Buber, M. "Distance and Relation," *Psychiatry* 20 (1957): 97–104.

Cissna, K. N. L. "Facilitative Communication and Interpersonal Relationships: An Empirical Test of a Theory of Interpersonal Communication." Doctoral dissertation, University of Denver, 1975.

Cissna, K. N. L. "Interpersonal Confirmation: A Review of Current/Recent Theory and Research." Paper presented at the Central States Speech Association Convention, Chicago, 1976, and the International Communication Association Convention, Portland, Oregon, 1976.

Cissna, K. N. L. *Interpersonal Confirmation: A Review of Current Theory, Measurement, and Research.* Saint Louis: Saint Louis University, 1976.

Cissna, K. N. L. "Gender, Sex, Type, and Perceived Confirmation: A Response from the Perspective of Interpersonal Confirmation." Presented at the International Communication Association Convention, Philadelphia, 1979.

Cissna, K. N. L., and S. Keating. "Speech Communication Antecedents of Perceived Confirmation," *Western Journal of Speech Communication* 43 (1979): 48–60.

Friedman, M. S. "Dialogue and the 'Essential We': The Bases of Values in the Philosophy of Martin Buber," *American Journal of Psychoanalysis* 20 (1960): 26–34.

Laing, R. D. *The Self and Others.* New York: Pantheon, 1961.

Laing, R. D. "Mystification, Confusion and Conflict," in *Intensive Family Therapy*, ed. I. Boszormenyi-Nagy and J. L. Framo. New York: Harper & Row, 1965.

Laing, R. D. *The Politics of Experience.* New York: Ballantine, 1967.

Laing, R. D. *The Self and Others.* 2nd ed. Baltimore: Penguin, 1969.

Laing, R. D. *Knots.* New York: Vintage, 1970.

Laing, R. D., and A. Esterson. *Sanity, Madness, and the Family.* Baltimore: Penguin, 1964.

Ruesch, J. "The Tangential Response," in *Psychopathology of Communication*, ed. P. H. Toch and J. Zuben. New York: Grune & Stratton, 1958.

Ruesch, J. and G. Bateson. *Communication: The Social Matrix of Psychiatry.* New York: Norton, 1951.

Sieburg, E. "Dysfunctional Communication and Interpersonal Responsiveness in Small Groups." Doctoral dissertation, University of Denver, 1969.

Sieburg, E. "Toward a Theory of Interpersonal Confirmation," Unpublished manuscript, University of Denver, 1972.

Sieburg, E. *Interpersonal Confirmation: A Paradigm for Conceptualization and Measurement.* San Diego: United States International University, 1975.

Sieburg, E. "Confirming and Disconfirming Organizational Communication," in *Communication in Organizations*. eds. J. L. Owen, P. A. Page, and G. I. Zimmerman. St. Paul: West Publishing, 1976.

Sieburg E. *Family Communication Systems* (in preparation).

Sieburg, E. and C. E. Larson. "Dimensions of Interpersonal Response." Paper presented at the annual convention of the International Communication Association, Phoenix, 1971.

Watzlawick, P. *An Anthology of Human Communication*. Palo Alto: Science and Behavior Books, 1964.

Watzlawick, P., J. Beavin, and D. D. Jackson. *Pragmatics of Human Communication: A Study of Interactional Patterns, Pathologies, and Paradoxes*. New York: Norton, 1967.

Review Questions

1. Give a one-sentence definition of the term "confirmation."
2. Discuss the distinctions between the four elements of confirmation that Cissna and Sieburg outline—existence, relating, significance, and validity of experience.
3. According to these authors, which are more important in the confirmation/disconfirmation process, verbal cues or nonverbal cues?
4. "The most extreme form of communication rejection is _____."
5. Which kind of disconfirmation is happening in the following example:
   Rae: "Damn! I wish that test wasn't tomorrow! That really ticks me off!"
   Kris: "You aren't mad, you're just scared because you haven't studied enough."
6. Give an example of a person "saying something without really saying it."
7. Explain the distinction between recognition and acknowledgment.

Probes

1. What makes the term "confirmation" appropriate for what's being discussed here? You can confirm an airplane reservation and in some churches young people are confirmed. How do those meanings echo the meaning of confirmation that's developed here?
2. Notice how, in the first paragraph under the heading "Dimensions of Confirmation," the authors emphasize the transactional or relational quality of the phenomenon. Paraphrase what you hear them saying there.
3. All of us experience disconfirmation, sometimes with destructive regularity. Give an example where you have given an *indifferent* response. Give an example where you've received one. Do the same for *imperviousness* and *disqualification*.
4. When a person is "impervious," what is he or she impervious *to?* Discuss.
5. Create an example of well-meant imperviousness, that is, imperviousness motivated by a genuine desire to comfort or to protect the other person. Do the same with a disqualifying response.
6. Identify five specific confirming communication events that you experienced in the last four hours.

Chapter 11

Friendship

riendship is a relationship that we all experience. At the same time, as these authors point out, it is not a well-defined phenomenon. In order to enrich the friendships we have, it can help to understand the nature of this type of relationship and to know how friendships develop over time. These are the two topics of this essay.

This essay is based on a great deal of research and reflection. Mac Parks, especially, has thought, studied, and written about close relationships for a number of years. So you can trust the generalizations that these authors make here.

After acknowledging the difficulty of defining something as pervasive and amorphous as friendship, the authors focus on five distinctive features of this kind of relationship: (1) voluntariness, (2) status equality, (3) assistance, (4) activity sharing, and (5) confidentiality and emotional support. Then they briefly discuss how each functions and, by the end of this discussion, we have a rather clear picture of the nature of friendship.

Their treatment of the development of friendship relations is equally thorough and helpful. They talk about the development toward increasing intimacy and attachment, toward increasing breadth or variety of interaction (friends can talk about almost anything almost anywhere), toward increasing interdependence, toward increasing communication code specialization (friends "speak the same language"), toward decreasing cognitive uncertainty (I can usually predict what my friend's going to do), and toward increasing network contact and overlap (My friends are your friends, your friends are my friends, and our friends are often friends). They also note that changes in each of these dimensions affect all the other factors. As with the first section of this essay, each dimension of relationship development the authors discuss is important and, when taken together, they cover just about all the crucial aspects of this topic.

Mara, Mac, and Teri don't try to tell you how to make friends or even specifically how to communicate with them. But they do provide a wealth of useful insights into this most common and often most important of all our relationships.

The Nature of Friendship and Its Development

Mara B. Adelman, Malcolm R. Parks, and Terrance L. Albrecht

The Nature of Friendship

Friendship is a slippery concept. Even if we limit the problem of defining friendship to North American and Western European models, consensus regarding the nature of friendship exists only at the most general level. Reisman (1979, p. 108), for example, defines a friend as "someone who likes and wishes to do well by someone else and who believes those feelings and good intentions are reciprocated." Argyle and Henderson (1985, p. 64) can be no more specific than to define friendship in this way:

> Friends are people who are liked, whose company is enjoyed, who share interests and activities, who are helpful and understanding, who can be trusted, with whom one feels comfortable, and who will be emotionally supportive.

The difficulty with such definitions, of course, is that they do not neatly differentiate friendship from other close relationships. In fact, most of the characteristics of friendship can, to one degree or another, be found in other close relationships (see Argyle & Henderson, 1985). Given this ambiguity, we believe that concepts like "friend" and "close friend" are best treated as social and cognitive labels. Their meaning is derived from the individual's act of labeling a relationship as a friendship rather than from some unique and theoretically specified conceptual domain.

Friendship is also a slippery concept because it is both a type of relationship and a quality that people attribute to other types of relationships. For example, people often view other types of close relationships as if they were friendships (e.g., "She's my cousin, but mostly she's my friend" or "My wife is my best friend"). People frequently count kin among their close friends. Conversely, people often treat close friends as if they were members of the family (e.g., "You're like a brother to me").

None of these observations should suggest that the vessel of friendship is an empty one, only that many other relationships also carry its cargo. Perhaps friendship can be distinguished from other relationships by negation. Marriage, for example, carries all of the expectations of friendship, but friendship does not carry all of the expectations of marriage. This naturally begs the question of what the expectations and characteristics of friendship are. Our admittedly nonexclusive manifest of characteristics include the following factors: (1) voluntariness, (2) status equality, (3) assistance, (4) activity sharing, and (5) confidentiality and emotional support.

Voluntariness   We are born into a family, but we choose our friends. The perception of choice distinguishes friendship from most family, kin, and work relationships. No other close relationship except marriage contains such a strong aura of voluntariness. The perception of voluntariness may give the support received from friends enhanced value just because the recipient knows that it was given more as a matter of choice than of obligation. However, even this perception is subject to restrictions. The amount of contact one has with kin becomes increasingly a matter of choice in adulthood (Argyle & Henderson, 1985). Moreover, because friendships are often developed within a network of other friendships, one's actual freedom of choice may be bounded by definite social pressures to either develop or to maintain a given friendship within the network.

Equality   Close friendships are usually based on the shared perception that the participants are social equals (Reisman, 1979, 1981). In her study of adult friendship choices in the United States and Germany, for instance, Verbrugge (1977) found that equality in social status was a major factor in close friendship choices. Less developed friendships, on the other hand, need not always be among equals. Many relationships growing out of work settings are "mixed friendships" in that they contain both elements of equality and inequality. Superiors and their favored subordinates, for example, often mix both a work relationship and a friendship. Elaborate rule systems are often needed to signal shifts from one relational domain to another. In general, however, the closer the friendship is perceived to be, the more equality the participants will perceive.

Assistance   Most studies of friendship emphasize that friends are people who help each other (e.g., Argyle & Henderson, 1985; Crawford, 1977; Parlee, 1979; Reisman, 1981; Reisman & Shorr, 1978). In contemporary U.S. and Western European cultures, however, there are definite limits to the amount of tangible and task assistance expected from friends. As Allan (1983) notes, friends typically "care about" rather than "care for" each other. While short-term and minor assistance can be expected, long-term and significant assistance must usually come from kin or public agencies. In a study of men who had suffered from myocardial infarctions, for example, Croog, Lipson, and Levine (1972) found that support from friends was more of a supplement to support from family rather than a primary or compensatory form of support.

Activity Sharing   Argyle & Henderson (1985, p. 84) observe that "above all we need friends to do things with, especially leisure activities, going out, and having fun." Obviously marital and family relationships also engage in activity sharing, but many of these shared activities are experienced with a sense of obligation rather than sharing for the joy of the activity alone. Shared leisure activities among friends can be more easily enjoyed purely for their intrinsic value. Friends also provide opportunities to share activities that are less enjoyable to the spouse or to other family members. Thus friends support us by giving us an outlet for activities not shared with family members and by giving us opportunities for enjoying activities without the larger relational implications so frequently a part of family life.

Confidentiality and Emotional Support   A major theme in the social support literature on friendship is the provision of emotional support, intimate confiding, and felt attachment (e.g., Allan, 1983; Argyle & Henderson, 1985; Bankoff, 1981; O'Conner & Brown, 1984; Quam, 1983). Friendships may serve as the primary sources of emotional support for unmarried persons, for adolescents experiencing the stresses of developing an independent identity, for men and women whose spouses are unsupportive, and for the elderly who have no kin living nearby (Argyle & Henderson, 1985). Friends may therefore at least partially compensate for inadequacies in other types of relationships. Even for those with many close family relationships, however, friends may serve as important sources of emotional support for at least two reasons. Because friendship networks tend to be less densely connected than family networks, individuals have a generally easier time keeping information confidential. Concerns for confidentiality and privacy figure prominently in people's subjective definitions of friendship (Argyle & Henderson, 1985; Crawford, 1977; Reisman & Shorr, 1978). In addition, friendships are sometimes more easily terminated than family and kin relationships. This fact provides individuals with a kind of "emergency exit" when the issues raised by the pursuit of emotional support become too disruptive to the relationship.

Dimensions of Relationship Development

. . . What does it mean to say that a relationship has "developed"? Relationships "develop" in several directions at the same time and so there is no one answer to such a question. However, we believe that the following six dimensions provide a relatively comprehensive view of relationship development. Personal relationships can be said to develop as (1) intimacy and emotional attachment increase, (2) the breadth or variety of interaction increases, (3) the degree of interdependence or contingency increases, (4) communication codes become specialized, (5) cognitive uncertainty about the self and other decreases, and (6) the participants' social networks become intertwined. Changes in each of these factors are presumed to affect the others. Moreover, while our primary concern is with the development of friendships, these dimensions of development are general ones that can be applied to the development of virtually any close relationship.

Increasing Intimacy and Attachment   The most obvious and researched aspect of relationship development is self-disclosure and intimacy. This is the "depth" dimension of relationship development (Altman & Taylor, 1973; Levinger & Snoek, 1972). As a relationship develops, the participants typically disclose more personal information, express more positive and negative feelings, and express praise and criticism more openly (Altman & Taylor, 1973; Huston & Burgess, 1979). At a general level, this implies that the value or magnitude of rewards and punishments exchanged tends to increase as a relationship develops (e.g., Altman & Taylor, 1973; Aronson, 1970; Hatfield, Utne, & Traupmann, 1979; Huesmann & Levinger, 1976). In a longitudinal study of friendship development, Hays (1984), for example, found that development was associated with increases in the intimacy of behaviors exchanged. At a more specific level, the depth dimension implies that the intimacy of participants' conversations increases as their friendship develops (e.g., Altman & Taylor, 1973; Naegele, 1958; Parks, 1976). Interaction becomes more oriented around the distinctive characteristics of the individual than around the more generalized characteristics they may stereotypically share with others (Miller & Steinberg, 1975).

Along with increases in the intimacy of interaction come increases in a series of affective variables such as liking and loving (e.g., Huston & Burgess, 1979) and a number of cognitive variables associated with them. In one recent study of friendship development, for instance, Eggert and Parks (1987) found strong positive correlations among measures of liking, love, intimacy, perceived similarity, satisfaction with communication, and the expectation that the friendship would continue into the future.

These findings suggest that the depth dimension of friendship development is reciprocally related to social support. As a relationship develops, the opportunities to provide the more intimate forms of social support such as emotional support increase and the participants place greater value on the support they receive. And as the opportunity for and value of support increases, the development of the relationship is spurred onward.

Increasing Breadth or Variety of Interaction   As a friendship develops, the participants come to interact not only about increasingly intimate concerns, but also about an increasing variety of concerns. This is the "breadth" dimension of relationship development (Altman & Taylor, 1973). Disclosure and conversation occur along a greater variety of topics (e.g., Altman & Taylor, 1973; Naegele, 1958; Parks, 1976). In the parlance of exchange theory the variety of resources exchanged increases as a relationship develops (e.g., Hatfield et al., 1979). This point is nicely illustrated by Hays's (1984) longitudinal study of same-sex friendship development. Hays found that pairs whose friendship developed tended to engage in more behaviors in more categories of interaction (i.e., activity sharing, task assistance, mutual disclosure, expressing emotion) than did pairs that terminated or failed to become closer over the three month period of the study. These findings suggest that closer friendships provide more different types of social support for the individual and that the ability to provide such variety contributes to the overall development of the relationship.

As a relationship develops, the participants also tend to interact in an increasing variety of settings and contexts (e.g., Huston & Burgess, 1979). Closer relationships are more portable, less dependent upon the particular situational context. This implies that close relationships can serve as sources of social support in a greater range of settings than can "weaker," less developed relationships.

Increasing Interdependence and Contingency   Relationships develop to the degree that the participants become increasingly interdependent (see Kelley, 1979; Kelley & Thibaut, 1978). What each receives becomes more contingent upon the actions of the other. Their individual goals and actions become more synchronized and intermeshed (e.g., Altman & Taylor, 1973; Huston & Burgess, 1979). Indeed, if the participants believe that the benefits of the relationship can also be obtained from a variety of other sources, the relationship is less likely to develop (Huston & Burgess, 1979).

Interdependence and contingency have several implications for the social support process. First, increasing interdependence creates increasing substitutability in the resources or types of social support. The individual who gives support in one area may be repaid by support in another area. Less developed or "weaker" social ties, on the other hand, tend to operate more often on a give and take of like resources (Hatfield et al., 1979). While this characteristic makes the coordination of a close relationship a more difficult task, it also increases the range of behaviors that can be used to reciprocate support and thereby decreases the probability that an inability to reciprocate with like resources will disrupt the overall relationship. In addition, increasing interdependence is usually associated with a lessening concern for immediate repayment of favors and assistance received. Close friends tend to be more tolerant of inequities in the support taken and given because, unlike those in less developed relationships, they can believe that they have a good deal of time and many ways to restore equity (Hatfield et al., 1979). Finally, these characteristics of interdependence imply that methodologies that examine only those support requests that are immediately reciprocated with similar resources will miss much of the richness of the support process in close relationships.

Increasing Communication Code Specialization   Relationship development is not only characterized by an increasing depth and breadth of communication, but also by changes in the structure of communication. Waller and Hill's (1951, p. 189) comments about the communication of courtship pairs apply equally well to the communication of close friends:

> As a result of conversations and experience, there emerges a common universe of discourse characterized by the feeling of something very special between two persons. . . . They soon develop a special language, their own idioms, pet names, and jokes; as a pair, they have a history and a separate culture.

Code specialization occurs at several levels (Bernstein, 1964; Hopper, Knapp, & Scott, 1981; Knapp, 1984). Private slang or jargon may be developed. Conventional language forms may be given new meanings that are fully understood only by the participants themselves. Verbal statements may become abbreviated, incomplete. Or that which used to be verbally communicated may become communicated nonverbally.

Code specialization has both methodological and substantive implications for the study of social support. Observers given the task of coding interaction for its support value may simply miss much of what is happening in a close relationship unless directly aided by the participants. Moreover, the presence of a specialized or "restricted" code implies that the conversation of close friends subtly reinforces and supports their relationship in an ongoing way that is independent of its overt content (see Bernstein, 1964). However, because so much is implicit in these codes, their presence can also be a barrier to renegotiation and change when partners have difficulty talking about their relationship (metacommunicating) at a more explicit level (see Adelman & Siemon, 1986).

Decreasing Cognitive Uncertainty Humans have a deeply set need to "make sense" of their social interactions (Heider, 1958). Much of what happens as a personal relationship develops is therefore contingent upon the participants' abilities to predict and explain each other's behavior; that is, to reduce uncertainty (Berger & Calabrese, 1975). Most theories of relationship development recognize the centrality of uncertainty reduction processes either explicitly or implicitly. As Parks and Adelman (1983, p. 56) point out, "No theory presumes that interpersonal relationships can develop when participants are unable to predict and explain each other's behavior." And, as we have emphasized elsewhere (see Albrecht & Adelman, 1984), uncertainty reduction processes are also at the heart of the process of social support.

Uncertainty reduction involves creating the sense that one knows how to act toward the other, knows how the other is likely to act toward the self, and understands why the other acts the way he or she does (Berger & Calabrese, 1975; Berger, Gardner, Parks, Schulman, & Miller, 1976; Parks, 1976). As uncertainty is reduced, predictive and attributional confidence grow. So, too, do most other dimensions of the relationship between the participants. Measures of uncertainty reduction have been empirically linked to increases in the breadth and depth of communication, the frequency of communication in general and metacommunication in particular, measures of emotional attachment and attraction, contact with and support from the partner's network, perceived similarity, relationship satisfaction, commitment to the future of the relationship, and even with the overall stability of personal relationships over time (e.g., Berger & Calabrese, 1975; Berger et al., 1976; Eggert & Parks, 1987; Parks, 1976; Parks & Adelman, 1983).

Increasing Network Contact and Overlap Whatever our inner experience of them may be, our personal relationships are also social objects existing within the broader context created by our surrounding social networks. How the participants in a developing relationship relate to those networks is therefore a vital dimension of the relationship itself.

The developmental course of a personal relationship is deeply influenced by network factors such as the extent to which the partners create an overlapping network of friends, perceive that each other's friends and family support their relationship, communicate with each other's networks, and are attracted to each other's friends and family. Research on friendship and romantic relationship development has shown that these factors are positively linked with the partners' emotional attachment for each other, their intimacy, commitment, perceived similarity, satisfaction, the frequency of their communication, and the stability of their relationship over time (e.g., Eggert & Parks, 1987; Lewis, 1973; Milardo, 1982; Parks & Adelman, 1983; Parks, Stan, & Eggert, 1983). . . .

Summary

Friendship is among the most malleable of human relationships. It is best understood as a social and cognitive label given to relationships that are characterized by relative voluntariness, perceived equality, the give and take of assistance, sharing activities, confidentiality, and emotional support.

References

Adelman, M. B., & Siemon, M. (1986). Communicating the relational shift: Separation among adult twins. *American Journal of Psychotherapy, 60,* 96–109.

Albrecht, T. L., & Adelman, M. B. (1984). Social support and life stress: New directions for communication research. *Human Communication Research, 11,* 3–32.

Allan, G. (1983). Informal networks of care: Issues raised by Barclay. *British Journal of Social Work, 13,* 417–433.

Altman, I., & Taylor, D. A. (1973). *Social penetration: The development of interpersonal relationships.* New York: Holt, Rinehart, & Winston.

Argyle, M., & Henderson, M. (1985). *The anatomy of relationships.* London: Heinemann.

Aronson, E. (1970). Some antecedents of interpersonal attraction. In W. J. Arnold & D. Levine (Eds.), *Nebraska Symposium on Motivation* (pp. 143–173). Lincoln: University of Nebraska Press.

Bankoff, E. A. (1981). Effects of friendship support on the psychological well-being of widows. In H. Z. Lapota & D. Maines (Eds.), *Research in the interweave of social roles: Friendship* (pp. 109–139), Greenwich, CT: JAI.

Berger, C. R., & Calabrese, R. J. (1975). Some explorations in initial interaction and beyond: Toward a developmental theory of interpersonal communication. *Human Communication Research, 1,* 99–112.

Berger, C. R., Gardner, R. R., Parks, M. R., Schulman, L., & Miller, G. R. (1976). Interpersonal epistemology and interpersonal communication. In G. R. Miller (Ed.), *Explorations in interpersonal communication* (pp. 149–171). Newbury Park, CA: Sage.

Bernstein, B. (1964). Elaborated and restricted codes: Their social origins and some consequences. *American Anthropologist, 66(2),* 55–69.

Crawford, M. (1977). What is a friend? *New Society, 42* (116–177).

Croog, S. H., Lipson, A., & Levine, S. (1972). Help patterns in severe illness: The roles of kin network, non-family resources, and institutions. *Journal of Marriage and the Family, 32,* 32–41.

Eggert, L. L., & Parks, M. R. (1987). Communication network involvement in adolescents' friendships and romantic relationships. In M. L. McLaughlin (Ed.), *Communication Yearbook 10.* Newbury Park, CA: Sage.

Hatfield, E., Utne, M. K., & Traupmann, J. (1979). Equity theory and intimate relationships. In R. L. Burgess & T. L. Huston (Eds.), *Social exchange in developing relationships* (pp. 99–133). New York: Academic Press.

Hays, R. B. (1984). The development and maintenance of friendship. *Journal of Social and Personal Relationships, 1,* 75–98.

Heider, F. (1958). *The psychology of interpersonal relations.* New York: John Wiley.

Hopper, R., Knapp, M. L., & Scott, L. (1981). Couples' personal idioms: Exploring intimate talk. *Journal of Communication, 32,* 23–33.

Huesmann, L. R., & Levinger, G. (1976). Incremental exchange theory: A formal model for progression in dyadic social interaction. In L. Berkowitz & E. Walster (Eds.), *Advances in experimental social psychology* (Vol. 9, pp. 191–229). New York: Academic Press.

Huston, T. L. & Burgess, R. L. (1979). Social exchange in developing relationships: An overview. In R. L. Burgess & T. L. Huston (Eds.), *Social exchange in developing relationships* (pp. 3–28). New York: Academic Press.

Kelley, H. H. (1979). *Personal relationships: Their structures and processes.* Hillsdale, NJ: Lawrence Erlbaum.

Kelley, H. H., & Thibaut, J. W. (1978). *Interpersonal relations: A theory of interdependence.* New York: John Wiley.

Knapp, M. L. (1984). *Interpersonal communication and human relationships.* Boston: Allyn & Bacon.

Levinger, G. & Snoek, J. D. (1972). *Attraction in relationship: A new look at interpersonal attraction.* Morristown, NJ: General Learning Press.

Lewis, R. (1973). Social reaction and the formation of dyads: An interactionist approach to mate selection. *Sociometry, 36,* 409–418.

Milardo, R. M. (1982). Friendship networks in developing relationships: Converging and diverging social environments. *Social Psychology Quarterly, 45,* 162–172.

Miller, G. R., & Steinberg, M. (1975). *Between people: A new analysis of interpersonal communication.* Science Research Associates.

Naegele, K. D. (1958). An exploration of some social distinction. *Harvard Educational Review, 28,* 232–252.

O'Connor, P., & Brown, G. W. (1984). Supportive relationships: Fact or fancy? *Journal of Social and Personal Relationships, 1,* 159–175.

Parks, M. R. (1976). Communication and relational change processes: Conceptualization and findings. Unpublished Ph.D. dissertation, Department of Communication, Michigan State University.

Parks, M. R., & Adelman, M. B. (1983). Communication networks and the development of romantic relationships: An expansion of uncertainty reduction theory. *Human Communication Research, 10,* 55–79.

Parks, M. R., Stan, C. M., & Eggert, L. L. (1983). Romantic involvement and social network involvement. *Social Psychology Quarterly, 46,* 116–131.

Parlee, M. B. (1979). The friendship bond. *Psychology Today, 13,* 43–54.

Quam, J. K. (1983). Older women and informal supports; Impact of prevention. *Prevention in Human Services, 3,* 119–133.

Reisman, J. M. (1979). *Anatomy of friendship.* New York: Irvington.

Reisman, J. M. (1981). Adult friendships. In S. W. Duck & R. Gilmour (Eds.), *Personal relationships 2: Developing personal relationships* (pp. 205–230). London: Academic Press.

Reisman, J. M., & Shorr, S. E. (1978). Friendship claims and expectations among children and adults. *Child Development, 49,* 913–916.

Verbrugge, L. M. (1977). The structure of adult friendship choices. *Social Forces, 56,* 576–597.

Waller, W., & Hill, R. (1951). *The family: A dynamic interpretation*. New York: Holt, Rinehart & Winston.

Review Questions

1. According to the authors, what makes friendship a "slippery concept"?
2. What's the relationship between the features of friendship called "assistance" and "activity sharing"? How do they overlap?
3. How is "contingency" the same as "interdependence?"
4. Give an example from your own experience of increasing communication code specialization between you and a friend.
5. What do the authors mean by "increasing network contact and overlap"?

Probes

1. The authors claim that "status equality" is one defining characteristic of friendship. But they also note that some friendships negotiate elements of equality and inequality. It strikes me that inequality may be more of the norm than equality. What do you think? Is social equality a defining characteristic of your friendships?
2. The authors note that changes in one dimension of development affect the other dimensions. Give an example of this phenomenon. For example, how is increasing the variety of interactions likely to affect a friendship's intimacy and attachment? How might increasing code specialization affect network contact and overlap?
3. Sometimes communication seems to increase rather than decrease cognitive uncertainty. The more we get to know a friend, for example, the less we take him or her for granted. Does that phenomenon or your own experience challenge what the authors say here about uncertainty reduction?
4. One implication of the network research is that, if my family and friends don't like a friend I have, the probability that we'll stay friends is significantly reduced. Does that tendency match your experience? Discuss.
5. Do you agree with the authors that friendship is "the most malleable of human relationships"? Why is this important?

teve Duck, an interpersonal communication professor at the University of Iowa, has written a number of books about how to understand and improve personal relationships. He begins this reading by explaining how "relationshipping" is a skill that each of us is taught—more or less effectively—and that we can learn to do better. He doesn't believe that building friendships is *nothing but* a mechanical process of applying certain skills, but he is convinced that skills are part of this process, just like they're part of the process of painting the Mona Lisa. As he suggests, the main advantage of treating relationshipping this way is that it can give you confidence in your ability to improve the ways you make and keep friends.

Duck talks about the general *features* that people expect friends to have and the friendship *rules* that people generally expect to be observed. Then he dedicates the bulk of this reading to a discussion of what he calls the "provisions" of friendships, that is, what they "provide" or do for us. He explains six reasons why we need friends: Belonging and sense of reliable alliance; emotional integration and stability; opportunities for communication about ourselves; assistance and physical support; reassurance of our worth and value and opportunity to help others; and personality support.

His discussion helps me understand important features of the friendships I enjoy. For example, as I write these words, Mason Brock, one of Kris's and my friends, is dropping Lincoln off at childcare—a clear example of Mason giving us "assistance and physical support." During the times Kris and I are around Mason, our friendship with him also gives both of us opportunities for communication about ourselves as we discuss how we share or differ with his priorities and values. Because Mason is younger and less established than we are, our friendship with him also provides us opportunities to help, which feel good because they provide reassurance of our worth and value. I can also sense some of what our friendship provides Mason, how we might change things to make our relationships even better. It's clear from just this brief example that the ideas in this reading can help you understand your friendships and even improve them.

Our Friends, Ourselves

Steve Duck

. . . 'Relationshipping' is actually a very complicated and prolonged process with many pitfalls and challenges. Relationships do not just happen; they have to be made—made to start, made to work, made to develop, kept in good working order and preserved from going sour. To do all this we need to be active, thoughtful and skilled. To suggest that one simply starts a friendship, courtship, romantic partnership or marriage and 'off it goes' is simple-minded. It is like believing that one can drive down the street merely by turning the ignition key, sitting back and letting the car take care of itself.

On the contrary, to develop a close personal relationship (with someone who was, after all, at first a stranger to us) careful adjustment and continuous monitoring are required, along with several very sophisticated skills. Some of these are: assessing the other person's needs accurately; adopting appropriate styles of communication; indicating liking and interest by means of minute bodily activities, like eye movements and postural shifts; finding out how to satisfy mutual personality needs; adjusting our behaviour to the relationship 'tango' with the other person; selecting and revealing the right sorts of information or opinion in an inviting, encouraging way in the appropriate style and circumstances; building up trust, making suitable demands; and building up commitment. In short, one must perform many complex behaviours. These necessitate proficiency in presenting ourselves efficiently, attending to the right features of the other person at the right time, and pacing the friendship properly.

Rather as learning to drive a car does, learning to steer a relationship involves a range of different abilities and these must be co-ordinated. Just as when, even after we have learned to drive, we need to concentrate harder each time we get into a new model, drive in an unfamiliar country or travel through unknown streets, so when

Excerpted from Chapter 1 of *Understanding Relationships* by Steve Duck. 1991 The Guilford Press, a Division of Guilford Publications, Inc.

entering unfamiliar relationships we have to relearn, modify or re-concentrate on the things that we do. All of us have pet stories about the strain, embarrassment and awkwardness that occurred in a first meeting with a new neighbour or a 'friend of a friend': some clumsy silence, an ill-judged phrase, a difficult situation. It is in such situations that the skills of friendship are bared and tested to the limits, and where intuition is so clearly not enough.

Because it is a skill, relationshipping—even in these novel situations—is something that can be improved, refined, polished (even coached and practised) like any other skill, trained like any other, and made more fluent. It can be taken right up to the level of expertise where it all flows so skillfully and automatically that we can metaphorically focus away from the position of the relational brakes or accelerator and devise ways to drive (the relationship) courteously, skilfully, carefully or enjoyably, so that the others in it can have a smoother ride!

Since we are not usually disposed to think of friendship and close relationships in this new kind of way, people sometimes feel irrationally resistant to doing so. 'How can you represent a close personal relationship as a simple mechanical skill?', they ask. 'Isn't it more mystical, more magical, more moral, less manipulative than you make it sound?' Such people seem happy to see relationships merely as pleasant, passive states: relationships just happen to us and we don't have to do anything particular—let alone do anything properly.

My answer is clear: I am not saying that friendship is all mechanical, any more than making a beautiful piece of furniture or playing an enchanting piano rhapsody or winning a sports championship is simply a mechanical exercise. But each of these activities has some mechanical elements that must be mastered before the higher level aspects of skill can be attempted. You can't paint the Mona Lisa until you know something about painting figures, using a canvas, holding a brush, mixing paints, and so on. Furthermore, research backs this up. Scholars now regard 'relationship work' as a process that continues right through the life of the relationship, with a constant and perpetual need for the right actions and activities at the right time to keep it all alive (for example, Baxter and Dindia, 1990). . . .

There are many advantages to this way of looking at relationships. It leads to a direct and useful form of practical advice for people who are unhappy with one or more of their relationships, or who are lonely or frustrated. It focuses on the things that one can do to improve relationships. It also runs counter to the common, but rather simplistic, assumption that relationships are based only on the matching of two individuals' personalities. This pervasive myth says that there is a Mr or a Ms Right for everyone or that friends can be defined in advance. If this were true, then we could all list the characteristics of our perfect partner—looking for a partner or being attractive to one would be like shopping for or making a checklist of things we liked. By contrast, the new approach adopted here will focus on performance, on behaviour, on the simple mistakes that people make at the various stages of friendship development.

Is it such a strange and unacceptable idea that people can be trained to adopt more satisfactory styles in relationships? Not really. Therapists, social workers, doctors and dentists nowadays receive instruction on the ways to establish rapport with patients and how to develop a reassuring and constructive 'bedside manner'. We know also that insurance or car sales staff are trained in how to relate to possible customers, that airline cabin crew and the police alike receive instruction on relating to the public, and that managers are now encouraged to spend time building up good personal relationships with employees. Such emphasis on skills takes us beyond the trite commonsense advice for lonely persons to 'go out and meet more people'. It focuses us on the fact that relationship problems derive in part, if not on the whole, from people 'doing relationships' wrongly rather than simply not getting enough opportunities to be in them.

The evidence suggests that all of us are probably missing out and not maximizing our potential for relationships. American research (Reisman, 1981) shows that people claim to have about fifteen 'friends' on average, although the numbers change with age (17-year olds claim about nineteen, while 28-year olds have only twelve; 45-year olds have acquired sixteen, while people in their sixties enjoy an average of fifteen). When people are asked to focus only on the relationships that are most satisfying, intimate and close, however, the number drops dramatically to around six (5.6 to be precise). . . .

The Nature of Friendship

A friend of mine once defined a 'friend' as someone who, seeing you drunk and about to stand up on a table and sing, would quietly take you aside to prevent you doing it. This definition actually embodies quite a few of the important aspects of friendship: caring, support, loyalty and putting high priority on the other person's interests. We shall see later in the book why these are important. However, when researchers have taken a more precise look at the meaning of friendship, they have focused on two specific things: the general *features* that humans expect friends to have and the *rules* of friendship that humans expect to be observed.

There are certain features that we find particularly desirable in friends and certain characteristics that everyone believes that being a friend demands. K.E. Davis and Todd (1985) found that we regularly expect a friend to be someone who is honest and open, shows affection, tells us his or her secrets and problems, gives us help when we need it, trusts us and is also trustworthy, shares time and activities with us, treats us with respect and obviously values us, and is prepared to work through disagreements. These are things that people *expect* a friend to do for them and expect to do for the friend in return. These features constitute a quite complex picture. However, when one looks at the *rules* of friendship that people actually adhere to, then the strongest ones are rather simple (Argyle & Henderson, 1985): hold conversations; do not disclose confidences to other people; refrain from public criticism; repay debts and favours. These researchers also demonstrate that emotional support, trust and confiding are among the rules that distinguish high quality friendships from less close ones.

In ideal circumstances, then, a friend is an open, affectionate, trusting, helpful, reliable companion who respects our privacy, carries out interactions with all due respect to the norms of behaviour and ourselves, does not criticize us in public, and both does us favours and returns those that we do. In the real world, friendship is unlikely to live up to this ideal and we all have some range of tolerance. However, it is a *voluntary* bond between two people and the above ideals can be seen as part of an unwritten contract between them, whose violation can become the grounds for the dissolution of the relationship (Wiseman, 1986).

Another important view of friendship has been offered by Wright (1984). He too stresses the 'voluntary interdependence' of friendship: it is important that people freely choose to be intertwined together in the relationship. He also places emphasis on the 'person qua person' element, or the extent to which we enjoy the person for his or her own sake, rather than for the things that he or she does for us. More recent research on this idea (Lea, 1989) finds indeed that 'self-referent rewards', or the way the other person makes us feel about ourselves, are just as important as these other things. The way in which the relationship helps us to feel about ourselves, and its voluntary nature, are crucial to the nature of friendship. There are good reasons why this is the case.

The 'Provisions' of Friendship

There are several ways to start answering the large question: 'Why do we need friends?'. We could just decide that everyone needs intimacy, possibly as a result of dependency needs formed in childhood, just as the psychoanalysts tell us. There may be something to this, as we shall see, but there is more to the need for friendships than a need for intimacy—and there is more to the need for intimacy than we may suppose, anyway. For instance, we might want to ask how intimacy develops, how it is expressed, what else changes when it grows, and so on. We might also note the curious finding (Wheeler *et al.*, 1983; R. B. Hays, 1989) that both men and women prefer intimate partners who are women! Indeed, Arkin and Grove (1990) show that shy men prefer to talk to women even when they are not in an intimate encounter. Not only this, but those people who talk to more women during the day have better health than those who talk to fewer women (Reis, 1986). Clearly the nature of needs for intimacy and friendship is rather intriguing and may be mediated by gender and other social contexts. . . .

Belonging and a Sense of Reliable Alliance

In writing about loneliness and the 'provisions' of relationships—what it is that they do for us—Weiss (1974) proposed that a major consequence of being in relationships is a sense of belonging and of 'reliable alliance'. He is touching on something very important about human experience. We all like to belong or to be accepted; even those who choose solitude want it to be the result of their own choice, not someone else's. No one wants to be an outcast, a pariah or a social reject. Indeed, the powerful effects of being made *not* to belong were long recognized as a severe punishment in Ancient Greece, where people could be ostracized and formally exiled or banished. The modern equivalent is found in the British trade union practice of 'sending someone to Coventry' when they break the union rules: the person's workmates, colleagues, neighbours and associates are instructed to refuse to speak to the person about anything. . . .

By contrast, relationships give us a sense of inclusion, a sense of being a member of a group—and, as the advertisers keep emphasizing, membership has its privileges. One of these privileges is 'reliable alliance'; that is to say, the existence of a bond that can be trusted to be there for you when you need it. To coin a phrase, 'A friend in need is a friend indeed'—or in our terms, the existence of a friendship creates a reliable alliance: one of the signs that someone is a true friend is when they help you in times of trouble.

Emotional Integration and Stability

Importantly, communities of friends provide a lot more than just a sense of belonging and reliable alliance (Weiss, 1974). They also provide necessary anchor points for opinions, beliefs and emotional responses. Friends are benchmarks that tell us how we should react appropriately, and they correct or guide our attitudes and beliefs in both obvious and subtle ways. As an example, consider how different cultures express grief differently. In some countries it is acceptable to fall to the ground, cover oneself with dust and wail loudly; in other cultures it is completely unacceptable to show such emotion, and the emphasis falls on dignified public composure. Imagine the reaction in Britain if the Queen were to roll on the ground as a way of demonstrating grief, or in the United States if the President and First Lady attended military funerals with their faces blacked and tearing their clothes. Humans have available many different ways of demonstrating grief but they typically cope with this strong emotion in a way particularly acceptable to their own culture.

Like cultures, friends and intimates develop their own sets of shared concerns, common interests and collective problems, as well as shared meanings, common responses to life and communal emotions. Friends are often appreciated exactly because they share private understandings, private jokes or private language. Indeed, communication researchers (Hopper *et al.*, 1981; Bell *et al.*, 1987) have shown that friends and lovers develop their own 'personal idioms' or ways of talking about such things as feelings, sex and bodily parts, so that they are obscure to third parties. By using a phrase with secret meaning, couples can communicate in public places about things that are private. Good examples are to be found in newspaper columns on St Valentine's Day. What, for example, are we to make of a message I found in the local student newspaper: 'Dinglet, All my dinkery forever, Love, Scrunnett'? Presumably it meant something both to the person who placed the advertisement and to the person who was the intended object of it. Be alert: the couple who announce that 'We are going home to make some pancakes' may in fact be planning to have a night of passion!

Such language is just a localized version of the fact that different cultures use different dialects or languages. Equally, friends have routines of behaving or beliefs that are not shared by everyone in a particular country or culture, but for that reason they are more important in daily life. Loneliness is, and isolation can be, wretched precisely because it deprives people of such psychological benchmarks and anchor points. Lonely people lose the stability provided by the chance to compare their own reactions to life with the reactions of other people that they know, like and respect. . . .

So loneliness and isolation are disruptive because they deprive the person of the opportunity for comfortable comparison of opinions and attitudes with other people— of close friends. People who are parted from friends become anxious, disoriented, unhappy and even severely destabilized emotionally; they may become still more anxious just because they feel themselves behaving erratically, or they may experience unusual mood swings. They often report sudden changes of temper and loss of control, sometimes resulting in violent outbursts; but in any case their judgment becomes erratic and unreliable, and they may become unusually vigilant, suspicious or jumpy in the presence of other unfamiliar people.

Another function of friendship, then, a reason why we need friends, is to keep us emotionally stable and to help us see where we stand *vis-à-vis* other people and whether we are 'doing OK'. It is particularly noticeable in times of stress and crisis. I remember an occasion when all the lights fused in a student residence block where I was an assistant warden. The rational thing to do was to find a flashlight and await the restoration of power. What we all actually did was to stumble down to the common-room and chatter amongst ourselves: the need to compare our reactions to the emergency was so powerful and so universal that even the warden, a medical researcher who had doctoral degrees from both Oxford and Cambridge, did the same. Such behaviour often happens after any kind of stress or crisis, from the crowd of people who gather to swap stories after a fire or a car accident, to the nervous chatter that schoolchildren perform when the doctor comes to inject them against measles or TB. . . .

Opportunities for Communication about Ourselves

There is a third reason why we need friends (Weiss, 1974). A centrally important need is for communication. This particular wheel was strikingly reinvented by the Quaker prison reformers several generations ago, who attempted to cut down communication between criminals in prison in order to stop them educating one another about ways of committing crime. Accordingly, one of their proposals was that prisoners should be isolated from one another. What occurred was very instructive: the prisoners spent much of their time tapping out coded messages on walls and pipes, devising means of passing information to one another, and working out other clever ways of communicating. Evidently, people who are involuntarily isolated feel a need to communicate. One additional function that healthy friendships provide, then, is a place for such communication to occur—communication about anything, not just important events but also trivial stuff as well as personal, intimate details about oneself. In a study at the University of Iowa, I and my students (S. W. Duck, *et al.*, 1991) have found that most conversations with friends last very short periods of time (about three minutes on average) and deal with trivialities. They are nonetheless rated as extremely significant. They revitalize the relationship, reaffirm it and celebrate its existence, through the medium of conversation.

A mild form of this overwhelming need to communicate is to be found on railway trains, planes and long-distance buses. Here many lonely people strike up conversations—but usually monologues—which allow them to communicate to someone or to tell someone about themselves and their opinions. A striking thing about this is the intimacy of the stories that are often told. Perfect strangers can often be regaled with the life history, family details and personal opinions of someone they have not seen before and will probably never see again. Indeed, that is probably a key part of it, for the listener who will not be seen again cannot divulge the 'confession' to friends or colleagues and so damage the confessor's reputation. (In cases where it is known that the listener and confessor will meet again, as in the case of doctors and patients, priests and parishioners, counsellors and clients, or lawyers and consultants, the listeners are bound by strict professional ethical codes not to reveal what they have been told. On the train, the 'ethics' are simply left to statistical chance, and the extreme improbability of the two strangers meeting one another's friends is a comfort in itself.) . . .

Provision of Assistance and Physical Support

Another 'provision' of relationships is simply that they offer us support, whether physical, psychological or emotional (Hobfoll and Stokes, 1988). This section focuses on physical support and assistance, which are often as significant to us as is any other sort of support.

For example, when people lose a friend or a spouse through bereavement, they report a lack of support—they are cut off from someone who has helped them to cope with life and to adjust to its problems, tasks and changing uncertainties. This can take one of two forms: physical support (such as help with day-to-day tasks) and psychological support (such as when someone shows that we are appreciated, or lets us know that our opinions are valued). Human beings need both of these types of support, but the types are significantly different.

This is very simply illustrated. When your friend gives you a birthday present you are supposed to accept it in a way that indicates your own unworthiness to receive it and also the kindness of the friend ('Oh you shouldn't have bothered. It really is very good of you'). In short, you repay your friend by accepting the gift as a token of friendship and by praising the friend. You 'exchange' the gift for love and respect, as it were. Imagine what would happen if you repaid by giving the friend the exact value of the gift in money. The friend would certainly be insulted by the ineptness: you would have altered the nature of the social exchange and also, in so doing, the nature of the relationship, by focusing on money rather than the gift as a symbol for friendship. Indeed, Cheal (1986) has shown that gift-giving as a one-way donation is rare and gift *reciprocity* is the norm, indicating that it serves an important relational function. Gift exchange serves the symbolic function of cementing and celebrating the relationship.

There are other clear examples of this point—that the nature of the exchange or support helps to define the degree and type of relationship. For instance, many elderly people get resentful of the fact that they gradually become more and more physically dependent on other people for help in conducting the daily business of their lives. The elderly cannot reach things so easily, cannot look after themselves and are more dependent physically, while at the same time they are less able to repay their friends by doing services in return. This, then, is one reason why many people dislike or feel uneasy with old age: they resent the feeling of helpless dependency coupled with the feeling of perpetual indebtedness that can never be paid off. For many elderly people, then, the mending of a piece of furniture, the making of a fruit pie or the knitting of a sweater can be traded off against dependency: elderly people *need to be allowed* to do things for other people as a way of demonstrating to themselves and to everyone else that they are valuable to others and can still make useful contributions to the world. . . .

Reassurance of Our Worth and Value, and Opportunity to Help Others

People who are lonely characteristically say that no-one cares about them, that they are useless, uninteresting, of low value and good for nothing. Studies of the conversation of severely depressed people invariably reveal indications that they have lost their self-respect or self-esteem (Gotlib and Hooley, 1988). In other words, they have come to see themselves as valueless, worthless and insignificant, often because that is how they feel that everyone else sees them. Furthermore, analysis of suicide notes shows that many suicide attempts are carried out as a way of forcing some particular friend to re-evaluate the person, or to shock the friend into realizing just how much he or she really does esteem the person making the attempt. For this reason, Alfred Adler has claimed, with characteristic insight, that every suicide is always a reproach or a revenge.

One reason, then, that we appreciate friends is because of their contribution to our self-evaluation and self-esteem. Friends can do this both directly and indirectly: they may compliment us or tell us about other people's good opinions of us. Dale

Carnegie's multimillion-seller book on *How to Win Friends and Influence People* stressed the positive consequences of doing this. Friends can also increase our self-esteem in other ways: by attending to what we do, listening, asking our advice and generally acting in ways that indicate the value that they place on our opinions. However, there are less obvious and more indirect ways in which they can communicate this estimation of our value. For one thing, the fact that they choose to spend time with us rather than with someone else must show that they value our company more than the alternatives.

There is a subtler version of these points too. Just as we look to friends to provide us with all of these things, so we can get from friendship one other key benefit. Because friends trust us and depend on us, they give us the chance to help them. That gives us the opportunity to take responsibility for them, to see ourselves helping them with their lives, to give them our measured advice and consequently to feel good. Friends provide us with these possibilities of taking responsibility and nurturing other people.

Undoubtedly, these things are important in the conduct of relationships and in making them satisfactory for both partners, and it is critical that we learn to evince them effectively. However, one important point to note is that those people who are poor at doing this (e.g., people who are poor at indicating interest, or who seem to have little time for other people, or never let them help or let them give advice) will find that other people are unattracted to relationships with them. All people need indications of their estimability and need chances to nurture just as we do, and if we do not adequately provide such signs then these people will reject us—just as we would do in their position. . . .

Personality Support

Yet there is something even more fundamental to close relationships than this. Recent research indicates that each feature mentioned above—sense of community, emotional stability, communication, provision of help, maintenance of self-esteem—in its own way serves to support and integrate the person's personality (S. W. Duck and Lea, 1982). Each of us is characterized by many thoughts, doubts, beliefs, attitudes, questions, hopes, expectations and opinions about recurrent patterns in life. Our personalities are composed not only of our behavioural style (for example, our introversion or extraversion) but also of our thoughts, doubts and beliefs. It is a place full of symbols, a space where we are ourselves, a system of interlocking thoughts, experiences, interpretations, expectancies and personal meanings. Our personality would be useless to us if all of these opinions and meanings were not, by and large, supported. We would simply stop behaving if we had no trust in our thoughts or beliefs about why we should behave or how we should behave, just as we stop doing other things that we are convinced are wrong. Some schizophrenics and depressives actually do stop behaving when their thought-world falls apart: they just sit and stare.

Each of us needs to be assured regularly that our thought-worlds or symbolic spaces are sound and reliable. A friend can help us to see that we are wrong and how we can change, or that we are right about some part of our thinking. We may have vigorous discussions about different attitudes that we hold—but our friends are likely to be very similar to us in many of our attitudes and interests, so that these discussions are more probably supportive than destructive. However, we all know the anger and pain that follow a really serious disagreement with a close friend—much more unpleasant than a disagreement with an enemy. What we should deduce from all this is that we seek out as friends those people who help to support our thought-world-personality, and we feel chastened, sapped or undermined when they do not provide this support.

What sorts of person best gives us the kind of personality support that I have described here? In the first instance, it is provided by people who share our way of thinking. The more of these 'thought-ways' that we share with someone, the easier it is to communicate with that person: we can assume that our words and presumptions will be understood more easily by someone who is 'our type' than by someone who is not—we shall not have the repetitious discomfort of perpetually explaining ourselves, our meanings and our jokes.

Yet there is much more to it than this, although it has taken researchers a long time to sort out the confusing detail of the picture. For one thing, the type of similarity that we need to share with someone in order to communicate effectively depends on the stage that the relationship has reached. At early stages it is quite enough that acquaintances are broadly similar, but at later stages the similarity must be more intricate, precise, refined and detailed. One of the skills of friend-making is to know what sorts of similarity to look for at which times as the relationship proceeds. General similarity of attitudes is fine at the early to middle stages, but matters much less later if the partners do not work at discovering similarities at the deeper level of the ways in which they view other people and understand their characters. Very close friends must share the same specific sorts of framework for understanding the actions, dispositions and characters of other people in general, and in specific instances of mutual acquaintance. Such similarity is rare and prized. For that reason, if for no other, it is painful and extremely significant to lose the persons who offer it.

Loss or absence of particular intimates or friends deprives us of some measure of support for our personality, and it is essential to our psychological health that we have the skill to avoid this. Losing an intimate partner or friend not only makes us die a little, it leaves floating in the air those bits of our personality that the person used to support, and can make people fall apart psychologically. Of course, this will depend on how much our personality has been supported by that partner, which particular parts are involved, how readily these parts are supported by others, how much time we have had to anticipate and adjust to the loss, and so on. But essentially the loss or absence of friends and of close, satisfying relationships does not merely cause anxiety, grief or depression; it can cause other, more severe, forms of psychological disintegration or deterioration, often with the physical and mental side-effects noted earlier. Many of the well-known psychosomatic illnesses and hysterical states are actually caused by relationship problems, although this has not been realized by as many doctors as one might expect (see Lynch, 1977). For too long the accepted medical folklore has assumed that the person's inner mental state is a given, and that it causes psychosomatic effects when it gets out of balance. It is now quite clear that the surest way to upset people's mental balance is to disturb their close relationships (Gerstein and Tesser, 1987). We need friends to keep us healthy both physically and mentally: therefore it is doubly important that we perfect the ways of gaining and keeping friends. An important first step is to recognize the different needs that each relationship can fulfill for us, and the means by which this can be achieved.

References

Argyle, M., & Henderson, M. (1985). *The Anatomy of Relationships*. London: Methuen.

Arkin, R., & Grove, T. (1990). Shyness, sociability and patterns of everyday affiliation. *Journal of Social and Personal Relationships* (7), 273–281.

Baxter, L. A., & Dindia, K. (1990). Marital partners' perceptions of marital maintenance strategies. *Journal of Social and Personal Relationships* (7), 187–208.

Bell, R. A., Buerkel-Rothfuss, N., & Gore, K. (1987). "Did you bring the yarmulke for the cabbage patch kid?": The idiomatic communication of young lovers. *Human Communication Research* (14), 47–67.

Cheal, D. J. (1986). The social dimensions of gift behaviour. *Journal of Social and Personal Relationships* (3), 423–39.

Davis, K. E., & Todd, M. (1985). Assessing friendship: Prototypes, paradigm cases, and relationship description, in S. W. Duck & D. Perlman (eds.), *Understanding Personal Relationships*. London: Sage.

Duck, S. W., & Lea, M. (1982). Breakdown of relationships as a threat to personal identity, in G. Breakwell (ed.), *Threatened Identities*. Chichester: Wiley.

Duck, S. W., Rutt, D. J., Hurst, M., & Strejc, H. (1991). Some evident truths about communication in everyday relationships: All communication is not created equal. *Human Communication Research* (18), 114–129.

Gerstein, I. H., & Tesser, A. (1987). Antecedents and responses associated with loneliness. *Journal of Social and Personal Relationships* (4), 329–63.

Gotlib, I. H., & Hooley, J. M. (1988). Depression and marital distress: Current and future directions, in S. W. Duck (ed.) with D. F. Hay, S. E. Hobfoll, W. Ickes, & B. Montgomery, *Handbook of Personal Relationships*. Chicester: Wiley.

Hays, R. B. (1989). The day-to-day functioning of close versus casual friendship. *Journal of Social and Personal Relationships* (1), 75–98.

Hopper, R., Knapp, M. L., & Scott, L. (1981). Couples' personal idioms: Exploring intimate talk. *Journal of Communication* (31), 23–33.

Lea, M. (1989). Factors underlying friendship: An analysis of responses on the acquaintance description form in relation to Wright's friendship model. *Journal of Social and Personal Relationships* (6), 275–292.

Lynch, J. J. (1977). *The Broken Heart: The Medical Consequences of Loneliness*. New York: Basic Books.

Reis, H. T. (1986). Gender effects in social participation: Intimacy, loneliness, and the conduct of social interaction, in R. Gilmour & S. W. Duck (eds.), *The Emerging Field of Personal Relationships*. Hillsdale, NJ: Lawrence Erlbaum.

Reisman, J. (1981). Adult friendships, in S. W. Duck & R. Gilmour (eds.), *Personal Relationships 2: Developing Personal Relationships*. London: Academic Press.

Weiss, R. S. (1974). The provisions of social relationships, in Z. Rubin (ed.), *Doing Unto Others*. Englewood Cliffs, NJ: Prentice-Hall.

Wheeler, L., Reis, H. T., & Nezelek, J. (1983). Loneliness, social interaction and sex roles. *Journal of Personality and Social Psychology* (35), 742–54.

Wiseman, J. P. (1986). Friendship: Bonds and binds in a voluntary relationship. *Journal of Social and Personal Relationships* (3), 191–211.

Wright, P. H. (1984). Self referent motivation and the intrinsic quality of friendship. *Journal of Social and Personal Relationships* (1), 114–30.

Review Questions

1. Define "relationshipping."
2. How many "satisfying, intimate, and close" relationships does the research say that people of your age typically have?
3. Duck lists four main "rules" that characterize friendship, according to the research. What are they?
4. Fill in the blank, explain, and tell whether you agree or disagree and why: "Both men and women prefer intimate partners who are _____."

5. What does it mean to have "a sense of reliable alliance"?
6. Paraphrase and give an example from your own experience of the reality-checking function of friendships.
7. Explain what Duck means when he says that sometimes elderly people need to be allowed to do things for others.
8. According to Duck, what is the relationship between friendship networks and personal mental health? Do you agree or disagree with this claim?

Probes

1. In what ways does Steve Duck's example of learning to drive a car fit your experience of learning how to "do" relationships? In what ways does it not fit?
2. Test Duck's claim about the average number of "friends" reported by people of your age and the average number of "satisfying, intimate, and close" relationships. Do you find any differences among the people you know?
3. What is the function in intimate relationships of private language and "personal idioms"? What does the presence of these private modes of expression suggest about the similarities between friendships and cultures?
4. What explanation does Duck give for the "stranger on the train (bus, plane)" phenomenon, where your seatmate, whom you don't know, tells you intimate details of his or her life? Why does this happen?
5. How do you respond to Duck's claim that, in some important ways, birthdays are times when many people give gifts *in exchange for* respect and love?
6. Paraphrase and respond to Duck's explanation of the role of similarities in friendship relationships.

T he author of this essay was, and may still be, a philosophy teacher at East Tennessee State University. The paper appeared in an unusual collection of readings that discusses several *philosophical* aspects of interpersonal relationships. As you'll see, John Hardwig's concern is that interpersonal contacts often raise important ethical issues, but that few people have thought or written about how ethics work in these situations. One of the reasons he offers for this neglect echoes a point Deborah Tannen makes in Chapter 9: Most philosophy has been written by men, and men typically favor impersonal topics over personal ones.

Whether or not you agree with this reason, notice how Hardwig outlines his ethics. He defines a *personal,* as contrasted with a quasi-personal or impersonal relationship, as one in which I want you as an end, and not as a means to an end, one in which I see "you and the realization of your goals as part of me and the realization of my goals." A personal relationship also involves wanting to be in relation with precisely you, not just wanting something that could be provided by you or somebody else. He contrasts this kind of relationship with a *quasi-personal* one in which I want to have "the kind of friend" or "the kind of wife" or husband that you might be. These relationships may appear to be personal, but they're actually not, because I've chosen the person who fits into a *category* of desire, rather than choosing the person because of who he or she is as an individual. Hardwig also says that hatred can define a truly personal relationship when I hate you, not just some of the things you are, do, or stand for.

This analysis makes it easier to understand the kind of relationship where I want precisely *you,* but "you simply want to be loved and protected or to have a certain kind of marriage." As Hardwig points out, "relationships are often made or broken by the issue of whether I want you or 'someone who. . . .'"

The main principle of Hardwig's ethics of personal relationships is that when attitudes or actions depersonalize personal relationships, they do violence to what these relationships are, and this kind of violence ought to be avoided. This principle heightens the importance of motives in personal relationships. Motives that are completely acceptable in some impersonal relationships—duty, obligation, and pity, for example—are often inappropriate in personal relationships. As he explains, "While it might be nice to feel yourself to be charitable, benevolent, or compassionate, who could endure being emotionally involved with someone who saw you essentially or *even very* often as an appropriate object of benevolence, charity, or pity?"

It follows that personal relationships between adults ought to be entered into and continued out of a shared sense of vitality and strength rather than weakness and need. I'm reminded of the person who said that, whenever I try to feed my friends from a cup that is anything other than overflowing, I feed them poison.

Another implication of Hardwig's central ethical principle is that people in personal relationships should act toward each other as purely as possible because they *want* to, not out of a sense of duty, obligation, or *quid pro quo* (you did it for me, so now I owe you). All this doesn't mean that motives such as duty, pity, and sympathy are *always* inappropriate in personal relationships, but only that they should be fallback positions, not the main focus of the relationship.

A third implication is that in personal relationships you can't really separate egoism and altruism—self-interest and interest in the other. This is because if the relationship is personal, "your ends are my ends too." So "the distinction between giving and receiving thus collapses." This is an important claim, and it's one I encourage you to try applying to your own personal relationships. It doesn't mean that there are *never* conflicts or that *all* interests are shared, but that mutuality is primary.

A fourth implication is that personal relationships can't and don't have to be justified by an appeal to some higher value such as love, pleasure, or social utility. They are ends in themselves, justified by their own existence. If you try to make them dependent on another value, you depersonalize them.

The final implication is that this ethics of personal relationships sees people not as individuals but as relational beings, intimately tied in with others. This doesn't make me *dependent* on your friendship or even your presence. But it does mean that if our relationship ends, I change—just as you do.

Hardwig concludes with an argument that when it's necessary to end a relationship, it is both possible and desirable to do so without depersonalizing it. Spouses and attorneys involved in divorces could usefully reflect on this claim.

I find this a thought-provoking essay, and I hope you do too. It raises some important questions about friendships and other relationships that aren't often discussed but that can provide helpful guidance when you are faced with a hard decision.

In Search of an Ethics of Personal Relationships

John Hardwig

Although it's been ten years, I can still see the student, hands on her hips, as she brought my beautiful lecture on Kant's ethics to a grinding halt: "Is Kant saying," she demanded, "that if I sleep with my boyfriend, I should sleep with him out of a sense of duty?" My response: "And when you're through, you should tell him that you would have done the same for anyone in his situation." What could I say?

We do not search for what we already have. Thus my title commits me to the thesis that we do not have an ethics of personal relationships. And that is in fact my view, a view grown out of incidents like this one.

More specifically, I believe that for at least the past 300 years or so, philosophers thinking about ethics have tacitly presupposed a very impersonal context. They have unconsciously assumed a context in which we mean little or nothing to each other and have then asked themselves what principles could be invoked to keep us from trampling each other in the pursuit of our separate and often conflicting interests. Consequently, I contend, what we now study and teach under the rubric of ethics is almost entirely the ethics of impersonal relationships.

Various explanations might be offered as to why philosophers have thought in terms of impersonal relationships. Philosophers have historically been almost exclusively males, and males have generally believed that the public realm where impersonal relationships predominate is much more important and worthy of study than the private and personal dimensions of life. Or perhaps the assumption that we are talking about impersonal relationships reflects the growing impersonality of modern society or an awareness of the increasing ability given us by our technology to affect the lives of people quite remote from us.

However, even if philosophers were not thinking about personal relationships when developing their ethics, it might seem that an ethics adequate to impersonal relationships should work at least as well in personal contexts. For in personal relationships there would be less temptation to callously ignore or to ride roughshod over each other's interests, owing to the greater meaning each has for the other. Thus it seems reasonable to assume that the principles constituting the ethics of impersonal relationships will work satisfactorily in personal contexts as well.

But this assumption is false. An ethics of personal relationships must, I try to show, be quite different from the ethics of impersonal relationships. Traditional ethics is, at best, significantly incomplete, only a small part of the story of the ethics of personal relationships. Often it is much worse: basically misguided or wrong-headed and thus inapplicable in the context of personal relationships. In fact, much of traditional

Excerpted from "In Search of an Ethics of Personal Relationships," by John Hardwig, Chapter 4 of *Person to Person*, ed. George Graham and Hugh Lafollette, © 1989 by Temple University. Reprinted by permission of Temple University Press.

ethics urges us to act in ways that would be inappropriate in personal contexts; and thus traditional ethics would often be dangerous and destructive in those contexts.

We do not search for what we already have. I do not have an ethics of personal relationships, though I offer some suggestions about what such an ethics would and would *not* look like. Since my views about the ethics of personal relationships depend, naturally enough, on what I take a personal relationship to be, I begin with a brief discussion of the nature and structure of personal relationships.

But I'm going to cheat some: Throughout, I speak of personal relationships as if they were static. Although this is obviously a gross oversimplification, limitations of space and understanding preclude a discussion of the beginnings and endings and dynamics of personal relationships.

I

So what's a personal relationship? Personal relationships, as opposed to impersonal relationships, are of course relationships such as love, being lovers, friends, spouses, parents, and so on. But these sorts of relationships aren't always very *personal*, since there are all sorts of marriages of convenience, Aristotle's "friendships of utility," Hobbesian power alliances, and many varieties of quite impersonal sexual relationships. Consequently, we need to distinguish what are commonly *called* personal relationships (love, friendship, marriage) from personal relationships in a deeper sense. Even when they are not *personal* in the deeper sense, relationships like love, friendship, and marriage are not exactly impersonal relationships either. So I use the phrase "quasi-personal relationships" to cover such cases, reserving the term "personal relationships" for those relationships which are personal in the deeper sense I hope to explicate. I thus work with a threefold distinction between personal, quasi-personal, and impersonal relationships.

Let us begin with the distinction between personal and impersonal relationships. I want to say two things by way of characterizing personal relationships: (1) If I have a personal relationship with you, I want you. You (and your well-being) are then one of my *ends*. This would seem to be part of what it means to care for or care about another person. (2) If my relationship to you is to be personal, this end must be you—precisely you and not any other person. The persons in personal relationships are not substitutable. . . .

First, then, the idea of having you as one of my ends is to be contrasted with both sides of the Kantian dichotomy between respecting you as an end in yourself and treating you as a means to my ends. Kant would have me respect you as a person, just as I would respect any person, simply because you (all) are persons. To respect you as an end in yourself is to recognize that you have value apart from whatever use I might be able to make of you. It is, moreover, to recognize that your goals and purposes have validity independent of whatever goals and purposes I may have and to acknowledge in my action that your goals and purposes have an equal claim to realization. Although respect for you and your goals is a part of a personal relationship, it is not what makes a personal relationship *personal*, valuable, or even a relationship. Instead, having you as one of my ends is valuing you in *relation* to me; it is seeing you and the realization of your goals as part of me and the realization of my goals. This is not, of course, to reduce you to a means to my ends. On the contrary, I want you. You are one of my *ends*.

The second characteristic of a personal relationship—that I want precisely *you*—serves to highlight the difference between this kind of relationship and impersonal relationships, and also to further elucidate the difference between seeing you as one of my ends and seeing you either as an end in yourself or as a means to my ends. The characteristic intentions in personal relationships are different from those in impersonal relationships. It is the difference between:

> wanting *to get* something (T) and wanting to get T *from you.*
> wanting *to give* T and wanting to give T *to you.*
> wanting *to do* T and wanting to do T *with you.*

The first set of intentions or desires structures impersonal relationships; the second, personal relationships. There is a big difference between wanting to be loved, for example, and wanting to be loved *by you*; a crucial difference between wanting to go to bed (with someone) and wanting to go to bed *with you*. This difference seems to retain its significance whether "T" ranges over relatively insignificant things like taking a walk, having your breakfast made, sharing a ride to a party, and going to a movie, or over crucially important things like baring your soul, receiving love and emotional support, sharing your living space, and having children.

If I want *something* (as opposed to wanting something *from you*), I depersonalize you, reducing you (in my eyes) to an X who is a possessor or producer of certain goods. For it's these good things I want, not you; anyone who could and would deliver these goods would do as well. The language captures the depersonalization nicely: I want "someone who. . . ." It is when I want *something* and you become for me a "someone who" is the possessor or producer of this good that I reduce you to a means to my ends. This kind of desire and the intentions it gives rise to structure an impersonal relationship, though many of what are usually called "personal relationships" are structured by precisely this sort of impersonal desire. . . .

Let us now turn to quasi-personal relationships. These are the relationships that are commonly *called* personal, but that are not personal relationships in the deeper sense I have discussed. Quasi-personal relationships can be analyzed along similar lines. Suppose that it's important to me to have *the kind of friend* or *the kind of wife* who will help me with my work. In such cases, my desire or our relationship is not simply impersonal, for it won't do for me just to get help with my work—I want help from a friend or from a wife. In this intermediate case, the kind of relationship you have to me (wife, lover, loved one, friend, child) is essential to the structure of my desire; a certain kind of relationship is one of my ends.

But our relationship is still abstract or impersonal in a sense. I want something from you *because you are my wife* (lover, friend, child). I'd want the same from *any* wife (lover, friend, kid). Thus *you* are not important to the structure of my desire, *you* are not one of my ends. In such cases, the relationship I want must be defined (by me) in terms of roles and rules for those roles. I call these relationships quasi-personal. They are important for an ethics of personal relationships, for we often get hurt in precisely these sorts of relationships, especially when we believe we are involved in a personal relationship.

Two additional points about personal relationships are important for the ethics of personal relationships. First, although I talk mainly about positive, healthy personal relationships, it is important to recognize that *hatred*, as well as love, can be a personal relationship. As can resentment, anger, contempt. Hatred is personal if I hate *you*, not just some of the things you are or do or stand for, not just "anyone who. . . ."

In cases of personal hatred, I may well desire your overall ill-being. Hatred that is personal rather than impersonal is much more thoroughgoing and often more vicious. Good sense suggests that we should get out of or depersonalize relationships dominated by intractable hatred, anger, or resentment. Interestingly, however, haters often don't get out of personal relationships with those they hate. And this calls for explanation. Such explanation must acknowledge that if I continue to hate *you* and to have your ill-being as one of my ends, there must be some sort of bond between you and me. *You* are important to me or I wouldn't devote my life to making *you* miserable. The opposite of love is not hatred; the opposite of love is indifference.

A second point important for the ethics of personal relationships is the possibility of one-sided personal relationships. Suppose I want *you* and you simply want to be loved and protected or to have a certain kind of marriage. Do I then have a personal relationship with you while you have an impersonal or quasi-personal relationship with me? Perhaps. But this surely is not the kind of relationship I will normally want. Such relationships are ripe for exploitation and tragedy. They are, in any case, almost always deeply disappointing, for we usually want *mutually* personal relationships. This means that not only do I want *you* and not just some producer of certain goods and services, but I want you to want *me*, not "someone who. . . ."

Although the logical structure of personal, quasi-personal, and impersonal relationships seems quite distinct, there can be tremendous . . . difficulties facing those of us who would know what kinds of relationships we have. Do I want *you* or do I want *something* (from you)? Do I want a relationship *with* you or do I want a *kind* of relationship with "someone who . . ."? Even if I think I want you, is it because I'm picking up on something that is *you*, or is it because you happen to resemble my childhood sweetheart, perhaps, or because you are so successful? If I cannot fathom my desires and intentions enough to make these discriminations accurately, it would be possible for me not to know whether I have a personal relationship with you, much less whether you have a personal relationship with me. These . . . difficulties notwithstanding, it may be *critically* important—both ethically and psychologically—to know what kinds of relationships we actually do have. Relationships are often made or broken by the issue of whether I want you or "someone who. . . ."

. . . Obviously, these characterizations of personal and quasi-personal relationships are based on my own intuitions, with which others may not agree. Fortunately, my argument does not require that my characterizations be accepted as necessary conditions, much less as necessary and sufficient conditions, for a personal relationship. It is enough for my purposes if it is admitted that many very healthy and beautiful personal relationships have the structure I have ascribed to them and that the reasons we often have for wanting personal relationships are expressed in my formulations.

II

Now for the ethics of personal relationships. My main contention and basic principle is that ethics must not depersonalize personal relationships, for doing so does violence to what these relationship are; to what is characteristically and normatively going on in them; and to the intentions, desires, and hopes we have in becoming involved in them. Particular persons figure essentially in personal relationships. But most ways of thinking about ethics invite or require us to treat ourselves or our loved ones as a "someone who. . . ." And this leads to many difficulties, both on the level of metaethical theory and on the practical level of ethical or moral prescription. . . .

III

"I don't want you to take me out," my wife exploded. "I just want you to want to go out with me. If you don't want to go out, let's just forget it." Motives, intentions, and reasons for acting play a *much* larger role in the ethics of personal relationships than they do in the ethics of impersonal relationships. In fact, the motivation of those who are close to us is often more important than the things which result from it. And even when actions are important in personal relationships, it is often because they are seen as symbols or symptoms of underlying feelings, desires, or commitments. Thus actions often seem worthless or even perverse if the motivation behind them is inappropriate.

In impersonal situations and relationships, on the other hand, we are much more content to allow people to do the right thing for the wrong reason and we are often even willing to provide incentives (for example, legal and financial) to increase the chances that they will do the right thing and also that they will do it for the wrong reason. I wouldn't, for example, be very much concerned about the motives of my congressman if I could be sure that he would always vote right. I believe that he should be well paid to increase the chances that he will vote right. But I would be deeply upset to learn that my wife is staying with me primarily for financial reasons. And I might be even more upset if her actions all along had been scrupulously wifelike. An ethics of personal relationships must, then, place more emphasis on motives and intentions, less on actions and consequences than most ethical theories have.

However, the motives that ethicists have found praiseworthy in impersonal contexts are usually inappropriate and unacceptable in personal contexts. Actions motivated by duty, a sense of obligation, or even a sense of responsibility are often unacceptable in personal relationships. A healthy personal relationship cannot be based on this sort of motivation; indeed, it cannot even come into play very often. . . . [It would be] devastating . . . to learn that your spouse of thirty-seven years had stayed in your marriage purely or even primarily out of a sense of obligation stemming from the marriage contract.

For similar reasons, motives of benevolence, pity, or compassion are also not acceptable as the characteristic or dominant motives in personal relationships. Acts of charity, altruism, and mercy are also, in general, out. As are sacrifices of important interests or a sense of self-sacrifice. Paternalism and maternalism are also generally unacceptable among adults in personal relationships. While it might be nice to feel yourself to be charitable, benevolent, or compassionate, who could endure being emotionally involved with someone who saw you essentially or even very often as an appropriate object of benevolence, charity, or pity? Of course, there always will be some occasions when you *are* an appropriate object of these attitudes, and it's desirable that they then be forthcoming . . . so long as they are viewed as exceptions. And yet, even in cases of great misfortune—if I contracted a debilitating disease, for example—I don't think I'd want my wife or friends to stay with me if they were motivated predominantly by pity or benevolence.

If even this much is correct, I think we can draw several lessons that point toward a deeper understanding of ethics in personal relationships. First, personal relationships between adults (and perhaps also between adults and children) are to be entered into and continued out of a sense of strength, fullness, and vitality, both in yourself and in the other, not out of a sense of weakness, need, emptiness, or incapacity.

Anything other than a shared sense of vitality and strength would lead to the unacceptable motives already discussed. Moreover, if I see myself primarily as a being in need, I will be too focused on myself and my needs. I will then tend to depersonalize you into a someone who can meet my needs. And I will also be generally unable to freely and joyously give: Since I see myself as not having enough as it is, my giving will seem to me a giving up. (Does this mean that those who most need a first-rate personal relationship will be unable to have one? I'm afraid that this might be true.)

The fact that giving characteristically must be free and joyous points to a second lesson about the ethics of personal relationships: Characteristically and normatively, the appropriate motive for action in personal relationships is simply that we want to do these things. Persons pursue whatever *ends* they have simply because they want to (that's what it means to say that something is an *end*, of course). And in a personal relationship, I and my well-being are ends of yours. From this vantage point it is easy to see why motives should play such a central role in personal relationships and also why *wanting* to do the things we do together is often the only acceptable motivation: That motivation is the touchstone of whether or not we have a personal relationship.

Of course, this is not to imply that personal relationships must rest simply on untutored feelings, taken as brute givens in the personalities of the participants. Indeed, it makes sense to talk about doing things, even for the wrong reasons, in order that doing those things will in time change you, your feelings, and your reasons. But it may be even more important to point out that continual attempts to create the right feelings in oneself are also not acceptable or satisfactory. If you must continually try to get yourself to want to do things with me, or for me, or for our relationship, we must at some point admit that I and my well-being are not among your ends and that we do not, therefore, have a personal relationship.

Nor am I claiming that actions motivated by a sense of duty or obligation, by altruism or self-sacrifice, by benevolence, pity, charity, sympathy, and so on *never* have a place in personal relationships. They may be appropriate in unusual circumstances. But such motives and actions are a fall-back mechanism which I compare to the safety net beneath a high wire act. We may be safer with a net, but the act is no good if the net actually comes into play very often. Similarly, the fall-back mechanisms may, in times of crisis, protect us and *some* of what we want, but they do not and cannot safeguard what is central to personal relationships. Thus when we find ourselves thinking characteristically or even very often in terms of the motives and concepts I have claimed are generally inappropriate in personal relationships, this is a symptom that our relationships are unsound, unhealthy, jeopardized, decayed, or that they never did become the personal relationships we wanted and hoped for. (Compare Hardwig, 1984.)

A third lesson about the ethics of personal relationships can be drawn from these reflections: The distinction between egoism and altruism is not characteristically applicable to personal relationships. Neither party magnanimously or ignominiously sacrifices personal interests, but the two interests are not independent, not really even two. For your ends are my ends too. The distinction between giving and receiving thus collapses. In impersonal contexts, if I respect your (independent) interests, that may be all you want of me. But in a personal context, you will want me to be interested in your interests. For if I am not interested in your interests, your well-being is not one of my ends.

This does not, of course, mean that all interests will be shared, but it means I am interested even in those of your interests I do not share. (I may have no appreciation of operas, but knowing how much they mean to you, it is important to me that your life include them. Operas for you are important to me in a way that operas for others who may love them just as much simply are not.) Nor, of course, am I claiming that there are *never* conflicts of interest in personal relationships. But such conflicts are set within the context of the meaning each has for the other and are therefore seen and handled differently. In personal relationships, conflicts of interest are conflicts within myself, a very different thing from a conflict of interest with someone separate from me.

A fourth lesson about ethics and personal relationships is this: Because personal relationships are ends—indeed, ultimate and incommensurable ends—they cannot and need not be justified by an appeal to some higher value such as love, pleasure, utility, or social utility. Any ethics that attempts to justify personal relationships in terms of more ultimate goods depersonalizes personal relationships. It construes us as wanting these higher goods, not each other.

Nor can the relative merits of personal relationships be adequately assessed in terms of abstract values. Each personal relationship is a good *sui generis*. Irreducibly involving the specific persons that they do, personal relationships cannot be reduced to common denominators that would permit comparison without depersonalizing them. Although persons caught in situations requiring choices between different personal relationships sometimes talk (and probably think) about comparing them in terms of abstract common denominators, evaluating relationships in this way Platonistically reduces our loved ones to mere instantiations of forms, thus depersonalizing them and our relationships to them.

A fifth and final lesson serves to summarize and conclude these reflections. The ethics of personal relationships must see persons in nonatomic terms; it must be based on a doctrine of internal relations. People see themselves in nonatomic terms if they see at least some other individuals not just as means to their well-being, but as part of their well-being. As I suggested earlier, there is no way to explain why I value a relationship with *you* (over and above the goods I desire from you and from this kind of relationship) except by saying that I feel a bond between us. I have come to see myself as a self that can only be fulfilled by a life that includes a relationship with you. Thus I see myself, in part, as part of a larger whole that is *us*. This does not mean that I see you as either a necessary or a sufficient condition for my well-being. If our relationship ends, my world will not fall apart and I may know that it won't. But if our relationship does end, I will have to alter my conception of myself and my well-being. . . .

Granted, we must remember that relationships can be viciously personal as well as gloriously personal. And it does seem plausible to maintain that we don't need an ethics for times when relationships are healthy and going smoothly. But again, I believe that the plausibility of this view reflects the limitations of the ways in which we have thought about ethics. I would contend, instead, that we *do* need an ethics for good times and for healthy, beautiful relationships—an ethics of *aspiration* that would serve to clarify what we aim for in personal relationships and to remind us of how they are best done.

Moreover, even when personal relationships become troubled, strained, or even vicious, it is not always possible or desirable to depersonalize the relationship. And an ethics must not tacitly urge or require us to depersonalize our relationships whenever serious conflicts arise. Within a personal relationship, the depersonalizing stance will often distort the issue beyond recognition. If we leave out my love for you, my turmoil over how often you drink yourself into oblivion vanishes, and with it, the issue that arises between us. For I can acknowledge with equanimity the drinking of others who are not personally related to me. My concern is simply not an impersonal concern that ranges indifferently over many possible objects of concern.

Depersonalizing (or ending) a relationship *may* be the appropriate final step in the face of intractable difficulties. But I would deny that depersonalizing is always the best course even here. For I think we should aspire to learn how to end relationships without depersonalizing them. If we can learn to continue to care and to care personally for our past loves, friends, and partners, we can be left happier, less bitter, wiser about the causes of the difficulties, and better able to go on to other relationships than if we end our relationships in hostility, anger, rejection, or even the kind of indifference characteristic of an impersonal stance.

What, then, is to be done? If we accept my position that we need an ethics of personal relationships and that such an ethics will have to be different from an ethics of impersonal relationships, the field of ethics opens up and ethical theory turns out to be a much less thoroughly explored domain than we might have thought. For my view implies that there are vast, largely uncharted regions beyond what we have come to know as ethics. I have tried to point to this region, but I have hardly begun to explore it.

1. We need to consider whether personal relationships are always better. If that view is correct, impersonal relationships would be only the result of the limitations of our sense of relatedness, and there would be a constant ethical imperative to personalize social contexts whenever possible and to expand our sense of connectedness. I suspect, however, that some relationships are better left impersonal and also that, because enmity, resentment, disgust, and many forms of conflict are much more bitter and intractable when they are personal, there are situations where depersonalizing is a good strategy. We must also understand more clearly exactly what depersonalizing a relationship involves.

2. We need an ethics for quasi-personal relationships (love, marriage, friendship) when these relationships are not also *personal* (in the sense I have been trying to explicate). For it is perhaps in such contexts that people are most devastatingly used, abused, and mistreated. Still, quasi-personal relationships have important roles to play, both when they do and when they do not involve a personal relationship: Marriage is also a financial institution; our concept of a parent seeks to insure that children will be protected and raised, even if not loved; even living together is in part an arrangement for sharing the chores of daily life.

3. We need some way to deal with the conflicts and tensions arising in situations involving both personal and impersonal relationships. Is it moral, for example, for me to buy computer games and gold chains for my son while other children are starving, simply because he is *my son* and I have a personal relationship with him? The issues about the extent to which one can legitimately favor those to whom one is personally related are, for me, deeply troubling and almost impenetrable to my ethical insight. . . .

4. Then, when we have all this in view, we should perhaps reexamine our "stranger ethics" to see if we need to revise our ethics of impersonal relationships in light of the ethics of personal and quasi-personal relationships.

5. Finally, we undoubtedly need a more precise understanding of what makes relationships personal, a better grasp on the values of such relationships, and a much more rigorous and developed account of the ethics of personal relationships. For even if the present paper succeeds beyond my wildest dreams, it has only scratched the surface.

Until we have done all these things, it will be premature to make pronouncements about what constitutes "the moral point of view."

Note

Acknowledgments: This paper was begun in 1978 at a National Endowment for the Humanities Summer Seminar directed by Amelie Rorty. It has, in various versions, benefited from many helpful criticisms and suggestions from the members of that NEH seminar, from the Philosophy Departments at East Tennessee State University and Virginia Commonwealth University, from the members of Kathy Emmett's seminar on personal relationships, from the editors of the present volume, and especially from Amelie Rorty and Mary Read English. My many benefactors have left me with a whole sheaf of powerful and important ideas for revising, amending, and qualifying what I've said, but unfortunately too often without the wit and wisdom needed to incorporate their suggestions into this paper.

References

Gilligan, C. 1982. *In a Different Voice: Psychological Theory and Women's Development.* Cambridge: Harvard University Press.

Hardwig, J. 1984. "Should Women Think in Terms of Rights?" *Ethics,* 94, 441–55.

Noddings, N. 1984. *Caring: A Feminine Approach to Ethics and Moral Education.* Berkeley: University of California Press.

Stocker, M. 1976. "The Schizophrenia of Modern Ethical Theories." *Journal of Philosophy,* 73, 453–66.

Williams, B. 1976. "Persons, Character, and Morality." In A. G. Rorty, ed. *The Identities of Persons.* Berkeley: University of California Press.

Review Questions

1. Why does Hardwig believe that we don't yet have an ethics of personal relationships?
2. Paraphrase Hardwig's two main characteristics of personal relationships.
3. What does the "quasi" mean in quasi-personal relationships?
4. State and explain the basic principle of Hardwig's ethics of personal relationships.
5. Fill in the blanks and explain: "First, personal relationships between adults (and perhaps also between adults and children) are to be entered into and continued out of a sense of _____ , _____ and _____, both in _____ and in _____ _____. . . ."
6. Explain what Hardwig means by his fifth lesson about the ethics of personal relationships; namely, that it's necessary to "see persons in nonatomic terms." Since this is such an important point, give a couple of examples of what it means to see persons as "nonatomic."

Probes

1. Explain the difference between treating a person as a means to an end and treating the person as an end in him or herself. Give an example to illustrate your explanation.
2. What is the link between Hardwig's second main characteristics of a personal relationship and my discussion of uniqueness or noninterchangeability in Chapter 2?
3. Why does Hardwig believe that a one-sided personal relationship is "ripe for exploitation and tragedy"?
4. Why do motives and intentions play so much larger a role in personal relationships than in impersonal relationships?
5. Why does Hardwig discourage—but not completely reject—the motives of duty, altruism, pity, and sympathy in personal relationships?

6. Hardwig claims that the distinction between egoism and altruism is not normally applicable to personal relationships. Paraphrase the argument he makes to support this claim, and tell whether you agree or disagree.
7. Hardwig says that we should learn to end a relationship without depersonalizing it. Think back to the last time you ended a relationship. Did either of you depersonalize it? What effects did that have? How might you have kept it personal and yet ended it?

Chapter 12

Families

Virginia Satir was a family therapist who always emphasized the crucial importance of effective communication. Besides writing several influential books and offering dozens of workshops and seminars, she helped hundreds of families improve their communication. This reading is taken from her book *The New Peoplemaking.* In it, she explains what a family network is and how making a map of your family network can help reveal a great deal about how the family communicates.

Like most of her work, this essay is practical and applied. Satir asks you to actually draw a map of your family network as you read the chapter. When you get to the point of specifying links between family pairs and role names for individuals, you'll begin to see how you can learn from this process. Then when you go to the next step—triangles—I suspect that additional insights will emerge. For example, I've often made one of Satir's points by noting that, although a triangle is the strongest geometric shape—it's widely used in bridges, house framing, cranes, and other structures—it is the weakest interpersonal shape. Why? Because, as Satir puts it, "A triangle is always a pair plus one and, since only two people can relate at one time, someone in the triangle is always the odd one out." This was a challenge for me to face when Kris's father died, leaving the triangle of me, Kris, and her mom; and the issue arose again 14 years later when Lincoln was born, creating a household of Kris, me, and Lincoln.

Satir offers several suggestions about how to handle the inevitable problems that arise from the triangles in a family. First, you need to understand that "no one can give equal attention to two people at the same time," but that if you are patient, the communication dynamic, like Texas weather, will change. A second step is to verbalize whatever concerns you have and to recognize that when you're the odd one out, it's because of the structure of the triangle, not because you are, or did something wrong.

In the case of the family Satir uses as an example—the Lintons—the network includes forty-five different units—five individuals, ten pairs, and thirty triangles. No wonder family communication can be frustrating!

In this reading Satir does not explain specifically how to deal with all the family communication problems you might face. But she does provide a way to begin to understand what's going on, and this is a major contribution.

Your Family Map

Virginia Satir

When I first started working with entire families, I was struck by the tremendous unrelated activity that went on in all directions: physically through bodily movement and psychologically through double messages, unfinished sentences, and so on. More than anything else I was reminded of the can of angleworms my father used to take as

From *The New Peoplemaking* by Virginia Satir, Chapter 13, pp. 182–193. 1988 Science and Behavior Books.

bait on fishing trips. The worms were all entangled, constantly writhing and moving. I couldn't tell where one ended and the other began. They really couldn't go anywhere except up, and down, around, and sideways, but they certainly gave the impression of aliveness and purpose. Had I been able to talk to one of those worms to see how he felt, it is my feeling that he would have told me the same kinds of things I have heard from family members over the years: *Where am I going? What am I doing? Who am I?*

The comparison between the way many families conduct themselves and the purposeless, tangled writhing of these worms seemed so apt that I termed the network that exists among family members a *can of worms*.

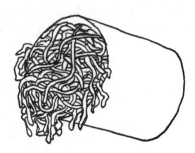

To show you what your family network is and how to map it will be the goal of this chapter. I think the best way to go about it is to take an imaginary family, the Lintons, and show you how their network works for and against them. No one can ever actually see this network, incidentally, but you can certainly feel it, as the exercises outlined in this and the following chapter will amply demonstrate to you.

All right. Here are the Lintons as individuals and as their family is today.

THE LINTON FAMILY NOW

ALICE
Adult Female
age 38

JOHN
Adult Male
age 40

JOE
Male Child
age 17

BOB
Male Child
age 16

TRUDY
Female Child
age 12

Tack a large sheet of paper to the wall where all of you can see it clearly. Begin the map of your family by drawing circles for each person, using a felt-tipped pen. Your family may now include a grandparent or other person as part of your household. If so, add a circle for that person on the row with the other adults.

If someone was once a part of your family but is gone now, represent her or him with a filled-in circle. If the husband or father is dead, has deserted the family or divorced his wife, and his wife has not remarried, your map would show it as follows:

If the woman has remarried, it would be shown thus:

If the second child died or was institutionalized, your map would look this way:

I believe that anyone who has ever been part of a family leaves a definite impact. A departed person is often very much alive in the memories of those left behind. Frequently, too, these memories play an important role—often a negative one—in what is going on in the present. This doesn't have to happen. If the departure has not been accepted, for whatever reason, the ghost is still very much around and often can disrupt the current scene. If, on the other hand, the departure has been accepted, then the present is clear as far as the departed one is concerned.

Each person is a separate self who can be described by name, physical characteristics, interests, tastes, talents, habits—all the qualities that relate to him or her as an individual.

So far our map shows the family members as islands, but anyone who has lived in a family knows that no one can remain an island for long. The various family members are connected by a whole network of ties. These links may be invisible, but they are there, as solid and firm as if they were woven of steel.

Let's add another strand to our network: pairs. Pairs have specific role names in a family. The illustration that follows shows the pairs in the Linton family with their *role names*.

Roles and pairs in the family fall into three major categories: marital, having the labels of husband and wife; parental-filial, having the labels of father-daughter, mother-daughter, father-son and mother-son; and sibling, having the labels of brother-brother, sister-sister, and brother-sister. Family roles always mean pairs. You can't take the role of a wife without a husband, nor father or mother without a son or daughter, and so on.

Beliefs about what different roles mean can differ. Each role evokes different expectations. It's important to find out what the various roles mean to each family member.

When families come to me a little mixed up, one of the first things I do is ask for each member's ideas about what his or her role means. I remember one couple very

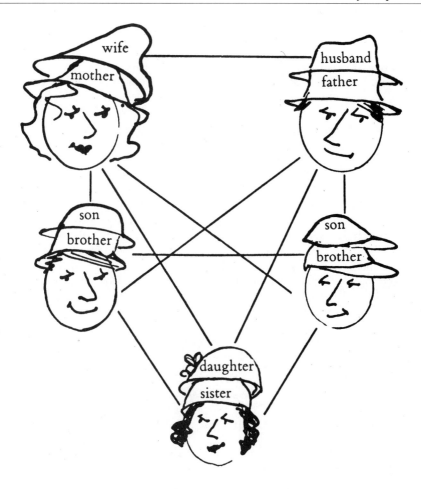

vivdly. She said, "I think being a wife means always having the meals on time, seeing that my husband's clothes are in order, and keeping the unpleasant things about the children and the day from him. I think the husband should provide a good living. He should not give the wife any trouble."

He said, "I think a husband means being the head of the house, providing income, and sharing his problems with his wife. I think a wife ought to tell her husband what's going on. She ought to be a pussycat in bed."

You can see that both were practicing what they thought the roles were; they didn't know how far apart they actually were in these important areas. Never having spoken about it, they had just assumed their views on their respective roles were the same. When they shared their ideas, some new understanding developed between them, and they achieved a much more satisfying relationship. I have seen this particular couple's experience over and over again in troubled families that come to me for help.

What about your family and your respective role expectations and definitions? Why not all sit down and share what you think your role is, and those of your spouse and your offspring as well? I think you'll be in for some surprises.

Now let's examine another facet of this role business. Alice Linton is a person who lives and breathes and wears a certain dress size. She is also a wife when she is with John, and a mother when she is with Joe, Bob, or Trudy. It might be helpful if we think of her roles as different hats she puts on when the occasion demands. Aside from her self-role, which she wears all the time, Alice uses a particular hat only when she is with the person who corresponds to the role-hat. So she is constantly putting on and taking off hats as she goes through her day. If she or John were to wear all their role-hats at once, they would look like this, and it could get a little top-heavy.

Now add the network lines to your family map, linking every member with every other member. As you draw each line, think for a moment about that particular relationship. Imagine how each of those two people involved feels about that connection. All of the family should share in this exercise, so each can try to feel what the different relationships are like.

So far I have presented the Lintons to you as selves and pairs—five selves and ten pairs. If this were all there were to the map, living in a family would be quite an easy matter. When Joe arrived, however, a triangle came into being. Here the plot begins to thicken, for the triangle is the trap in which most families get caught. I'll talk more about triangles later, but first let's add the network of triangles to the Linton family map.

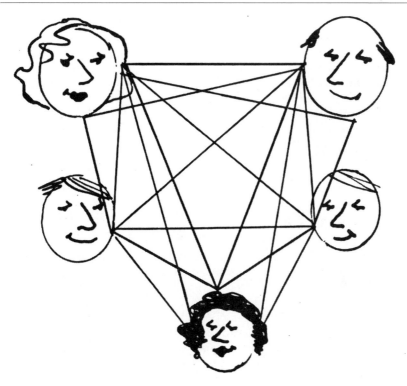

Now the Lintons' network looks like this. It's pretty hard to see any one part of it clearly, isn't it? You can see how the triangles obscure and complicate things. In families we don't live in pairs; we live in triangles.

When Joe was born, not one, but three triangles were formed. A triangle is always a pair plus one and, since only two people can relate at one time, someone in the triangle is always the odd one out. The whole nature of the triangle changes depending on who is odd one out, so what looks like one triangle actually is three (at different times).

The three triangles above consist of John, Alice, and Joe. In the first, John is the odd one, watching the relationship of his wife and son. In the second, Alice watches her husband and son together. In the third, little Joe watches his father and mother together. How troublesome any particular triangle is may depend on who is the odd one out at the moment and whether he or she feels bad about being left out.

There is truth to the old saying, "Two's company, three's a crowd." The odd person in a triangle always has a choice between breaking up the relationship between the other two, withdrawing from it, or supporting it by being an interested observer. The odd person's choice is crucial to the functioning of the whole family network.

All kinds of games go on among people in triangles. When a pair is talking, the third may interrupt or try to draw their attention. If the pair disagrees about something, one may invite the third to become an ally; this changes the triangle by making one of the original pair the odd one out.

Can you remember a time recently when you were with two other people? How did you handle that triangle? How did you feel? How are triangles handled in your family?

Families are full of triangles. The Linton family of five has thirty triangles:

John/his wife/his first son
John/his wife/his second son
John/his wife/his daughter
John/his first son/his second son
John/his first son/his daughter
John/his second son/his daughter
Alice/her husband/her first son
and so on.

Triangles are extremely important because the family's operation depends in large part on how triangles are handled.

The first step toward making a triangle bearable is to understand very clearly that no one can give equal attention to two people at the same time. Maybe the best idea is to approach the inevitable triangle as people do with Texas weather: stick around awhile, and it will change.

The second step, when you are the odd person, is to put your dilemma into words so that everyone can hear. The third step is to show by your own actions that being the odd one out isn't a cause for anger or hurt or shame. Problems arise when people feel that being on the outside means they are no good. Low self-worth!

To live comfortably in a triangle, it seems to me that one needs certain feelings about oneself. An individual has to feel good about him- or herself and be able to stand on two feet without leaning on someone else. He or she can be the odd one temporarily without feeling bad or rejected. She or he needs to be able to wait without feeling abused, talk straight and clearly, let the others know what she or he is feeling and thinking, and not brood or store up bad feelings.

If you glance again at the Lintons' family map and triangles, you can appreciate how complex family networks are. The concept of the can of worms may be more understandable to you, too.

Draw your family's can of worms by adding all the triangles to your family map. Using a different colored pencil or ink may help distinguish the triangles from the pairs. Again, as you draw, think of the relationship that each line represents. Among any three people you will be drawing only one triangle, although three actually exist. Think of how that triangle looks from each person's point of view.

The Lintons' network did not develop overnight. It took six years to gather the people now represented in the network—possibly eight years, if you consider the two years John and Alice courted. Some families take fifteen or twenty years to assemble their casts. Others take one or two years, and some never finish because the core (the couple in charge) keeps changing.

Whenever the Lintons are all together, forty-five different units are operating: five individuals, ten pairs, and thirty triangles. Similar elements exist in your family. Each person has his or her own mental picture of what each of these units is like. John may look very different to his wife Alice than to his son Bob. Alice may see her relationship to Bob one way; Bob would see it differently. John's picture is probably quite different from either of theirs. All these varying pictures are supposed to fit together in the family, whether or not the individuals are aware of them. In nurturing families, all of these elements and everyone's interpretation of them are out in the open and can easily be talked about. On the other hand, troubled families are either not aware of their family pictures or are unwilling or unable to talk about them.

Many families have told me they feel frustrated, physically tight, and uncomfortable when the whole family is assembled. Everyone feels constant movement, being pulled in many directions. If family members could be made aware of the can of worms in which they are trying to function, they wouldn't be so puzzled and uncomfortable.

When families see their network for the first time and fully realize how tremendously complicated family living really is, they often tell me they feel great relief. They realize they don't need to be on top of everything all the time. Who can keep track or control of forty-five units at once? Individual members can have a much easier time together because they didn't feel the necessity to control things; they became more interested in observing what is happening and in planning creative ways to make the family function better.

The challenge in family living is to find ways each individual can participate or be an observer of others without feeling he or she doesn't count. Meeting this challenge involves not being a victim of our old villain: low self-esteem.

A family's can of worms exerts tremendous push-pull pressures on the individual. It puts great demand on each one. In some families it is difficult to be an individual at all. The larger the family, the more units to be dealt with, the more difficult it is for each family member to get a share of the action. I certainly don't mean to imply that big families are always failures. On the contrary, some of the most nurturing families I know have large numbers of children.

Even so, the more children that come into the family, the more pressure on the marital relationship. A family of three has only three self-pair triangles; a family of four has twelve; a family of five has thirty; and a family of ten has 280 triangles! Each time a new person is added, the family's limited time and other resources have to be divided into smaller portions. A larger house and more money may be found, but the parents still have only two arms and two ears. And the airwaves can still carry only one set of words at a time without total bedlam.

What often happens is that the pressure of parenting gets so overwhelming that very little of the self of either parent finds expression, and the marital relationship grows weak with neglect. At this point many couples break up, give up, and run away. They have starved as individuals, failed as mates, and probably aren't doing very well as parents, either. Frustrated, turned off, emotionally dying adults don't make good family leaders.

Unless the marital relationship is protected and given a chance to flower and unless each partner has a chance to develop the family system becomes crooked and the children are bound to be lopsided in their growth.

Being good, balanced parents is not impossible. It is just that parents must be particularly skillful and aware to maintain their selfhood and keep their marriage partnership alive when the can of worms is so full. Such parents will be in charge of nurturing families. They are living examples of the kind of family functioning that channels pressures in the family network into creative, growth-producing directions.

Review Questions

1. What are Satir's three major categories of roles and pairs in the family?
2. What's the relationship between family roles and expectations?

3. Satir's family (the Lintons) is made up of five people who comprise thirty triangles. How many triangles are there in your family?
4. What main points does Satir make about the tremendous complexity of family relationships?

Probes

1. Why does Satir suggest that you include family members who have died or been institutionalized on your family map?
2. Why does Satir say that "family roles always mean pairs"?
3. What important feature is added to your family map when you move from pairs to triangles (besides the obvious additional person)?
4. Satir's map shows pairs and triangles linking *all* the members of a family. Do you think this is always true of family networks? Are there ever family members who are *not* connected as a pair or as part of a triangle?
5. Paraphrase Satir's main piece of advice to parents.

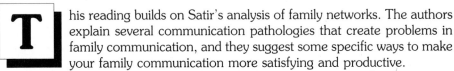

This reading builds on Satir's analysis of family networks. The authors explain several communication pathologies that create problems in family communication, and they suggest some specific ways to make your family communication more satisfying and productive.

The reading begins with a list of unhealthy rules that distort family communication, for example the rules that it is wrong to ask for help, to express anger at your parents, to talk about your sexual needs or feelings, or to express fear. There are also families with specific rules about perceptions, for example that children shouldn't notice that dad or mom is drunk and disfunctional, or that there is hostility at the dinner table. When such perception or communication rules exist, they lead family members to four toxic responses or "major communication disorders": denial, deletion, substitution, or incongruent messages. Denial means rejecting what someone is afraid to express. Deletion means leaving out parts of a message that directly express the speaker's awareness and needs. Substitution involves the indirect expression of feelings, often by taking them out on family members. Incongruent messages are ones in which the words don't match the nonverbal elements, such as the person who shrieks, "I'M NOT MAD!!"

When family members are denying, deleting, substituting, or using incongruent messages, others in the family have to engage in "mind reading" in order to figure out what's going on. And, as the authors point out, "All this guesswork results in just one thing: mistakes." These mistakes can worsen as "Your inappropriate response then creates a chain reaction like the proverbial falling dominoes." McKay, Davis, and Fanning offer two specific ways to combat this problem. As a speaker you can work to create congruent, unified messages, and as a listener you can remember to check out all ambiguous messages.

Satir's main point about triangles is repeated as these authors talk about family alliances. They suggest a family contract as a way to combat the negative effects of alliances.

Then McKay, Davis, and Fanning explain eight covert manipulation strategies that are common in families, and in each case they indicate how family members can change their communication to avoid these strategies. The reading ends with two exercises designed to help family members create and sustain a healthy communication climate.

Family Communications

Matthew McKay, Martha Davis, and Patrick Fanning

There is one major difference between communication within a family setting and communication with the world at large. The stakes are a lot higher with your family. You can escape from conflicts with a neighbor down the street, the union rep, or your auto mechanic, but you can't get away from your family; you still have to go home every night. A family with chronic, poor communications becomes a pressure cooker. Each member is vulnerable to emotional devastation. The children, especially, are susceptible to a range of physical and psychological symptoms.

Families get into trouble when members are prohibited from expressing certain feelings, needs, or awarenesses. Rules for what can't be asked for, talked about, or noticed are learned from your parents. They become unconscious inhibitors that prevent you from sharing important parts of your experience. Here are some examples of unhealthy rules that distort family communication. It's wrong to:

1. Ask for help
2. Talk about your hopes and dreams
3. Express anger at your parents
4. Seek acknowledgment or recognition for work
5. Ask for emotional support
6. Show that you've been hurt
7. Show your emotional pain
8. Talk about your sexual needs or feelings
9. Notice or comment on mistakes and problems
10. Voice disagreement or bring conflicts into the open
11. Directly express your anger (unless you can prove that the other person is horrible and disgusting)
12. Express fear
13. Express ambivalence, reservations, uncertainty
14. Show affection
15. Ask for attention

In addition to the general rules, families may have very specific regulations limiting perception. They govern what can and can't be seen and talked about. These rules are particularly stringent for the children, who have not yet been socialized into blocking their awarenesses. The following are typical for this category of family rules.

1. Don't notice that daddy is drunk and disfunctional
2. Don't notice hostility at the dinner table
3. Don't mourn or talk about grandmother's death
4. Don't express your fears of a Martian invasion
5. Don't ask for hugs or reassurance
6. Don't notice mom's affair

To survive in a family you have to follow the rules. The rules are created and continually reinforced by the fear of rejection. If your father reacted angrily when you were anxious as a chlid, you quickly learned that anxiety should not be expressed. You were conditioned to expect being hurt if you talked about your fears. Eventually the rule dropped out of your awareness and became a hidden influence. As an adult, you remain uncomfortable with fear and may become irritated with your children for expressing it. Your spouse may also accept your rule because it has reciprocal benefits: "I won't show my fear, if I don't have to deal with yours."

For most people, the powerful rules that limit their expression are completely unconscious. In the family therapist's office, when finally asked to communicate their hurt or fear or need for support, they feel strangely paralyzed. It all seems very dangerous, but they don't know why. That sense of danger, of course, derives from conditioning long ago, when their parents rejected them for saying what they felt, needed, or observed.

Family Communication Disorders

The rules limiting expression within families result in four major communication disorders. Restricted from direct expression, you must either deny, delete, substitute, or incongruently communicate aspects of your experience.

Denial

People tend to deny what they are afraid to express. Your needs and feelings can be denied overtly or covertly. Overt denial involves statements such as "I don't care." "No problem." "Whatever you want." "I'm fine." "Who's angry?" "Who's upset?" "I don't need you to do anything." Covert denial is harder to spot, but often involves shrugging, speaking in a monotone, slouching or withdrawing contact. The message is "It doesn't matter, I don't feel anything."

Deletion

Deletion involves leaving parts of a message out, particularly the parts that directly express your needs and awareness. Instead of saying "I'd like to go to a movie," you may catch yourself saying "It's sure a lousy TV night isn't it?" With deletions you have to say everything roundabout. Statements don't specify who, what, where, or when. The following are some typical examples:

- "It's been a little lonely." (*Meaning:* "I've missed you the three nights a week you've been in class, and I hope you take fewer night classes next quarter.")
- "There's a new French restaurant down the street." (*Meaning:* "Let's eat out tonight.")

- "Damn, the threads are stripped, I'll never get this running." (*Meaning:* "Give me a little sympathy and bring me a cup of coffee.")
- "Now what do you want me to do?" (*Meaning:* "Leave me alone right now, this is the first time I've relaxed all day.")
- "I guess you're a little tired." (*Meaning:* "How come you're so angry all of a sudden?")

Deletions are usually constructed in one of three ways:

1. *Statements in the form of a question.* "Are you still here?" (*Meaning:* "I would like to be alone for a few hours.")
2. *Requests in the form of neutral observations.* "It's a gorgeous day." (*Meaning:* "Let's take a drive to the country.")
3. *Deleted references.* The message is vague and doesn't say who feels what about whom. "There's been some anger lately." (*Meaning:* "I have been angry at *you* because of all the extra work since you fired the housekeeper.") "There hasn't been much contact." (*Meaning:* "*I've* felt out of contact with my *husband* and oldest *daughter.*")

Substitution

Feelings have to come out sometime, and substitution allows them to be expressed in a safer way or with a safer person. Substitution lets you express your feelings indirectly. If you have a rule against showing hurt, you might channel the hurt feelings into anger. If it's forbidden for you to express anger toward your wife, you might attack your son about his chores. The following are some typical examples of substitution.

1. Your boss criticizes your work. You're angry, you attack your wife for mismanaging the food money.
2. You're frightened when you see your boy run into the street. You angrily attack him as "stupid and crazy."
3. You feel hurt and a little lonely when your daughter spends three hours a night on the phone. You attack her for leaving the milk out of the refrigerator.
4. You're hurt and angry when your spouse announces the desire to take a vacation without you. Your rule against expressing anger forces you to convert the feeling to depression.
5. You are unable to express your secret happiness that the children will spend the summer with your ex-spouse. You express the feeling as anxiety about their health and safety.

Incongruent Messages

Incongruent communications occur when the messages carried by your posture, facial expression, tone of voice, and tempo of speech don't match the content of what you are saying. A woman says to her daughter, "I'm not upset that you were out late." But her voice has a strident, harsh quality, she talks quickly, she's pointing her finger, while her other hand is on her hip. The words simply don't match what the body and voice are saying. "I'm very sad that we can't pull this family together," a man announces at the dinner table. His eyes bore into those of his son, his jaws are clenched, one hand forms a fist around the napkin. He says he's sad, but he's also communicating something else. It may be anger, or it may be a kind of agitated despair.

When messages don't match, family members are forced to decide which message is the true one. They have to mind-read and try to guess what the speaker is really saying. The following examples of incongruent communication are divided into four parts: (1) words, (2) voice and body language, (3) listener's interpretation, and (4) real message.

Words: "I'm terrifically glad to see you home."

Voice and body language: Flat monotone, eyes looking at the floor, a half-smile, body turned slightly sideways.

Listener's interpretation: Chooses to respond to voice and body language. Assumes that the speaker is uncomfortable and disappointed. Listener feels hurt.

Real message: "I'm glad you're home. Unfortunately I couldn't finish the work I wanted to do, and I'm afraid I won't complete it now that you're back." The speaker has a rule against expressing anything but joy at a reunion. The result is incongruent communication.

Words: "I don't mind not going, there are lots of things to do around the house."

Voice and body language: A bright smile that fades unnaturally fast, stooped shoulders, neck bowed, a high, placating voice.

Listener's interpretation: Chooses to respond to the reassuring words, but feels anxiety and discomfort because the body language shows extreme disappointment.

Real message: "I'm extremely disappointed that we couldn't go to the movies tonight."

Words: "I just want some more support, the feeling that you care about me."

Voice and body language: Voice high and loud, almost whining, mouth drawn out in a flat line, shoulders and arms shrugging, looking over the top of glasses.

Listener's interpretation: Chooses to respond to the voice and body language. "He sometimes shrugs like that and stares over his glasses when he's angry. He must be angry." The listener experiences the message as a demand.

Real message: A request for help and a feeling of hopelessness that any will be forthcoming. The speaker's body language for expressing hopelessness is apparently similar to that used for anger. The listener, confused by incongruent messages, assumes that the speaker is hiding irritation.

Words: "I worry terribly about you when you're late like this."

Voice and body language: Arms crossed, weight on one leg, mouth drawn in a thin line, voice harsh and loud.

Listener's interpretation: Chooses to respond to the words. Feels vaguely uneasy that the words don't match the body language.

Real message: "I waited for you and worried about you. I'm angry that you didn't have the courtesy to call."

Words: "Why don't you get the kid a couple more toys?"

Voice and body language: Voice slightly high and singsong, torso leaning forward, head shaking from side to side, finger pointing.

Listener's interpretation: Chooses to respond to the voice and body language. The voice and finger pointing are interpreted as critical, taunting.

Real message: "It worries me that she has nothing to play with at your house. I'm afraid she'll stop wanting to be with you because she's bored there." Because the speaker has used finger pointing and a singsong voice in the past to express annoyance, the listener mindreads annoyance and responds by getting angry.

Incongruent messages form the basis of much family pathology. People usually assume that the voice and body language communications are the true ones. But these messages are easily misinterpreted because of *overgeneralization*. This is the tendency to believe that a particular posture or intonation *always* means the same thing. "When Harry shrugs that always means he's upset with me." "When Jane frowns and points her finger, that always means she's making a demand." "When Natasha has a high strident voice that always means she's anxious." Overgeneralization cancels out any other meanings the gesture could have. It increases the opportunity for misinterpretation.

Family Pathology

Mind Reading

Because family members have rules about what can and cannot be expressed, they are forced to communicate covertly. Through deletions, substitutions, and incongruent messages family members say what they need to say. But often no one understands them. When you try to interpret covert messages you are forced to mind-read. You have to make a guess as to what the covert request or feeling really is. Take the example of the man who remarks that the house is infested with fleas. Since he has deleted his feelings and needs about the matter, his wife must try to divine if his hatred for the cat has surfaced again, he wants her to have the house flea-bombed, or wants her to acknowledge and commiserate about the problem. If he has a history of substitutions, she may be worried that he brought up the flea business because he's angry about her purchasing new drapes. The matter is further complicated if there are incongruent messages. If he stands with his hands on his hips and talks very rapidly, the wife may conclude by virtue of overgeneralization that her husband is violently angry.

All this guesswork results in just one thing: mistakes. If you are mind-reading, you are going to be wrong a certain percentage of the time. You will respond to what you think is going on, rather than the real message. Your inappropriate response then creates a chain reaction like the proverbial falling dominoes. Consider the following interaction: Margaret, whose husband demands peace and quiet when he arrives home, hastily ends a fight with her son as she hears his keys in the front door. She's anxious when she greets him. Her voice is high and clipped. She avoids eye contact. By virtue of overgeneralization, Al assumes that the clipped, high-pitched voice means that his wife is angry. He mind-reads that she is irritated with him for being late. He makes himself angry by telling himself that she doesn't care about the long hard hours he works. Al can't express the anger, and instead substitutes by complaining about the toys left on the floor. Margaret feels hurt, but substitutes by complaining that he's late again. The ensuing melee is entirely a result of mind reading.

There are two ways to break out of the mind-reading trap.

1. As a speaker, you have to ask yourself these questions: "What feeling, request, or awareness have I left out of my message? Do my tone of voice and body

language match the content of my message?" If you find that you are simultaneously communicating more than one message, break it down into two separate communications. Suppose, for example, that you have a rule against expressing anger. You're telling your child to clean up his room, but you notice a lot of anger in your voice and that you are pointing your finger. You might separate and express the messages in this way: "I want you to clean up your room by an hour from now. I asked you to do it this morning and now I find myself a little frustrated and angry that it's still not done."

2. As a listener, you can combat mind reading by checking out all ambiguous messages. If you notice that the content doesn't match the voice or body language, describe in a nonjudgmental way what you observe. Ask if there is more that needs to be said. "I notice your shoulders were kind of hunched and you were staring at the floor while we talked about the kitchen remodeling. Is there something more that you feel about that?" You need to catch yourself when you make assumptions about the needs and feelings of others. A red flag has to go up inside when you mind-read. As you catch yourself, you'll notice that certain assumptions typically come up over and over again. You may be prone to imagining that people are angry, disappointed, or making covert demands on you. These typical assumptions derive from overgeneralization, in which you invariably read certain gestures or tones of voice as anger, disappointment, or demands.

Alliances

Family alliances are formed to help you express forbidden feelings and needs. If dad gets angry when his son discusses problems in school, maybe mom will listen. And perhaps mom will also share some of her negative feelings about dad. As the mother-son alliance develops, Dad becomes more and more isolated. He doesn't hear the anger and the hurt, and he is also cut off from any warmth or support. Dad, as he feels increasingly peripheral, may seek an alliance with his daughter. They may complain to each other about how cold mom is, and secretly collude to support each other in family conflicts.

Sibling alliances are a good way to deal with a punitive parent who focuses more on rules than on the particular needs of his children. Parent-child alliances are helpful when a parent has been dying on the vine emotionally and feels trapped in a dead marriage. In general, alliances are very useful short-term strategies for getting support and acknowledgment. But they are death on family happiness. The feuding camps continue to attack and hurt each other, often until the children leave home or the parents separate.

A family contract for directness is the antidote for the alliance. Feelings and wants are expressed to the person who needs to hear them. Secrets (an implied alliance) are not allowed. For example, a mother-son alliance that would keep dad from knowing about the boy's poor grades is prevented by a contract for openness. A dad-mom alliance, in which dad bitterly gripes about his daughter's laziness, is likewise prevented. The contract for directness says that gripes are expressed to the offending person. With such a contract, the whole family enters an alliance. They agree to support each other in expressing and hearing important messages. They agree that feelings and needs that two of them share should be shared by all.

Covert Manipulation Strategies

All communication has an implied request built into it. You're always trying to influence people in some way, even if it's only to listen and give your attention. The problem is that many people have rules against asking for things. If you have such rules, you can't openly request support, help, or acknowledgment. Nobody knows what you want. As a consequence, you are forced to use covert manipulative strategies to get the things you need. The following eight manipulative strategies are widely used in pathological families.

1. Blaming and judging   The blamer attacks other family members for not meeting his needs. They should be more supportive, more loving, more helpful around the house. If they really cared they would get home earlier, do more things with the kids. A blamer's weapon is the prejorative attack. He aims at people's vulnerable self-esteem in the way a Doberman goes for the jugular. Certain blamers have refined their strategy to an art. Some attack with a needling sarcasm that ostensibly seems funny, but cuts deeply. Others make unreasonable demands, then explode with "justifiable" rage after they are turned down. Through judicious fault-finding the blamer can push family members to give him some of what he wants. He can get grudging attention and help. The problem is that the strategy only works for awhile. Though it is initially successful, and people are quite responsive to the fear of being hurt, the blamer's knives grow dull. Family members can become thick-skinned and oblivious to assaults. The blamer's once effective strategy for getting his way loses power. He is left with a simmering, impotent rage.

2. Pulling for guilt   This strategy banks on everyone's need to feel like a good person. Good people care for others, giving time and energy. They sacrifice themselves. Pulling for guilt involves subtly, sadly, letting family members know that you're in pain. If they cared they would do something about it. If they were good people they would stay home with you instead of going to the movies; if they really loved they would keep the lawn mowed. The best way to pull for guilt is to sigh a lot, refer bleakly to past sins and mistakes, tell everyone you're fine while looking miserable. Pulling for guilt is very effective. People secretly resent you, but they will often do what you want.

3. Pulling for pity   This strategy is designed to arouse sympathy rather than guilt. The demeanor is helpless and pathetic. There are sad stories, hopeless shrugs, all filling in the portrait of a victim. Pulling for pity has a period of maximum effectiveness. After a while exhaustion sets in, and family members begin to lose patience with the seemingly endless stream of problems.

4. Blackmail   Blackmailing involves threats to withold something other family members need. Overtly or covertly the suggestion gets made that there will be no more sex, dinner won't be cooked, forget that birthday party. Some blackmailers play for high stakes by continually threatening to leave the family. As every parent who has threatened to take away a child's allowance knows, blackmail quickly becomes ineffective if you don't make good on the threats. This puts the blackmailer in a difficult bind. He's either making empty threats (which are soon ignored) or he must follow through on his spiteful and destructive schemes. If he follows through, and family members are damaged, he is courting the possibility of real hatred.

5. Bribery This strategy involves insincere use of flattery, favors, or affection to induce other family members to change. Sex is turned on and off like a spigot. Attention and support are forthcoming only when the briber is in need. Like most of the covert manipulative strategies, bribery has short-term benefits. In the long-run, however, family members cease to trust the integrity and authenticity of the briber. Resentment sets in.

6. Placating Placators are nice. They fear conflict and avoid it at all costs. They try to please, to ingratiate, to garner approval. They are always quick to apologize. The placator gets his way by making people like him and owe him things. He's so agreeable, he's done so much for everyone, how could family members deny him the things he needs? Surely they will be as nice and as sacrificing as he has been. The problem for the placator is that people take him for granted. In the end he becomes a martyr with a long list of hidden resentments. He thought he had made a deal: "I'll be nice if you'll be nice." But other family members don't keep their end of the unspoken bargain.

7. Turning cold This strategy turns on the eloquent silence, the clenched jaw, the back turned in bed. The message is "You're getting nothing from me." It's a powerful strategy because it frightens people. Children in particular, who depend for their very survival on a parent's love, are enormously vulnerable to sudden coldness. But the withdrawal of love is more than a way of influencing behavior: it is a weapon that makes scars. Both children and spouse become distrusting. And a secret rage develops that anyone would take away the most precious and necessary of human resources: emotional energy.

8. Developing symptoms When all else fails, and people have no other way of getting what they want, they develop symptoms. They get headaches, they begin to drink, they have dark bouts of depression or impulsive spending sprees, they become unfaithful. Children get into fights at school, try to run away, develop asthma, attack their siblings. The symptoms are a covert attempt to get certain needs met. Headaches may get dad some time off work. Vaginismus may help a woman get time off from a sexually aggressive mate. A child may get important attention needs met with asthma. Symptoms are extremely useful, but they can also mutilate the family member who suffers them. A depressed woman finally gets her husband to take her on a vacation. But she's paid for that vacation with months of pain.

Covert manipulative strategies are only necessary when people have rules against the expression of needs, feelings, or awarenesses. If two or more family members have rules limiting what they can say, the resulting covert strategies are called a family system. . . .

How To Keep Family Communications Healthy

The best way to keep a family healthy is to allow each member the freedom to say what he feels, what he sees, and what he wants. Here are two exercises to help you reach those goals.

1. Checking out   Each time a family member says something that disturbs or confuses you, write down the following:

    a. *Words:* The actual content of the message.

    b. *Voice and body language:* Write down your memory of the pitch and tone of voice, the posture and facial expression. What gestures were used?

    c. *Your interpretation:* Notice whether the words match the voice and body language. If they seem to be saying different things, which do you believe? What do you assume to be the true message?

    d. *Real message:* Ask the family member for further clarification. Describe in a nonjudgmental way any discrepancies you see between the words and the nonverbal message. Ask if some feeling or need might have been left out. Now compare what you've learned with the previous assumptions you made.

This exercise helps you to combat mind reading by soliciting the information you need to accurately hear a message. Do this exercise at least once a day for two weeks. At the end of that time you'll get an idea of how much or how little you are distorting what family members say to you.

Remember that the tendency to mind-read is a natural one. Because important feelings or needs are often deleted, or show up only in body language, you may have developed a habit of guessing at the "real" message. The problem is that your guesses will not always be accurate. Just as Henrietta tortured herself by assuming that Jack was trying to escape their marriage, your mind reading may be adding fuel to a painful family system.

2. Hearing yourself   This exercise is designed to help you uncover your own deletions, substitutions, and incongruent messages. Whenver you take part in a painful or problematic bit of communication, write down the following:

    a. *Words:* Write down the first four or five sentences you said.

    b. *Voice and body language:* As you remember, how did your voice sound, what was your posture, what were your hands doing? What were you saying with your voice, your posture, your hands?

    c. What *feeling* did you leave out of your communication?

    d. What *implied request* was hidden in your communication?

    e. *Review the covert manipulation strategies:* Notice if there is anything in your message which indicates the use of one of those strategies.

    f. *Rewrite your message:* Include the original content of your message (if it was accurate), plus what your body and voice were saying. Include any feelings or needs that you are now aware that you deleted.

Review Questions

1. According to these authors, what is the one major difference between communication in a family setting and communication with the world at large?
2. What's the difference between deletion and substitution?
3. An incongruent message is one in which there is a lack of congruence or "fit" between what and what?
4. List and give a real-life example of the two ways these authors say we can break out of the mind-reading trap.
5. What's the difference between "pulling for guilt" and "pulling for pity"?

Probes

1. Individually review the twenty-one toxic family rules that these authors list. Did any exist in your family (or do they still)? Are there any rules in your family that are closely related to these? How do you believe these rules have affected your family's communicating? *If you are comfortable doing so,* discuss your responses to this question with a classmate.

2. The authors indicate that deletion is often expressed in statements that are in the form of a question. How might denial, substitution, and incongruent messages also get expressed as statements in the form of a question?

3. It seems to me that one kind of message that these authors believe can help solve problems created by denial, deletion, and so on is I-messages made up of the first-person pronoun followed by a present-tense verb and a concrete specific—for example, "I'd like us to be able to talk for a few minutes right when you get home, rather than having you read the newspaper first." What *other* kinds of messages do you think authors are advising people to use?

4. What's the relationship between these authors' discussion of family alliances and Satir's discussion of networks?

5. Which of the eight covert manipulation strategies are your favorites? Which do you almost never use? What kind of messages could you substitute for the ones you do use?

Chapter 13

Intimate Partners

This excerpt comes from the fifth edition of an unusual book designed to help people of any age expand their self-awareness and explore the choices available to them in significant areas of their lives. I've included it because it focuses on some of the most difficult and important topics to discuss—for example, what does it mean to be in an "intimate" relationship or to "love" someone—and it addresses these topics personally rather than impersonally. One author—Jerry—is a professor of human services and counseling, and the other—Marianne—is a marriage and family therapist.

One of the first really important points they make is that "we have the power to bring about change [in our relationships] if we ourselves change and do not insist that the other person make quick and total changes." This means that the rule of "quid pro quo" (I only give something when I get something in return) should *not* be applied in personal relationships. The only part of the relationship that I have any control over is my own part. And, although changes by one person almost always precede changes in the other (just because a relationship is a system in which everything affects everything else), it doesn't work to focus your change efforts on anyone but yourself. With this in mind, the authors emphasize, "you can choose the kinds of relationships you want to experience."

The first major section of this chapter discusses nineteen characteristics of a meaningful relationship. I won't repeat the whole list here, but I think several are worth paying close attention to. For example, they emphasize that intimacy doesn't mean losing your sense of self; people in healthy close relationships maintain their own separate identities. This is often experienced and discussed as the difference between "wanting" the other person and "needing" him or her. Another is that, as Steve Duck emphasizes in Chapter 11, each person in a healthy relationship is willing to work at keeping the relationship alive. If the relationship includes a sexual component, this also means that each person also makes some attempt to keep the romance alive. Another feature is that each person finds meaning and nourishment outside the relationship, rather than being totally dependent on the other, and both avoid manipulating, exploiting, or using the other. Healthy relationships are also marked by the partners' abilities to deal with the anger that inevitably surfaces. And, perhaps most fundamentally, in a healthy intimate relationship, each person has a commitment to the other, an investment in their future together which can tide them over times of conflict and crisis.

The second major section of the reading discusses how to deal with barriers to effective communication that inhibit the developing and maintaining of intimate relationships. Poor listening is one of the major barriers, which means that the materials in Chapter 7 apply to this chapter, too. Awareness of different gender styles is also important. In this section the Coreys discuss some of the ideas Deborah Tannen brought up in Chapter 9. The Coreys acknowledge that there are important cultural differences in what makes personal communication "effective," and they list nine characteristics of this kind of communication in Euro-American cultures.

The final major section discusses inauthentic and authentic love. The Coreys note that each of our love relationships is sometimes partly inauthentic, but they also urge us to avoid actions that lead to inauthentic love, for example, attaching strings to the relationship, withholding trust, refusing to disclose, and resorting to manipulation.

Then they offer a discussion of some meanings of authentic love. I wish I could have read this section when I was in high school and was first wondering what it really means to be "in love." The Coreys explain that authentic love nourishes rather than suffocates the other, that it is grounded in respect and responsibility, and that it means growth for both myself and the person I love. It also means commitment and vulnerability. Interestingly, they also maintain that "Love is *selfish*." This means that I can't love another person unless and until I genuinely love, value, appreciate, and respect myself. At the end of this section they emphasize that love means letting go of the illusion that you can *control* the other person, yourself, or your environment. I've found this to be consistently true— and one of the most important points in this reading.

Intimate Relationships and Love

Gerald Corey and Marianne Schneider-Corey

Introduction

Although this chapter focuses mainly on the role that relationships play in our lives, we deal with relationships from a broad perspective, and also with a range of lifestyles. The chapter deals with friendships, marital relationships, intimacy between people who are not married, dating relationships, relationships between parents and children, same-gender relationships as well as opposite-gender relationships, alternative lifestyles, and other meaningful personal relationships.

Marriage is still the dominant relationship in our society, particularly if the term *marriage* is construed broadly to include the many couples who consider themselves committed to each other even though they are not legally married as well as those who are creating relationships that are different in many respects from the traditional marriage. Bellah and his colleagues (1985) found that in today's society most people still want to marry, even though many of them no longer see it as a life requirement. For increasing numbers of people it is not considered disgraceful to be unmarried, and more people are remaining single by choice. There is less pressure to have children, and starting a family tends to be more of a conscious decision than was true in the past. Most of those interviewed believe in love as a basis for an enduring relationship. Love and commitment appear to be highly valued, although maintaining these qualities is difficult. Most people value spontaneity and solidity, freedom and intimacy, and the sharing of thoughts, feelings, values, and life goals. They feel freer than in the past to leave a marriage that is not working, and divorce is seen as one (but not the only) solution to an unhappy marriage.

Whether you choose to marry or not, or whether your preference is a same-gender or an opposite-gender primary relationship, you probably have many different types of relationships. What is true for marriage is largely true for these other relationships as well. Allowing for the differences in relationships, the signs of growth and meaningfulness are much the same, and so are the problems. Consequently, whatever lifestyle you choose, you can use the ideas in this chapter as a basis for thinking about the role relationships play in your life. The aim of the chapter is to stimulate your reflection on what you want from all of your special relationships, and also to invite you to take an honest look at the quality of these relationships.

Types of Intimacy

[Psychologist Erik] Erikson maintains that the challenge of forming intimate relationships is the major task of early adulthood. Intimacy implies that we are able to share significant aspects of ourselves with others. The issues we raise concerning barriers to intimacy and ways of enhancing intimacy can help you better understand the many different types of relationships in your life. The ideas in this chapter are useful tools in rethinking what kind of relationships you want, as well as in clarifying some new choices that you may want to make. You can take a fresh look at these relationships, including both their frustrations and their delights, and you can think about initiating some changes.

Consider the case of Donald, who told us about how little closeness he had experienced with his father. He saw his father as uncaring, aloof, and preoccupied with his own concerns. Yet Donald deeply wished that he could be physically and emotionally closer to him, and he had no idea how to bring this about. He made the difficult decision to talk to his father and tell him how he felt and what he wanted. His father appeared to listen, and his eyes moistened, but then without saying much he quickly left the room. Donald reported how hurt and disappointed he was that his father had not been as responsive as he had hoped he would be. What Donald was missing were subtle, yet significant, signs that his father had been touched and was not as uncaring as he had imagined. That his father listened to him, that he responded with even a few clumsy words, that he touched Donald on the shoulder, and that he became emotional were all manifestations that Donald's overtures had been received. Donald needs to understand that his father is probably very uncomfortable in talking personally. His father may well be every bit as afraid of his son's rejection as Donald is of his father's rebuffs. Donald will need to show patience and continue "hanging in there" with his father if he is really interested in changing the ways they relate to each other.

The experience Donald had with his father could have occurred in any intimate relationship. We can experience feelings of awkwardness, unexpressed desires, and fears of rejection with our friends, lovers, spouses, parents, or children. A key point is that we have the power to bring about change if we ourselves change and do not insist that the other person make quick and total changes. It is up to us to teach others specific ways of becoming more personal. It does little good to invest our energy in lamenting all the ways in which the other person is not fulfilling our expectations, nor is it helpful to focus on remaking others. . . . When you take a passive stance and simply hope the other person will change in the ways that you would like, you are giving away a sense of your power.

The intimacy we share with another person can be emotional, intellectual, physical, spiritual, or any combination of these. It can be exclusive or nonexclusive, long-term or brief. . . .

When we avoid intimacy, we only rob ourselves. We may pass up the chance to really get to know neighbors and new acquaintances, because we fear that either we or our new friends will move and that the friendship will come to an end. Similarly, we may not want to open ourselves to intimacy with sick or dying persons, because we fear the pain of losing them. Although such fears may be natural ones, too often we allow them to cheat us of the uniquely rich experience of being truly close to another person. We can enhance our life greatly by daring to care about others and fully savoring the time we can share with them now.

The idea that we most want to stress is that you can choose the kinds of relationships you want to experience. Often, we fail to make our own choices and instead fall into a certain type of relationship because we think "This is the way it's *supposed* to be." For example, some people marry who in reality might perfer to remain single—particularly women who often feel the pressure to have a family because it's "natural" for them to do so. Sometimes people choose a heterosexual relationship because they think that it is what is expected of them, when they would really prefer a homosexual relationship. Instead of blindly accepting that relationships must be a certain way or that only one type of lifestyle is possible, you have the choice of giving real thought to the question of what types of intimacy have meaning for you.

Meaningful Relationships: A Personal View

In this section we share some of our ideas about the characteristics of a meaningful relationship. Although these guidelines pertain to couples, they are also relevant to other personal relationships, such as those between parent and child and between friends of the same or opposite gender. Take, for example, the guideline "The persons involved are willing to work at keeping their relationship alive." Sometimes parents and children take each other for granted and rarely spend time talking about how they are getting along. Either parent or child may expect the other to assume the major responsibility for their relationship. The same principle applies to friends or to partners in a primary relationship. As you look over our list, adapt it to your own relationships, keeping in mind your particular cultural values. Since the values that are a part of your cultural background play an influential role in your relationships, you will need to adapt them in appropriate ways. As you review our list, ask yourself what qualities you think are most important in your relationships.

We see relationships as most meaningful when they are dynamic and evolving rather than fixed or final. Thus, there may be periods of joy and excitement followed by times of struggle, pain, and distance. As long as the persons in a relationship are growing and changing, their relationship is bound to change as well. The following are some of the qualities of a relationship that seem most important to us.

• *Each person in the relationship has a separate identity.* Kahlil Gibran (1923) expresses this thought in *The Prophet:* "But let there be spaces in your togetherness, and let the winds of the heavens dance between you" (p. 16). In *The Dance of Anger,* Harriet Goldhor Lerner (1985) says that making long-term relationships work is difficult because it is necessary to create and maintain a balance between separateness and togetherness. If there is not enough togetherness in a relationship, people in it typically feel isolated and do not share feelings and experiences. If there is not enough separateness, they give up a sense of their own identity and control. They also devote much effort to becoming what the other person expects.

- *Although each person desires the other, each can survive without the other.* This characteristic is an extension of the prior one, and it implies that people are in a relationship by choice. They are not so tightly bound together that if they are separated, one or the other becomes lost and empty. Thus, if a young man says "I simply can't live without my girlfriend," he is indeed in trouble. His dependency should not be interpreted as love but as the seeking of an object to make him feel complete.

- *Each is able to talk openly with the other about matters of significance to the relationship.* The two persons can openly express grievances and let each other know the changes they desire. They can ask for what they want, rather than expecting the other to intuitively know what they want and give it to them. For example, assume that you are not satisfied with how you and your mother spend time together. You can take the first step by letting her know, in a nonjudgmental way, that you would like to talk more personally. Rather than telling her how she is, you can focus more on telling her how you feel in your relationship with her.

- *Each person assumes responsibility for his or her own level of happiness and refrains from blaming the other if he or she is unhappy.* Of course, in a close relationship or friendship the unhappiness of the other person is bound to affect you, but you should not expect another person to *make* you happy, fulfilled, or excited. Although the way others feel will influence your life, they do not create or cause your feelings. Ultimately, you are responsible for defining your goals and your life, and you can take actions to change what *you* are doing if you are unhappy with a situation.

- *The persons involved are willing to work at keeping their relationship alive.* If we hope to keep a relationship vital, we must reevaluate and revise our way of being with each other from time to time. Consider how this guideline fits for your friendships. If you take a good friend for granted and show little interest in doing what is necessary to maintain your friendship, she may soon grow disenchanted and wonder what kind of friend you are.

- *The persons are able to have fun and to play together, they enjoy doing things with each other.* It is easy to become so serious that we forget to take the time to enjoy those we love. One way of changing drab relationships is to become aware of the infrequency of playful moments and then determine what things are getting in the way of enjoying life. Again, think of this guideline as it applies to your close friends.

- *Each person is growing, changing, and opening up to new experiences.* When you rely on others for your personal fulfillment and confirmation as a person, you are in trouble. The best way to build solid relationships with others is to work on developing your own personality. But do not be surprised if you encounter resistance to your growth and change. This resistance can come from within yourself as well as from others.

- *If the relationship contains a sexual component, each person makes some attempt to keep the romance alive.* The two persons may not always experience the intensity and novelty of the early period of their relationship, but they can devise ways of creating a climate of romance and closeness. They may go places they haven't been to before or otherwise vary their routine in some ways. They recognize when their life is getting dull and look for ways to eliminate its boring aspects. In their lovemaking they are sensitive to each other's needs and desires; at the same time, they are able to ask each other for what they want and need.

- *The two persons are equal in the relationship.* People who feel that they are typically the "givers" and that their partner is usually unavailable when they need him or her might question the balance in their relationship. In some relationships one person may feel compelled to assume a superior position relative to the other—for example, to be very willing to listen and give advice yet unwilling to go to the other person and show any vulnerability or need. Lerner (1985) says that women often define their own wishes and preferences as being the same as those of their partner. In this case there surely is no equality in the relationship. Both parties need to be willing to look at aspects of inequality and demonstrate a willingness to negotiate changes.

- *Each person actively demonstrates concern for the other.* In a vital relationship the participants do more than just talk about how much they value each other. Their actions show their care and concern more eloquently than any words. Each person has a desire to give to the other. They have an interest in each other's welfare and a desire to see that the other person is fulfilled.

- *Each person finds meaning and sources of nourishment outside the relationship.* Sometimes people become very possessive in their friendships. A sign of a healthy relationship is that each avoids assuming an attitude of ownership toward the other. Although they may experience jealousy at times, they do not demand that the other person deaden his or her feelings for others. Their lives did not begin when they met each other, nor would their lives end if they should part.

- *Each avoids manipulating, exploiting, and using the other.* Each respects and cares for the other and is willing to see the world through the other's eyes. At times parent-child relationships are strained because either or both parties attempt to manipulate the other. Consider the father who brags about his son, Roger, to others and whose affection is based on Roger's being an outstanding athlete. Roger may feel used if his father is able to talk only of sports. What if he were to decide to quit playing sports? Would he still be earning his father's approval?

- *Each person is moving in a direction in life that is personally meaningful.* They are both excited about the quality of their lives and their projects. Applied to couples, this guideline implies that both individuals feel that their needs are being met within the relationship, but they also feel a sense of engagement in their work, play, and relationships with other friends and family members. Goldberg (1987) makes some excellent points pertaining to these issues:

> Probably the best or healthiest relationships begin without intensely romantic feelings, but where there is a genuine basis for being with each other on a friendship level and where there is enjoyment of each other's company without concern over commitment or future. Add to that a balanced flow of power, healthy conflict resolution free of blaming guilt, a sense of being known for who you are and knowing your partner, and a relaxed desire to be fully present with little need to escape or avoid through distraction, and you have a fine potential for growth in a good relationship. (p. 89) . . .

- *If they are in a committed relationship, they maintain this relationship by choice, not simply for the sake of any children involved, out of duty, or because of convenience.* They choose to keep their ties with each other even if things get rough or if they sometimes experience emptiness in their relationship. They share some common purposes and values, and therefore, they are willing to look at what is lacking in their relationship and to work on changing undesirable situations.

- *They are able to cope with anger in their relationship.* Couples often seek relationship counseling with the expectation that they will learn to stop fighting and that conflict will end. This is not a realistic goal. More important than the absence of fighting is learning how to fight cleanly and constructively, which entails an ongoing process of expressing anger and frustrations. It is the buildup of these emotions that creates trouble. If anger is not expressed and dealt with constructively, it will sour a relationship. Stored-up anger usually results in the target person getting more than his or her share of deserved anger. At other times bottled-up anger is let out in indirect ways such as sarcasm and hostility. If the parties in a relationship are angry, they should try to express it in a direct way.

• *Each person recognizes the need for solitude and is willing to create the time in which to be alone.* Each allows the other a sense of privacy. Because they recognize each other's individual integrity, they avoid prying into every thought or manipulating the other to disclose what he or she wants to keep private. Sometimes parents are guilty of not respecting the privacy of their children. A father may be hurt if his daughter does not want to talk with him at any time that he feels like talking. He needs to realize that she is a separate person with her own needs and that she may need time alone at certain times when he wants to talk.

• *They do not expect the other to do for them what they are capable of doing for themselves.* They don't expect the other person to make them feel alive, take away their boredom, assume their risks, or make them feel valued and important. Each is working toward creating his or her own autonomous identity. Consequently, neither person depends on the other for confirmation of his or her personal worth; nor does one walk in the shadow of the other.

• *They encourage each other to become all that they are capable of becoming.* Unfortunately, people often have an investment in keeping those with whom they are intimately involved from changing. Their expectations and needs may lead them to resist changes in their partner and thus make it difficult for their partner to grow. If they recognize their fears, however, they can challenge their need to block their partner's progress.

• *Each has a commitment to the other.* Commitment is a vital part of an intimate relationship. It means that the people involved have an investment in their future together and that they are willing to stay with each other in times of crisis and conflict. Although many people express an aversion to any long-term commitment in a relationship, how deeply will they allow themselves to be loved if they believe that the relationship can be dissolved on a whim when things look bleak? Perhaps, for some people, a fear of intimacy gets in the way of developing a sense of commitment. Loving and being loved is both exciting and frightening, and we may have to struggle with the issue of how much anxiety we want to tolerate. Commitment to another person involves risks and carries a price, but it is an essential part of an intimate relationship.

Dealing with Communication Blocks

A number of barriers to effective communication can inhibit the developing and maintaining of intimate relationships. Some of these barriers are failing to really listen to another person; selective listening—that is, hearing only what you want to hear; being overly concerned with getting your point across without considering the other's views; silently rehearsing what you will say next as you are "listening"; becoming defensive, with self-protection your primary concern; attempting to change others rather than first attempting to understand them; telling others how they are, rather than telling them how they affect you; bringing old patterns into the present and not allowing the other person to change; overreacting to a person; failing to state what your needs are and expecting others to know intuitively; making assumptions about another person without checking them out; using sarcasm and hostility instead of being direct; and speaking in vague terms such as "You manipulate me!"

In most of these cases you tend to be so concerned with getting your point across, defending your view of yourself, or changing another person that you cannot appreciate what the other person is thinking and feeling. These blocks make it very difficult to have what are called I-Thou encounters, in which two persons are open with themselves and each other, expressing what they think and feel and making genuine contact. Instead, the persons who are attempting to communicate typically feel distant from each other.

Deborah Tannen has written two best-selling books on the subject of communication between women and men. In *That's Not What I Meant* (1987), Tannen focuses on how conversational styles can make or break a relationship. She maintains that male-female communication can be considered cross-cultural. The language we use as we are growing up is influenced by our gender, ethnicity, class and cultural background, and location. Boys and girls grow up in different worlds, even if they are part of the same family. Furthermore, they carry many of the patterns they established in childhood into their transactions as adults. For Tannen, these cultural differences include different expectations about the role of communication in relationships. These factors make up our conversational style, and the subtle differences in this style can lead to overwhelming misunderstandings and disappointments. In her other book, *You Just Don't Understand* (1991), Tannen develops the idea that conversational style differences do not explain all the conflicts in relationships between women and men, but many problems result because partners are expressing their thoughts and feelings in different ways. She believes that if we can sort out these differences based on conversational style, then we are better able to confront real conflicts and find a form of communication that will allow for a negotiation of these differences.

[Carl R.] Rogers (1961) has written extensively on ways to improve personal relationships. For him, the main block to effective communication is our tendency to evaluate and judge the statements of others. He believes that what gets in the way of understanding another is the tendency to approve or disapprove, the unwillingness to put ourselves in the other's frame of reference, and the fear of being changed ourselves if we really listen to and understand a person with a viewpoint different from our own.

One of Rogers's suggestions for testing the quality of our understanding of someone is as follows: The next time you get into an argument with your partner, your friend, or a small group of friends, just stop the discussion for a moment and, for an experiment, institute this rule: "Each person can speak up for himself only after he has restated the ideas and feelings of the previous speaker accurately, and to that speaker's satisfaction" (p. 332). Carrying out this experiment implies that you must strive to genuinely understand another person and achieve his or her perspective. Although this may sound simple, it can be extremely difficult to put into practice. It involves challenging yourself to go beyond what you find convenient to hear, examining your assumptions and prejudices, not attributing to statements meanings that were not intended, and not coming to quick conclusions based on superficial listening. If you are successful in challenging yourself in these ways, you can enter the subjective world of the significant person in your life; that is, you can acquire empathy, which is the necessary foundation for all intimate relationships. Rogers (1980) contends that the sensitive companionship offered by an empathic person is healing and that such a deep understanding is a precious gift to another.

Effective Personal Communication

Your culture influences both the content and the process of your communication. Some cultures prize direct communication, while other cultures see this behavior as rude and insensitive. In certain cultures direct eye contact is as insulting as the avoidance of eye contact is in other cultures. Harmony within the family is a cardinal value in certain cultures, and it may be inappropriate for adult children to confront their parents. As you read the following discussion, recognize that variations do exist among cultures. Our discussion has a Euro-American slant, which makes it essential that you adapt the principles we present to your own cultural framework. You need to examine the ways that your communication style has been influenced by your culture and then decide if you want to modify certain patterns that you have learned. For example, your culture might have taught you to control your feelings. You might decide to become more emotionally expressive if you discover that this pattern is restricting you in areas of your life where you would like to be freer.

From our perspective, when two persons are communicating meaningfully, they are involved in many of the following processes:

- They are facing each other and making eye contact, and one is listening while the other speaks.
- They do not rehearse their response while the other is speaking. The listener is able to summarize accurately what the speaker has said. ("So you're hurt when I don't call to tell you that I'll be late.")
- The language is specific and concrete. (A vague statement is "I feel manipulated." A concrete statement is "I don't like it when you bring me flowers and then expect me to do something for you that I already told you I didn't want to do.")
- The speaker makes personal statements instead of bombarding the other with impersonal questions. (A questioning statement is "Where were you last night, and why did you come home so late?" A personal statement is "I was worried and scared because I didn't know where you were last night.")
- The listener takes a moment before responding to reflect on what was said and on how he or she is affected. There is a sincere effort to walk in the shoes of the other person. ("It must have been very hard for you when you didn't know where I was last night and thought I might have been in an accident.")
- Although each has reactions to what the other is saying, there is an absence of critical judgment. (A critical judgment is "You never think about anybody but yourself, and you're totally irresponsible." A more appropriate reaction would be "I appreciate it when you think to call me, knowing that I may be worried.")
- Each of the parties can be honest and direct without insensitively damaging the other's dignity. Each makes "I" statements, rather than second-guessing and speaking for the other. ("Sometimes I worry that you don't care about me, and I want to check that out with you, rather than assuming that it's true.")
- There is a respect for each other's differences and an avoidance of pressuring each other to accept a point of view. ("I look at this matter very differently than you do, but I understand that you have your own opinion.")
- There is a congruency (or a matching) between the verbal and nonverbal messages. (If she is expressing anger, she is not smiling.)
- Each person is open about how he or she is affected by the other. (An ineffective response is "You have no right to criticize me." An effective response is "I'm very disappointed that you don't like the work I've done.")
- Neither person is being mysterious, expecting the other to decode his or her messages.

These processes are essential for fostering any meaningful relationship. You might try observing yourself while you are communicating, and take note of the degree to which you practice these principles. Decide if the quality of your relationships is satisfying to you. If you determine that you want to improve certain relationships, it will be helpful to begin by working on one of these skills at a time. . . .

Inauthentic and Authentic Love

"Love" That Stifles

It isn't always easy to distinguish between authentic love, which enhances us and those we love, and the kind of "love" that diminishes ourselves and those to whom we attempt to give it. Certainly, there are forms of pseudolove that parade as real love but that cripple not only ourselves but also those we say we love.

The following are some characteristics that indicate a type of love that stifles. This list isn't rigid or definitive, but it may give you some ideas you can use in thinking about the quality of your love. A person whose love is inauthentic

- needs to be in charge and make decisions for the other person
- has rigid and unrealistic expectations of how the other person must act in order to be worthy of love
- attaches strings to loving and loves conditionally
- puts little trust in the love relationship
- perceives personal change as a threat to the continuation of the relationship
- is possessive
- depends on the other person to fill a void in life
- lacks commitment
- is unwilling to share important thoughts and feelings about the relationship
- resorts to manipulation as a way of getting the other person to respond in a predetermined manner

Most of us can find some of these manifestations of inauthentic love occurring in our relationships, yet this does not mean that our love is necessarily fraudulent. For instance, at times we may be reluctant to let another person know about our private life, may have excessive expectations of the person, and may attempt to impose our agenda. What is essential is to be honest with ourselves and to recognize when we are not expressing genuine love, for then we can change these patterns.

Some Meanings of Authentic Love

So far, we've discussed mostly what we think love is *not*. Now we'd like to share some of the positive meanings love has for us.

Love means that I *know* the person I love. I'm aware of the many facets of the other person—not just the beautiful side but also the limitations, inconsistencies, and flaws. I have an awareness of the other's feelings and thoughts, and I experience something of the core of that person. I can penetrate social masks and roles and see the other person on a deeper level.

Love means that I *care* about the welfare of the person I love. To the extent that it is genuine, my caring is not a smothering of the person or a possessive clinging. On the contrary, my caring liberates both of us. If I care about you, I'm concerned about your growth, and I hope you will become all that you can become. Consequently, I don't put up roadblocks to what you do that enhances you as a person, even though it may result in my discomfort at times.

Love means having *respect* for the *dignity* of the person I love. If I love you, I can see you as a separate person, with your own values and thoughts and feelings, and I do not insist that you surrender your identity and conform to an image of what I expect you to be for me. I can allow and encourage you to stand alone and to be who you are, and I avoid treating you as an object or using you primarily to gratify my own needs.

Love means having a *responsibility* toward the person I love. If I love you, I'm responsive to most of your major needs as a person. This responsibility does not entail my doing for you what you are capable of doing for yourself; nor does it mean that I run your life for you. It *does* imply acknowledging that what I am and what I do affects you, so that I am directly involved in your happiness and your misery. A lover does have the capacity to hurt or neglect the loved one, and in this sense I see that love entails an acceptance of some responsibility for the impact my way of being has on you.

Love means *growth* for both myself and the person I love. If I love you, I am growing as a result of my love. You are a stimulant for me to become more fully what I might become, and my loving enhances your being as well. We each grow as a result of caring and being cared for; we each share in an enriching experience that does not detract from our being.

Love entails *letting go of fear*. In *Love Is Letting Go of Fear*, Jampolsky (1981) writes about ways that worrying about past guilts and future fears allows little room to enjoy and savor the present. Not judging others is one way that I can let go of fear and experience love. Acceptance means that I am not focused on changing others so that they will conform to my expectations of how they should be.

Love means making a *commitment* to the person I love. This commitment does not entail surrendering our total selves to each other; nor does it imply that the relationship is necessarily permanent. It does entail a willingness to stay with each other in times of pain, uncertainty, struggle, and despair, as well as in times of calm and enjoyment.

Love means that I am *vulnerable*. If I open myself up to you in trust, then I can experience hurt, rejection, and loss. Since you aren't perfect, you have the capacity to hurt me; and since there are no guarantees in love, there is no security that your love will endure. Loving involves a sharing with and an experiencing with the person I love. My love for you implies that I want to spend time with you and share meangingful aspects of your life with you. It also implies that I have a desire to share significant aspects of myself with you. As Maier (1991) reminds us, one of the dimensions of love is our willingness to reveal ourselves to those whom we love. Reverend Maier indicates that Jesus provided us with a good role model for loving. Not only did Jesus share his beautiful sayings, but he shared his own frustrations and struggles, his hopes and fears, and his joys and pains as well. Maier believes that it is a challenge for us to love the way Jesus did, for doing so makes us vulnerable. After all, if we show who and what we are, people could reject us. "So it is difficult, even dangerous, to love by revealing ourselves. It is much easier to pretend to be what we are not and hide the parts that are not so lovely" (Maier, 1991, p. 42).

Love means *trusting* the person I love. If I love you, I trust that you will accept my caring and my love and that you won't deliberately hurt me. I trust that you will find me lovable and that you won't abandon me; I trust the reciprocal nature of our love. If we trust each other, we are willing to be open to each other and can shed masks and pretenses and reveal our true selves.

Love can tolerate *imperfection*. In a love relationship there are times of boredom, times when I may feel like giving up, times of real strain, and times I experience an impasse. Authentic love does not imply perpetual happiness. I can stay during rough times, however, because I can remember what we had together in the past, and I can envision what we will have together in our future if we care enough to face our problems and work them through. We agree with Maier (1991) when he writes that love is a spirit that changes life. Love is a way of life that is creative and that transforms. However, Maier does not view love as being reserved for a perfect world. "Love is meant for our imperfect world where things go wrong. Love is meant to be a spirit that works in painful situations. Love is meant to bring meaning into life where nonsense appears to reign" (p. 47). In other words, love comes into an imperfect world to make it livable.

Love is *freeing*. Love is freely given, not doled out on demand. At the same time, my love for you is not contingent on whether you fulfill my expectations of you. Authentic love does not imply "I'll love you when you become perfect or when you become what I expect you to become." Authentic love is not given with strings attached. There is an unconditional quality about love. Maier (1991, pp. 68–69) believes that the prayer of Saint Francis of Assisi is illustrative of a heart that is filled with unconditional love:

> O Lord, make me an instrument of Thy peace.
> Where there is hatred, let me sow love;
> Where there is injury, pardon;
> Where there is discord, union;
> Where there is despair, hope;
> Where there is darkness, light;
> Where there is sadness, joy;
> O Lord, grant that we seek not to be consoled, but to console;
> not to be understood, but to understand;
> not to be loved but to love.
> For it is in giving that we receive,
> in forgetting that we find ourselves,
> in pardoning that we are pardoned,
> and in dying that we are born to eternal life.
> Amen.

Love is *expansive*. If I love you, I encourage you to reach out and develop other relationships. Although our love for each other and our commitment to each other might preclude certain actions on our parts, we are not totally and exclusively wedded to each other. It is a pseudolove that cements one person to another in such a way that he or she is not given room to grow. Casey and Vanceburg (1985) put this notion well:

> The honest evidence of our love is our commitment to encouraging another's full development. We are interdependent personalities who need one another's presence in order to fulfill our destiny. And yet, we are also separate individuals. We must come to terms with our struggles alone. (Meditation of February 21)

Love means having a *want* for the person I love without having a *need* for that person in order to be complete. If I am nothing without you then I'm not really free to love you. If I love you and you leave, I'll experience a loss and be sad and lonely, but

I'll still be able to survive. If I am overly dependent on you for my meaning and my survival, then I am not free to challenge our relationship; nor am I free to challenge and confront you. Because of my fear of losing you, I'll settle for less than I want, and this settling will surely lead to feelings of resentment.

Love means *identifying* with the person I love. If I love you, I can empathize with you and see the world through your eyes. I can identify with you because I'm able to see myself in you and you in me. This closeness does not imply a continued "togetherness," for distance and separation are sometimes essential in a loving relationship. Distance can intensify a loving bond, and it can help us rediscover ourselves, so that we are able to meet each other in a new way.

Love is *selfish*. I can only love you if I genuinely love, value, appreciate, and respect myself. If I am empty, then all I can give you is my emptiness. If I feel that I'm complete and worthwhile in myself, then I'm able to give to you out of my fullness. One of the best ways for me to give you love is by fully enjoying myself with you.

Love involves *seeing the potential* within the person we love. In my love for another, I view her or him as the person she or he can become, while still accepting who and what the person is now. Goethe's observation is relevant here: by taking people as they are, we make them worse, but by treating them as if they already were what they ought to be, we help make them better.

Love means *letting go* of the illusion of total *control* of ourselves, others, and our environment. The more I strive for complete control, the more out of control I am. Loving implies a surrender of control and being open to life's events. It implies the capacity to be surprised.

A while ago a friend surprised me (Jerry), which jarred me into considering the value of surrendering control. I thought that my friend and I were going on an early morning hike up a mountain trail to watch the sunrise. When we got to the trailhead, to my total surprise, we climbed into a hot-air balloon for a ride that he had arranged. As we floated up into the skies at dawn, we saw the sunrise above the clouds and the mountains. Just before I climbed into the basket of the balloon, I felt a need to allay my anxiety, so I asked the pilot how long he had been doing this and if these balloons ever fell down. Calmly he let us know that he had been doing this for eighteen years and that these balloons fall out of the sky only if the pilot wants them to! With that reassurance, I was able to be present and absorb the beauty of the spectacular mountains, the rising sun, and the peacefulness of being taken by the current. I had absolutely no control over which direction we would move and I learned that the pilot had to allow the wind to move us. It dawned on me that living an overly controlled existence shuts out surprises such as this, and that I could not have experienced this majestic ride unless I was willing to be taken by the current and to trust the pilot and the forces of nature.

We conclude this discussion of the meanings that authentic love has for us by sharing a thought from Fromm's *The Art of Loving* (1956). His description of mature love sums up the essential characteristics of authentic love quite well:

> Mature love is union under the condition of preserving one's integrity, one's individuality. In love this paradox occurs that two beings become one and yet remain two. (pp. 20–21)

References

Bellah, R. N., Madsen, R., Sullivan, W. M., Swidler, A., & Tipton, S. M. (1985). *Habits of the Heart: Individualism and Commitment in American Life*. New York: Harper & Row.

Casey, K., & Vanceburg, M. (1985). *The Promise of a New Day: A Book of Daily Meditations*. New York: Harper/Hazelden.

Gibran, K. (1923). *The Prophet*. New York: Knopf.

Goldberg, H. (1987). *The Inner Male: Overcoming Roadblocks to Intimacy*. New York: New American Library.

Jampolsky, G. D. (1981). *Love Is Letting Go of Fear*. New York: Bantam Books.

Lerner, H. G. (1985). *The Dance of Anger: A Woman's Guide to Changing the Patterns of Intimate Relationships*. New York: Harper & Row.

May, R. (1973). *Man's Search for Himself*. New York: Dell.

Moustakas, C. (1975). *Finding Yourself, Finding Others*. Englewood Cliffs, NJ: Prentice-Hall.

Rogers, C. R. (1961). *On Becoming a Person*. Boston: Houghton Mifflin.

Rogers, C. R. (1980). *A Way of Being*. Boston: Houghton Mifflin.

Tannen, D. (1987). *That's Not What I Meant: How Conversational Style Makes or Breaks Relationships*. New York: Ballantine.

Tannen, D. (1991). *You Just Don't Understand: Women and Men in Conversation*. New York: Ballantine.

Review Questions

1. Give an example from your own experience of a relationship where the persons involved do not have very strong individual identities. Give an example of another relationship where they do.
2. What do the Coreys say about fault-finding and blaming in relationships?
3. Explain the conflict management suggestion by Carl Rogers that the Coreys include in their discussion about communication blocks.
4. What do the Coreys mean when they say that effective communication involves "specific and concrete" language and "personal statements instead of impersonal questions"?
5. Based on your own experience, which of the ten features of inauthentic love is most damaging or toxic?
6. Paraphrase: "Authentic love does not imply perpetual happiness."
7. Paraphrase: "Love means *letting go* of the illusion of total *control* of ourselves, others, and our environment."

Probes

1. How do you respond to these authors' comments about same-gender relationships? How might your response be reflected in your own communication with lesbian and homosexual individuals?
2. The Coreys say that in a meaningful relationship, "Each is able to talk openly with the other about matters of significance to the relationship." Are they suggesting that you need to be *completely* open and honest? What are some important limitations on this feature?
3. What might be the Coreys' rationale for beginning their discussion of "communication blocks" with a comment about *listening*? Why do they start at this end of the communication process?

4. Review the Coreys' eleven suggestions about effective communication from the perspective of a non-Euro American culture. What differences do you believe characterize effective communication in another culture?
5. The Coreys say that love means "having a *responsibility* toward the person I love," but that this does *not* mean running the other person's life or doing for the other person what he or she can do alone. So what does "responsibility" mean here?
6. How might the *vulnerability* that the Coreys discuss surface in interpersonal communication?

When I was looking for a brief but useful discussion of the couple relationship, I found the next reading in a book by Dolores Curran called *Stress and the Healthy Family.*

Curran learned the information that's reprinted here by interviewing thirty-two sets of spouses and eight single parents. She focused on how the couples handled stress, and my assumption is that the ability to handle stress is one feature of a healthy, strong relationship.

Curran identifies five characteristics of couples who handle stress in a healthy way: (1) they view stress as a normal part of family life, (2) they share feelings as well as words, (3) they develop conflict-resolution skills and creative coping skills, (4) they make use of support people and systems, and (5) they are adaptable. As Curran discusses each of these characteristics, you will probably notice similarities between what she found and what Adelman, Parks, and Albrecht found in their research on friendship in Chapter 11.

Curran makes two key points about the first characteristic. One is that healthy couples expect stress; they don't have an unrealistically romantic view of "the perfect relationship." A related point is that stress is usually generated by expectations. When you can manage your expectations, you can often manage your stress.

Her discussion of the second trait emphasizes the importance of what other authors discuss in Chapter 8, self-disclosure. Healthy couples were willing to take the risk of openness, and they developed nonthreatening ways to communicate feelings. Curran also notes that these couples' relationships typically developed into intimate *friendships*.

I omitted some parts of Curran's discussion of characteristic 3 because it overlaps material in this book's chapter on conflict. But Curran's treatment is useful because it reminds us of the central importance of conflict in all long-term, healthy relationships. Curran notes the importance of both conflict-resolution and coping skills.

Characteristic 4 echoes a point Adelman, Parks, and Albrecht made earlier: healthy couples pay attention to and use their networks to help them cope with stress. Frequently couples with short histories and newlyweds overlook the importance of strong support systems. They believe that their love can "conquer all" and that the two of them should be able to survive just fine on a desert island. The first really difficult problem or conflict reminds them of the truth of what Curran discusses here.

The final characteristic is adaptability. Given the pervasiveness of change in couple relationships—job change, geographic change, economic change, the changes caused by children, etc.—couples have to relax whatever white-knuckled grip they have on future plans so they can adapt to the circumstances that confront them.

Once again, the goal is not to lay out a prescription for the "perfect" couple relationship. But the guidelines suggested here can help you work toward a relationship that deals creatively rather than destructively with the problems you encounter.

The Couple Relationship

Dolores Curran

"I notice that when things are going well between us, other pressures disappear. But if we're not clicking, even the cat becomes a stress."

—FORTY-ONE-YEAR-OLD HUSBAND

"Clicking" is an apt word to use in looking at the basic factor in controlling everyday stress in the family. What makes couples click? What goes on inside the healthy spousal relationship that enables some couples to deal more effectively with time, money, work, and children than others? In an attempt to isolate commonalities among stress-effective couples, I interviewed and studied thirty-two couples and eight single parents identified as healthy by professionals who responded to my earlier research for *Traits of a Healthy Family*. Certain attitudes and characteristics surfaced among these families that give a clue to the dynamic which enables them to control normal stress well in their families.

Because the word *couple* in this book is necessary in discussing the two-parent family structure, I have used it frequently. However, the discussion applies to single-parent families as well. I suggest single parents substitute the word *family* where couple is used because in the single-parent family, the couple interaction usually transfers into a parent/children interaction, a parent/grandparent interaction, or a parent/friend interaction. I leave it to the single-parent reader to substitute whichever grouping is most appropriate. At times, of course, the use of couple is fitting for the single parent if the former spouse is involved in the issue under discussion.

The following are five characteristics of couples who handle stress in a healthy way:

- They view stress as a normal part of family life.
- They share feelings as well as words.
- They develop conflict-resolution skills and creative coping skills.
- They make use of support people and systems.
- They are adaptable.

1. The Healthy Couple Views Stress as a Normal Part of Family Life.

Healthy couples do not equate family life with perfection. Their expectations and goals are frequently lower than those of other couples. These couples don't link problems with self-failure, but rather anticipate stresses like children's behavior and occasional disagreements over money as a normal part of married life, and they develop ways of coping that are both traditional and unique.

Expectations in marriage play a foundational role in a couple's satisfaction with marriage. For example, if he expects her to be satisfied with his role as a good provider while finding his primary need for intimacy satisfied in his work, and she expects him to find his primary intimacy needs satisfied within the family, stress is predictable. Family scholars are bending their attention to this expectation factor in marriage to predict marital satisfaction. A recent paper delivered before the National Council on Family Relations provides an instrument to measure the degree of contrast between couple expectations in their relationship and complaints about the relationship.[1] If such an instrument becomes commonplace, couples may eventually be able to name their expectations before marriage rather than presume they share the same ones.

Couples often have very different expectations of what marriage and marriage roles mean. [One] woman said, "When we got married I was expected to stay home and be ready to be 'together' with my husband at a moment's notice. We had many arguments when I wanted to go back to school for a degree in social work; he deeply believed it was an insult to his masculinity and pride to have a wife who worked. Then it was OK with him if I worked—in fact, he was secretly very proud of me—as long as I didn't make much money or question the priority of his career." This couple had to renegotiate their expectations in order to deal with the normal stresses change brought. Later on, she ruefully reported, "Now I think he'd be happy to let me support him!"[2]

Couples with a strong spousal relationship expect change as part of growth and expect stress to result as part of this change. The first skill, then, in dealing with family stress springs from the couple's expectations and their ability to express them to one another.

2. The Healthy Couple Shares Feelings as Well as Words.

"In a survey, 5,000 German husbands and wives were asked how often they talked to each other. After two years of marriage, most managed two or three minutes of conversation at breakfast, more than 20 minutes over dinner, and a few minutes in bed. By the sixth year, the total was down to 10 minutes a day. A state of 'almost total speechlessness' was reached by the eighth year of marriage."[3]

Lack of communication is not an exclusively German phenomenon. "Whenever my husband is in a deep gloom, I have to play search and destroy," said an American wife. "Why won't he share his feelings? The more I search, the gloomier he gets." . . .

When I interviewed the couples who communicated effectively, I was struck by the many nonthreatening techniques they developed to get in touch with their own and their partners' feelings. "I learned early in our marriage not to say, 'What's bothering you?'" one woman said. "His answer was always, 'Nothing.' And if I pushed he became angry or silent. One day I told him, 'I feel so lonely when something's bothering you and you won't tell me . . . like I've failed.' And I meant it.

"He was astonished at my reaction. He said, 'I don't want you to feel like that. The reason I don't tell you my worries is because I don't want to worry you.'

"Here we were, both concerned about the other's feelings but I was accusing him of being unfeeling and he was accusing me of intruding. I convinced him that hiding his feelings was more painful to me than any worry he could share. We agreed that when I felt he was shutting me out, I would say to him, 'I'm feeling lonely,' and he'd try to be more open. It's taken a long time for us but it works. Sometimes it's a risk, though."

Risk is a word we hear often from couples when they talk about feelings. "He won't risk confrontation." "I can't risk telling her." Yet, intimacy is built upon risk. It implies being able to risk one's vulnerability by sharing feelings that might not be acceptable to the other. When partners risk and there's belittlement or no response at all, another layer of protection is built around feelings. Some couples have such thick walls that the only time feelings emerge is in explosive anger.

In an article, "The Stresses of Intimacy," Michael Griffin writes, "If there is going to be deep intimacy, there will be stress. There can be no deep intimacy between a couple unless there is a great deal of fighting about what is important. Two people who care deeply about what is important to them are bound to come into conflict. If intimacy is the most important thing in life then the price must be paid to achieve this in conflict and struggle. But the rewards can be enormous."[4]

Love and intimacy don't come easily, however. We know how to work and how to cook because these skills were prized in an earlier economic model of family. We accepted honorable labels like the "hardworking man" and the "good little mother" as applied to husbands and wives. As a consequence, persons who fit such labels became enshrined as the underpinning of successful marriages.

Today we find ourselves seeking intimacy at its deepest level in a highly technological society, but we (particularly men) don't know how to be intimate. Intimacy is a skill to be learned and to share, and yet we're novices as far as understanding it. How often I hear a wife say, "He's a wonderful provider, a good father, and never unfaithful *but* . . . ," and then she indicates that they can't talk or share feelings.

Psychiatrist Harold Lief, director of the Institute for Marital and Sexual Health in Philadelphia, believes that many people never learn to recognize and express feelings. "Fearful of sounding foolish or of bruising another's feelings, they're also tongue-tied by the risks of exposing themselves, of being vulnerable, of getting hurt. It *is* scary," Dr. Lief concedes, "but, if you play it too safe, your relationship will suffer. In effect, every couple truly committed to staying together have to create a language, a special code of words, gestures and actions that only they fully understand."[5]

I found that many healthy couples create their own code. Certain words give permission to open up while others warn, "Stay away." A letter from a reader of an article I wrote on family communication caused me to reflect on fear and lack of adequate language. She wrote, "I just finished reading your article and just have to tell you how much I enjoyed it. I only wish my husband would read it. *I intend to cut it out and mail it to his office* and hope he will take the time to read it as we could benefit from it." What an obvious communication problem right there. She has to mail the article to his office to get his attention. Their level of communication has become so impersonalized that it takes place through the U.S. mail, even though they live together. . . .

When couples begin to share feelings, they begin to become friends, not just spouses or lovers. This element of friendship is mentioned frequently by couples in good relationships. "We're good friends. We can talk about anything." Because most marriages begin with a sexual attraction rather than friendship, some couples never become good friends. . . .

I see a reluctance on the part of many young people today to cross the line from a friendship to a dating relationship. They realize that the nature of the relationship will change, and they don't want to jeopardize the friendship. It's a sad commentary on our cultural attitudes toward marriage—that spouses can't be friends. . . .

Thousands of "unmarried" marrieds in the world are lonely in their couple lives. For reasons of their own, they choose to remain in a relationship that began with love but deteriorated through the years. Carin Rubinstein and Phillip Shaver, authors of *In Search of Intimacy,* found that one out of every four Americans suffers from loneliness and that 13 percent of married people say they are lonely and not in love. Their research also showed that men need women more than women need men because women are intimacy-givers while men tend to be intimacy-takers.[6]

Even within couples who develop friendship, life is not always smooth because one may not enjoy what the other enjoys. I worked with a couple who had very different social preferences. He hated parties and socializing, and she loved them. "At first I tried to change him," she admitted. "I'd drag him to a cocktail party where he'd head for a corner and stand there while I flitted around having a wonderful time. Then I'd be angry with him on the way home for being antisocial."

He nodded and said, "It was a no-win situation. I didn't want to go in the first place because I knew I would fail her and get scolded for it. We had an argument after every party. What she didn't know was how I envied her ability to talk with strangers and have a good itme. I'm not good at that but I wish I was."

How did they deal with the stress affecting their relationship? He gathered the courage to tell her his real feelings—not that he disliked parties but that he was intimidated by them. A basic shyness, which she perceived as antisocial behavior, underlay his reluctance to attend that particular kind of social function. Once he risked his vulnerability to tell her he felt insecure in chatting with strangers, she reacted differently to his social needs.

"I felt awful," she said. "I didn't know he was shy and intimidated because he isn't that way with me or with our close friends."

Here is a common attitudinal change that takes place in healthy couples once they dare to risk sharing feelings. He risked, and she followed through with an important response to that risk: She accepted his feelings rather than discounting them by reacting with, "Nonsense. What's there to be shy about? Nobody's going to hurt you. Just get out there and start talking." . . .

We behave similarly with teenagers, and it drives *them* crazy, too. When they share with us that they're fat or ugly, we tell them they're not. Then we wonder why they become angry with such a loving response. If they feel fat and ugly, our words inflame them because we're actually telling them their feelings are worthless. (Besides, they expect parents to say such things. Didn't we tell them their kindergarten artwork was beautiful?)

A more effective response would be, "I know how you feel . . . I feel that way at times, too," or, "I'm sorry you feel ugly because I see such a lovely person in front of me." This doesn't discount their feelings but lets us share ours in a reassuring and supportive way. . . .

How did the couple with the party stress respond ultimately to their diverse social needs? Once the wife realized the basis for her husband's dislike of cocktail parties, she didn't insist they attend as many, and she no longer left him alone in a corner but led him into conversations. She also no longer criticized him for his antisocial behavior. They gravitated toward smaller functions, inviting close friends with whom he was comfortable.

In talking about it, they indicated they both tried harder to collaborate, he attempting to join in more and she expecting less. They dealt with the actual stress—his shyness—to change the perceived stress—parties. In order to do this, they had to risk sharing some deep feelings of insecurity and compassion. . . .

3. The Healthy Couple Develops Conflict-Resolution Skills and Creative Coping Skills.

Quite simply, the couples best able to deal with everyday stresses are those who develop workable ways of solving their disagreements and a fat supply of coping skills. Resolving conflict and coping are related, but not identical, skills.

Conflict-resolution skills depend largely on communication, while *coping skills* depend upon creativity, ingenuity, and perseverance. Some couples can have one set of skills and not the other. I met a couple who had excellent conflict-resolution skills. They could talk anything to death, share feelings, and emerge feeling good about themselves, but their family life was chaotic because they never *did* anything about the stresses attacking them. They just talked about them. The stresses went on and multiplied, and the couple finally sought help.

On the other hand, there are families in which stresses are addressed but not the conflict their resolution engenders. Maybe insufficient money stress is resolved by a husband's taking a second job, but the resentment this instills in him can be explosive. Such couples are constantly putting out brush fires as a response to stress rather than dealing with the dry prairie.

Let's look at *conflict resolution* first. Philip Blumstein and Pepper Schwartz, authors of *American Couples: Money, Work, Sex,* an exhaustive study on how couples interact, explained their purpose in studying how American couples deal with stresses: "Today's marriages require a new level of awareness and more commitment to problem solving. When marriage was forever, issues could be left alone because there was the understanding that the couple had a lifetime together to work them out. Because this is no longer the case, we hope that a little information can help people to spot vulnerabilities and give their marriage the best chance it has to be a satisfying lifetime experience."[7]

All stressors do not lead to conflict, but many do, particularly those that have to do with money, sex, children, and shared responsibility in the family. When these reach a high stress level, they can damage the spousal relationship if the couple lacks the skills needed to resolve conflict. . . .

And single parents, too, suffer increased stress if they are in continual conflict with former spouses. Robert E. Emery reviewed research findings that suggest that children's behavior may be affected more by the level of "family turmoil" surrounding the divorce than the separation itself; that many of the problems evident in the children of divorced parents were present long before the divorce occurred; and most significant, *that children of divorced parents whose family members are not in conflict exhibit fewer problems than those from two-parent families in which discord does exist.* From his evidence, the author suggests that parents try to keep children out of their conflicts and do everything they can to keep their individual relationships with their children supportive ones.[8]

Osolina Ricci, family therapist and author, says that divorced parents should get away from the idea that only mothers are important. "The parent who ends up with the least amount of time with the child is just as important to the child as the parent with the most amount of time," she says. The good divorce is not a mystery, even though there are a lot of hard feelings . . . It's hard work to have a good divorce, but the amount of time the parents spend to make it a good divorce the first couple years will come back to reward them one hundred-fold three and four years down the line."[9] . . .

Coping skills are discussed throughout this book so I will not develop them in depth here other than to say that the effective parents tend to collect, devise, and use a variety of coping skills rather than to depend upon the one or two most commonly used in our culture. For example, they don't automatically turn to grounding for every adolescent infraction but work out other consequences. When money gets tight, they don't automatically send a wife to work but try other methods of simplifying their life-style or share goods and services with others. Instead of automatically saying no to a child, they develop other responses. I loved the reaction of the mother whose eleven-year-old daughter wanted to use eye makeup. "You can use it as long as I can't see it," she said. It was a creative solution to a common family stressor.

Families who deal most effectively with stresses have hundreds of little solutions to share on allowances, television, sibling fighting, time pressures, and shared responsibility, and I will pass them on to you in the chapters ahead.

4. The Healthy Couple Makes Use of Support People and Systems.

"We couldn't have survived without our friends . . ."; "If I didn't have my family nearby . . ."; "The neighbors were there when we needed them . . ."; "I couldn't get over the support I got from our church . . ."

Stress-effective families and stressed families view support systems quite differently from one another. Stress-effective families see relatives, friends, groups, and community as valuable supports in dealing with stresses, while highly stressed families view them as evidence of their own inability to deal with stresses. Culturally, we came to believe that a good family was one that could handle its own problems. If it had to call upon relatives or neighbors for help in other than an emergency, it was not quite as "good" as other families.

Whatever the origin of this myth, I am appalled to find it still operating within pockets of our culture. We find, for example, cases of child abuse in which parents refuse to ask for help because they see such a request as a sign of weakness. The supports are there for them—loving family, hot lines, church mother's-day-out programs, friendly neighbors, a good community social service system which offers preventive skills—but even so these parents will risk abusing their children when stresses get too high rather than admit they need support and help.

Clearly, the most stress-effective families make the most use of support systems. When they need sudden childcare or when there's an illness or a problem, they have people to call upon, people who will call upon them as freely in return. I know a single mother, never married, who has a ten-year-old daughter. When she decided to keep her baby, her disapproving parents told her not to come to them if she needed help.

"I tried to prove to them that I could do it alone," she told me, " and as a result I nearly collapsed in stress overload. My therapist suggested a support group of other single parents and it has been my salvation. We call each other when we need support. We sit each other's children, loan dishes, furniture, even money. But most of all, we're family to one another. They are far more family to me than my own family."

Her experience is echoed in many studies of family support systems, particularly one by Nancy Colletta (1981), who found that those parents with high levels of support were more affectionate toward, closer to, and more positive with their children, while those with low levels of support were more hostile to, indifferent toward, and rejecting of their children.[10]

In today's highly mobile and technological society, we're not likely to find our relatives and old friends nearby. They may be a thousand miles away and available as support in an emergency but not in an everyday stress situation.

But we find the structured support group stepping in to meet the need for close family and friend networking. In the past few years, I have worked with support groups for families of Vietnam veterans, parents of unwed teenage mothers, bereaved parents, single-parent and stepparent families, pregnant women, parents of chronically ill family members, parents of adolescents, and others. I have great respect for these groups and often encourage stressed couples to consider becoming part of a support group to give them affirmation and confidence in their parenting. . . .

5. The Healthy Couple Is Adaptable.

Although many of these couples speak of entering marriage with set ideas of marriage and family life, they then mention—often with humor—how quickly they came to recognize and negotiate individual differences. Some spouses marry intending to change their partner to their own way of thinking.

Healthy couples adapt and borrow each other's techniques in resolving conflict and dealing with stress. One couple I interviewed spoke laughingly of their attitude toward sleeping late on Saturday morning. "When we married I was up at 6:00 A.M. to get at the housework," admitted the wife. "My husband slept until noon and I thought that was immoral. Now we both sleep until nine. We never made a conscious agreement about it—we just sort of evolved into it."

Whether or not to sleep late on Saturday is hardly a major point of stress, but the example does show how couples gradually come to respect each other's habits and needs. Adaptability is a feature found in stress-effective families.

When faced with a stress, adaptable couples are able to modify attitudes and habits to best meet it. An example of this ability may occur when a couple's employment conditions change. "When Peter lost his job, I was concerned, of course. But I knew we could scale down and get through it," reported one wife. "Our biggest problem was relatives who thought the world was going to end. We ended up reassuring them rather than the reverse."

Recently there has been intensive study on the family life cycle, particularly as it relates to stress and change. Dr. Hamilton I. McCubbin and Dr. Charles R. Figley invited top family scholars to contribute their insights and research on families and the stresses families experience as they move along the life cycle from courtship to old age. These scholars came from many different perspectives. But, according to the authors, "In spite of these differences in perspective, it is remarkable how much similarity these scholars see in how families respond to different stressors. The methods of functional coping are very similar across the different transitions and demands. These coping strategies include seeking information and understanding of the stressor event; seeking social support from relatives, friends, neighbors, others in similar situations, and professionals; being flexible about family roles, taking an optimistic view of the situation; and improving family member communication."[11]

Notes

1. Ronald M. Sabatelli, "The Marital Comparison Level Index: A Social Exchange Measure of Marital Satisfaction," unpublished paper.
2. Carol Tavris, "The Myth of the 50/50 Marriage," *Woman's Day*, March 6, 1984.
3. "Around the Network," *Family Therapy NetWorker*, March–April 1984.
4. Michael Griffin, O.C.D., "The Stresses of Intimacy," *Spiritual Life*, 1979.
5. Diane Hales, "Marriages That Get Better and Better," *McCall's*, January 1983.
6. Carin Rubinstein and Phillip Shaver, *In Search of Intimacy* (New York: Delacorte Press, 1982).
7. Philip Blumstein and Pepper Schwartz, "What Makes Today's Marriages Last?" *Family Weekly*, November 13, 1983.
8. Robert E. Emery, "Interpersonal Conflict and the Children of Discord and Divorce," *Psychological Bulletin* (92) 2.
9. Mary Meitus, "Therapist Supports Shared Parenting," *Rocky Mountain News*, February 12, 1984.
10. Hamilton I. McCubbin and Charles R. Figley, eds., *Stress and the Family: Coping with Normative Transitions*, vol. I (New York: Brunner/Mazel, 1983).
11. Ibid.

Review Questions

1. According to Curran, what's the relationship between expectations and stress?
2. What's the relationship between intimacy and risk?
3. Give an example from your own experience of a time you and a close friend created your own code.
4. According to Curran, what's the relationship between stress and conflict in a couple relationship?
5. Which kind of support system does Curran believe is most helpful for a couple, an informal system of friends, or a more formal group?

Probes

1. What are some weaknesses in Curran's research methods? To what degree do those weaknesses undermine the validity of the points she makes? How does your own experience lead you to verify or to challenge what she says?
2. Ask a married person you know to keep track over a one-week period of the number of minutes per day that person spends communicating with his or her spouse. How do your results compare with the ones Curran cites?
3. How do you view the connection between a dating relationship and a friendship? Which has to come first? Do they both need to go together?
4. Recall when you were a teenager. How do you respond to what Curran says about how parents behave with teenagers?
5. In your opinion, what is the most important/useful kind of support system for a couple?

This reading offers a fairly complete outline of how to think about and prepare for a productive, rather than a destructive conflict. The authors have a long connection with *Bridges Not Walls.* In 1972, when I was working on the first edition of this book, I wrote Hugh Prather asking for permission to reprint excerpts from his book *Notes to Myself.* I was struck by how his brief, journallike notations captured several of the central points I wanted this book to make. He generously agreed to let me use some of his material, and his selections have appeared prominently in this book ever since. Now Hugh and his wife Gayle have written *A Book for Couples,* and I believe their discussion of conflict is among the best I've read.

They begin with an example of a typical everyday conflict that reveals how many issues are often buried in an argument between friends or intimates. It starts as an argument about the cat window and only lasts a couple of minutes, but the Prathers identify seventeen separate issues that get raised. No wonder arguments like this create more problems that they solve!

The next important point that's made in this reading is that discussions like the one about the cat window "create the relationship's terrain." In other words, the way these discussions are carried out defines the quality of the couple's relationship. This means that *process* is vital. *How* an argument happens is more important than the outcome that emerges. Process is literally more important than product.

With their tongues firmly planted in their cheeks, the Prathers then offer seven "magic rules for ruining any discussion." You can probably recognize some of your favorite fighting moves in this list—I know I do. The point of the list is to contrast the main features of productive and destructive conflict.

Then the authors explicitly highlight the point about process that they introduced earlier. They urge you to recognize that when you are in a conflict with a person you're close to, "to agree is not the purpose." Rather, "The only allowable purpose" for this kind of discussion "is to bring you and your partner closer." This, it seems to me, is a profoundly simple but important idea. It challenges one primary assumption most of us carry into our conflicts with people we care about: that the point is to get my way, be sure the other knows how I feel, or make the other feel bad. What might happen if couples could actually internalize this idea: that the real point of our argument is to get closer?

The rest of this reading builds on this foundation. The Prathers offer five steps for preparing to argue. All these guidelines make good sense and, taken together, as I mentioned earlier, they provide a fairly comprehensive outline of how to prepare to "do" conflict well. I won't repeat what they say here, but I do want to highlight some points.

Preparation step 2 is to "try to let go" of the issue you're thinking of raising. Although I don't think it's good to suppress genuinely felt emotions, I do believe that couples could frequently profit from applying this suggestion. I've found that it can frequently be relaxing, freeing, and empowering simply to let an irritation go.

Preparation steps 4 and 5 operationalize the Prathers' point about the only allowable purpose for a conflict. It's revealing to ask about a conflict whether "communication is your aim" rather than winning or venting. It is also helpful for me to try to be clear that "the problem is the relationship's and not your partner's."

As I read some sections of their essay I am a little frustrated by what can sound like oversimplification and rose-colored naivete. The real tough arguments are much more intense and difficult than these two authors seem to realize. But when I look again at their advice, I recognize that they understand well enough how gut-wrenching a fight with a loved one can be. They are simply convinced, as have been a great many wise people over the ages, that returning anger for anger doesn't help. Ultimately love, which in this case means the often unromantic commitment to a relationship, is stronger than defensiveness and bitterness.

How to Resolve Issues Unmemorably

Hugh and Gayle Prather

Unfinished Arguments Accumulate

It's not that issues don't get resolved. Indeed they are settled but settled like ketchup settles into a carpet. An uncleaned carpet can triple in weight within five years, and most relationships get so laden with undigested arguments that they collapse into a dull, angry stupor and cease to move toward their original goal.

"Albert, you've just got to install the cat window. I woke up again at 3 A.M. with Runnymede standing on my chest staring at me. I'm not getting enough alpha sleep."

"Sorry about that, Paula. I'll get to it this weekend."

"But Albert, you've been saying that for a month."

"Well, you know, honey, we could just put the cat out at night like everyone else."

"Oh, sure, and then what if he needed to get in? What if something was after him? What then?"

"What difference will the cat window make? He can still stay out all night if he wants to."

"Yes, Albert, but he can *also* get in if he *needs* to. You know, if you're not going to be a responsible pet owner, you shouldn't have a pet."

"Now there's a thought."

"I see. And I guess you don't mind breaking Gigi's heart."

"That's another thing, Paula, her name is Virginia, not Gigi. Why do we have to have a cat named Runnymede and a daughter named Gigi? Besides, I'll buy her a nice stuffed Garfield after the cat is comfortably settled in at the animal shelter."

"You know, Albert, this conversation is opening my eyes to something I've felt for a very long time."

"What's that, Paula?"

"You only care about mixed soccer. Since joining that team with the silly name you haven't been playing horsey with Gigi and you haven't been scratching Runnymede under the chin where he can't lick. You certainly pretended to like Runnymede well enough when we were dating."

"You were the one who insisted I join the team. You were the one who said it would be good for me to 'get out of the house for a change.' I like the cat. I love my daughter. But I don't want to spend my Saturdays ruining a window with a perfectly good view."

"I guess you don't really care about me either, Albert. And you can stand there calmly peeling your Snickers while wanting Runnymede to be gassed. If I didn't know how much emotion you devote to *mixed* soccer I would say you have become psychotically insensitive and unfeeling. Perhaps you should seek help."

Here Albert, proving that he is neither insensitive nor unfeeling, flings his Snickers at the window in question, grabs his soccer gear, and storms from the house, where in an afternoon match playing goalie for the Yuma Yuccas he fractures the middle three phalanges in his right hand, thus ending the question of installing anything.

Each New Issue Resurrects the Old

We wish we could say that this dialogue was a transcript but it is a composite. If we reprinted verbatim some of the typical arguments we have heard during counseling, they would be dismissed as overwrought fiction. The large number of digressions seen here is actually commonplace and illustrates the typical residue of unsettled questions found in most long-term relationships. The difference between this and the average disagreement is that some of these words might have been thought but left unspoken. Yet the feeling of estrangement by the end of the argument would have been the same.

On this Saturday morning Paula is upset because her sleep continues to be interrupted by the cat asking to be put out. That is the sum of the issue. If the couple had sat down together instead of using the problem as a means of separating still further, they could easily have solved this one difficulty in any of a hundred different mutually acceptable ways. But a hive of older discord lies just beneath their awareness, and therefore settling just one problem in peace is harder than it would seem.

The cry of unresolved issues is strong and persistent. Any couple will feel their failure to have joined. They yearn to bridge the old gaps and fear the potential of further separation more than they welcome the opportunity to reverse the process. To bring up former differences during a discussion is not blameworthy, it is in fact a call for help, but it is mistimed.

Without realizing it—because most arguments are conducted with no deep awareness—Albert and Paula allude to seventeen other issues, none of which had to be brought up to solve *this* problem. In the order they appear, here are the questions they have left unanswered in the past, a small fraction of the total residue if you consider all the others that will be mentioned in future arguments: (1) Why has Albert's promise gone unfulfilled for a month? (2) Should the cat be left out overnight? (3) Is

Albert irresponsible? (4) Should the family continue having this pet? (5) Is Albert insensitive to his daughter? (6) Should Paula continue calling Virginia "Gigi"? (7) Should the cat be renamed? (8) Would a stuffed animal sufficiently compensate? (9) Is mixed soccer affecting Albert's attitude toward his daughter and pet? (10) Does the team have a silly name? (11) Is Albert being sufficiently attentive to Paula or has he changed in some fundamental way? (12) Does Paula want Albert around the house? (13) How important is the window view to Albert's happiness? (14) Does Albert still love Paula? (15) Should Albert eat Snickers? (16) Is Albert's contact with other women on Saturdays the root cause of his, in Paula's view, wavering commitment to his family? (17) Does Albert have serious psychological problems?

As can be seen here, it is not easy for most couples to concentrate on a single issue. Nevertheless it is certainly possible and, in itself, to practice doing so will begin giving them a new kind of evidence: that within this relationship there are still grounds for unity and happiness. If one of the partners deviates from this guideline, the other should not make still another issue of this or get caught up in the irrelevant point raised, but should see instead the real desire behind the digression and treat it gently and answer it with love.

Discussions Create the Relationship's Terrain

. . . To resolve issues in the usual way is as damaging to a relationship as not resolving them at all, because the gap is not truly bridged and the unsuccessful attempt merely adds more weight to the couple's doubts about each other. In the argument over the cat window, Paula's concern about the health of her marriage surfaces, a question of far greater importance to her than how she will manage to get more sleep, and yet without fully realizing it she exacerbates this larger problem and works against her own interests. By arguing in the manner they did, this couple, as do most, merely manufactured new issues between them. Albert probably did not mean to take that hard a stand on getting rid of the cat—he may actually have wanted to keep it. And Paula did not have real doubts about Albert's mental health.

The past that drives so many relationships into the ground is built piece by piece, smallness fitted to smallness, selfishness answered with selfishness. Yet the process is largely unconscious. Each couple quickly settles into a few sad methods of conducting arguments, but seldom is the means they use thought through or the results closely examined. One person nags, the other relents. One person reasons, the other becomes silent. One person flares, the other backs down. One person cajoles, the other gives in. But where are the joy and grandeur, where is the friendship that was supposed to flourish, the companionship that through the years was to fuse an invulnerable bond, a solace and a blessing at the close of life? Instead there is a bitter and widening wedge between the two, and even the briefest of discussions contains a hundred dark echoes from the past.

No matter how entrenched are our patterns of problem solving, they can be stepped away from easily once we see that they do not serve our interests. The only interest served in most discussions is to be right. But, truly, how deep is this? Do we actually want to make our partner wrong, to defeat a friend, and slowly to defeat a friendship? It certainly may feel that way. Caught up once again in the emotions of a disagreement, we stride doggedly toward our usual means of concluding every argument: adamant silence, crushing logic, patronizing practicality, collapsed crying, quelling anger, martyred acquiescence, loveless humor, sulking retreat.

These postures and a thousand more are attempts to prove a point other than love, and as with all endeavors to show up one's partner, the friendship itself is the victim, because the friendship becomes a mere tool, a means of making the other person feel guilty. The love our partner has for us is now seen as leverage, and in our quiet or noisy way we set about making the relationship a shambles, not realizing that we ourselves are part of the wreckage.

The Magic Rules for Ruining Any Discussion

. . . The dialogue with which we began this chapter incorporates a few of but not all the rules for disastrous communication—yet only one or two are needed to neutralize the best of intentions. Follow these guidelines, even a little sloppily, and you are guaranteed a miserable time:

1. *Bring the matter up when at least one of you is angry.*

   Variations: Bring it up when nothing can be done about it (in the middle of the night; right before guests are due; when one of you is in the shower). Bring it up when concentration is impossible (while driving to a meeting with the IRS; while watching the one TV program you both agree on; while your spouse is balancing the checkbook).

2. *Be as personal as possible when setting forth the problem.*

   Variations: Know the answer before you ask the question. While describing the issue, use an accusatory tone. Begin by implying who, as usual, is to blame.

3. *Concentrate on getting what you want.*

   Variations: Overwhelm your partner's position before he or she can muster a defense (be very emotional; call in past favors; be impeccably reasonable). Impress on your partner what you need and what he or she must do without. If you begin losing ground, jockey for position.

4. *Instead of listening, think only of what you will say next.*

   Variations: Do other things while your partner is talking. Forget where your partner left off. In other words, listen with all the interest you would give a bathroom exhaust fan.

5. *Correct anything your partner says about you.*

   Variations: Each time your partner gives an example of your behavior, cite a worse example of his or hers. Repeat "That's not what I said" often. Do not accept anything your partner says at face value (point out exceptions; point out inaccuracies in facts and in grammar).

6. *Mention anything from the past that has a chance of making your partner defensive.*

   Variations: Make allusions to your partner's sexual performance. Remind your husband of his mother's faults. Compare what your wife does to what other women do, and after she complains, say, "I didn't mean it that way."

7. *End by saying something that will never be forgotten.*

Variations: Do something that proves you are a madman. Let your parting display proclaim that no exposure of your partner could be amply revealing, no characterization too profane, no consequence sufficiently wretched. At least leave the impression you are a little put out.

To Agree Is Not the Purpose

All couples believe they know how to hold a discussion, and yet it is not an exaggeration to say that in most long-term relationships there has rarely been one wholly successful argument. Obviously they are filled with disagreements that end in agreements, but when these are examined, it can be seen that at least a small patch of reservation had to be overlooked in order for accord to be reached.

We believe this is simply how differences are settled, and so even though we sense that our partner is still in conflict, we barge ahead with our newly won concession, thinking the bad moment will pass. Later it becomes painfully clear that it has not and we judge our partner irresolute. Or if we are the one who complied, we count our little sacrifice dear and wait for reparation—which never comes or is never quite adequate, and we cannot understand why our partner feels such little gratitude.

The aim of most arguments is to reach outward agreement. Until that is replaced with a desire for friendship, varying degrees of alienation will be the only lasting outcome. Couples quickly develop a sense of helplessness over the pattern that their discussions have fallen into. They believe they are sincerely attempting to break out of it and are simply failing. They try different responses, going from shouting to silence, from interminable talking to walking out of the room, from considering each point raised to sticking tenaciously to one point, but nothing they do seems to alter the usual unhappy ending.

There is no behavioral formula to reversing the habitual course of an argument. It requires a shift in attitude, not in actions, even though actions will modify in the process. No more is needed than one partner's absolute clarity about the purpose of the argument. This is not easy but it is simple. Therefore let us look again at what the aim should be. . . .

The only allowable purpose for a discussion is to bring you and your partner closer. Minds must come together to decide instead of backing away in order to apply pressure. How is this possible, given the fact that you and your partner are deeply selfish! Fortunately, the selfishness is compartmentalized and your hearts remain unaffected. You need not eliminate it; merely bypass it because you recognize that it is not in your interests to be selfish. To the ego, this concept is insane because it sees no value in love. But love is in your interests because you *are* love, or at least part of you is, and thus each discussion is a way of moving into your real self.

A little time is obviously needed to see one's true interests. If you rush into a discussion you will operate from your insensitivity by habit and aim for a prize your heart cares nothing about. Do not kid yourself. You *do* know whether the discussion is ending with the two of you feeling closer. The selfish part of your mind will tell you that the little sadness and sense of distance you may now feel was a small price to pay for the concession you won or the point you made. Or it will argue that it was all unavoidable. This may happen many times before you begin reversing your ordinary way of participating. This transition is an important stage of growth and entails looking more and more carefully at selfish impulses and their aftermath. Is how you feel really worth it? Was the way it went truly unavoidable?

Thus you will come to see the result you want, and this deeper recognition will begin to eclipse your pettiness in the midst of an argument. Gradually you will catch the mistakes sooner, and eventually you will learn to avoid them from the start. For you *do* want these times of deciding to warm your hearts and lighten your steps. So persist in the guidelines we will give, and these little defeats to your relationship will slowly give way to friendship.

We are so used to thinking of a discussion as a symbol of separation that it can often be helpful to change its form enough that something new will appear to be happening and thus the old mind set is undercut. To take the usual process, break it into steps and put them in order is usually all that is needed to accomplish this.

An issue could be said to pass through five stages in reaching resolution. First, it must be thought of by at least one of the partners as an issue. Second, a moment is chosen to bring the matter up. Third, a decision is made as to the manner in which it will be presented. Fourth, there is an exchange of thoughts and feelings. And fifth, the discussion is concluded.

Most couples give very little thought to the first three stages. They simply find themselves in the thick of a so-called spontaneous argument and no one is certain at what point it began. Obviously you must become more conscious of the subjects you bring up so carelessly. Any sign of fear over what you are about to say is a very useful indicator. If you see you have a question about whether to say it, let this be your cue to break these preliminary choices into conscious steps. Do not begrudge the time, remember instead how strongly you want to begin building a real friendship.

Five Steps in Preparing to Argue

First, you might ask yourself if the issue you are thinking of is actually a present issue or merely one you have been reminded of. In other words, be certain this is currently a problem and not one the relationship may already be on its way to solving. Many people habitually rake over their marriage for signs of imperfection and naturally they find a great many, but it can be far more disrupting to friendship to be constantly questioning and comparing than to wait to see if the problem continues in any severe way. Meanwhile, enjoy what is already between you without telling yourself what this is. . . .

If the issue is unquestionably a present one, the second step you might try is to let go of it. Letting go is not "better," but it is an option that current values tend to underrate. However, it must be accomplished thoroughly and honestly or the issue will grow like mold in a dark unseen place. If it is done consciously dismissal is not denial. Essentially it entails examining in detail what you do not like and then making a deliberate effort to identify with another part of you that never "takes issue" with any living thing, that is still and at ease, that acts only from peace. . . .

If a couple espouses world energy consciousness or is on a tight budget, for one of the partners to habitually leave the hot water running, not turn off lights, or keep the refrigerator door open may be grating or even shocking to the other partner. Yet the spectacle of someone wasting energy and money is *not* grating or shocking. The interpretation we assign it, and not the act itself, determines the emotions we feel. Jordan, age two, is "shockingly irresponsible." He has even been known (yesterday, in fact) to flush a toilet five times in a row and then run to tell his big brother about the accomplishment. "John, I flush, I flush!" "That's nice." said John, blatantly contributing to the delinquency of a minor. The reason Jordan didn't tell his father (who is the family's conscience in these matters) was that he was the very one who kept showing him how it was done, thereby encouraging him to waste over fifteen gallons of water (plus six more his father used researching that figure). . . .

So here we have four reactions issuing from four interpretations: pride from the father, support from the seven-year-old, excitement from the two-year-old and, having no originality, curiosity from the cat. Clearly no uniform effect was produced by an external and unreachable cause. How then might you let go of your reaction to your spouse's wasteful habits in lieu of bringing it up one more time? Certainly you would not try dishonestly to convince yourself that the practice was not costing money or energy. Or that it did not really matter to you. Neither would you attempt to assign some motive to your partner's acts that you did not believe, such as not knowing any better or really trying hard but being unable to stop. Dishonesty does not end an unhappy line of thought. That is why reinterpretation is generally not effective. . . .

If in your moment of consideration you are able to see these facts deeply enough, you may open your eyes to your partner's innocence and no longer feel compelled to understand why he or she does these things. But if after making the attempt to free your mind you see that you have not let the issue go, then perhaps to bring it up would be the preferable course, for undoubtedly that is better than storing anger or fear. . . .

The third step is to consider if this is the time. If you feel an urge to bring it up quickly, be very alert to anger. Your heart is willing to wait but your ego is not, especially if it senses an opportunity to strike back. The ego is merely our love of misery, of withdrawal and loneliness, and it can feel like our own deep impulse even though it exists on the most superficial level of the mind.

For too long now our relationships have been jerked around by our own lack of awareness. There is more to your mind than selfishness. So be still a moment and let peace arise from you. Is this the time? A simple question. There need not be great soul-searching and hand-wringing over it. If your partner has just done something and this is the issue, clearly he or she is likely to be more defensive if instantly called on it. If your partner is not in a particularly happy frame of mind, is hostile, worried or depressed, a more receptive state will surely come and nothing is lost by waiting. Is this the time? Merely look and know the answer. The urge to attack when you are angry is very strong, but if you will allow yourself time to reflect on your genuine feelings, this will do more to relieve your frustration.

The fourth step is to be certain that communication is your aim. Trying to get someone to change is not communication because you have already decided what change is needed. Your partner is therefore left with nothing to say and will definitely feel your unwillingness to consider, to listen, to appreciate. So before you speak take time to hear your heart.

You are not two advocates arguing a case. You are interested in joining, not in prevailing. You are like the directors of a business you both love coming together to help it over a difficult situation. You don't care from whose lips the solution comes. You welcome the *answer*. To this end what are you willing to do if your partner becomes defensive? Are you prepared, and have you prepared, to carry through your love of the relationship? . . .

The final point to consider is whether you are clear that the problem is the relationship's and not your partner's. In our example the problem was not Paula's, because her lack of sleep was affecting Albert also. One person's jealousy, appetite, hypersensitivity, frigidity, phobia or any other characteristic that has become an issue cannot successfully be viewed as more one's responsibility than the other's because friendship is always a mutual sharing of all burdens. . . .

You must understand that unless you make a specific effort to see through the fallacy, you *will* go into a discussion thinking one of you is more to blame than the other, and this will make it very hard to listen and be open. Learn to treat every issue as an impersonal and neutral enemy and to close ranks against it. An addiction, for example, can be viewed as you would a hurricane or a deluge—you need each other's help to survive the storm. Our dog, Sunny Sunshine Pumpkin Prather (whose very name is a masterpiece of family compromise), gets sprayed by a skunk about once a month and the smell is everyone's problem. What good would it do to blame the dog? And yet we have seen other families get angry at their dog "for being so stupid.". . .

These preliminary steps, which should only take an instant or two to complete, will at least make it possible for a discussion to begin with some chance of success. Now you are ready for a *real* argument, one in which your minds can join rather than separate.

Review Questions

1. What point are the Prathers making by listing seventeen issues that were brought up in the argument between Albert and Paula?
2. What do the authors mean when they say that discussions "create the relationship's terrain"?
3. Paraphrase this statement: "The only allowable purpose for a discussion is to bring you and your partner closer." Do you agree or disagree with it? Explain.
4. What do the authors mean when they say that you should "Learn to treat every issue as an impersonal and neutral enemy and to close ranks against it"?
5. What keeps the "protect your gains" step from being selfish?

Probes

1. What alternative do the authors offer to "being right" in a conflict?
2. What general principle or principles are violated by the seven "Magic Rules for Ruining any Discussion"? In other words, what general attitudes makes these moves destructive?
3. Which of the five steps for preparing to argue do you *least* often follow? What does that fact tell you about your way of "doing" conflict?
4. A fundamental, perhaps even a radically different perspective or point of view is behind just about everything the Prathers say about "resolving issues unmemorably." By "different," I mean different from the attitude we normally carry into a conflict. How would you describe this alternative point of view or perspective?

This next reading comes from a best-selling book called *Fire in the Belly: On Being a Man.* Its author, Sam Keen, has a theology degree from Harvard and a PhD from Princeton, and was a longstanding consulting editor of the popular journal, *Psychology Today.* One of Keen's goals here is obviously to spearhead the growing "men's movement." But another is to separate what he calls the "false mystification of gender" from the "authentic mystery of gender."

Keen points out that he uses the term *mystery* in order to underscore the fact that there are no simple, open-and-shut answers to the problems all of us experience in our intimate partnerships. As he puts it, "The mystery of our sexual being is not something that can be settled by science." One point of his argument is to warn readers to be wary of claims that "biology is not destiny," as if we could learn completely to overcome patterns we follow because we are male or female.

As you might expect from a peson with his background, Sam Keen argues that, if you're going to understand the mystery of the genders, you'll need to recognize that "the language of sexuality and spirituality mingle." In other words, he claims, the sexual and the sacred are connected. What does this mean? In part it means that "Love increases the mystery of the self and the other. In love we learn," just as we learn in our spiritual lives, "to respect and adore what is beyond understanding, grasping, or explanation."

Keen's discussion of marriage emphasizes that it is *not* "a lifelong romance." Instead, most married people discover that they respond to this level of intimacy in part by rediscovering or reinventing patterns of relating that were learned unconsciously in our families of origin. He illustrates the love-hate tensions that often surface for married men in a letter addressed, "Dear Jananne." He also discusses how many men respond to the inevitable tests of marriage vows and the problem of maintaining fidelity. The key, he concludes, is to be able to look on the same woman with "both respect and desire."

Keen's comments about cocreation begin with the important claim that "Sex may teach a man and woman the delight of coming together; marriage may suffuse us with the comfort and healing that comes from knowing and being known; but it takes a child to tutor us in the virtue of hope." One of his main points is that it is both blind and foolish to think or talk about heterosexual sex without taking into consideration the potential triad of man-woman-child. This is a profound truth that much of the thinking about men's liberation (and women's) seems to overlook. With the help of his own personal experience, Keen explains the truth that's in the politically and religiously conservative claim, "Nothing makes up for failure in the family." On this point, in fact, this highly-educated liberal agrees with the conservative sentiment: "For better and for worse, the family is the first line of defense against dehumanization and misplaced loyalty." "The only revolution that will heal us," Sam Keen believes, "is one in which men and women come together and place the creation of a rich family life back in the center of the horizon of our values." He acknowledges that abusive, alcoholic, and otherwise addicted families are often worse than no families at all. But, he insists, no other institution can be substituted for this one. His advice to contemporary men is to help build healthy families by "becoming the kind of fathers we wanted but did not have." Unmarried, childless, and gay men can participate in this quest, too.

You will probably find this reading provocative—maybe even angering. You certainly don't have to agree with everything Sam Keen writes. But, especially if you're male, I hope you'll approach this excerpt with an open mind. Men have some issues to face in our relationships that are as profound as those that define women's liberation.

Men and Women: Becoming Together

Sam Keen

The Mystery of Man and Woman

Once we have stripped away all the false mystification of gender, an authentic mystery of gender remains. Beneath the facade of socially constructed differences between men and women, there is a genuine mystery of biological and ontological differences.

Gabriel Marcel proposed a distinction between problem and mystery that is helpful in thinking about gender. A problem involves questions that can be solved because the observer can gain objective distance, pose crucial experiments, and verify hypotheses. We know how to discover whether there is life on Mars or whether the AIDS virus responds to a specific medicine. A mystery at first appears to be merely a problem that is difficult to solve. Am I free, or is my life predetermined? What are the essential—noncultural—differences between men and women? A little reflection shows that in a genuine mystery the distinction between subject and object breaks down. A mystery is something in which I am involved. If, for instance, I ask: Should I commit myself to this marriage? or, Is there any meaning in life? there is no objective, scientific standpoint I can occupy to answer such questions. I cannot separate myself from my life—my will, my values, my sense of meaning, my gender—in order to get a definitive, verifiable answer to any of these questions. There are more and less intelligent ways to explore and clarify the mystery of our lives but we cannot reduce the great mythic questions—"Where did I come from? What should I do? For what may I hope? What is a heroic man? What is a heroic woman?"—to problems that can be solved.

The question of gender is penultimately a problem, but ultimately a mystery. The social sciences can tell us how different societies structure gender roles, how they define heroes and heroines, how they educate, condition, and initiate boys into the status of manhood and girls into the condition of womanhood. In this sense we can strip away the false mystification that surrounds gender. But underneath the stereotypes lies a true mystery. God did not make persons,—chairpersons, mailpersons, or spokespersons—only men and women. Peel away the layers of the social conditioning and there remains the prime fact of the duality of men and women. Throughout the eons of history we move toward becoming fully human only through a sexual dance of men and women. Each sex is one side of a Möbius strip, a fragment necessary to create a whole.

The mystery of our sexual being is not something that can be settled by science. It is who we are and where we come from. It is deeper than our ability to abstract and objectify. We know more about it than we can ever explain or articulate. Every theory is more simplistic than the facts. Anthropology, sociology, psychology, etc., can show us how we self-limit and give social definition to the genders, how we form and deform.

But it can never reduce the preconscious, presocial duality of the sexes to an adequate explanation.

There is a contemporary mind-set that wants to reduce gender to a problem we can solve, an inconvenience we can overcome, a mistake we can, finally, set right. The battle flag of this movement carries the slogan: "Biology is not destiny." Its hope is that, with proper social and biological engineering, women can be "liberated" from bondage to their wombs and from the degrading work of raising children.

Science fiction writers have best seen the logical consequence of this project to free human beings from "bondage" to biology. When gender becomes a problem to be solved rather than a mystery to be reverenced, science and technology can be counted on to produce a solution that will encourage human beings to become more like machines, computers, robots. As we engineer our way out of the bondage to gender, the values of the marketplace replace those of the family and efficiency triumphs over compassion. The encompassing arms of the mother and the muscular arms of the father are replaced by incubators and the care of professional, anonymous child-handlers. In due course, a world without gender makes obsolete those names we have invested with a numinous power only a little less than God's—Mother and Father. The unfortunate byproduct of such a technologically rationalized, centrally planned, economically oriented society is that it destroys all the forms of love—friendship, erotic love, and worshipful—that make our lives sweet.

So, what's the difference between a man and a woman? I can't say, but that doesn't mean that I can't recognize the difference. A genuine mystery is protected by silence that remains after analysis and explanation. We approach the mystery of our being by respectful listening, by recollecting our experience, by cherishing paradox and, above all, by loving what we cannot reduce to understanding.

There is a way for man and woman to come together that does not depend on correct explanations, a language in which we celebrate the communion of opposites—in love and sex. When we penetrate to the deepest level of our experience of gender, we inevitably come to a point where the language of sexuality and spirituality mingle. Since the beginning of recorded human history, the phallus and vulva have been metaphors for the sacred. Carnal knowledge and spiritual awareness, the mystery of sexuality and the mystery of being, have been joined tongue in groove. Sexuality teaches us about the sacred, and vice versa.

> "They try to say what you are, spiritual or sexual?
> They wonder about Solomon and all his wives.
> In the body of the world, they say, there is a Soul
> and you are *that*
> But we have ways within each other
> that will never be said by anyone."
>
> "At night we fall into each other with such grace.
> When it's light, you throw me back
> like you do your hair.
>
> Your eyes now drunk with God
> mine with looking at you,
> one drunkard takes care of another."
>
> —RUMI, *OPEN SECRET**

*John Moyne and Coleman Barks, trans., *Open Secret: Versions of Rumi* (Putney, VT: Threshold Books, 1984).

The sexual and the sacred both shatter the categories of our understanding. After thirteen pages of careful reasoning about how we may give names to God, Thomas Aquinas concludes, "But finally we remain joined to Him as to one unknown." In the same way, man and woman are joined to each other as beings unknown, and we commune within a mystery that encompasses us. The love between us is a coming together and a going apart in which the fragments we are as sexual beings move together within the economy of an unseen whole.

Love increases the mystery of the self and the other. In love we learn to respect and adore what is beyond understanding, grasping, or explanation. Together we play our separate parts in the drama of creation. Strangers in the night, opposites joined in a passionate dance, keeping step to an echo of a distant harmony we must strain to hear. Moving toward and away from each other; two becoming one becoming two becoming one, ad infinitum.

Paean to Marriage: The Conjunction of the Opposites

Marriage is: an aphrodisiac for the mature; a great yoga; a discipline of incarnate love; a task that stretches a man and a woman to the fullest; a drama in which a man and woman must gradually divest themselves of their archetypes and stereotypes and come to love each other as perfectly flawed individuals.

As a spiritual path, a dance of individuation and communion, marriage begins on the far side of romance.

If you consider marriage a lifelong romance, you are certain to be disillusioned. The shallowest of complaints is that marriage destroys romance. Of course it does. Marriage is designed to allow two people to fall out of love and into reality.

In romance two people plant a seed in a common pot, fertilize it, water it, turn it toward the sun, rejoice when it buds and blossoms. When it flowers they believe it will last foever. But the greater the passion, the more the affair hastens toward its predestined climax. The plant is stifled by its own growth; it becomes rootbound. To continue to flourish it needs more room to grow. The time for decision arrives. Does the couple invest in a larger pot and transplant what has begun to flower between them, or do they abandon the plant and begin again? One way leads toward the deepening commitments of marriage, the other toward an addiction to romance that requires the changing of partners whenever passion, excitement, and intensity fade.

Recently I cleared a flat place by the stream that had been overgrown with thimbleberries and small alders. After cutting the underbrush, I pulled up plants and roots and cultivated the soil until it was fine and soft. I planted clover, watered it, and waited. Within a week the clover sprouted. Two weeks later thimbleberries charged out like bullies in a schoolyard. Impossible! I had destroyed their entire root system, ground them up into little pieces. I pulled up the offending youngsters by the ears and found that each had sprouted from a disconnected fragment of the original, and that the separate plants were already reaching out to form an interconnected network.

Love may blossom in romance, but in marriage we return to our deep psychic roots that are mysteriously alive no matter how many times they have been severed. Many of us—separated and alienated from our families of origin, divorced, veterans of many love affairs—are surprised when we approach intimacy and commitment to find infantile feelings, needs, expectations we had exiled or repressed come flooding back.

Why does marriage and the threat-promise of intimacy put our souls in a pressure cooker?

Romance is all "yes" and heavy breathing—an affair built around the illusion of unbroken affirmation. Marriage is "yes" and "no" and "maybe"—a relationship of trust that is steeped in the primal ambivalence of love and hate.

> Dear Jananne. I love and hate you: find you desirable and terrible, satisfying and maddening, a helpmate and a saboteur. I was rich and wounded in history long before I knew you. You are a nectarine grafted onto an apricot branch grafted onto peach root stock that goes deep into the ground of my being. In you I taste generations of women who have nurtured and injured me—my ex-wife, past lovers, my mother, my grandmother. One moment I am encompassed in your earth-mothering arms, tendered and warmed. A moment later I look into your face and see bloody Kali ready to devour me. I know you as a woman who can take up a flute and improve on the music of the spheres, and an hour later play the shrill bitch. Light-bringer and shadow monster, creator and destroyer. You delight me, except for those times I could wring your neck and dance a jig on your grave.

But marriage and the family may provide the best hospital for our ancient wounds. When we vow to marry for better and worse, we implicitly pledge our willingness to reopen the terror and beauty of innocence. The promise of childhood, the birthright each child genetically claims in its flesh, the cry of life is, "I deserve to be loved unconditionally." Our innate sense of our own goodness carries with it the innocent expectation that we are lovable in our entirety. But this promise is inevitably broken. All parents, all cultures, systematically stunt the young. Love is given on the condition that we are pleasing, that we perform well, that we obey the "oughts." Every child is expelled from the paradise of perfect love. We compromise and become adults. But the hope for unconditional love does not die, it only lies dormant. When we marry it springs to life again. Before God we vow the impossible secret hope of our heart, to love and cherish, without condition, so long as we both shall live.

Inevitably marriage vows are put to the test. Will she really love me when she sees the worst; when she sees my sadness, my insecurity, my domineering, my little-boyish whining and bullying ways? Will he really love me when he sees my anger, my aggressive demands, my guilt-tripping manipulations, my seductive little-girl ways? Sure as night follows day, when the trust deepens between a man and a woman, their infantile selves will come out of hiding. I will play the brat I was forbidden to be, you will play the bitch. We will cease being "nice" to each other. All the unfinished business I have with women in general and Mother in particular, all the unfinished business you have with men in general and Father in particular, all of the credits and debits of the Keen and the Lovett clans, become psychic soil that we two must turn over, plow, and tend together.

The alchemy of unconditional love that heals us only takes place when a man and a woman, knowing the best and worst of each other, finally accept what is unacceptable in the other, burn their bridges, and close off their escape routes.

As a rule, men fare better in marriage than when single. Studies show that married men live longer, are healthier, and make more money. But fidelity seems to come harder to us than to women. Common wisdom tells us that we are phobic about commitment, and that even when we are well married we continue to desire many women.

Maybe we want sexual variety because we are programmed by evolution to sow our seed as widely as possible. Maybe we want numerous women to bolster our sense of our own masculinity. Whatever the reasons for our resistance to monogamy, the great virtue of marriage is that it presents us with a chance to heal the split within ourselves, between passion and tenderness, between our schizophrenic images of woman as whore or virgin. Until a man can look on the same woman with both respect and desire, he remains the victim of his own ambivalence—a boy-child, a playboy.

Cocreation: Familial Love and the Fatherhood of Men

In the last generation, far too much of our thinking about men and women circled around sexual skills, romantic love, and the changing dynamics of marriage in the era of the two-career family. Both men and women have increasingly divorced the discussion of gender from our biological and spiritual destiny as the bearer, nurturers, and initiators of children. To try to distance ourselves from the only creative act that requires the unique endowments of a man and a woman is certain to cause us confusion.

Sex may teach a man and woman the delight of coming together; marriage may suffuse us with the comfort and healing that comes from knowing and being known; but it takes a child to tutor us in the virtue of hope. In sex we forget ourselves and inhabit the present moment; in marriage we remember and heal the wounds of the past; in creating a child we invest all that we are in a future that extends beyond our days.

The starting point for thinking about the mystery of gender, for cherishing the ineradicable differences between the sexes, for celebrating the coming together of the opposites, is the procreation of a child. It would be folly to try to return to the silly and repressive medieval notion that only heterosexual acts between partners desiring to conceive a child are justified. But it seems to me equally foolish to think that we can explore manhood and womanhood, male or female sexuality, without placing children at the center of our attention. To retain our humanity we need to preserve something of the ancient feeling of the awful-sweet mystery of sexuality that is reflected in the worship of the creative phallus and the fertile womb. Primitive peoples know what we are beginning to forget—sexuality is wonderful and terrible because it is our link with the creative power of being, itself. If ever we lose sight of the ontological fact that human sexuality is defined by a situation that implicitly involves the triad of man-woman-child, we neglect something of the spiritual dimension of sexuality.

A strange kind of forgetfulness seems to affect much of the recent writing and thinking about men's liberation. The men's movement has allowed men to talk about how much we have been wounded by the missing father, how we long for the fathers we never knew, how insecure we feel because our fathers never initiated us into manhood. But then, strangely, the family is seldom mentioned as a major arena within which virility is exercised. Often men who suffer from the father vacuum resolve to be intimate with their sons and spend quality time with them, but somehow the family remains on the outer edge of men's circle of values.

I had been divorced for five years when I saw a billboard, smack in the middle of the smoggy, industrial section of Richmond, with the dire message: "Nothing makes up for failure in the family." My immediate reaction was to start an argument with the billboard evangelist, to defend myself and the multitude of my fellow divorcés who had broken up families for what we considered the best of reasons. "That's asinine! What a guilt trip! A good divorce is better for the kids than a bad marriage. And, anyway, divorce is not necessarily the sign of 'failure.' And, besides that, my kids are living with me and I am 'making up' their loss to them. And, and, and . . ." Not until I had exhausted my self-defense did I simmer down and let the full weight of the proposition sink in and think about it in a calm manner.

It has now been twelve years since I saw the billboard. My daughter and son from my first marriage are grown and lovely. I am remarried and I have a ten-year-old daughter. After considerable meditation on the matter, I have come to believe that the message of the billboard is both true and prophetic. In watching my children struggle with the hurts and discontinuities that are the inevitable result of the irreconcilable differences between their parents, I have learned what many men learn only after divorce. There is nothing more precious than our children. In the quiet hours of the night, when I add up the accomplishments of my life in which I take justifiable pride—a dozen books, thousands of lectures and seminars, a farm built by hand, a prize here, an honor there—I know that three that rank above all the others are named Lael, Gifford, and Jessamyn. In the degree to which I have loved, nurtured, and enjoyed them, I honor myself. In the degree to which I have injured them by being unavailable to them because of my obsessive preoccupations with myself or my profession, I have failed as a father and as a man.

The health, vitality, and happiness of the family is the yardstick by which a man, a woman, a society should measure success and failure. I suggest that the decline of honor in family is directly related to the continuing cold war between the sexes, the escalating climate of violence and the sense of the vacuum of meaning that haunts our time. As far as I can see, there is no way for men and women to recover wholeheartedness, to become passionate and truly free, without rediscovering the central importance of the family. A man or woman without an abiding investment in family, children, and generations yet to come is a straw blowing in the wind.

To understand how crucial the existence of strong families is to the cultivation of free spirits we might meditate on the odd fact that the first target of tyrants and utopians of the political right and left is always the family. From Plato to Marx to Mao, all those thinkers who want society organized so individuals will fit into some overarching five-year plan for the ideal republic, the ideal socialist or religious state, inevitably try to replace the family and place the education of the young in the hands of state-run institutions. Under the banner of freeing women for productive work, or liberating the young from the prejudices of the old, or instilling the values necessary for an ideal commonwealth, parents and children are separated or allowed minimal contact. The motive behind this antipathy toward the family is not difficult to find. So long as men's and women's prime loyalty is to family and kin, they cannot be controlled by the state or any other institution. But if they can be convinced to switch their loyalty to some "higher" cause or institution, they will obey the dictates of their leaders.

For better and for worse, the family is the first line of defense against dehumanization and misplaced loyalty. Within the privacy of the home, we may think, speak, and worship as we please. We may educate our children in the values we cherish and teach them respect for the traditions we uphold. Because it is easiest to love our own children unconditionally, the family is the natural school of love. Loving our kin, we may gradually learn to extend kindness to strangers. And because children incarnate our hopes, they are our visceral evidence of the wisdom of investing our time and care in the lives of others.

Almost without noticing it, we are voluntarily eroding the freedoms and surrendering the loyalties that no tyrant could take from us without a fight. By our increasingly slavish devotion to the economic order, we are destroying the cradle of freedom. The iron law of profit is best served by those who are willing to depersonalize themselves by valuing efficiency above compassion, and devotion to the competitive goals of the corporation over loyalty to family.

A history of the word "economics" contains a parable that illuminates our present dilemma and offers a challenge to men and women. Originally "economics" meant "the art of managing a household" and it contained the notion of thrift and voluntary simplicity. Later, under the impact of the industrial revolution, "economics" came to mean the system of production, distribution, and consumption of commodities. When factory, store, office, and bank usurped the loyalties of men and replaced the home as the center of economic activity, women who chose to give serious attention to homemaking were given the condescending title of "home economists." And the final transformation, which is to say degradation, of the dignity of the home, is symbolized by a recent change made at the University of Iowa. What was once the College of Home Economics has now been renamed the College of Consumer Sciences.

The only revolution that will heal us is one in which men and women come together and place the creation of a rich family life back in the center of the horizon of our values. A letter I got recently from a woman makes the point: "Perhaps the real shift will come when men fully realize, in the gut and not just in the head, that they are equally responsible, with women, for the creation, nurturing, and protection of children—that children are not simple sex objects, ego trips, or nuisances, but their first responsibillity—before war, money, power, and status."

You may object: "All of this is well enough in theory, but unfortunate in fact, for many people the family was a vicious trap and a cruel destiny. The place that should have been a sanctuary was often a torture house. The arms that should have held us often pushed us away. Many flee the family because it was the place of injury, captivity, disappointment, abuse. The children of alcoholics and abusive parents fear marriage and family and find their solace in becoming solitary. There are so many bad marriages and dysfunctional families it sometimes seems only reasonable to junk the institution or invent a replacement." True enough, but hopes of replacing the family with some more perfect institution, like hi-tech pipe dreams of creating space colonies into which we can escape when we have polluted the earth, have proven to be both dangerous and deluded. It is within the bonds of what is familial that we must live or perish.

Fortunately, the profusion of dysfunctional families does not necessarily predict a grim future for the family. One of the standard themes in mythology is the promise of the wounded healer. In our hurt lies the sources of our healing. The bird with the broken and mended wing soars the highest. Where you stumble and fall, there you find the treasure.

One of men's greatest resources for change is our wound and our longing for the missing father. We can heal ourselves by becoming the kind of fathers we wanted but did not have. Create out of the void, out of the absence. Our best map for parenting is outlined like a photographic negative in the shadow side of our psyches. Get in touch with your disappointment, your rage, your grief, your loneliness for the father, the intimate touching family you did not have, and you will find a blueprint for parenting.

Become the father you longed for. We heal ourselves by learning to give to our children what we did not receive.

If you are not married, do not have children, or are gay, find a friend's child who needs nurturing and become a part-time substitute parent. It strikes me that the lack of substantial manliness one finds in some gay communities is a result not of a homoerotic expression of sexuality, but of the lack of a relationship of nurturance to the young. To be involved in creating a wholesome future, men, gay or straight, need an active caring relationship to children. A man who takes no care of and is not involved in the process of caring for and initiating the young remains a boy no matter what his achievements. This generation of men knows by its longing for fathers who were absent that nothing fills the void that is created when men abandon their families, whether out of selfishness, dedication to work, or devotion to "important" causes. When anything becomes more important to a society than the welfare of its children, it is a sure sign of spiritual disintegration.

There is a felicitous match between what men need to learn for their own wholeness, and attitudes and skills that are necessary for fathering. The child-within-the-man can best be healed by caring for a child who is to become a man. Children are our playmates and teachers. These days many men, lamenting that they experienced no rites of initiation into manhood, are gathering in small groups and experimenting with creating new rites and rituals. This is well and good, but we need to remember that a solid sense of manhood is not something we can ultimately get from any ceremony. Male initiation may involve a ceremony, but the reality in back of it is what happens day by day in the nitty-gritty contact between a boy and the significant men in his life, especially his father. A boy naturally learns how to be a man by observing how his father treats women, how he deals with illness, failure, and success, whether he shares in the household chores, whether he cuddles and plays. We first and forever [or not at all] learn our infinite worth from the look of adoration we see in our parents' eyes. We learn the delights of sensuality from their enjoyment of our innocent bodies—cuddling, wrestling, tickling. We learn to trust in a world that contains evil when we come crying with a skinned knee and are held, hurting, in arms; and the voice that is forever assuring us, "Everything is going to be all right." We learn to give ourselves generously to create a better future that we will not live to see by the sacrifices our parents make on behalf of our becoming.

The second time around with marriage and fatherhood, I learned that the most important thing I can do as a father is to create a sense of welcome. By allowing my delight to overflow, I imprint a message on my child's psyche: "I welcome you, the world welcomes you. We appreciate your being and take joy in your becoming." Erik Erikson said in *Identity and the Life Cycle* that the first developmental task of childhood is achieving a sense of basic trust. I would rather think of the first necessity as achieving a sense of basic delight. A child whose sheer existence is a joy to its parents will begin life with a sense that it is desired, its being is a gift, the world will welcome its creativity. And one of the best ways to do this is to get down and get physical. In the beginning most of my ideas of what would be fun for Jessamyn were far too complex. I finally discovered that what she liked most was rough wrestling, and stories invented on the spot. When someone asked her what she liked about me her reply was, "I like his wrestle." It is hard to overemphasize children's need for touch, cuddling, and holding.

I am also learning to talk to children, not at them. First time round as a father I had truckloads of rules, oughts, ideals, and explanations—all of which kept me at arm's

length from my chidren. I thought it was my responsibility to overse
experience from my superior position, to protect them from comp
and from the harsh realities of the world until they were ready to c
I have come to believe that the best thing I can give my children is an
of what I feel, think, and experience, to invite them into my inner world, te
stories that will give them some sense of my pilgrimage as a man.

The other night I had a dream in which my father slipped, fell down the stairs, and hurt himself. As he started to get up I said to him, "You always try to be so large and tough, even when you are hurt, and you never let anybody hold you." He turned to me, curled up in my arms, and allowed me to hold him. I woke from the dream with a heaviness in my heart, a refrain from an old hymn on my lips, and a question in my mind. The line was from the hymn, "When we are strong, Lord, leave us not alone, our refuge be." The question was: Who holds the father? I have learned to allow the little boy in myself to be held. Women have often done that for me. But who nurtures and comforts the strong man when he is hurt or weary? Three days after the dream I got the answer to my question. My son, Gifford, arrived in Sonoma to help me build our house. He is the head builder. I am contractor and general workman. The circle of familiar love begins to complete itself. His coming of age ritual marks my passage into autumn. The father who once held the small boy within his arms is now tended by the strong arms of his manchild.

Review Questions

1. According to Sam Keen (and Gabriel Marcel), what's the difference between a "problem" and a "mystery"? Why is this difference significant in this discussion?
2. What does it mean to say that the sexual and the sacred overlap, that is, that you can't understand the mystery of sex except by grappling with the mystery of the spiritual?
3. What does Keen mean when he says that marriage is *not* "a lifelong romance"?
4. Paraphrase Keen's discussion of the problem and the promise of fidelity for a man.
5. Keen agrees with many of his contemporaries that it's silly to believe that only heterosexual sex between partners desiring to conceive a child is justified. But he also believes that there's some truth in that point of view. Explain his position.
6. Some people argue that families are the source of many of the *problems* men and women experience today, not of the *solution*. How does Keen respond to this point?
7. What are some specific communication suggestions that Keen offers to fathers?

Probes

1. *Why* does this author believe that "science" cannot teach us everything we need to know about relationships between the sexes?
2. Keen suggests that the way to approach a genuine mystery is "by respectful listening, by recollecting our experience, [and] by cherishing paradox. . . ." I think that these same principles can be applied to our *communication* with someone we love. If they were applied, what do you think it would mean you should do as a communicator?
3. What point about marriage is Keen's thimbleberry story meant to illustrate?
4. Keen's letter to Jananne is pretty intense. If you're married—or have been—does it capture part of your experience of your partner? What point do you think Keen is trying to make with this letter?
5. How do you respond to Keen's comments about the importance and value of the family?
6. This excerpt presents only a few of only one person's views of "the men's movement," or "men's liberation." But based on what is here, how would you describe this part of the men's movement's approach to interpersonal communication?

Bridging
Differences

Chapter 14

Conflict

T his reading comes from the first chapter of a conflict management textbook written by three speech communication teachers. It lays out some of the basic ideas that I think it's important to understand if you're going to approach conflict constructively and effectively.

The authors begin with a "textbook case" that illustrates both the bad side and the potentially good side of conflict. Although they don't emphasize this point, the case shows how your view of conflict can strongly affect the ways you deal with it. For example, many people view conflict as always painful. From this point of view, unless you enjoy being blamed, put down, and shouted at, it's hard to be positive about conflicts. But if you see conflict as something entirely negative, you'll behave accordingly and will probably help create a self-fulfilling prophecy—the more you believe it's awful, the worse it will get. As the case study shows, there are actually some benefits to conflict. Feelings get out in the open where they can be dealt with, and often people discover creative solutions to problems that had stumped them. So the first step toward handling conflict effectively is to be open to the positive values of conflict so you can, as these authors suggest, analyze "both the specific behaviors and interaction patterns involved in conflict and the forces that influence these patterns."

Folger, Poole, and Stutman define conflict as "the interaction of interdependent people who perceive incompatible goals and interference from each other in achieving those goals." This means that struggles inside one person's head are not "conflict" as it's defined here. Conflict always involves communication. The definition also emphasizes that conflict doesn't happen unless the people involved are interdependent. It only happens when one person's beliefs or actions have some impact on the other's. Otherwise the parties could just ignore each other.

The central section of this chapter distinguishes productive from destructive conflict interaction. One difference is that productive conflicts are *realistic*, which means that they focus on substantive problems the parties can potentially solve, while *nonrealistic* conflicts are mainly expressions of aggression designed to defeat or hurt the other. Productive conflict attitudes and behaviors are also *flexible*, while destructive ones are *inflexible*. In addition, productive conflict management is grounded in the belief that all parties can realize at least some of their goals, while destructive conflict is thoroughly win/lose. Finally, productive conflict happens when the parties are committed to "working through" their differences, rather than either avoiding them or simply favoring one position over the other.

In the final section the authors develop the idea that *every* move made in a conflict has impact on the other parties, and that this is why conflicts often degenerate into destructive cycles or patterns. These cycles can only be understood as unified wholes, and they can often be self-reinforcing. This means that, if you want to manage conflict effectively, you have to (a) look for the cycles, and (b) be willing and able to take unilateral action to break the destructive pattern. Subsequent readings in this chapter suggest what you can do *after* this to handle conflicts more effectively.

Conflict and Interaction

Joseph P. Folger, Marshall Scott Poole, and Randall K. Stutman

The Potential of Conflict Interaction

It is often said that conflict can be beneficial. Trainers, counselors, consultants, and authors of conflict textbooks point to the potential positive functions of conflict: conflicts allow important issues to be aired; they produce new and creative ideas; they release built-up tension; they can strengthen relationships; they can cause groups and organizations to reevaluate and clarify goals and missions; they can also stimulate social change to eliminate inequities and injustice. These advantages, and others, are raised in order to justify conflict as a normal, healthy occurrence and to stress the importance of understanding and handling it properly.

But why must such an argument be made? Everyone has been in conflicts, and almost everyone would readily acknowledge at least some benefits. Why then do social scientists, popular authors, and consultants persist in attempting to persuade us of something we already know? Perhaps the answer can be found by studying an actual conflict. The twists and turns of a specific case often reveal why negative views of conflict persist. Consider the fairly typical case study of a conflict in a small work group in Case I.1.

Case I.1   The Women's Hotline Case

Women's Hotline is a rape and domestic crisis center in a medium-sized city; the center employs seven full- and part-time workers. The workers, all women, formed a cohesive unit and made all important decisions as a group; there were no formal supervisors. The Hotline had started as a voluntary organization and had grown by capturing local and federal funds. The group remained proud of its roots in a democratic, feminist tradition.

The atmosphere at the Hotline was rather informal. The staff saw each other as friends, but there was an implicit understanding that people should not have to take responsibility for each other's cases. Since the Hotline's work was draining, having to handle each other's worries could create an unbearable strain. This norm encouraged workers to work on their own and keep problems to themselves.

The conflict arose when Diane, a new counselor who had only six months' experience, was involved in a very disturbing incident. One of her clients was killed by a man who had previously raped her. Diane had trouble dealing with this incident. She felt guilty about it; she questioned her own ability and asked herself whether she might have been able to prevent this tragedy. In the months following, Diane had increasing difficulty in coping with her feelings and began to feel that her co-workers were not giving her the support she needed. Diane had no supervisor to turn to, and, although her friends outside the Hotline were helpful, she did not believe they could understand the pressure as well as her co-workers.

Since the murder, Diane had not been able to work to full capacity, and she began to notice some resentment from the other counselors. She felt the other staff were more concerned about whether she was adding to their work loads than whether she was recovering form the traumatic incident. Although Diane did not realize it at the time, most of the staff felt she had been slow to take on responsibilities even before her client was killed. They thought Diane had generally asked for more help than other staff members and that these requests were adding to their own responsibilities. No one was willing to tell Diane about these feelings after the incident, because they realized she was very disturbed. After six months, Diane believed she could no longer continue to work effectively. She felt pressure from the other women at the center, and she was still shaken by the tragedy. She requested two weeks off with pay in order to get away from the work situation for a while, reduce the stress she felt, and come back with renewed energy. The staff, feeling that Diane was slacking off, denied this request. They responded by outlining, in print, what they saw as the responsibilities of a full-time staff worker. Diane was angry when she realized her request had been denied, and she decided to file a formal work grievance.

Diane and the staff felt bad about having to resort to such a formal, adversarial procedure. No staff member had ever filed a work grievance, and the group was embarrassed by its inability to deal with the problem on a more informal basis. This added to tension between Diane and the staff. The staff committee who received Diane's grievance suggested that they could handle the problem in a less formal way if both Diane and the staff were willing to call in a neutral third party mediator. Everyone agreed that this suggestion had promise, and a third party was invited to a meeting where the entire staff would address the issue.

At this meeting, the group faced a difficult task. Each member offered reactions they had been unwilling to express previously. The staff made several pointed criticisms of Diane's overall performance. Diane expressed doubts about the staff's willingness to help new workers or to give support when it was requested. Although this discussion was often tense, it was well directed. At the outset of the meeting, Diane withdrew her formal complaint. This changed the definition of the problem from the immediate work grievance to the question of what levels of support were required for various people to work effectively in this difficult and emotionally draining setting. Staff members shared doubts and fears about their own inadequacies as counselors and agreed that something less than perfection was acceptable. The group recognized that a collective inertia had developed and that they had consistently avoided giving others the support they needed to deal with difficult rape cases. They acknowledged, however, the constraints on each woman's time; each worker could handle only a limited amount of stress. The group recognized that some level of mutual support was essential and felt they had fallen below that level over the past year and a half. One member suggested that any staff person should be able to ask for a "debriefing contract" whenever they felt they needed help or support. These contracts would allow someone to ask for ten minutes of another person's time to hear about a particularly disturbing issue or case. The group members adopted this suggestion because they saw it could allow members to seek help without overburdening each other. The person who was asked to listen could assist and give needed support without feeling that she had to "fix" another worker's problem. Diane continued to work at the center and found that her abilities and confidence increased as the group provided the support she needed.

This is a "textbook" case in effective conflict management because it resulted in a solution that all parties accepted. It does, however, exhibit several features in common with even the most destructive conflicts and could easily have turned in a destructive direction. First, the situation was **tense** and **threatening**. The weeks during which the incident evolved were an extremely difficult time for the workers. Even for "old hands" at negotiation, conflicts are often unpleasant and frightening. Second, participants experienced a great deal of **uncertainty**. They were unable to understand many aspects of the conflict and how their behavior affected it. Conflicts are confusing; our actions can have consequences quite different from those we intend because the situation is more complicated than we assume. Diane did **not** know her co-workers thought she was slacking. So when she asked for time off, she was surprised at their refusal, and her own angry reaction nearly started a major battle. Third, the situation was extremely **fragile**. If even one worker had acted differently at several crucial points, the conflict might have gone differently. If, for example, the staff had chosen to fire Diane, the conflict might have been squelched, or it might have festered and undermined relationships among the remaining members. If, on the other hand, Diane had won allies, the staff might have split over the issue and ultimately dissolved the Hotline.

The members of this group were walking a tightrope throughout the conflict. Luckily, they managed to avoid a fall. The tension, unpleasantness, uncertainty, and fragility of conflict situations make them hard to face. Because these problems make it difficult to deal with issues in a constructive way, conflicts are often terminated by force, by uncomfortable suppression of the issues, or by exhaustion after a prolonged fight—all outcomes that leave at least one party dissatisfied. Entering a conflict is often like making a bet against the odds: you can win big if it turns out well, but so many things can go wrong that few people are willing to chance it. It is no wonder then that many writers feel a need to reassure us. They feel compelled to remind us of the positive outcomes of conflict because all too often the destructive results are all that people remember.

We believe that the key to working through conflict is not to minimize its disadvantages, or even to emphasize its positive functions, but to accept both and to try to understand how conflicts move in destructive or productive directions. Such an understanding requires a conception of conflict that calls for a careful analysis of both the specific behaviors and interaction patterns involved in conflict and the forces that influence these patterns. Moreover, we can only grasp the fragility of conflicts and the effects that tension and misunderstandings have in their development if we work at the level at which conflicts unfold—specific interactions among the parties.

Definition of Conflict

Conflict is the **interaction of interdependent people who perceive incompatible goals and interference from each other in achieving those goals** (Hocker & Wilmot, 1985). This definition has the advantage of providing a much clearer focus than definitions that view conflict simply as disagreement, as competition, or as the presence of incompatible interests (Fink, 1968). The most important feature of conflict is that it is based on **interaction**. Conflicts are constituted and sustained by the behaviors of the parties involved and their reactions to one another. Conflict interaction takes many forms and each form presents special problems and requires special handling. The most familiar type of conflict interaction is marked by shouting matches or open competition where each party tries to defeat the other. But conflicts can also be more subtle. Often people react to conflict by suppressing it. They interact in ways that allow them to avoid confrontation, either because they are afraid of possible changes the conflict may bring about or because the issue "isn't worth fighting over." This response is as much a part of the conflict process as the open struggles most of us associate with conflict. . . . We believe conflicts can best be understood and managed by concentrating on specific behavioral patterns and the forces shaping them.

People in conflict perceive that they have incompatible goals or interests and that others are a source of interference in achieving their goals. the key word here is "perceive." Regardless of whether goals are actually incompatible or if the parties believe them to be incompatible, conditions are ripe for conflict. Regardless of whether an employee really stands in the way of a co-worker or if the co-worker interprets the employee's behavior as interference, the co-worker may move against her or feel compelled to skirt certain issues. Thus the parties' interpretations and beliefs play a key role in conflicts. This does not mean that goals are always conscious as conflict develops. People can act without a clear sense of what their goals or interests are (Coser, 1961). Sometimes people find themselves in strained interactions but are unsure why. They realize afterward what their implicit goals were and how their goals were incompatible with those held by others (Hawes & Smith, 1973). Communication looms large because of its importance in shaping and maintaining the perceptions that guide conflict behavior.

Indeed, communication problems are sometimes the cause of conflicts. Tension or irritation can result from misunderstandings that occur when people interact with very different communication styles (Tannen, 1986; Grimshaw, 1990). One person's inquisitive style may be seen by someone else as intrusive and rude. One person's attempt to avoid stepping on another's toes may be seen by someone else as distant and cold. Style differences create difficult problems that are often related to differences in cultural backgrounds (Kochman, 1981). We do not, however, agree with the old adage "most conflicts are actually communication problems." The vast majority of conflicts would not exist without some real difference of interest. This difference may be hard to uncover, it may be redefined over time, and occasionally it may be trivial, but it is there nonetheless. Communication processes constitute conflicts and can easily [worsen] them, but they are rarely the sole source of the difficulty.

Conflict interaction is colored by the **interdependence** of the parties. For a conflict to arise, the behavior of one or both parties must have consequences for the other. So, by definition, the parties involved in conflict are interdependent. The conflict at the Hotline would not have occurred if Diane's behavior had not irritated the other workers and if their response had not threatened Diane's position. Furthermore, any action taken in response to the conflict affects both sides. The decision to institute a "debriefing contract" required considerable change by everyone. If Diane had been fired, that too would have affected the other workers; they would have had to "cover" Diane's cases and come to terms with themselves as co-workers who could be accused of being unresponsive or insensitive.

But interdependence implies more than this: when parties are interdependent they can potentially aid or interfere with each other. For this reason, conflicts are always characterized by a mixture of incentives to cooperate and to compete. Any comment during conflict interaction can be seen either as an attempt to advance the speaker's own interest or as an attempt to promote a good outcome for all involved. A party may believe that having their own point accepted is more important, at least for the moment, than proposing a mutually beneficial outcome. When Diane asked for two weeks off, she was probably thinking not of the group's best interest but of her own needs. In other cases, a participant may advance a proposal designed to benefit everyone, as when the staff member suggested the "debriefing contract." In still other instances, a participant may offer a comment with a cooperative intent, but others may interpret it as one that advances individual interests. Regardless of whether the competitive motive is intended by the speaker or assigned by other members, the interaction unfolds from that point under the assumption that the speaker may value only his/her own interests. Subsequent interaction is further likely to undermine incentives to cooperate and is also likely to weaken members' recognition of their own interdependence. The balance of incentives to compete or cooperate is important in determining the direction the conflict interaction takes.

Arenas of Conflict Interaction

Conflict occurs in almost all social settings. Most of us learn at a very young age that conflicts arise in families, playgrounds, classrooms, Little League fields, ballet centers, scout troops, and cheerleading teams. As we enter more complex relationships and become involved in more diverse and public settings, we often find that conflicts remain remarkably similar to those in our early lives. (Indeed, some argue that our early experiences shape our involvement in conflict throughout our lives.) As adults, we find conflict as we enter casual work relationships or emotionally intense, intimate relationships. We find it in close friendships or in political rivalries. We encounter it as we interact in decision-making groups, small businesses, large corporations, church organizations, and doctors' offices. Given the diversity of conflicts we typically encounter, what often is of most concern is how much is at stake in any conflict. We assess whether conflicts are pedestrian or profound, whether their effects on our lives will be trivial or tremendous, whether they are major or minor maelstroms. Our estimate of the significance of any conflict often influences the time and effort we invest in strategizing or in developing safeguards or fallbacks. . . .

Productive and Destructive Conflict Interaction

As we have noted, people often associate conflict with negative outcomes. However, there are times when conflicts must be addressed regardless of the apprehension they create. When differences exist and the issues are important, suppression of conflict is often more dangerous than facing it. The psychologist Irving Janis points to a number of famous political disasters, such as the Bay of Pigs invasion and the failure to anticipate the Japanese attack on Pearl Harbor, where poor decisions can be traced to the repression of conflict by key decision-making groups (Janis, 1972). The critical question is: what forms of conflict interaction will yield the obvious benefits without tearing a relationship, a group, or an organization apart?

Years ago the sociologist Lewis Coser (1956) distinguished **realistic** from **nonrealistic** conflicts. **Realistic** conflicts are conflicts based in disagreements over the means to an end or over the ends themselves. In realistic conflicts, the interaction focuses on the substantive issues the participants must address in order to resolve their underlying incompatibilities. **Nonrealistic** conflicts are expressions of aggression in which the sole end is to defeat or hurt the other. Participants in nonrealistic conflicts serve their own interests by undercutting those of the other party. Coser argues that because nonrealistic conflicts are oriented toward the expression of aggression, force and coercion are the means for resolving these disputes. Realistic conflicts, on the other hand, foster a wide range of resolution techniques—force, negotiation, persuasion, even voting—because they are oriented toward the resolution of some substantive problem. Although Coser's analysis oversimplifies things somewhat, it is insightful and suggests important contrasts between productive and destructive conflict interaction (Deutsch, 1973). What criteria could one use to evaluate whether a conflict is productive? In large part, productive conflict interaction depends on flexibility. In constructive conflicts, members engage in a wide variety of behaviors ranging from coercion and threat to negotiation, joking, and relaxation in order to reach an acceptable solution. In contrast, parties in destructive conflicts are likely to be much less flexible because their goal is more narrowly defined: they are trying to defeat each other. Destructive conflict interaction is likely to have protracted, uncontrolled escalation cycles or prolonged attempts to avoid issues. In productive conflict, on the other hand, the interaction in the group will change direction often. Short cycles of escalation, de-escalation, avoidance, and constructive work on the issue are likely to occur as the participants attempt to manage the conflict.

Consider the Hotline case. The group exhibited a wide range of interaction styles, from the threat of a grievance to the cooperative attempt to reach a mutually satisfactory solution. Even though Diane and the members engaged in hostile or threatening interaction, they did not persist in this mode, and when the conflict threatened to escalate, they called in a third party. The conflict showed all the hallmarks of productive interaction. In a destructive conflict the members might have responded to Diane's grievance by suspending her, and Diane might have retaliated by suing or by attempting to discredit the center in the local newspaper. Her retaliation would have hardened others' positions and they might have fired her, leading to further retaliation. Alternatively, the Hotline conflict might have ended in destructive avoidance. Diane might have hidden her problem and the other members might have consciously or unconsciously abetted her by changing the subject when the murder came up or by avoiding talking to her at all. Diane's problem would probably have grown worse, and she might have had to quit. The center would then revert back to "normal" until the same problem surfaced again. While the damage done by destructive avoidance is much less serious in this case than that done by destructive escalation, it is still considerable: the Hotline loses a good worker, and the seeds of future losses remain. In both cases, it is not the behaviors themselves that are destructive—neither avoidance nor hostile arguments are harmful in themselves—but rather the **inflexibility** of the parties that locks them into escalation or avoidance cycles.

In productive conflicts, interaction is guided by the belief that all factions can attain important goals (Deutsch, 1973). The interaction reflects a sustained effort to bridge the apparent incompatibility of positions. This is in marked contrast to destructive conflicts where the interaction is premised on participants' belief that one side must win and the other must lose. Productive conflict interaction results in a solution satisfactory to all and produces a general feeling that the parties have gained something (e.g., a new idea, greater clarity of others' positions, a stronger sense of solidarity). In some cases, the win-lose orientation of destructive conflict stems from fear of losing. People attempt to defeat alternative proposals because they believe that if their positions are not accepted they will lose resources, self-esteem, or the respect of others. In other cases, win-lose interaction is sparked, not by competitive motives, but by the parties' fear of **working through** a difficult conflict. Groups that rely on voting to reach decisions often call for a vote when discussion becomes heated and the members do not see any other immediate way out of a hostile and threatening situation. Any further attempt to discuss the alternatives or to pursue the reasons behind people's positions seems risky. A vote can put a quick end to threatening interaction, but it also induces a win-lose orientation that can easily trigger destructive cycles. Members whose proposal is rejected must resist a natural tendency to be less committed to the chosen solution and may try to "even the score" in future conflicts. Productive conflict interaction is sometimes competitive; both parties must stand up for their own positions if a representative outcome is to be attained. A great deal of tension and hostility may result as people struggle with the conflict. Although parties in productive conflicts hold to their positions strongly, they are also open to movement when convinced that such movement will result in the best decision. The need to preserve power, save face, or make the opponent look bad does not stand in the way of change. In destructive conflict, parties often become polarized, and the defense of a nonnegotiable position becomes more important than working out a viable solution. This description of productive and destructive conflict interaction is obviously an idealization. We rarely observe a conflict that exhibits all the constructive or destructive qualities just mentioned; indeed, many conflicts exhibit both productive and destructive interaction. We maintain, however, that better conflict management will result if parties can sustain productive conflict interaction patterns.

Conflict As Interactive Behavior

Conflict is, by nature, interactive. It is never wholly under one person's control (Kriesberg, 1973). The other party's reactions and the person's anticipation of the other's response are extremely important. Any comment made during a conflict is made with some awareness or prediction about the likely response it will elicit. This predictive basis for any move in interaction creates a strong tendency for conflict interaction to become cyclic or repetitive. Suppose Robert criticizes Susan, an employee under his supervision, for her decreasing productivity. Susan may accept the criticism and explain why her production is down, thus reducing the conflict and moving toward a solution. Susan may also shout back and sulk, inviting escalation, or she may choose to say nothing and avoid the conflict, resulting in no improvement in the situation. Once Robert has spoken to Susan and she has responded, the situation is no longer totally under Robert's control: his next behavior will be a response to Susan's reaction. Robert's behavior, and its subsequent meaning to Susan, is dependent on the interchange between them. A behavioral cycle of initiation-response-counterresponse results from the conflict interchange. This cycle cannot be understood by breaking it into its parts, into the individual behaviors of Robert and Susan. It is more complex than the individual behaviors and, in a real sense, has a "life" of its own. The cycle can be self-reinforcing, if, for example, Susan shouts back at Robert, Robert tries to discipline her, Susan become more recalcitrant, and so on, in an escalating spiral. The cycle could also limit itself if Robert responds to Susan's shouting with an attempt to calm her and listen to her side of the story. Conflict interaction cycles acquire a momentum of their own. They tend in a definite direction—toward escalation, toward avoidance and suppression, or toward productive work on the conflict. The situation becomes even more complex when we remember that Robert formulated his criticism on the basis of his previous experience with Susan. That is, Robert's move is based on his perception of Susan's likely response. In the same way, Susan's response is based not only on Robert's criticism, but on her estimate of Robert's likely reaction to her response. Usually such estimations are "intuitive"—that is, they are not conscious—but sometimes parties plot them out ("If I shout at Robert, he'll back down and maybe I won't have to deal with this"). They are always based on the parties' perceptions of each other, on whatever theories or beliefs each holds about the other's reactions. Because these estimates are only intuitive predictions, they may be wrong to some extent. They will be revised as the conflict unfolds, and this revision will largely determine what direction the conflict takes. The most striking thing about this predictive process is the extraordinary difficulties it poses for attempts to understand the parties' thinking. When Susan responds to Robert on the basis of her prediction of Robert's answer, from the outside we see *Susan* making an estimate of *Robert's* estimate of what she means by her response. If Robert reflects on Susan's intention before answering, we observe *Robert's* estimate of *Susan's* estimate of *his* estimate of what *Susan* meant. This string of estimates can increase without bounds if we try to pin down the originating point, and after a while the prospect is just as dizzying as a hall of mirrors.

Several studies of arms races (Richardson, 1960; North, Brody, & Holsti, 1963) and of marital relations (Watzlawick, Beavin, & Jackson, 1967; Rubin, 1983; Scarf, 1987) and employee-supervisor interactions (Brown, 1983) have shown how this spiral of predictions poses a critical problem in conflicts. If the parties do not take the spiral into account, they run the risk of miscalculation. However, it is beyond the capacities of any of us to calculate all the possibilities. At best, people have extremely limited knowledge of the implications their actions hold for others, and their ability to manage conflicts is therefore severely curtailed. Not only are parties' behaviors inherently interwoven in conflicts, but their thinking and anticipations are as well. The key question [to address] is: **how does conflict interaction develop destructive patterns—radical escalation, prolonged or inappropriate avoidance of conflict issues, inflexibility—rather than constructive patterns leading to productive conflict management?** Conflict interaction is always poised on a precipice: one push can send it in a negative direction while another can send it in a positive direction. This [chapter] considers several major forces that direct conflicts and examines the problems people encounter in trying to control these forces in order to regulate their own conflict interaction.

References

Brown, L. D. (1983). *Managing conflict at organization interfaces*. Reading, MA: Addison-Wesley.

Coser, L. (1956). *The functions of social conflict*. New York: Free Press.

Coser, L. (1961). The termination of conflict. *Journal of Conflict Resolution, 5*, 347–353.

Deutsch, M. (1973). *The resolution of conflict.* New Haven: Yale University Press.

Fink, C. F. (1968). Some conceptual difficulties in the theory of social conflict. *Journal of Conflict Resolution, 12,* 412–460.

Grimshaw, A. D. (Ed.). (1990). *Conflict talk: Sociolinguistic investigations of arguments in conversations.* Cambridge: Cambridge University Press.

Hawes, L. & Smith, D. H. (1973). A critique of assumptions underlying the study of communication in conflict. *Quarterly Journal of Speech, 59,* 423–435.

Hocker, J. L. & Wilmot, W. W. (1985). *Interpersonal conflict.* Dubuque: Wm. C. Brown.

Janis, I. (1972). *Victims of groupthink.* Boston: Houghton Mifflin.

Kochman, T. (1981). *Black and white styles in conflict.* Chicago: The University of Chicago Press.

Kriesberg, L. (1973). *The sociology of social conflicts.* Englewood Cliffs, NJ: Prentice-Hall.

North, R. C., Brody, R. A., & Holsti, O. (1963). Some empirical data on the conflict spiral. *Peace Research Society; Papers I.* Chicago Conference, pp. 1–14.

Richardson, L. F. (1960). *Arms and insecurity.* Pittsburgh: The Boxwood Press.

Rubin, L. (1983). *Intimate strangers.* New York: Harper & Row.

Scarf, M. (1987). *Intimate partners: Patterns in love and marriage.* New York: Ballantine.

Tannen, D. (1986). *That's not what I meant.* New York: William Morrow.

Watzlawick, P., Beavin, J., & Jackson, D. (1967). *Pragmatics of human communication.* New York: W. W. Norton.

Review Questions

1. Describe what the authors mean when they say that the case study about Diane and her coworkers shows how conflict situations are *tense and threatening, uncertain,* and *fragile.*
2. Explain what is significant about each of the following terms in the authors' definition of conflict: "interaction," "interdependent," "incompatible goals," "interference."
3. Why do the authors disagree with the old adage, "most conflicts are actually communication problems"?
4. Distinguish between "realistic" and "nonrealistic" conflict.

Probes

1. As you read the case study about Diane and her coworkers, what single feature of the situation strikes you as the most important positive move that was made? In other words, what one thing most helped resolve this conflict productively?
2. Give an example from your own experience of the difference between a "realistic" and a "nonrealistic" conflict.
3. At one point the authors argue about the wisdom of resolving a conflict by voting. (a) What is their rationale for discouraging voting? (b) How do you respond; that is, do you agree or disagree, and why?
4. The authors end this excerpt with "the key question" about how conflicts develop destructive patterns. After you've read the other three readings in this chapter, what is your response to this "key question"?

 n the next selection, Jack Gibb shares some insights about how conflict happens and what you can do to promote a supportive rather than a defensive climate for communication.

As Gibb points out, when you anticipate or perceive that you are threatened by a person or a situation, you will usually react defensively and so will the other persons involved. When any combination of the six "defensiveness-producing" elements are present, a spiral usually begins, a spiral that starts with a little discomfort and often escalates into all-out conflict.

But, Gibb notes, you can also start a spiral in the other direction. The more supportive you can be, the less other people are likely to read into the situation distorted reactions created by their own defensiveness. So when you can manifest any combination of the six alternative attitudes and skills, you can help reduce the defensiveness that's present. You don't have to "give up" or "give in." You just have to stop trying so hard to demean, control, and impose your hard-and-fast superiority on the others.

Most of the people I work with find this article very useful. They discover that they can apply Gibb's analysis of the six characteristics of defensive and supportive communication climates to their own experience. They also find that Gibb is right when he says that most people are much more aware of being manipulated or deceived than the manipulators or deceivers think and that such awareness creates defensiveness. They are usually able to perceive quite accurately another's communication strategy or "gimmicks." Whey they learn that sometimes it's their own transparently manipulative behavior that creates defensiveness in others, they get one step closer to communicating interpersonally.

This is a "classic" essay, written before authors understood that it's inappropriate to refer to people in general as "he" and "him." I hope you'll be able to read beyond the sexist language for Gibb's excellent ideas.

Defensive Communication

Jack R. Gibb

One way to understand communication is to view it as a people process rather than as a language process. If one is to make fundamental improvement in communication, he must make changes in interpersonal relationships. One possible type of alteration—and the one with which this paper is concerned—is that of reducing the degree of defensiveness.

Definition and Significance

Defensive behavior is defined as that behavior which occurs when an individual perceives threat or anticipates threat in the group. The person who behaves defensively, even though he also gives some attention to the common task, devotes an appreciable portion of his energy to defending himself. Besides talking about the topic, he thinks about how he appears to others, how he may be seen more favorably, how he may win, dominate, impress, or escape punishment, and/or how he may avoid or mitigate a perceived or an anticipated attack.

Such inner feelings and outward acts tend to create similarly defensive postures in others; and, if unchecked, the ensuing circular response becomes increasingly

From Jack R. Gibb, "Defensive Communication," *Journal of Communication* 11, no. 3 (September 1961): 141–148. Reprinted by permission of the *Journal of Communication* and the author.

destructive. Defensive behavior, in short, engenders defensive listening, and this in turn produces postural, facial, and verbal cues which raise the defense level of the original communicator.

Defense arousal prevents the listener from concentrating upon the message. Not only do defensive communicators send off multiple value, motive, and affect cues, but also defensive recipients distort what they receive. As a person becomes more and more defensive, he becomes less and less able to perceive accurately the motives, the values, and the emotions of the sender. The writer's analyses of tape recorded discussions revealed that increases in defensive behavior were correlated positively with losses in efficiency in communication.[1] Specifically, distortions became greater when defensive states existed in the groups.

The converse, moreover, also is true. The more "supportive" or defense reductive the climate the less the receiver reads into the communication distorted loadings which arise from projections of his own anxieties, motives, and concerns. As defenses are reduced, the receivers become better able to concentrate upon the structure, the content, and the cognitive meanings of the message.

Categories of Defensive and Supportive Communication

In working over an eight-year period with recordings of discussions occurring in varied settings, the writer developed the six pairs of defensive and supportive categories presented in Table 1. Behavior which a listener perceives as possessing any of the characteristics listed in the left-hand column arouses defensiveness, whereas that which he interprets as having any of the qualities designated as supportive reduces defensive feelings. The degree to which these reactions occur depends upon the personal level of defensiveness and upon the general climate in the group at the time.[2]

Table 1
Categories of Behavior Characteristic of Supportive and Defensive Climates in Small Groups

Defensive Climates	*Supportive Climates*
1. Evaluation	1. Description
2. Control	2. Problem orientation
3. Strategy	3. Spontaneity
4. Neutrality	4. Empathy
5. Superiority	5. Equality
6. Certainty	6. Provisionalism

Evaluation and Description

Speech or other behavior which appears evaluative increases defensiveness. If by expression, manner of speech, tone of voice, or verbal content the sender seems to be evaluating or judging the listener, then the receiver goes on guard. Of course, other factors may inhibit the reaction. If the listener thought that the speaker regarded him as an equal and was being open and spontaneous, for example, the evaluativeness in a message would be neutralized and perhaps not even perceived. This same principle applies equally to the other five categories of potentially defense-producing climates. The six sets are interactive.

Because our attitudes toward other persons are frequently, and often necessarily, evaluative, expressions which the defensive person will regard as nonjudgmental are hard to frame. Even the simplest question usually conveys the answer that the sender wishes or implies the response that would fit into his value system. A mother, for example, immediately following an earth tremor that shook the house, sought for her small son with the question:"Bobby, where are you?" The timid and plaintive "Mommy, I didn't do it" indicated how Bobby's chronic mild defensiveness predisposed him to react with a projection of his own guilt and in the context of his chronic assumption that questions are full of accusation.

Anyone who has attempted to train professionals to use information-seeking speech with neutral affect appreciates how difficult it is to teach a person to say even the simple "who did that?" without being seen as accusing. Speech is so frequently judgmental that there is a reality base for the defensive interpretations which are so common.

When insecure, group members are particularly likely to place blame, to see others as fitting into categories of good or bad, to make moral judgments of their colleagues, and to question the value, motive, and affect loadings of the speech which they hear. Since value loadings imply a judgment of others, a belief that the standards of the speaker differ from his own causes the listener to become defensive.

Descriptive speech, in contrast to that which is evaluative, tends to arouse a minimum of uneasiness. Speech acts which the listener perceives as genuine requests for information or as material with neutral loadings is descriptive. Specifically, presentations of feelings, events, perceptions, or processes which do not ask or imply that the receiver change behavior or attitude are minimally defense producing. The difficulty in avoiding overtone is illustrated by the problems of news reporters in writing stories about unions, communists, Blacks, and religious activities without tipping off the "party" line of the newspaper. One can often tell from the opening words in a news article which side the newspaper's editorial policy favors.

Control and Problem Orientation

Speech which is used to control the listener evokes resistance. In most of our social intercourse someone is trying to do something to someone else—to change an attitude, to influence behavior, or to restrict the field of activity. The degree to which attempts to control produce defensiveness depends upon the openness of the effort, for a suspicion that hidden motives exist heightens resistance. For this reason attempts of nondirective therapists and progressive educators to refrain from imposing a set of values, a point of view, or a problem solution upon the receivers meet with many barriers. Since the norm is control, noncontrollers must earn the perceptions that their efforts have no hidden motives. A bombardment of persuasive "messages" in the fields of politics, education, special causes, advertising, religion, medicine, industrial relations, and guidance has bred cynical and paranoidal responses in listeners.

Implicit in all attempts to alter another person is the assumption by the change agent that the person to be altered is inadequate. That the speaker secretly views the listener as ignorant, unable to make his own decisions, uninformed, immature, unwise, or possessed of wrong or inadequate attitudes is a subconscious perception which gives the latter a valid base for defensive reactions.

Methods of control are many and varied. Legalistic insistence on detail, restrictive regulations and policies, conformity norms, and all laws are among the methods. Gestures, facial expressions, other forms of nonverbal communication, and even such simple acts as holding a door open in a particular manner are means of imposing one's will upon another and hence are potential sources of resistance.

Problem orientation, on the other hand, is the antithesis of persuasion. When the sender communicates a desire to collaborate in defining a mutual problem and in seeking its solution, he tends to create the same problem orientation in the listener; and, of greater importance, he implies that he has no predetermined solution, attitude, or method to impose. Such behavior is permissive in that it allows the receiver to set his own goals, make his own decisions, and evaluate his own progress—or to share with the sender in doing so. The exact methods of attaining permissiveness are not known, but they must involve a constellation of cues and they certainly go beyond mere verbal assurances that the communicator has no hidden desires to exercise control.

Strategy and Spontaneity

When the sender is perceived as engaged in a stratagem involving ambiguous and multiple motivations, the receiver becomes defensive. No one wishes to be a guinea pig, a role player, or an impressed actor, and no one likes to be the victim of some hidden motivation. That which is concealed, also, may appear larger than it really is with the degree of defensiveness of the listener determining the perceived size of the suppressed element. The intense reaction of the reading audience to the material in *Hidden Persuaders* indicates the prevalence of defensive reactions to multiple motivations behind strategy. Group members who are seen as "taking a role," as feigning emotion, as toying with their colleagues, as withholding information, or as having special sources of data are especially resented. One participant once complained that another was "using a listening technique" on him!

A large part of the adverse reaction to much of the so-called human relations training is a feeling against what are perceived as gimmicks and tricks to fool or to "involve" people, to make a person think he is making his own decision, or to make the listener feel that the sender is genuinely interested in him as a person. Particularly violent reactions occur when it appears that someone is trying to make a stratagem appear spontaneous. One person has reported a boss who incurred resentment by habitually using the gimmick of "spontaneously" looking at his watch and saying, "My gosh, look at the time—I must run to an appointment." The belief was that the boss would create less irritation by honestly asking to be excused.

Similarly, the deliberate assumption of guilelessness and natural simplicity is especially resented. Monitoring the tapes of feedback and evaluation sessions in training groups indicates the surprising extent to which members perceive the strategies of their colleagues. This perceptual clarity may be quite shocking to the strategist, who usually feels that he had cleverly hidden the motivational aura around the "gimmick."

This aversion to deceit may account for one's resistance to politicians who are suspected of behind-the-scenes planning to get his vote, to psychologists whose listening apparently is motivated by more than the manifest or content-level interest in his behavior, or to the sophisticated, smooth, or clever person whose "oneupmanship" is marked with guile. In training groups the role-flexible person frequently is resented because his changes in behavior are perceived as strategic maneuvers.

In contrast, behavior which appears to be spontaneous and free of deception is defense reductive. If the communicator is seen as having a clean id, as having uncom-

plicated motivations, as being straightforward and honest, and as behaving spontaneously in response to the situation, he is likely to arouse minimal defense.

Neutrality and Empathy

When neutrality in speech appears to the listener to indicate a lack of concern
for his welfare, he becomes defensive. Group members usually desire to be perceived as
valued persons, as individuals of special worth, and as objects of concern and affection.
The clinical, detached, person-is-an-object-of-study attitude on the part of many psy-
chologist-trainers is resented by group members. Speech with low affect that communicates little warmth or caring is in such contrast with the affect-laden speech in social
situations that it sometimes communicates rejection.

Communication that conveys empathy for the feelings and respect for the worth
of the listener, however, is particularly supportive and defense reductive. Reassurance
results when a message indicates that the speaker identifies himself with the listener's
problems, shares his feelings, and accepts his emotional reactions as face value.
Abortive efforts to deny the legitimacy of the receiver's emotions by assuring the
receiver that he need not feel bad, that he should not feel rejected, or that he is overly
anxious, though often intended as support giving, may impress the listener as lack of
acceptance. The combination of understanding and empathizing with the other person's emotions with no accompanying effort to change him apparently is supportive at
a high level.

The importance of gestural behavioral cues in communicating empathy should
be mentioned. Apparently spontaneous facial and bodily evidences of concern are
often interpreted as especially valid evidence of deep-level acceptance.

Superiority and Equality

When a person communicates to another that he feels superior in position,
power, wealth, intellectual ability, physical characteristics, or other ways, he arouses
defensiveness. Here, as with the other sources of disturbance, whatever arouses feelings
of inadequacy causes the listener to center upon the affect loading of the statement
rather than upon the cognitive elements. The receiver then reacts by not hearing the
message, by forgetting it, by competing with the sender, or by becoming jealous of him.

The person who is perceived as feeling superior communicates that he is not willing to enter into a shared problem-solving relationship, that he probably does not
desire feedback, that he does not require help, and/or that he will be likely to try to
reduce the power, the status, or the worth of the receiver.

Many ways exist for creating the atmosphere that the sender feels himself equal
to the listener. Defenses are reduced when one perceives the sender as being willing to
enter into participative planning with mutual trust and respect. Differences in talent,
ability, worth, appearance, status, and power often exist, but the low defense communicator seems to attach little importance to these distinctions.

Certainty and Provisionalism

The effects of dogmatism in producing defensiveness are well known. Those who
seem to know the answers, to require no additional data, and to regard themselves as
teachers rather than as co-workers tend to put others on guard. Moreover, in the
writer's experiment, listeners often perceived manifest expressions of certainty as con-
noting inward feelings of inferiority. They saw the dogmatic individual as needing to
be right, as wanting to win an argument rather than solve a problem, and as seeing his

ideas as truths to be defended. This kind of behavior often was associated with acts which others regarded as attempts to exercise control. People who were right seemed to have low tolerance for members who were "wrong"—i.e., who did not agree with the sender.

One reduces the defensiveness of the listener when he communicates that he is willing to experiment with his own behavior, attitudes, and ideas. The person who appears to be taking provisional attitudes, to be investigating issues rather than taking sides on them, to be problem solving rather than debating, and to be willing to experiment and explore tends to communicate that the listener may have some control over the shared quest or the investigation of the ideas. If a person is genuinely searching for information and data, he does not resent help or company along the way.

Conclusion

The implications of the above material for the parent, the teacher, the manager, the administrator, or the therapist are fairly obvious. Arousing defensiveness interferes with communication and thus makes it difficult—and sometimes impossible—for anyone to convey ideas clearly and to move effectively toward the solution of therapeutic, educational, or managerial problems.

Notes

1. J. R. Gibb, "Defense Level and Influence Potential in Small Groups," *Leadership and Interpersonal Behavior*, ed. L. Petrullo and B. M. Bass (New York: Holt, Rinehart and Winston, 1961), pp. 66–81.
2. J. R. Gibb, "Sociopsychological Processes of Group Instruction," *The Dynamics of Instructional Groups*, ed. N. B. Henry (Fifty-ninth Yearbook of the National Society of the Study of Education, Part II, 1960), pp. 115–135.

Review Questions

1. How does Gibb define "defensiveness"?
2. What does "defensiveness" defend? What does "supportiveness" support?
3. How can description accomplish the same purpose as evaluation?
4. Based on what you've already read about empathy, how is neutrality the opposite of empathy?

Probes

1. Does Gibb see defensiveness as a relational thing—something that's created *between* persons—or does he see it as something one person or group creates and forces on another person or a group?
2. Gibb cautions us about the negative effects of evaluation. But is it possible actually to be nonevaluative? Or is that what Gibb is asking us to do?
3. Although most of Gibb's examples use verbal cues, each of the categories of defensiveness and supportiveness is also communicated nonverbally. Can you identify how you nonverbally communicate Evaluation? Control? Strategy? Superiority? Spontaneity? Empathy? Equality?
4. Self-disclosing is one way to communicate spontaneity. Can you identify communication behaviors that help create the other kinds of supportive climate?
5. Which categories of defensive behavior are most present in your relationship with your lover or spouse? Your employer? Your parents? Which categories of supportive behavior characterize those relationships?

T here's probably no greater interpersonal communication challenge than what to do with your anger. On the one hand, anger seems to be a pervasive emotion; we all feel it at one time or another almost every day. On the other hand, it seems like any expression of anger drives a wedge between us and the other person. So what are we supposed to do? Suppress our anger all the time? Or just give up and expect to go around making other people mad at us?

In this next reading, John Amodeo and Kris Wentworth apply some of what they've learned about anger in their work as family counselors. They begin by admitting that it's a powerful but little-understood emotion. Then they suggest that we begin working with anger by recognizing that it is natural and not necessarily bad. Bottled-up anger often is bad, as is anger that is destructively expressed. In fact, unexpressed anger surfaces in what's called "passive-aggressive" behavior such as arriving late, withholding affection, or forgetting appointments. It can also contribute to such stress-related physical symptoms as backache, headaches, and hypertension.

But effectively expressed anger can actually increase, not decrease, both your own sense of well-being and your intimacy with someone else. The first step is to accept anger as normal and natural. Most anger is not evidence of some deep psychological maladjustment or childhood trauma. It's simply one of our natural responses to things not going our way.

Then the key to dealing with it is, in their words, to learn to express "clean" anger. When you express clean anger, you reveal your own feelings and unmet needs in ways that are uncontaminated by blame or guilt-producing statements. This communication skill can be a difficult one both to practice and to hear. When you're angry, you need to learn to substitute "I don't like those dishes in the sink!" for statements like, "How many times have I told you not to leave your dirty dishes in the sink?" or 'Why do you always leave such a mess in the sink?" The difference between these two kinds of statements may sound subtle, but it's enormously important. In the first case you're forcefully expressing your *own* anger— which is an accurate reflection of what you're feeling. In the second two cases you're blaming the other person, attributing your own anger to his or her actions. The first is much cleaner than the second two.

Even "clean" expressions of anger, though, are often interpreted as blaming statements. Naturally enough—as we learned above in Chapter 4—people respond to the nonverbal aspects of volume and tone of voice. So even though you might have *said*, "I'm angry!" they *hear*, "You screwed up!" There is no easy solution to this problem, but in this essay the authors make several suggestions about how to cope with it.

For example, they emphasize the importance of both people involved learning that others do not cause our feelings. It also helps to learn to express and to hear anger as an emphatic "I don't like this!" of "No!" rather than an attack on someone else. The way anger is expressed often reveals a great deal about how power is distributed in a relationship. And it can also echo what we learned from watching and listening to our parents and other family members.

The authors conclude this reading by sketching some of the benefits that you can experience when you learn to express anger cleanly. One of the most obvious is catharsis, the feeling of release, that you don't have to carry around a bottled-up emotion any more. But it can also help you discover important insights about yourself. If you can learn simply to notice anger rather than judging it good or bad, you can sometimes discover what's under the surface of your own every-day emotions. For example, as they say, "we may realize that just below the sur-face of our anger about the dishes not being washed lies a deeper concern about whether we are really loved."

Another important benefit of the "clean" expression of anger is that it can increase intimacy. When you express anger directly and nondefensively, you place yourself in a vulnerable position. You've given the other person an insight into how you really feel about something important. If both of you can deal with this anger as a clean expression, your vulnerability can get translated into enhanced intimacy. Obviously it won't work that way every time. But there is the genuine potential in work, friend, family, and intimate relationships that, as the authors conclude, "The mutual sharing of anger in clean, self-revealing ways can lead to a process of communication that can help two individuals feel closer to one another."

Working with Anger

John Amodeo and Kris Wentworth

Anger is a powerful, yet little understood human emotion. Our inability to deal with it effectively is a frequent cause of problems in our relationships. A major factor that contributes to this difficulty is the common misconception that anger is somehow "bad," destructive or inappropriate. It is true that the way in which resentments are expressed can lead to a great deal of hurt in relationships and violence in the world. However, it would be a grave error to conclude that anger, in itself, is responsible for the destructiveness, and should therefore be avoided.

Rather than maintain a simplistic good/bad perception of anger, it is more useful to adopt a non-judgmental attitude toward it. If it is true that growth involves learn-ing to love ourselves, then it follows that we must learn to fully accept ourselves, including our anger. The unfortunate alternative is to turn the anger inward against ourselves. In other words, unacknowledged and unexpressed anger gets held in the body, creating tension that may be experienced as frustration or anxiety. Or, when resentments have no healthy outlet, our bodily held anger may be felt as a chronic fatigue or depression—the anger turns against us, suppressing our energy and vitality. Internalized anger may also be partially responsible for those times when we feel con-fused—resentments fuse with other emotions and unproductive thoughts that then overwhelm us.

Bottled-up anger can also lead to physical symptoms such as headaches, ulcers,

Excerpts from "Working with Anger," from *Being Intimate: A Guide to Successful Relationships* by John Amodeo and Kris Wentworth. 1986 Viking Penquin.

and an array of other illnesses whose causes we are only beginning to understand. In the years ahead, we may recognize that an accumulation of unacknowledged anger coupled with an inability to deal with it responsibly contributes significantly to the origin of many common diseases.

A key to our physical as well as emotional well-being involves allowing the experience of anger to simply be, without either judging it or trying to get rid of it due to our fear or aversion. Opening to our anger can then become a way to unlock suppressed energy and vitality. Dealing with it responsibly can enliven our relationships and rejuvenate those that have become stagnant or boringly comfortable.

Once we accept anger as a neutral energy, rather than morally judge it, we are in a position to differentiate between its responsible expression, and the impulse to vent it in destructive, hurtful ways. The need to communicate it in healthy ways becomes particularly obvious once we realize that we cannot *not* express our anger. There is some kind of inner intelligence within our organism that wants to express it. This healthy urge manifests in unhealthy, indirect ways when our belief system does not permit a direct experience of the anger.

It is the indirect expression of anger that has harmful, insidious effects upon relationships. Psychologists call this "passive-aggressive" behavior because, instead of expressing the anger or communicating about it, we act it out in passive ways. For example, if we fear the consequences of sharing our resentment directly, we may express anger indirectly by missing appointments, arriving late, withholding affection, or acting in a variety of spiteful ways. One client, for instance, stated that she took great satisfaction in running up her husband's charge accounts. At the time, she was not even aware of her anger, but upon closer exploration of her motives, she realized what she was actually feeling. She had experienced some relief (a re-emergence of her sense of power) by "getting back" at her husband for not giving her the caring and affection she wanted. But the relationship suffered because the anger did not have a chance to be expressed openly and explored in terms of its deeper meaning. Once the wisdom of the anger was understood, some resolution occurred as she became more willing to express her need for affection.

While some people disguise their anger through its passive expression, others vent it in an exaggerated fashion through unpredictable explosions. We sometimes read stories about the "nice guy" on the block who kills his wife and children. While the neighbors are left puzzled, it is no wonder to those who know that when resentments are repressed, they go underground and amass greater force for a future eruption. This pattern is familiar in relationships where one has a self-image of not being an angry person. For example, one individual who was deeply involved with spiritual practices had a strong conviction that it was wrong to get angry. One day, however, she exploded in a fierce rage. Being uncomfortable with her anger, she tried to cover it up by being sweet and forgiving. But, as inevitably occurs when anger is submerged, her fury erupted despite her best efforts to keep it under control.

Once we can acknowledge and feel our anger, we can begin to differentiate between its responsible expression and the impulse to vent it in destructive ways. It is not the anger that hurts others, but rather the blaming, judgmental ways in which it is often communicated. Gaining greater control over our anger does not mean suppressing it, but rather learning how to channel it in a way that can lead to greater intimacy and communication.

Learning to Express "Clean" Anger

The expression of anger can be distinguished by whether it is "clean" or "destructive." Destructive anger is very hurtful because it is tinged with personality attacks or judgmental criticisms. For example, through choice of words, tone of voice, or movements of the body, we may convey a message such as "You're pretty stupid," or "You're really selfish," or "You're wrong, don't you know anything!?" These and similar invalidating communications constitute an attack on the other person. They say, in effect, "You are not a worthwhile human being; you do not deserve love and respect." Such messages are especially hurtful because they reinforce the bad feelings we may already have about ourselves.

Receiving hurtful communications from another, we instinctively protect ourselves by either attacking or withdrawing. We may withdraw in a number of ways, such as by watching television, compulsively eating, drinking, going to sleep, refusing to talk, or threatening to end the relationship. Or, rather than withdrawing, we may retaliate by blaming or verbally attacking the other—becoming self-righteous and mentally deciding that the other person is wrong, bad, selfish, or immature. This leads to a spiraling escalation of tensions. Whether we withdraw or attack, the relationship suffers because one or both parties are left feeling hurt, defensive, or isolated. Surprisingly, this toxic pattern can continue indefinitely, leading to a painful negativity toward relationships and bitterness toward life.

Clean anger, on the other hand, does not focus on making the other person wrong for their behavior, feelings, or opinions. Instead of blaming or analyzing the other person ("you're too needy" or "you're so depressed!"), or assuming to know their motives ("you're just trying to get back at me," or "you only care about yourself!"), a clean communication reveals one's own feelings and unmet needs, uncontaminated by blame or guilt-producing statements. For example, clean anger could be expressed in the following manner: "I'm angry about these dishes in the sink!" Included in this communication may be an emotional intensity in one's voice, but it is clean because the individual is merely expressing his or her feeling without implying (through words, tone of voice, or gestures) that the other person is wrong or suspect in some way. In contrast, a destructive communication would involve saying something like, "How many times do I have to tell you not to leave your dirty dishes in the sink!" At first, the distinction may appear to be a subtle one, but there is a crucial difference. Receiving the clean expression of anger, we hear, "This person is angry about dishes in the sink." Since we do not feel attacked, we may feel inclined to respond in an accommodating way. In the destructive communication, we feel nagged at and hear, "I'm bad for doing something wrong." As a result, we may withdraw in order to remove ourselves from a hurtful situation. Or we may give voice to our anger through an ineffectual, sarcastic remark such as, "Yes, dear," or "There you go complaining again. . . ."

Feeling entitled to experience anger and express it in a clean, self-revealing way provides a direct, psychologically healthy outlet for it. As a result, there is less of a tendency for it to leap out later in irrational, hurtful ways (whether passively or actively). Our anger, plus other issues surrounding it, have a greater chance of being resolved through a simple, guiltless expression in the moment. Daniel Wile, a couples therapist, describes this clearly:

> An angry feeling or impulse, experienced and expressed in a direct and straightforward manner, often has a clarifying and beneficial effect...when anger is warded off, it reappears in regressive forms, as sudden rage, sadistic fantasies, or chronic irritability. If fear or self-

criticism (guilt) prevent people from being assertive, the impulse goes underground and re-emerges in sudden blatant expressions (aggression) or subdued, inhibited ones (nonassertion).[1]

In addition, by releasing anger, our genuine love for the other can continue to grow, rather than be smothered by ever-increasing layers of resentment.

A clean expression of anger reflects the understanding that others do not cause our feelings. The common statement, "You make me so angry," depicts how anger is often blamed on the one toward whom we feel it. While another's words or actions can certainly bring up our anger, the other person cannot be held fully responsible for it. Our present upset is often the result of many factors, such as our unmet need for love, a re-stimulation of unresolved past hurts, feelings of unworthiness, fears of rejection, as well as the present anger-provoking situation. Our present feeling cannot be reduced simply to past causes or only to the present circumstance. Rather, our feeling is usually created by both. Growth comes through honoring our emotion as it arises, expressing it cleanly, and exploring it further internally if it seems particularly charged or out of proportion to the current situation.

The expression of anger need not be seen as threatening when expressed responsibly. In effect, it states, "I do not like this!" or "I won't accept that!" Anger sends a big "No!" message to the other: "No! I won't stand for this!" Through our anger, we stand up for ourselves, recover our self-esteem, and express our unwillingness to be abused, ignored, or depreciated by another. Even if we feel powerless to change the actual circumstances, expressing our anger enables us to release bodily held frustrations and energies, which can lead to a welcome change of attitude toward the situation. And, perhaps surprisingly, the situation itself may change once we have dealt with our feelings about it.

While it is important to be mindful of our felt experience, we are not suggesting that anger be expressed without regard for another's feelings or needs. As we grow more intimate with ourselves—becoming better acquainted with our true feelings and discovering patterns that no longer serve us—it becomes more possible to express ourselves while having an awareness of another's experience and a sensitivity to his or her feelings and well-being. Once the anger has subsided, we can demonstrate concern about the impact that our anger may have had by asking how the other person is feeling as a result of our communication. We can then be available to receive their response in a caring way.

One of the most difficult and challenging aspects of skillful communication is to integrate a sense of personal power with compassion—developing an ability to assert our own feelings and needs while maintaining a genuine caring for others. If we attend only to our own feelings, we become narcissistic. Preoccupied with ourselves, out of touch with the world around us, we feel disconnected from intimacy and therefore undernourished in our very being. It is one of the great paradoxes of life that when we are focused only upon our own needs, they cannot possibly be fully met. On the other hand, if we pay exclusive attention to other people's feelings and reactions, we abandon our own genuine needs. This pattern may be reinforced by becoming identified with the self-image of being a compassionate or loving person. Seeing ourselves as more "evolved" than others and obliged to care for them regardless of personal needs, we will again be left undernourished and disconnected from the interdependence that is natural to human existence. Eventually we may experience an angry outrage resulting from an accumulated sense of deprivation and self-neglect.

We grow up in a society that teaches us to conceal our anger. As a result, we hold it back, and may justify this through statements such as, "I don't want to hurt him," or "I don't want her to feel badly." What seems like a noble concern for protecting others is frequently a hidden fear of being disliked. The fear or rejection, and subsequent fear of feeling isolated and alone, is a major reason for withholding our anger and failing to be completely honest with one another. However, taking the risk to be authentic in this way can often lead to the growth of trust when we are relating to a person who appreciates such honesty.

Taking care of ourselves by expressing clean anger can be done in a variety of ways. "Getting angry" without blame is the most intense way, as in shouting, "I want to have a say in what movie we see tonight!" This vocal anger may be especially appropriate in situations where we have stifled resentments and felt unheard for a long time.

As we work with our anger and release some of the charge that may have been accumulating, we can eventually learn to stand up for ourselves without becoming irate. Becoming comfortable with our right to say "no," or to stand up for what we want, we can begin to embody an assertiveness that appropriately matches the situation. Doing so, we learn to simply state how we feel, what is bothering us, or what we want, untinged by leftover anger that we may still be carrying from the past.

Experiencing anger and learning to express it cleanly can lead to other important insights about ourselves. For instance, we may discover a sense of hurt or fear beneath a more obvious layer of resentment. For example, we may realize that just below the surface of our anger about the dishes not being washed lies a deeper concern about whether we are really loved. In this case, our reactive anger is precariously sitting atop a storehouse of hurt of which we may only be vaguely aware. However, if anger is our most distinct feeling, then that is where we must begin to access our deeper level of experience. If we avoid the anger entirely (for example, by believing that we should just forgive and forget), than we may rob ourselves of a vital opportunity to follow the wisdom of our felt process to its natural outcome. As a result, we bypass a chance to learn more about ourselves and become more intimate with another person.

Expressing anger cleanly and non-defensively can place us in a vulnerable position in relation to the person with whom we are angry. In order to help us feel safer in beginning new patterns of behavior in a relationship, we may wish to agree to the basic ground rule that each person has permission to cleanly express anger. This implies a willingness to make clearer discrimination between clean and destructive anger. Perceiving this distinction is not always easy. Individuals with a commitment to their own growth and to one another's well-being can sensitively explore how to communicate their anger in ways that lead to a resolution of conflicts.

Another factor that can support productive communication concerns how we relate to others' anger. Can we simply receive it? Can we hear how they are feeling without counter-attacking or defending ourselves? We certainly have a right to respond, but can we first hear their feelings and point of view? Responding differs from reacting. Reactions tend to be automatic and habitual, and are often triggered by underlying fears, such as feeling unloved. Responding occurs after we have received their communication, allowed it to touch us in some way, and taken time to notice the fresh feelings and meanings that then arise within us. Can we hear them without assuming that it means something negative about ourselves, or that the person no longer loves us simply because they are feeling angry? The simple act of hearing others' resentments can go a long way toward resolving it. People feel better when they sense that their anger is heard rather than avoided, received rather than judged as being wrong or inappropriate. The process of receiving others' anger and opening to the meaning it holds for them can lead to a precious moment of interpersonal contact.

A relationship that has love and trust as its context can become stronger through its ability to accommodate a wide range of human emotions. If trust is tenuous or uncertain, a wave of anger can jeopardize it. However, as trust grows, then, instead of being a threat, anger can be seen as conveying a crucial message that is calling for attention. If we really care about another, then we want to hear his or her anger and understand what it is really all about. Perhaps, for example, we gradually discover that they are feeling misunderstood, unappreciated, or unloved.

Learning to acknowledge our anger and hold a healthy respect for the wisdom it contains is an important step toward the development of meaningful intimacy. The mutual sharing of anger in clean, self-revealing ways can lead to a process of communication that can help two individuals feel closer to one another. As normally suppressed energies are released and we more intimately touch one another, our relationships can flourish in unexpected ways.

Note

1. D. Wile, *Couples Therapy—a Nontraditional Approach* (New York: John Wiley, 1981), p. 12.

Review Questions

1. True or false: The authors believe that anger is good for relationships. Discuss
2. What is "passive-aggressive behavior"?
3. What is the primary difference between "clean" and "destructive" expressions of anger?
4. Explain what the authors mean when they say that "others do not cause our feelings."
5. What do they say about power and the expression of anger?
6. Paraphrase what the authors say in the third from the last paragraph in the article, where they talk about how we *hear* anger.

Probes

1. Have you ever experienced a physical symptom—headache, backache, etc.—that you later discovered was due to anger? What did you discover from that experience?
2. It's one thing to urge people, as the authors do, not to "judge" anger but just to notice it when it occurs. It's quite another thing to follow that advice, especially when your anger is intense. Create two or three practical, helpful suggestions for people who want to learn to stop evaluating their own anger.
3. Try illustrating the differences between "clean" and "destructive" anger by making a column of five or six different "destructive" expressions of anger. For example, throwing dishes or spitting in someone's face. Put as much variety in this column as you can. Then write out clean expressions to correspond with each different destructive one. What characteristics of clean expressions emerge from your lists?
4. The authors claim that our society teaches us not express anger. Has that been true in your experience? How has that proscription affected you?
5. What do you hear these authors saying about what other authors have called the difference between "assertiveness" and "aggressiveness"?
6. I believe that anger is clean or destructive not because of what one person does but because of what happens *between* persons. Like all other aspects of communication, I believe anger is a relational phenomenon. As a result, I don't think this essay pays enough attention to how anger is *heard*. What is your opinion on this issue?

ther cultures have lessons to teach white Westerners about emotions like anger and revenge. Hugh and Gayle Prather capture one of these lessons in the following brief excerpt from their book, *Parables from Other Planets: Folktales of the Universe.*

The central lesson here is this: "To take hate personally—that is, to take it into my heart and see the attacker with the same eyes with which he sees me— is to inflict pain on myself and to extend the world's ancient wound."

You might be thinking that this sentiment doesn't apply to every conflict, especially those that are much less intense. And it might also sound like this is one of those hopelessly idealistic and impractical ways to cope with real-world problems. But if anger is as big a problem as it seems to be in our cities, schools, families, and businesses, maybe the Prathers' advice is too relevant to dismiss so quickly. Think about it.

Dancing Arrow

Hugh and Gayle Prather

This fragment is all that remains of what is believed to be the last interview with Saguano, called by many on the planet of Iom the "dancing arrow," because of his unequivocal philosophy and joyous temperament. Oddly, Saguano granted this interview to The Disbeliever, *a small periodical that throughout its publishing history had harshly attacked Saguano and his followers.*

TD: The facts of your life are widely known: how you were a common farmer married to a local woman who bore you seven daughters, how you sought for no more than the warm winds and rains to nurture your crops and then how, during The War, just before you returned home, your wife and daughters were tortured and brutally slaughtered, even the youngest, who was only seven years old. My question to you is this: If you had really loved them, how could you have come home to that gruesome scene and then spent the rest of your life teaching the importance of understanding and even of humor?

SAGUANO: Would the crime have offended you less, and would you have thought that I had loved my family more, if it had not been brutal, if only my wife and elder daughters had been killed, and if they had been quickly shot but not beaten? Are you surprised that I chose not to extend the same anger that killed them?

TD: You found them that day—tortured, having spent their final hours in agony—and what did you think, that your God had honored them by wanting them with him? Or that his divine plan was to spare you?

SAGUANO: No, that day I believed that I had been cursed by God.

TD: Yet you are still smiling. Haven't you taught this planet to forsake vengeance so that you can continue to deny what happened to you? You don't seem to recognize that your teachings have placed many people in grave danger.

SAGUANO: My son, I have simply tried to give to others what saved me from over-whelming pain. I never asked for a follower.

TD: But all examples teach and everyone is a teacher. The effect of your conspicuous example is that most people now will not fight back. You have eliminated war but not aggression.

SAGUANO: Yes. And perhaps that is not entirely good. Evil must be resisted and it is extremely difficult to see how to do this in each situation. Kind does not mean weak, and I have never taught martyrdom. I only know that to take hate per-sonally—that is, to take it into my heart and see the attacker with the same eyes with which he sees me—is to inflict pain on myself and to extend the world's ancient wound. I could have spent my life hunting down the attackers and killing them one by one. Indeed, as I laid my beloved wife and children into their graves, as I covered their faces with cold earth, I was consumed with just this thought.

TD: Anyone would be. It's right to be consumed with hatred in such circumstances.

SAGUANO It is certainly not wrong to feel this way—but how could hatred have made the situation better? Would it have assuaged my sorrow? Would it have honored my loved ones? And if I had followed its leadings, would it have set for me a con-structive destiny?

TD: Revenge is natural. It is a form of control. It is an inherent emotion that marshals our defensive energies. You would have served justice and your family better by seeing to it that these savages never did this to anyone else. As it is, your family has died a meaningless death. Evil must be punished and eradicated by everyone who can reach it.

SAGUANO: Attack simply fans the fires of counterattack. If the evildoer is struck down in anger, another rises to take his place. It is good to bring criminals to justice, and there are those who are well equipped to do this with fairness. However, pur-suing my enemies is not my function in life. I did not want to extend my pain. I did not want one mother or father of the attackers to experience my suffering. And if I had sought to punish, where would the punishment have stopped?

TD: With those who committed the crime, of course.

SAGUANO: And what of those who drove them to this act of depravity, and those who in turn drove them? We are all connected, you see, and we can no longer deny this connection. My choice, as I began to recover a little from the death of all that I had ever loved, was to remain eternally damaged, the living proof of their guilt, or to rise out of it and shake the anger from me. Do not forget that it took me many years to accomplish this, and certainly no one is to be condemned if it takes them even longer. And I will admit to you one other thing: it is equally dif-ficult for me to respond to the hundreds of *little* provocations that arise every day, to respond, that is, from something within me besides irritation.

TD: Let us turn from your tragedy—which you have already dealt with in your own peculiar way—to the tragedy of others. You have said before that "laughter is the loveliest sound on the planet," that "humor is vision," that "a laughing heart accomplishes all," and other such pronouncements. However, *your* pain came from your association with, your connection to, the far greater pain of your fam-ily. You did not experience what they did. What of the millions of others who suffer directly? Are these people to laugh also?

SAGUANO: One who is truly laughing is *never* laughing at horror. To do so would be heartless. Instead, he is laughing in oneness with what he sees beyond horror.

Such laughter really never ends. One does not mock or even slight another's pain. One should not even question another's fears. Laughter is merely the happy and often silent recognition of what could help and of how it will all turn out someday. It extends a hand into the waters of pain but remains standing on firm ground.

TD: Seriousness and realism have accomplished far more for society than laughter. In fact, aside from a temporary lifting of spirits, not one historical change can be attributed to laughter.

SAGUANO You of course are right. And the reason is that it has never been tried. And yet, for all the humorless changes we have had, is our world really any different from what it has always been?

Review Questions and Probes

1. Summarize in your own words the two sides' arguments. I've started the process below. Then read over your summary and discuss with a classmate how you respond to this debate.

TD (*The Disbeliever*)

Your refusal to pursue vengeance is irresponsible and unrealistic.

Your teaching-by-example has eliminated war, but people are still suffering from aggression.

Saguano

I have only tried to give others the insight that spared me from overwhelming pain.

Chapter 15

. . .

Communicating Across Cultures

e more we learn about the ways people differ, the more we under-
:and that a great deal of our everyday communication is actually
ntercultural." For example, communication scholar and best-selling
ıthor Deborah Tannen makes a convincing argument that men and
tute distinct cultures, so that the best way to approach each
ınstance of male-female communication is to realize that you're in an *intercultural* situation. Especially in the United States, peoples' ethnic awareness is also
increasing, which means that individuals want to be recognized as members of
distinct cultures—African-American, Taiwanese, handicapped, Puerto Rican,
Laotian, or gay, for example. Regardless of your own cultural identity, it can get
more and more difficult to know how to deal with all the diversity.

Bill Gudykunst and Young Yun Kim are two speech communication teachers and researchers who have devoted their careers to studying intercultural communication. In the following pages they lay out a basic approach to intercultural
communication that is broad enough to apply not only to U.S.-Japanese and
Canadian-Mexican contacts, but also to encounters between African Americans
and Asian Americans, Laotian refugees and Caucasian bureaucrats, heterosexu-
als and lesbian women, and "a new bride visiting the groom's family."

There are two keys to this breadth. The first is the idea that "culture is communication and communication is culture." In other words, verbal and nonverbal
communicating is the place where the "culture" rubber hits the road. Cultural
abstractions become concrete in communication behaviors. The second key is the
concept of "the stranger," which can be used to talk about "aliens, intruders, foreigners, outsiders, newcomers, and immigrants, as well as any person who is
unknown and unfamiliar." When we encounter someone we define as "a
stranger," we experience some predictable difficulties and tend to respond in
some predictable ways. Gudykunst and Kim outline these tendencies and suggest
how we can become aware of them, and when it's desirable, change them.

First we can recognize the three levels of data that people use in making
predictions about others—cultural, sociological, and psychological. When we
mainly notice cultural data, the dangers are that we are unaware of the complexity of other persons' cultural experiences and/or that we interpret what they
do *ethnocentrically*, that is, as if only our own culture knows how to "do things
right." When we base our predictions on sociological, or group membership,
information, we often overlook the number of groups a stranger may belong to
and misinterpret which group's norms and values are influencing them. When we
base predictions on psychological data, we take into consideration each other
person's individual differences. Since all three levels of data involve some cultural
information, Gudykunst and Kim rename them "cultural," "sociocultural," and
"psychocultural."

When we make inferences on the basis of the first two levels of data—cultural and sociocultural—we engage in categorization that can become stereotyping. Unfortunately, many of these categorizing processes are also "mindless,"
which means that they operate below our level of awareness. One way to become
a more effective intercultural communicator is to move from what these authors
call mindless "unconscious incompetence" through "conscious incompetence"
and "conscious competence" to "unconscious competence."

The best way to begin making this set of moves is to learn how to reduce our uncertainty about the strangers we encounter. Gudykunst and Kim discuss three general sets of uncertainty reduction strategies—passive ones, active ones, and interactive ones. They illustrate how these operate in an example using Hiroko, a Japanese you've just been introduced to.

Anxiety is another barrier to intercultural communication that these authors discuss. They explain where it comes from and suggest how to cope with it. Then Gudykunst and Kim explain some of the attributional processes that occur in intercultural contacts—how the people involved make attributions based on each other's behavior. This section is useful because it illustrates the choices we have. We don't have to jump to the conclusion, for example, that what we hear as an insult is grounded in hostility.

This reading provides a general way to think about the many intercultural contacts you experience every day. It also suggests some initial ways to deal with the problems you might encounter. The following readings develop many of the suggestions made here.

Communicating with Strangers: An Approach to Intercultural Communication

William B. Gudykunst and Young Yun Kim

Greetings. I am pleased to see that we are different. May we together become greater than the sum of both of us.

VULCAN GREETING (*STAR TREK*)

In the past most human beings were born, lived, and died within a limited geographical area, never encountering people of other faces and/or cultural backgrounds. Such an existence, however, no longer prevails in the world. Even members of once isolated groups of people like the Tasadays in the Philippines now frequently have contact with members of other cultural groups. McLuhan (1962) characterized today's world as a "global village" because of the rapid expansion of worldwide transportation and communication networks (e.g., airplanes, communication satellites, and telephones). It is now possible for any person from an industrialized country to communicate with any person in another industrialized country within minutes by phone or within hours face-to-face. In fact, we are at a point in history when important or interesting events (wars, U.S. presidential debates, major sporting events, royal weddings,

Excerpts from Chapters 1 and 2 of *Communicating with Strangers: An Approach to Intercultural Communication*, 2/e by William B. Gudykunst and Young Yun Kim. 1992 McGraw-Hill.

and so forth) in one country are often transmitted simultaneously to more than 100 different countries. . . .

In a world of international interdependence, the ability to understand and communicate effectively with people from other cultures takes on extreme urgency. The need for intercultural understanding, however, does not begin or end with national boundaries. Within any nation a multitude of racial and ethnic groups exist, and their members interact daily. Legislation and legal rulings in the United States on affirmative action, school busing, and desegregation underscore the importance of nondiscriminatory contact between members of different racial and ethnic groups. The importance of good intergroup relations also is apparent when current demographic trends are examined. It is projected, for example, that in the near future the workplace will change from a place dominated by white males to a place dominated by women, immigrants, and nonwhite ethnics (Hudson Institute, 1987). For work to be accomplished effectively in the multicultural organization, people of different racial and ethnic groups need to understand one another's cultures and patterns of communication.

It is recognized widely that one of the characteristics separating humans from other animals is our development of culture. The development of human culture is made possible through communication, and it is through communication that culture is transmitted from one generation to another. Culture and communication are intertwined so closely that Hall (1959) maintains that "culture is communication" and "communication is culture." In other words, we communicate the way we do because we are raised in a particular culture and learn its language, rules, and norms. Because we learn the language, rules, and norms of our culture by a very early age (between five and ten years old), however, we generally are unaware of how culture influences our behavior in general and our communication in particular.

When we communicate with people from other cultures, we often are confronted with languages, rules, and norms different from our own. Confronting these differences can be a source of insight into the rules and norms of our own culture, as well as being a source of frustration or gratification. Although the presence of cultural differences may suggest the need for accommodation in our communication, it cannot be taken automatically as either a barrier or a facilitator of effective communication (Ellingsworth, 1977). Communication between people from different cultures can be as effective as communication between people from the same culture (Taylor & Simard, 1975). Stated in another way, communicating with a person from another culture may be either easier or more difficult than communicating with someone from the same culture.

One of the major factors influencing our effectiveness in communicating with people from other cultures is our ability to understand their culture. It is impossible to understand the communication of people from other cultures if we are highly ethnocentric. Sumner (1940) characterizes ethnocentrism as the "view of things in which one's own group is the center of everything, and all others are scaled and rated with reference to it" (p. 27). Ethnocentrism leads us to see our own culture's way of doing things as "right" and all others as "wrong." While the tendency to make judgments according to our own cultural standards is natural, it hinders our understanding of other cultures and the patterns of communication of their people. Becoming more culturally relativistic, on the other hand, can be conducive to understanding.

Cultural relativism suggests that the only way we can understand the behavior of others is in the context of their culture. Herskovits (1973) succinctly summarizes this position when he says evaluations must be "relative to the cultural background out of which they arise" (p. 14). No one cultural trait is "right" or "wrong"; it is merely "different" from alternative cultural traits. This is not to say we must never make value judgments of people in other cultures. Making them is often necessary. . . . Postponing these value judgments, or recognizing their tentative nature, until adequate information is gathered and we understand the people from the other culture, however, greatly facilitates understanding and effective communication. . . .

An Approach to the Study of Intercultural Communication

> See at a distance an undesirable person;
> See close at hand a desirable person;
> Come closer to the undesirable person;
> Move away from the desirable person.
> Coming close and moving apart,
> how interesting life is.
>
> GENSHO OGURA

It commonly is accepted that cultural variability in people's backgrounds influences their communication behavior. This "fact" leads many scholars studying intercultural communication to view it as a unique form of communication, differing in kind from other forms of communication (e.g., communication between people from the same culture). This point of view, however, is not accepted widely. Sarbaugh (1979) points out that

> there appears to be a temptation among scholars and practitioners of communication to approach intercultural communication as though it were a different process than intracultural communication. As one begins to identify the variables that operate in the communication being studied, however, it becomes apparent that they are the same for both intracultural and intercultural settings. (p. 5)

We agree with Sarbaugh; not only are the variables the same, but the underlying communication process is also the same.

We believe that any approach to the study of intercultural communication must be consistent with the study of intracultural communication. In this chapter . . . we lay out a perspective for the study of communication that is useful not only for understanding our communication with people from other cultures or subcultures but also for understanding our communication with people from our own culture or subculture. We first turn our attention to the linking concept in our view of communication—the concept of the stranger as a social phenomenon.

The Concept of the Stranger

To understand communication between people from different cultures, it is necessary to recognize that when people are confronted with cultural differences (and other forms of group differences, such as racial, ethnic, or class differences), they tend to view people from the group that is different as strangers. The term *stranger* is somewhat ambiguous in that it is often used to refer to aliens, intruders, foreigners, outsiders, newcomers, and immigrants, as well as any person who is unknown and unfamiliar. Despite this ambiguity "the concept of the stranger remains one of the most powerful sociological tools for analyzing social processes of individuals and groups confronting new social orders" (Shack, 1979, p. 2). . . .

Strangers do not have the knowledge necessary to fully understand their new environment or the communication of the people who live in it. Further, members of the host group do not possess information regarding individual strangers, even though they may have some information about the group or culture from which the strangers come. Since we do not have information regarding individual strangers, our initial impression of them must be largely an abstract or categoric one (i.e., a stereotypical one). Strangers are classified on the basis of whatever information we can obtain. If the only information we have is their culture, we base our initial impression on this information. If we have additional information (e.g., their race, ethnicity, gender, class), we use that as well.

Strangers, as we conceive of them, are people who are different and unknown and have come in contact with our group for the first time. It should be obvious that strangerhood is a figure-ground phenomenon—a stranger's status is always defined in relation to a host, a native, or some existing group. A person from the United States visiting another country and a person from another country visiting the United States, for example, are both strangers. A white teacher in a predominantly black school, a Native American working in a predominantly white organization, a Vietnamese refugee in the United States, a new bride visiting the groom's family, and a Chicano moving into a predominantly white neighborhood are all examples of strangers. In general, we include anyone entering a relatively unknown or unfamiliar environment under the rubric of stranger. . . .

Obviously, not everyone we meet for the first time is truly unknown and unfamiliar. Sometimes we are familiar with or know something about people we meet for the first time. Following Cohen (1972), we can say our social interactions, not just our interactions with people we meet for the first time, vary with respect to the degree of strangeness and/or familiarity present in the interaction. Our interactions with close friends and relatives involve a high degree of familiarity, while our interactions with acquaintances and coworkers involve less familiarity and more strangeness. When we meet people for the first time, there may be any degree of strangeness and/or familiarity. When we meet a close friend of our best friend for the first time, for example, we may be somewhat familiar with that person already. When we meet a person from another subculture of our culture (e.g., a person from another race or ethnic group), in contrast, our interaction with that person usually involves more strangeness than familiarity. Because they do not share the same culture, our interactions with people from other cultures often involve the highest degree of strangeness and the least degree of familiarity.

Our use of the term stranger . . . refers to those relationships where there is a relatively high degree of strangeness and a relatively low degree of familiarity. Since our interactions with people from other cultures tend to involve the highest degree of strangeness and the lowest degree of familiarity, we focus on these interactions, but we also examine other interactions involving a relatively high degree of strangeness (e.g., those with members of different races or ethnic groups).

In looking at the general process of communication with strangers, we are able to overcome one of the major conceptual problems of many analyses of intercultural communication. The problem to which we refer involves the drawing of artificial distinctions among intracultural, intercultural, interracial, and interethnic communication. While some variables may take on more importance in one situation than in another (e.g., our racial prejudices may be more important in interracial communication than in intraracial communication), each of the situations is influenced by the same variables (e.g., our prejudice also influences our intraracial communication, but it may be other prejudices, for example, sexism). If the variables influencing each situation and the underlying process of communication are the same, it does not make sense to draw artificial distinctions among them. By using the stranger as a linking concept, we can examine a general process, communicating with strangers, which subsumes intracultural, intercultural, interracial, and interethnic communication into one general framework.

An Overview of Communication With Strangers

Levels of Data Used in Making Predictions

Whenever we communicate with strangers, we make predictions about the outcome of our communication behavior. Of course, we are not always aware of making these predictions. Our awareness of making predictions varies with the degree to which we are aware of alternative outcomes in a particular situation (Miller & Steinberg, 1975). If we are aware of alternative outcomes, we are more aware of making predictions about the effects of our behavior. When we communicate with strangers, we tend to be more aware of alternative outcomes than when we communicate with someone we know, or someone who is familiar.

Miller and Steinberg (1975) argue that we use three levels of data when we make predictions about other people's behavior. The first level of data we use is "cultural." The people in any culture generally behave in a regular fashion because of their postulates, norms, and values. It is this regularity that allows us to make predictions on the basis of cultural data. Miller and Sunnafrank (1982) point out that

> knowledge about another person's culture—its language, dominant values, beliefs, and prevailing ideology—often permits predictions of the person's probable responses to certain messages. . . . Upon first encountering a stranger, cultural information provides the only grounds for communicative predictions. This fact explains the uneasiness and perceived lack of control most people experience when thrust into an alien culture: they not only lack information about the individuals with whom they must communicate, they are bereft of information concerning shared cultural norms and values. (pp. 226–227)

Two major factors influence our predictive accuracy using cultural data. First, the more experiences at the cultural level we have, the better our predictive accuracy is. When we are confronting someone from our own culture, the experiences to which we refer are in our culture. When we are communicating with strangers, on the other hand, our accuracy depends on our experiences with their culture. If we know little or nothing about the strangers' culture, our predictions will be less accurate than if we know a lot about their culture. Second, errors in predictions are made either because we are not aware of the strangers' cultural experiences or because we try to predict the behavior of strangers on the basis of cultural experiences different from the ones they have had—for example, when we make ethnocentric predictions on the basis of our own cultural experiences (Miller & Steinberg, 1975).

The second level of data used in making predictions is "sociological." Sociological level predictions are based on strangers' memberships in or aspirations to particular social groups. "Knowledge of an individual's membership groups, as well as the reference groups to which he or she aspires, permits numerous predictions about responses to various messages" (Miller & Sunnafrank, 1982, p. 227). Membership in social groups may be voluntary, or strangers may be classified as a member of a group because of certain characteristics they possess. Our predictions at the sociological level, for example, include those based on strangers' memberships in political or other social groups, the roles they fill, their gender, or their ethnicity. Miller and Sunnafrank (1982) argue that sociological level data are the principal kind used to predict the behavior of people from the same culture. The major error in making predictions using sociological level data stems from the fact that strangers are members of many groups, and when we communicate with other people it is not always possible to be sure which group's norms and values are influencing their behavior (Miller & Steinberg, 1975).

The final level of data used in making predictions about the outcomes of our communication behavior is "psychological." At the psychological level predictions are based on the specific people with whom we are communicating. At this level we are concerned with how these people are different from and similar to other members of their culture and the groups to which they belong. When predictions are based on psychological data, "each participant relates to the other in terms of what sets the other apart from most people. They take into consideration each other's individual differences in terms of the subject and the occasion" (Dance & Larson, 1972, p. 56).

It is important to keep in mind that our predictions are rarely made at only one level. Once we have some psychological information about a stranger with whom we are communicating, we use this information and combine it with our cultural and sociological data to make predictions about her or his behavior. Most of our predictions are some combination of the three levels of data, but one level often predominates.

For the purpose of the present analysis, we modify the labels for the three levels of data used in making predictions. Since all three levels are highly interrelated, we use labels reflecting the interrelations: cultural, sociocultural, and psychocultural. Our modification of the last two labels is intended only to emphasize that the three levels of data are interrelated, not to reflect a disagreement with Miller and Steinberg's (1975) conceptualization.

Categorization and Particularization

Making predictions based on cultural and/or sociocultural data can be likened to stimulus generalization, or looking for sameness when making predictions about other communicators, according to Miller and Steinberg (1975). They go on to point out that "stimulus generalization is closely akin to abstraction: One observes a group of objects and notes aspects they have in common. . . . Stimulus generalization necessarily ignores the characteristics on which objects and events differ" (p. 24). If predictions based on cultural and/or sociocultural data can be likened to stimulus generalization, then making predictions based on psychocultural data can be likened to stimulus discrimination, or looking for differences among communicators (Miller & Steinberg, 1975).

Stimulus generalization involves the process of categorization. Much of the work in social psychology on social cognition is based on the assumption that categorization is the fundamental process in thought. Cantor, Mischel, and Schwartz (1982), for example, contend that categorization is a fundamental quality of cognition. They go on to suggest that categorization is important because it allows "us to structure and give coherence to our general knowledge about people and the social world, providing expectations about typical patterns of behavior and the range of likely variation between types of people and their characteristic actions and attributes" (p. 34).

Billig (1987) does not deny that we engage in categorization, but he also believes that we engage in particularization. While categorization is the process whereby stimuli are placed in a general category, particularization is the process whereby stimuli are separated or differentiated from members of a category.

Billig contends that categorization and particularization are highly interrelated, "so much so that the ability to categorize presupposes the ability to particularize" (p. 133). He points out that

> the paradox is that these two processes seem to pull in opposite cognitive directions: the one pulls toward the aggregation of things and the other toward the uniqueness of things. The result is that the human mind is equipped with two contrary skills of being able to put things into categories and treat them as special. (p. 134).

Billig goes on to argue that "categorization does not provide the basis of thinking in a simple sense. The automatic application of categories is the negation of thinking, in that it is essentially a thoughtless process" (p. 140).

To summarize, anytime we communicate with strangers we engage in both categorization and particularization. Categorization, however, often predominates. When the process of categorization predominates we do not recognize strangers as individuals and communicate with them based on our stereotypes (i.e., the "pictures" of their groups we have in our heads) and attitudes toward their group. . . . Since our stereotypes often are inaccurate and/or do not apply to particular strangers, our predictions of their behavior often are inaccurate. This leads to misunderstandings and ineffective communication. To communicate effectively, we must be thoughtful and particularize incoming messages from strangers. That is, we must look closely at the unique attributes, attitudes, and behaviors of strangers before making predictions about them. We must be mindful.

Mindfulness

As indicated above, we engage in both categorization and particularization. Engaging in categorization is essentially a "thoughtless" process and engaging in particularization involves thought. Further, we are not always aware of our cognitive processes. Another way of stating this is that we vary in the degree that we are mindful of, consciously aware of, or pay attention to, our communication behavior.

There are several conditions under which we do not think much about our behavior. Much of our communication behavior, for example, is habitual. When we are communicating habitually, we are following a script—"a coherent sequence of events expected by the individual involving him [or her] either as a participant or an observer" (Abelson, 1976, p. 33). According to Langer (1978), when we first encounter a new situation, we consciously seek cues to guide our behavior. As we have repeated experiences with the same event, we have less need to consciously think about our behavior. "The more often we engage in the activity, the more likely it is that we rely on scripts for the completion of the activity and the less likely there will be any correspondence between our actions and those thoughts of ours that occur simultaneously" (Langer, 1978, p. 39).

As indicated above, when we are engaging in habitual or scripted behavior, we are not highly aware of what we are doing or saying. To borrow an analogy from flying a plane, we are on "automatic pilot." In Langer's (1978) terminology, we are "mindless." Recent research, however, suggests that we do not communicate totally on automatic pilot. Rather, we pay sufficient attention so that we can recall key words in the conversations we have (Kitayama & Burnstein, 1988).

Another condition that contributes to being mindless is the use of categories. Categorization often is based on physical (e.g., gender, race) or cultural (e.g., ethnic background) characteristics, but we also can categorize others in terms of their attitudes (e.g., liberal-conservative) or approaches to life (e.g., Christian or Buddhist: Trungpa, 1973). In order to particularize stimuli, we must become mindful of our thought processes. Langer (1989) isolates three qualities of mindfulness: "(1) creation of new categories; (2) openness to new information; and (3) awareness of more than one perspective" (p. 62). She points out that "categorizing is a fundamental and natural human activity. It is the way we come to know the world. Any attempt to eliminate bias by attempting to eliminate the perception of differences is doomed to failure" (p. 154).

Langer argues that being mindful involves making more, not fewer, distinctions. To illustrate, Langer uses an example of people who are in the category "cripple." If we see all people in this category as the same, we start treating the category in which we place them as their identity—cripple. If we draw additional distinction within this category (i.e., create new categories), on the other hand, it stops us from identifying the person as a category. If we draw an additional distinction and see a person with a lame leg, we do not necessarily regard her or him as a member of that category "cripple," thereby making it possible to see the person as an individual.

We become more conscious of our behavior when we enter new situations such as communicating with strangers. The situations under which we are aware of our behavior, however, must be delineated more fully. Berger and Douglas (1982) list five conditions under which we are highly cognizant of our behavior:

> (1) in novel situations where, by definition, no appropriate script exists, (2) where external factors prevent completion of a script, (3) when scripted behavior becomes effortful because substantially more of the behavior is required than is usual, (4) when a discrepant outcome is experienced, or (5) where multiple scripts come into conflict so that involvement in any one script is suspended. In short, individuals will enact scripted sequences whenever those sequences are available and will continue to do so until events unusual to the script are encountered. (pp. 46–47)

From Berger and Douglas' summary of these conditions, it can be inferred we are more aware of our behavior when communicating with strangers than we are when communicating with people who are familiar.

Improving the effectiveness of our communication with strangers requires that we become aware of how we communicate. Howell (1982) argues that awareness and competence can be thought of as a four-stage process: (1) unconscious incompetence, where we misinterpret others' behavior, but are not aware of it; (2) conscious incompetence, where we are aware that we misinterpret others' behavior, but we do not do anything about it; (3) conscious competence, where we think about our communication behavior and consciously modify it to improve our effectiveness (we refer to this stage as mindfulness above); and (4) unconscious competence, where we have practiced the skills for effective communication to the extent that we no longer have to think about them to use them.

Because of our socialization in our culture, most of us misinterpret strangers' behavior and are not aware of it (i.e., we are unconsciously incompetent). One of the purposes of this [chapter] is to help readers become consciously competent. To accomplish this goal, we present material designed to illustrate the factors that lead to our misinterpretation of strangers' behavior. Once we are consciously incompetent (i.e., understand that we misinterpret strangers' behavior), we can consciously (i.e., mindfully) try to improve our effectiveness. . . .

Uncertainty in Interactions with Strangers

The predictions we make when we are communicating are aimed at reducing the uncertainty present whenever we communicate with strangers. Berger and Calabrese (1975) point out that the primary concern anytime we meet someone new is uncertainty reduction. Berger (1979) modified this position, arguing that we try to reduce uncertainty when the person we meet will be encountered in the future, provides rewards to us, or behaves in a deviant fashion. Given that strangers, especially those from other cultures or ethnic groups, are likely to behave in a deviant fashion, it is reasonable to say we try to reduce uncertainty when we communicate with strangers more than we do when we communicate with people who are familiar.

Berger and Calabrese (1975) point out there are at least two distinct types of uncertainty present in our interactions with strangers. First, there is the uncertainty we have about strangers' attitudes, feelings, beliefs, values, and behavior. We need to be able, for example, to predict which of several alternative behavior patterns strangers will choose to employ. An illustration is the situation when we meet a person we find attractive at a party. Assuming we want to see this person again after the party, we try to think about different ways we can approach this person in order to convince him or her to see us again. The different approaches we think about are the predictions of alternative behaviors that reduce our uncertainty. The second type of uncertainty Berger and Calabrese (1975) isolate involves explanations of strangers' behavior. Whenever we try to figure out why strangers behaved the way they did, we are engaging in explanatory uncertainty reduction. The problem we are addressing is one of reducing the number of possible explanations for the strangers' behavior. This is necessary if we are to understand their behavior and, thus, be able to increase our ability to predict their behavior in the future.

It appears that there is greater uncertainty in our initial interactions with strangers than with people who are familiar (Gudykunst, 1991). This does not mean, however, that we will be motivated to actively reduce uncertainty more when we communicate with strangers than when we communicate with people who are familiar. While strangers may behave in a "deviant" fashion (e.g., not follow *our* norms or communication rules) they rarely are seen as sources of rewards and we may not anticipate seeing them again in the future. When we do not actively try to reduce our uncertainty regarding strangers' behavior, we rely on our categorizations of strangers to reduce our uncertainty and guide our predictions. As indicated earlier, this often leads to misunderstandings.

If we choose to reduce our uncertainty about strangers, there are several strategies we can use. Berger (2979) isolates three general sets of strategies: passive, active, and interactive. When we use passive strategies we take the role of unobtrusive observers (i.e., we do not intervene in the situation we are observing). To illustrate this process, assume that we want to find out about Hiroko, a Japanese to whom we have just been introduced.

Obviously, the type of situation in which we observe Hiroko influences the amount of information we gain about her. If we observe Hiroko in a situation where she does not have to interact with others, we will not gain much information about her. Situations in which she is interacting with several people at once, in contrast, allow us to make comparisons of how Hiroko interacts with the different people.

If we know any of the people with whom Hiroko is interacting, we can compare how Hiroko interacts with the people we know and how she might interact with us. It also should be noted that if other Japanese are present in the situation, we can compare Hiroko's behavior with theirs to try to determine how she is similar to and different from other Japanese.

There is one other aspect of the situation that will influence the amount of information we obtain about Hiroko's behavior. If the situation is a formal one, her behavior is likely to be a function of the role she is filling in the situation and we will not learn much about Hiroko as an individual. Situations where behavior is not guided by roles or social protocol, on the other hand, will provide useful information on Hiroko's behavior.

The preceding examples all involve our taking the role of an observer. The active strategies for reducing uncertainty require us to do something to acquire information about Hiroko. One thing we could do to get information about Hiroko is to ask questions of someone who knows her. When we ask others about someone we need to keep in mind that the information we receive may not be accurate. The other person may intentionally give us wrong information, or the other person may not really know Hiroko well.

We can also gather information about other groups by asking people who have had contact with those groups or by gathering information from the library. In this example, we could gather information on Japan by questioning someone we know who has lived in Japan or by reading a book on Japanese culture. This would give us information about Hiroko's cultural background that would allow us to make cultural level predictions about her behavior.

When we use active strategies to gather information we do not actually interact with the people about whom we are trying to gather information. The interactive strategies of verbal interrogation (question asking) and self-disclosure, in contrast, are used when we interact with the other person.

One obvious way we can gather information about others is to ask them questions. When we are interacting with someone who is similar, there are limitations to this strategy that have to be kept in mind. First, we can ask only so many questions; we always know when we have asked too many. Second, our questions must be appropriate to the nature of the interaction we are having and the relationship we have with the other person.

When we are communicating with strangers, the same limitations are present, and there are others. The number and type of questions that strangers consider acceptable may not be the same as what we consider acceptable. Strangers also may not be able to answer our questions, especially if our questions deal with why they behave the way they do [the ultimate answer is to "why" questions is "because!" (that is the way we do it here)].

The other way we can gather information about another person when interacting with her or him is through self-disclosure—telling the other person information about ourselves. Self-disclosure works as an information gathering strategy because of the reciprocity norm (Gouldner, 1960). Essentially, the reciprocity norm states that if I do something for you, you will reciprocate and do something for me. The reciprocity norm appears to be a cultural universal; it exists in all cultures.

In conversations between people who are not close (e.g., people we meet for the first time, acquaintances), we tend to reciprocate and tell each other the same information about ourselves that the other person tells us. If Hiroko discloses her opinion on a topic, you will probably tell her your opinion on the same topic. There will, however, be some differences when we communicate with strangers than when we communicate with people from our own group. The topics that are appropriate to be discussed, for example, vary from culture to culture and ethnic group to ethnic group. If we self-disclose on a topic with a stranger and she or he does not reciprocate, there is a good chance we have found an inappropriate topic of conversation in that person's group. Since the timing and pacing of self-disclosure vary across cultures and ethnic groups, it is also possible that our timing is off or we have tried to self-disclose at an inappropriate pace.

Anxiety in Interactions with Strangers

When we communicate with strangers we not only have a high level of uncertainty, we also have a high level of anxiety. The anxiety we experience when we communicate with strangers usually is based on negative expectations. Research indicates, for example, that actual or anticipated interaction with a member of a different ethnic group leads to anxiety. . . . Stephan and Stephan (1985) argue we fear four types of negative consequences when interacting with strangers.

First we fear negative consequences for our self-concepts. In interacting with strangers, we worry "about feeling incompetent, confused, and not in control . . . anticipate discomfort, frustration, and irritation due to the awkwardness of intergroup interactions" (Stephan & Stephan, 1985, p. 159). We also may fear that we will lose self-esteem, that our social identities will be threatened, and that we will feel guilty if we behave in ways that offend strangers.

Second, we may fear negative behavioral consequences will result from our communication with strangers. We may feel that strangers will exploit us, take advantage of us, or try to dominate us. We also may worry about performing poorly in the presence of strangers or worry that physical harm or verbal conflict will occur.

Third, we fear negative evaluations of strangers. We fear rejection, ridicule, disapproval, and being stereotyped negatively. These negative evaluations, in turn can be seen as threats to our social identities. Recent research suggests that we perceive communication with people who are familiar as more agreeable and less abrasive than communication with strangers (Hoyle, Pinkley, & Insko, 1989).

Finally, we may fear negative evaluations by members of our ingroups. If we interact with strangers, members of our ingroups may disapprove. We may fear that "ingroup members will reject" us, "apply other sanctions," or identify us "with the outgroup" (Stephan & Stephan, 1985, p. 160).

Stephan and Stephan (1985) point out that the anxiety we experience when we communicate with strangers "often has a basis in reality. People sometimes do make embarrassing mistakes, are taken advantage of, and are rejected by ingroup and out-group members" (p. 160) when communicating with strangers. One of the emotional reactions we have to our expectations of strangers being disconfirmed is that we become frustrated. "Frustration involves feelings of intense discomfort stemming from the blockage of paths toward goals. . . . Frustration, in turn, often leads to aggressive behavior or people try to vent their negative feelings" (Brislin, Cushner, Cherrie, & Yong, 1986, p. 250).

Several factors appear to be associated with the amount of anxiety we experience when we communicate with strangers. Thinking about the behavior in which we need to engage when communicating with strangers, for example, can reduce our anxiety about interacting with them (Janis & Mann, 1977). Further, if we focus on finding out as much as we can and on forming accurate impressions of strangers as well as the biases we have, our anxiety and negative expectations will be reduced (Leary, Kowalski, & Bergen, 1988; Neuberg, 1989). Stephan and Stephan (1989) also found that the more intergroup contact we have experienced, the less ethnocentric we are, and the more positive our stereotypes are, the less the intergroup anxiety we experience.

Attributional Processes

A problem closely related to uncertainty and anxiety reduction is the question of how we utilize information about strangers to reach inferences about their behavior. Attribution theory is instructive concerning this process.

Jones and Nisbett (1972) argue that people performing behavior interpret their behavior differently than do people observing it. Specifically, they suggest people usually attribute their own behavior to situational factors, whereas observers attribute the behavior to qualities of the people being observed. Nisbett, Caputo, Legant, and Marecek (1973) offer two probable explanations for these divergent perspectives. The first is simply a perceptual one. The attention of the people engaging in the behavior is focused on situational cues with which their behavior is coordinated. It therefore appears to people engaging in behavior that their behavior is a response to these situational cues. For observers, however, it is not the situational cues that are salient, but rather the behavior. Observers are more likely to perceive the cause of others' behavior to be a trait or quality inherent in the person exhibiting it. This view suggests that when we communicate with strangers our retroactive explanations of their behavior are likely to focus on characteristics of the strangers (e.g., their cultural background or group membership). The second explanation suggested by Nisbett et al. for the differential bias of people engaging in behavior and observers stems from a difference in the nature and extent of information possessed. In general, the people engaging in behavior know more about their own past behavior and present experiences than do observers. This difference in information may prevent people engaging in behavior from interpreting their behavior in terms of personal characteristics, while allowing observers to make such an interpretation:

> If an actor [or actress] insults another person, an observer may be free to infer that the actor [or actress] did so because the actor [or actress] is hostile. The actor [or actress], however, may know that he [or she] rarely insults others and may believe that his [or her] insult was a response to the most recent in a series of provocations from the person he [or she] finally attacked. The difference in information available to the actor [or actress] and observer is, of course, reduced when the actor [or actress] and observer know one another well but is always present to a degree. (Nisbett et al., 1973, p. 155)

When we are communicating with strangers, there is an increased likelihood we will attribute the cause of their behavior to one particular characteristic—namely, their cultural background or group membership. Stated differently, we are not likely to attribute the cause of others' behavior to their culture if they come from the same culture we do, but since strangers often come from another culture or ethnic group, their origin or background is a plausible explanation for their behavior. . . .

Summary

Communication with people from our own culture, with people from other races or ethnic groups, and with people from other cultures shares the same underlying process. While communication in these different situations differs in degrees, it does not differ in kind. Various names are available to label communication in these different situations, but ambiguity exists as to which label is appropriate for certain situations. Communication between a white person from South Africa and a black person from the United States, for example, can be labeled as either intercultural or interracial communication. Given the similarity of the underlying process of communication and the confusion in applying the various labels, we believe what is needed is a way to refer to the underlying process without referring to a particular situation. Talking about communication with strangers is a way to accomplish this end. Strangers can be conceived of as people who are unknown and unfamiliar and are confronting a group for the first time. A black student in a mainly white school, a Mexican student studying at a university in the United States, a groom meeting the bride's family for the first time, and a manager from the United States working in Thailand are all examples of strangers.

Our communication with strangers is influenced by our conceptual filters, just as their communication with us is influenced by their filters. Our conceptual filters can be placed into four categories: cultural, sociocultural, psychocultural, and environmental. Each of these influences how we interpret messages encoded by strangers and what predictions we make about strangers' behavior. Without understanding the strangers' filters, we cannot accurately interpret or predict their behavior.

References

Berger, C. (1979). Beyond initial interaction. In H. Giles & R. St. Clair (Eds.), *Language and Social Psychology*. Oxford, England: Blackwell.

Berger, C., & Calabrese, R. (1975). Some explorations in initial interaction and beyond. *Human Communication Research, 1*, 99–112.

Berger, C., & Douglas, W. (1982). Thought and talk: "Excuse me, but have I been talking to myself?" In F. Dance (Ed.), *Human communication theory*. New York: Harper & Row.

Billig, M. (1987). *Arguing and thinking*. Cambridge, England: Cambridge University Press.

Brislin, R., Cushner, K., Cherrie, C., & Young, M. (1986). *Intercultural interactions*. Beverly Hills, CA: Sage.

Cantor, N., Mischel, W., & Schwartz, J. (1982). Social knowledge. In A. Isen & A. Hastorf (Eds.), *Cognitive social psychology*. New York: Elsevier North-Holland.

Cohen, E. (1972). Toward a sociology of international tourism. *Social Research, 39*, 164–182.

Dance, F., & Larson, C. (1972). *Speech communication*. New York: Holt, Rinehart & Winston.

Ellingsworth, H. (1977). Conceptualizing intercultural communication. In B. Ruben (Ed.), *Communication yearbook 1*. New Brunswick, NJ: Transaction.

Gouldner, A. (1960) The norm of reciprocity. *American Sociological Review, 25,* 161–179.

Gudykunst, W. B. (1991). *Bridging differences*. Newbury Park, CA: Sage.

Hall, E. T. (1959). *The silent language*. New York: Doubleday.

Herskovits, M. (1973). *Cultural relativism*. New York: Random House.

Howell, W. (1982). *The empathic communicator*. Belmont, CA: Wadsworth.

Hoyle, R., Pinkley, R., & Insko, C. (1989). Perceptions of social behavior. *Personality and Social Psychology Bulletin, 15,* 365–376.

Hudson Institute. (1987). *Workforce 2000*. Washington, DC: United States Department of Labor.

Janis, I., & Mann, L. (1977). *Decision making*. New York: Free Press.

Jones, E., & Nisbett, R. (1972). *The actor and the observer*. Morristown, NJ: General Learning Press.

Kitayama, S., & Burnstein, E. (1988). Automaticity in conversations. *Journal of Personality and Social Psychology, 54,* 219–224.

Langer, E. (1978). Rethinking the role of thought in social interaction. In J. Harvey, W. Ickes, and R. Kidd (Eds.), *New directions in attribution research* (Vol. 2). Hillsdale, NJ: Lawrence Erlbaum.

Langer, E. (1989). *Mindfulness*. Reading, MA: Addison-Wesley.

Leary, M., Kowalski, R., & Bergen, D. (1988). Interpersonal information acquisition and confidence in first encounters. *Personality and Social Psychology Bulletin, 14,* 68-77.

McLuhan, M. (1962). *The Gutenberg galaxy*. New York: New American Library.

Miller, G., & Steinberg, M. (1975). *Between people*. Chicago: Science Research Associates.

Miller, G., & Sunnafrank, M. (1982). All is for one but one is not for all: A conceptual perspective of interpersonal communication. In F. Dance (Ed.), *Human communication theory*. New York: Harper & Row.

Nisbett, R., Caputo, C., Legant, P., & Marecek, J. (1973). Behavior as seen by the actor and as seen by the observer. *Journal of Personality and Social Psychology, 27,* 154–165.

Sarbaugh, L. (1979). *Intercultural communication*. Rochelle Park, NJ: Hayden.

Shack, W. (1979). Open systems and closed boundaries. In W. Shack & E. Skinner (Eds.), *Strangers in African society*. Berkeley: University of California Press.

Stephan, W., & Stephan, C. (1985). Intergroup anxiety. *Journal of Social Issues, 41,* 157–166.

Sumner, W. G. (1940). *Folkways*. Boston: Ginn.

Taylor, D. M., & Simard, L. M. (1975). Social interaction in a bilingual setting. *Canadian Psychological Review, 16,* 240–254.

Trungpa, C. (1973). *Cutting through spiritual materialism*. Boulder, CO: Shambhala.

Review Questions

1. What does it mean to say we inhabit a "global village"? What's the significance of this idea?
2. What's the significance of the idea that "communication is culture and culture is communication"?
3. In your own words, define "ethnocentrism."
4. Why do these authors change the labels "sociological data" and psychological data" to "sociocultural data" and psychocultural data"?
5. What's the difference between "stimulus generalization" and "stimulus discrimination"?

6. Distinguish among unconscious incompetence, conscious incompetence, conscious competence, and unconscious competence.
7. What are the two types of uncertainty that Berger and Calabrese say we have about the strangers we encounter?
8. Paraphrase the four fears that these authors say contribute to the anxiety we often experience when communicating with strangers.

Probes

1. These authors' use of the concept "the stranger" significantly broadens their conception of intercultural communication. List ten different contacts that you might have in a typical week that qualify as "intercultural" under this definition.
2. If you're using this book in a college or university course, think back to the first time you came into contact with your teacher. As you perceived him or her for the first time (the first class period, for example), which kind(s) of data did you rely on to build your first impression—cultural, sociocultural, or psychocultural? How did your perceptions affect your communication with your teacher?
3. What do these authors say about what stereotyping is and how to avoid it? How applicable do you find their advice to be? Does it help you avoid the pitfalls of stereotyping in your own intercultural communication?
4. Think of a specific "stranger" that you would like to know better. List nine strategies that you could use to reduce your uncertainty—three passive, three active, and three interactive ones.
5. Some other authors who write about attributional processes label the natural tendency to attribute another's behavior to internal causes—hostility, incompetence, prejudice, and so on—rather than to situational factors—lack of time, other commitments, and so on— "the fundamental attribution error." (a) Explain the *cultural* version of this error that Gudykunst and Kim describe. (b) Test it against your own experience with a stranger. Do your attributions tend to fall into this pattern?

I n 1987 Letty Cottin Pogrebin published an exhaustive book on friendship based on two very thorough friendship surveys, many additional published research reports, and interviews with almost 150 people ranging in age from early adolescence to eighty-two years and representing most of the spectrum of cultures and subcultures in the United States. The following reading consists of excerpts from Chapter 11 of her sixteen-chapter book. As the title indicates, the chapter deals with friendship across a variety of cultural boundaries including color, culture, sexual preference, disability, and age. As with other readings, I chose this one because it blends sound research and straightforward writing, credible theory, and solid practice.

This rigorous but accessible flavor or Pogrebin's work emerges in the section right after the introduction. She begins with the obvious but important point that if you're going to cross a boundary, you'll find yourself doing a lot of explaining—to yourself, to each other, and to your respective communities. Then she takes a couple of pages to elaborate on what that "explaining" will probably consist of.

The next major section develops another potentially profound theme: intercultural relationships consistently have to deal with the reality that the two persons might be "the same," but that they're also "never quite the same." She illustrates the point with examples from black/redneck white, Jewish/Irish-

Catholic, Puerto Rican/white, and Spanish/Jewish relationships. Pogrebin's discussion of "moving in one another's world" extends the notion of "the same but never quite the same" to include challenges introduced by second and third languages and fundamental cultural values. She also discusses several "hazards of crossing" that emerge when fundamental differences in cultural values meet.

Under the heading "The Problem with 'Them' Is 'Us,'" Pogrebin discusses gay/straight, disabled/nondisabled, and young/aged relationships. All three topics became current only in the past decade as the minority rights movement spread to include gays and lesbians, the disabled, and "senior citizens," and government regulations made these groups increasingly visible. As the author notes, these groups warrant separate discussions in part because, "To a large degree, our society still wants to keep them out of sight—the gays and lesbians for 'flaunting their alternative life-styles,' the disabled for not 'getting better,' and the old for reminding us of our eventual fate."

Pogrebin's outline of the kinds of "explaining" one has to do about his or her gay/straight relationships accurately captures the last ten years or so of my experience communicating with gays and lesbians. The strong relationship Kris and I have with Bill and John Paul, our "married" next-door neighbors, is one example of some of the problems and much of the potential Pogrebin discusses. I also appreciate her summary of the contrasts between gay and straight views on homophobia, AIDS, lesbian politics, and acceptance.

Until recently, disabled persons in the United States made up perhaps an even more invisible subculture than gays. Thanks in part to major changes in building codes affecting all public construction, wheelchair-bound, deaf, and blind persons are becoming increasingly visible. Pogrebin explains some of the unique problems the nondisabled can have establishing and maintaining relationships with these persons. As one quadriplegic succinctly puts it, "We need friends who won't treat us as weirdo asexual second-class children or expect us to be 'Supercrips'—miracle cripples who work like crazy to make themselves whole again. . . . We want to be accepted the way we are." Many nondisabled persons are guilty of exactly these charges and can be shocked to hear them expressed so bluntly.

In the final section of this reading, Pogrebin discusses cross-age friendships. She cites some studies that indicate that three-year-olds already have developed "ageist" perceptions of the elderly—believing that old people are sick, tired, and ugly. Other studies reveal the stereotypes older people have of children and teenagers. She discusses some of the typical reasons for cross-age miscommunication and then suggests some reasons why age can be immaterial to developing friendships. As the average age of the U.S. populace continues to increase, Pogrebin's comments will become more and more applicable and important.

I like the way this reading extends the general theoretical ideas Gudykunst and Kim outline. I also appreciate the breadth of application that's here. I believe that Pogrebin is writing about some "cutting-edge" aspects of interpersonal communication and that her ideas are going to become increasingly important between now and the turn of the century.

The Same and Different: Crossing Boundaries of Color, Culture, Sexual Preference, Disability, and Age

Letty Cottin Pogrebin

On August 21, 1985, as they had done several times before, twenty-one men from a work unit at a factory in Mount Vernon, New York, each chipped in a dollar, signed a handwritten contract agreeing to "share the money equaly [sic] & fairly to each other," and bought a ticket in the New York State Lottery. The next day, their ticket was picked as one of three winners of the largest jackpot in history: $41 million.

The story of the Mount Vernon 21 captivated millions not just because of the size of the pot of gold but because of the rainbow of people who won it. Black, white, yellow, and brown had scribbled their names on that contract—Mariano Martinez, Chi Wah Tse, Jaroslaw Siwy, and Peter Lee—all immigrants from countries ranging from Paraguay to Poland, from Trinidad to Thailand.

"We're like a big family here," said Peter Lee. "We thought by pooling our efforts we would increase our luck—and we were right."[1]

The men's good fortune is a metaphor for the possibility that friendships across ethnic and racial boundaries may be the winning ticket for everyone. This is not to say that crossing boundaries is a snap. It isn't. There are checkpoints along the way where psychic border guards put up a fuss and credentials must be reviewed. We look at a prospective friend and ask, "Do they want something from me?" Is this someone who sees personal advantage in having a friend of another race at his school, in her company, at this moment in history? Is it Brotherhood Week? Does this person understand that "crossing friendships" require more care and feeding than in-group friendship, that it takes extra work?

Explaining

Most of the extra work can be summed up in one word: *explaining*. Whatever the boundary being crossed—race, ethnicity, or any other social category—both partners in a crossing friendship usually find they have to do a lot of explaining—to themselves, to each other, and to their respective communities.

Explaining to Yourself

One way or another, you ask yourself, "What is the meaning of my being friends with someone not like me?"

In his classic study, *The Nature of Prejudice*, Gordon Allport distinguishes between the in-group, which is the group to which you factually belong, and the reference group, which is the group to which you relate or aspire.[2] Allport gives the example of Blacks who so wish to partake of white skin privilege that they seek only white friends, disdain their own group, and become self-hating. One could as easily cite Jews who assume a WASP identity or "Anglicized Chicanos" who gain education and facility in English and then sever their ties of kinship and friendship with other Mexican-Americans.[3]

When you have a friend from another racial or ethnic group, you ask yourself whether you are sincerely fond of this person or might be using him or her as an entrée into a group that is your unconscious reference group. The explaining you do to yourself helps you understand your own motivations. It helps you ascertain whether the friend complements or denies your identity, and whether your crossing friendships are in reasonable balance with your in-group relationships.

Explaining to Each Other

Ongoing mutual clarification is one of the healthiest characteristics of crossing friendships. The Black friend explains why your saying "going ape" offends him, and the Jewish friend reminds you she can't eat your famous barbecued pork. Both of you try to be honest about your cultural sore points and to forgive the other person's initial ignorance or insensitivities. You give one another the benefit of the doubt. Step by step, you discover which aspects of the other person's "in-groupness" you can share and where you must accept exclusion with grace.

David Osborne, a white, describes his close and treasured friendship with an American Indian from Montana: "Steve was tall and athletic—the classic image of the noble full-blooded Indian chief. We were in the same dorm in my freshman year at Stanford at a time when there were only one or two other Native Americans in the whole university. He had no choice but to live in a white world. Our friendship began when our English professor gave an assignment to write about race. Steve and I got together to talk about it. We explored stuff people don't usually discuss openly. After that, we started spending a lot of time together. We played intramural sports. We were amazingly honest with each other, but we were also comfortable being silent.

"When I drove him home for spring vacation, we stopped off at a battlefield that had seen a major war between Chief Joseph's tribe and the U.S. Cavalry. Suddenly it hit me that, had we lived then, Steve and I would have been fighting on opposite sides, and we talked about the past. Another time, an owl flew onto our windowsill and Steve was very frightened. He told me the owl was a symbol of bad luck to Indians. I took it very seriously. We were so in touch, so in sync, that I felt the plausibility of his superstitions. I was open to his mysticism."

Mutual respect, acceptance, tolerance for the faux pas and the occasional closed door, open discussion and patient mutual education, all this gives crossing friendships—when they work at all—a special kind of depth.

Explaining to Your Community of Origin

Accountability to one's own group can present the most difficult challenge to the maintenance of crossing friendships. In 1950 the authors of *The Lonely Crowd* said that interracial contact runs risks not only from whites but from Blacks who may "interpret friendliness as Uncle Tomism."[4] The intervening years have not eliminated such group censure.

In her article "Friendship in Black and White," Bebe Moore Campbell wrote: "For whites, the phrase 'nigger lover' and for Blacks, the accusation of 'trying to be white' are the pressure the group applies to discourage social interaction."[5] Even without overt attacks, people's worry about group reaction inspires self-censorship. Henry, a Black man with a fair complexion, told me he dropped a white friendship that became a touchy subject during the Black Power years. "We'd just come out of a period when many light-skinned Negroes tried to pass for white and I wasn't about to be mistaken for one of them," he explains. "My racial identity mattered more to me than any white friend."

Black-white friendships are "'conducted underground,'" says Campbell, quoting a Black social worker, who chooses to limit her intimacy with whites rather than fight the system. "'I'd feel comfortable at my white friend's parties because everybody there would be a liberal, but I'd never invite her to mine because I have some friends who just don't like white people and I didn't want anybody to be embarrassed.'"

If a white friend of mine said she hated Blacks, I would not just keep my Black friends away from her, I would find it impossible to maintain the friendship. However, the converse is not comparable. Most Blacks have at some point been wounded by racism, while whites have not been victimized from the other direction. Understanding the experiences *behind* the reaction allows decent Black people to remain friends with anti-white Blacks. That these Blacks may have reason to hate certain whites does not excuse their hating all whites, but it does explain it. . . .

Historically, of course, the biggest enemies of boundary-crossing friendships have not been Blacks or ethnic minorities but majority whites. Because whites gain the most from social inequality, they have the most to lose from crossing friendships, which, by their existence, deny the relevance of ethnic and racial hierarchies. More important, the empowered whites can put muscle behind their disapproval by restricting access to clubs, schools, and businesses.

If you sense that your community of origin condemns one of your crossing friendships, the amount of explaining or justifying you do will depend on how conformist you are and whether you feel entitled to a happiness of your own making. . . .

The Same but Never Quite the Same

"I go coon hunting with Tobe Spencer," said former police officer L. C. Albritton about his Black friend in Camden, Alabama. "We're good friends. We stay in town during the day for all the hullabaloo and at night we go home and load up the truck with three dogs and go way down into the swamps. We let the dogs go and sit on a log, take out our knives and a big chew of tobacco . . . and just let the rest of the world go by."

Looking at a picture of himself and Spencer taken in 1966, Albritton mused: "It's funny that a police officer like me is standing up there smiling and talking to a nigger because we were having marches and trouble at that time. . . . Old Tobe Spencer—ain't nothing wrong with that nigger. He's always neat and clean as a pin. He'll help you too. Call him at midnight and he'll come running just like that."[6]

Two friends with the same leisure-time pleasures, two men at ease together in the lonely night of the swamps. Yet race makes a difference. Not only does the white man use the derogatory "nigger," but he differentiates his friend Tobe from the rest of "them" who, presumably, are not neat and clean and helpful. The *same but never quite the same.*

Leonard Fein, the editor of *Moment*, a magazine of progressive Jewish opinion, gave me "the controlling vignette" of his cross-ethnic friendships: "An Irish-Catholic couple was among our dearest friends, but on that morning in 1967 when we first heard that Israel was being bombed, my wife said, 'Who can we huddle with tonight to get through this ordeal,' and we picked three Jewish couples. Our Irish friends were deeply offended. 'Don't you think we would have felt for you?' they asked. 'Yes,' we said, 'but it wasn't sympathy we wanted, it was people with whom, if necessary, we could have mourned the death of Israel—and that could only be other Jews.'

"The following week, when the war was over, my wife and I went to Israel. The people who came to live in our house and take care of our children were our Irish friends. They had understood they were our closest friends yet they could never be exactly like us.". . .

For Raoul, a phenomenally successful advertising man, crossing friendships have been just about the only game in town. He reminisced with me about growing up in a Puerto Rican family in a Manhattan neighborhood populated mostly by Irish, Italians, and Jews:

"In the fifties I hung out with all kinds of guys. I sang on street corners—do-wopping in the night—played kick the can, and belonged to six different basketball clubs, from the Police Athletic League to the YMCA. My high school had 6000 kids in it—street kids who hung out in gangs like The Beacons, The Fanwoods, The Guinea Dukes, The Irish Lords, and The Diablos from Spanish Harlem and Jewish kids who never hung out because they were home studying. The gang members were bullies and punks who protected their own two-block area. They wore leather jackets and some of them carried zip guns and knives. I managed to be acceptable to all of them just because I was good at sports. I was the best athlete in the school and president of the class. So I was protected by the gangs and admired by the Jewish kids and I had a lot of friends."

Raoul's athletic prowess won him a scholarship to a large midwestern university where he was the first Puerto Rican to be encountered by some people. "They wanted me to sing the whole sound track of *West Side Story*. They asked to see my switchblade. And I was as amazed by the midwesterners as they were by me. My first hayride was a real shock. Same with hearing people saying 'Good morning' to each other. Every one of my friends—my roommate, teammates, and fraternity brothers, Blacks from Chicago and Detroit and whites from the farms—they were all gentle and nice. And gigantic and strong. Boy, if one of them had moved into my neighborhood back home, he'd have owned the block.

"After graduation, a college friend went to work in a New York City ad agency that played in a Central Park league and needed a softball pitcher. He had me brought in for an interview. Even though I knew nothing about advertising, I was a helluva pitcher, and the owner of the agency took sports seriously. So he hired me. I always say I had the only athletic scholarship in the history of advertising. I pitched for the agency, I played basketball with the owner, and I learned the business. So I found my friends and my career through sports. Even though I may have been a Spic to most everyone, sports opened all the doors."

The same but never quite the same. . . .

"At the beginning, because of difficulties of adaptation, we immigrants protect ourselves by getting together with people from the same culture who speak the same language," says Luis Marcos, a psychiatrist, who came to the United States from Seville, Spain. "Next, when we feel more comfortable, we reach out to people who do the same work we do, mostly those who help us or those we help in some way. Then we have a basis for friendship. My mentor, the director of psychiatry at Bellevue, is a native-born American and a Jew. He helped me in my area of research and now he's one of my best friends. I also began to teach and to make friends with my medical students as they grew and advanced."

That Marcos and his friends have the health profession in common has not prevented misunderstandings. "When we first went out for meals together, my impulse was to pay for both of us," he says of another doctor, a Black woman who taught him not to leave his own behavior unexamined. "It wasn't that I thought she couldn't afford to pay; we were equally able to pick up the check. It was just that the cultural habit of paying for a woman was ingrained in my personality. But she misconstrued it. She felt I was trying to take care of her and put her down as a Black, a professional, and a woman. In order for our friendship to survive, she had to explain how she experiences things that I don't even think about."

Moving in One Another's World

Ethnotherapist Judith Klein revels in her crossing friendships. "My interest in people who are different from me may be explained by the fact that I'm a twin. Many people look to be mirrored in friendship; I've had mirroring through my sister, so I can use friendship for other things. One thing I use it for is to extend my own life. People who aren't exactly like me enhance my knowledge and experience. They let me be a vicarious voyager in their world."

As much as friends try to explain one another's world, certain differences remain particular barriers to intimacy.

Luis Marcos mentions the language barrier. "No matter how well I speak, I can never overcome my accent," he says. "And some people mistake the way I talk for lack of comprehension. They are afraid I won't understand an American joke, or if I choose to use aggressive words, they don't think I mean it, they blame my 'language problem.'"

While many Americans assume people with an accent are ignorant, many ethnics assume, just as incorrectly, that someone *without* an accent is smart. Some Americans have a habit of blaming the other person for doing or saying whatever is not understandable to Americans. Ethnics also have been known to blame their own culture—to use their "foreignness" as an excuse for behavior for which an American would have to take personal responsibility. "I can't help it if we Latins are hot-tempered" is a way of generalizing one's culpability.

Of course, the strongest barrier to friendship is outright resistance. After two years of off-and-on living in Tokyo, Angie Smith came to terms with the fact that "the Japanese do not socialize the way we do." She found, as many have, that in Japan friendship is considered an obligation more than a pleasure and is almost always associated with business.[7]

"Three times I invited two couples for dinner—the men were my husband's business associates—and three times the men came and the women didn't," Smith recalls. "They sent charming little notes with flowers, but they would not have been comfortable in our house for an evening of social conversation. Yet these same Japanese women would go out to lunch with me and tell me more intimate things than they tell each other. While we were in Japan, I just had to get used to sex-divided socializing and not having any couple friendships."

When people's differences are grounded in racism rather than alien styles of socializing, it can be especially painful to move in the other person's world.

"I felt myself a slave and the idea of speaking to white people weighed me down," wrote Frederick Douglass a century ago.[8] Today, most Blacks refuse to be weighed down by whites. They do not "need" white friends. Some doubt that true friendship is possible between the races until institutional racism is destroyed. Feminists of every shade have debated the question "Is Sisterhood Possible?" Despite the issues that affect *all* women, such as sexual violence, many Black women resist working together for social change or organizing with white women because they believe most whites don't care enough about welfare reform, housing, teen pregnancies, or school dropouts—issues that are of primary concern to Blacks.

Bell Hooks, a writer and a professor of Afro-American studies, wrote: "All too frequently in the women's movement it was assumed one could be free of sexist thinking by simply adopting the appropriate feminist rhetoric; it was further assumed that identifying oneself as oppressed freed one from being an oppressor. To a very great extent, such thinking prevented white feminists from understanding and overcoming their own sexist-racist attitudes toward black women. They could pay lip service to the idea of sisterhood and solidarity between women but at the same time dismiss black women."[9]

Phyllis Marynick Palmer, a historian, says white women are confounded by Black women's strong family role and work experience, which challenge the white stereotype of female incapacity. White women also criticize Black women for making solidarity with their brothers a priority rather than confronting Black men's sexism. In turn, Black women get angry at white women who ignore "their own history of racism and the benefits that white women have gained at the expense of black women."[10] With all this, how could sisterhood be possible? How can friendship be possible?

"I would argue for the abandonment of the concept of sisterhood as a global construct based on unexamined assumptions about our similarities," answers Dill, "and I would substitute a more pluralistic approach that recognizes and accepts the objective differences between women."

Again the word "pluralistic" is associated with friendship. An emphasis on double consciousness, not a denial of differences. The importance of feeling both the same and different, of acknowledging "the essence of me," of understanding that friends need not *transcend* race or ethnicity but can embrace differences and be enriched by them. The people who have managed to incorporate these precepts say that they are pretty reliable guidelines for good crossing friendships. But sometimes it's harder than it looks. Sometimes, the "vicarious voyage" into another world can be a bad trip.

The Hazards of Crossing

"Anglo wannabes" are a particular peeve of David Hayes Bautista. "These are Anglos who wanna be so at home with us that they try too hard to go native. For instance, Mexicans have a certain way that we yell along with the music of mariachi band. When someone brought along an Anglo friend and yelled 'Yahoo, Yahoo' all night, every Chicano in the place squirmed."

Maxine Baca Zinn gives the reverse perspective: of a Chicano in an Anglo environment. "Once, when I was to speak at the University of California, a Chicana friend who was there told me that the minute I walked into that white academic world my spine straightened up. I carried myself differently. I talked differently around them and I didn't even know it." Was Zinn just nervous about giving her speech or did she tighten up in anticipation of the tensions Chicanos feel in non-Hispanic settings? She's not certain.

When Charlie Chin, a bartender, started work in a new place, a white coworker quipped, "One thing you have to watch out for, Charlie, are all the Chinks around here." I winced when Chin said this, but he told me, "I just smiled at the guy. I'm used to those jokes. That's the way whites break the ice with Asians. That's the American idea of being friendly.". . .

For another pair of friends, having different sensitivities did not destroy the relationship but did create a temporary misunderstanding. Yvonne, a Black woman, was offended when her white friend, Fran, came to visit, took off her shoes, and put her feet up on the couch. "I felt it showed her disregard for me and I blamed it on race," says Yvonne. "Black people believe the way you behave in someone's home indicates the respect you have for that person. Also, furniture means a lot to us because we buy it with such hard-won wages." Weeks later, Yvonne saw one of Fran's white friends do the same thing while sitting on Fran's couch. Yvonne realized that the behavior had nothing to do with lack of respect for Blacks. "For all I know millions of whites all over America put their feet up when they relax—I'd just never seen that part of their world before."

What Bill Tatum discovered about a couple of his white friends was not so easy to explain away. When the couple asked Tatum to take some food to Helen, their Black housekeeper who was sick, he asked her name and address. They knew her only as "Helen" but were able to get her address from their 6-year-old who had spent a week at her apartment when they had been on vacation.

"I arrived to find a filthy, urine-smelling building, with addicts hanging out on the front stoop. Rags were stuffed in the broken windows in Helen's apartment. She was wearing a bag of asafetida around her neck, a concoction made by southern Blacks to ward off bad luck and colds. She was old, sick, and feverish. She said she'd never been sick before and her employers—my friends—had provided her with no health insurance. Obviously, they'd never imagined where or how this poor woman might live—or else they wouldn't have left their little girl with her. They treated their Black housekeeper with none of the respect and concern they showed me, their Black *friend* and a member of their economic class."

Until that experience, if anyone had ever accused the couple of racism, Tatum says he'd have gone to the mat defending them. Now he has to square what he's seen with his old love for them and he is finding it very, very difficult.

He makes another point about moving in the world of white friends. "Some whites make me feel completely comfortable because they say exactly what they think even if it contradicts whatever I've said. But other whites never disagree with me on anything. They act as if Blacks can't defend their positions, or they're afraid it would look like a put-down to challenge what I say even though they would challenge a white person's opinion in a minute."

While Tatum resents whites' misguided protectiveness, he also finds fault with "many Blacks who are climbing socially and are too damned careful of what *they* say. They won't advance an opinion until they have a sense of what the white friend is thinking." Not only is that not good conversation, he says, "that's not good friendship."

The Problem with "Them" Is "Us"

If you're a young, heterosexual, nondisabled person and you do not have one friend who is either gay, old, or disabled, there might be something wrong with *you*. If you're gay, old, or disabled and all your friends are just like you, it may not be because you prefer it that way.

Gay people, the elderly, and disabled people get the same pleasure from companionship and intimacy and have the same problems with friendship as does anyone else. They merit a separate discussion in this book for the same reason that class, race, and ethnicity required special discussion: because on top of the usual friendship concerns, they experience additional barriers.

In essence, the barriers exist because we don't *know* each other. Many people— some of whom are homophobic (have a fear of homosexuality)—reach adulthood without ever to their knowledge meeting a homosexual or a lesbian. Many have neither known someone who is blind or deaf or who uses a wheelchair nor spent time with an old person other than their grandparents. That there are such things as Gay Pride marches, disability rights organizations, and the Gray Panthers does not mean that these groups have achieved equal treatment under the law or full humanity in the eyes of the world. To a large degree, our society still wants to keep them out of sight—the gays for "flaunting their alternative life-styles," the disabled for not "getting better," and the old for reminding us of our eventual fate.

As a result of our hang-ups, these populations may be even more segregated than racial or ethnic minorities. When these groups are segregated, "we" don't have to think about "them." Out of sight, out of mind, out of friendship. People told me they had no gay, elderly, or disabled friends because "we live in two different worlds" or because "they" are so different—meaning threatening, unsettling, or strange. Closer analysis reveals, however, that we *keep* them different by making this world so hard for them to live in and be defining human norms so narrowly. It is our world—the homophobic, youth-worshipping, disability-fearing world—that is threatening, unsettling, and strange to them. In other words, their biggest problem is us.

To make friends, we have to cross our self-made boundaries and grant to other people the right to be both distinctive and equal.

Gay-Straight Friendship

Forming relationships across gay-straight boundaries can be as challenging as crossing racial and ethnic lines because it too requires the extra work of "explaining":

- Explaining to yourself why, if you're gay, you need this straight friend ("Am I unconsciously trying to keep my heterosexual credentials in order?"), or why, if you're straight, you need this gay friend ("Am I a latent homosexual?")
- Explaining to each other what your lives are like—telling the straight friend what's behind the words "heavy leather" or explaining to the gay friend just why he *cannot* bring his transvestite lover to a Bar Mitzvah
- Explaining to your respective communities why you have such a close relationship with one of "them"

Gay-straight friendship is a challenge not only because the heterosexual world stigmatizes gays but because homosexual society is a culture unto itself. Straights who relate comfortably with their gay friends say they get along so well because they respect the distinctive qualities of gay culture—almost as if it were an ethnic group. Interestingly enough, a Toronto sociologist has determined that gay men have the same institutions, "sense of peoplehood," and friendship networks as an ethnic community; all that gays lack is the emphasis on family.[11] All in places where lesbians congregate, such as San Francisco, there are women's bars, music, bookstores, publications, folklore, and dress styles—an elaborate self-contained culture.[12]

Since gay men and lesbians have to function in a straight world during most of their lives, it's not too much to ask a straight friend to occasionally accommodate to an environment defined by homosexuals. But even when both friends accommodate, gay-straight relations can be strained by disagreements over provocative issues.

Gay-Straight Debate

The Gay's View
On Homophobia

The Straight's View

The Gay's View	The Straight's View
You're not relaxed with me. You think gayness rubs off or friendship might lead to sex. You act like every gay person wants to seduce you. You fear others will think you're gay. You are repulsed by gay sex though you try to hide it. You bear some responsibility for the discrimination against gays and if you're my friend, you'll fight it with me.	I am the product of a traditional upbringing. I cannot help being afraid or ignorant of homosexuality. My religion taught me that homosexuality is a sin. I'm trying to overcome these biases and still be honest with you about my feelings. I support gay rights, but I cannot be responsible for everyone else's homophobia.

On AIDS

Ever since the AIDS epidemic, you have not touched me or drunk from a glass in my house. I resent your paranoia. I shouldn't have to watch my gay friends die and at the same time feel that my straight friends are treating me like a leper. If I did get AIDS, I'm afraid you would blame the victim and abandon me. Can I trust a friend like that?	I *am* afraid. I don't know how contagious the AIDS virus is or how it's transmitted. From what I read, no one does. All I know is that AIDS is fatal, homosexuals are the primary victims, and you are a homosexual. I'm caught between my affection for you and my terror of the disease. I don't know what's right and you're in no position to tell me.

On Lesbian Politics

Lesbianism is not just sexual, it's political. Every woman should call herself a lesbian, become woman-identified, and reject everything masculinist. Women who love men and live in the nuclear family contribute to the entrenchment of patriarchal power and the oppression of women. Authentic female friendship can only exist in lesbian communities. If you don't accept "lesbian" as a positive identity, it will be used to condemn all women who are not dependent on men.	I support lesbian rights and even lesbian separatism if lesbians choose it. I believe lesbian mothers must be permitted to keep their children. I oppose all discrimination and defamation of lesbians. I believe that lesbian feminists and straight women can work together and be friends, *but* I resent lesbian coercion and political strong-arming. I also resent your more-radical-than-thou attitude toward heterosexuals. Like you, what I do with my body is my business.

On Acceptance

You want me to act straight whenever having a gay friend might embarrass you. I'm not going to tone down my speech or dress to please your friends or family. I do not enjoy being treated as a second-class couple when my lover and I go out with you and your spouse. If you can kiss and hold hands, we should be able to show affection in public. If straights ask each other how they met or how long they have been married, they should ask us how we met and how long we've been together.

You refuse to understand how difficult it is to explain gay life-styles to a child or an 80-year-old. You make me feel like a square in comparison with your flashy gay friends. You treat married people like Mr. and Mrs. Tepid, as if the only true passion is gay passion. Your friends make me feel unwanted on gay turf and at political events when I'm there to support gay rights. You put down all straights before you know them. It's hard to be your friend if I can't introduce you to other people without your feeling hostile or judging their every word. . . .

Disabled and Nondisabled Friendship

About 36 million Americans have a disabling limitation in their hearing, seeing, speaking, walking, moving, or thinking. Few nondisabled people are as sensitive to the experiences of this population as are those with close friends who are disabled.

"Last week," recalls Barbara Spring, "I went to have a drink at a midtown hotel with a friend who uses a wheelchair. Obviously it's not important to this hotel to have disabled patrons because we had to wait for the so-called accessible elevator for thirty minutes. Anyone who waits with the disabled is amazed at how long the disabled have to wait for everything."

"In graduate school, one of my friends was a young man with cerebral palsy," says Rena Gropper. "Because he articulated slowly and with great difficulty, everyone thought he was dumb and always interrupted him, but if you let him finish, you hear how bright and original his thinking was."

Terry Keegan, an interpreter for the deaf, has become friends with many deaf people and roomed for two years with a coworker who is deaf. "If they don't understand what we're saying it's not because they're stupid but because we aren't speaking front face or we can't sign." Keegan believes all hearing people should learn 100 basic words in Ameslan, American Sign Language. "Historically, this wonderful language has been suppressed. Deaf people were forced to use speech, lipreading, and hearing aids so they would not look handicapped and would 'fit in' with the rest of us. Their hands were slapped when they tried to sign. This deprived them of a superior communication method. Deafness is not a pathology, it's a difference. When we deny deaf people their deafness, we deny them their identity."

Many nondisabled people have become sensitized to idioms that sound like racial epithets to the disabled, such as "the blind leading the blind" or "that's a lame excuse." Some find "handicapped" demeaning because it derives from "cap in hand." A man who wears leg braces says the issue is accuracy. "I'm not handicapped, people's attitudes about me handicap me." Merle Froschl, a nondisabled member of the Women and

Disability Awareness Project, points out that the opposite of "disabled" is "*not* disabled"; thus, "nondisabled" is the most neutral term. Disabled people are infuriated by being contrasted with "normal" people—it implies that the disabled are "abnormal" and everyone else is perfect. And the term "able-bodied" inspires the question, Able to do what: Run a marathon? See without glasses? Isn't it all relative?

"Differently abled" and "physically challenged" had a brief vogue, but, says Harilyn Rousso, those terms "made me feel I really had something to hide." Rousso, a psychotherapist who has cerebral palsy, emphasizes, "Friends who care the most sometimes think they're doing you a favor by using euphemisms or saying 'I never think of you as disabled." The reason they don't want to acknowledge my disability is that they think it's so negative. Meanwhile, I'm trying to recognize it as a valid part of me. I'm more complex than my disability and I don't want my friends to be obsessed by it. But it's clearly there, like my eye color, and I want my friends to appreciate and accept me with it."

The point is not that there is a "right way" to talk to people who are disabled but that friendship carries with it the obligation to *know thy friends*, their sore points and their preferences. That includes knowing what words hurt their feelings as well as when and how to help them do what they cannot do for themselves.

"Each disabled person sends out messages about what they need," says Froschl. "One friend who is blind makes me feel comfortable about taking her arm crossing the street, another dislikes physical contact and wants to negotiate by cane. I've learned not to automatically do things for disabled people since they often experience help as patronizing."

"I need someone to pour cream in my coffee, but in this culture, it's not acceptable to ask for help," say Rousso, adding that women's ordinary problems with dependence are intensified by disability. "I have to feel very comfortable with my friends before I can explain my needs openly and trust that their reaction will not humiliate both of us. For some people it raises too many anxieties."

Anxieties that surround the unknown are dissipated by familiarity. Maybe that explains why so many disabled-nondisabled friendships are composed of classmates or coworkers who spend a lot of time together.

"There are those who can deal with disability and those who can't," says Phil Draper, a quadriplegic whose spinal cord was injured in a car accident. "If they can't— if they get quiet or talk nervously or avoid our eyes—the work of the relationship falls entirely on us. We need friends who won't treat us as weirdo asexual second-class children or expect us to be 'Supercrips'—miracle cripples who work like crazy to make themselves whole again. Ninety-nine percent of us aren't going to be whole no matter what we do. We want to be accepted the way we are."

To accept friends like Phil Draper, the nondisabled have to confront their unconscious fears of vulnerability and death. In one study, 80 percent of nondisabled people said they would be comfortable having someone in a wheelchair as their friend. But "being in a wheelchair" came immediately after "blind" and "deaf-mute" as the affliction they themselves would least want to have.[13] If we fear being what our friend *is*, that feeling is somewhere in the friendship.

Nondisabled people also have to disavow the cult of perfectability. Disabled people are not going to "get better" because they are not "sick"; they are generally healthy people who are not allowed to function fully in this society—as friends or as anything else.

"Friendship is based on people's ability to communicate," says Judy Heumann, the first postpolio person to get a teacher's license in New York City and now a leader of the disability rights movement. "But barriers such as inaccessible homes make it hard for disabled people to just drop in. Spontaneity is something disabled people enjoy infrequently and the nondisabled take for granted.

"While more public places have ramps and bathrooms that accommodate wheelchairs, many parties still occur in inaccessible spaces. If I have to be carried upstairs or if I can't have a drink because I know I won't be able to use the bathroom later, I'll probably decide not to go at all. One way I measure my friends is by whether they have put in the effort and money to make their houses wheelchair-accessible. It shows their sensitivity to me as a person.

"Good friends are conscious of the fact that a movie theater or concert hall has to be accessible before I can join them; they share my anger and frustration if it's not. They understand why I'm not crazy about big parties where all the non-disabled are standing up and I'm at ass-level. It makes me able to function more as an equal within the group if people sit down to talk to me. I can't pretend I'm part of things if I can't hear anyone. I don't want to *not* be invited to large parties—I just want people to be sensitive to my needs.

"I always need help cooking, cleaning, driving, going to the bathroom, getting dressed. I pay an attendant to do most of those things for me but sometimes I have to ask a friend for help, which presents a lot of opportunities for rejection. Often, the friends who come through best are other disabled people whose disabilities complement mine. I can help a blind woman with her reading, child care, and traveling around town; she can do the physical things I need. And we don't have to appreciate each other's help, we can just accept it.". . .

Cross-Age Friendship

I am now 46, my husband is 51. Among our good friends are two couples who are old enough to be our parents. One woman, a poet, can be counted on for the latest word on political protests and promising writers. She and I once spent a month together at a writers' colony. The other woman—as energetic and as well-read as anyone I know—is also involved in progressive causes. Although the men of both couples have each had a life-threatening illness, the one with a heart condition is a brilliant civil liberties lawyer and the one who had a stroke is a prize-winning novelist with stunning imaginative powers. The lawyer taught our son to play chess when he was 5. The novelist has encouraged our daughters to write stories ever since they could read. The men have been fine surrogate grandfathers.

When I described these couples to someone my own age, he said, "Ah, it's easy to be friends with *interesting* old people, but what about the dull ones?" The answer is, I am not friends with dull young or middle-aged people so why should I want to be friends with dull old people? And why does he immediately think in terms of old people *not* being interesting? Perhaps the crux of the problem with cross-generational friendship is this *double* double standard. First, to think we "ought" to be friends with the elderly—as a class—denies old people the dignity of individuality and devalues their friendship through condescension. But second, to assume that those who are young or in mid-life will necessarily be more interesting and attractive than those over 65 maintains a double standard of expectation that cheats younger people of friends like ours.

Ageism hurts all ages. And it begins early: Studies show that 3-year-olds already see old people as sick, tired, and ugly and don't want to associate with them.[14] Older people also have their biases about youthful behavior. Some 70-year-olds think children are undependable, unappreciative, ask too many questions, and must be told what to do. They believe teenagers are callow, impatient, and unseasoned.[15]

The authors of *Grandparents/Grandchildren* write, "We shouldn't blame adolescents for not being adults. To become adults, the young need to be around adults."[16] But age segregation keeps us apart. Without benefit of mutual acquaintance, stereotypes mount, brick by brick, until there is a wall high enough to conceal the real human beings on either side.

Another big problem is miscommunication. Conversations between young and old often founder because "sensory, physical, or cognitive differences" cause "distortion, message failure, and social discomfort."[17] That's a fancy way of saying they can't understand each other. And anyone who has ever talked with a young person whose span of concentration is the length of a TV commercial or with an old person whose mind wanders to the blizzard of '48 when asked how to dress for today's weather will understand how each generation's communication style can be a problem for the other.

But stereotypes and miscommunication do not entirely account for the gulf between young and old. Homophily—the attraction to the similar self—is the missing link. Those who are going through the same thing at the same time find it comforting to have friends who mirror their problems and meet their needs, and, usually, people of similar chronological age are going through parallel experiences with wage-earning, setting up house, child-rearing, and other life-cycle events.

Age-mates also tend to have in common the same angle of vision on history and culture. Two 65-year-olds watching a film about the Depression or World War II can exchange memories and emotional responses that are unavailable to a 30-year-old who did not live through those cataclysms. And while a person of 18 and one of 75 might both love Vivaldi, their simultaneous appreciation for Bruce Springsteen is unlikely.

Claude Fischer's studies reveal that more than half of all friend-partners are fewer than five years apart. But the span is reduced to two years if their relationship dates back to their youth when age gradations matter the most and the places where youngsters meet—school, camp, military service, and entry-level jobs—are more age-segregated. Contrary to popular wisdom, elderly people, like the rest of us, prefer friends of their own age. The more old people there are in a given community the more likely it is that each one will have a preponderance of same-age friends. And, believe it or not, a majority of old people say they think it's more important for them to have age-mates than family as their intimates.

Given this overwhelming preference for homophily at every age, why am I on the bandwagon for cross-generational friendship? Because when it's good, it's very, very good—both for friends of different ages who are undergoing similar experiences at the same time and for friends of different ages who are enjoying their differences.

- A 38-year-old woman meets 22-year-olds in her contracts class at law school.
- A couple in their early forties enrolled in a natural childbirth course make friends with parents-to-be who are twenty years younger.
- Three fathers commiserate about the high cost of college; two are in their forties, the third is a 60-year-old educating his second family.

Age-crossing friendships become less unusual as Americans follow more idiosyncratic schedules for marrying, having children, and making career decisions.

But there are other reasons for feeling that age is immaterial to friendship. Marie Wilson, a 45-year-old foundation executive who has five children of high school age or older, told me, "My friends are in their early thirties, and they have kids under 8. But these women are where I am in my head. We became close working together on organizing self-help for the poor. Most women my age are more involved in suburban life or planning their own career moves."

Sharing important interests can be as strong a basis for friendship as is experiencing the same life-cycle events. However, without either of those links, the age difference can sit between the young and the old like a stranger. I'm not asking that we deny that difference but that we free ourselves from what Victoria Secunda calls "the tyranny of age assumptions"[18] and that we entertain the possibility of enriching ourselves through our differences. . . .

As we cross all these lines and meet at many points along the life cycle, people of diverse ages, like people of every class and condition, are discovering that we who are in so many ways "the same and different" can also be friends.

Notes

1. L. Rohter, "Immigrant Factory Workers Share Dream, Luck and a Lotto Jackpot," *New York Times*, August 23, 1985.
2. G. Allport, *The Nature of Prejudice*, Doubleday, Anchor Press, 1958.
3. J. Provinzano, "Settling Out and Settling In." Papers presented at annual meeting of the American Anthropological Association, November 1974.
4. D. Riesman, R. Denney, and N. Glazer, *The Lonely Crowd: A Study of the Changing American Character*, Yale University Press, 1950.
5. B. M. Campbell, "Friendship in Black and White," Ms., August 1983.
6. B. Adelman, *Down Home: Camden, Alabama*, Times Books, Quadrangle, 1972.
7. R. Atsumi, "Tsukiai—Obligatory Personal Relationships of Japanese White Collar Employees," *Human Organization*, vol. 38, no. 1 (1979).
8. F. Douglass, *Narrative of the Life of Frederick Douglass, an American Slave*, New American Library, Signet, 1968.
9. B. Hooks, *Ain't I a Woman: Black Women and Feminism*, South End Press, 1981.
10. P. M. Palmer, "White Women/Black Women: The Dualism of Female Identity and Experience in the United States," *Feminist Studies*, Spring 1983.
11. S. O. Murray, "The Institutional Elaboration of a Quasi-Ethnic Community," *International Review of Modern Sociology*, vol. 9, no. 2 (1979).
12. J. C. Albro and C. Tully, "A Study of Lesbian Lifestyles in the Homosexual Micro-Culture and the Heterosexual Macro-Culture," *Journal of Homosexuality*, vol. 4, no. 4 (1979).
13. L. M. Shears and C. J. Jensema, "Social Acceptability of Anomalous Persons," *Exceptional Children*, October 1969.
14. R. K. Jantz et al., *Children's Attitudes Toward the Elderly*, University of Maryland Press, 1976.
15. A. G. Cryns and A. Monk, "Attitudes of the Aged Toward the Young," *Journal of Gerontology*, vol. 1 (1972); see also, C. Seefeld et al., "Elderly Persons' Attitude Toward Children,": *Educational Gerontology*, vol. 8, no. 4 (1982).
16. K. L. Woodward and A. Kornhaber, *Grandparents, Grandchildren: The Vital Connection* (Doubleday, Anchor Press, 1981), quoted in "Youth Is Maturing Later," *New York Times*, May 10, 1985.

17. L. J. Hess and R. Hess, "Inclusion, Affection, Control: The Pragmatics of Intergenerational Communication." Paper presented at the Conference on Communication and Gerontology of the Speech Communication Association, July 1981.
18. V. Secunda, *By Youth Possessed: The Denial of Age in America*, Bobbs-Merrill, 1984.

Review Questions

1. According to the author, when we engage in a cross-cultural relationship, what do we typically need to "explain" about it to ourselves? To each other? To our friends?
2. What is meant by Pogrebin's label, "the same but never quite the same"?
3. In the paragraph before the heading "The Hazards of Crossing," the author distinguishes "double consciousness" from "a denial of differences." What do those two terms mean?
4. The essay includes a story about a white couple asking their black friend, Bill Tatum, to take some food to their black housekeeper who lived in Harlem and was sick. Tatum was shocked to discover the housekeeper living in a filthy slum. What was racist about the white couple's "generosity"?
5. How accurate is Pogrebin's summary of each side's views in the section titled "Gay-Straight Debate"?
6. What is the point of the author's discussion of the words we use to label disabled persons?
7. Paraphrase the following comment by Pogrebin: "If we fear being what our friend *is*, that feeling is somewhere in the friendship."

Probes

1. Which of the three kinds of "explaining" that Pogrebin describes has been most difficult for you?
2. That author claims that "many Americans assume people with an accent are ignorant" and that "many ethnics assume, just as incorrectly, that someone *without* an accent is smart." How is this distorted value mirrored in the major television networks' choice of news anchors and reporters?
3. You may be surprised to read a discussion of gay/straight relationships here. What might justify putting a discussion of this topic in this book?
4. Do you commonly think about relationships with disabled persons as examples of "intercultural communication"? What happens when you do?
5. What problems have you encountered in your relationships with older persons? What is the most helpful thing Pogrebin says about these relationships?

hen I was planning this chapter, I first thought that I'd like to include readings about the specific communication patterns of each of the major cultures present in the United States. That thought lasted about two seconds. There are so many identifiable cultures that no single book—let alone one chapter—could ever include such a collection. So I decided to settle for a couple of helpful examples.

This first one is written by a professor in the Afro-American Studies Department of San Diego State University. It describes some features of black language as spoken in the United States. Black language, or what some people call black English, has been studied for several decades now, but aspects of it change so rapidly that no study can capture the details of its most current form.

Here Shirley Weber describes some of the features that change more slowly—its history, some of the forms it has taken, and the ways it functions in black culture.

First, she agrees with the point Gudykunst and Kim made that communication is culture and culture is communication. As she puts it, "the study of language is a study of the people who speak that language and of the way they bring order to the chaos of the world." Historically, black language grew as a "creole," which is a blend of two or more languages. In this case the creole was a blend of English and languages spoken on the west coast of Africa. Thus from the beginning, the language reflected some of the philosophical concepts found in African cultures.

One concept is that Nommo, the power of the word, makes humans uniquely powerful. This helps explain why vivid and imaginative language is still viewed among many African Americans as a special mark of effectiveness and community status. It also helps explain the call-and-response pattern in some black language. As Weber puts it, "an audience listening and responding to a message is just as important as the speaker, because without their 'amens' and 'right-ons' the speaker may not be successful." This call-and-response pattern also reflects the African world view that all elements in nature work together to accomplish a common goal.

Weber then discusses four forms black language commonly takes: rappin', runnin' it down, the dozens, and proverbial wisdom. Obviously the meaning of "rap" has changed in the past half-dozen years as it has become a dominant form of popular culture. But even gangsta rap and other current manifestations are rooted in the male-female, often sexually-explicit mating dance that, as Weber explains, was rap's original home. Runnin' it down is a form of rap without such strong sexual overtones, but with a similar emphasis on vivid detail. The dozens is a verbal battle of insults between speakers, often played in jest. Like other forms, it also frequently appeals to a nearby audience, who evaluates each comment with remarks about its quality and impact. The final form Weber discusses is proverbial wisdom, where speakers work into their talk such proverbs as "God don't like ugly," and "Don't let your mouth write a check you ass can't cash."

This reading emphasizes how black language reflects the importance that speech and speaking play in its speakers' lives. As Weber puts it, "To say someone is 'all jawed up,' or 'smacking on some barnyard pimp,' or 'ready to hat,' is more imaginative and creative than saying they had 'nothin to say,' or 'eating chicken,' or 'ready to leave.'" It also underscores the fact that black language continues to be spoken because its speakers continue to experience their identity as a culture. So long as black experiences continue to be unique—especially because they continue to be subject to oppression and discrimination—there will be a need for black language and it will continue to grow and change.

On this basis, Weber concludes that whites and others should *not* try to learn black language. Instead, nonblacks should recognize the language for what it is—an expression of cultural identity, not evidence of hostility or lack of education. "The beginning of racial understanding is the acceptance that difference is just what it is: different, not inferior. And equality does not mean sameness."

The Need to Be:
The Socio-Cultural Significance
of Black Language

Shirley N. Weber

"Hey blood, what it is? Ah, Man, ain't notin to it but to do it."
"Huney, I done told ya', God, he don't lak ugly."
"Look-a-there. I ain't seen nothin like these economic indicators."

From the street corners to the church pew to the board room, black language is used in varying degrees. It is estimated that 80 to 90 percent of all black Americans use the black dialect at least some of the time.[1] However, despite its widespread use among blacks at all social and economic levels, there continues to be concern over its validity and continued use. Many of the concerns arise from a lack of knowledge and appreciation for the history of black language and the philosophy behind its use.

Since the publication of J. L. Dillard's book *Black English* in 1972, much has been written on the subject of black language. Generally, the research focuses on the historical and linguistic validity of black English, and very little has been devoted to the communications and cultural functions black language serves in the black community. It seems obvious that given the fact that black English is not "formally" taught in schools to black children and, yet, has widespread use among blacks, it must serve some important functions in the black community that represents the blacks' unique experience in America. If black language served no important function, it would become extinct like other cultural relics because all languages are functional tools that change and adapt to cultural and technological demands. If they cease to do this, they cease to exist as living languages. (The study of the English language's evolution and expansion over the last hundred years, to accommodate changing values and technological advancements, is a good example.) This article looks at the "need to be," the significance of black language to black people.

One's language is a model of his or her culture and of that culture's adjustment to the world. All cultures have some form of linguistic communications; without language, the community would cease to exist. To deny that a people has a language to express its unique perspective of the world is to deny its humanity. Furthermore, the study of language is a study of the people who speak that language and of the way they bring order to the chaos of the world. Consequently, the study of black language is really an examination of African people and of their adjustment to the conditions of American slavery. Smitherman says that black English (dialect) is

By Shirley N. Weber, pp. 220–225 from *Intercultural Communication: A Reader*, 7/e, by Larry A. Samovar and Richard E. Porter, 1994 Wadsworth Publishers.

an Africanized form of English reflecting Black America's linguistic-cultural African heritage and the conditions of servitude, oppression and life in America....
> *(It) is a language mixture, adapted to the conditions of slavery and discrimination, a combination of language and style interwoven with and inextricable from Afro-American culture.[2]*

Much has been written about the origins of black language, and even though the issue seems to be resolved for linguists, the rest of the world is still lingering under false assumptions about it. Basically, there are two opposing views: one that says there was African influence in the development of the language and the other that says there was not. Those who reject African influence believe that the African arrived in the United States and tried to speak English. And, because he lacked certain intellectual and physical attributes, he failed. This hypothesis makes no attempt to examine the phonological and grammatical structures of West African languages to see if there are any similarities. It places the African in a unique position unlike any other immigrant to America. Linguistic rationales and analyses are given for every other group that entered America pronouncing words differently and/or structuring their sentences in a unique way. Therefore, when the German said *zis* instead of *this*, America understood. But, when the African said *dis*, no one considered the fact that consonant combinations such as *th* may not exist in African languages.

Countering this dialectical hypothesis is the creole hypothesis that, as a result of contact between Africans and Europeans, a new language formed that was influenced by both languages. This language took a variety of forms, depending on whether there was French, Portuguese, or English influence. There is evidence that these languages were spoken on the west coast of Africa as early as the sixteenth century (before the slave trade). This hypothesis is further supported by studies of African languages that demonstrate the grammatical, phonological, and rhythmic similarities between them and black English. Thus, the creole hypothesis says that the African responded to the English language as do all other non-English speakers: from the phonological and grammatical constructs of the native language.

The acceptance of the creole hypothesis is the first step toward improving communications with blacks. However, to fully understand and appreciate black language and its function in the black community, it is essential to understand some general African philosophies about language and communications, and then to see how they are applied in the various styles and forms of black communications.

In Janheinz Jahn's *Muntu*, basic African philosophies are examined to give a general overview of African culture. It is important to understand that while philosophies that govern the different groups in Africa vary, some general concepts are found throughout African cultures. One of the primary principles is the belief that everything has a reason for being. Nothing simply exists without purpose or consequences. This is the basis of Jahn's explanation of the four basic elements of life, which are Muntu, mankind; Kintu, things; Hantu, place and time; and Kuntu, modality. These four elements do not exist as static objects but as forces that have consequences and influence. For instance, in Hantu, the West is not merely a place defined by geographic location, but a force that influences the East, North, and South. Thus, the term "Western world" connotes a way of life that either complements or challenges other ways of life. The Western world is seen as a force and not a place. (This is applicable to the other three elements also.)

Muntu, or man, is distinguished from the other three elements by his possession of Nommo, the magical power of the word. Without Nommo, nothing exists. Consequently, mankind, the possessor of Nommo, becomes the master of all things.

> *All magic is word magic, incantations and exorcism, blessings and curse. Through Nommo, the word, man establishes his mastery over things....*
>
> *If there were no word all forces would be frozen, there would be no procreation, no changes, no life....For the word holds the course of things in train and changes and transforms them. And since the word has this power every word is an effective word, every word is binding. And the muntu is responsible for his word.*[3]

Nommo is so powerful and respected in the black community that only those who are skillful users of the word become leaders. One of the main qualifications of leaders of black people is that they must be able to articulate the needs of the people in a most eloquent manner. And because Muntu is a force who controls Nommo, which has power and consequences, the speaker must generate and create movement and power within his listeners. One of the ways this is done is through the use of imaginative and vivid language. Of the five canons of speech, it is said that Inventio or invention is the most utilized in black American. Molefi Asante called it the "coming to be of the novel," or the making of the new. So that while the message might be the same, the analogies, stories, images, and so forth must be fresh, new, and alive.

Because nothing exists without Nommo, it, too, is the force that creates a sense of community among communicators, so much so that the speaker and audience become one as senders and receivers of the message. Thus, an audience listening and responding to a message is just as important as the speaker, because without their "amens" and "right-ons" the speaker may not be successful. This interplay between speaker and listeners is called "call and response" and is a part of the African world view, which holds that all elements and forces are interrelated and indistinguishable because they work together to accomplish a common goal and to create a sense of community between the speaker and the listeners.

This difference between blacks and whites was evident, recently, in a class where I lectured on Afro-American history. During the lecture, one of my more vocal black students began to respond to the message with some encouraging remarks like "all right," "make it plain," "that all right," and "teach." She was soon joined by a few more black students who gave similar comments. I noticed that this surprised and confused some of the white students. When questioned later about this, their response was that they were not used to having more than one person talk at a time, and they really could not talk and listen at the same time. They found the comments annoying and disruptive. As the lecturer, I found the comments refreshing and inspiring. The black student who initiated the responses had no difficulty understanding what I was saying while she was reacting to it, and did not consider herself "rude."

In addition to the speaker's verbal creativity and the dynamic quality of the communication environment, black speech is very rhythmic. It flows like African languages in a consonant-vowel-consonant-vowel pattern. To achieve this rhythmic effect, some syllables are held longer and are accented stronger and differently from standard English, such as DE-troit. This rhythmic pattern is learned early by young blacks and is reinforced by the various styles it complements.

With this brief background into the historical and philosophical foundation of black language, we can examine some of the styles commonly employed and their role in African-American life. Among the secular styles, the most common is *rappin'*. Although the term *rappin'* is currently used by whites to mean simply talking (as in *rap sessions*), it originally described the dialogue between a man and a woman where the main intention is to win the admiration of the woman. A man's success in rappin' depends on his ability to make creative and imaginative statements that generate interest on the part of the woman to hear more of the rap. And, although she already knows his intentions, the ritual is still played out; and, if the rap is weak, he will probably lose the woman.

To outsiders, rappin' might not appear to be an important style in the black community, but it is very important and affects the majority of black people because at some time in a black person's life, he or she will be involved in a situation where rappin' will take place. For, in the black community, it is the mating call, the introduction of the male to the female, and it is ritualistically expected by black women. So that while it is reasonable to assume that all black males will not rise to the level of "leader" in the black community because only a few will possess the unique oral skills necessary, it can be predicted that black men will have to learn how to "rap" to a woman.

Like other forms of black speech, the rap is rhythmic and has consequences. It is the good *rapper* who *gets over* (scores). And, as the master of Nommo, the rapper creates, motivates, and changes conditions through his language. It requires him to be imaginative and capable of responding to positive and negative stimuli immediately. For instance:

R: Hey Mama, how you doing?
L: Fine.
R: Yeah, I can see! (looking her up and down) Say, you married?
L: Yes.
R: Is your husband married? (bringing humor and doubt)

The rap requires participation by the listener. Thus, the speaker will ask for confirmation that the listener is following his line of progression. The rap is an old style that is taught to young men early. And, while each male will have his own style of rappin' that will adapt to the type of woman he is rappin' to, a poor, unimaginative rap is distasteful and often repulsive to black women.

Runnin' it down is a form of rappin' without sexual overtones. It is simply explaining something in great detail. The speaker's responsibility is to vividly recreate the event or concept for the listener so that there is complete agreement and understanding concerning the event. The speaker gives accurate descriptions of the individuals involved, describing them from head to toe. Every object and step of action is minutely described. To an outsider this might sound boring and tedious. However, it is the responsibility of the speaker to use figurative language to keep the listener's attention. In a narrative of a former slave from Tennessee, the following brief excerpt demonstrates the vivid language used in runnin' it down:

> *I remember Mammy told me about one master who almost starved his slaves. Mighty stingy I reckon he was.*
>
> *Some of them slaves was so poorly thin they ribs would kinda rustle against each other like corn stalks a-drying in the hot winds. But they gets even one hog killing time, and it was funny, too, Mammy said.*[4]

Runnin' it down is not confined to secular styles. In C. L. Franklin's sermon, "The Eagle Stirreth Her Nest"—the simple story of an eagle, mistaken for a chicken, that grows up and is eventually set free—the story becomes a drama that vividly takes the listener through each stage of the eagle's development. And even when the eagle is set free because she can no longer live in a cage, she does not simply fly away. Instead, she flies from one height to the other, surveying the surroundings, and then flies away. The details are so vivid that the listener can "see" and "feel" the events. Such is the style and the effect of runnin' it down.

Another common style of black language is *the dozens*. The dozens is a verbal battle of insults between speakers. The term dozens was used during slavery to refer to a selling technique used by slavers. If an individual had a disability, he was considered "damaged goods" and was sold with eleven other "damaged" slaves at a discount rate. The term dozens refers to negative physical characteristics. To an outsider, the dozens might appear cruel and harsh. But to members of the black community, it is the highest form of verbal warfare and impromptu speaking. The game is often played in jest.

When the dozens is played, there is usually a group of listeners that serves as judge and jury over the originality, creativity, and humor of the comments. The listeners encourage continuation of the contest by giving comments like "Ou, I wouldn't take that," "Cold," "Rough," "Stale," or any statement that assesses the quality of the comments and encourages response. The battle continues until someone wins. This is determined by the loser giving up and walking away, or losing his cool and wanting to fight. When a physical confrontation occurs, the winner is not determined by the fight, but by the verbal confrontation. The dozens is so popular that a rock n' roll group made a humorous recording of insults between friends. Some of the exchanges were:

Say Man, your girlfriend so ugly, she had to sneak-up on a glass to get a drink of water.

Man, you so ugly, yo mamma had to put a sheet over your head so sleep could sneak up on you.

The dozens, like other forms of black language, calls on the speaker to use words to create moods. More than any other form, it pits wit against wit, and honors the skillful user of Nommo.

The final secular style to be discussed is proverbial wisdom. Sayings are used in the black community as teaching tools to impart values and truths. Their use demonstrates the African-American's respect for the oral tradition in teaching and socializing the young. Popular phrases, such as "what goes around comes around," "if you make you bed hard you gon lay in it," "God don't like ugly," and "a hard head make a soft behind," are used in everyday conversation by blacks from all social, economic, and educational strata. At some time in a black child's life, the sayings are used to teach them what life expects of them and what they can expect in return. It is also used to expose the truth in an artful and less offensive manner, such as "you don't believe fat meat is greasy." In this saying the listener is being put down for having a narrow or inaccurate view of things. And while it might appear that proverbial wisdoms are static, they are constantly changing and new ones are being created. One of the latest is said when you believe someone is lying to you or "putting you on." It is, "pee on my head and tell me it's raining." Or, if someone is talking bad about you, you might say, "don't let your mouth write a check your ass can't cash." Proverbial wisdom can be found on every socioeconomic level in the black community, and it is transmitted from generation to generation. Listening to speech that is peppered with proverbial sayings might seem strange to nonblacks. But, because proverbial sayings are generally accepted as "truths" because they are taught to children at a very early age, they effectively sum up events and predict outcome.

Like the secular, the nonsecular realm places a tremendous emphasis on the creative abilities of the speaker. The speaker (preacher) creates experiences for his listeners, who are participants in the communication event. The minister calls and his audience responds, and at some point they become one. The minister actively seeks his audience's involvement and when he does not receive it, he chides and scolds them. The audience also believes that the delivery of a good sermon is dependent upon them encouraging the minister with their "amens" and "right-ons." And if the minister preaches false doctrine, the audience also feels obliged to tell him, "Uh, oh Reb, you done gone too far now!"

The language used by the minister, who is probably very fluent in standard English, is generally seasoned with black English. Seldom will you hear the term *Lord* used, but you will hear *Lawd* because the *Lord* is the man in the big house who is an overseer, but the *Lawd* is a friend who walks, talks, and comforts you. The relationship between the *Lawd* and his people is more personal than the *Lord's*.

Also, the speaker may overaccent a word for black emphasis. In C. L. Franklin's sermon, he said, "*extra*-ordinary sight." He then came right back and said *extraordinary*, to demonstrate that he knew how to "correctly" enunciate the word. The nonsecular style of speech is generally the most dramatic of all forms and has the highest degree of audience participation. It encompasses all the elements of black language, and of all the styles it is the most African in form.

Black language and the numerous styles that have been developed are indications of the African-American's respect for the spoken word. The language has often been called a hieroglyphic language because of the vivid picture created by the speaker for the listener about the activities or feelings taking place. To say someone is "all jawed up," or "smacking on some barnyard pimp," or "ready to hat," is more imaginative and creative than saying they had "nothin to say," or "eating chicken," or "ready to leave." The responsibility of the speaker and the listener to participate in the communication event also emphasizes the African world view, which stresses the interrelatedness of all things to each other. And finally, the dynamics of the communication, and the responsibility of man as the user of Nommo, places communication and the spoken word in the arena of forces and not static objects. The rhythm and flow of the language approximates the style and flow and unity of African life.

Despite all of the explanation of the Africanness found in black language, many continue to ask, why use it? Why do blacks who have lived in America for hundreds of years continue to speak "black"? Why do those who posses degrees of higher learning and even write scholarly articles and books in standard English continue to talk "black"?

There are many reasons for the continued use of black language. A language expresses an experience. If the experiences of a group are culturally unique, the group will need a different vocabulary to express them. If white folks in white churches don't get *happy* because they have been socialized to be quiet listeners in church, then they don't have the vocabulary that blacks have to describe levels of spiritual possession. And if they do not have curly hair, they probably do not *press* their hair or worry about *catching up* their *kitchins*. Thus, because blacks experience the world differently from other groups in America, there is a need for a language that communicates that experience.

Secondly, black language reaches across the superficial barriers of education and social position. It is the language that binds, that creates community for blacks, so that the brother in the three-piece Brooks Brothers suit can go to the local corner where folks "hang out" and say, "hey, blood, what it is?", and be one with them. Additionally, the minister's use of black language reminds the listeners of their common experiences and struggles (for example, "I been thur the storm"). Through black language, barriers that separate blacks are lowered and they are finally "home" with each other. So, for cultural identity, the code is essential to define the common elements among them.

Finally, black language usage stands as a political statement that black people are African people who have not given up a vital part of themselves in slavery: their language. They have retained the cultural link that allows them to think and to express themselves in a non-European form. As an old adage says, The namer of names is the father of things. Thus, the ability of blacks to maintain and sustain a living language shows their control over that aspect of their lives, and their determination to preserve the culture. The use of black language is the black man's defiance of white America's total indoctrination. The use of black language by choice is a reflection not of a lack of intelligence, but of a desire to retain and preserve black life styles.

The purpose of this discussion is to help others understand and appreciate black language styles and the reasons blacks speak the way they do, in hopes of building respect for cultural difference. Now the question may be asked, what does the general society do about it? Some might ask, should whites learn black English? To that question comes a resounding *no!* Black language is, first of all, not a laboratory language and it cannot be learned in a classroom. And even if you could learn definition and grammar, you would not learn the art of creative expression that is taught when you're "knee high to a duck." Thus, you would miss the elements of rhythm and style, and you would sound like invaders or foreigners.

What one should do about the language is be open-minded and not judge the speaker by European standards of expression. If you're in a classroom and the teach is *gettin down*, don't *wig out* because the black student says "teach." Simply realize that you must become listening participants. If some *bloods* decide to use a double negative or play *the dozens*, don't assume some social theory about how they lack a father image in the home and are therefore culturally and linguistically deprived. You just might discover that they are the authors of your college English text.

The use of black language does not represent any pathology in blacks. It simply says that, as African people transplanted to America, they are a different flower whose aroma is just as sweet as other flowers. The beginning of racial understanding is the acceptance that difference is just what it is: different, not inferior. And equality does not mean sameness.

Notes

1. Geneva Smitherman. *Talkin' and Testifyin'*. (1972). Boston: Houghton Mifflin Company, p. 2.
2. Ibid, p. 3.
3. Janheinz Jahn. *Muntu*. (1961). New York: Grove Press, Inc., pp. 132–133.
4. Smitherman, *Talkin' and Testifyin'*, p. 156.

Review Questions

1. What does Weber mean by the phrase in her title, "The Need to Be"?

2. What point does Weber make when she contrasts the ways many people respond to "this" being pronounced "zis" versus "dis"?
3. In the African philosophy Weber reviews, what is the relationship between Muntu and Nommo?
4. What feature of African philosophy is exemplified in the call-and-response pattern of black language?
5. According to Weber, what parts of African culture does the *rhythm* of black language grow out of?
6. What is the significance of the term *dozens*?
7. Explain in your own words the three reasons why Weber says black language continues to be spoken.

Probes

1. The definition of black English that Weber cites emphasizes its roots in "the conditions of servitude, oppression and life in America." Given what she says about this language and your own experience with it, what features of black language do you think especially reflect these roots in "servitude and oppression"?
2. The first reading in Chapter 2 reviews three approaches to the study of language: as a system of symbols, as an action, and as a soup. Which of these three most closely approximates the approach to language reflected in African philosophy— "For the word holds the course of things in train and changes and transforms them"?
3. Weber emphasizes the *oral* focus of much African culture. This contrasts with the *print* focus of many European cultures. How do you believe Euro-Americans' print focus surfaces in their speaking? (Hints: Consider rhythm. Also think about the role of logic.)
4. For many years, people believed that the United States could become a great "melting pot," where cultural differences would disappear as we all became assimilated into one "people." Then it became obvious that that wasn't going to happen, so people turned instead to a philosophy of "diversity" rather than "assimilation." In what specific ways does Weber's article support the goal of "diversity" over "assimilation"? How do you respond to this part of her position? Do you agree that nonblacks should give up any plans they might have to learn and then try to speak black language?

The next selection comes from a small book that describes the experiences of a young, Jewish-American anthropologist who went to Morocco to live and study the culture there. I discovered this excerpt in a conversation with Tamar Katriel, an Israeli who was studying interpersonal communication in our department. Tamar noticed how the event Rabinow describes here is an excellent intercultural example of confirmation and disconfirmation, which we were discussing in class.

Confirmation basically means acknowledging the other person's existence and significance. It happens when a person verbally and/or nonverbally says, "I notice you. You count." One question we had discussed was whether confirmation is important in all cultures or just in Western ones. We know, for example, that the direct eye contact that can be so confirming to whites can often be inappropriate and uncomfortable for persons from Japanese or other nonwhite cultures. And there are many other differences.

Tamar noticed that Rabinow's description of his confrontation with Ali suggested that confirmation is also vital in nonwhite cultures but that it is communicated in radically different ways. Rabinow thought he could affirm Ali as a person by being passive, accepting, and deferent. When he blew up at Ali he thought he'd ruined their relationship. But he discovered that in Ali's culture it was more confirming to be confronted than to be treated gently and with total acceptance. It impressed me to read that only *after* their argument and the strong mutual confirmation it established were Rabinow and Ali able to talk about Ali's involvement in a radical religious group and prostitution, two very private topics.

This article reinforces the point that the basic elements of effective interpersonal communication—contact, confirmation, understanding, clarity, responsiveness—are important in all cultures, but the way you communicate each of these differs significantly from culture to culture. In other words, the mode of communicating described in this book is not restricted just to Western white majority cultures; it applies to all human contacts, so long as it is adapted to the cultural setting.

Confrontation with Ali

Paul Rabinow

Ali promised to take me to a wedding in the village of Sidi Lahcen Lyussi. I had already been to several urban weddings. The best Moroccan food, music, and ceremonial were displayed on these occasions. It was a nice change of pace, a break in the routine. The wedding would be an excellent opportunity for me to see the village, and for the villagers to see me.

That afternoon, Ali came by. I told him I wasn't sure I would be able to go with him because I was suffering from a stomach virus. The prospect of being in a strange and demanding situation where I wanted to please, for such a long period, seemed overwhelming, especially in my present condition. Ali expressed keen disappointment at this. He had clearly counted on transportation in my car and the mixed prestige of arriving with the most auspicious guest (if not the guest of honor).

When he returned the next day I was feeling a bit better. He assured me that we would stay only for a short time. He stressed all the preliminary politicking and arranging he had done; if I didn't show up it would not be good for either of us. So I agreed, but made him promise me that we would stay only an hour or so because I was still weak. He repeated his promise several times saying we would leave whenever I felt like it.

Ali and Soussi came to my house around nine that evening and we were off. I was already somewhat tired and repeated clearly to Soussi, a renowned partygoer in his own right, that we would stay only for a short time and then return to Sefrou. *Waxxa*, O.K.?

It was already growing dark as we left Sefrou. By the time we turned off the highway onto the unpaved road which leads to the village, it was nearly pitch black, depriving me of a sense of the countryside, while adding to my feelings of uncertainty about the whole affair. Nonetheless, on arriving in the village I was exhilarated.

The wedding itself was held in a set of connected houses which formed a com-pound. A group of sons had built simple mud and mortar houses next to each other as they married, and by now these formed an enclosed compound. Each part of the enclo-sure was made up of a two-story building. The facilities for the animals and cooking areas were downstairs, the sleeping quarters were on the top level, connected by a rick-ety staircase. That night the center of the compound area had been covered with straw for the dancing. We were welcomed and ushered up the stairs into a long narrow room furnished with thin cushions along the perimeters. Perhaps five tables were arranged parallel to each other, running the length of the room. I told myself it was a good thing we had come, a wise decision. Everyone was friendly and seemed to know who I was. We had tea, then after perhaps an hour of chatting and banter, dinner was served on battered but polished metal trays. The hour of talk had passed amicably enough, even though my minimal Arabic did not permit much expansive conversation. I still had a beard at this point, and there was much friendly but insistent joking that this was improper for such a young man. The dinner was simple but nicely prepared, consisting of goat meat in a sort of olive oil stew with freshly baked bread, still warm from the oven.

After we ate and drank more tea, we went down to the courtyard, where the dancing began. I watched from a corner, leaning against a pillar. The dancers were all men, of course, and they formed two lines facing each other, their arms draped over one another's shoulders. Between the two lines was a singer with a crude tambourine. He sang and swayed back and forth. The lines of men responded in turn to his direct, insistent beat, answering his verses with verses of their own. The women were peeping out from another part of the compound where they had eaten their dinner. They were all dressed in their best clothes, brightly colored kaftans. They answered the various verses with calls of their own, enthusiastically urging the men on. Since I did not understand the songs and was not dancing, my excitement wore off rapidly. Ali was one of the most dedicated of the dancers, and it was difficult to catch his attention. During a break when the central singer was warming his tambourine over the fire to restretch the skin, I finally got Ali's ear and told him politely but insistently that I was not feel-ing well, that we had been here three hours already. It was midnight, could we leave soon after the next round of dances maybe? Of course, he said, just a few more min-utes, no problem, don't worry, I understand.

An hour later I tried again and received the same answer. This time, however, I was getting angrier and more frustrated; I was feeling truly ill. The mountain air was quite cold by now, and I had not dressed warmly enough. I felt entirely at Ali's mercy. I didn't want to antagonize him, but neither did I want to stay. I continued to grumble to myself but managed to smile at whoever was smiling at me.

Finally, at three in the morning, I could stand it no longer. I was feeling terrible. I was furious at Ali but loath to express it. I was going to leave, regardless of the con-sequences. I told Soussi, let's go; if you want a ride, get Ali and that's it. Ali at this point was nowhere in sight. Soussi went off and returned to the car with a smiling and contented Ali. I was warming the engine up, publicly announcing my readiness to leave. They climbed in, Soussi in the front and Ali in the back, and we were off. The road for the first five miles is little more than a path—untarred, pitted, and winding and steep in places. I was a novice driver and unsure of myself, so I said nothing, con-centrating all my energy on staying on the road and keeping the car going. I managed to negotiate this stretch of road successfully and heaved a sigh of relief when we reached the highway.

Soussi had been keeping up a steady flow of chatter as we bumped over the country road. I had kept my silence, ignoring Ali in the back, who said little himself. When we reached the highway and began rolling smoothly toward Sefrou, he asked in a nonchalant manner, *wash ferhan?*, are you happy? I snickered and said no. He pursued this. Why not? In simple terms I told him that I was sick, that it was three-thirty in the morning, and all I wanted to do was go home to bed—adding that I sincerely hoped he had enjoyed himself. Yes, he said, he had enjoyed himself, but if I was unhappy then the whole evening was spoiled, he was getting out of the car. Please, Ali, I said, let's just get back to Sefrou in peace. But why are you unhappy? I reminded him of his promise. If you are unhappy, he said, then I will walk back. This exchange was repeated several times, Soussi's vain attempts at mediation being ignored by both sides. Finally I told Ali he was acting like a baby, and yes, I was unhappy. He never offered any specific excuses but only insisted that if I was unhappy he would walk. He started to lean over and open the door on Soussi's side, scaring Soussi witless. We were traveling at forty miles an hour, and it scared me too, and I slowed down to ten. He challenged me again asking me if I was happy. I just could not bring myself to answer yes. My superego told me I should. But the events of the evening combined with the frustration of not being able to express myself fully to him in Arabic got the better of me. After another exchange and bluff on his part, I stopped the car to let him get out, which he now had to do. He did, promptly, and began striding down the dark highway in the direction of Sefrou. I let him get about one hundred yards ahead and then drove up alongside and told him to get in the car. He looked the other way. Soussi tried his luck with the same results. We repeated this melodrama two more times. I was confused, nauseous, and totally frustrated. I stepped on the gas and off we went to Sefrou, leaving Ali to walk the remaining five miles.

I went to sleep immediately, but woke from a fitful night saying to myself that I had probably made a grave professional mistake, because the informant is always right. Otherwise I was unrepentant. It was quite possible that I had ruined my relationship with Ali and that I had done irreparable damage to my chances of working my way into the village. But there were other things worth studying in Morocco, and it was something I would just have to make the best of. I took a walk through the tree-lined streets of the Ville Nouvelle and remembered a story a friend had told me before we took our doctoral exams; he had had nightmares for a week before the exams in which he saw himself as a shoe salesman. I mentally tried several occupations on for size as I drifted aimlessly among the villas. I felt calm; if this was anthropology and if I had ruined it for myself, then it simply wasn't for me.

The parameters seemed clear enough. I had to clarify for myself where I stood. If the informant was always right, then by implication the anthropologist had to become a sort of non-person, or more accurately a total persona. He had to be willing to enter into any situation as a smiling observer and carefully note down the specifics of the event under consideration. If one was interested in symbolic analysis or expressive culture, then the more elusive dimensions of feeling tone, gesture, and the like would be no exception. This was the position my professors had advocated: one simply endured whatever inconveniences and annoyances came along. One had to completely subordinate one's own code of ethics, conduct, and world view, to "suspend disbelief," as another colleague was proud of putting it, and sympathetically and accurately record events.

All of this had seemed simple enough back in Chicago (where, more accurately, no one paid more than lip service to these problems), but it was far from simple at the wedding. Ali had been a steady companion during the previous month and I had established a real rapport with him, more as a friend than as an informant; I was getting acclimated to Sefrou, and my Arabic was still too limited for us to do any sustained and systematic work together. I found the demands of greater self-control and abnegation hard to accept. I was used to engaging people energetically and found the idea of a year constantly on my guard, with very little to fall back on except the joys of asceticism, productive sublimation, and the pleasures of self-control, a grim prospect. . . .

At the wedding Ali was beginning to test me, much in the way that Moroccans test each other to ascertain strengths and weaknesses. He was pushing and probing. I tried to avoid responding in the counter-assertive style of another Moroccan, vainly offering instead the persona of anthropologist, all-accepting. He continued to interpret my behavior in his own terms; he saw me as weak, giving in to each of his testing thrusts. So the cycle continued: he would probe more deeply, show his dominance, and exhibit my submission and lack of character. Even on the way back to Sefrou he was testing me, and in what was a backhanded compliment, trying to humiliate me. But Ali was uneasy with his victories, and shifted to defining the situation in terms of a guest-host relationship. My silence in the car clearly signaled the limits of my submission. His response was a strong one: Was I happy? Was he a good host?

The role of the host combines two of the most important of Moroccan values. As throughout the Arabic world, the host is judged by his generosity. The truly good host is one whose bounty, the largesse he shows his guests, is truly neverending. One of the highest compliments one can pay to a man is to say that he is *karim*, generous. The epitome of the host is the man who can entertain many people and distribute his bounty graciously. This links him ultimately to Allah, who is the source of bounty.

If the generosity is accepted by the guest, then a very clear relationship of domination is established. The guest, while being fed and taken care of, is by that very token acknowledging the power of the host. Merely entering into such a position represents an acceptance of submission. In this fiercely egalitarian society, the necessity of exchange or reciprocity so as to restore the balance is keenly felt. Moroccans will go to great lengths, and endure rather severe personal privation, to reciprocate hospitality. By so doing, they reestablish their claim to independence.

Later in the day, I went down to Soussi's store in search of Ali to try and make amends. At first he refused even to shake hands, and was suitably haughty. But with the aid of Soussi's mediation and innumerable and profuse apologies on my part, he began to come round. By the time I left them later that afternoon it was clear that we had reestablished our relationship. Actually, it had been broadened by the confrontation. I had in fact acknowledged him. I had, in his own terms, pulled the rug out from under him—first by cutting off communication and then by challenging his gambit in the car. There was a fortuitous congruence between my breaking point and Moroccan cultural style. Perhaps in another situation my behavior might have proved irreparable. Brinkmanship, however, is a fact of everyday life in Morocco, and finesse in its use is a necessity. By finally standing up to Ali I had communicated to him.

Indeed, from that point on, we got along famously. It was only after this incident that he began to reveal to me two aspects of his life which he had previously concealed: his involvement in an ecstatic brotherhood, and his involvement in prostitution.

Review Questions

1. What professional mistake did Rabinow think he had made with Ali? What "rule all good anthropologists should follow" did he think he had violated?

2. Why does Rabinow talk about enduring annoyances and inconveniences as "suspending disbelief"?
3. What does it mean in the Moroccan culture to be *karim*? What is the significance of this characteristic?

Probes

1. Notice how space is organized and used in the Moroccan village Rabinow describes. For example, how are the houses arranged and built? Where are the men and the women during the dancing? What messages about culture do you get from these uses of space?
2. How do you account for the radical response Rabinow first had to the argument with Ali—he actually considered having to become a shoe salesperson or something other than an anthropologist. Why do you suppose he responded so strongly?
3. What does Rabinow's experience say about the relationship between theory and practice?
4. Paraphrase Rabinow's explanation of the guest-host, dominant-submissive dynamic he found in Moroccan culture.
5. Notice that, for Rabinow, the key outcome of the confrontation with Ali was that "I had in fact acknowledged him." What does he mean by that?

Part 6

Approaches to Interpersonal Communication

Chapter 16

A Teacher's Approach

This final section of *Bridges Not Walls* is made up of three "approaches" to interpersonal communication, one by a teacher, one by a psychotherapist, and one by a philosopher. These readings are meant to illustrate three different ways in which the concepts and skills discussed in the first fifteen chapters can be organized into a coherent whole. Each of the final readings develops one way to approach communication with others interpersonally, that is, *as contact between persons.* None of the three includes *every* single concept and skill, but all reflect a commitment to the basic beliefs that are reflected in the other readings; namely, that communication is a reciprocal and mutual process, not something one person does "to" some-body else; that communication is more than instrumental and expressive because it affects our personal identity; that communication is as complex as the humans who engage in it; and that there's a direct link between the quality of our communication and the quality of our lives.

Each approach reflects the main agenda of its author. C. Roland Christensen is a teacher at the Harvard Business School who wants his students to learn by communicating interpersonally with him and with each other. Carl R. Rogers was a psychotherapist who wanted his clients—and readers of his books—to experience the quality of communication that he knew could help make them healthier. And Martin Buber was a philosopher who wanted to help people deeply understand the profound connection between the quality of their communication and the quality of their existence.

I encourage you to use these three readings to give some *unity* to your experience with the first fifteen chapters. Interpersonal communication is complex enough that it can be easy to get lost in the details of verbal cues, nonverbal cues, self-awareness, person perception, listening, disclosure, gender differences, conflict, and intercultural complexities. So you might want to read these final chapters as a respite from work on the specifics, or as a way to reconnect with the forest after having concentrated on the trees, or even as a preview before you've jumped into the other chapters. But in any case I encourage you to notice how these three people have synthesized the other ideas into a whole that works for them. They can be a guide to your efforts to do the same thing.

As I mentioned, C. Roland Christensen is a teacher at the Harvard Business School and senior editor of a book called *Education for Judgment: The Artistry of Discussion Leadership.* The book is a collection of essays by teachers who have given up lecturing in favor of collaborative learning through focused discussion. I like his book and use it as a text partly because its title acknowledges that facilitating a good classroom discussion is an *art* not a *science,* which is to say that it includes some *unmeasurable* aspects and some *mystery.* Christensen is a teacher who clearly recognizes this, and who applies to his teaching large chunks of the approach to interpersonal communication that's been laid out in the earlier chapters of *Bridges Not Walls.*

One of these "chunks" is the commitment to the idea that communication is a relational thing, something that happens mutually, *between people.* Christensen expresses his version of this idea as the "fundamental insight" that "teaching and learning are inseparable, [a] reciprocal giving and receiving." As he discovered firsthand, when you apply this insight to an eighty-student classroom, the results can create cognitive overload. But they can also be gratifying as you find that students are deeply involved "both intellectually and with their guts." As a result of his first experiences, Christensen reports, he wanted to find out how this electrifying-yet-overwhelming process works.

When other teachers could only tell him, "Play it by ear," he went to those responsible for his survival, his students. He discovered that, directly or indirectly, they would let him know what worked and what didn't. He also figured out that the complex process could be understood in terms of three basic activities: questioning, listening, and responding to student responses. He explains some of the insights students taught him about these activities under six headings. First, students can play a significant role in constructing the day's agenda. Second, student logic can be different from—but nonetheless as useful as—the teacher's logic. Third, timing is crucial, and fourth, the types of questions affect how the discussion goes. Fifth, students can often communicate more effectively than the instructor because of their "rough and ready emotional profiles of one another," and finally, students build a class *culture* which affects all the class activities. These are all specific ways students contribute materially to the "teaching" process, and, Christensen believes, successful teaching begins when you recognize them.

In the major section of this essay, Christensen discusses five main "lessons" that he has learned about this approach to teaching. I could spend pages on each, but since he discusses them well, I'll just summarize them here. (1) *A teacher's openness and caring increase the student's learning opportunities.* Caring teachers don't just "coddle" students; they actually help them *learn*. (2) *Effective discussions require the classroom to become a learning space.* Intellectual hospitality and the safety that encourages risk-taking are two of its main features. (3) *Modest expectations are the most powerful of all.* Rather than trying to cover every possible topic or every possible reading, it works best to just help everybody learn a few ideas well. What a revolutionary idea! (4) *Instructors' patience promotes students' learning.* Inquiry and growth flourish under low pressure. The story in this section about the butterfly is super. (5) *Faith is the most essential ingredient in good teaching practice.* And to flesh out this idea, Christensen concludes with ten items of "faith" that guide his teaching. I'll just mention a couple: "Involvement is critical to enduring learning." "Teaching is a moral act." "What my students become is as important as what they learn." "Fun has a critical place in teaching."

It's hard to read this essay without wishing that all of your classes could be taught by Christensen, or somebody who approached teaching and learning as he does. But I hope you can also see how this approach to classroom discussion is one exciting way to synthesize this book's approach to interpersonal communication.

Every Student Teaches and Every Teacher Learns: The Reciprocal Gift of Discussion Teaching

C. Roland Christensen

It has been said that we live life forward but understand it backward. Looking back over years of discussion teaching, I see how intensely its process has intrigued, baffled, and intellectually nourished this practitioner—and the fascination shows no signs of abating. At its core lies a fundamental insight: teaching and learning are inseparable, parts of a single continuum—more Möbius strip than circle—of reciprocal giving and receiving. In discussion pedagogy students share the teaching task with the instructor and one another. All teach, and all learn. This view of the dynamic has implications for every aspect of discussion teaching, from fundamental assumptions to the finest points of classroom behavior. I make no claim to understand them all. But looking at teaching through the prism of reciprocity has allowed me to discern certain components of the process than can be named, described, studied, and communicated.

The reader should not be surprised to find "what I know," and, in particular, my descriptions of how I think while teaching, in the form of questions rather than statements. Four decades of discussion teaching leave their mark—in my case, an aversion to divorcing knowledge from challenge, dialogue, emotional engagement, and personal development. The quest for wisdom, as distinct from knowledge, will always remain open-ended.

This essay will present insights I have collected about the discussion teaching process with some details about the context that allowed me to see them. It will begin in the past, with my very first discussion class and fledgling efforts to learn how to learn about its mysteries. It will then continue with hypotheses about the nature of the process and the very powerful role students play in sharing its leadership with their instructors. And it will conclude in the present, with overarching "lessons learned" about values and the essential ingredient in all good teaching: faith.

Early Years: How I Learned to Learn About Discussion Teaching

Exploring the discussion process has been a wondrous adventure, a long journey within the confines of classroom walls. Like any productive educational enterprise, mine was aided by a fortunate synergy between instructor and institution. My colleagues on the faculty of the Harvard Business School honored teaching as a legitimate subject to be studied, as well as an action to be performed—an attitude that affected

Pages 99–119 of *Education for Judgment: The Artistry of Discussion Leadership*, ed. C. Roland Christensen, David A. Garvin, and Ann Sweet. 1991 Harvard Business School Press.

my perspective on everything that I saw, heard, and sensed as I taught, and my decisions on the best investment of my own intellectual resources.

My personal chain of discovery began with the first discussion class I ever taught: Tuesday, February 14, 1947. Yesterday. Remembered painfully, it was a bit like a session with a dental surgeon, sans novocaine. I was to teach an eighty-student section of the required second-year Business Policy course. The course mission was complex: to help students learn the functions, roles, and knowledge requirements of a general manager, with emphasis on the qualitative intricacies of strategic decision making. Underlying all this was the more basic goal of promoting the development of essential personal qualities: judgment, wisdom, and ethics.

Promptly at 8:30 A.M., having sweated through the weekend and Monday, I opened the door to Baker Library 101. It was a thin, cold room, with windows that rattled in the northeast wind and metal blinds stuck in various positions of closure. A slightly curved amphitheater format barely allowed space at the front for a platform, replete with brass rail and curtain that but partially hid the instructor's chair and desk. My suit coat over one arm—army exercise had changed my body frame and Harvard's salary did not allow for wardrobe refurbishment—and a folder of class notes in the other, I walked to the small platform, started up the three steps, tripped, and fell.

I blushed a bright red and knelt to gather my scattered papers. The room was quiet, except for an embarrassed half-laugh from the right, so brief it must have been squelched. I took a deep breath and, finally, stood up to look around at "them": scores of almost indistinguishable faces. A few smiled at me, thank heavens. My opening question—"Mr. Adams [you can imagine my reason for selecting him to start off], what is your diagnosis of the Consolidated Vultee situation?"—went well. But the remainder of the eighty minutes was a blur. My carefully prepared teaching plan, crafted to direct the group through an efficient analysis of the case that would reveal both the principles of Business Policy and my own indispensability to the discussion process, had minimal impact.

We were discussing a case about a company organizing for rapidly expanded military production during wartime, a topic still of high interest in 1947. The students wanted to pursue their own concerns and questions in ways that were meaningful to them. They agreed, disagreed, expressed confidence in (or incredulity at the naiveté of) their associates' suggestions. Infrequently, someone would admit confusion—a predicament appreciated and shared by the instructor. A few seemed bored, but most were deeply involved in the case, both intellectually and with their guts. There was no antagonism—all were polite—but the group permitted neither plan nor professor to get in its way.

When the class was over, I had heard hundreds and hundreds of words—verbal exchanges between and among the students, a multiplicity of conclusions, and an explosion of suggestions as to what the president of Consolidated Vultee should do. For me, it had been an academic Tower of Babel, a throw of conversational confetti. Most puzzling, however, was the reaction of the students. Seemingly, the class had made sense to them. Small groups stayed in the classroom after the discussion. Others left still carrying on their dialogue with an intensity that would have been difficult to contrive. Several commented, "Good class, professor." I thought, "Good class? Come on!"

The few steps back to my office felt like a stroll through a sandstorm. All I could remember of what had happened but minutes before were a few major themes and some dramatic statements. Students' comments fused; I couldn't recall who had said what or the responses those comments had triggered. A psychologist might have diagnosed my condition as cognitive overload: too much information to process too fast. How could I lead such a confusing process as this discussion had been? "It can't be done," I thought. "It simply can't be done!"

The only sensible course of action was to get help. Our faculty was the best, artists of the classroom, the teaching equivalents of Monet, Miró, and Jasper Johns. I asked senior colleagues to explain the discussion teaching process to me. Unfortunately, mastery of a creative activity does not guarantee the ability to explain it or help another master it. "Play it by ear, just play it by ear," was a typical response. For all their classroom genius, my colleagues treated teaching like the proverbial "black box": a container full of powerful mechanisms, but sealed.

During that first year of teaching, succeeding classes continued to listen much like the first one. The weeks marched by: dozens of class meetings, three times a week, with two eighty-person class groups. The discussion were spirited—decibels galore, dialogue, orations, even disquisitions. Crisp comments and pauses, murmurs, and mumbles. Themes did emerge in class, and the group often obtained reasonable consensus by the end of the session. Assumptions were tested and points proved. I had a good notion that cooperation powered the process, but even so, its dynamic eluded me. It was still a noisy mystery "out there." I felt like a stranger in the midst of the familiar. Nietzsche somewhere notes that all that is profound wears a mask. I wanted to look behind the mask that the learning process wore every day in the classroom.

Getting help became a puzzle, a pedagogical Rubik's cube. By now I had guessed that the students were responsible for my survival, thus far, in the classroom. Slowly this realization became a clue to learning about the mysterious process of discussion teaching. If colleagues couldn't "give" me the answer, perhaps I might find it with the students. After all, they were the reason it was working. I wondered if, somehow, those whom I supposedly led could help me learn how to lead. Perhaps I could work out a way to study what we all did in discussions and discover order in the apparent chaos. This would mean observing other teachers' classes and, as far as possible, my own.

I soon learned that mastery of course content wasn't the key. At the very beginning, I had, like most instructors, assumed that my job was to devise the clearest, most insightful analysis of the material possible, compose a list of questions to elicit that analysis in class, and then lead the students through my list in a courteous but authoritative manner. How starkly that assumption clashed with what I observed in class! When I tried to figure out what distinguished higher- from lower-quality discussion classes, I noticed that the better discussions were those in which the students asked particularly good questions—questions that often eclipsed those I had prepared. And the best discussions often modified or completely abandoned my neatly sequenced teaching plans. I was intrigued to realize that this aspect of good classes lay largely beyond my control, as did another common feature of productive discussions: students' listening to one another with attention and care. Good discussions frequently took paths that the group found reasonable but I had not foreseen. It seemed increasingly obvious that I neither could nor should try to control the discussion process. The students were my co-teachers.

Over time, such glimmers of insight brightened to beams of light that illuminated at least a portion of the contents of the black box of the discussion process. My early, overwhelmed conclusion, "It can't be done," evolved to, "It *can* be done, but not alone." But if the students were teaching, what was my job? To help them teach better. This meant that I needed not only to master the skills of leading the discussion process but also to devise ways to describe and explain the process to others.

Self-knowledge is the beginning of all knowledge. I had to find the teacher in myself before I could find the teacher in my students and gain understanding of how we all taught one another. Slowly, I learned to make my classroom observations more productive by focusing them. I started to try out tiny experiments. Instead of waiting for the class to assemble before making my appearance, for example, I tried arriving early to see what that might teach me about my students. The exercise proved valuable. Talking with students and watching them enter the room revealed much about their lives and interests—who played sports before class, who was under the weather or visibly fatigued that day, who had special interest in the day's topic (or, conversely, an apparent desire to hide). Coming to class early also allowed me to prepare a genial, cooperative atmosphere by welcoming students by name, and it gave me an opportunity to note students' subgroups.

Some other early experiments: I dropped my initial practice of calling opening speakers in alphabetical order and made choices based on some knowledge of students' backgrounds and interests. And I took a tip from a student who noted a preponderance of "whats" among my questions and tried more "whys." Simple, simple steps, rooted in practicality. But these were my first glimpses of the workings of the black box.

Finding time to reflect on the discussion as it unfolded in class was still like trying to meditate on a speeding fire engine. The after-class reprise was equally difficult. But I now had some ideas about why certain classes seemed more productive than others. Much of what we teachers do in the classroom seems intuitive. My task was to examine this apparently automatic behavior, show its workings, and identify areas in which judgment might play a part. "Process," whatever it might be, was clearly going to be the major focus of my attention.

Like most academics, I assumed that abstract principles of some sort would be my best guides. But my initial attempts, directed at understanding "process" in its purest sense, brought little practical reward. It seemed that the farther down the "abstraction ladder" I climbed, the closer I came to my real goal, an ever-deeper understanding of process. Near the bottom of the ladder, on the operational (how to) level, I began to make observations that truly dispelled confusion. When I came to class with a simple, practical teaching experiment in mind—something like evaluating the effect of calling on students seated in different parts of the room—I got results. Sometimes I focused on the art of questioning. What happens when I ask the same question of two students in succession? What is the effect of asking a delayed question—one to be answered after a moment of reflection—compared with asking the same question "cold"? Sometimes I concentrated on phrasing. What is the difference between using a student's name and simply gesturing? Or I concentrated on timing: How long can a silence last before restlessness sets in? I repeated these experiments from class to class, year to year, trying, like any researcher, to hold as many things constant as possible each time in order to evaluate the variable element.

Once I learned to focus on what a teacher says and does in the classroom, possibilities for experimentation and learning began to proliferate. The classroom proved to be a perfect laboratory for my nuts-and-bolts experiments with the discussion process. As an observer, of myself and other instructors in action, I truly began to learn. My experimental approach to the discussion process revealed that all participants, instructor included, spent most of their time either asking questions, listening to people's answers, or making some sort of response to those answers. I began to appreciate that these activities—questioning, listening, and response—were the most basic "stuff" of process. I also realized that every discussion produced rehearsals of data, analysis, questions, challenges, and syntheses, but not necessarily in a predictable sequence. This insight suggested that one of the instructor's most crucial tasks is linking—explicitly relating, and helping the students to relate, current points of argument to others that may have appeared earlier that day or in a previous discussion. This point, I realized, had important implications for teaching preparation as well as discussion management.

What I found inside the black box of the discussion process was an ever-changing flow of activities that resisted abstract analysis but yielded to disciplined observation and the application of very specific skills. To some extent, all of the essays in [*Education for Judgment*] examine aspects of these skills from the points of view of experienced practitioners, teachers at work. And what is our work? To create a favorable learning climate, to set a teaching/learning contract, to ask and respond to questions, listen to contributions, and promote the formation of groups in which students can teach themselves and one another. All these are practical approaches to a process that cannot be abstracted without substantial loss of identity, for the discussion process is a true slice of life. Guiding it takes skill, patience, and a basic faith that one may learn, with time and effort, to preside over disorder without disorientation.

Some Insights about Process and Students' Role in Its Leadership

Seen in retrospect, my attempts to understand the workings of the discussion teaching process have much in common with the process itself. Both exhibit the disorderliness of discovery: even the most steadfast explorer cannot march straight through a jungle. Most attempts to capture the essence of the discussion process produce frustrations as well as insights. The very meaning of the phrase, for example, still teases our profession. The totality of a discussion includes the intellectual and emotional experiences of a whole roomful of people: material to occupy psychologists, neurologists, sociologists, anthropologists, and philosophers for years to come. My own quest for an enlightening definition produced little to help me choose which of ten vigorously waving hands to recognize. All processes are flows, either of activities or thoughts, but this basic definition gives one no handle on why some opening questions inspire lively debate while others trigger alienation or apathy, or why the comments of "student experts" sometimes help and sometimes hinder a discussion. Nor does it distinguish what happens in a discussion classroom from what happens on an assembly line.

I found the exercise of drawing distinctions more fruitful. Contrasting process with content provided practical help. Confusing mastery of material with mastery of the discussion process produces a common error: a controlling teaching style that creates bilateral frustration when students inevitably try to go their own ways. This lesson became clear to me as my students continued to offer polite, but stubborn resistance to my attempts to shepherd them through the meticulous analyses that had cost me so many hours of preparation. And when I examined my own initial inclination to choose opening speakers alphabetically from my class list, I found that it showed another typical novice's confusion: the failure to distinguish process from procedure. Procedures are logical and rigid sequences of actions, indispensable in making an arrest, performing an appendectomy, or accessing a computer file—but fatal to leading a meaningful group discussion. Discussions are liquid. They do not move in straight lines; they undulate.

Over the years, I have found the use of metaphor enriching to my understanding of the discussion process. What is a discussion, if not a voyage of exploration, with the leader as both captain and crew member? To appreciate the frequent reversals and indirections of the process, one may imagine a discussion class as a mountain climb, where even apparent reversals produce ascent. In the discussion process, "wrong" can be more helpful than "right"; an obtuse statement can spark a charged, enlightening debate that straightforward analysis could never provoke.

Discussion teaching is noisy. Messy, too. It greets an observer with a verbal cacophony—an unnerving scene for teachers unprepared for its energy. Good discussions unfold in unexpected ways that modify the programmed logic of a teaching plan. They pose new questions, uncover and gnaw away at sanctified assumptions, rejuvenate old topics with fresh insights, broaden perspectives, and create new paths of inquiry. But focused observation and systematic analysis can reveal meaning in the noise and logic in the disorder. The rough-and-tumble of classroom interchange contains opportunities that enhance the learning of both students and instructors. What unsettles a teacher may energize the students: less disorder, than new order. Discussion teaching demands a milieu of freedom, an openness that encourages students to share power over, and responsibility for, the leadership and conduct of a class.

In discussion teaching, tidiness can tyrannize. Messiness can work miracles. To succeed, the enterprise requires the active contribution, not merely cooperation, of the discussion group. Mutual collaboration—reciprocity of effort—is not only engaging and exciting for students, it is also imperative for the discussion leader. However impressive your experience or skills, you will have difficulty in questioning, listening, and responding while simultaneously observing, synthesizing, reflecting, and evaluating the discussion dialogue, and planning for the rest of the class. A teacher would need more than one pair of eyes and ears to carry out such a task—it really *can't* be done alone!

This realization suggests a further point: a great deal of essential information—factors that condition the instructional choices of the moment—emerges only in action as the process unfolds. Should an idea be explored in greater depth or overviewed in a hurry? Should the class move on to another topic? Would it be helpful to raise or lower the abstraction level of the argument? What does the group understand? What is missing? What topics need to be covered again? What questions are bothering or intriguing the group? What new avenues of exploration should we investigate now? It helps to remember that the teacher does not bear the sole responsibility for answering these questions. Students control a surprisingly large part of the turf of discussion leadership. They participate in critical "framework" decisions by influencing the agenda, sequence of topics, and allocation of time to various topics. They help determine the minute-by-minute direction of the discussion process and the quality of the dialogue. They contribute to the creation of a class culture, accept responsibility for their own involvement, and teach their peers. They develop and practice the skills of leading and following. Without their co-leadership, there is no true discussion.

I have found it helpful to consider students' contribution to the leadership of the discussion process under six broad categories. First, when responsibility is collective, the students play a significant role in constructing the agenda of the day. The instructor may find his or her preclass teaching plan influenced by the addition of new topics of interest to student, suggestions for restating issues in ways that provoke different questions, or requests that materials from previous discussions be combined with the dialogue of the day. Sometimes the class will simply reject the instructor's program. In these cases capitulation is advisable, if not inevitable. Teaching is difficult enough when students want to learn, virtually impossible if they are uninterested. Given these circumstances, discussion teachers do not, like lecturers, set the agenda; they manage its emergence, direction, and evolution.

Second, the students affect the sequence in which topics of the day are discussed. Teachers and students prepare differently. Instructors' plans exploit a flow of inquiry that seems logical to them, consistent with course objectives, and built on past experience with the material and students. But the instructor's teaching logic may not match the students' learning logic. In discussion leadership, efficiency does not always equal effectiveness. Last year's—or last hour's—discussion of a particular topic will never exactly predict the one that's about to begin. Even very experienced instructors, who have been teaching longer than their students have been studying (sometimes longer than their students have been alive), have an inferior command of one essential topic: their students' agendas and learning styles. As a result, questions that an instructor may wish to consider early may well be out of sync with the students' wishes and needs.

Accordingly, a wise instructor prepares twice: both from his or her point of view and, more important, from the students' point of view. How will participants be likely to approach the material? What paths of inquiry might they follow? When the instructor's approach differs from that of the students, the discussion may well tilt in the students' direction. The professor proposes, but the class disposes.

The third aspect of the discussion that students influence is timing. When their involvement in a question or topic is intense, it will be difficult for an instructor to redirect their energy. One can force a shift in topic, but students' interests, though denied, do not disappear. They reemerge, deftly inserted into their responses to the instructor's new questions. The sensitive instructor will "hear" the discontinuity and act accordingly.

Fourth, the types of questions students ask of one another and of the instructor play a critical role in directing the minute-by-minute flow of dialogue. Their questions may be directionally neutral— "Where do we go next?"—or may shift the discussion to another topic. The phrasing, tone, and delivery of their questions and comments influence the mood and tempo of the class, encourage conflict, excitement, resolution, or reflection. The astute instructor will listen carefully, and on several levels, to students' questions and also respectfully note the directive power in the students' choice of which individual or subgroup to address. This choice is another, crucial contribution students make to determining both the style and content of discussion.

Working and playing together over a period of time, students get to know their associates better than the instructor can—their itches and ouches, blind spots, areas of experience and wisdom, cares and concerns. And students possess current information about their peers to augment this background information. They are familiar with Rosa's or Juan's circumstances today, this minute. They know Herman's special interest in the topic and his mood. Was he worked over in an earlier class today? Is there a family crisis going on? This sort of student intelligence (in the military sense) lies mainly beyond an instructor's reach. But its power to maintain continuity or produce radical change in the direction of dialogue will show up in the classroom.

Such information can improve the quality of the group's communication. Effective communication—in which words encourage and advance understanding for others as well as the speaker—is difficult to achieve under the best of circumstances. Indeed, as the late Fritz Roethlisberger observed, the first law of communication is to expect miscommunication. Communication is even more complex in crowded classrooms, where dialogue is rapid-fire, personal commitment—even passion—accompanies many comments, and reflection time is limited. In such situations, students' intelligence does more to influence the flow of dialogue than the instructor's directions can.

Fifth, because students relate to one another as peers, they can often communicate more effectively than the instructor in class. Why? Not because they are more rigorous in thought, skilled in semantics and phonetics, or expert in their artistry of explanation. Rather, because they possess rough and ready emotional profiles of one another. In what fields does Ms. Peterson feel confident, have the knack of explaining, and the interest, patience, and ingenuity to state her message in a variety of ways? What are the barriers, the ignorance, bias, lack of interest, that limit Mr. Ripley's understanding and ability to listen?

Students also tend to share the language system of their generation, a common idiom of "go" and "no go" words and relevant metaphors ("needle in a haystack" might resonate less well than "contact lens in a swimming pool," for example). This, plus their knowledge of fellow students, brings them swiftly to the core of effective communication, speaking *to*, not *at*, one another.

Equally important, it is simpler and less threatening for participants to check and recheck each other's meaning than for the instructor to do so. They can accept "I don't understand what you said" more easily from a friend than a potential judge. Correction of the inevitable miscommunication is less complicated when it comes from a classmate than a teacher. When a fellow student says, "You didn't read me right. I meant this," or "Give me that again, Bill. Your assumptions are off base," the remark is less likely to be perceived as an accusation of ignorance or error, and more likely to be seen as a low-key request for help.

Finally, the sixth aspect of the discussion process that students influence heavily is class culture. Discussion groups derive tone and character from the way students work together in the daily routines of class. What is to be the balance between cooperation and competition? Where are the boundaries? What is acceptable and nonacceptable behavior? What are the responsibilities of a class member to himself or herself and the group? Obviously, all students should prepare, attend, and participate. It is difficult to experience a discussion in absentia. But what more? How will these particular participants work out the fundamental challenges of a member of a discussion group—when to stand out, when to blend in, when to lead, when to follow? How members of the group help one another through these complexities affects the context in which the discussions take place. The resolution of these problems contributes to the quality of the learning milieu.

The apparent disorder of a discussion class is, then, but a mask for a complicated teaching and learning process in which students play a vital, but far from obvious role in leadership. Only appreciation of, and attention to, process can help us teachers understand students' essential teaching contribution—a key understanding for effective educational discussions. Most important, the mask blinds us, as teachers, to a fundamental fact: we not only teach a course, but also simultaneously help the students learn how to teach one another. It is not enough to ask "good questions"; we must understand the art of questioning, listening, and responding constructively; model those skills in class for our students and, by so doing, demonstrate our respect for their importance.

Lessons Learned

Years after that first disorienting class, I still regard the mysterious power of discussion teaching with awe. I have shed the youthful naiveté that led me to search for "the answer," but I still work away at pedagogical questions. Accommodation is the order of the years, but the decades have brought a measure of understanding. My belief in the essential magnificence of teaching grows ever stronger. What I have learned about the abiding conundrums of discussion pedagogy makes me even more certain that teaching is a great learning experience. And for the study of teaching, what better research laboratory than the classroom, where the teacher can experiment with the real "stuff" and test, modify, and retest all hypotheses? I have stressed the rewards of this pursuit, but I am also aware of its price. The gains in depth and specificity that come from "knowing more" increase the pressure for yet higher standards. As hands-on classroom knowledge builds, one can no longer turn to easy excuses—the students just didn't like the material; another course had a long report due this week; or (most common of all) I just had a bad day. None of these explanations works when one grasps the dynamics of classroom process. Higher standards are a constant reminder to do better.

In working up a "wish I had learned this earlier" list, I asked myself: Does my experience suggest one quintessential lesson? Perhaps the answer is yes. Teaching is a human activity. Intellect does not teach intellect; people teach people. No matter how factually accurate and time-tested our data, how clear cut and disciplined our analytical methods, or how practiced and skillful our pedagogical techniques, true learning emerges only when we honor the human factor. One measure of pedagogical maturity is the ability to augment technical expertise with attention to people.

Given this overarching proposition, I would like to offer some lessons learned from students, colleagues, and day-to-day classroom practice. Some of these lessons have been purchased at substantial personal cost. Many lessons had to be both learned and relearned. On reflection, I find none of them surprising. Why didn't I think of them earlier? No one reason. But is a lifetime in the classroom really long enough to figure out what effective teaching is all about?

1. A teacher's openness and caring increase the students' learning opportunities. When students perceive the instructor at the front of the room as distant and impersonal—a figurehead, not a friend—their learning opportunities suffer. "He lives in another world, guys; I don't know what turns his flame up. . . . I'm just line twelve on the class list." Enduring learning needs a human context, an emotional matrix, in which to grow. The teacher who provides that context and encourages it in the learning group must let students know him or her as more than an intellectual resource or mobile data base.

Our educational conventions put distance between teachers and students. Without sacrificing propriety or relinquishing our role as guides, we teachers need to open our worlds to students. Far too many people in public view become, as Dr. Grete

Bibring put it, "individuals with faces that have never been lived in." Our students want and need to know what we stand for. The opposite side of this coin is our need to understand students as people. What are their ambitions, uncertainties, blind spots, and areas of excellence? When we open our wider worlds and appear "in the round," we also maximize our possibilities for learning about them. Openness brings mutual advantage because it permits mutual learning.

But openness is not enough. We must combine it with caring. Teachers must do more than feel concerned; we must actively look after and provide for the welfare of students. We must not only appreciate, but also become personally involved in, their progress. By so doing, we measurably enhance the potential for learning on both sides. One experienced associate noted that most students want to know how much you care before they care how much you know. His judgment, though paradoxical, makes sense to me. Caring converts impersonal offers of academic assistance into gifts, and every gift of learning enriches the giver as much as the recipient. Students sense the difference between perfunctory offers of help and true personal willingness to teach and learn with them. Openness increases a discussion leader's opportunities to help students. Caring makes the process work.

2. Effective discussions require the classroom to become a learning space. As a novice instructor I would have defined "learning space" physically, as the classroom. Baker 101 was an adequate room—satisfactory acoustics, lights in working order, enough chairs. I looked for nothing more. Over the years, however, my view of the classroom has grown metaphorical and far more demanding. A true learning space is psychological, not physical, and the teacher bears the primary responsibility for creating it.

I now view the discussion classroom as a joining ground where students, instructor, and ideas meet and commingle; a space where, as Henri Nouwen suggests, "students and teachers can enter into a fearless communication with each other and allow their respective life experiences to be their primary and most valuable source of growth and maturation."[1] The creation of such space requires a mutual trust in which teachers and learners (those shifting roles) can present themselves as colleagues in a common quest for truth. A genuine learning space is more than a container for this quest; it is a place where all feel free to question one another constructively and where an aggregation of competitive individuals, dedicated to personal goals, can become a learning group.

When we teachers create and support an atmosphere of intellectual hospitality, we help students believe that they have something of value to contribute. This belief, in turn, encourages them to risk trying out ideas—the risk that makes learning possible. Perhaps most important, it is only within a welcoming classroom space that we can obtain students' active involvement in discussions. Discussions that take place in true learning spaces engage students verbally and reflectively, intellectually and emotionally.

Above all, such spaces make risk-taking safe—as safe as it can be, that is. And safety—students' anticipation of aid and comfort in tough situations—is the greatest antidote to the discussion leader's ever-present, always unsettling challenge: silence. Joe isn't contributing very much anymore. What's going on? Is he reflecting on points made earlier, contemplating new questions to ask, wrestling with uncertainty, just feeling turned off—or is he scared? We teachers sometimes forget how difficult it is for students to develop the capacity for what Donald Schön calls cognitive risk-taking. A glance backward at our own student days may help us remember. Didn't we use silence to protect ourselves from questions—by peers, instructors, or ourselves (these last often the most painful)? In a safe space, members of a group with especially complex needs and concerns (that includes most of us, doesn't it?) can reveal their sensitivities and needs. When this happens, community is strengthened, and all benefit.

The creation and maintenance of a safe space is not very arduous, and its rewards are bountiful. David Riesman's metaphor of the teacher as host, or welcomer of guests, may serve as a useful guide. There is little cost but great value in learning something about students' backgrounds and current circumstances in time to welcome them personally to the upcoming dialogue. Similarly, the few moments we instructors devote to weaving "safety nets"—techniques for supporting students who run into trouble by taking on complex or unpopular points of argument—are well spent. Safety nets enable participants to walk the high wire of adventuresome thought and argument with daring bolstered by a sense of security.

When the instructor fosters the creation of a learning space in the classroom, everyone gains. The class becomes a community. A working partnership emerges between teacher and students, and risk-taking increases on both sides. We sometimes forget that instructors are as risk-averse as students. We hesitate to reveal our own uncertainties and areas of ignorance. We hold back from presenting positions in their early stages of development. We resist challenging popular points of view. But in a safe learning space, we can reveal what we know and need to know, and also what we are and would like to be.

3. Modest expectations are the most powerful of all. Teachers select their life's work for complex reasons, unique in every case. But one basic circumstance of our vocation unites us all: our work simultaneously allows us to serve the wider community and make significant contributions to the lives of the individual students entrusted to our care. Stories about master teachers give us pictures of what the great can do. Each of us has had some personal experience of the impact a teacher can make on a life by stimulating interest in a topic or field of study, providing a role model, or molding our basic values and beliefs. Teachers can accomplish so much of importance. But the contemplation of that accomplishment can overwhelm as well as inspire.

As my years in the classroom have multiplied, I have made the paradoxical discovery that modest expectations, particularly in the realm of content, trigger more effective learning than ambitious ones. Material learned in depth—with heart as well as head—stays with students, but broad-based lists of facts, techniques, and theories tend to fade. J. D. Salinger noted that the mark of immaturity is a desire to die nobly for a cause, but maturity brings the willingness to live humbly for one. Our colleague Abby Hansen suggests that discussion leaders' best songs are anthems of modest expectations. I have found that teaching practice improves when I fit my expectations about how much the group should cover in a given period to a quite modest standard. Thoroughness and depth compensate abundantly for the sacrifice of breadth. Retention of a few crucial things over time brings far more benefit than superficial mastery.

There are few tasks more difficult than evaluating the effect of our teaching. Trying to gauge success is like tossing coins into the Grand Canyon and waiting to hear the clink. How can we ever know just what we have contributed to a student's education? Teachers have much in common with performing artists, but our applause (or boos and hisses) may not come for years, if ever. Who knows what students retain a day, week, year, or decade after a seminar? It is chastening to be thanked by an alumnus for all you taught him only to realize, as the conversation continues, that he is praising a colleague, not you.

Gradually I have abandoned my interest in final outcomes—whatever they may be—and begun to derive satisfaction from the act of teaching itself. When I consider the innumerable gradations that intervene between success and failure, the complex natures of the parties involved, and the magnitude of the daily efforts that go unevaluated, I marvel at the imponderability of long-term effects. I have learned that wisdom and effectiveness lie in a constant struggle for improvement, rather than a quest for final results. Like virtue, teaching is its own reward. For me this means that if I practice and hone my skills, welcome observation and constructive criticism, and experiment and grow, my efforts may very well have an impact. Minor miracles do happen—often enough, in fact, to justify this hope.

4. Instructors' patience promotes students' learning. Patience, though a virtue of restraint, has the effect of energizing students. Inquiry, growth, and learning flourish under low pressure. Concepts and ideas are difficult to plant in our intellectual garden. They have erratic, individualized growing circles, and harvesting is always under the student's control—exam schedules to the contrary notwithstanding. Yet I found this simple lesson difficult to learn. Patience is not readily acquired.

Impatience comes more easily. Having worked through the process of understanding the applicability and limits of the ideas under study, we feel we know our subjects. The material is ours, and we forget the missteps we took on the way to this possession. But discussion teaching is not a straightforward dispensing of knowledge. Students have their own missteps to make; their journeys will not necessarily parallel ours. Discussion leaders who fail to appreciate the constructiveness of inefficiency make a serious error. Efficient teaching does not always equate with effective learning. On the contrary, students often discover valuable lessons at the ends of blind alleys—lessons that we teachers cannot anticipate before they unfold in the discussion. What seems like a digression may link the challenge of the moment to prior explorations. Apparent tangents examine questions of the students' creation, not because of any obvious link to the assignment of the day, but because they hold high, continuing intellectual interest for the students.

The syllabi we develop contribute to our impatience. There is always more to be taught than time to teach. A rigid, daily roster of material to cover pressures us to ignore crucial elements of context—school events, local and national circumstances, and personal matters. A colleague tells of a friend, a Civil War historian, who puts the point well: "In my class Grant has to arrive at Richmond before Thanksgiving, no matter what!"

The costs of such rigidity can be high, even cruel. As an unknown poet once said, "All the flowers of all the tomorrows are planted in the seeds of today." We need to nurture, tend, and let them mature at their own pace. Forcing can kill. Nikos Kazantzakis makes the point tellingly in *Zorba the Greek*:

> I remembered one morning when I discovered a cocoon in the bark of a tree, just as a butterfly was making a hole in its case and preparing to come out. I waited awhile, but it was too long appearing and I was impatient. I bent over it and breathed on it to warm it. I warmed it as quickly as I could and the miracle began to happen before my eyes, faster

than life. The case opened, the butterfly started slowly crawling out and I shall never forget my horror when I saw how its wings were folded back and crumpled; the wretched butterfly tried with its whole trembling body to unfold them. Bending over it, I tried to help it breathe. In vain.

It needed to be hatched out patiently and the unfolding of the wings should be a gradual process in the sun. Now it was too late. My breath had forced the butterfly to appear, all crumpled before its time. It struggled desperately and a few seconds later, died in the palm of my hand.

That little body is, I do believe, the greatest weight I have on my conscience. For I realize today that it is a mortal sin to violate the great laws of nature. We should not hurry, we should not be impatient, but we should confidently obey the eternal rhythm.[2]

This lesson has special meaning for teachers. We must bring to each class infinite patience, and moderate our critical judgments about students' progress. Walter Jackson Bate reminds us, in his biography of Samuel Johnson, how difficult it is to appreciate "the actual process and daily crawl of other people's experience."[3] But it is precisely this "daily crawl" that we must respect, protect, and honor. And we must, I submit, do it in a context of positive belief in students.

5. Faith is the most essential ingredient in good teaching practice.   Thus far I have discussed in depth two essentials of discussion teaching: knowledge of pedagogical concepts and mastery of process skills. It is now time to consider the third essential: faith. Faith in the fundamental worth of our vocation, in the values that govern our relations with individual students and classes, and in the likelihood that at least some of the results we desire will be achieved. To me, faith is the indispensable dimension of teaching life. Why, then, is it so rarely mentioned? Perhaps because academicians may feel more comfortable with hard facts, logical analysis, and readily observable skills than with intangibles like belief. But without these intangibles—the "soul," if you will, that animates that mechanism inside the black box of discussion teaching—technique becomes mechanical, skills manipulative, and attitudes suspect.

Can faith be codified? I have found that certain insights have not only endured but assumed increasing significance for my teaching practice while other observations and theoretical constructs have faded or been replaced. I offer these articles of faith—so meaningful to me—not as prescriptions or dogma, but as a purely personal testament: *credo*, after all, means "*I* believe."

• I believe that the profession of teaching is crucial to the maintenance and advancement of civilization. Only our most talented—master crafts-people who perform to the highest possible standards—should undertake it. As Theodore Roethke put it in "Words for Young Writers," we need "more people that specialize in the impossible,"[4] and that is what teachers do. To me, teaching carries an awesome responsibility to encourage students to want to know, to show them how to know, and to insist that they ask and answer the question "For what purpose do *I* need to know?"

• I believe in the teachability of teaching. For the past two decades my pedagogical research, statements, and teaching objectives have centered on this fundamental conviction: good teachers are made, not born. We can observe, analyze, and communicate the artistry of discussion leadership to other practitioners. Effective teachers both practice and constantly search and research their own activities; their classrooms are both instructional arenas and laboratories.

• I believe that active involvement is critical to enduring learning. In discussion classes, students and teachers alike must give of themselves. Without involvement, the discussion of the day is but noise and its leadership a charade. There's a world of difference between a lackadaisical game of "Simon Says" and the muscle-building that takes place when a committed coach leads an eager team through a workout. Involvement transforms passive, received knowledge into the active ability to apply that knowledge effectively.

• I believe that discussion leaders need to master both process skills as well as the substantive knowledge of their course. Without knowledge of process, instructors are limited in their effort to help students discover, assimilate, and retain course content. It is through command of process that the primacy of content is realized.

• I believe that teaching is a moral act. Ethical commitment must temper the balance we strike in selecting materials and working with them in class. Morality must shape our treatment of students—David Riesman calls teaching "power, with sympathy"—and the values we develop for the classroom community. As the late Professor Lon Fuller suggested, we must distinguish between a morality of duty—that which is formally and/or legally appropriate—and a morality of aspiration—a striving for excellence and idealism. The latter must govern.

• I believe that what my students become is as important as what they learn. The endpoint of teaching is as much human as intellectual growth. Where qualities of person are as central as qualities of mind—as is true in all professional education—we must engage the whole being of students so that they become open and receptive to multiple levels of understanding. And we must engage our whole selves as well. I teach not only what I know, but what I am.

• I believe that, in the words of Professor Charles Gragg, "teachers must also learn!"[5] We cannot truly teach unless we let ourselves experience the vicissitudes and exhilaration of exploration—the mastery and communication of ideas, coupled with the reception of new insights, and the never-ending desire to know more. Teaching and learning are inseparable; the process of education is a reciprocal gift.

• I believe that fun has a critical place in teaching. Great classes include multiple moods—verbal pyrotechnics, moments of stillness, measured, cadenced analyses, and flights of fancy—but always in a context of celebration. Fun permits breakouts from routine. It enlivens the humdrum and sustains generosity as all participants give and receive enjoyment along with wisdom. And fun can heal: it is difficult to dislike someone with whom you share a laugh. Humor can broaden the scope of the possible, but, as Samuel Johnson noted, "Nothing is more hopeless than a scheme of merriment."[6] In a context of good nature, fun will emerge unplanned from the inevitable incongruities of all extended conversations: the extrapolations that take comments to maximum exaggeration and the implosions that carry words and images to absurdity.

• I believe that the teacher's challenge in evaluating students is less to separate the gifted from the ordinary than to find the gifts of the ordinary. And I believe that we must communicate our evaluations in a manner that helps students understand their competence, or lack thereof, without destroying their confidence. Robert Frost said it well: "No figure [or letter] has ever caught the whole of it." At best, grades are imprecise measures even of academic achievement. They do not weigh the worth of a student as a person, now or in the future.

• I believe in the unlimited potential of every student. At first glance they range, like instructors, from mediocre to magnificent. But potential is invisible to the superficial gaze. It takes faith to discern it, but I have witnessed too many academic miracles to doubt its existence. I now view each student as "material for a work of art."

If I have faith, deep faith, in students' capacities for creativity and growth, how very much we can accomplish together. If, on the other hand, I fail to believe in that potential, my failure sows seeds of doubt. Students read our negative signals, however carefully cloaked, and retreat from creative risk to the "just possible." When this happens, everyone loses.

One student—call him Andy—was tottering between Low Pass and Unsatisfactory in my Business Policy course. Together we devised a remedial program. He would write five "dry run" exams before a "make-or-break" final that could determine whether he would graduate with his class. After each remedial exam, we would meet to discuss what he had written. Andy worked hard, but progress came slowly. At our last meeting, somewhat discouraged, I asked, "Andy, do you think you can handle the exam tomorrow?" He looked at me and said, oh so softly, "Professor Christensen, Professor Christensen, that's not it. The question is, do *you* think I can handle the exam? *Do you believe in me?*" His comment hit home—helped me. It reminded me of his strengths and the gains he had made. "Andy," I said, "would I spend this much time on a hopeless cause? Yes, I think you can pass this exam and take your degree. What's more, I know you will have a wonderful career. *I believe in you.*"

My words affected him visibly. He smiled, and I thought I could seen his back straighten a bit as he left my office. He passed the final exam, graduated with his class, and went on to great success, in both business and civic affairs. Many people have benefited from Andy's capability and generosity—his family, our school, his community, and society in general.

We learn so much from our students. Andy and others like him taught me that if I round out my knowledge of Business Policy and skill at discussion management with faith in them, they can accomplish the improbable and enable me to do the same. For the reciprocity of teaching and learning—their inseparability—makes us share in our students' successes, just as we share in their failures. To give up on students is to give up on ourselves, and that I have never done.

Notes

1. Henri J. M. Nouwen, *Reaching Out* (Garden City, NY: Image Books, 1986), p. 85.
2. Nikos Kazantzakis, *Zorba the Greek*, tr. Carl Wildman (New York: Simon & Schuster, 1952), p. 120.
3. Walter Jackson Bate, *Samuel Johnson* (New York: Harcourt Brace Jovanovich, 1977), p. 233.
4. Theodore Roethke, *Straw for the Fire: From the Notebooks of Theodore Roethke, 1943–63*, selected and arranged by David Wagoner (Garden City, NY: Doubleday, 1972), p. 185.
5. Charles I. Gragg, "Teachers Also Must Learn," *Harvard Educational Review*, vol. 10 (1940), pp. 30–47.
6. Samuel Johnson, "The Idler," in vol. 2, no. 58, *The Works of Samuel Johnson*, ed. Robert Lynam (London: George Cowre, 1825).

Review Questions

1. What is a "Möbius strip"? How does it help make Christensen's point in the first paragraph?
2. Christensen says he "soon learned that mastery of course content wasn't the key" to effective teaching. What was?
3. Describe the difference Christensen makes between "content" and "process" and between "process" and "procedures."
4. Paraphrase: "In discussion teaching, tidiness can tyrannize. Messiness can work miracles."
    "In discussion leadership, efficiency does not always equal effectiveness."

5. Explain the connection Christensen makes between a teacher's "openness" and his or her "caring."
6. Give two clear examples of what Christensen means by "patience."
7. What does it mean to say that "teaching is a moral act?"

Probes

1. It was relatively easy for Christensen to build this approach in a business-school class based on the case-study method. But other chapters of the book this essay appears in discuss applications of discussion teaching in political science, literature, and medical school (microscopic anatomy class). How might this approach be applied to each of the courses you are registered for this term?
2. On the one hand, Christensen emphasizes the application of specific, even "mechanical" skills—like asking questions of students in various parts of the room or using the students' name in the question versus not using his or her name. On the other hand, he clearly believes that excellent teaching involves more than just "mechanics." How would you describe his view of this tension between "mechanics" or "rules" and "intuition" or "art"?
3. What do you believe makes up the "class culture" Christensen talks about near the end of the essay? How does this culture affect what goes on in the classroom?
4. I think one of Christensen's most important insights is this: "Teaching is a human activity. Intellect does not teach intellect; people teach people." Paraphrase what you think this means and then respond. What would you expect the teacher who believes this to do, for example, with a syllabus, required readings, tests, office hours, and grading?
5. Give an example from your own experience of the importance of the classroom being a space where it is safe to take a cognitive risk.
6. Christensen says that he has gradually given up any interest in final outcomes—the degree to which his students achieve some particular goal in their education or in the "real world." What is his rationale for giving this up, and what has he substituted for it? How do you respond to this part of his essay?
7. How do you respond to all Christensen's talk about "faith"? Isn't this a pretty imprecise, abstract, and maybe even dangerous topic for something as concrete and practical as teaching? What justifies his discussion of it?

Chapter 17

A Psychotherapist's Approach

C arl Rogers was a psychotherapist and communication theorist who influenced many of the authors represented in this book. I highly recommend that you read at least one of his books—for example, *On Becoming a Person, Person to Person: The Process of Becoming Human,* or his most recent book, *A Way of Being.* In the 1950s Rogers was one of the half-dozen persons responsible for moving psychology away from an exclusive focus on Freudian psychodynamics and quantifiable variables to a concern with the whole person and communication relationships. By the time of his death in the late 1980s, he was known all over the world as a psychotherapist, group facilitator, and teacher.

This reading is made up of excerpts from a chapter in *A Way of Being.* Like many of his writings, this one was originally a talk he gave, in this case an invited speech at the California Institute of Technology. Rogers reports that as he prepared for the occasion, he became frustrated at his own efforts to describe what he believed about communication. So he decided to demonstrate rather than simply discuss, to endeavor, as he put it, "to *communicate,* rather than just to speak *about* the subject of communication."

In another place, Rogers wrote that over his lifetime he had discovered that "What is most personal is most general." This talk is evidence of this same insight. Rogers tries to stick close to his personal experiences with communication, and as he describes them he finds himself talking about my experience—and probably yours, too. So this essay demonstrates how "what is most personal is most general."

One of the reasons I like much of what Rogers says is that he begins discussing communication by focusing not on talk but on listening. He describes what it means really to hear someone and to be heard, to be listened to by another. Over his forty years as a psychotherapist, Rogers learned that complete hearing—listening, clarifying, and responding to all the levels at which the other is communicating—is one key to a therapeutic, growth-promoting relationship. The therapist, he argues, doesn't primarily need to be able to administer psychometric tests or interpret dreams. The most important thing is that he or she needs to make contact, to communicate interpersonally. As Rogers summarizes, "a creative, active, sensitive, accurate, emphatic, nonjudgmental listening is for me terribly important in a relationship."

The second of Rogers's three main points involves what he calls "congruence." This is his label for the state where "my experiencing of this moment is present in my awareness and when what is present in my awareness is present in my communication." As he explains in other writings, this does not mean that you impulsively blurt out every thought that enters your mind. Especially when you're experiencing mixed feelings, it's important to reflect on the dimensions of experience that deserve communicating. Rogers also believes that incongruence is often an outgrowth of fear.

The flip side of congruence, of course, is allowing and encouraging the other to be congruent too. As Rogers says, this is often the ultimate test for the leader, teacher, and parent. But when at least some measure of congruence characterizes both sides of a relationship, the communication is enriched by it.

Rogers's third learning is that what he's called unconditional positive regard or nonpossessive warmth is also vital to effective communication. People typically experience so much evaluation and criticism that when they feel accepted for who they are, they often blossom. As he notes, people can be appreciated just as we appreciate a sunset.

In other writings, Rogers has also clarified that he doesn't mean we should go around in a naive pink fog, loving every terrorist, rapist, and sociopath who makes the front page. He worked extensively with "sick" persons, and he knew what it was like to apply the principle of unconditional positive regard to his communication with them. Often the key is to separate the person and the behavior so that you can accept the former while rejecting the latter. It is also important to remember that persons act in ways that make the most sense to them at the time they act. Observers may not be able to fathom the sense that some actions make, but if we want to communicate with these persons—without necessarily condoning what they do—positive regard helps.

When Rogers gave this talk it was remarkable to hear a person being so open and straightforward in such a relatively "formal" situation. Rogers was often disarmingly direct in just that way. I hope his directness enables you to hear what he has to say. Carl Rogers had an approach to interpersonal communication that is very much worth getting to know.

Rogers is another "classic" writer who used "he" to mean "everyone." As with the essays by Gibb and Buber, I hope you can read beyond this sexist language for the good ideas that are here.

Experiences in Communication

Carl R. Rogers

. . . What I would like to do is very simple indeed. I would like to share with you some of the things I have learned for myself in regard to communication. There are personal learnings growing out of my own experience. I am not attempting at all to say that you should learn or do these same things but I feel that if I can report my own experience honestly enough, perhaps you can check what I say against your own experience and decide as to its truth or falsity for you. . . . Another way of putting this is that some of my experiences in communicating with others have made me feel expanded, larger, enriched, and have accelerated my own growth. Very often in these experiences I feel that the other person has had similar reactions and that he too has been enriched, that his development and his functioning have moved forward. Then there have been other occasions in which the growth or development of each of us has been diminished or stopped or even reversed. . . .

The first simple feeling I want to share with you is my enjoyment when I can really *hear* someone. I think perhaps this has been a long-standing characteristic of mine. I can remember this in my early grammar school days. A child would ask the teacher a question and the teacher would give a perfectly good answer to a completely different question. A feeling of pain and distress would always strike me. My reaction was, "But you didn't hear him!" I felt a sort of childish despair at the lack of communication which was (and is) so common.

I believe I know why it is satisfying to me to hear someone. When I can really hear someone, it puts me in touch with him; it enriches my life. It is through hearing people that I have learned all that I know about individuals, about personality, about interpersonal relationships. . . .

When I say that I enjoy hearing someone, I mean, of course, hearing deeply. I mean that I hear the words, the thoughts, the feeling tones, the personal meaning, even the meaning that is below the conscious intent of the speaker. Sometimes too, in a message which superficially is not very important, I hear a deep human cry that lies buried and unknown far below the surface of the person.

So I have learned to ask myself, can I hear the sounds and sense the shape of this other person's inner world? Can I resonate to what he is saying so deeply that I sense the meanings he is afraid of yet would like to communicate, as well as those he knows?

I think, for example, of an interview I had with an adolescent boy. Like many an adolescent today he was saying at the outset of the interview that he had no goals. When I questioned him on this, he insisted even more strongly that he had no goals whatsoever, not even one. I said, "There isn't anything you want to do?" "Nothing. . . . Well, yeah, I want to keep on living." I remember distinctly my feeling at that moment. I resonated very deeply to this phrase. He might simply be telling me that, like everyone else, he wanted to live. On the other hand, he might be telling me—and this seemed to be a definite possibility—that at some point the question of whether or not to live had been a real issue with him. So I tried to resonate to him at all levels. I didn't know for certain what the message was. I simply wanted to be open to any of the meanings that this statement might have, including the possibility that he might at one time have considered suicide. My being willing and able to listen to him at all levels is perhaps one of the things that made it possible for him to tell me, before the end of the interview, that not long before he had been on the point of blowing his brains out. This little episode is an example of what I mean by wanting to really hear someone at all the levels at which he is endeavoring to communicate. . . .

I find, both in therapeutic interviews and in the intensive group experiences which have meant a great deal to me, that hearing has consequences. When I truly hear a person and the meanings that are important to him at that moment, hearing not simply his words, but him, and when I let him know that I have heard his own private personal meanings, many things happen. There is first of all a grateful look. He feels released. He wants to tell me more about his world. He surges forth in a new sense of freedom. He becomes more open to the process of change. . . .

Let me move on to a second learning that I would like to share with you. I like to *be heard*. A number of times in my life I have felt myself bursting with insoluble problems, or going round and round in tormented circles or, during one period, overcome by feelings of worthlessness and despair. I think I have been more fortunate than most in finding at these times individuals who have been able to hear me and thus to rescue me from the chaos of my feelings, individuals who have been able to hear my meanings a little more deeply than I have known them. These persons have heard me without judging me, diagnosing me, appraising me, evaluating me. They have just listened and clarified and responded to me at all the levels at which I was communicating. I can testify that when you are in psychological distress and someone really hears you without passing judgment on you, without trying to take responsibility for you, without trying to mold you, it feels damn good! At these times it has relaxed the tension in me. It has permitted me to bring out the frightening feelings, the guilts, the despair, the confusions that have been a part of my experience. When I have been listened to and when I have been heard, I am able to reperceive my world in a new way and to go on. It is astonishing how elements that seem insoluble become soluble when someone listens, how confusions that seem irremediable turn into relatively clear flowing streams when one is heard. I have deeply appreciated the times that I have experienced this sensitive, empathic, concentrated listening.

I dislike it myself when I can't hear another, when I do not understand him. If it is only a simple failure of comprehension or a failure to focus my attention on what he is saying or a difficulty in understanding his words, then I feel only a very mild dissatisfaction with myself. But what I really dislike in myself is not being able to hear the other person because I am so sure in advance of what he is about to say that I don't listen. It is only afterward that I realize that I have heard what I have already decided he is saying; I have failed really to listen. Or even worse are those times when I catch myself trying to twist his message to make it say what I want him to say, and then only hearing that. This can be a very subtle thing, and it is surprising how skillful I can be in doing it. Just by twisting his words a small amount, by distorting his meaning just a little, I can make it appear that he is not only saying the thing I want to hear, but that he is the person I want him to be. Only when I realize through his protest or through my own gradual recognition that I am subtly manipulating him, do I become disgusted with myself. I know too, from being on the receiving end of this, how frustrating it is to be received for what you are not, to be heard as saying something which you have not said. This creates anger and bafflement and disillusion.

This last statement indeed leads into the next learning that I want to share with you: I am terribly frustrated and shut into myself when I try to express something which is deeply me, which is a part of my own private, inner world, and the other person does not understand. When I take the gamble, the risk, of trying to share something that is very personal with another individual and it is not received and not understood, this is a very deflating and a very lonely experience. I have come to believe that such an experience makes some individuals psychotic. It causes them to give up hoping that anyone can understand them. Once they have lost that hope, then their own inner world, which becomes more and more bizarre, is the only place where they can live. They can no longer live in any shared human experience. I can sympathize with them because I know that when I try to share some feeling aspect of myself which is private, precious, and tentative, and when this communication is met by evaluation, by reassurance, by distortion of my meaning, my very strong reaction is, "Oh, what's the use!" At such a time, one knows what it is to be alone.

So, as you can readily see from what I have said thus far, a creative, active, sensitive, accurate, empathic, nonjudgmental listening is for me terribly important in a relationship. It is important for me to provide it; it has been extremely important, especially at certain times in my life, to receive it. I feel that I have grown within myself when I have provided it; I am very sure that I have grown and been released and enhanced when I have received this kind of listening.

Let me move on to another area of my learnings.

I find it very satisfying when I can be real, when I can be close to whatever it is that is going on within me. I like it when I can listen to myself. To really know what I am experiencing in the moment is by no means an easy thing, but I feel somewhat encouraged because I think that over the years I have been improving at it. I am convinced, however, that it is a lifelong task and that none of us ever is totally able to be comfortably close to all that is going on within our own experience.

In place of the term "realness" I have sometimes used the word "congruence." By this I mean when my experiencing of this moment is present in my awareness and when what is present in my awareness is present in my communication, then each of these three levels matches or is congruent. At such moments I am integrated or whole, I am completely in one piece. Most of the time, of course, I, like everyone else, exhibit some degree of incongruence. I have learned, however, that realness, or genuineness, or congruence—whatever term you wish to give it—is a fundamental basis for the best of communication.

What do I mean by being close to what is going on in me? Let me try to explain what I mean by describing what sometimes occurs in my work as a therapist. Sometimes a feeling "rises up in me" which seems to have no particular relationship to what is going on. Yet I have learned to accept and trust this feeling in my awareness and to try to communicate it to my client. For example, a client is talking to me and I suddenly feel an image of him as a pleading little boy, folding his hands in supplication, saying, "Please let me have this, please let me have this." I have learned that if I can be real in the relationship with him and express this feeling that has occurred in me, it is very likely to strike some deep note in him and to advance our relationship. . . .

I feel a sense of satisfaction when I can dare to communicate the realness in me to another. This is far from easy, partly because what I am experiencing keeps changing every moment. Usually there is a lag, sometimes of moments, sometimes of days, weeks or months, between the experiencing and the communication: I experience something; I feel something, but only later do I dare to communicate it, when it has become cool enough to risk sharing it with another. But when I can communicate what is real in me at the moment that it occurs, I feel genuine, spontaneous, and alive.

I am disappointed when I realize—and of course this realization always comes afterward, after a lag of time—that I have been too frightened or too threatened to let myself get close to what I am experiencing, and that consequently I have not been genuine or congruent. There immediately comes to mind an instance that is somewhat painful to reveal. Some years ago I was invited to be a Fellow at the Center for Advanced Study in the Behavioral Sciences at Stanford. The Fellows are a group of brilliant and well-informed scholars. I suppose it is inevitable that there is a considerable amount of one-upmanship, of showing off one's knowledge and achievements. It seems important for each Fellow to impress the others, to be a little more assured, to be a little more knowledgeable than he really is. I found myself doing this same thing— playing a role of having greater certainty and greater competence than I really possess. I can't tell you how disgusted with myself I felt as I realized what I was doing: I was not being me, I was playing a part.

I regret it when I suppress my feelings too long and they burst forth in ways that are distorted or attacking or hurtful. I have a friend whom I like very much but who has one particular pattern of behavior that thoroughly annoys me. Because of the usual tendency to be nice, polite, and pleasant I kept this annoyance to myself for too long and, when it finally burst its bounds, it came out not only as annoyance but as an attack on him. This was hurtful, and it took us some time to repair the relationship.

I am inwardly pleased when I have the strength to permit another person to be his own realness and to be separate from me. I think that is often a very threatening possibility. In some ways I have found it an ultimate test of staff leadership and of parenthood. Can I freely permit this staff member or my son or my daughter to become a separate person with ideas, purpose, and values which may not be identical with my own? I think of one staff member this past year who showed many flashes of brilliance but who clearly held values different from mine and behaved in ways very different from the ways in which I would behave. It was a real struggle, in which I feel I was only partially successful, to let him be himself, to let him develop as a person entirely separate from me and my ideas and my values. Yet to the extent that I was successful, I was pleased with myself, because I think this permission to be a separate person is what makes for the autonomous development of another individual.

I am angry with myself when I discover that I have been subtly controlling and molding another person in my own image. This has been a very painful part of my professional experience. I hate to have "disciples," students who have molded themselves meticulously into the pattern that they feel I wish. Some of the responsibility I place with them, but I cannot avoid the uncomfortable probability that in unknown ways I have subtly controlled such individuals and made them into carbon copies of myself, instead of the separate professional persons they have every right to become.

From what I have been saying, I trust it is clear that when I can permit realness in myself or sense it or permit it in another, I am very satisfied. When I cannot permit it in myself or fail to permit it in another, I am very distressed. When I am able to let myself be congruent and genuine, I often help the other person. When the other person is transparently real and congruent, he often helps me. In those rare moments when a deep realness in one meets a realness in the other, a memorable "I-thou relationship," as Martin Buber would call it, occurs. Such a deep and mutual personal encounter does not happen often, but I am convinced that unless it happens occasionally, we are not living as human beings.

I want to move on to another area of my learning in interpersonal relationships—one that has been slow and painful for me.

I feel warmed and fulfilled when I can let in the fact, or permit myself to feel, that someone cares for, accepts, admires, or prizes me. Because of elements in my past history, I suppose, it has been very difficult for me to do this. For a long time I tended almost automatically to brush aside any positive feelings aimed in my direction. My reaction was, "Who, me? You couldn't possibly care for me. You might like what I have done, or my achievements, but not me." This is one respect in which my own therapy helped me very much. I am not always able even now to let in such warm and loving feelings from others, but I find it very releasing when I can do so. I know that some people flatter me in order to gain something for themselves; some people praise me because they are afraid to be hostile. But I have come to recognize the fact that some people genuinely appreciate me, like me, love me, and I want to sense that fact and let it in. I think I have become less aloof as I have been able to take in and soak up those loving feelings.

I feel enriched when I can truly prize or care for or love another person and when I can let that feeling flow out to that person. Like many others, I used to fear being trapped by letting my feelings show. "If I care for him, he can control me." "If I love her, I am trying to control her." I think that I have moved a long way toward being less fearful in this respect. Like my clients, I too have slowly learned that tender, positive feelings are not dangerous either to give or to receive. . . .

I think of one governmental executive in a group in which I participated, a man with high responsibility and excellent technical training as an engineer. At the first meeting of the group he impressed me, and I think others, as being cold, aloof, somewhat bitter, resentful, and cynical. When he spoke of how he ran his office, it appeared that he administered it "by the book," without any warmth or human feeling. In one of the early sessions he was speaking of his wife, and a group member asked him, "Do you love your wife?" He paused for a long time and the questioner said, "O.K. That's answer enough." The executive said, "No. Wait a minute. The reason I didn't respond was that I was wondering, 'Have I ever loved anyone?' I don't really think I have ever *loved* anyone."

A few days later, he listened with great intensity as one member of the group revealed many personal feelings of isolation and loneliness and spoke of the extent to which he had been living behind a facade. The next morning the engineer said, "Last night I thought and thought about what he told us. I even wept quite a bit myself. I can't remember how long it has been since I have cried, and I really felt something. I think perhaps what I felt was love."

It is not surprising that before the week was over, he had thought through different ways of handling his growing son, on whom he had been placing very rigorous demands. He had also began to really appreciate the love his wife had extended to him—love that he now felt he could in some measure reciprocate.

Because of having less fear of giving or receiving positive feelings, I have become more able to appreciate individuals. I have come to believe that this ability is rather rare; so often, even with our children, we love them to control them rather than loving them because we appreciate them. One of the most satisfying feelings I know—and also one of the most growth-promoting experiences for the other person—comes from my appreciating this individual in the same way that I appreciate a sunset. People are just as wonderful as sunsets if I can let them *be*. In fact, perhaps the reason we can truly appreciate a sunset is that we cannot control it. When I look at a sunset as I did the other evening, I don't find myself saying, "Soften the orange a little on the right hand corner, and put a bit more purple along the base, and use a little more pink in the cloud color." I don't do that. I don't *try* to control a sunset. I watch it with awe as it unfolds. I like myself best when I can appreciate my staff member, my son, my daughter, my grandchildren, in this same way. I believe this is a somewhat Oriental attitude; for me it is a most satisfying one.

Another learning I would like to mention briefly is one of which I am not proud but which seems to be a fact. When I am not prized and appreciated, I not only *feel* very much diminished, but my behavior is actually affected by my feelings. When I am prized, I blossom and expand, I am an interesting individual. In a hostile or unappreciative group, I am just not much of anything. People wonder, with very good reason, how did he ever get a reputation? I wish I had the strength to be more similar in both kinds of groups, but actually the person I am in a warm and interested group is different from the person I am in a hostile or cold group.

Thus, prizing or loving and being prized or loved is experienced as very growth enhancing. A person who is loved appreciatively, not possessively, blooms and develops his own unique self. The person who loves nonpossessively is himself enriched. This, at least, has been my experience.

I could give you some of the research evidence which shows that these qualities I have mentioned—an ability to listen emphatically, a congruence or genuineness an acceptance or prizing of the other—when they are present in a relationship make for good communication and for constructive change in personality. But I feel that, somehow, research evidence is out of place in a talk such as I have been giving.

Review Questions

1. What does Rogers mean by "hearing deeply"?
2. According to Rogers, what is the primary outcome of someone being fully or deeply heard?
3. What does "congruence" mean? What does it *not* mean?
4. How does the fact that I am changing from moment to moment affect my being congruent?
5. At what points in his talk does Rogers suggest that the communication he is discussing is appropriate in nonintimate—that is, business or professional—settings?

Probes

1. Which discussion of listening in Chapter 7 is closest to Rogers's description of hearing another and being heard?
2. How is Rogers's concept of congruence related to what John Amodeo and Kris Wentworth say about self-revealing communication in Chapter 8?
3. Do you think congruence helps create a defensive or a supportive communication climate (see Chapter 14).
4. What is the relationship between what Rogers says about suppressing feelings and the discussion of anger in Chapter 14?
5. Did you ever feel uncomfortable as you read Rogers's words? What do those feelings tell you about the topic of Chapter 8, self-disclosure?
6. How do you think Neil Postman, the author of "The Communication Panacea" in Chapter 8, would respond to what Rogers says here?

Chapter 18

A Philosopher's Approach

Martin Buber, a Jewish philosopher and teacher, was born and raised in what is now part of the Soviet Union, and died in 1965 in Israel. Throughout his life, Buber was both a "scholar" or "intellectual" and an intensely practical person interested in everyday life experiences. As an intellectual, he was hungry to learn and to write all he could about how humans relate with one another. As a practical person, he was determined to keep all of his theorizing and scholarship firmly based on the concrete events he experienced every day. Because he was raised by his grandparents in Europe during the late nineteenth and early twentieth centuries (Buber's parents were divorced), lived through both world wars, was active in several political movements, and was a well-known, even famous, citizen of Israel, his life experiences are different in many ways from yours and mine. But for me, Buber's peculiar genius is that he can sense the part of his experience that is universal and can project that universal knowledge about human meetings through his European heritage and his "foreign" native language in such a way that he talks to me directly. In other words, even though he is in many ways very different from me, he says, "this is my experience; reflect on it a little and you might find that it's your experience too." Sometimes I stumble over Buber's language, the way he puts things. For example, like some other older authors in this book, Buber uses "man" when he means "human." But when I listen to him and do what he asks, I discover that he's right. It *is* my experience, only now I understand it better than I did before.

I don't know whether this one excerpt from Buber's writing will work this way for you. But the possibility is there if you will open yourself to hear him.* That's one thing about Buber's writings. Although he's a philosopher, he has been criticized because he doesn't state philosophical propositions and then try to verify and validate them with "proof." Instead, Buber insists that his reader try to meet him in a *conversation,* a dialogue. The main thing is for the reader to see whether his or her life experiences resonate with Buber's. This resonance is the only "proof" of the validity of Buber's ideas that the reader will receive. So far, millions of persons have experienced this resonance. Books by and about Buber, especially his *I and Thou,* have been translated into over twenty languages and are read around the world.

In almost all his writing, Buber begins by observing that each of us lives a twofold reality. He describes the two "folds" in the section of *I and Thou* I paraphrased in my essay in Chapter 2. One "fold" is made up of our interaction with objects—human and otherwise—in the world. In this model of living, we merely need to develop and maintain our ability to be "objective," to explain ourselves and the world with accurate theories and valid cause-and-effect formulations. But the other "fold" occurs when we become fully human *persons* in genuine rela-

---

* You might also be interested in other things written by or about Buber. For starters I recommend Aubrey Hodes, *Martin Buber: An Intimate Portrait* (New York: Viking, 1971); or Hilary Evans Bender, *Monarch Notes: The Philosophy of Martin Buber* (New York: Monarch, 1974). Maurice Friedman has written the definitive Buber biography, and I'd especially recommend the third volume, *Martin Buber's Life and Work: The Later Years, 1945–1965* (New York: Dutton, 1983). Buber's most important and influential book is *I and Thou,* trans. Walter Kaufmann (New York: Scribner, 1970).

tionships with others, when we meet another and "make the other present as a whole and as a unique being, as the person that he is."

The genuine relationship Buber talks about is the "highest form" of what I've been calling interpersonal communication. You've probably heard of Buber's term for it—an *"I-Thou* relationship."* According to Buber, the individual lives always in the world of *I-It; the person* can enter the world of *I-Thou.* Both worlds are necessary. You can't expect to communicate interpersonally with everyone in every situation. But you can only become a fully human person by sharing genuine interpersonal relationships with others. As Buber puts it, without *It* the person cannot live. But he who lives with *It* alone is not a person.

This article is taken from a talk Buber gave when he visited the United States in 1957. It's especially useful because it is a kind of summary of much of what he had written in the first seventy-nine years of his life (he died when he was eighty-seven).

I've outlined the article to simplify it some and to show how clearly organized it actually is. As you can see from the outline, Buber's subject is interpersonal relationships, which he calls "man's personal dealings with one another," or "the interhuman." Like the rest of this book, Buber's article doesn't deal with some mystical spirit world in which we all become one. Rather, he's writing about communication between today's teachers and students, politicians and voters, preachers and parishioners, and between you and me. First, he explains some attitudes and actions that keep people from achieving "genuine dialogue." Then he describes the characteristics of this dialogue, or *I-Thou* relationship. In the outline I've paraphrased each point that he makes.

When you read the essay, you'll probably be able to see where several of the other writers in this book got some of their ideas. For example, compare Carl Rogers's explanation of "congruence" with what Buber says about "being and seeming."

Whether or not you note that kind of thing, however, read this article as thoughtfully as you can. It sums up everything in this book. And I know from the experience I have lived that it's worth understanding.

A reminder about sexist language: I pointed out in the Introduction that a few of the readings in *Bridges Not Walls* were written before we had learned about the destructive potential of the male bias in the English language. This is one of these readings. When I paraphrase Buber I remove this bias, and I have tried to soft-pedal it when I quote him. But it's still part of his writing, at least as it is now translated. Given what he believed about human beings—and given the strong intellectual influence his wife, Paula, had on him—I am sure that Buber would have been quick to correct the gender bias in his language if he had lived long enough to have the opportunity. I hope you can overlook this unfortunate part of his writing and can hear his insights about *persons.*

---

*As I noted in Chapter 2, Buber's translators always point out that this "thou" is not the religious term of formal address. It is a translation of the German *Du,* the familiar form of the pronoun "you." As Walter Kaufmann, one of Buber's translators, explains, "German lovers say *Du* to one another and so do friends. *Du* is spontaneous and unpretentious, remote from formality, pomp, and dignity."

Outline of Martin Buber's "Elements of the Interhuman"

I. Interhuman relationships are not the same as "Social Relationships."
   A. Social relationships can be very close, but no *existential* or person-to-person relation is necessarily involved.
   B. This is because the collective or social suppresses individual persons.
   C. But in the interhuman, person meets person. In other words, "the only thing that matters is that for each of the two [persons] the other happens as the particular other, that each becomes aware of the other and is thus related to him in such a way that he does not regard and use him as his object, but as his partner in a living event, even if it is no more than a boxing match."
   D. In short, "the sphere of the interhuman is one in which a person is confronted by the other. We [i.e., Buber] call its unfolding the dialogical."

II. There are three problems that get in the way of dialogue.
   A. The first problem is the duality of *being* and *seeming*. Dialogue won't happen if the people involved are only "seeming." They need to try to practice "being."
      1. "Seeming" in a relationship involves being concerned with your image or front—with how you wish to appear.
      2. "Being" involves the spontaneous and unreserved presentation of what you really are in your personal dealings with the other.
      3. These two are generally found mixed together. The most we can do is to distinguish between persons in whose essential attitude one or the other (being or seeming) predominates.
      4. When seeming reigns, real interpersonal communication is impossible: "Whatever the meaning of the word 'truth' may be in other realms, in the interhuman realm it means that [people] communicate themselves to one another as what they are."
      5. The tendency toward seeming, however, is understandable.
         a. We *essentially* need personal confirmation, i.e., we can't live without being confirmed by other people.
         b. Seeming often appears to help us get the confirmation we need.
         c. Consequently, "to yield to seeming is [the human's] essential cowardice, to resist it is his [or her] essential courage."
      6. This view indicates that there is no such thing as "bad being," but rather people who are habitually content to "seem" and afraid to "be." I have never known a young person who seemed to me irretrievably bad."
   B. The second problem involves the way we perceive others.
      1. Many modern fatalists, such as Jean-Paul Sartre, believe that we can ultimately know *only* ourselves, that "man has directly to do only with himself and his own affairs."
      2. But the main prerequisite for dialogue is that you get in direct

touch with the other, "that each person should regard his partner as the very one he is."

   a. This means becoming aware of the other person as an essentially unique being. "To be aware of a [person] . . . means in particular to perceive his wholeness as a person determined by the spirit: it means to perceive the dynamic centre which stamps his every utterance, action, and attitude with the recognizable sign of uniqueness."

   b. But this kind of awareness is impossible so long as I objectify the other.

  3. Perceiving the other in this way is contrary to everything in our world that is scientifically analytic or reductive.

   a. This is not to say that the sciences are wrong, only that they are severely limited.

   b. What's dangerous is the extension of the scientific, analytic method to all of life, because it is very difficult for science to remain aware of the essential uniqueness of persons.

  4. This kind of perception is called "personal making present." What enables us to do it is our capacity for "imagining the real" of the other.

   a. Imagining the real "is not a looking at the other but a bold swinging—demanding the most intensive stirring of one's being—into the life of the other."

   b. When I *imagine* what the other person is *really* thinking and feeling, I can make direct contact with him or her.

C. The third problem which impedes the growth of dialogue is the tendency toward imposition instead of unfolding.

  1. One way to affect a person is to impose yourself on him or her.

  2. Another way is to "find and further in the soul of the other the disposition toward" that which you have recognized in yourself as right.

   a. Unfolding is not simply "teaching," but rather *meeting.*

   b. It requires believing in the other person.

   c. It means working as a helper of the growth processes already going on in the other.

  3. The propagandist is the typical "imposer"; the teacher *can* be the correspondingly typical "unfolder."

  4. The ethic implied here is similar to Immanuel Kant's, i.e., persons should never be treated as means to an end, but only as ends in themselves.

   a. The only difference is that Buber stresses that persons exist not in isolation but in the interhuman, and

   b. for the interhuman to occur, there must be:

    (1) as little seeming as possible.

    (2) genuine perceiving ("personal making present") of the other, and

    (3) as little imposing as possible.

III.   Summary of the characteristics of genuine dialogue:
A.   Each person must turn toward and be open to the other, a "turning of the being."
B.   Each must make present the other by imagining the real.
C.   Each confirms the other's being; however, confirmation does not necessarily mean approval.
D.   Each must be authentically himself or herself.
1.   Each must say whatever she or he "has to say."
2.   Each cannot be ruled by thoughts of his or her own effect or effectiveness as a speaker.
E.   Where dialogue becomes genuine, "there is brought into being a memorable common fruitlessness which is to be found nowhere else."
F.   Speaking is not always essential; silence can be very important.
G.   Finally, all participants must be committed to dialogue; otherwise, it will fail.

Again, Buber's language sometimes can get in the way of understanding him. But if you listen carefully to him, I think you will be able to resonate with at least some of what he says.

Elements of the Interhuman

Martin Buber

The Social and the Interhuman

It is usual to ascribe what takes place between men to the social realm, thereby blurring a basically important line of division between two essentially different areas of human life. I myself, when I began nearly fifty years ago to find my own bearings in the knowledge of society, making use of the then unknown concept of the interhuman, made the same error. From that time it became increasingly clear to me that we have to do here with a separate category of our existence, even a separate dimension, to use a mathematical term, and one with which we are so familiar that its peculiarity has hitherto almost escaped us. Yet insight into its peculiarity is extremely important not only for our thinking but also for our living.

We may speak of social phenomena wherever the life of a number of men, lived with one another, bound up together, brings in its train shared experiences and reactions. But to be thus bound up together means only that each individual existence is enclosed and contained in a group existence. It does not mean that between one member and another of the group there exists any kind of personal relation. They do feel that they belong together in a way that is, so to speak, fundamentally different from every possible belonging together with someone outside the group. And there do arise, especially in the life of smaller groups, contacts which frequently favour the birth of individual relations, but, on the other hand, frequently make it more difficult. In no case, however, does membership in a group necessarily involve an existential relation between one member and another. It is true that there have been groups in history which included highly sensitive and intimate relations between two of their members—as, for instance, in the homosexual relations among the Japanese samurai or among Doric warriors—and these were countenanced for the sake of the stricter cohesion of the group. But in general it must be said that the leading elements in groups, especially in the later course of human history, have rather been inclined to suppress the personal relation in favour of the purely collective element. Where this latter element reigns alone or is predominant, men feel themselves to be carried by the collectivity, which lifts them out of loneliness and fear of the world and lostness. When this happens—and for modern man it is an essential happening—the life between person and person seems to retreat more and more before the advance of the collective. The collective aims at holding in check the inclination to personal life. It is as though those who are bound together in groups should in the main be concerned only with the work of the group and should turn to the personal partners, who are tolerated by the group, only in secondary meetings.

The difference between the two realms became very palpable to me on one occasion when I had joined the procession through a large town of a movement to which I did not belong. I did it out of sympathy for the tragic development which I sensed was at hand in the destiny of a friend who was one of the leaders of the movement. While the procession was forming, I conversed with him and with another, a good-hearted "wild man," who also had the mark of death upon him. At that moment I still felt that the two men really were there, over against me, each of them a man near to me, near even in what was most remote from me; so different from me that my soul continually suffered from this difference, yet by virtue of this very difference confronting me with authentic being. Then the formations started off, and after a short time I was lifted out of all confrontation, drawn into the procession, falling in with its aimless step; and it was obviously the very same for the two with whom I had just exchanged human words. After a while we passed a café where I had been sitting the previous day with a musician whom I knew only slightly. The very moment we passed it the door opened, the musician stood on the threshold, saw me, apparently saw me alone, and waved to me. Straightway it seemed to me as though I were taken out of the procession and of the presence of my marching friends, and set there, confronting the musician. I forgot that I was walking along with the same step; I felt that I was standing over there by the man who had called out to me, and without a word, with a smile of understanding, was answering him. When consciousness of the facts returned to me, the procession, with my companions and myself at its head, had left the café behind.

The realm of the interhuman goes far beyond that of sympathy. Such simple happenings can be part of it as, for instance, when two strangers exchange glances in a crowded streetcar, at once to sink back again into the convenient state of wishing to know nothing about each other. But also every casual encounter between opponents belong to this realm, when it affects the opponent's attitude—that is, when something, however imperceptible, happens between the two, no matter whether it is marked at the time by any feeling or not. The only thing that matters is that for each of the two men the other happens as the particular other, that each becomes aware of the other and is thus related to him in such a way that he does not regard and use him as his object, but as his partner in a living event, even if it is no more than a boxing match. It is well known that some existentialists assert that the basic factor between men is that one is an object for the other. But so far as this is actually the case, the special reality of the interhuman, the fact of the contact, has been largely eliminated. It cannot indeed be entirely eliminated. As a crude example, take two men who are observing one another. The essential thing is not that the one makes the other his object, but the fact that he is not fully able to do so and the reason for his failure. We have in common with all existing things that we can be made objects of observation. But it is my privilege as man that by the hidden activity of my being I can establish an impassable barrier to objectification. Only in partnership can my being be perceived as an existing whole.

The sociologist may object to any separation of the social and the interhuman on the ground that society is actually built upon human relations, and the theory of these relations is therefore to be regarded as the very foundation of sociology. But here an ambiguity in the concept "relation" becomes evident. We speak, for instance, of a comradely relation between two men in their work, and do not merely mean what happens between them as comrades, but also a lasting disposition which is actualized in those happenings and which even includes purely psychological events such as the recollection of the absent comrade. But by the sphere of the interhuman I mean solely actual happenings between men, whether wholly mutual or tending to grow into mutual relations. For the participation of both partners is in principle indispensable. The sphere of the interhuman is one in which a person is confronted by the other. We call its unfolding the dialogical.

In accordance with this, it is basically erroneous to try to understand the interhuman phenomena as psychological. When two men converse together, the psychological is certainly an important part of the situation, as each listens and each prepares to speak. Yet this is only the hidden accompaniment to the conversation itself, the phonetic event fraught with meaning, whose meaning is to be found neither in one of the two partners nor in both together, but only in their dialogue itself, in this "between" which they live together.

Being and Seeming

The essential problem of the sphere of the interhuman is the duality of being and seeming. Although it is a familiar fact that men are often troubled about the impression they make on others, this has been much more discussed in moral philosophy than in anthropology. Yet this is one of the most important subjects for anthropological study.

We may distinguish between two different types of human existence. The one proceeds from what one really is, the other from what one wishes to seem. In general, the two are found mixed together. There have probably been few men who were entirely independent of the impression they made on others, while there has scarcely existed one who was exclusively determined by the impression made by him. We must be content to distinguish between men in whose essential attitude the one or the other predominates.

This distinction is most powerfully at work, as its nature indicates, in the inter-human realm—that is, in men's personal dealings with one another.

Take as the simplest and yet quite clear example the situation in which two persons look at one another—the first belonging to the first type, the second to the second. The one who lives from his being looks at the other just as one looks at someone with whom he has personal dealings. His look is "spontaneous," "without reserve"; of course, he is not uninfluenced by the desire to make himself understood by the other, but he is uninfluenced by any thought of the idea of himself which he can or should awaken in the person whom he is looking at. His opposite is different. Since he is concerned with the image which his appearance, and especially his look or glance, produces in the other, he "makes" this look. With the help of the capacity, in greater or lesser degree peculiar to man, to make a definite element of his being appear in his look, he produces a look which is meant to have, and often enough does have, the effect of a spontaneous utterance—not only the utterance of a physical event supposed to be taking place at that very moment, but also, as it were, the reflection of a personal life of such-and-such a kind.

This must, however, be carefully distinguished from another area of seeming whose ontological legitimacy cannot be doubted. I mean the realm of "genuine seeming," where a lad, for instance, imitates his heroic model and while he is doing so is seized by the actuality of heroism, or a man plays the part of a destiny and conjures up authentic destiny. In this situation there is nothing false; the imitation is genuine imitation and the part played is genuine; the mask, too, is a mask and no deceit. But where the semblance originates from the lie and is permeated by it, the interhuman is threatened in its very existence. It is not that someone utters a lie, falsifies some account. The lie I mean does not take place in relation to particular facts, but in relation to existence itself, and it attacks interhuman existence as such. There are times when a man, to satisfy some stale conceit, forfeits the great chance of a true happening between I and Thou.

Let us now imagine two men, whose life is dominated by appearance, sitting and talking together. Call them Peter and Paul. Let us list the different configurations which are involved. First, there is Peter as he wishes to appear to Paul, and Paul as he wishes to appear to Peter. Then there is Peter as he really appears to Paul, that is, Paul's image of Peter, which in general does not in the least coincide with what Peter wishes Paul to see; and similarly there is the reverse situation. Further, there is Peter as he appears to himself, and Paul as he appears to himself. Lastly, there are the bodily Peter and the bodily Paul. Two living beings and six ghostly appearances, which mingle in many ways in the conversation between the two. Where is there room for any genuine interhuman life?

Whatever the meaning of the word "truth" may be in other realms, in the interhuman realm it means that men communicate themselves to one another as what they are. It does not depend on one saying to the other everything that occurs to him, but only on his letting no seeming creep in between himself and the other. It does not depend on one letting himself go before another, but on his granting to the man to whom he communicates himself a share in his being. This is a question of the authenticity of the interhuman, and where this is not to be found, neither is the human element itself authentic.

Therefore, as we begin to recognize the crisis of man as the crisis of what is between man and man, we must free the concept of uprightness from the thin moralistic tones which cling to it, and let it take its tone from the concept of bodily uprightness. If a presupposition of human life in primeval times is given in man's walking upright, the fulfillment of human life can only come through the soul's walking upright, through the great uprightness which is not tempted by any seeming because it has conquered all semblance.

But, one may ask, what if a man by his nature makes his life subservient to the images which he produces in others? Can he, in such a case, still become a man living from his being, can he escape from his nature?

The widespread tendency to live from the recurrent impression one makes instead of from the steadiness of one's being is not a "nature." It originates, in fact, on the other side of interhuman life itself, in men's dependence upon one another. It is no light thing to be confirmed in one's being by others, and seeming deceptively offers itself as a help in this. To yield to seeming is man's essential cowardice, to resist it is his essential courage. But this is not an inexorable state of affairs which is as it is and must so remain. One can struggle to come to oneself—that is, to come to confidence in being. One struggles, now more successfully, now less, but never in vain, even when one thinks he is defeated. One must at times pay dearly for life lived from the being; but it is never too dear. Yet is there not bad being, do weeds not grow everywhere? I have never known a young person who seemed to me irretrievably bad. Later indeed it becomes more and more difficult to penetrate the increasingly tough layer which has settled down on a man's being. Thus there arises the false perspective of the seemingly fixed "nature" which cannot be overcome. It is false; the foreground is deceitful; man as man can be redeemed.

Again we see Peter and Paul before us surrounded by the ghosts of the semblances. A ghost can be exorcized. Let us imagine that these two find it more and more repellent to be represented by ghosts. In each of them the will is stirred and strengthened to be confirmed in their being as what they really are and nothing else. We see the forces of real life at work as they drive out the ghosts, till the semblance vanishes and the depths of personal life call to one another.

Personal Making Present

By far the greater part of what is today called conversation among men would be more properly and precisely described as speechifying. In general, people do not really speak to one another, but each, although turned to the other, really speaks to a fictitious court of appeal whose life consists of nothing but listening to him. Chekhov has given poetic expression to this state of affairs in *The Cherry Orchard*, where the only use the members of a family make of their being together is to talk past one another. But it is Sartre who has raised to a principle of existence what in Chekhov still appears as the deficiency of a person who is shut up in himself. Sartre regards the walls between the partners in a conversation as simply impassable. For him it is inevitable human destiny that a man has directly to do only with himself and his own affairs. The inner existence of the other is his own concern, not mine; there is no direct relation with the other, nor can there be. This is perhaps the clearest expression of the wretched fatalism of modern man, which regards degeneration as the unchangeable nature of *Homo sapiens* and the misfortune of having run into a blind alley as his primal fate, and which brands every thought of a breakthrough as reactionary romanticism. He who really knows how far our generation has lost the way of true freedom, of free giving between I and Thou, must himself, by virtue of the demand implicit in every great knowledge of this kind, practice directness—even if he were the only man on earth who did it—and not depart from it until scoffers are struck with fear and hear in his voice the voice of their own suppressed longing.

The chief presupposition for the rise of genuine dialogue is that each should regard his partner as the very one he is. I become aware of him, aware that he is different, essentially different from myself, in the definite, unique way which is peculiar to him, and I accept whom I thus see, so that in full earnestness I can direct what I say to him as the person he is. Perhaps from time to time I must offer strict opposition to his view about the subject of our conversation. But I accept this person, the personal bearer of a conviction, in his definite being out of which his conviction has grown—even though I must try to show, bit by bit, the wrongness of this very conviction. I affirm the person I struggle with: I struggle with him as his partner, I confirm him as creature and as creation, I confirm him who is opposed to me as him who is over against me. It is true that it now depends on the other whether genuine dialogue, mutuality in speech arises between us. But if I thus give to the other who confronts me his legitimate standing as a man with whom I am ready to enter into dialogue, then I may trust him and suppose him to be also ready to deal with me as his partner.

But what does it mean to be "aware" of a man in the exact sense in which I use the word? To be aware of a thing or a being means, in quite general terms, to experience it as a whole and yet at the same time without reduction or abstraction, in all its concreteness. But a man, although he exists as a living being among living beings and even as a thing among things, is nevertheless something categorically different from all things and all beings. A man cannot really be grasped except on the basis of the gift of the spirit which belongs to man alone among all things, the spirit as sharing decisively in the personal life of the living man, that is, the spirit which determines the person. To be aware of a man, therefore, means in particular to perceive his wholeness as a person determined by the spirit; it means to perceive the dynamic centre which stamps his every utterance, action, and attitude with the recognizable sign of uniqueness. Such an awareness is impossible, however, if and so long as the other is the separated object of my contemplation or even observation, for this wholeness and its centre do not let themselves be known to contemplation or observation. It is only possible when I step into an elemental relation with the other, that is, when he becomes present to me. Hence I designate awareness in this special sense as "personal making present."

The perception of one's fellow man as a whole, as a unity, and as unique—even if his wholeness, unity, and uniqueness are only partly developed, as is usually the case—is opposed in our time by almost everything that is commonly understood as specifically modern. In our time there predominates an analytical, reductive, and deriving look between man and man. This look is analytical, or rather pseudo analytical, since it treats the whole being as put together and therefore able to be taken apart—not only the so-called unconscious which is accessible to relative objectification, but also the psychic stream itself, which can never, in fact, be grasped as an object. This look is a reductive one because it tries to contract the manifold person, who is nourished by the microcosmic richness of the possible, to some schematically surveyable and recurrent structures. And this look is a deriving one because it supposes it can grasp what a man has become, or even is becoming, in genetic formulae, and it thinks that even the dynamic central principle of the individual in this becoming can be represented by a general concept. An effort is being made today radically to destroy the mystery between man and man. The personal life, the ever-near mystery, once the source of the stillest enthusiasms, is levelled down.

What I have just said is not an attack on the analytical method of the human sciences, a method which is indispensable wherever it furthers knowledge of a phenomenon without impairing the essentially different knowledge of its uniqueness that transcends the valid circle of the method. The science of man that makes use of the analytical method must accordingly always keep in view the boundary of such a contemplation, which stretches like a horizon around it. This duty makes the transportation of the method into life dubious; for it is excessively difficult to see where the boundary is in life.

If we want to do today's work and prepare tomorrow's with clear sight, then we must develop in ourselves and in the next generation a gift which lives in man's inwardness as a Cinderella, one day to be a princess. Some call it intuition, but that is not a wholly unambiguous concept. I prefer the name "imagining the real," for in its essential being this gift is not a looking at the other, but a bold swinging—demanding the most intensive stirring of one's being—into the life of the other. This is the nature of all genuine imagining, only that here the realm of my action is not the all-possible, but the particular real person who confronts me, whom I can attempt to make present to myself just in this way, and not otherwise, in his wholeness, unity, and uniqueness, and with his dynamic centre which realizes all these things ever anew.

Let it be said again that all this can only take place in a living partnership, that is, when I stand in a common situation with the other and expose myself vitally to his share in the situation as really his share. It is true that my basic attitude can remain unanswered, and the dialogue can die in seed. But if mutuality stirs, then the interhuman blossoms into genuine dialogue.

Imposition and Unfolding

I have referred to two things which impede the growth of life between men: the invasion of seeming, and the inadequacy of perception. We are now faced with a third, plainer than the others, and in this critical hour more powerful and more dangerous than ever.

There are two basic ways of affecting men in their views and their attitude to life. In the first a man tries to impose himself, his opinion and his attitude, on the other in such a way that the latter feels the psychical result of the action to be his own insight, which has only been freed by the influence. In the second basic way of affecting others, as man wishes to find and to further in the soul of the other the disposition toward what he has recognized in himself as the right. Because it is the right, it must also be alive in the microcosm of the other, as one possibility. The other need only be opened out in this potentiality of his; moreover, this opening out takes place not essentially by teaching, but by meeting, by existential communication between someone that is in actual being and someone that is in a process of becoming. The first way has been most powerfully developed in the realm of propaganda, the second in that of education.

The propagandist I have in mind, who imposes himself, is not in the least concerned with the person whom he desires to influence, as a person; various individual qualities are of importance only in so far as he can exploit them to win the other and must get to know them for this purpose. In his indifference to everything personal the propagandist goes a substantial distance beyond the party for which he works. For the party, persons in their difference are of significance because each can be used according to his special qualities in a particular function. It is true that the personal is considered only in respect of the specific use to which it can be put, but within these limits it is recognized in practice. To propaganda as such, on the other hand, individual qualities are rather looked on as a burden, for propaganda is concerned simply with *more*—more members, more adherents, an increasing extent of support. Political methods, where they rule in an extreme form, as here, simply mean winning power over the other by depersonalizing him. This kind of propaganda enters upon different relations with force; it supplements it or replaces it, according to the need or the prospects, but it is in the last analysis nothing but sublimated violence, which has become imperceptible as such. It places men's souls under a pressure which allows the illusion of autonomy. Political methods at their height mean the effective abolition of the human factor.

The educator whom I have in mind lives in a world of individuals, a certain number of whom are always at any one time committed to his care. He sees each of these individuals as in a position to become a unique, single person, and thus the bearer of a special task of existence which can be fulfilled through him and through him alone. He sees every personal life as engaged in such a process of actualization, and he knows from his own experience that the forces making for actualization are all the time involved in a microcosmic struggle with counterforces. He has come to see himself as a helper of the actualizing forces. He knows these forces; they have shaped and they still shape him. Now he puts this person shaped by them at their disposal for a new struggle and a new work. He cannot wish to impose himself, for he believes in the effect of the actualizing forces, that is, he believes that in every man what is right is established in a single and uniquely personal way. No other way may be imposed on a man, but another way, that of the educator, may and must unfold what is right, as in this case it struggles for achievement, and help it to develop.

The propagandist, who imposes himself, does not really believe in his own cause, for he does not trust it to attain its effect of its own power without his special methods, whose symbols are the loudspeaker and the television advertisement. The educator who unfolds what is there believes in the primal power which has scattered itself, and still scatters itself, in all human beings in order that it may grow up in each man in the special form of that man. He is confident that this growth needs at each moment only that help which is given in meeting and that he is called to supply that help.

I have illustrated the character of the two basic attitudes and their relation to one another by means of two extremely antithetical examples. But wherever men have dealings with one another, one or the other attitude is to be found to be in more or less degree.

These two principles of imposing oneself on someone and helping someone to unfold should not be confused with concepts such as arrogance and humility. A man can be arrogant without wishing to impose himself on others, and it is not enough to be humble in order to help another unfold. Arrogance and humility are dispositions of the soul, psychological fact with a moral accent, while imposition and helping to unfold are events between men, anthropological facts which point to an ontology, the ontology of the interhuman.

In the moral realm Kant expressed the essential principle that one's fellow man must never be thought of and treated merely as a means, but always at the same time as an independent end. The principle is expressed as an "ought" which is sustained by the idea of human dignity. My point of view, which is near to Kant's in its essential features, has another source and goal. It is concerned with the presuppositions of the interhuman. Man exists anthropologically not in his isolation, but in the completeness of the relation between man and man; what humanity is can be properly grasped only in vital reciprocity. For the proper existence of the interhuman it is necessary, as I have shown, that the semblance does not intervene to spoil the relation of personal being to personal being. It is further necessary, as I have also shown, that each one means and makes present the other in his personal being. That neither should wish to impose himself on the other is the third basic presupposition of the interhuman. These presuppositions do not include the demand that one should influence the other in his unfolding; that is, however, an element that is suited to lead to a higher stage of the interhuman.

That there resides in every man the possibility of attaining authentic human existence in the special way peculiar to him can be grasped in the Aristotelian image of entelechy, innate self-realization; but one must note that it is an entelechy of the work of creation. It would be mistaken to speak here of individuation alone. Individuation is only the indispensable personal stamp of all realization of human existence. The self as such is not ultimately the essential, but the meaning of human existence given in creation again and again fulfills itself as self. The help that men give each other in becoming a self leads the life between men to its height. The dynamic glory of the being of man is first bodily present in the relation between two men each of whom in meaning the other also means the highest to which this person is called, and serves the self-realization of this human life as one true to creation without wishing to impose on the other anything of his own realization.

Genuine Dialogue

We must now summarize and clarify the marks of genuine dialogue.

In genuine dialogue the turning to the partner takes place in all truth, that is, it is a turning of the being. Every speaker "means" the partner of partners to whom he turns as this personal existence. To "mean" someone in this connection is at the same time to exercise that degree of making present which is possible to the speaker at that moment. The experiencing senses and the imagining of the real which completes the findings of the senses work together to make the other present as a whole and as a unique being, as the person that he is. But the speaker does not merely perceive the one who is present to him in this way; he receives him as his partner, and that means that he confirms this other being, so far as it is for him to confirm. The true turning of his person to the other includes this confirmation, this acceptance. Of course, such a confirmation does not mean approval; but no matter in what I am against the other, by accepting him as my partner in genuine dialogue I have affirmed him as a person.

Further, if genuine dialogue is to arise, everyone who takes part in it must bring himself into it. And that also means that he must be willing on each occasion to say what is really in his mind about the subject of the conversation. And that means further that on each occasion he makes the contribution of his spirit without reduction and without shifting his ground. Even men of great integrity are under the illusion that they are not bound to say everything "they have to say." But in the great faithfulness which is the climate of genuine dialogue, what I have to say at any one time already has in me the character of something that wishes to be uttered, and I must not keep it back, keep it in myself. It bears for me the unmistakable sign which indicates that it belongs to the common life of the word. Where the dialogical word genuinely exists, it must be given its right by keeping nothing back. To keep nothing back is the exact opposite of unreserved speech. Everything depends on the legitimacy of "what I have to say." And of course I must also be intent to raise into an inner word and then into a spoken word what I have to say at this moment but do not yet possess as speech. To speak is both nature and work, something that grows and something that is made, and where it appears dialogically, in the climate of great faithfulness, it has to fulfill ever anew the unity of the two.

Associated with this is that overcoming of semblance to which I have referred. In the atmosphere of genuine dialogue, he who is ruled by the thought of his own effect as the speaker of what he has to speak has a destructive effect. If, instead of what has to be said, I try to bring attention to my *I*, I have irrevocably miscarried what I had to say; it enters the dialogue as a failure and the dialogue is a failure. Because genuine dialogue is an ontological sphere which is constituted by the authenticity of being, every invasion of semblance must damage it.

But where the dialogue is fulfilled in its being, between partners who have turned to one another in truth, who express themselves without reserve and are free of the desire for semblance, there is brought into being a memorable common fruitfulness which is to be found nowhere else. At such times, at each such time, the word arises in a substantial way between men who have been seized in their depths and opened out by the dynamic of an elemental togetherness. The interhuman opens out what otherwise remains unopened.

This phenomenon is indeed well known in dialogue between two persons; but I have also sometimes experienced it in a dialogue in which several have taken part.

About Easter of 1914 there met a group consisting of representatives of several European nations for a three-day discussion that was intended to be preliminary to further talks. We wanted to discuss together how the catastrophe, which we all believed was imminent, could be avoided. Without our having agreed beforehand on any sort of modalities for our talk, all the presuppositions of genuine dialogue were fulfilled. From the first hour immediacy reigned between all of us, some of whom had just got to know one another; everyone spoke with an unheard-of unreserve, and clearly not a single one of the participants was in bondage to semblance. In respect of its purpose the meeting must be described as a failure (though even now in my heart it is still not a certainty that it had to be a failure); the irony of the situation was that we arranged the final discussion for the middle of August, and in the course of events the group was soon broken up. Nevertheless, in the time that followed, not one of the participants doubted that he shared in a triumph of the interhuman.

One more point must be noted. Of course it is not necessary for all who are joined in a genuine dialogue actually to speak; those who keep silent can on occasion be especially important. But each must be determined not to withdraw when the course of the conversation makes it proper for him to say what he has to say. No one, of course, can know in advance what it is that he has to say; genuine dialogue cannot be arranged beforehand. It has indeed its basic order in itself from the beginning, but nothing can be determined, the course is of the spirit, and some discover what they have to say only when they catch the call of the spirit.

But it is also a matter of course that all the participants, without exception, must be of such nature that they are capable of satisfying the presuppositions of genuine dialogue and are ready to do so. The genuineness of the dialogue is called in question as soon as even a small number of those present are felt by themselves and by the others as not being expected to take any active part. Such a state of affairs can lead to very serious problems.

I had a friend whom I account one of the most considerable men of our age. He was a master of conversation, and he loved it: his genuineness as a speaker was evident. But once it happened that he was sitting with two friends and with the three wives, and a conversation arose in which by its nature the women were clearly not joining, although their presence in fact had a great influence. The conversation among the men soon developed into a duel between two of them (I was the third). The other "duelist," also a friend of mine, was of a noble nature; he too was a man of true conversation, but given more to objective fairness than to the play of the intellect, and a stranger to any controversy. The friend whom I have called a master of conversation did not speak with his usual composure and strength, but he scintillated, he fought, he triumphed. The dialogue was destroyed.

Review Questions

1. What distinction does Buber make between the "social" and the "interhuman"?
2. What feature of interpersonal contact does Buber say can characterize even "a boxing match"?
3. What does Buber mean when he says that "it is basically erroneous to try to understand the interhuman phenomena as psychological"?
4. Does Buber say that a person can practice "being" consistently, all the time? Explain.
5. Paraphrase the last sentence in the first paragraph under the heading, "Personal Making Present." What is Buber challenging his reader to do here?
6. Identify three possible things that a person who is "imposing" could impose on his or her conversational partner. In other words, what is (are) imposed when a person is "imposing"? What is "unfolded" when a person is "unfolding"?
7. What does Buber mean when he says that "To keep nothing back is the exact opposite of unreserved speech"?

Probes

1. What does it mean to you when Buber says that social contacts don't involve an *existential* relation, but that interhuman contacts do?
2. How is Buber's discussion of "being" and "seeming" similar to and different from Rogers's discussion of "congruence" (Chapter 17)?
3. For Buber, does "being" mean total honesty? Is "seeming" lying?
4. What circumstances make it difficult for you to "be"? How can you best help others to "be" instead of "seem"?
5. How do Buber's comments about the way we perceive others relate to the discussion of person perception in Chapter 6?
6. It sounds as if Buber is saying that science *cannot* be used to study human life. Is he saying that? Do you agree with him? Why or why not?
7. How is Buber's discussion of "imagining the real" related to what Brownell (Chapter 7) and Rogers (Chapter 17) say about empathy? How does it fit what Milt and I say about sculpting mutual meanings (Chapter 7)?
8. Which teacher that you've had has functioned most as an "imposer"? Which teacher has been most consistently an "unfolder"?
9. What does "personal making present" mean to you? What do you need to do in order to perceive someone that way?
10. Have you ever experienced a silent "dialogue" of the kind Buber mentions here? What happened?

Ideas are clean. They soar in the serene supernal. I can take them out and look at them, they fit in books, they lead me down that narrow way. And in the morning they are there. Ideas are straight—
But the world is round, and a
messy mortal is my friend.
Come walk with me in the mud. . . .

Hugh Prather

Index